THE
ENCYCLOPEDIA
of the
SRI LANKAN
DIASPORA

INTERNATIONAL ADVISORY PANEL

EDITORIAL MANAGEMENT

EDITORIAL TEAM

SPONSORS

The publisher would like to thank the following companies and organisations for their generous support.

Platinum Sponsors

Other Sponsors

SINGAPORE CEYLON TAMILS' ASSOCIATION • **SAT PAL KHATTAR**

© Editions Didier Millet 2013

First published in 2013 by
Editions Didier Millet
121 Telok Ayer Street, #03-01, Singapore 068590

www.edmbooks.com

In association with **Institute of South Asian Studies, National University of Singapore**

Colour separation by Pica Digital, Singapore
Printed in Singapore by Tien Wah Press Pte Ltd

ISBN 978-981-4260-83-1

THE
ENCYCLOPEDIA
of the
SRI LANKAN
DIASPORA

General Editor
PETER REEVES

Editor
RAJESH RAI

Assistant Editor
HEMA KIRUPPALINI

EDITIONS
DIDIER
MILLET

in association with

NUS
National University
of Singapore

ISAS
Institute of South Asian Studies

FOREWORD

T HE STORY OF how generations of people from Sri Lanka have ventured out and contributed far beyond the island's shores has been largely untold. This book, the first comprehensive study of the Sri Lankan diaspora, fills an important gap in social history.

The project was initiated soon after the decades-long civil war in Sri Lanka came to an end in 2009. It was, for this fact, both significant and complex. Against that background, *The Encyclopedia of the Sri Lankan Diaspora* has approached its task inclusively and with considerable sophistication.

It seeks to provide a carefully researched, objective account of the Sri Lankan diaspora in all its major strands: across time, from migration during the colonial period to the contemporary; across vastly different host countries; and across the distinct and yet overlapping ethno-political identities of the diaspora. It dissects the migration of the island's Tamils, starting with flows from colonial Ceylon to other parts of the British Empire, with notable impact in Malaya and Singapore—flows that largely reflected pull rather than push factors, and hence distinguished from the surge of migrants to North America, Europe and Australia after the 1970s. The book also captures the unique and poignant accounts of migration among the other sub-ethnic communities over time— the Sinhalese, the Burghers who with their European ancestries were able to move to Australia soon after independence, and the Moors, Malays and other Muslims—all adding to a complex but potent story.

The *Encyclopedia* is a fascinating study of how people of Sri Lankan origin, as small minorities in all the countries they settled in, achieved and contributed out of proportion to their numbers. They have made their mark especially in medicine, the judiciary, science and engineering; among academia and educationists; in politics and public administration; in leadership of various religious faiths; and in literature, culture and the arts. The book tells of the reverence for education, that began in Sri Lanka and has stayed on with the diaspora. It is well recognised that the island had one of the most developed school and university systems in Asia during colonial times. Scholars also point to the greater fluidity of its caste and social structures during the period when compared to India; plus the earlier shift away from making income off the land, among its middle and upper social strata; and the correspondingly greater emphasis on education as a way to do well in life.

As important as this social and cultural legacy was, however, the diaspora have also relied on opportunities in the countries that they settled in. They have done best and contributed most where they have been able to climb the ladder of meritocracy in education and jobs.

It is notable too that the generations of Sri Lankans who emigrated during colonial times had a sense of fellowship with each other, regardless of sub-ethnic identities. In what was then Malaya and Singapore, the Tamils, Sinhalese, Burghers, Moors and others played sports and otherwise got along well together. They also made a determined effort to integrate with the broader community. Current-day Singaporeans who trace their roots to Sri Lanka view themselves as Singaporeans first, even as they retain a sense of their ancestral past and cultural identities linked in different ways to Sri Lanka and South Asia.

Time will tell if what we have seen in Singapore, a small, multicultural nation, will be repeated amongst those who migrated in more recent times to places like North America and Europe. But identities among and within the Sri Lankan diaspora will surely evolve, shaped by developments and interactions in their host societies as well as in Sri Lanka.

The Encyclopedia of the Sri Lankan Diaspora brings together a spectrum of reputed international scholars, from various specialisations. I commend them and the editorial team led by Emeritus Professor Peter Reeves for putting together this challenging volume, and raising international understanding of an important part of the broader South Asian diaspora. The *Encyclopedia* has also benefitted from the guidance of the International Advisory Panel chaired by Sir Sabaratnam Arulkumaran. The project was coordinated by the Institute of South Asian Studies at the National University of Singapore, together with Editions Didier Millet. I also wish to acknowledge the various sponsors whose support has ensured the project's completion.

I hope that the *Encyclopedia* will serve a positive and constructive purpose; certainly not accentuating a sense of differences, but recognising that we are not only shaped by the twists and turns of history but have the ability and responsibility, wherever we belong, to shape the history that will be.

THARMAN SHANMUGARATNAM
Deputy Prime Minister and Minister of Finance
Singapore

CONTENTS

OPPOSITE: *Sri Lanka Unites (SLU) is an organisation that aims to foster reconciliation and unity. The 'Sri Lanka Unites School Relations Tour of 2011' pictured here inspired young people to be leaders and agents of change in their own communities. The SLU also organises the 'Future Leaders' Conference' that involves substantial participation from their diaspora chapters.*
ABOVE: *An abstract image depicting Sri Lankan migration.*
RIGHT: *The Ceylon Pavilion in London was influenced by the old Kandyan style of architecture. The panels and circular moonstones of the doorway were brought from Ceylon to London in 1924.*

EDITORIAL COMMITTEE

Peter Reeves is Emeritus Professor of South Asian History, Curtin University in Perth (Western Australia) and Fellow of the Academy of the Humanities in Australia. He was Head of the South Asian Studies Programme at the National University of Singapore from 1999 to 2005 and has also taught at Sussex, Western Australia and Michigan. He specialises in the modern political and socio-economic history of South Asia. Reeves' current work concerns the history of fisheries in colonial South Asia and fisheries and aquaculture in post-colonial South Asia.

Rajesh Rai (PhD., Birmingham) is Assistant Professor at the South Asian Studies Programme at the National University of Singapore. His research interests are in the fields of Indian and Hindu transnationalisms, nationalisms, and the postcolonial history and politics of South Asia. Rai has edited several books on the South Asian diaspora and his scholarship has been published in premier journals, including: *Modern Asian Studies, South Asia: Journal of South Asian Studies, Journal of Southeast Asian Studies*, and *South Asian Diaspora*. His book, *Indians in Singapore, 1819–1945: Diaspora in the Port-City*, is forthcoming.

Hema Kiruppalini, Research Associate at the Institute of South Asian Studies at the National University of Singapore (NUS). She obtained her BA (Hons) in History and Masters in South Asian Studies from NUS. Her Master's thesis on the Nepali diaspora in Singapore was amongst the pioneering scholarship on the Gurkha community in Singapore and several of her works on this topic have been published. Her research interests are in the areas migration, diaspora studies, ethnic conflicts and identity politics in South Asia and Southeast Asia.

Contributors

ALEX VAN ARKADIE, *Freelance journalist and media correspondent; Consultant, Food and Agriculture Organization of the United Nations, Rome, Italy.*

AMEER ALI, *Visiting Fellow, Murdoch Business School, Murdoch University, Australia.*

ANNE BLACKBURN, *Professor, Department of Asian Studies, Cornell University, USA.*

ANNETTE WILKE, *Professor, Study of Religion, Westphalian Wilhelms–University Muenster, Germany.*

BACHAMIYA ABDUL HUSSAINMIYA, *Associate Professor, Historical Studies Programme, Universiti Brunei Darussalam.*

BRIAN STODDART, *Emeritus Professor and former Vice-Chancellor, La Trobe University, Australia.*

CAMILLA ORJUELA, *Associate Professor, Peace and Development Research, School of Global Studies, University of Gothenburg, Sweden.*

CHAN E. S. CHOENNI, *Professor, Indian Migration and Diaspora, Free University Amsterdam, the Netherlands.*

CHANDRA RICHARD DE SILVA, *Professor of History and Vice Provost, Old Dominion University, USA.*

CHRISTOPHER McDOWELL, *Reader, Political Anthropology, Department of International Politics, City University London, UK.*

D. MITRA BARUA, *INSTRUCTOR, Department of Religion and Culture, University of Saskatchewan, Canada.*

DAVID GELLNER, *Professor, Social Anthropology, University of Oxford, UK.*

DELON MADAVAN, *PhD, Geography, Laboratoire Espaces, Natures et Cultures, Université Paris-Sorbonne, France.*

DENNIS McGILVRAY, *Professor, Anthropology, University of Colorado, USA.*

ERIC MEYER, *Emeritus Professor, South Asian History, Inalco, Université Paris-Cité, France.*

GAËLLE DEQUIREZ, *PhD, Political Science, Centre d'Etudes et de Recherches Administratives, Politiques et Sociales, France.*

HEMA GOONETILEKE, *Honorary Editor, Royal Asiatic Society of Sri Lanka.*

HEMA KIRUPPALINI, *Research Associate, Institute of South Asian Studies, National University of Singapore.*

IGOR KOTIN, *Senior Research Fellow, Peter the Great Museum of Anthropology and Ethnography of the Russian Academy of Sciences; Professor, Saint Petersburg State University, Russia.*

JEFFERY SAMMUELS, *Associate Professor, Religious Studies and Coordinator of Asian Studies, Western Kentucky University, USA.*

KAMALA GANESH, *Professor, Department of Sociology, University of Mumbai, India.*

LARRY MARSHALL, *Lecturer, Community Development, University of Melbourne, Australia.*

LESLEY JEFFERY, *born in Colombo and educated at St Christopher's School, Canberra; Holy Family Convent, Bambalapitiya; St Vincent's College, Potts Point; and Sydney University, Australia.*

MAHINDA DEEGALLE, *Senior Lecturer, School of Humanities and Cultural Industries, Bath Spa University, UK.*

MARIANNE C. QVORTRUP FIBIGER, *Associate Professor, Religious Studies, The Institute of Culture and Society, Faculty of Arts, Aarhus University, Denmark.*

MARTIN BAUMANN, *Professor, Study of Religions, University of Lucerne, Switzerland.*

MENUSHA DE SILVA, *PhD candidate, Department of Geography, National University of Singapore.*

MICHELE RUTH GAMBURD, *Professor, College of Liberal Arts and Sciences, Portland State University, USA.*

NINA G. KRASNODEMBSKAIA, *Leading Research Fellow, Peter the Great Museum of Anthropology and Ethnography of the Russian Academy of Sciences, Russia.*

ØIVIND FUGLERUD, *Professor, Social Anthropology, Museum of Cultural History, Oslo, Norway.*

P. SAHADEVAN, *Professor, School of International Studies, Jawaharlal Nehru University, New Delhi, India.*

PALITHA GANEWATTA, *Executive Producer, Sinhalese Language Program, Special Broadcasting Service, Australia.*

PATRICK MENDIS, *American Commissioner of the National Commission for UNESCO; Distinguished Senior Fellow and Affiliate Professor, Public and International Affairs, George Mason University School of Public Policy, USA.*

PATRICK PEEBLES, *Emeritus Professor of History, University of Missouri–Kansas City, USA.*

PETER REEVES, *Emeritus Professor, South Asian Studies, Curtin University, Australia; former Head, South Asian Studies Programme, National University of Singapore.*

RAFAELA EULBERG, *PhD candidate, Department for the Study of Religions, University of Lucerne, Switzerland.*

RAJESH RAI, *Assistant Professor, South Asian Studies Programme, National University of Singapore.*

RANJITH HENAYAKA LOCHBIHLER, *Writer, social worker and political activist, Italy.*

RAZEEN SALLY, *Visiting Associate Professor, Lee Kuan Yew School of Public Policy and Institute of South Asian Studies, National University of Singapore.*

ROSHINI JAYAWEERA, *Research Officer, Institute of Policy Studies of Sri Lanka.*

SAMAN KELEGAMA, *Executive Director, Institute of Policy Studies of Sri Lanka.*

SHARANYA JAYAWICKRAMA, *Postdoctoral Fellow, Department of English, University of Macau, China.*

SHIHAN DE SILVA JAYASURIYA, *Senior Fellow, Institute of Commonwealth Studies, University of London, UK.*

SHIRLEY PULLE TISSERA, *Board Member of the Global Fund in Geneva; retired CEO of a marketing company in Sri Lanka.*

SIDDHARTHAN MAUNAGURU, *Newton International Fellow, Department of Anthropology, University of Edinburgh, UK.*

SINNAPOO APPUTHURAI, *Fellow, Chartered Institute of Transport and Logistics, Malaysia.*

SITHY ZULFIKA, *Executive Director, Muslim Women's Research and Action Forum, Sri Lanka; Psychosocial Counselor, Toronto, Canada.*

SUHARSHINI SENEVIRATNE, *Author of Exotics Tastes of Sri Lanka, Virginia, USA.*

SUVENDRINI PERERA, *Professor, School of Media, Culture and Creative Arts, Curtin University, Australia.*

UMME SALMA, *Research Assistant, Centro em Rede de Investigação em Antropologia/ Faculdade de Ciências Sociais e Humanas da Universidade Nova de Lisboa, Portugal.*

V. SURYANARAYAN, *Former Director, Centre for South and Southeast Asian Studies, University of Madras, India.*

VASUGI KAILASAM, *PhD candidate, Department of English Language and Literature, National University of Singapore.*

VISAKA NITHIYANANDAM, *Retired Senior Lecturer, Economics, Massey University, New Zealand; former Professor of Economics, University of Jaffna, Sri Lanka.*

VISVAN NAVARATNAM, *PhD, Former Head of Anatomy Department, University of Cambridge and Life Fellow of Christ's College.*

Guide to the Use of the Encyclopedia and Editorial Conventions

STRUCTURE OF THE VOLUME

The encyclopedia has been divided into several sections. Part I—Context—surveys the Sri Lankan setting, providing a sense of the land, the nature of connections and relations with the outside world; and the historical experience of the island. The classical period reveals the myriad early migration streams to the island, the emergence of agrarian society, the development of polities, and the evolving patterns of social norms and religious practices in Sri Lanka prior to the advent of European rule. The colonial period (circa 16th century to 1948) accounts for developments during the Portuguese, Dutch and British rule over the island—in terms of key administrative, social and economic changes, the opening up of new educational opportunities, and the evolving political frame till independence. The post-colonial phase examines the development of nationalism in the independent state, the nature of successive governments, key constitutional changes, the factors leading to the outbreak of ethnic conflict and the ramifications of the civil war on the Sri Lankan polity, society and diaspora.

Part II of the encyclopedia deals thematically with the cultural, social and economic life of the diaspora: the ways in which Sri Lanka's food traditions have been transplanted in the diaspora and changes that have come about in culinary practices; the wide range of sports, which both link different areas of the diaspora and reconnect people in the diaspora with Sri Lanka; how transnational marriage patterns have evolved and played a role in peopling the diaspora; and of religious life, in terms of institutions and practices but as well of the evolution of Sri Lankan Buddhist relations with neighbouring states. This section also features key icons of popular culture—in music, cinema, dance and theatre—and successful entrepreneurs, and analyses the impact of temporary migrant labour remittances on the Sri Lankan economy.

Part III, the final section of the encyclopedia's contextual segment, studies the evolution and character of the creative literature of the diaspora, and examines how this distinguished corpus of literary works have addressed key aspects of the diasporic experience.

The largest section of the volume, Part IV—'Communities'—provides country or in some cases regional profiles of the Sri Lankan diaspora. Widely dispersed across the globe, significant Sri Lankan diasporic communities have emerged in Asia, North America, Europe and Australasia. Various trajectories of migration account for the formation of these communities. In the second half of the 19th and the early 20th centuries, the search for better economic opportunities saw many educated personnel and traders migrating to colonial outposts in Southeast Asia. In the latter half of the 20th century, as Western countries gradually opened their borders to non-White immigrants, Sri Lankans ventured to new destinations, in North America, Europe and Australasia. The large scale movement of refugees following the outbreak of the civil war in Sri Lanka further augmented the size of the diaspora in these locations. In recent times, a significant number of Sri Lankans have also come to be employed in the Gulf States, albeit on contractual terms that ensure only a temporary residence. The 'Communities' section thus accounts for the specific Sri Lankan experience in specific locations, providing a synoptic view of their historical origins, migration process and evolution, demographic change, their social, economic and political experience, and their contemporary concerns and challenges. Important episodes and events which capture the essence of the community's experience have been highlighted. There are some common threads across certain clusters—in Malaysia and Singapore, for example, where the history of Sri Lankan emigration spans well over a century, and was closely connected to the spread of colonial power in the region. Sri Lankan diasporic communities in the West also share certain commonalities, in terms of their encounters with the culture of their countries of residence, and as well a manifest concern with political developments in Sri Lanka. It is the individual distinctiveness of the various diasporic communities, however, that stands out and underlines the enormous complexity and variation in experience.

THE MATERIALS PRESENTED

The encyclopedia contains signed articles by the authors, who are in the list of contributors. The largest body of material in both the 'Context' (Parts I–III) and 'Communities' (Part IV) sections of the volume is presented in essay form. In these sections there are also boxed features, which allow certain topics or illustrative examples to be looked at closely. Each authorial signature relates to all the text in the article or boxed feature—some small, others quite large—with which it is associated, except where indicated.

Every attempt has been made to ensure that the structure and content of the encyclopedia are clear by arranging the material according to both chronological and geographical indicators. Moreover, the volume has a comprehensive and detailed thematic index.

The encyclopedia is illustrated with a wide-ranging selection of photographs, both historical and contemporary, and examples of documents, dust jackets and other illustrative materials. Statistical data are presented throughout in figures and tables. In addition, there is a full set of maps—both to locate communities in terms of region and territory and to illustrate historical aspects of the growth and development of the community or the contextual factors to do with migration, settlement and socio-economic activities. For the maps, the intention has been to mark and name places mentioned in the accompanying text, together with additional features, to assist in terms of context and reference. The key to the features used in all the modern maps is as follows:

Area/areas under discussion	—— International boundary
Area/areas beyond scope of discussion	······ Provincial/state boundary

The bibliography is intended purely as a source for further reading on the subjects of each of the main sections of the 'Context' and 'Communities' sections of the volume. This means that rather than being presented as a single, consolidated list of bibliographical material (books, book chapters, articles and, where appropriate, websites), the bibliography is divided into relevant sections following the structure of the encyclopedia. Therefore, some titles may appear more than once.

LANGUAGES, MATERIALS AND AIDS

The editorial approach has been to use English as far as possible. However, the nature of the material is such that romanised non-English vocabulary, including Sri Lankan terms and idioms with no exact English equivalents, occasionally appear. We have included a glossary which defines a large number of Sinhala and Tamil words and names, along with some variants. Besides Sri Lankan languages, there is a sprinkling of Asian (Bahasa Melayu, Hindi, Thai and Chinese), Middle Eastern and European (French, Portuguese, Dutch, German and Russian) terms. There are also words and phrases from the creole languages of some territories, and words arising from the diasporic versions of Sri Lankan languages carried to their new homes by migrants; these are usually explained in the text.

The spelling of English words is based on *The Concise Oxford Dictionary* (12th Edition), which does not regard as foreign, and, therefore, does not italicise many words which have been absorbed into English from other languages, including Sri Lankan languages.

INTRODUCTION

Diasporic communities are significant for their cultural and economic contributions to host countries and quite often to their 'homeland' as well. The Sri Lankan diaspora is an important example of a diasporic community spread throughout the world, which developed over time and for a variety of reasons. The Sri Lankan heritage is visible in diverse places, often overlapping or confused with other South Asian contributions. This volume documents the when, where, what and how of the development of the Sri Lankan diaspora and the elements in many cultures that can be traced to the movement of people to and from the island.

The Sri Lankan diaspora numbers about three million world-wide, with significant communities now settled in Europe, the Americas, Asia and Australasia. In the context of the global movements of South Asians, the number of Sri Lankans living overseas pales in comparison to the Indian, Pakistani and Bangladeshi diasporas. Yet, given that Sri Lanka's population only just exceeds 21 million (2011), effectively one in eight Sri Lankans are based overseas—a remarkable diaspora-to-population ratio that is not matched by any of its South Asian counterparts.

It is important to note that the Sri Lankan diaspora was not created by a single movement of one group of people. Rather, different groups moved at different times and because of particular circumstances, so that it is not so much a question of a 'Sri Lankan diaspora' as it is a question of identifying discrete groups which have had the effect of planting, in different parts of the world, groups of people who can be traced originally to Sri Lanka. In many cases they have kept linkages with people from that group in Sri Lanka and operate as a diaspora of those particular communities. It would be more accurate, therefore, to distinguish as separate elements communities from Sri Lanka which occupy the diasporic ground, such as a 'Sinhala diaspora', the 'Tamil diaspora', the 'Burgher diaspora' or the 'Moor diaspora'. An understanding of their movements, and the development of these diaspora(s) requires, as a preliminary, a 'preview' of Sri Lanka—the land and its people, and the dynamics of social and political change in the country.

Sri Lanka: Island and Resources

The island previously known as Ceylon and now known as Sri Lanka has had many other names throughout recorded history. In the 2nd century BCE it was known to the Greeks as Taprobane, a corruption of the local name Thambapanni. It was called Lanka in the Indian epic poem *Ramayana*, at other times Ratnadvipa and Serendib, and then Ceilao by the Portuguese. Some of these names were reflections of the perceived natural beauty of the island: a gem, paradise or heaven. The island is located at latitude north 5° 55′ – 9° 50′ and longitude east 79° 42′ – 81° 53′ close to Tamil Nadu, the south-eastern coastal state of India. It is 65,610 square kilometres in extent rising in the central south to its highest point at 2,527 metres, an area known as the hill country which was famous as Kandy, the seat of the last Sinhalese kings, and which became distinctive as the tea plantation area in the late 19th and 20th centuries. The climate is subtropical and the monsoons bring rainfall, which in some areas is over 150 inches per year and overall averages 75 inches *per annum*, which is adequate except in the north and north-central regions where irrigation is important.

Historically, agriculture centred on rice production but also included important industries from coconut products (coir and oil) derived from coconut plantations. Tea plantations became significant as the basis of the so-called 'Dual Economy', a mix of peasant cultivation and capital ventures which, in the last century of British colonial rule, saw limited industrialisation through the medium of plantations employing British investment and migrant ('indentured') labour from South India. Other important resources were spices, especially cinnamon, mace and pepper, precious and semi-precious gemstones, graphite, pearls and *chank*. Given the island's central location on the trade routes across the Indian Ocean, maritime trade was important for the use that Arab, Indian and occasional Chinese ships made of the Sri Lankan ports for reprovisioning. This drew the island's own commodities into trade.

Rice remains an important commodity in domestic agriculture. Tea is still an export crop although the large plantations have been much divided and much reduced in size. Stemming from government initiatives during the 1960s and 1970s, construction and industries such as the production of textiles, garments and electronics have become important.

Sri Lanka: People and Culture

Essentially, the island was a plural society from the initial migration in the 6th century BCE of the Sinhalese conquerors from northern India, who took a great part of the island from the Vedda people and established their settlements in the north of the island. Their Sinhala language came with the settlers and some centuries later they brought Buddhism to the island—and, importantly, preserved it when it disappeared as a vital part of Indian culture. The proximity of the Hindu states in south India also led to a process of south Indian migration and conquest in the north and the east, which resulted in the addition of the Tamil language and Saivite Hinduism to the life of the island.

Further social and cultural development came from the impact of transient or colonising people: the Moors and their Islamic faith came from the intermarriage of women from the island and Arab merchants sailing and trading on the Indian Ocean routes from the 12th to 13th centuries CE. Roman Catholicism and Protestant Christianity followed in the 16th to 17th centuries from conversions and liaisons between island people, and Portuguese and Dutch trading and colonising invaders. These Portuguese and Dutch periods on the island also saw the in-migration of males from the European homelands who married with islander women and built the basis of the Burgher communities. British colonisation in the 19th and 20th centuries added further variety to forms of Christian allegiance and also brought the English language, which became a major feature of education, administration and politics on the island.

Sri Lankan Political and Social Change

Sinhala and Tamil kings ruled the island until Portuguese and Dutch traders and colonisers took control of the coasts. The end of indigenous royal rule came with British colonial rule, which in the early 19th century displaced the last dynasty, the 'Kings of Kandy'. British rule also meant the tightening of administrative order across the island as a territorial whole, with an ordered civil service working in English—a regime which enabled those islanders educated in English, and in tune with British practice, to look to careers in administration and management. Firstly this took place in all parts of the island and then, in other parts of the British colonial empire in South and Southeast Asia. This latter development was important for the growth of a diaspora of Ceylonese civil servants. It was in part responsible for a relatively free colonial political record that led to its characterisation as 'the model colony'. That, in turn, made political reform leading towards popular political participation and freedom possible for the colony. The 1931 constitutional settlement, which was based on universal adult franchise, gave virtual home rule to the Ceylonese and thereby strengthened the role of Sinhala elite politicians in the period immediately before independence. This laid the basis for Sinhala-Tamil political tension after independence was granted in 1948, tension which centred around questions of language, religion, educational opportunity and political power, and played a large part in building the political role of the diasporic communities linked to the island.

Modern Migration Processes

Migration had been a significant part of the history of South Asia since the earliest times. At different periods and under different economic and political pressures, migration constituted the basis for the development of regional South Asian societies down to the early 21st century. Such migratory movements included 'folk movements'; organised or spontaneous pressures from local community leaders; conquest by migrating warrior groups; and efforts to move the people of one area by enslaving them or organising systems of labour transfer such as transportation or indenture. Each system had different effects on the regional societies which emerged in the areas in which the migration took place.

Against such a backdrop, the present volume seeks to particularly study the effects of migration from the island which was itself an example of such a regional entity. It aims to provide a global account of those people living and working around the world, who regard themselves (or whose forebears regarded themselves), as people whose 'homeland' was the island state or some portion of the island known in colonial times as Ceylon. For some, this was only a temporary absence from Sri Lanka, but in many cases, those who began as 'sojourners' stayed on and became the founders of overseas communities.

As already mentioned, the Sri Lankan diaspora was not the result of emigration by a single movement of one group of people. The contextual section elaborates on the contributions which these various groups and their heritages have made to national and international literature, sport, cuisine, popular culture, the arts, business and professions. Elements of diasporic culture are now embedded in host communities as well. Religion is particularly evident. Some places of worship serve people long removed from the island, others have been constructed by recent arrivals.

As we will see from the discussion of the Sri Lankan case, earlier migrants and settlers who transferred under a wide range of schemes and movements from the colonial territory have an important part to play in the ways in which the independent nation can meet the challenges that it faces in the post-colonial situation.

Remittances are critical to the family's economic and social standing. Moreover, the importance of remittance payments to the national economy of Sri Lanka means that the standing of the disapora can be quantified. It plays a significant part in the formulation of political programmes to do with both the new state and other global partners which can be crucial in international relations.

There is also a very personal aspect to the question of identity as will be seen in many of the following articles. Many of the people who have moved abroad see themselves today as Sri Lanka's 'diaspora' and they are seen in that way by others who are familiar with Sri Lanka. However, there are sizeable communities who do not identify themselves as part of this diaspora—chief among whom are Tamils who have sought residence outside Sri Lanka and who refer to themselves as members of the 'Tamil diaspora' or in some cases the 'Ceylon Tamil' or the 'Jaffna Tamil' diaspora.

THE DEVELOPMENT OF SRI LANKAN DIASPORIC COMMUNITIES

The 'communities' section of this volume looks at the history and development of these individual diasporic communities in specific countries, in an attempt to show how they developed particular characteristics and contributions, and what these particular developments have meant for the ongoing linkage with Sri Lanka—or not, as the case may be.

Throughout the historical period covered there is evidence of people moving in, out and around the island for a variety of reasons, bringing change wherever they settled. Two significant areas of movement and contact can be seen in pre-colonial times. The first of these comprises the religious contacts, particularly of Buddhist groups, in South, Southeast and East Asia. The second pre-colonial strand is migration linked to economic developments; for example, the opening of new lands and new sectors in the economy which attracted migrants like the Karava fisherfolk from South India to Ceylon in the 16th century CE.

The earliest centres of the modern diaspora began in the movements from Ceylon to British colonial possessions in Malaya and Singapore, along with older religious and cultural connections. Such linkages continued through the colonial period and were augmented as Sri Lanka grew in importance as a colony. Sri Lankan merchants began operations in the wider South and Southeast Asian regions. This 'modernisation' gave the island a place in the global economy. This involved plantations, which used cheap land in the hills, readily available British capital and an exploitable south Indian labour force, especially in the production and marketing of tea.

A range of migratory contexts were established in the mid to late 19th and early 20th centuries. These included religious, especially Buddhist, linkages in South and Southeast Asia. At the same time, there were movements of merchants and financiers. Increasingly, as education expanded, there were also movements within the British empire for civil administrators, teachers and students or professionals following career opportunities overseas, as in the case of doctors, lawyers and managers.

POST-COLONIAL DEVELOPMENTS

Ceylon's independence in 1948 saw movements by relatively small minorities, especially the Burghers and the Moors, who foresaw difficulties in holding their positions under the political dominance of the Sinhala-speaking majority. There was also a growth in the number of educators, professionals and students who took up positions in Europe, North America and Australasia. Alongside these developments there were the earliest signs of skilled worker involvement in contract labour, which was to develop strongly in the last three decades of the 20th century.

The two major areas of post-colonial migration which developed after the 1970s concern, firstly, the opening of a contract labour market in the Middle East, Singapore and East Asia; and, secondly, the migration, especially of Tamils, during the time of the insurgency from 1983 to 2009.

With regard to the contract labour market, there were quite large movements of both men and women who faced economic difficulties in Sri Lanka from the 1970s. Sri Lanka was able to provide both male labour for construction and other industries, and female labour for domestic service, nursing, child carers and the like, in the Middle East, the Gulf and the rapidly-developing Southeast and East Asian economies, in order to support their families in Sri Lanka with remittances.

Pressures in the post-colonial period produced a political structure in the island nation that handed power to the Sinhala-speaking majority who were overwhelmingly Buddhist and constituted some 74 per cent of the population. Politically, the other ethnic groups were in a markedly inferior position. Post-colonial policies emphasised the dominance of the Sinhala-speaking majority by insisting that 'Sinhala-only' was the official national language; by determining that Buddhism had the 'foremost place' in the nation's religious affairs; and by granting Sinhala students special status, with regard to educational opportunities. Constitutional decisions made in 1972 and 1977 defined Sri Lanka as a republic with a president having executive powers and a unicameral parliament. This meant the ethnic minorities had little chance of exercising regional or local control even if they were a majority in some areas. Tamils were in such a position in the north and east of the country (in the area they designate as 'Tamil Eelam'), but the possibility of providing regional autonomy was ruled out by a refusal to provide for a 'federal' system within the state. The result of this political settlement was to position the Sinhala majority and the Tamil minority as rivals in national and local political affairs. That rivalry became more and more militant and violent over the decades from the 1950s to 1970s, and burst into a sustained 'civil war' from 1983 to the defeat of the Tamil forces in 2009. This led to a substantial movement of Tamils seeking protection as refugees and asylum seekers from the 'civil war', as well as those who sought opportunities to work for the Tamil cause, by developing support and assistance for Tamil militant movements between 1983 and 2009. In parallel, the economic fallout of the conflict also augmented Sinhala emigration from the island.

This volume attempts to do justice to the large number of men, women and children who have contributed over time to the development of the Sri Lankan diaspora, paying attention to the historical and political backgrounds that made the undertaking either desirable or essential. Whatever the reasons, the richness of the culture from which the diaspora has evolved has benefited us all.

Peter Reeves

THE CONTEXT

Parts I–III of the encyclopedia contextualises the basis for understanding the development, character and functioning of the Sri Lankan diaspora. It does this through an overview of the historical formation of Sri Lankan society in the classical, colonial and postcolonial periods; and an account of key aspects of life in the diaspora such as cuisine, sport, popular culture, religion, entrepreneurship and literature.

This turn of the 20th century photograph depicts a ship docked at the Borneo wharf of the Tanjong Pagar dock in Singapore—at the time the main disembarkation point for Sri Lankan emigrants to the island. Many Sri Lankans came to be employed at the Tanjong Pagar railway station, which was constructed adjacent to the dock in 1932.

View of the Wharf

THE SRI LANKAN CONTEXT

The Sri Lankan diaspora is the product of several journeys. Long before the advent of colonial rule, Buddhist monks and nuns who crossed the Bay of Bengal influenced religious developments in Southeast Asia. In the 19th and early 20th centuries, large numbers of educated Sri Lankan personnel were procured to develop the frontiers of the British Empire. While the flow of professionals continued well after Sri Lankan independence, new movements from the island emerged in the late 20th and early 21st centuries—of refugees escaping the civil war and of semi-skilled and unskilled labourers seeking economic opportunities abroad.

Wherever the people of the Sri Lankan diaspora settled, they have carried with them the social norms, cultural 'artefacts', religious traditions, ideas and values, political thought and ethical suppositions from their country of origin. An understanding of the Sri Lankan diaspora thus requires a sense of Sri Lanka—its history, peoples, values and politics.

SRI LANKA HAS a glorious ancient past noted for its technologically advanced irrigation system, the great city of Anuradhapura, and the preservation of Theravāda Buddhism. A cosmopolitan society located on the trade routes of the Indian Ocean, the island was well-known to Romans, Chinese and Arabs. Centuries of European colonialism shaped modern Sri Lankan society. British colonialism in particular created a prosperous plantation economy, from which emerged a wealthy Anglicised elite. Independence came to the colony without a struggle, and the elites who inherited power were unprepared to deal with the religio-ethnic differences that had been exacerbated under colonialism. Slow economic growth and majoritarian politics resulted in the spread of both Sinhala Buddhist nationalism and Tamil separatism. After 1983, twenty-six years of civil war appeared to create two de facto nations until the separatist Liberation Tigers of the Tamil Eelam (LTTE) was suppressed in 2009. Sri Lanka's economy is now growing, but political uncertainties continue.

HISTORICAL FORMATION AND PRE-COLONIAL DEVELOPMENT

A SINHALESE BUDDHIST kingdom flourished in the north-central plains, or 'Dry Zone', of Sri Lanka for more than a millennium. Large irrigation reservoirs and canals allowed intensive agricultural production and supported a large population. When the ancient civilisation declined, these deteriorated, and the former breadbasket depopulated. The population grew on the coasts and the rain-fed southwest (the 'Wet Zone'), enhanced by substantial migration, particularly from

The Vedda community were an indigenous, forest-dwelling people who practised traditional hunting and gathering. British colonial anthropologists fostered this image of scantily clad wild men.

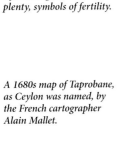

Nagas persisted in ancient Anuradhapura as pairs of guardians of Buddha at the foot of the stairs leading to the platform of a stupa (large domed reliquary). This nagaraja, or snake-deity, holds a flowering stem and a vase of plenty, symbols of fertility.

A 1680s map of Taprobane, as Ceylon was named, by the French cartographer Alain Mallet.

LEFT: *A wall fresco in Kandy depicts a Sri Lankan prince examining jewellery in his palace.*
RIGHT: *Stairs through the 'Lion's Paws' lead to ruins of a palace built by King Kassapa (CE 477–95) at the summit of the colossal rock formation of Sigiriya.*

South India. The people of Sri Lanka are grouped into a number of ethnic identities, which are rooted in the early history of the island but took their current form in the 19th and 20th centuries.

Early humans settled on the island (then connected to the mainland) at least 125,000 years ago. The oldest fossil remains of modern humans in South Asia have been dated to 36,000 BCE, and possibly earlier. These discoveries have influenced the idea that South Asia was initially settled by migrants from Africa along the coasts of the Indian Ocean rather than through the interior of the Middle East. Although the early population has been identified with the contemporary *Vädda* community, much of the population in the early historic period descended from these settlers.

Rising sea levels separated Sri Lanka from South India about 5000 BCE. Even then, people could cross the shallow gap near Mannar island or the string of islands west of the Jaffna Peninsula in the simplest waterborne craft. Early seafaring merchants probably sailed from the highly developed west coast of India. According to legend, they left trade goods on the shore, which were exchanged at night by the inhabitants. The major port, Mātoṭa (Sinhala Mantai and Tamil Mātōṭṭam) was on the northwest coast, opposite Mannar island. Sea traffic between western and eastern India passed by Mātoṭa because it was located near the deepest channel between Sri Lanka and India. The Gulf of Mannar was the source of Sri Lanka's major export—pearls. The island may also have exported gems, *chanks* (seashells used as money), elephants and later iron and copper. There were two other main ports: Jambukolapaṭṭana at the northern tip of the Jaffna Peninsula was the closest port to East and North India, and Gokaṇṇa was located on the great bay of Trincomalee on the east coast. Gokaṇṇa was near the sources of the copper mines at Seruwila.

There is some evidence of copper refining and pottery manufacture before the introduction of iron, but in general there seems to have been a rapid transition from the Mesolithic era (late Stone Age) to the Megalithic era (early Iron Age) in Sri Lanka. Early Iron Age sites in South India and Sri Lanka are associated with urn and cist burial sites from the 17th century BCE. Based on the large number of these sites, there was probably an urban settlement at Pomparippu near the mouth of the Kala Oya on the west coast. It is generally believed that the 'Nāgas' referred to in later literature point to these early iron users. The name Nāga continued to appear in the Anurādhapura kingdom in the names of rulers up to the 3rd century CE and of donors to the Buddhist monks in inscriptions.

Genetic evidence suggests that the people of Sri Lanka were physically similar to one another, distinct from the people of South India, but more closely related to them than to North Indians. Genetic studies so far are inconclusive, however. Despite its close connections with South India, the separation by sea enabled Sri Lanka to maintain a distinct culture. The dominant group on the island spoke a North Indian Prakrit, which became Sinhala, belonging to the Indo-Aryan language family rather than the Dravidian language family of South India. The Sinhala language, like Sinhalese kinship, caste and other institutions shows heavy Dravidian influence.

The legendary explanation for the North Indian cultural dominance is that the founder of the Sinhalese people, Prince Vijāya, was exiled from North India and settled in Sri Lanka. He first married a daughter of a local chief, then abandoned her to marry a princess from South India, where he found brides for his followers and craftsmen. According to legend, Vijāya's nephew arrived from India to establish the dynasty based in Anurādhapura.

Archaeological evidence has shown that urban culture began well before the traditional dates of this putative founder. Prehistoric peoples migrated up the rivers of the Dry Zone to the site in the interior of north-central Sri Lanka where Anurādhapura is today. By 800 BCE the site of Anurādhapura covered 10 hectares; by 600 BCE it had spread over 50 hectares. The earliest records in the Brāhmī script, graffiti inscribed on pottery shards, have been found there and are dated to the 6th century BCE.

The Thuparama in Anuradhapura is one of the oldest stupas in the world. Sri Lankans believe that it enshrines the right collarbone of the Buddha.

Known as the Golden Temple of Dambulla, the Kandyan King Kirti Sri Raja Singha filled the cave temple with statues and paintings of the Buddha and his attendant deities.

Stone pillars in the ruins of Anuradhapura that suggest the grandeur of the city during its thousand-year history. These pillars are all that remain of the Loha Prasada (Brazen Palace, so-called because of its copper roof), believed to have been a monastery housing monks in nine stories of 100 rooms each.

The heavy soils, forests and tropical rainfall made agriculture difficult until iron tools were used in the clearing of forests and wet-rice cultivation was introduced. Anurādhapura was an ideal location for irrigated rice cultivation: gently sloping terrain, ample supplies of water from the monsoons and runoff from the mountains to the south, and rich nutrients in the soil—natural deposits of phosphate appear to have made the land exceptionally fertile. The introduction of rice cultivation was accompanied by the construction of many small-scale reservoirs. Later these were extended to take advantage of the favourable terrain until massive reservoirs supplied by technologically advanced canals and sluices watered the plain.

At some point before the 3rd century BCE the island became a favoured location for Buddhist, Jaina and Ājīvika ascetics. In particular, *bhikkhus* (monks), following the teachings of the Buddha (traditionally 563–483 BCE but probably later), sought *nirvana* (enlightenment, a release from the cycle of birth and rebirth and a cessation of any consciousness of self). Over the following centuries monks took up residence in *leṇa* (caves, often overhanging rocks) throughout the island. Local chieftains, immigrant traders and village leaders donated caves to the *sangha* (community of monks) and carved drip ledges to keep the caves dry. There are over 2,000 such caves, with 1300 Brāhmī inscriptions carved on them from the 3rd century BCE to the 2nd century CE.

Over time, monks formed into communities to transmit Buddha's teachings. The Chinese pilgrim Fa Hien claimed that the largest monastery, Abhayagirivihāra, consisted of 5,000 monks. Sri Lanka remained a centre of Buddhism when Buddhism was gradually absorbed into Hinduism on the continent.

Buddhist monks in Sri Lanka maintained a tradition of historiography that is unique in South Asia. The earliest surviving historical texts are two narratives, *Dīpavamsa* (4th century CE) and *Mahāvamsa* (5th century CE). Written in Pāli, the language of Buddhist scholarship, they provide the most complete histories of early Buddhism and the Sinhalese kingdom until about 300 CE. These and later chronicles are invaluable for Sri Lankan as well as Indian history, but the *Mahāvamsa* is also a partisan account that emphasises the Sinhalese community, the Mahāvihara *nikāya* (monastic order), the Theravāda school as practised by that order, and the relationship of the *sangha* with the kings.

The *Mahāvamsa* begins with magical accounts of the connections of Buddha with Sri Lanka and the origins of the Sinhalese kingdom. According to the

The Tooth Relic is housed in the shrine room of Sri Dalada Maligawa (The Temple of the Sacred Tooth Relic) in Kandy.

Mahāvamsa, the great Indian emperor Ashoka sent one of his many foreign missions to Sri Lanka in 250 BCE. It was led by his son Mahinda, who ordained monks who joined the Mahāvihara monastery established by King Devānampiyatissa. Ashoka's daughter brought a branch from the bodhi tree under which Buddha attained enlightenment; it took root within the Mahāvihara monastery, where it became a shrine and survives today. The *Mahāvamsa* claims that the doctrines brought to Sri Lanka were the authoritative decisions of a 'Third Council' summoned by Ashoka.

The Anurādhapura city-state extended its control over the centuries after Devānampiyatissa, as kingship passed between his successors and at least nine rulers identified as 'Damiḷa' (Tamils) by the *Mahāvamsa*. Anurādhapura was ideally located to control the long-distance trade. According to the chronicle, the island was divided into numerous principalities until it was unified by Duṭṭagāmiṇī (161–137 BCE). He defeated the Damiḷa (Tamil) Eḷāra (presumably of South Indian origin), who had ruled in Anurādhapura for 44 years. The succeeding centuries saw invasions from South India, provincial revolts and heterodox sects. The *Mahāvamsa* refers to these in passing, but in the absence of other accounts, the history remains unclear.

The Lambakanna dynasty founded by Vasabha (67–111 CE) brought stability; inscriptions suggest that no serious rivals challenged his authority and the kingdom seems to have been relatively peaceful and prosperous for nearly four centuries. Sri Lanka became part of a cultural and political region with Tamil Nadu and Kerala. By this time South India had passed through a cultural revolution known as the Sangam Age, and the Pāṇḍya kingdom at Madurai had become a regional power.

Buddhist monasteries became a source of strength for the kings, who patronised the *sangha*, built Buddhist monuments and venerated Buddhist relics, particularly the Tooth Relic (*daladā*), an object believed by Sri Lankan Buddhists to be a tooth of the Buddha. The monasteries administered widespread networks of village temples through extensive land holdings. The stability of this kingdom came to an end with an invasion from South India, after which Damiḷa kings ruled in Anurādhapura from 429 to 455.

Anurādhapura was a cosmopolitan city, visited by merchants and other travellers from Rome to China. In addition to huge and technologically advanced irrigation works, the city was filled with magnificent Buddhist architectures, particularly the great *stūpa* (domed reliquaries), some of the largest architectural monuments of the ancient world after the Egyptian pyramids. They

The ancient Hindu temple Nalanda Gedige was built some time between the 8th and 10th centuries, when the Pallavas were allies of the Anuradhapura kingdom.

have a circular base, and a hemispherical dome with a miniature railing on top. They were built of brick, sometimes covered with plaster and white paint, and often enlarged and restored by later kings. Texts refer also to palaces of wood and metal that have now disappeared.

The last phase in the history of the Anurādhapura kingdom coincides with the rise of strong kingdoms in South India. From the 7th century onwards, its international position declined from internal conflict, the shift of the Indian Ocean trade to new centres, and increased competition from South India. South India had a larger population base than Sri Lanka, and the growth of aggressive kingdoms there posed a threat to the security of the Sinhalese kingdom. Mānavarma, a Sinhalese prince unable to succeed to the throne, took power in 684 with the aid of a Pallava army, and his successors allied with the Pallavas against the Pāṇḍyas.

The Theravāda Buddhism of the *Mahāvamsa* faced competition within the network of South Indian kingdoms from other Buddhist doctrines and then Śaivism, which eventually prevailed on the mainland. The Sanskrit inscription of Sena I (833–853 CE), founder of the Okkāka dynasty, at the Jetavanā monastery dedicated a hall for the veneration of four major sectarian divisions of the Buddhist world. He was allied with the Pallavas, but Pāṇḍyas invaded Anurādhapura and forced him to flee to the south. The Pāṇḍyas sacked the kingdom, looted its treasures, forced Sena I to support Śaivism. His successors, however, enlisted the support of the Mahāvihāra doctrines (Theravāda) to strengthen their hold on the island kingdom and began to see themselves as Bodhisattvas (Buddhist saints). Sena I's son, Sena II, conquered Madurai while the Pāṇḍyas, who were threatened by the rising Cōḷas, returned the treasures and restored Buddhism. According to the Mahāvihāra version, Sena II supported Theravādins against the Sarvāstivādins and Lokottaravādins of the Abhayagiri and Jetavanā monasteries.

At the height of the Anurādhapura kingdom, an estimated four to seven million people lived in the northern Dry Zone, perhaps 90 per cent of the population of the island. By the 9th century there was some settlement in the lower valleys of the mountainous interior, and an increase of coconut cultivation along the eastern and southwestern coasts. Inscriptional evidence suggests that at this time, the population centres of the Sinhalese kingdom were moving to the southwest while Tamil settlements spread to the northern peninsula, the east coast, and in pockets within the kingdom. The area to the southwest of the core of the Anurādhapura kingdom

This bronze gilded figure of Tara (cast in Sri Lanka circa 8th century CE)—prominently displayed in the British Museum—is clear evidence of the presence of Mahayana Buddhism in Anuradhapura during that period. According to Buddhist mythology, the goddess Tara was the consort of Avalokiteshvara, the bodhisattva of compassion.

Ruvanvelisaya Dagoba in Anuradhapura, built by King Dutugemunu (circa 140 BCE), is renowned for its architectural qualities.

Founded in 10th century CE, the Nallur Kandasamy Temple in Jaffna once functioned as a fort. The shrine continues to be an important pilgrimage site for Sri Lankan Hindus.

The few thousand surviving Veddas are assimilating to modern society, but retain much of their unique culture. Some Veddas still act the role of primitive hunter-gatherers as a tourist attraction. Other than the traditional bow and arrow, this man dresses much like many other Sri Lankan villagers.

King Nissanka Malla (1187–96), of South Indian origin, recorded his exploits on a stone slab weighing 25 tonnes called the Gal-Pota (stone book), which is located in Polonnaruwa.

was administered by the heir to the throne and came to be known as Māyāraṭa in contrast to the Rājāraṭa, or king's division of the kingdom.

The Okkāka rulers of the 9th and 10th centuries promoted and regulated Buddhism. They had become a regional power and seemed to try to restore Buddhism on the continent in the 10th and 11th centuries through military expeditions and Buddhist missionaries. The threat of invasion from the South Indian kingdoms was ever present, however, particularly as the imperialist Cōḷas defeated the Pallavas and drove the Sinhalese and Pāṇḍyas into a defensive alliance. When the Cōḷas strengthened, the Sri Lankan alliance with the Pāṇḍyas strengthened. When the Rāṣṭrakūtas attacked the Cōḷas from the north, the Sinhalas allied with them.

Early in the 10th century, the Cōḷas occupied the Pāṇḍyan capital at Madurai and the king took refuge in Sri Lanka. The Cōḷas invaded the island at least three times in the 10th century. During the last of these in 993, Mahinda V (982–1029 CE) abandoned Anurādhapura to the Cōḷas. The Cōḷas governed the heartland of the Anurādhapura kingdom as a province of the Cōḷa empire until 1070, when warfare elsewhere forced them to withdraw from the island.

Caste was an Indian institution brought to the island at an early period. It may have facilitated the spread of Sinhala and Buddhism by incorporating local communities into the new society, similar to the way Vedic culture appears to have done in North India. Groups became hereditary, endogamous, occupational castes (*jāti*), which would have been ranked into a hierarchy as they are today. There are mentions in the literature of the Indian division of society into the four *varna* categories of *brahman*, *kshatriya* (rulers), *vaisya* (merchants) and *sudra* (labourers) but with the influence of Buddhist ideas, their hold was limited. Sri Lankan kings, like Indian kings, claimed the status of the *kshatriya* royal caste, but the few Brahmins were unable to enforce the *varna* system. There are also references to 'untouchables,' people outside the *varna*s, called *caṇḍalā*, but they do not appear to have ever been included in the sizable numbers they do in India.

Sri Lanka's caste system evolved much like South India's, with a broad distinction between higher (*kulina*) and lower (*hina*) castes. The large cultivating caste (*govigama* in Sinhala and *veḷḷāḷa* in Tamil) was considered the highest caste. People owed the king compulsory labour service (*rājakāriya*) based on caste obligations. This service probably provided the labour for the construction of irrigation works.

The Cōḷas moved the capital from Anurādhapura 100 kilometres southeast to Poḷonnaruwa. In spite of the construction of monumental architecture and massive irrigation works in the 11th and 12th centuries, Poḷonnaruwa appears not to have been a major population centre. Unlike Anurādhapura, the ruins are close together, as they would have been in a primarily ceremonial centre. Moreover, the territory to the south and east of the capital is infertile and apparently, *Vädda* hunter-gatherers inhabited the area then, as they do now. The Cōḷas promoted Saivite Hinduism, which continued to influence Sri Lankan religious practices.

The Cōḷas ruled from Poḷonnaruwa for most of the 11th century until Vijayabāhu I (1055–1110) restored a Sinhalese monarchy. He was consecrated at Anurādhapura, but made Poḷonnaruwa his capital. After his death, Rohaṇa and Māyāraṭa became independent of Rājāraṭa, although acknowledging the supremacy of the Poḷonnaruwa king. Parākramabāhu I (1153–86), who originally ruled Māyāraṭa, subdued Rohaṇa after succeeding to the Poḷonnaruwa throne, and thereafter ruled the two regions directly, rather than through governors.

Sinhalese Buddhist culture flourished under Parākramabāhu I. The earliest surviving Sinhalese literature dates from this period, and Parākramabāhu and his successors reorganised the *sangha* on lines much as it is today, patronising Theravāda Buddhism. The Poḷonnaruwa kingdom maintained an alliance with the Pāṇḍyas against the Cōḷas until the end of the 12th century, when Parākramabāhu invaded the Pāṇḍyan kingdom. Although the *Cūlavamsa*, a continuation of the *Mahāvamsa*, claims unbroken victories in South India, it is clear from South Indian records that the war ended in defeat and a Pāṇḍyan invasion of Sri Lanka. Parākramabāhu I also raided the coasts of Burma. Parākramabāhu I and Nissanka Malla both invaded South India, allied with other enemies of the Cōḷas.

The Poḷonnaruwa era came to an end after the invasions of a series of adventurers who pillaged the countryside without restoring order. The *Cūlavamsa* singles out Māgha of Kalinga (1215–55) for cruelty and

The 7-metre standing Buddha is the oldest sculpture at the Gal Vihara, and the 14-metre reclining Buddha is the most superbly carved of the group—an image copied in many Buddhist temples in Sri Lanka.

oppression, accusing him of forcing people to convert to Hinduism. A Damiḷa king, Jayabāhu, ruled the northern Rājaraṭa in alliance with Māgha. A deposed Buddhist Malay king, Chandrabhānu, raised an army in India in 1247 and demanded to be given the kingdom's Buddhist relics, clearly hoping to use them to establish his legitimacy. He appears to have succeeded Māgha in the north of the island as the dominant figure and to have been followed by Pāṇḍyan overlordship.

Sinhalese rulers abandoned the Rājaraṭa in the 13th century. The Rājaraṭa fell into the hands of chieftains known as *vanniyā*. They held local power in the Rājaraṭa in the 13th and 14th centuries, entering into feudal relations with the conqueror of the day. There were both Sinhalese and Tamil *vanniyā* chieftains in the Rājaraṭa, although ethnic identity was certainly less important than it became in the Sinhalese and Tamil kingdoms that emerged outside the area. Vanni has come to mean the name for the Dry Zone as a whole.

Foreign invasions may have been more a result of the decline of the Dry Zone civilisation than a cause of it. Parākramabāhu's administration was more centralised than in previous centuries, and local institutions that maintained and repaired reservoirs and canals may have deteriorated. Inscriptions show that the weak rulers after Parākramabāhu I attempted ineffectually to repair irrigation works. Other factors may have affected the irrigation system, such as global climate change (the 'medieval warm period', when world temperatures rose) and the long-term effects of deforestation. At some point malaria made the Rājaraṭa virtually uninhabitable until recent times.

Sinhalese principalities arose in Māyāraṭa and Rohaōa. They built fortresses (*giri durga*) in locations where high rock formations gave the rulers a vantage point, such as Yāpahuva, Dambadeniya, and Kurunägala. New invasions, administrative collapse, endemic malaria and perhaps climatic change appear to have destroyed the irrigation system and brought about a precipitous

decline in the population. Inscriptions suggest that Tamils had also taken control of small territories.

A Sinhalese monarchy was restored by the short-lived dynasty that ruled at Dambadeniya, 75 miles southwest of Polonnaruwa. Parākramabāhu II (1236–70) is the hero of one section of the *Cūlavamsa*, which devotes eight chapters to his career. He seems to have been a chieftain of South Indian origin in the Vanni where he built up a following. With no strong hereditary claim to the monarchy, he established himself as a patron of Buddhism to win support from the *sangha*. The histories say he built a temple for the Tooth Relic and Alms Bowl Relic, which had become potent symbols of the Sinhalese-Buddhist state, repaired monasteries, founded new *vihāra*s, reformed the *sangha*, and promoted learning.

The Nelum Pokuna (Lotus bath)—an exquisitely designed stone bath built in tiers of eight-petalled lotuses—is one of the few remaining sites of the Jetavana monastery at the northern edge of Polonnaruwa.

Parakramabahu I built the magnificent Polonnaruwa vatadage (circular relic house) to hold the Tooth Relic. The main entrance is ornately carved with nagaraja *guard stones, a moonstone threshold with bands of animals, rows of dwarfs, and flowers.*

Parakramabahu I built the unusual Lankatilaka (ornament of Lanka) north of the city of Polonnaruwa.

Stone anchors dating back to the 13th century were used by Arab ships that visited the port of Galle at that time, when there was a large Arab population in Sri Lanka.

The death of Māgha and the defeat of Chandrabhānu enabled Parākramabāhu to extend his territorial control over the Vanni chieftains, and eventually reoccupied Anurādhapura and Poḷonnaruwa. He strengthened the link between the Dambadeṇiya kingdom and ancient Sri Lanka by performing a consecration ritual in Poḷonnaruwa in 1262. He restored villages to the *sangha* that Māgha had confiscated and enjoyed a period of relative peace. Although he does not seem to have remained long in Poḷonnaruwa—a hoard of buried Chinese coins with the later date of 1265 may signal the end of his occupation—the histories say he repaired its buildings, and returned the Tooth Relic. His long reign did not restore Poḷonnaruwa to its previous glory, but it enabled his kingdom to claim a magnificent heritage, one appropriated by subsequent rulers.

After the 13th century, the division between the Sinhala-speaking regions and the Tamil-speaking north and east became stronger. There is little evidence of migration within Sri Lanka during this period, and the shift in the population seems to have been brought about primarily by the natural increase of the population and immigration from South India and their assimilation to the two cultures.

Migration from South India was driven by many factors. The spread of Hinduism compelled some Buddhists and Jains to emigrate; drought and famine drove people to the island, as they continued to do into the 12th century; the opening of new lands in the interior of the Wet Zone invited cultivators; mariners from small ports along the east and west coasts of South India participated in the vigorous Indian Ocean trade from Sri Lanka; and political disunity encouraged adventurers and their retinues to seek their fortunes there. Some new settlers were organised into gangs of labourers

under the leadership of foremen or *kanganis*. These eventually became a regular part of Sinhalese society, as Low Country Sinhalese castes divided into caste grades along occupational lines.

With the exception of Parākramabāhu VI (1411–66), Sinhalese kings were only the strongest among several competitors. Parākramabāhu IV (1302–26) presided over a literary revival before the dynasty ended a few years later. Sinhalese rulers became little more than warring chieftains, and the kingdom at Jaffna was the only strong kingdom in the latter 14th century. Bhuvanekabāhu IV (1341–51) built his capital in the Kandyan hills at Gampola. His reign is notable for the construction of the important temples at Laṅkātilaka and Gadalādeniya, which show both the attempt to recapture the grandeur of Poḷonnaruwa and also the religious and architectural influence of South India. Another ruler, Parākramabāhu V (1344–59) ruled less than 30 miles away in Dādigama. He may have been Bhuvanekabāhu IV's son, and he succeeded him at Gampola.

Life in the new population centres of the southwest differed greatly from ancient society. Cultivators faced poorer soils, heavy but uncertain rainfall and hilly terrain. The Sinhalese peasant learned to terrace steeply sloping fields and plant tree crops and 'dry grains' such as millet (*kurakkan*) where rice would not grow well; unirrigated rice culture was supplemented by shifting cultivation (*chēna*). Coconut cultivation was extended, and coconut became the main source of vegetable oil in place of sesame seed oil. Internal trade and the circulation of money decreased as productivity declined. Communication became difficult in the tropical rainforest; cities were reduced to local market towns.

The Indian Ocean trade flourished during this period, and Sri Lanka had

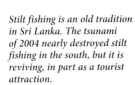

Stilt fishing is an old tradition in Sri Lanka. The tsunami of 2004 nearly destroyed stilt fishing in the south, but it is reviving, in part as a tourist attraction.

become an important link in it by the 14th century. Cinnamon was the island's major export, along with other spices, arecanuts, gemstones and elephants. Colombo and Galle (where the Chinese inscribed a trilingual inscription in 1411 in Chinese, Persian and Tamil) were ports for external trade. Smaller ports engaged in coastal trade between India and Sri Lanka. The island imported rice, sugar, textiles and spices.

The new immigrants brought new elements into Sri Lankan culture. On the east coast, matrilineal kinship is the result of migrations from Kerala. Hindu deities such as Vishnu and Pattini became part of Sinhalese worship, sometimes as Bodhisattvas. Three new Sinhalese castes found only on the southwest coast—*karāva*, *salāgama*, and *durāva*—came into existence. The *karāva* (like their Jaffna Tamil counterparts, the *kariyār*) came to be associated with fishing. The *salāgama*, apparently originating with the Tamil *chālia* caste, were drafted into the growing cinnamon export industry. All three castes have origin myths which recognise their Indian origins, but also attempt to connect the modern castes with the ancient civilisation.

The most important merchants were Muslims, who did not convert to Buddhism or Hinduism. Arab traders had come to the island from about the 10th century. Muslim settlements on the southwest coast of India had become the centre of the Indian Ocean trade in the 13th century, and Muslim colonies at Colombo, Pānadura, Beruwala and Hambantota connected the island to this trade. The traveller Ibn Battuta mentions a Muslim ruler at Kurunāgala in 1344 who claimed to be the principal ruler of the island. Legend says that this ruler, Vathimi Raja, was the son of Bhuvanekabāhu I by the daughter of a Muslim chieftain.

Rulers no longer had the land revenue made possible by rice surpluses. Kings increasingly depended on universal compulsory service (*rājakāriya*) to cultivate royal land, pay officials, maintain public works and supply trade goods. External trade became a royal monopoly and a major source of revenue. Kings dealt directly with seafaring merchants, which discouraged the development of local trade.

The Pāndyans dominated the north of Sri Lanka as they did the south in the second half of the 13th century under Jatavarman Sundara Pāndya (1251–72). Their fortunes declined in the early 14th century, which enabled the Tamil rulers of the north to establish their independence. A Pāndyan general called Āryachakravarti led an invasion about the year 1284. He may have remained in northern Sri Lanka following the invasion,

and he or a family member declared their independence as the Pāndyas declined. Sinhalese texts of the 13th and 14th centuries refer to the King of Jaffna by the same title.

A later Tamil text, the *Yālppānavaipavamālai*, suggests that the *vellāla* caste played a central role in the creation of a Tamil state. The kings brought colonists from South India—Brahman priests, *vellāla* administrators, and the 'eighteen *kuñis*'—castes that were subordinate to the *vellāla*. Subordinates, *vellāla añikars*, or chieftains, advised the king. The *Yālppānavaipavamālai* emphasises that the kings had both Tamil and Sinhalese subjects, the latter sometimes rebellious. Vanni chieftains paid tribute to the Āryachakravartis, continuing the feudal relations they maintained with previous rulers.

Ibn Battuta visited the Jaffna Kingdom in 1344. The king had a large merchant fleet and was heavily involved in the export of cinnamon—which may have been the reason for his aggressive intentions toward the southwest coast. Mārttānta Cinkaiyāriyan appears to have levied tribute from Vikramabāhu III (1356–74) of Gampola in 1359, collected customs duties in the Rājarata, and established military bases along the west coast as far south as Colombo, taking advantage of dynastic disputes among the Sinhalese. They met sterner resistance, however, from the de facto ruler of the west coast, Nissanka Alagakkōnāra. The Hindu kingdom of Vijayanagara claimed sovereignty over the Āryachakravartis in 1385 and may have assisted them to invade the Sinhalese kingdom.

By the latter part of the 14th century, ministers of South Indian origin became the major power brokers in Southwestern Sri Lanka. South Indian immigrants had come to the island in substantial numbers during the previous two centuries. One of them, Sēnalankādikāra, was adviser to Parākramabāhu V and Vikramabāhu III, a nephew of Bhuvanekabāhu IV who ruled at Peradeniya. The Alagakkōnāra family were originally merchants from Kerala who had settled in Rayigama near the coastal ports. They had become so rich and powerful that Ibn Battuta mistakenly identified the Alagakkōnāra as the principal rulers on the island. Nissanka Alagakkōnāra, reportedly the tenth in succession as head of the family, married the sister of Parākramabāhu V and later succeeded Sēnalankādikāra as the chief adviser to Vikramabāhu III. He lived at Peradeniya with his patron, and continued to advise his successor Bhuvanekabāhu V (1374–1408), who may have been a member of the same family.

Patrick Peebles

Sri Lanka is a major exporter of cinnamon. This sketch shows cinnamon barks peeled by a caste for whom it was a hereditary duty.

This 1409 CE slab in three different languages—Persian, Chinese and Tamil—was brought to Sri Lanka from China by Admiral Zheng He. The slab was discovered in Galle around 1911.

Dedicated to the deity Skanda-Murugan, the Kataragama Temple in southeastern Sri Lanka is a multi-religious site.

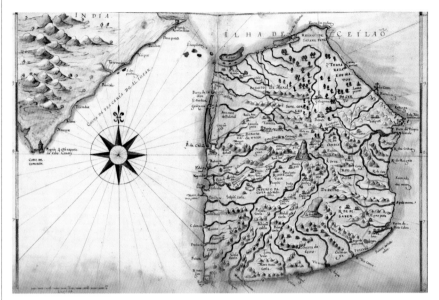

Portuguese Map of Ceylon (circa 1630).

AN
Historical Relation
Of the Island
CEYLON,
IN THE
EAST-INDIES:
TOGETHER,
With an ACCOUNT of the Detaining
in Captivity the AUTHOR and divers other
Englishmen now Living there, and of the
AUTHOR'S Miraculous ESCAPE.

Illustrated with Figures, and a Map of the ISLAND.

By ROBERT KNOX, a Captive there
near Twenty Years.

LONDON,
Printed by *Richard Chiswell*, Printer to the
ROYAL SOCIETY, at the *Rose* and *Crown* in
St. *Paul's* Church-yard, 1681.

English sailor Robert Knox (1641–1720) wrote an account of his experiences in Ceylon.

COLONIAL DEVELOPMENT

THE EUROPEAN COLONIAL impact was deeper in Sri Lanka than in any other country in South Asia, largely because a significant part of the country was under colonial rule for three and a half centuries. The colonial impact laid the foundations for the Sri Lankan diaspora in the post-colonial era. Prolonged resistance to colonial dominance also led to modifications of indigenous traditions and practices, and major changes in its economy.

THE COLONIAL CONQUEST: THE PORTUGUESE, THE DUTCH AND THE BRITISH

Sri Lanka's first contact with a colonial power came in the early 16th century. The Portuguese, who sought to control trade in the Indian Ocean, established a presence in Colombo and, almost immediately, began to involve themselves in Sri Lanka's internal political conflicts. Efforts to convert indigenous peoples to Roman Catholicism accelerated in the 1540s, but met with limited success until the end of the century. Portuguese control over the coastal plains of Southwest Sri Lanka lasted for about 60 years after the collapse of the kingdoms of Kotte and Sitawaka and their rule over the north, after the conquest of the kingdom of Jaffna in 1621, was limited to less than 40 years. Moreover, Portuguese control of almost a third of the country was challenged from time to time by rebellions and by the kingdom of Kandy. Nevertheless, the Portuguese socio-economic impact was substantial.

The Dutch East India Company came to Sri Lanka as allies of the ruler of Kandy, the only independent kingdom of Sri Lanka which survived the Portuguese onslaught. The joint forces of the allies drove out the Portuguese in a series of campaigns between 1638 and 1658. Thereafter, the Dutch set themselves up as rulers of the coastal areas until they were ousted by the British in a brief campaign. The Dutch faced occasional uprisings but they managed to keep the peace with the kingdom of Kandy, except for two brief periods of conflict in the 1660s and the 1760s.

British interest in Sri Lanka stemmed partly from the need for a good natural harbour for the British fleet in the Indian Ocean (which Trincomalee, on the east coast of Sri Lanka, provided). Between 1796–98, during the French Revolutionary Wars, the English East India Company provided the forces which took over the Dutch possessions in Sri Lanka after token resistance. After some experimentation in sharing administrative control of Sri Lanka with the Company from 1796 to 1802, the British Government converted Sri Lanka to a Crown Colony, administered directly from London. In 1815, the British, profiting from internal divisions within Kandy, invaded that kingdom and deposed its king. The Kandyan chieftains accepted British rule by signing a convention in which the British promised to preserve the laws and institutions of the kingdom. Three years later, in 1818, some of the chiefs rose in rebellion. That attempt at challenging colonial authority was crushed. From then on, the interior of the country became increasingly exposed to colonial impact.

RESISTANCE AND ADAPTATION

Changes during this period also emerged both through resistance and adaptation to the colonial impact as well as due to autonomous indigenous developments. A good example of the latter was the spread of the cultivation of coconut as a garden crop throughout the southwestern plains, though its emergence as a plantation crop in the 19th century was partly due to changes brought about by British rule. Resistance also reformulated indigenous identities. For instance, Portuguese attacks on Buddhist monks and institutions led to a stronger identification of Buddhism with indigenous rule and left a tradition that identified Christianity with colonial dominance.

ECONOMIC CHANGES

Portuguese rule in the coastal areas marked the emergence of a 'colonial economy' under which the state became more dependent on revenue from the export of agricultural products, cinnamon and elephants than on land revenue. This change and destruction due to frequent warfare led to a decline in population and in agricultural production, which was reversed only in the long period of peace after the 1660s. Dutch rule in coastal areas contributed to the continued monetisation of the economy, partly because of their somewhat fitful encouragement of new commercial garden crops such as coffee and tobacco, and also the successful cultivation of cinnamon (formerly harvested from the jungle) enabled them to relax restrictions on land settlement. The major economic changes came in the 19th century. The British constructed a network of roads to the interior and encouraged the cultivation of cash crops especially from the 1830s. Coffee became Sri Lanka's major export in the 1840s and retained that position till it was devastated

Copper engraving of the Town of Colombo from a Dutch book (circa 1775) after the original engraving by Johannes Kip in 1680.

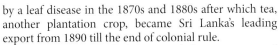

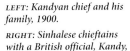

by a leaf disease in the 1870s and 1880s after which tea, another plantation crop, became Sri Lanka's leading export from 1890 till the end of colonial rule.

The emergence of plantations led to a continued expansion of the road network and the construction of a railway from the port of Colombo to Kandy (completed in 1867). The extension of road and rail connections led to greater mobility. One of the effects of the improvement in transportation was to increase pilgrimage travel. This also encouraged further commercialisation. The social impact of these changes was profound.

Coffee plantations were modelled after those of the West Indies, on which Tamil workers from South India replaced slave labour when the Kandyans rejected plantation labour. Labour gangs were brought by *kanganies*, who were foremen as well as recruiters. The immigrant workforce grew steadily. The labour demand increased with the ascendancy of tea, which involved harvesting the leaves throughout the year. Tamil residents in plantations grew to almost a quarter million by 1891 and to over 750,000 (or 14.5 per cent of the population of Sri Lanka) in 1931. Continued immigration from India during this period raised concerns among the indigenous Sinhala population in the highlands, who feared that they would become an impoverished minority with limited land for agricultural use. This had an impact on political tensions during and after the transition from British rule.

RELIGION

Colonial rule also had a profound impact on the religious mosaic of Sri Lanka. At the beginning of colonial rule, the majority of the people in Sri Lanka saw themselves as followers of the teachings of the Buddha while most of the people in the north were devotees of Siva (and other gods). In addition, there were a few Muslims, mostly traders living in the ports. The introduction of a militant form of Roman Catholicism by the Portuguese and the confiscation of temple lands seems to have increased religious

consciousness among non-Christian religious groups. Muslims, expelled from Portuguese territories in 1626, mostly took refuge in the Buddhist kingdom of Kandy. By the 1630s, Roman Catholic Christianity had been accepted by at least half the people living under Portuguese rule, but these numbers fell steeply after the ascendency of the Dutch, who forbade Roman Catholic services in their territory. Subsequently, Buddhist Kandy provided a safe-house for Roman Catholic missionary priests, but it was only in the 19th century under a more tolerant British regime that Roman Catholic Christianity revived substantially. At independence, the vast majority of Christians in Sri Lanka (just over 9 per cent of the total population) were Roman Catholics because few were converted to Calvinist Christianity propagated by the Dutch, or to Anglican Christianity favoured by the British.

Religious change during the colonial period was not simply in the introduction of various versions of Christianity but in perceptions of religious identity. Buddhist identity became the focus of resistance to colonialism led by the kingdom of Kandy up to 1815. Consequently, the nationalist movement among the Sinhalese increasingly took on Buddhist concepts and imagery. The use of newspapers and journals to advocate Buddhist causes and values, the establishment of western-style Buddhist schools and eventually, the emergence of plays and novels with Buddhist themes, led to the strengthening of a Sinhalese-Buddhist identity among the majority group (Sinhala Buddhists were 64.5 per cent of the population in 1946). Christian attacks on Buddhism as 'heathen' led to an emphasis on the more rational elements of Buddhist teachings. A series of public debates between Christians and Buddhists, the establishment of two centres of oriental learning, the support by members of the Theosophical Society of America (which was critical of Christianity) and the increase in the currency of Buddhist

LEFT: Kandyan chief and his family, 1900.

RIGHT: Sinhalese chieftains with a British official, Kandy, 1880.

The entrance to the Star Fort in the southern town of Matara showcasing the Dutch VOC emblem.

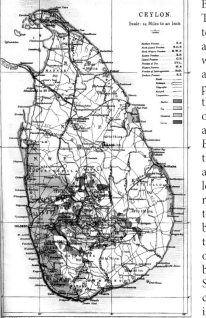

An early 20th century map of areas in Ceylon with tea, rubber, cocoa and coconut plantations.

LEFT: *Ceylonese Christian clergymen during the colonial period.*

RIGHT: *The British played a key role in the development of railways in Ceylon. This 1905 postcard depicts a scene of the Ceylonese government railways.*

The St Lucia Cathedral in Colombo is one of the oldest Parish cathedrals in Sri Lanka.

newspapers and books marked a greater self-awareness of identity among Sinhalese Buddhists that grew from the 1860s to the 1880s. The establishment of Buddhist schools and the development of a temperance movement continued a trend towards criticising Christian and Western values. The rise in Hindu consciousness started even earlier, but was more internally focused in terms of strengthening indigenous religious values through education. The Muslim revival took a similar turn but occurred later and was more limited in scope. The significance of these changes included the growth of an anti-colonial nationalist movement as well as the strengthening of religio-ethnic identities that would continue to divide Sri Lankans in the 20th century.

CASTE AND ETHNICITY

Existing ethnic identities had been reinforced by the British practice of using ethnicity as a means of political representation for a century prior to 1931. They were also strengthened by colonial censuses and forms that forced individuals to make choices relating to their ethnic identity. However, throughout the colonial period, ethnic identity was modified by both caste and class. The traditional dominant caste in pre-colonial Sri Lanka had been the farmer/landholder caste (the Sinhalese *govigama* and the Tamil *vellala*) although other caste

groups had gained influence in certain localities. The conversion of fishermen (Sinhalese *karava* and Tamil *karaiyar*) to Christianity and their exposure to Western values provided them with opportunities for economic progress, and by the late 19th century the *karava* were challenging *govigama* claims to primacy. A similar effort to improve their social position came from the Sinhalese *salagama* (cinnamon-peeler) caste. The Portuguese and Dutch had recognised traditional caste distinctions when it was convenient to them (for example, requiring all of the *salagama* to peel cinnamon) but the British, after initially accepting caste distinctions in government appointments, began to move away from that policy. Thus, for example, after 1843, caste distinctions were disregarded in jury selection. The efforts of the dominant castes to enforce distinctions in dress collapsed with time. However, caste remained important, especially because marriage continued to be within each caste. Among the Sinhalese, caste disputes became muted after universal franchise enabled the *govigama* to use their numbers to reassert dominance. The Tamil *vellala*, who did not face as strong a challenge from other castes continued to deny entry to Hindu temples to the 'outcaste' groups up to the end of colonial rule.

European settlers in Sri Lanka were few but they were influential throughout the colonial era. Portuguese male

LEFT: *Artistic impression of Sinhalese chiefs and their spouses, Kandy, 1880.*

RIGHT: *Antique hand-coloured print of Jaffnese women in their finest traditional clothing.*

settlers generally lived near ports and often inter-married with indigenous women. Some of them continued to live in Sri Lanka after the end of Portuguese rule and eventually merged into the local population. Dutch settlers, generally known as Dutch Burghers, tried to maintain their ethnic identity and after the end of Dutch rule, adapted themselves by learning English and dominated the medical and legal professions for much of the 19th century. It was the improvement of education facilities in the 20th century that diminished their relative dominance in these fields.

Social changes during colonial times also included the emergence of a wealthy indigenous elite. This group gained wealth through participation in coconut and rubber plantations, supply and transport contracts, and the mining of gems and graphite. Many of the second generation acquired an education and some entered the professions. This group became an influential westernised elite group that captured the leadership of the nationalist movement despite a degree of alienation from indigenous values. One of the major achievements of the elite in the last two decades of colonial rule was the further development of an effective system of state health care that dramatically reduced infant and maternal mortality rates, leading to rapid population growth by the mid-20th century. This was accompanied by a number of other welfare measures that included subsidies for basic food items (1943), a free mid-day meal for poor school children and free milk for infants and expectant mothers. These measures helped to moderate the impact of inflation during World War II and in its aftermath.

CHANGES IN EDUCATION

Sri Lanka's system of Buddhist monastic education suffered under colonial rule due to wars and the lack of state patronage, although there were revivals of monastic scholarship in the Kandyan kingdom in the 18th century and in the southwest in the late 19th century. British patronage of a reformed system of monastic education

An 1879 photograph of Buddhist monks conducting a prayer.

facilitated the development of some Buddhist tertiary educational institutions in the 20th century. However, the major transformation in the educational sphere came with the development of western-style schools. Early schools of this type were run by missionaries who mostly wished to enable converts to read the scriptures.

Changes were introduced under the British in the mid-19th century when, apart from setting up a few state schools, the colonial government began to provide regular financial assistance to missionary organisations that established schools. Most of these schools taught in local languages and much of the development came in the 20th century when literacy rates rose from 26.4 per cent in 1901 to 57.8 per cent in 1946. Literacy in English, however, was just over 3 per cent in 1901 and about 6 per cent in 1946. This meant that access to the more lucrative professions was limited to a small proportion of the population, most of whom were from urban centres and disproportionately Christian.

In the last few years before independence, with elected Sri Lankan politicians sharing power with the British, the state established new secondary schools offering instruction in English and also abolished tuition fees in

Precious metal work in Ratnapura (circa 1900–1920).

THE CHETTIES OF SRI LANKA

The Chetties are a relatively small community, numbering approximately 175,000, most of whom live in the western, north-western and southern provinces of Sri Lanka. According to the 1824 Ceylon Census, of a total population of 851,940, Chetties numbered 8,471. In 1871, however, the census showed that the Chetty number was down to 3,114. That decline was largely due to assimilation with the other major communities of Sri Lanka. For a long time after that, Sri Lankan census exercises tended to include the Chetties into the Sinhala, Tamil and Burgher populations. It was only from the 2001 Sri Lankan census that the Chetties have come to be enumerated as a separate and distinct ethnic group.

The term Chetty is referred to as *setti* or *setthi* in Pali; *hetti, situ* or *sitana* in Sinhalese; and as *etti* in Tamil. Said to be of Tana *vaisya* trading caste, which inhabited areas in and close to Coorg and Benares in India, many purportedly moved to Southern India following the Muslim invasion of the north. Over time the Chetties commenced trade with Lanka and this eventually gave rise to large scale immigration. As wealthy traders, they were able to establish deep connections to the

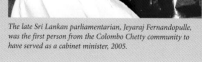

The late Sri Lankan parliamentarian, Jeyaraj Fernandopulle, was the first person from the Colombo Chetty community to have served as a cabinet minister, 2005.

Sinhala and Tamil nobility. Their movement from Southern India to the island continued well into the Portuguese and Dutch periods, and they were also able to forge close ties with the colonial rulers.

Chetties are recognised for their immense contribution to the economic development of Sri Lanka. They were among the first importers and exporters of traditional and non-traditional goods, and are said to have pioneered teak plantations in Sri Lanka. Chetties have always played an important role in religious affairs. During the Portuguese and Dutch periods, many Chetties adopted Christianity, and financed the building of churches in Colombo, Thoppu, Veyangoda, Kelaniya and Nuwaraeliya.

Since 1983, many Chetties have emigrated from Sri Lanka to Australia, Canada and the United Kingdom. That movement was in part due to concerns over mistaken identity as many Chetties possessed Tamil sounding names. In recent times Chetties in Sri Lanka have moved from being merchants, financiers, bankers and land-owners to being professionals—lawyers, doctors, and accountants—who hold distinguished positions in the public and private sectors.

Shirley Pulle Tissera

THE BURGHERS OF CEYLON: THE HYBRID PEOPLE IN-BETWEEN

*The fair-skinned relics of colonial trespass,
eminently usable by the British.*

Sri Lankan writer Carl Muller

The Burghers are the racially mixed descendants of the Portuguese, Dutch and British colonialists who occupied old Ceylon for four and a half centuries. However, the identity of the Burgher and the definition of who has a right to claim membership in this clan are highly contested issues.

The Portuguese Period (1505 to 1658)
Miscegenation thrived under European rule. The early colonialists themselves were in fact ethnically heterogeneous. The poor of Europe and North Africa, eager to escape either the Inquisition or abject poverty, would take their chances on a rough voyage to the new world. This was almost exclusively a male adventure.

The descendants of 'mixed unions' between these colonial males and local women were called *Mechanics* or *Tupass*—often poor labourers and fisher folk. The increasing numbers of mixed race children did not reflect Portuguese racial tolerance or acceptance. And yet, while native Sri Lankans were deemed inferior, these mixed race people (*mestizo*) were given higher status and responsibility in the colonial system.

Notions of cultural and racial superiority become part of the complex, conflicted inheritance of Ceylon's Burgher minority. The colonial power believed that the mixture of European blood somehow 'improved and elevated' these people. This was echoed by many of the *mestizos* themselves in their general disdain for their native forebears and native culture. Portuguese

The wedding of Henrietta Edith (Rita) Robertson to Victor Percy Mervyn Marshall on 12 April 1947 in Colombo. Both were from railway families and the two young people met as their fathers were transferred around the country. The couple had five children, all born in Sri Lanka. The family migrated to Melbourne, Australia in 1966. All of their 14 siblings eventually migrated to Australia as well. The Marshall/Robertson clan now numbers well over 100 people.

Wolvendaal Church in Pettah, Colombo (circa 1860), is considered an important church for the Burgher community.

A 1956 photograph of the Rosario and Atton family taken at Kiribathgoda, Kelaniya.

Creole came to be adopted as the lingua franca of the *Tupass*, while Sinhalese and Tamil were eschewed.

The Dutch Period (1658 to 1796)
It was the Dutch who began to use the word Burghers (a Dutch descriptor for 'townsfolk', left over from feudal times) to describe the children of mixed unions.

Dutch colonial society existed under the umbrella of the powerful United Netherlands East India Company (VOC), run out of Batavia in Indonesia. Europeans were classified either as servants of the company (soldiers or merchants) or as 'free burghers' (*vrijburgers*) who were former servants of the company who had decided to marry locally and settle in the colony.

Within the general category of 'the Dutch' (*Hollandsche*) in Ceylon, distinctions were made between Europeans born in Europe, Europeans born in Ceylon and the 'mixties'—offspring of a European father and either a native or a *mestizo* mother—the latter group was easily the largest.

Amongst the Burghers there was a hierarchy established which sought to distinguish Burghers of Dutch descent from those of Portuguese descent. The 'Dutch Burghers' sought to trace their genealogy carefully and claimed special privileges for themselves ahead of their poorer, more numerous and darker skinned cousins. Under patriarchal laws, Burgher identity was exclusively determined by paternal descent, and social scientists such as Kumari Jayawardene have written eloquently about the 'erasure' of the Euro-Asian women from Burgher history.

In 1912, the Goan linguist Tavares de Mello noted that 'It has become fashionable in Ceylon for all the Burghers... to have Dutch ancestors of whom, with rare exceptions, they don't possess the name, colour or even the language.' Of course not all Burghers supported making these racial distinctions. Responses from others in the middle class were even more cutting and the production of satirical poems and limericks expressed this resentment. Here is a poem by lawyer Edmund de Livera, 'Dutch Burgher' penned in 1908:

> *All the people you know – all the people you see*
> *Aren't Burgher you know – Dutch Burgher you know*
> *The Tamil, Mechanic, Malay, Cingalee*
> *Aren't Burgher – Dutch Burgher, you know.*
> *But born in this Island are some with a touch*
> *Of a dram or a teaspoon of blood that is Dutch –*
> *'Tis a hard thing to tell you – how little, how much*
> *They're Burgher, Dutch Burgher, you know.*

Yet for all this noise and self-importance, the Burghers as a whole have never exceeded even

1 per cent of the island's population, and the proportion of Burghers with a fully documented Dutch pedigree was only a tiny fraction of that.

The English Period (1796 to 1947)
Under the British administration, missionary school education was favoured by Burgher parents who saw the link between a good education and safe employment in the developing public services. The British too saw great value in employing this hybrid community that acted as a buffer between them and the indigenous population.

The Burghers had developed their own hybrid culture and cuisine. Instilled with Western concepts of civic responsibility, they could contribute to the capitalistic development of the colonial society. They soon adopted English as their language, many became Anglicised and over time, they eagerly embraced English culture and traditions.

Burgher workers administered the railways, police departments and the courts. They were the ubiquitous clerks. By the 1850s, they formed a majority of the rising middle class in all the towns in Ceylon and held important positions in the administration. Increasingly they saw themselves as a Westernised elite and the heirs apparent to the British. A counterpoint to this elitism was evident amongst some Burghers with spokesmen such as C. A. Lorenz writing patriotically about 'us Ceylonese', joining the Burgher and the natives under one umbrella.

The racism at the heart of British exclusiveness was, however, practised in turn by many Burghers. Within the Burgher community the small, generally lighter skinned, Dutch Burgher elite, acquired their status and influence at the expense of their darker skinned cousins and the indigenous population. This arrogance elicited angry responses at times. Some in the native population began to regard the Burghers as 'outsiders'. The epithet '*suddo lansi karapotha*' (white Burgher cockroach) cast the Burghers as aliens compared to the true 'people of the soil'.

The appearance of the Dutch Burgher Union (DBU) in 1908 marked a turning point in the socio-political history of the Burgher people. In the 19th century, one seat in the Governor's legislative council had been reserved for a Burgher representative (invariably a Dutch Burgher). Leading up to the constitutional reforms of 1910, ethnic representation was set to become a matter of democratic choice within communal electorates. The DBU lobbied strongly for a restricted electorate to be comprised solely of the only 'true Burghers'—the Dutch Burghers. The request was denied, and from that point on the political and economic privileges of the Dutch Burghers was steadily

This picture (circa 1920) shows the pupils and teachers (mainly Dutch Burghers) of the Wolvendaal School which was part of the Dutch Reformed Church of Ceylon.

eroded by the democratic reforms and nationalist movements which led to independence in 1948.

Even by the 1920s, the Burghers were a fading force as the majority moved to the right of the political spectrum and into the political margins. There were concerns that the process of political devolution, which was on the horizon, would further weaken their position. These fears were heightened with the arrival of the universal franchise in 1931 which confirmed their minority status. The Burghers' fear was not just ethnically specific; it was part of a general fear amongst the privileged conservative faction of the middle class that the country would swing to the Left.

The Post-Independence Period: Exodus after 1956

The sudden death of the first Prime Minister D. S. Senanayake in 1952, followed closely by the emergence of the Sri Lanka Freedom Party (SLFP) as an agent of Sinhala Buddhist nationalism, confirmed the fears of many Burghers about their lack of status and influence in the new dispensation. The death knell came in 1956 with the massive political victory of Bandaranaike, and the passage of the Official Language Act which made Sinhala the only official language of the island. This was not just a victory of linguistic nationalism, it was also a victory of the 'brown sahibs' against the Anglophile elite.

English was not maintained even as a link language and the Burgher community felt severely disadvantaged. They lost their social status, employment opportunities and their privileges. Most importantly, it struck at their children's birth right to this same privileged position. Now the exodus began in earnest with Australia as the preferred destination for the majority.

Diaspora

In Australia, over the past 50 years since the great exodus began, the Burgher diaspora's love story with old Ceylon—the dream state of a Garden of Eden—continues. There still exist many Sri Lanka-Australia Associations and the evocative identity markers of old boys' and old girls' school associations. Burgher

Members of the Roberton family (from left: Herbert Robertson, Mrs June Robertson and Fiona Robertson) in Sydney, Australia.

migrants continue to sponsor annual dances, inter-school cricket matches and raise funds to maintain these links and reaffirm their identity as Sri Lankan Australians. Once again, far from the islands shores, they wish to claim their contested birth right.

The Dutch Burgher Union (DBU) in Colombo.

Larry Marshall

Margaret Ootschorn's grandniece on the day of her wedding in Batticaloa, 2012.

The Portuguese Burghers still celebrate their weddings in style with their unique blend of Kaffrinha music, dancing and wine.

PORTUGUESE BURGHERS—LANGUAGE, MUSIC AND DANCE

The Portuguese Burghers have, unconsciously, been the guardians of Portuguese legacies in Sri Lanka. Although the official Portuguese presence in Batticaloa and Trincomalee was only towards the end of the Portuguese era, Portuguese Burgher communities now live in these enclaves. They have sustained a Portuguese-based Creole language, which was called Indo-Portuguese of Ceylon at the end of the 19th century and nowadays known as Sri Lankan Portuguese Creole. Indo-Portuguese was the lingua franca for about 350 years during the colonial period. Some Portuguese Burghers, mainly in the eastern province, still speak this historically important language, which once served as the bridging tongue between all three colonial powers and the indigenous peoples.

Being immersed in a multilingual set up, the ability to speak Indo-Portuguese is now diminishing but the vestiges of an endangered language are embedded in the lyrics of songs. The longevity of this once important language is due to the fidelity of the mother-tongue speakers, the Portuguese Burghers,

Margaret Ootschorn, a 92 year-old Portuguese Burgher, is very likely the oldest living member of the community in Batticaloa. Displaced from the Dutch Bar after the 2004 tsunami, she now lives with her daughter in Thiraaimadu, a new settlement developed especially for the community.

who consider Indo-Portuguese an important part of their Portuguese heritage and identity. Their songs (*cantigas*), influenced by the Portuguese ballads (*romanceiros*), convey the harmonies of European melodies. Harmony, where several notes are played simultaneously, added an extra dimension to Sri Lankan popular music, a genre known as *baila*. Weddings and other social occasions reinforced these traditions. Portuguese Burgher wedding ceremonies are not complete until the bride and groom dance the *kaffrinha* to the lively music of the orchestra. Violins, guitar, drum and tambourine play on whilst the *kaffrinha* is danced by four couples. The bride and groom open the dance, the bridesmaid and bestman follow and the other two couples follow suit. The dance, which continues for about two hours, is in five parts with alternating fast and slow movements, the opening and the finale being rapid.

Although in the big cities and towns, they blend into the multicultural social fabric of Sri Lankan society, language, music and dance differentiates the Portuguese Burghers from other groups on the island.

Shihan de Silva Jayasuriya

A girls' school in Galagadera, western province of Ceylon (circa 1902).

all secondary schools. This began a spurt in enrolment growth at the secondary education level that continued after independence.

ADMINISTRATIVE AND LEGAL STRUCTURES

A diverse legal legacy evolved during colonial times. By the 19th century, Roman Dutch Law came to be applied in civil matters when laws applicable to specific groups (e.g. Muslim law, *tesavalamai* for northern Tamils, and Kandyan law) were silent. Criminal law was derived from English law. Although the Dutch established a rudimentary system of courts, and indigenous kingdoms had officials exercising judicial powers, the court structure at the end of the colonial period came largely from the British. Provincial boundaries drawn up by the British in the 19th century survived until the end of colonial rule.

THE MOVEMENT TOWARDS INDEPENDENCE

The end of colonial rule in Sri Lanka was greatly influenced by external factors, including the changed attitude and ideology of the colonial power, the impact of World War II and the influence of the Indian nationalist movement. Within Sri Lanka, in the late 19th century and the early decades of the 20th, popular agitation at the grassroots level was more important than elite efforts to seek constitutional change through memorials and petitions. The temperance movement gave the English educated elite some common ground with local leaders, linkages that were strengthened due to the strong British reaction to the riots of 1915; riots by Sinhalese against Muslims precipitated by insistence by the latter that Buddhist processions passing by mosques should silence their drums. Nevertheless, political progress was slow. Despite the inauguration of public elections in Sri Lanka for three seats on a limited electorate in 1912 and the founding of the Ceylon National Congress in 1919 (successor to the Ceylon National Association formed in the late 19th century), progress in devolving power to local politicians lagged far behind neighbouring India. By 1924, 34 of the 71 seats in the Legislative Council were filled through election (11 of them through exclusive ethnic constituencies) but the right to vote was confined to 4 per cent of the population.

Some of these political changes occurred also because of pressure from below. Trade unions organised in the port of Colombo and in the transportation sector in the 1920s were soon joined by unions of plantation workers. Union demands led to some progress in terms of the fixing of a minimum wage and some benefits for workers, but unions were divided on ethnic and political grounds. However, efforts to strengthen the trade union movement were adversely affected by the effects of the Great Depression (1929–33).

The next major step came in 1931 when, following a special commission of inquiry on political changes, the British decided to allow universal franchise (for which there was only limited support among the Sri Lankan elite), the end of exclusive ethnic constituencies and a measure of internal self-government. The ethnic minorities became apprehensive of an electoral system that would enable Sinhalese politicians to gain a majority of seats, especially as the prospect of the end of colonial rule came closer in the 1940s. This led, in 1944, to the

formation of the Tamil Congress, a party designed to protect the rights of Tamil-speaking peoples. Sinhalese Buddhist interests were advocated by numerous groups, including the Sinhala Maha Sabha.

The more conservative elements of the elite worked with the British during World War II. They were seen more favourably by the colonial power than the Marxist leaders who formed the Lanka Sama Samaja Party in 1935. At the end of the war, these elites persuaded the British to fashion a new constitution (1946) that devolved powers relating to internal affairs to Sri Lankan politicians.

The new political structure involved a bicameral legislature with a Senate of 30 members (15 of whom were nominated by the British Governor and the rest selected by the lower house), and a House of Representatives with 101 members (six being similarly nominated and the others elected). Extra representation was provided for sparsely populated areas and a few multi-member constituencies were created to enable minority representation in the legislature in urban

LEFT: *A World War II poster of the 'Ceylon Garrison Artillery'.*

RIGHT: *A poster—London Calling on 13 February 1941—showcasing the efforts to raise funds for the war.*

Postcard illustrating the view from the Colombo Harbour (circa 1905). The Port of Colombo, previously known as the Port of Kolomthota, continues to be a pivotal point for traders.

Inaugurated in the 1930s, the Jaffna Library was a key educational institution in Asia, home to rare collections of books and manuscripts. The civil war in Sri Lanka witnessed the burning of the library that has since been rebuilt.

Colombo Harbour and Shipping.

AFRICANS IN SRI LANKA

African migration in the Indian Ocean was both voluntary and involuntary. It occurred over a wide geographical area and over a long period of time. Ethiopians were trading in Mannar (northeast of Sri Lanka) in the 6th century. Ibn Battuta, the 14th-century Moroccan traveller, found 500 Ethiopians in the force of Jalasti, the ruler of Colombo.

Understandably, there have been several waves of African migration eastwards and the history of Afro-Sri Lankans is multi-layered. Three colonial powers—Portuguese, Dutch and British—swept over the shores of Sri Lanka and empire building demanded manpower. Africans performed a variety of tasks as soldiers, road-builders, water carriers, servants and nannies.

Africans came from various parts of the continent and they were, ethno-linguistically, not a homogeneous group. Most of them came from Mozambique, Madagascar and Mauritius, but others came via Asian ports (Goa and Mumbai). This widens the geographical roots of their ultimate African origins, which could have been Tanzania, Kenya or other locations, not necessarily from the coastal regions because slaves were obtained from the interior once the stock in the maritime areas ran out. A lucrative slave trade was operating in the Indian Ocean and private ventures were also involved. This increased the sources of supply and the ethnicity of the slaves. As slaves did not arrive at their final destination in a single voyage or journey, at times it led to acculturation by Asians who purchased them. These factors are important in considering the cultural heritage of the Afro-Sri Lankans.

Over the centuries, Africans have assimilated with the local population. However, there still exists an Afro-Sri Lankan community in the village of Sirambiyadiya, a few miles inland of the west coast town of Puttalama. They are associated with the Portuguese mainly due to religious and linguistic reasons. They are Roman Catholics. Regardless of the African language spoken by their ancestors, when they arrived in Sri Lanka, they learnt Indo-Portuguese, the lingua franca for about three and a half centuries of the colonial era.

Nowadays it is the elderly Afro-Sri Lankans in Sirambiyadiya who speak Indo-Portuguese, while everyone else speaks Sinhala. In terms of clothing, food habits and housing, the Afro-Sri Lankans are not different to others on the island. It is music, song and dance that differentiates them from the other ethnic groups. Their un-choreographed dancing links them to an imagined homeland. Reverberating rhythms produced by a combination of homemade and local instruments, echo the sounds of Africa. Coconut halves beaten on a piece of wood, a metal vessel beaten with wooden sticks and a glass bottle beaten with a metal spoon complement the drum rhythms and singing.

The community know the context of their songs, called *Manhas*, which they have learnt through an oral tradition. Having resisted recording for several years, they brought out their debut album—*Kaffir Strelas* ('African Stars')—in 2011, which features a selection of their songs. The word *Kaffir* was borrowed by the British, who in turn borrowed the Portuguese word *cafre*, in itself an adapation of the Arabic word *qafr* meaning 'non-believer'. This can be misleading because the genre of popular music called *kaffrinha* is associated entirely with Africans. *Kaffrinha* indicates a bit of *kaffir*, *nha* being the Portuguese diminutive. Some Afro-Sri Lankans would have known *kaffrinha* as a late 19th century manuscript of Indo-Portuguese songs from the eastern province containing "*Cantiga De Purtiegese—Kaffrein—Neger Song Portigiese*" ('Songs of the Portuguese—*Kaffrinha*—Portuguese Negro Songs') testifies.

Kaffrinha is also associated with the Portuguese Burgher traditions. These two communities are co-religionists (Roman Catholics) and share a common language (Indo-Portuguese) and perhaps it is not surprising that their artistic traditions are also entangled.

Recently there has been a renewed interest in the Afro-Sri Lankans due to the work of academics and journalists. This has been complemented by increased and more professional performances of *Manhas* in fashionable locations.

In the 1970s, the nation was able to see the Sirambiyadiya Afro-Sri Lankan community in a programme telecasted by Rupavahini, a Sri Lankan television station. The grand matriach of the community at that time, Ana Miseliya, predicted that out-marriage would dilute their physiognomic features, but that their descendants could be identified in the future only through their musical ability.

In Sirambiyadiya, a village proximate to the town of Puttalama, Afro-Sri Lankans have managed to sustain a distinct community.

The Afro-Sri Lankans are now assimilating into wider Sri Lankan society. This is largely due to their small number. Nevertheless, their vibrant music and dance signal their presence on the island. These are representations of their links to a distant 'homeland', albeit through their imagination of a place they have long been detached from.

Shihan de Silva Jayasuriya

Members of the Afro-Sri Lankan community came together and formed a musical group they call 'Kaffir Manja'. The group has performed around the country, including this concert at the Barefoot Gallery in 2009.

Afro-Sri Lankans playing their music—Manja—inside their home. Music, song and dance comprise an integral part of Afro-Sri Lankan identity.

Ignesia, 82 years old, is one of the few Afro-Sri Lankans who still speaks the lyrical Creole. Her family believes that they are descendants of slaves brought over by the British to Ceylon in the 19th century.

Radio Ceylon which began in the early 1920s is one of South Asia's oldest radio stations.

A Sinhalese wedding photo taken during the colonial period.

A stamp commemorating Ceylon's independence on 4 February 1948.

constituencies. Elections under the new constitution were held in September 1947. By that time, however, even more significant political changes had occurred in the neighbouring sub-continent. India and Pakistan had gained their independence in August 1947.

Sri Lankan politicians pressed for similar status and received a promise of 'full responsible status within the British Commonwealth of Nations.' Strong ties with Britain were maintained through various agreements in 1947 that assured the former colonial power the right to use airports and the Trincomalee harbour. On 4 February 1948, Sri Lanka, the 'model colony', became an independent country.

Chandra R. de Silva

Postcolonial Development

SRI LANKA'S TUMULTUOUS experience in the postcolonial period is starkly in contrast to the expectation at the time of independence in 1948, that the process of nation-building and national regeneration would be peaceful. In 2012, 64 years after its independence from British rule, the task remains unsuccessful. At the same time, the protracted ethnic conflict that attained a civil war dimension during 1983–2009 has severely battered the society. Yet, the Sri Lankan state has emerged victorious in preserving its sovereignty and territorial integrity, albeit at a heavy human cost. The chronic instability and disorder, though manifestly produced by the ethnic conflict, is fundamentally rooted in the nature of postcolonial politics and policies pursued by the state. In comparison, colonial Sri Lanka enjoyed relative peace. Considered as a 'model British colony', the country had an advanced welfare state which ensured greater electoral participation after the introduction of universal adult suffrage (1931), relied on the police to enforce public order, maintained rudimentary armed forces, secured people's greater compliance with constitutionality and, above all, created propitious conditions for a consensual, peaceful and orderly transfer of power, that too, without a movement or struggle for independence.

Nature of the Polity and Governments

If the contemporary Sri Lankan polity owes its creation to British colonialism, its growth has occurred under the tremendous influence of the Westminster model of democracy that the country adopted in the first thirty years (1948–77) of its independence. Even after the change over to the presidential system in 1978, some of the legacies and experiences of parliamentary democracy have not been completely dispensed with. But the peculiar characteristics the polity has developed over the years are the outcomes of the manner in which it has functioned and responded to some of the national issues under pressure from political parties. Ethnic nationalism is a dominant issue, which has divided the polity in a notional sense into south and north along ethnic lines. In spatial terms, the southern polity encompasses the Sinhalese-dominated provinces and the northern polity denotes the Sri Lankan Tamil-concentrated areas in the northern and eastern provinces. Ethnicity is the single most important source of electoral mobilisation. Electoral issues centre on ethnic interests of communities and the forces contesting for power seek to promote them in an exclusive manner.

Sri Lanka has a two-party dominant multi-party system. Its evolution has been influenced by the plural social structure and competing ideological issues. The United National Party (UNP) and the Sri Lanka Freedom Party (SLFP) are the mainstream political formations; they enjoy maximum support of the majority of Sinhalese community. The electoral history shows that power alternates periodically between them alone, even though they often rely on smaller parties. The two major traditional Tamil parties had been the All Ceylon Tamil Congress (ACTC) and the Federal Party (FP); both remained wedded to Sri Lankan Tamil nationalism but differed on the issue of citizenship to the Indian Tamils during 1948–49. In the 1970s, the Tamil United Liberation Front (TULF) became a popular force that had mobilised the Sri Lankan Tamils for a separate Eelam. Following the July 1987 India-Sri Lanka peace accord, most of the Tamil militant organisations, such as the Eelam People's Democratic Party (EPDP) and the Eelam People's Revolutionary Liberation Front (EPRLF), joined the political mainstream and successfully contested elections. Presently, the EPRLF is an important constituent of the Tamil National Alliance (TNA), the largest Sri Lankan Tamil group in parliament. The Muslims are represented by various factions of the Sri Lanka Muslim Congress (SLMC) and the majority of the Indian Tamils have traditionally been the supporters of the Ceylon Workers Congress (CWC). Clearly, ethnicity is the dominant ideology of these parties whose primary goal is to protect the ethnic interests and welfare of their respective communities. The political agenda of most of them is focused on promoting a particularistic ethnic nationalism either to counter the majoritarian Sinhalese nationalism (by the Sri Lankan Tamil parties) or the minoritarian Sri Lankan Tamil nationalism (in case of the Sinhalese and Sri Lankan Muslim parties).

The Sinhalese parties largely share the characteristics of the minority ethnic parties. Both the UNP and SLFP are considered national parties, but their orientations, policies and programmes are strongly linked to Sinhalese Buddhist nationalism. Until the 1990s, the ideological differences between them remained strong. The UNP held the right-of-centre position and the SLFP was known for its left-of-centre views—a 'middle path' between the rightist UNP and the leftist Marxists. While being pro-West and anti-Communism during the early decades of independence, the UNP's economic policy remained tilted in favour of the private sector. After the introduction of liberalisation in 1977, it has changed itself from being democratic-socialist to democratic-capitalist. In contrast, the SLFP advocated the idea of a socialist society and diversified the country's foreign relations with countries in the West and in the East. It was deeply committed to the protection of Buddhism and Sinhalese culture, favoured the parliamentary system, and opposed the liberal economic policy. Now, these differences are less evident. Both parties share similar views on many issues. Even the left parties, divided into traditionalists and revolutionaries, do not challenge the UNP or the SLFP on ideological grounds. They have lost their ideological position because of their support to chauvinistic and anti-minority policies of the government. The decline of left politics is an outcome of ethnicisation of the polity. The Lanka Sama Samaja Party (LSSP—Sri Lanka Equal Society Party), the oldest traditional leftist party, changed its ideology from Marxism to Trotskyism in the late 1930s. Its breakaway group, the Communist Party (CP), formed in 1943, identified itself ideologically with the former Soviet Union. The Janatha Vimukthi Peramuna (JVP—People's Liberation Front) is a major revolutionary leftist group whose ideology of Marxism-Leninism is blended with Sinhalese chauvinism. In recent years, the polity has seen the swift rise of a radical religious party, the Jathika Hela Urumaya (JHU—National Heritage Party). Established in 2004, this all-Buddhist monk party's active mobilisation of support for a righteous Buddhist society has formalised the radical role of religion in politics.

The multi-party system and the competing interests of the ethnic communities have made the polity a vibrant arena for a fierce contest for power. Its outcomes are twofold: first, in their determination to win elections the local party leaders and cadres have used violence. The result has been the institutionalisation of political violence. Almost all the elections since 1960s are marred by violence; the number of such incidents has increased in the recent decades. Second, heightened political as well as ethnic consciousness and greater interest of people in the political process are reflected in the high level of electoral participation. None of the elections since 1947 had turnouts of less than 60 per cent; in many elections the recorded turnout exceeded 75 per cent. This shows that the rural electorates have been thoroughly politicised. The vehicles of their mobilisation are collective identities such as religion, ethnicity and caste.

Sri Lanka has evolved a strong coalition culture. The first government in independent Sri Lanka itself was a coalition as the 1947 elections gave a fractured verdict in favour of the UNP. Coalition politics continued in the subsequent decades. Except the short-lived UNP government of March–July 1960 and the SLFP of July 1960-June 1964, all others from 1956 to 1977 were coalitions. In the 1977 elections, the UNP secured a massive 5/6 majority in parliament. It ruled the island uninterruptedly for 17 years until the SLFP-led People's Alliance (PA) was voted to power in 1994. Incidentally, all the governments since 1994 have been coalitions; most of them enjoyed a slender majority. The SLFP has headed all of them except the one that the UNP-led coalition formed in December 2001. It was a cohabitation government, under which the UNP Prime Minister, Ranil Shriyan Wickremasinghe, and President Chandrika Bandaranaike Kumaratunga of the SLFP shared power until it was dismissed by the latter in February 2004. The short-lived governments and snap polls in the early 2000s, which indicated political instability, were symptomatic of political decay afflicting the polity. Since 2010, however, the regime has become stable. In the April 2010 general elections, the ruling SLFP-led United People's Freedom Alliance (UPFA) won a 'near 2/3 majority' (144 out of 225 seats in parliament).

CONSTITUTIONAL DEVELOPMENT

The two dominant constitutional traditions in Sri Lanka are parliamentary democracy and presidential system. Though both of them have a long history and have had strong influence on the political system, in relative terms the former is more popular than the latter in the country. The first two constitutions (of 1948 and 1972) established a Westminster form of government under which the parliament became supreme. But the executive presidential system introduced by the 1978 Constitution has signified a radical change. While all three constitutions have maintained the unitary structure of the state, the political system has become highly centralised under the Constitutions of 1972 and 1978. Cumulatively, the constitutional development has contributed to a majoritarian democracy since 1956.

The 1948 Constitution was essentially the by-product of British colonialism. It was based on the Soulbury Constitution (1946), recommended by the Commission on Constitutional Reform and adopted by the State Council. The colonial influence remained strong on the political system as Sri Lanka, under the constitution, had maintained symbolic links with Britain. The parliament was composed of two houses—the House of Representatives and the Senate—and the British Queen. Under the Royal Titles Act of 1953, she was the Queen of Ceylon as well, represented by the Governor-General (a nominal executive), whom she appointed on the Prime Minister's advice. Importantly, the first two Governor-Generals—Sir Henry Monck-Mason Moore (1944–49) and The Viscount Soulbury (1949–54)—were Englishmen. Aimed at establishing a multi-racial democracy, the constitution created a liberal secular state and incorporated a provision under Section 29(2) to prohibit the legislature from enacting any law to discriminate against the ethnic minorities. At the same time, it did not include a Bill of Rights. This was a notable omission. The left-wing forces termed the country's independence as spurious because of the continued colonial connection and influence, and therefore demanded for a constituent assembly to draft a new autochthonous constitution.

It took 25 years for the Sri Lankans to make an indigenous constitution. In 1972, the country, known as Ceylon since 1505, was renamed Sri Lanka (resplendent land), and the constitutional order was changed substantially and negatively too by the first republican

Don Stephen Senanayake was the first Prime Minister of Ceylon. His son, Dudley Shelton Senanayake succeeded him as Prime Minister in 1952.

The hammer and sickle flies over a rally on 16 May 1950. Sri Lanka has had a long history of leftist parties.

The ceremonial opening of Sri Lanka's first parliament six days after independence from Britain. Prime Minister Don Stephen Senanayake is seated on the extreme left while the Duke of Gloucester presides.

The parliament building on a postage stamp.

Crowds of Ceylonese lining the streets to welcome Queen Elizabeth II, 1954.

Voters in a remote village wait to cast their votes in the General Election, 22 March 1960.

constitution. It broke the island's symbolic relations with the British Queen, abolished the minority safeguards provided in the previous constitution, converted the legislature into a unicameral chamber—the National State Assembly (NSA)—and changed the state's secular character by according primacy and patronage to the Buddhist religion. The prime minister's position became strong, especially in view of the emergency powers vested in him. The principle of separation of powers was done away with; instead a mere recognition was given to separation of functions between all three government organs—executive, legislature and judiciary. The constitution incorporated fundamental rights and freedoms, but the power of judicial review earlier enjoyed by the judiciary was abolished. In its place, a Constitutional Court was empowered to give its opinion on the constitutional validity of bills introduced in parliament. In the process, the parliament was made 'the supreme instrument of state power'.

The constitution-making in Sri Lanka has been a partisan affair. Each mainstream party, the SLFP or the UNP, used its electoral strength in parliament to design a constitution of its choice. The 1972 Constitution represented the political ideology and objectives of the United Front regime led by SLFP leader Sirimavo Bandaranaike. Whereas the UNP voted against the constitution, the FP boycotted the Constituent Assembly since its demand for parity of status for the Tamil language was rejected.

Similarly, the 1978 Constitution was the brainchild of UNP leader J. R. Jayewardene who emphasised the need for a strong and stable government to achieve economic development. This provided the political logic for a powerful executive presidential system under the 1978 Constitution, which was rejected by almost all opposition parties including the SLFP and the TULF. The UNP could afford to ignore the opposition because it enjoyed a massive majority in parliament. But the lack of bipartisan approach, on both occasions, virtually questioned the credibility of the two constitutions.

The 1978 Constitution is a 'hybrid' in the sense that it borrowed the principles of both the French and British constitutions. It retained some of the core provisions (relating to Buddhism, judicial review, separation of functions, unicameralism, unitary state, etc.) of the earlier constitution but shifted power from the parliament to people and made them supreme. The President's direct election by them for a six-year term makes him a popular leader with supreme and overarching powers over other institutions. The two-term limit imposed on his election was removed in favour of an unlimited term by the 18th constitutional amendment passed in 2010. Being a real executive, the President enjoys a unique position as both the head of the state and the government, and the commander-in-chief of the armed forces. In the absence of a system of checks and balances, the President is able to effectively centralise state powers, particularly when his party commands an absolute majority in parliament. The lack of judicial review has contributed to increasing executive control of the legislative. Critics maintain that the provision for mere consultation of the Supreme Court prior to any legislative enactment and, consequently, its diminished role has made the judiciary a 'third house' of parliament. Finally, the constitution has replaced the first-past-the-post system by the proportional representation system, under which the country is divided into twenty-two electoral districts, from where 196 members are elected directly to the 225-member NSA and another 29 members are nominated on the national basis of the votes obtained by each party or group.

From 1995 to 2000, the People's Alliance government under Kumaratunga made serious efforts to change the 1978 Constitution into a liberal-democratic one that would redefine the nature of the state, democratise and strengthen the institutions, protect fundamental rights, and devise a structure of power-sharing between the centre and the proposed regions. More strikingly, the proposed constitution did not retain the term 'unitary' to characterise the state; nor did it use the term 'federal'. It sought to replace the presidential form of government by the parliamentary system. The provisions pertaining to devolution formed the core of the state-reform project as the government acknowledged that the powers devolved under the 13th Amendment to the Provincial Councils established in 1987, were deficient in meeting the Sri Lankan Tamils' autonomy aspirations.

In August 2000, the constitutional proposals were introduced as a bill in parliament. The process, however, was suspended amidst opposition from political parties. Amongst the dissenters included the UNP and Sinhalese chauvinistic groups. Finally, the bill lapsed when the parliament was dissolved on 18 August 2000.

The State and Nationalism

Development of the state and nationalism is a dominant theme in Sri Lanka's postcolonial political history. Both the state as the core institution of governance and nationalism as its ideology have formed critical factors to influence political development. In turn, politics has made negative contributions to their drastic transformation, leading to the breakdown of legitimacy of the state while making its ideology inherently flawed. Thus, both of them have become a prime source and objective of protracted conflict and endemic violence.

In contrast, the British colonial state was by and large popular even though it appeared to have tilted its political balance towards the Sinhalese community. Much to its chagrin, the state's religious policy deterred the growth of Buddhism to become a pivotal religion on the island. Consequently, it worked to assure the ethnic minorities of their rights and privileges. Also, the state's welfare policies and benign political approach towards order-maintenance in the society had enhanced its standing. In the process, its inherent desire to exercise domination by employing a wide range of control mechanisms and strategies did not evoke resistance from the society. However, the situation changed in the postcolonial period when the state altered the entire ideological framework of politics and chose to become an ethnocratic entity, seeking to represent the aspirations of the Sinhalese community and promoting its interests at the cost of ethnic minorities.

The postcolonial state continued to pursue the welfare-oriented social democratic policy till the 1970s. It was disbanded in the wake of introduction of economic liberalisation policy by the UNP government since 1977, leading to a radical change in the fundamental nature of the state from being socialist to capitalist. Resultantly, while forsaking its role in regulating the market, it has come to rely heavily on the foreign capital. Under pressure from the international financial institutions, the state has cut down subsidies to the social sector. In comparison, the state's political ideology came under drastic revision in the mid-1950s; when SLFP leader S. W. R. D. Bandaranaike successfully mobilised the Sinhalese Buddhist forces to challenge the idea of pluralism that the UNP government, particularly under D. S. Senanayake (1948–52), sought to promote by developing

a broader Sri Lankan nationalism. Under this, religious and linguistic identities became subordinate to the greater composite national culture, and the state maintained distance from religion to become secular. For the Sinhalese Buddhist nationalists, however, a national ideology grounded in pluralism was anathema to their belief that Sri Lanka was the Sinhadipa (the island of the Sinhalese). Therefore, it was not surprising that majoritarian nationalism that Bandaranaike framed and promoted became enormously popular among the Sinhalese. They worked on the state to recognise and adopt their ethnic nationalism as an ideology of the whole nation. It was achieved at least in two ways.

First, in 1956, the state's mono-linguistic identity was established by making Sinhala the only official language of the country. Since Buddhism provides an ideological framework or base for Sinhalese nationalism the next significant step was to forge a link between the state and the majority religion. This task was accomplished in 1972 when the constitution gave the 'foremost place' to Buddhism and underlined the duty of the state to 'protect and foster the Buddha Sasana'. The 1978 Constitution provides a greater continuity in the state's formal association with Buddhism. Besides, the principle of unitarianism has been enforced as a state ideology by all three constitutions. The unitary political system ensures that power is vested solely in the Sinhalese community, which is the permanent majority, on whom the minorities depend for power on a shared basis. Thus, the unitary political system, the Sinhala language, the Buddhist religion and the historicity as well as the perception of the Sinhalese as the 'chosen people' have collectively contributed to the political construction of Sinhalese nationalism.

Since 1956, Sri Lankan Tamils have contested the majoritarian state and nationalism by emphasising their separate ethnic identity and constructing their own nationalism. The contest has resulted in a protracted conflict. In response, the state has militarised the entire society and employed violent coercion to ensure its cohesion and survival. In the process it has become a typical national security institution.

Another major challenge to the state was posed by the JVP in the form of an insurrection, launched in two phases (in 1971 and 1987–89), to capture power. Its first insurrection saw the mobilisation largely of educated unemployed Sinhalese youths who felt alienated from the state. The JVP, under a non-elite Sinhalese leadership, was ill-prepared to challenge the state militarily. Yet its attacks lasting for weeks mainly on police stations caused disorder. The unprepared state's weak armed forces could not stop them until friendly countries, including India, extended military support. Thousands of youths lost their lives and many of the JVP leaders including Rohana Wijeweera were captured, tried and imprisoned. For a brief period in the early 1980s, the JVP tried to test its popularity in parliamentary politics by contesting the 1982 presidential election. But in a matter of five years, it re-launched the insurrection in 1987, aimed at removing the UNP regime of J. R. Jayewardene for signing a peace

The Prime Minister of Ceylon, Solomon Bandaranaike, with his wife Sirimavo Bandaranaike, arriving in New York (circa 1956). After his assassination, Sirimavo Bandaranaike became the world's first woman Prime Minister in 1960.

Born in Ipoh, Malaysia, lawyer Samuel James Veluppillai Chelvanayakam championed the rights of the Tamil minority in independent Sri Lanka. He was regarded as 'Thanthai (Father) Chelva' by the Tamil community.

Janatha Vimukthi Peramuna (JVP) supporters push carts with portraits of communist leaders (Karl Marx, Friedrich Engels, Vladimir Lenin and Rohana Wijeweera) during May Day celebrations in Colombo, 2012.

'Self-defence training' in the LTTE-controlled village of Uthayanagar East, 23 May 2006.

Soldiers of the Indian Peace Keeping Force (IPKF) in Sri Lanka, 1989.

LTTE leader Velupillai Prabhakaran (centre), leader of the political wing P. Thamilselvan (left), and chief negotiator and political strategist, Anton Balasingham (right), in a meeting with Norwegian peace envoy Eric Solheim in Kilinochchi, 2006. Norwegian peace brokers played a key role in these negotiations.

Sri Lankan army soldiers patrol the frontline at Nagarkovil in the Jaffna Peninsula, 2008.

36

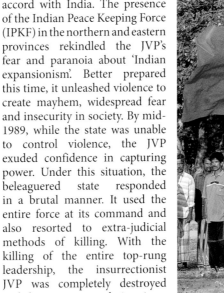

accord with India. The presence of the Indian Peace Keeping Force (IPKF) in the northern and eastern provinces rekindled the JVP's fear and paranoia about 'Indian expansionism'. Better prepared this time, it unleashed violence to create mayhem, widespread fear and insecurity in society. By mid-1989, while the state was unable to control violence, the JVP exuded confidence in capturing power. Under this situation, the beleaguered state responded in a brutal manner. It used the entire force at its command and also resorted to extra-judicial methods of killing. With the killing of the entire top-rung leadership, the insurrectionist JVP was completely destroyed and the state emerged victorious. But the cost of its victory was prohibitively high: there were reports that suggested that thousands of young people suspected of being JVP supporters were brutally and mercilessly massacred in the process of quelling the formidable insurrection.

ETHNIC CONFLICT AND CIVIL WAR

The single most important development with its pervasive effect on the polity and society has been the protracted conflict between the Sinhalese and the Sri Lankan Tamils. In fact, it covers the greater part of postcolonial Sri Lankan history. Though the conflict is anchored in ancient history, its primary causes are rooted in postcolonial politics in that nationalism has been a key issue. It marks a violent expression of two endangered nationalisms, with diametrically opposed goals. While Sinhalese nationalism seeks to establish 'supremacy', Sri Lankan Tamil nationalism insists on 'equality'.

The Indian Tamils, who had migrated to Sri Lanka as plantation labour during the British colonial period, were the first minority group to have suffered severely in the postcolonial period due to the state's ethnic-exclusive nation-building policy. The crux of the issue was that a large number of them became stateless because of the stringent citizenship laws enacted in 1948–49. Though this problem in itself did not turn the Sri Lankan Tamils against the state, the FP factored the Indian Tamils' grievances in its political agenda in the 1950s. The 1956 Sinhala-only Act touched a raw nerve among the Sri Lankan Tamils who were, for the first time, legally denied equal linguistic rights. In the subsequent years successive governments had pursued policies to discriminate them further in education, employment, resource allocation, and land colonisation. In the 1970s, the Sri Lankan Tamil students' representation in science education at universities declined sharply due to the standardisation policy, which fixed different credits for Tamil and Sinhalese students. Similarly, in government employment, while the Sinhalese continued to increase their share, the Sri Lankan Tamils experienced a steady decline. Their leaders complained that while concentrating on the development in the Sinhalese areas, the government deliberately neglected the northern and eastern provinces and allocated very limited resources for them. Since the 1950s, the settlement of a large number of landless Sinhalese, under the state-aided colonisation schemes, brought about a significant change in the demographic structure of the northern and eastern provinces—claimed by the Sri Lankan Tamils as their 'traditional homeland'. Their grievances grew strong, creating a deep sense of 'relative deprivation' and 'powerlessness' when successive governments failed to address their problems. Under the circumstances, Tamils sought to change and redefine their relations with the state by, initially, demanding federal autonomy (till 1976) and a separate Eelam thereafter.

The FP spearheaded the autonomy movement until the Tamil United Front was formed in 1972, as a result of the unity forged among the Tamil parties. The latter rechristened itself as the TULF in 1976, when secession became the declared goal. Its popular leader, S. J. V. Chelvanayakam, who was revered as *thanthai* (father) by the Sri Lankan Tamils, justified the Eelam demand and exuded confidence in achieving it. After his death in March 1977, Appapillai Amirthalingam (who became the Opposition leader in parliament in 1977) led the Eelam movement until the mid-1980s. Simultaneously, since the mid-1970s, a number of militant groups came into existence. The dominant one among them was the Liberation Tigers of Tamil Eelam (LTTE). Under Velupillai Prabhakaran's leadership, the LTTE emerged as the most powerful of these groups. It was able to control the Eelam movement from 1986 by virtue of its armed strength and after eliminating or weakening most of its rival organisations. Known for its ruthlessness, the LTTE unrealistically developed a steely determination to achieve the Eelam goal.

The year 1983 was a watershed in the movement. In that year, two major incidents changed the nature of the conflict. First, the LTTE's ambush of an army patrol in Tinneveli (Jaffna Peninsula) on 23 July 1983 killed 13 Sinhalese soldiers. This triggered large-scale military operations, which effectively marked the beginning of a long civil war. Second, when the soldiers' bodies were brought to Colombo, the worst-ever anti-Tamil riots broke out in the capital. The city and its suburbs were

the worst-hit. Approximately 2000 Tamil civilians were killed and their properties pillaged or destroyed.

Both the civil war and ethnic riots led to the internationalisation of the conflict. The government secured direct military assistance from a number of countries including China and Pakistan, and used foreign agencies such as Israel's Mossad and Shin Bet to strengthen its intelligence and impart military training. With a view to befriending the West and countering the perceived Indian threat, Colombo offered naval base facilities to the US. India, under both Indira Gandhi and Rajiv Gandhi, sought to counter the extra-regional powers' influence on the island which became controversial and futile in the end. Its twin role as a mediator-cum-militant-supporter led to a peace accord between Indian Prime Minister Rajiv Gandhi and Sri Lankan President Jayewardene in July 1987. While all other Tamil groups had willy-nilly accepted the accord, the LTTE rejected it and fought the IPKF, which went to the island on the invitation of the Sri Lankan President to restore peace and normalcy. The IPKF's withdrawal under Sri Lanka's pressure in March 1990, without fulfilling the objectives laid down in the peace accord, ended India's 'direct role' in the conflict. Thereafter, it has maintained its strong 'interest' in the conflict, but sought to play an 'indirect role'.

The second phase of internationalisation of the conflict happened in the early 2000s when the government of Wickremasinghe invited Norway to facilitate its peace process (2002–03) with the LTTE. It also involved the US, Japan and the European Union—all of them, together with Norway, formed the Co-Chairs of the Sri Lanka Donor Group. They held two major international donor conferences in Oslo and Tokyo, and a preparatory meeting in Washington to mobilise economic support for peace-building. At the Tokyo conference in June 2003, the international community pledged US$4.5 billion for the reconstruction of the war-ravaged north and east. Six rounds of negotiations between the government and the LTTE focused on confidence-building measures, but they did not result in a peace accord. The LTTE withdrew from the peace process in April 2003; yet 'negative peace' continued until the military hostilities were resumed in 2006. This caused an irreversible breakdown of the international community's agenda for liberal peace-building.

The Eelam war had a primary goal of controlling territories in the north and east. Whereas the state wanted to establish its sovereign authority and quell the armed movement, the Tamil militants considered that taking control of both provinces would not only make the state's sovereignty truncated, but also increase their power to eventually realise their Eelam goal. Fought in four different phases, the brutal war lasted for 26 years. During the first Eelam war (1983–90) about half-a-dozen militant groups challenged the security forces. Of them, the LTTE proved to be a formidable force that, in 1987, unsuccessfully attempted to adopt conventional war strategies. The second half of this phase (1987–90) entailed direct military hostilities between the IPKF and the LTTE. The Indian forces chased the Tigers out of the Jaffna Peninsula to the Vavuniya and Mullaitivu jungles and hideouts in the east. But the LTTE regained their lost territories once the IPKF was withdrawn. This led to the second Eelam war (1990–94), in which the government forces captured areas in the east, but the LTTE maintained its control over the north. In the third Eelam war (1995–2002), both the adversaries experienced territorial loss and gains. The LTTE lost the Jaffna Peninsula but retained its control over a vast stretch of lands in the north, while maintaining its influence in the east. But the fourth Eelam war (2006–09)—considered as a war of attrition—saw the massive and indiscriminate use of air power and artillery by the government. At the end of the war, the government forces were able to achieve a decisive victory not only by capturing territories, but also by killing the entire LTTE leadership, including Prabhakaran.

Thus, the brutal war eventually became a zero-sum game. Its cumulative human and economic cost has been phenomenally high. The war has left an indelible scar in society, whose members presently include a strong community of widows, orphans, refugees, and internally displaced persons. Besides, a vast Sri Lankan Tamil diaspora settled worldwide has formed a transnational community. This conflict-produced 'new' diaspora is a politically active component of the deeply segmented Sri Lankan diaspora.

P. Sahadevan

A Sri Lankan soldier walks past a map in the northern town of Pandivirichchan depicting parts of the island's north and east, which the LTTE claimed as their homeland, 2008.

Sri Lankans celebrate the end of over 25 years of civil war in the country, May 2009.

LIFE AND PEOPLE IN THE DIASPORA

The social, cultural and economic features of the diverse communities that comprise the Sri Lankan diaspora, is integrally connected to their migratory experience and the new situations they confront in the 'host' society. While this may give rise to differences, wherever Sri Lankans have migrated they have carried with them social, religious and cultural identities of the 'homeland', which they have actively sought to preserve. In 'Life and People in the Diaspora' we look at ways in which cuisine and popular culture have evolved in the diasporic context, and study how sports, marriage and religious practices link the diaspora and connect the people of the diaspora with Sri Lanka. Also important are aspects of the economic life of those who have ventured overseas—the experience of entrepreneurs who have made their mark in the global village, and contract labourers whose remittances have yielded considerable developmental benefits for Sri Lanka as well.

During the Pongal festival, Sri Lankan Hindu devotees prepare a ritual dish, comprising rice mixed with pulses and sugar.

CUISINE AND FOOD CULTURE

THE SRI LANKAN diaspora, alongside eclectic ethnic communities, are globally most prevalent in major cities and their immediate suburbs. Among its diaspora, Sri Lankan cuisine, a natural choice, is a tremendous source of cultural pride and identity. Sri Lankan fare essentially retains its authenticity throughout the diaspora, while marked and subtle variations contribute further diversity. Best integrated from the authentic cuisine to the diasporic repertoire of daily meals are the cultural comfort foods, special-occasion foods and snacks. The flavours of Sri Lanka are best described as a convergence of Indian, Thai and Indonesian cuisines. However, the unique blends of exotic spices and the use of ingredients like *gamboge* (sour-blackish-wrinkled cloves, of a dried-fleshy fruit) and *Maldive-fish* (sun-dried tuna flakes) give the cuisine its distinct flavour. Authentic Sri Lankan

cuisine encompasses an amazing variety of indigenous dishes and cooking styles. A typical Sri Lankan meal revolves around the nation's primary staple, rice, or a choice of other exquisite staples such as *hoppers* (small wok-shaped crepes with a crispy edge and soft spongy centre), stringhoppers (steamed, thin rice noodles, curled into flat-spiral stacks) and coconut *roti* (flat bread). Staple dishes are accompanied by classic combinations of seafood, meat or poultry, and vegetable dishes. Sri Lankans, in general, revel in their capacity to savour the 'heat' a preparation offers. However, not all dishes are 'fiery' hot. The culinary spread offers a wide array of mild dishes; and meals are often planned to include one, or several, to complement the 'fiery' hot preparations. The lavish use of aromatic and flavourful herbs (mint, lemongrass, curry leaves, etc.) and spices (cardamom, cloves, cinnamon, etc.) is evident in Sri Lankan fare.

Sri Lanka's geographic proximity to India has inevitably influenced the island's cuisine. South Indian culinary influences are typically evident in certain Northern Sri Lankan-Tamil dishes. In particular, *urad-dhal* (black lentils) based dishes such as *thosai* (crepe made with fermented black lentils), *masala vadai* (doughnut-shaped, fried, soft, black-lentil dumpling)

The myriad colours of traditional Sri Lankan cuisine.

and tamarind-based preparations like *pulichatham* (tamarind rice). Historically, Sri Lanka's strategic location as a trading post, along with its flourishing spice gardens, enticed European colonists and Arab traders to the isle. During their consecutive periods of occupation, the Portuguese, Dutch and British greatly influenced native Sri Lankan cuisine by the introduction of innovative cooking techniques and recipes. Sweetmeats such as *boroa* (semolina-coconut cookie) and preparations like *lamprais* (a special rice and curry combination, parcelled in a banana leaf and oven baked) have Portuguese and Dutch origins respectively. In addition, the dramatically varying terrain of the country influences the regional cultivar and indigenous plant species, consequently resulting in northern, southern and central regional fare. The distinct flavours and uniquely varied conventional preparations thus contribute a rich heritage and diversity to the exotic cuisine. Northern recipes such as *pittu* (a steamed granular mixture of coconut and rice flour) and *vara* (a sauté of flaked-cooked fish, grated coconut, onion and green chillies); southern recipes like *kiri bath* (milk rice), *seeni sambol* (sweet and spicy onion sauté onions fried with dried prawns or *Maldive-fish*) and *fish ambul thiyal* (a sour, dry preparation of fish); and central recipes like *bibikkan* (a jaggery [unrefined-brown sugar, made from palm sap] infused coconut cake) and *konda kavum* (fried mini cakes made of rice flour, treacle and coconut-milk) are signature regional dishes. As a tropical-island nation, Sri Lanka has an abundant supply of fresh coconut and seafood. The most illustrious ingredient in Sri Lankan cuisine is evidently coconut. Used in numerous forms (freshly grated, coconut milk, coconut oil, etc.), coconut lends its unique depth of flavour and texture to both savoury and sweet dishes. Sri Lankan cuisine has an impressive repertoire of seafood dishes that range from spicy crab curry and stuffed calamari, to salted dry-fish *theldala* (sauté).

A melting pot of cultures and faiths, the predominant communities of the country have been instrumental in enriching and developing the cuisine. The people of Sri Lanka are of diverse ethnicities (Sinhalese, Tamil, Muslim, Burgher, and Malay) and religions. Presumably, Sri Lankan Hindus and Buddhists played pivotal roles in refining vegetarian dishes; Christians and Catholics in beef and pork recipes; and Muslims in the preparation of mutton and lamb menus. Special occasion foods are plenty in the Sri Lankan repertoire. Made from the humblest of ingredients, *kiri bath* is a must-have on all

auspicious occasions. This versatile dish makes a fabulous breakfast staple and is a favourite comfort food. *Pongal* (sweetened milk rice), a Tamil recipe, equivalent in significance to *kiri bath*, is made in Tamil homes. An array of sweetmeats grace the tables, especially during the Sinhala-Tamil New Year celebrations in April. During Ramadan and Id, *biryani* and *watalappam* (coconut-jaggery, steamed pudding) are must-haves in Muslim homes. These dishes are generally more elaborate and complex in preparation style.

As a natural progression, the Sri Lankan diaspora gravitate toward and draw influence from cuisines with similar flavour-traits. South and Southeast Asian cuisines have the closest ties to Sri Lankan cuisine. As in the homeland, rice is a popular staple in these regions, and the lavish use of familiar ingredients such as coconut, spices, curry powders, garlic and ginger is common. In addition, the abundant supply and use of exotic fruit, vegetables and seafood builds further kinship to the homeland cuisine. Sri Lankan cuisine and food culture is steadily evolving to meet the requirements of its diasporic populace. Global trends, such as busy lifestyles, economic status, availability of ingredients, healthy choices and palatable 'heat levels', dictate the direction of this movement. Within the Sri Lankan diaspora, the most obvious variation to the authentic cuisine is the significant reduction in 'heat' level. The 'heat' of a dish is typically dependent on the amount of chilli (fresh, ground, whole, dry-crushed), curry powders (Jaffna curry powder, roasted Sinhala curry powder) and black pepper used, and is readily adjusted to taste, without compromising the integrity of the dish. The Sri Lankan diaspora, while

Rathu Kekulu (red rice), deviled prawns, coconut sambol, dhal and polos curry (green jackfruit) served at the Sri Lankan Association of Washington D.C. (SLAWDC) 'Sports Day' celebrations in 2009.

At the New Zealand Sri Lanka Foundation's food fair, members of the Sri Lankan diaspora and others had the opportunity to taste the rich flavours of traditional Sri Lankan cuisine.

shying from the overuse of chilli, is progressively using spices and herbs to subtly enhance dishes, and learning to value the inherent flavours of key ingredients, such as vegetables and seafood.

An increasing appreciation and adherence to healthy dietary practices is observed within the diaspora. High calorific ingredients like coconut is used sparingly, reserved for special occasions and successfully substituted with healthier alternatives (e.g. lite-canned coconut-milk). Coconut oil is rarely used in the diaspora, and often substituted with vegetable oil, olive oil or non-stick cooking sprays. Deep-frying is frequently replaced with healthier options such as baking and grilling. When preparing traditional 'twice-cooked' recipes, like eggplant *moju*, where the eggplant pieces are first deep-fried and then simmered in a blend of ingredients, the deep-frying step is successfully replaced by baking the eggplant (with a drizzle of oil). The concept of preserving nutrients, by not overcooking (especially delicate ingredients like vegetables and seafood), is a growing acceptance within the diaspora. In the hot summer months, chilled raw-vegetable soups like *gazpacho* is introduced. Furthermore, the perception and role of 'salads', is at a revolutionary turning point in the diaspora. In conventional Sri Lankan cuisine, salads are never considered a meal by itself, but a side dish. The Western world, especially the United States, takes salad to great heights, by mixing complementary textures and flavours, and making it an appetising meal option. When finances permit, skinless, lean cuts of meat

are excellent healthy options, valued for significantly lower saturated fat content. In the diaspora (especially beyond the first generation), rice is prepared less often and more whole grains, in breads, pasta and cereal, are incorporated into meals.

Basic ingredients for cooking the most traditional Sri Lankan fare are readily available at ethnic grocers and markets. Specialised ingredients such as roasted Sinhala curry powder, Jaffna curry powder, *kithul* treacle and roasted red-rice flour are mainly available at Sri Lankan grocery stores and online sites. Sri Lankan grocers offer a wide range of frozen pre-cooked traditional staples, such as *godamba roti* (flat bread, made of dough balls soaked in oil) and stringhoppers, freshly made snacks,

COOKBOOKS OF JAFFNA CUISINE IN THE DIASPORA

The Recipes of Jaffna Tamils (2003) by Australian-based Nese Eliezer and Rani Thangarajah.

The *Recipes of Jaffna Tamils* (2003), translated and edited by Nese Eliezer and compiled by Rani Thangarajah, offers readers an insight into Jaffna cuisine. Of Sri Lankan Tamil origin, Nese Eliezer is a freelance writer who grew up in Malaysia. Rani Thangarajah is a Tamil poet who has been active in various cultural productions.

Catering to the Tamils in the diaspora, the book consists of an array of Jaffna Tamil recipes such as *idiyappam* (stringhoppers) and *sothi* (coconut-based gravy), *pittu, thenggai paal kanchi* (coconut milk porridge), *manchal choru* (yellow rice) and a variety of *pachadis* and *chambals*.

Another poignant book that illustrates the culinary traditions of Jaffna Tamils is *Celebrating 100 Years: The Singapore Ceylon Tamils' Association* (2011) by Indra Rani Lavan Iswaran. The author is a Jaffna Tamil Singaporean who was born in Perak, Malaysia. The chapter on 'Favourite Flavours from Jaffna Cusine' contains important recipes such as *palchura varai* (baby shark flake), *kool* (seafood dish made with palmyrah root flour, jackfruit, dried chillies, etc), *raasavali kelangu kanchi* (purple yam porridge), *paitham paniyaram* (snack made with green gram flour), *chippi* (bite-sized crispy snack made with black gram, coconut milk and sugar), and *mothagam* (sweetmeat made of moong dhal, jaggery and desiccated coconut commonly seen during special occasions).

Hema Kiruppalini

Of Sri Lankan-Austrian heritage, London-born Peter Kuruvita is an Australian celebrity chef, restaurateur and media personality. His early childhood in Sri Lanka significantly influenced his culinary expertise.

Idiyappam served with sothi. In Singapore and Malaysia, it is common for locals to eat stringhoppers with orange sugar.

Paitham paniyaram, a snack made with moong (green gram flour), is a favourite among Jaffna Tamils who prepare this on special occasions.

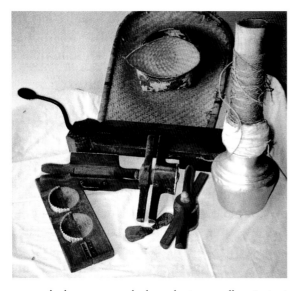

Traditional Sri Lankan utensils brought by emigrants to Malaysia and Singapore in the early 20th century. They include the grinding stone and roller (ammi and kulavi), dhal grinder (aatukallu), rice-pounding equipment (ulakkai) and murukku (savoury crunchy snack) maker (ural).

pre-cooked vacuum-packed products as well as instant mixes (imported from the homeland). Assorted products, including condiments, are available in many familiar brands such as MD (Marketing Department), Larich, Nikado and Maharaja. Various blends of the world-renowned 'Ceylon' tea are always available at Sri Lankan grocers. Unfortunately, there are not enough Sri Lankan grocers, cafes, and restaurants, even in major cities, to satisfy the culinary demands of the diaspora. Toronto is an exception, where there is a significant number of Sri Lankan proprietors catering to the diaspora. Accessibility to Sri Lankan grocery items can be limited by economics, for most items cost at least double the price compared to the homeland.

Within the Sri Lankan diaspora, a progressively faster-paced lifestyle dictates a burgeoning food culture of semi-homemade meals, take-out and dining-out. Modern amenities (microwaves, blenders, food processors, pressure cookers, etc.) are often used, hastening preparation and cooking times; and one-pot meals, like casseroles, are ideal time saving options. When preparing semi-homemade meals, every dish is not made from basic ingredients. One or more ingredients are purchased (pre-cooked or as an instant-mix) and combined with other homemade preparations. For instance, a traditional staple like stringhoppers is bought fresh, or a frozen batch is defrosted and paired with a homemade fish or chicken curry. The fast-food culture in the United States is catching on in the rest of the world. Convenient, tasty and relatively affordable fast-food chains like McDonalds', KFC (Kentucky Fried Chicken) and Pizza Hut are attractive alternatives to a home-cooked meal. The gastronomical practices, among the Sri Lankan diaspora, is highly dependent on the level of assimilation with the resident country. In Europe, North America and the Pacific (Australia and New Zealand), wine and cheese are an important part of a meal, especially during dinner, when dining out or entertaining guests. Cheese is especially important for diaspora in Northern and Western European countries. Drawing inspiration from the resident countries, interesting pairings for wine, such as olives, smoked salmon, herring (raw or pickled), seasonal fruit and prosciutto have been adopted in the diaspora. In European countries, a culture of cafes and patisserie is popular, where sweet croissants and tarts accompanied with a cup of coffee or espresso is a must. Sweetbreads or a bowl of cereal with milk make a popular breakfast in the West, whereas in the homeland, breakfast is mainly a 'savoury' meal. The bar and pub culture offers an entirely different experience, where an array of local and imported beer and finger-foods (buffalo wings, barbecue ribs, fries, etc.) are at hand. Irish and British pubs introduce Shepherd's Pie and fish and chips to the culinary repertoire. The popular culture of summer grilling is adopted, especially from the contagiously zesty lifestyles of the Americans, Australians and New Zealanders. Meat, seafood, vegetables and fruit are grilled to perfection outdoors, seasoned by many marinades and herbs.

As a result of the diasporic intercultural-social experiences, the emergence of Sri Lankan fusion recipes and recipe variations is evident. A burgeoning concept in the diaspora, Sri Lankan fusion recipes stem from an interest in pairing familiar flavours and textures with the intriguing new, or by simply substituting ingredients in classic recipes. The staples, seasonings and cooking practices of inspirational cuisines are more commonly adopted and integrated into the diasporic culinary repertoire. Staples such as *chapatti* (flat bread) and *poori* (deep-fried flat bread), and seasonings such as Madras curry powder, Tandoori paste and *garam masala*, are favourites borrowed from Indian cuisine. Here, cilantro and yogurt are used more readily, and seafood preparations are enhanced with mustard oil.

'Jaffna House', a restaurant in London is well-known for both Sri Lankan and Indian cuisine.

Ceylon Spices and Cargo Services in Adelaide, Australia, offers a range of spices and produce from South Asia, Fiji and Africa.

'Hopper Night', organised by the Melbourne-based Sri Lankan Study Centre for the Advancement of Technology and Social Welfare (SCATS), raises funds for a community centre.

In Saskatoon, Canada, Sri Lankan men take charge of preparing kottu roti, *a popular street food delicacy in Sri Lanka.*

Members of the New Zealand Sri Lanka Foundation prepare appam *for the annual food fair.*

American-born hip-hop journalist, S.H. Fernando Jr, returned to Sri Lanka in 2006 where he learnt how to cook various traditional delicacies. His book 'Rice and Curry: Sri Lankan Home Cooking' was published in 2008.

Practices such as simmering key ingredients in tomato-based gravies and the use of roasted coconut and ground nuts to thicken and flavour dishes are all enticing possibilities. Indonesian cuisine offers *sambal olek* (fresh red chilli paste in vinegar), peanut sauce and shrimp paste, as well as delicious preparations such as *satay* and fish in banana leaf parcels. Chinese cuisine introduces an array of noodles, soy sauce, Chinese mustard, horseradish, chilli paste, Hoisin sauce and hot-oil, while practices like wok-stir frying, steaming fish, balancing hot and sour flavours, and cooking vegetables to crunchy perfection are lessons well learnt. Italian cuisine offers staples (pasta, pizza and calzones), sauces (pesto, marinara and alfredo) and delicious cheeses (mozzarella, ricotta, etc). The abundant use of basil and extra virgin olive oil are further attributes of this type of cuisine. In the United States, the Sri Lankan diasporic cuisine progresses towards the use of herbs like rosemary, thyme, dill and sage. Potato, couscous, pasta, casseroles, tortillas, rice and beans; seasonings such as spice rubs (Cajun, creole, Mexican), sauces (Tabasco and barbecue sauce), salad dressings and marinades, open the adventurous to further diversity. Middle Eastern cuisines offer versatile staples such as pita bread and couscous, and preparations like *kabobs, falafel* and hummus. Mint, yogurt, lamb, lemon and olive oil are also tasteful additions to the diasporic culinary repertoire.

Special occasions in the resident country do influence the Sri Lankan diasporic food culture. For instance, Thanksgiving in the United States is a holiday marked by a roast turkey with stuffing, gravy and cranberry sauce, followed with a decadent dessert of pumpkin pie. Most

Sri Lankans in the United States celebrate Thanksgiving in similar fashion.

Typically conventional, there is a tendency for the Sri Lankan diaspora to avoid what they perceive as 'extreme' foods, such as frogs' legs, pigs' trotters, certain insects, escargots (snails), even if these may be considered local delicacies in some countries. *Sushi* has become increasingly popular within the Sri Lankan community, and some have even mastered the art of eating with chopsticks. However, other Japanese preparations (except vegetables) that are served raw, such as oysters and *sashimi*, are usually given a pass. The Sri Lankan diasporic cuisine and food culture is broadening its scope, embracing diversity, making the cuisine further relevant in modern society.

Suharshini Seneviratne

BURGHER CUISINE

Burgher cuisine in old Ceylon included menus derived from the community's European connections. Portuguese and Dutch cakes and pastries, veal cutlets, stews and potatoes regularly appeared on Burgher tables. It was relatively easy therefore for Burgher families to adopt the cuisines of countries they migrated to since the 1950s. However, long-standing ideals of elaborate ingredients and pungent tastes remained.

The Burgher community in Australia is perhaps one of the largest Burgher communities today. The food that has been treasured and eaten by this community is based on the traditions of families and owes little to published cookbooks, apart from bedraggled copies of the *Daily News Cookery Book*. It does owe much to the efforts of grandmothers, mothers and aunts to teach their progeny how particular *short-eats*, curries, desserts and drinks should taste. 'Now what should the sour be in this curry?' was the question that constantly rang in my ears when my grandmother, fearful that I was spending too much time on study and would never be married, descended on us to teach me how to cook. 'Is it lime, vinegar, tamarind or *billing*?' (Even though that last ingredient does not grow in Australia). Since these tastes and skills were particular to families, ingredients are hotly debated. Sadly, many of these have also been abandoned.

However, many Burghers are united in the belief that there are certain essentials to good eating. Any decent party should have *short-eats*. These consist of fish or meat patties, some version of cheese straws (long cheese biscuits) meat balls and asparagus rolls.

Vegetable curries must be flavoured with flakes of *Maldive-fish*, and *dhal* must have these and mustard seeds. *Seeni sambol*, or lime pickle, made with preserved limes, chopped onions, chilli, and *Maldive-fish* or a mustard pickle ought to accompany any rice meal. Contrary to the current obsession with freshly ground herbs and spices, the Marketing Board's double roasted curry powder with curry leaves, *rampa*, lemon grass already in the mix was a must for meat curries except chicken curry.

Crabs must be seen alive and moving before they are cooked—and some families insist this can only be done in a curry flavoured with *murunga* or drumstick leaves. *Rissoles* are comfort food, as is coconut sambol. A roast chicken should be accompanied by a stuffing made of liver, cashew nuts, sultanas and sweet spices. *Seer* fish is regarded as a food for the gods.

Stalls retailing Sri Lankan food preparations are a common feature of the Annual Sri Lanka Day that is celebrated at the Gardner Field Recreation Park, Denville, New Jersey, 2010.

On special occasions, stringhoppers and *mulligatawny* (made properly with cleaned prawn heads and shells, fried liberally with chilli) or *lamprais* are a big treat. *Lamprais* are individual packages that can be held in the palm of a hand. A mound of rice, cooked in meat stock, is placed on a banana leaf and embellished with a curry of chopped beef, chicken, lamb, pork and liver, eggplant, a dab each of prawn blachang, and *seeni sambol*, two *frikkadels* or breaded meatballs, and, if it can be obtained, ash plantain vegetable. The leaf is then folded into a parcel and baked or steamed so that all flavours are infused. Dessert on such an occasion should be *wattalappam*.

Christmas would not be Christmas without *breudher*—a buttery cake with raisins, baked in a jelly mould and eaten with more butter, Edam cheese and long, green skinned bananas. This must be eaten for breakfast. Guests who have 'come to wish' must be served slices of two essential cakes. *Love cake*, made of cashew nuts, 25 eggs, semolina, lemon peel and sweet spices. This is then baked so that it emerges in three layers: thin crisp top, gelatinous middle and biscuit bottom. Elderly ladies remark, in horror,

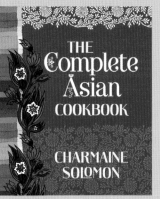

Charmaine Solomon, of Burgher origin, migrated to Australia in 1959. The Complete Asian Cookbook comprises some 800 recipes and is considered one of the most influential cookbooks in Australia.

about cakes which, sadly, did not have three layers. 'She could not have beaten in each yolk for 20 minutes. It was such a disgrace.' Small parcels of wrapped fruit cake, iced with almond paste, are quite simply called Rich Cake. Rich Cake must have cashew nuts, sultanas, raisins, candied peel, preserved ginger, pumpkin preserve, pineapple jam, rose water and, of course, 25 egg yolks, each beaten in separately. *Chow chow* preserve is now difficult to get and seldom added. In certain families, the fruit is marinated for three weeks before baking, in a glass of brandy and one of Benedictine. Accompanying this should be a small glass of *milk wine*, arrack mulled with milk and sweet spices.

Lost to most of the current generation are pastries like *bola fiado* and *fogguett* and many of the younger members of the community struggle to find the time and the will to carry on all or any of their culinary heritage. Consequently, today, small businesses have sprung up from which members of the community order stringhoppers, the Christmas cakes and milk wine. The hopper man at a dinner party is a luxury indulged in by some.

Lesley Jeffery

Sri Lankan Burgher crab curry flavoured with murunga leanves.

Love cakes — often served during festive occassions.

Lamprais served at the 'Lakruwana' Sri Lankan restaurant in the Staten Island, New York.

SPORTS

AS WITH ALL colonial-into-postcolonial conditions, the social contours of sport for Sri Lanka and its diaspora were, and remain drawn, by the circumstances and conditions in which they were formed and from which they emerged. In the specific Sri Lankan case, those contours were further nuanced by the evolving social interactions between the Sinhala, Burgher and Indian elements of the community.

The predominant patterns of modern sport (and the term here excludes the hunting of animals so prominent in British South Asia) emerged through the mid- to late-19th century when the British predilection for organised sport as moral metaphor and social training regime took strong root.

In one sense the Ceylon impact began quickly. In 1878 Patrick Frank Hadow went 'Home' to England on holiday from his tea estate. Hadow was the son of the Chairman of the Peninsular & Oriental (P&O) shipping line, and his brother perished on the descent following Edward Whymper's conquering the Matterhorn. A Harrow School man, Frank Hadow played cricket for Middlesex, the MCC, the Gentlemen of England and Ceylon. The folklore is that Hadow became taken with tennis, and entered for Wimbledon, then in its second year. He won the all-comers section to reach the final against reigning champion, Spencer William Gore, whom he beat by a judicious use of the lob. Hadow remains the only champion never to have lost a set—he refused to return to defend his title, allegedly because tennis should only be for women!

Similarly, George Bailey, born in Colombo in the mid-19th century, was educated in England where he developed excellent cricket skills. By 1874 he was in Launceston, Tasmania, where he went into business but kept his cricket to such a level that he toured England with the 1878 Australian side, winning a reputation as a leading batsman. He never toured again but was still playing around the turn of the century. He died in Tasmania in 1927 but his great-great-grandson, also George Bailey, now captains Tasmania and has followed his ancestor into the Australian side.

Hadow and Bailey reaffirmed the importance of what was considered to be the strong connection between sport and Sri Lankan social development, by underlining the idea of sport and social growth being linked. Organised interschool cricket was introduced in 1879 and this competition effectively grafted sport onto the island's extant and complex social systems, and was driven quintessentially through the schools. In particular, it began with the intense sporting contests, especially cricket, between the Colombo-based St Thomas' and Royal colleges, reinforced by the arrival of English teaching staff who themselves emerged from the then strong 'muscular Christian' ethos of the Greater Public Schools, Oxford and Cambridge. In 1896, the Reverend W. A. Buck was appointed Warden of St Thomas'. Buck was educated at Merchant Taylors' then Peterhouse, Cambridge. He was an accomplished rugby player through to county level, played cricket for the Gentlemen of Essex, was an oarsman and an athlete. He brought to St Thomas' a strong games ethic, and visitors to the school noticed immediate improvements in cricket pitch quality.

Sri Lankan fans cheered their team on in the final of the one-day cricket series in Adelaide, 8 March 2012.

The Canadian Tamil Sports Association (CTSA) established in 1995 has been an umbrella organisation for various sporting activities. Pictured here are youth members who took part in the annual Track and Field event, 2010.

Among Buck's charges, James Arthur Scharenguivel became one of Ceylon's first major sports exports. Born in Kandy in 1879, Scharenguivel, tall and strong, proved outstanding of mind and at games. A left hand bat, he set all kinds of records before going to Aberdeen University where he completed a medical degree. Resident in Aberdeen for several years, he became the first Sri Lankan to score a century overseas. He had an outstanding record for the university's cricket club and while he never gained a full cap for Scotland, he did play against the Australians in 1905 alongside outstanding players like Monty Noble, Clem Hill and the ferociously fast bowler Tibby Cotter.

Scharenguivel then set the pattern for many later Sri Lankan sports people, going to the Straits Settlements where he practiced medicine for several years. He was a regular feature on Singapore's cricket ground for both club and representative games into the 1920s. In 1909 he played for the Straits Settlements against Monty Noble's Australian side, renewing his friendship from the Scotland match, and by the 1920s (then in his 40s) was still playing at a good level. He returned to Ceylon and in 1930 turned out for Panadura against the Maharajkumar of Vizianagram's Indian XI. In the 1940s he looked to emigrate to Tasmania, but went instead to Perth where he died in 1958.

Throughout his life there was a strong sense that the connection between sport, social service and social training was an essential element in community growth. His younger cousin, Douglas Scharenguivel, became one of Ceylon's first Davis Cup tennis players and was for several years based at the Bristol Tennis Club in England, from where he was a regular if unsuccessful Wimbledon player. Another descendant was a recent Sri Lankan cricket captain, Marvan Atapattu.

The sport-social growth and service nexus lasted well into the 20th century, encouraged by the presence, in Ceylon, of people like the wonderfully named Banner Carruthers Johnstone. Born in 1883, Johnstone was educated at Eton then Trinity, Cambridge, where he was among the leading rowers of his day. He rowed in the Oxford-Cambridge boat race from 1904 to 1907; represented Cambridge against Harvard in 1906; and was a leading contender at Henley through those years. His standing was demonstrated through his election as President of the Cambridge University Boat Club, and more so by his appointment as Captain of Leander, the premier rowing club. In 1908, Johnstone reached the pinnacle of his rowing career, winning an Olympic Gold medal in the eights along with the legendary Guy Nickalls. At the same time 'Bush', his nickname derived from his luxuriant moustache, served in the Black Watch militia, and later in World War I served with the Black Watch in France. Again, the link between sport and social service was exemplified.

In 1909, Banner Johnstone joined the Government Survey Office in Colombo. He stayed there for four years before shifting to Zanzibar, but while on the island he epitomised the role played by sport in forming what were considered to be the desired and desirable social mores in the colonial setting.

At that time Ceylon had another interesting sports export, Alfred Holsinger. Born in 1880, Holsinger was also a St Thomas' man and was said to be the fastest bowler on the island. He was a prolific wicket taker in schoolboy and senior cricket, then around the turn of the century became Ceylon's first professional cricketer, travelling to England in search of fame and fortune. He never really found either. While Scharenguivel studied and played in Scotland, Holsinger, pointedly referred to as a 'coloured' player, struggled away in the county leagues. He may have even played first on the Isle of Wight because he married there in 1901. Sadly, he lost his newborn son in 1905, but was soon trooping his wife and daughters through the Yorkshire and other leagues.

In 1907–08 Holsinger played several matches for Lincolnshire in the Minor Counties championship. His best bowling came in a 1908 match against Staffordshire for whom former England player S. F. Barnes appeared—

Sinhavalokanaya, a Sri Lankan film based on cricket, screened at Monash University, in aid of the Sinhala Cultural and Community Services Foundation in Melbourne.

At the Beijing 2008 Olympic Games, Pradeeban Peter-Paul represented Canada in table tennis.

Holsinger took 6/37 off 27 overs. In some of his earlier appearances he did not bowl, inexplicably, raising questions about how he was treated as a 'coloured' player long before they became common in the leagues. He also played against William Tyldesley who would later die in Belgium towards the end of World War I, and who was the brother of England player Dick Tyldesley.

At the 1911 census, though, Viola Holsinger was recorded as residing in Mirfield in the Yorkshire West Riding, with at least three daughters and a male (presumably her husband, Alfred) also in residence. Alfred Holsinger was certainly playing for Mirfield in 1915 because he took six wickets against local rivals Hopton Mills, for which team he also played at some point. By then Holsinger had played for many teams including Burnley St Andrews in the Lancashire League, Liverpool Nomads, Lincoln Lindrum, Llanelly in Wales and would also play for Eppleton in the Durham League.

Holsinger spent 20 years pursuing this tough life, taking his family into what must have been frequently an uncomfortable, unwelcoming environment. Upon retirement, however, he stayed in the area and passed away in the Spen Valley in 1942, the first case of a Sri Lankan turning what was thought to be a social training tool into a working life, even if a precarious one.

Carl Theodore van Geyzel, from a prominent Burgher line, had a very different trajectory. Born in 1902 he attended Royal College and, like his father and brother, became a prominent cricketer—one first-class match for Ceylon and another for Cambridge against the MCC. A tall, stylish batsman he was far better known as an athlete. An athletics Blue at Cambridge in 1924–25, he was one of the outstanding contemporary high jumpers. He won the English Amateur Athletic Association championship in 1926, had a personal best of over 6' 2", and represented Great Britain at the 1928 Amsterdam Olympics. He performed poorly, jumped under 6' and missed qualification, watching the gold medal won at a height below his personal best. Carl van Geyzel returned to Sri Lanka and set national records. He was appointed President of the Ceylon Amateur Atheletic Association between 1952 and 1966 before his death in 1971.

There were clear patterns in these cases: sports predominantly as part of an education and upbringing, and generally part of a social training but with the appearance of a 'professional' career option. That pattern held for most classes and communities for a very long time, but began to fragment as political

change escalated and further social alteration began.

The Tamil elements in Sri Lankan society, for example, showed the potential variations. As they moved for work and opportunity, particularly across the Indian Ocean to Singapore and Malaysia, they brought many practices with them, including sport. The controversial Mahadevan Sathasivam provided a later case in point. Born in 1915 he became a skilled and elegant batsman, and a controversial personality. He was well regarded by world cricket figures like Gary Sobers who thought him to be the best batsman in the world at the time, a huge compliment. Satha was appointed Ceylon captain to face Sir Donald Bradman's 1948 team en route to England, an unpopular decision because a Sinhalese player was reckoned more senior. In part, this reflected doubts about Satha's alleged off-field behaviours but was also a sign of the inter-community tensions surfacing around that time. As with all other social spheres in Sri Lanka and around the British Empire, sport was often used to exclude rather than include. In the 1950s, Satha went off to Singapore where he captained the side there, before going to Malaysia where he also became captain. He returned to Sri Lanka later in his life and died there in 1977.

Before, but especially after independence, the Tamils and the Burghers alike contributed to a steady flow of sports influence around the world. It is often said, for example, that Malaysian cricket developed out of the railway towns where Sri Lankan Tamil engineers and workers were notable. Sathasivam, for example, was later followed as Malaysian captain by R. Ratnalingam, the Rhodes Scholar physicist who became a leading Malaysian educationist. One of Malaysia's leading athletes and administrators has been Mani Jegathesan, born in Perak of Sri Lankan Tamil origin. Women sprint stars M. Rajamani and G. Shanti similarly dominated athletics.

With the onset of independence that spread with the Sri Lankan sports, influence gathered pace, accelerated later by the rise in playing power of Sri Lankan cricket. Leading up to and beyond February 1948, a steady stream of sportspeople left Sri Lanka, adding to the already strong patterns of influence developed over the preceding 50 years. Immediately after independence, for example, former Royal College cricket player Pat McCarthy arrived in Western Australia and played for that state in 1950–51 and 1953–54. Western Australia was not the cricket power it later became but was still competitive, so McCarthy's inclusion was notable. In one of his later appearances he made 98 against New South Wales, then the leading side, falling to Richie Benaud but playing well against Ray Lindwall, Bill O'Reilly and Keith Miller. He was in heady company, a

SPORTS IN SINGAPORE AND MALAYSIA

Ceylonese pioneers who migrated to Malaya showed a keen interest in sports and established early institutions in both Malaysia and Singapore during the 20th century. Among them emerged sporting talents who represented their country at state, national and international arenas. Ceylonese from both Malaysia and Singapore have long shared a strong sporting fraternity; the Ceylon Sports Club (CSC) in Singapore and the Tamilians' Physical Culture Association (TPCA) in Kuala Lumpur have served as key venues for joint activities.

S. N. Arseculeratne informed about the existence of a Selangor Sinhalese Sports Club during the early 1920s and some prominent sporting figures from the Sinhalese diaspora in Malaysia included Felix Perera, who represented Malaya in the national cricket team; Noel Monerasinghe notable in both cricket and hockey; Cyril Perera, who in 1958 captained the Malayan Contingent at the South East Asian Peninsular Games and won for Malaya a gold for the pole vault at the Decathlon; Frederica 'Winnie' Tallalle, who in 1927 founded the first Women's Hockey team in Malaya, among others.

Over the years, the sporting institutions that were established by the multi-ethnic pioneers from Ceylon have developed to include the various racial groups that make up Malaysia and Singapore.

Ceylon Sports Club (CSC), Singapore

The Lanka Union, which was formed in 1920 and later renamed as the Ceylon Sports Club (CSC) in 1928, garnered the support and participation of Ceylonese Tamils, Sinhalese, Burghers and Malays. The club was founded by early Ceylonese professionals and students of King Edward VII College of Medicine who were keen to form a sporting club that would unite various groups of Ceylonese students. The CSC is one of the oldest sporting clubs in Singapore. In 1951, the foundation stone for the new building was laid by the Prime Minister of Ceylon, Dudley S. Senanayake, and the official inauguration was held in 1954. Since its founding, the club has achieved considerable success in sports, especially cricket. It remains an important venue for cricket tournaments and holds the record for organising 72 hours of continuous cricket matches. Apart from sporting activities, the CSC is also used as a venue for the Sri Lankan diaspora in Singapore to hold social functions.

In December 2001, Tharman Shanmugaratnam, Singapore's then Senior Minister of State for Education and Trade and Industry, applauded the CSC for its role in bringing together the Ceylonese community and, as well, for reaching out to fellow Singaporeans and expatriates:

The Ceylon Sports Club in Singapore, 2013.

… Through the years, the CSC has retained the ability to make any Ceylonese feel at home and part of a common fraternity, notwithstanding the political travails of post-independence Sri Lanka. Second, the Club has increasingly brought in Singaporean and expatriate members of other races. Almost two-thirds of the club's members today are not of Ceylonese descent…

Lanka Lions Cricket Club, Singapore

Registered in 2006, the Lanka Lions Cricket Club commonly known as the 'Lanka Lions' comprises of a team of Singaporeans and expatriates of Sri Lankan origin. Members of Sri Lankan origin include Tamils, Sinhalese and Muslims, most of whom emigrated to Singapore in recent years. The club has been active in organising and participating in international events. They have also developed links with prominent Sri Lankan international cricket stars.

The Tamilians' Physical Culture Association (TPCA), Malaysia

The Tamilians' Physical Culture Association (TPCA) in Kuala Lumpur formed in 1914 remains an important sporting club in Malaysia. R. Rajakrishnan informs that the association grew from the Ceylon Tamil Atheletics Club formed in 1906. The stadium at the TPCA has hosted several national and international sporting events. Many distinguished sportsmen from the Ceylonese diaspora in Malaysia were members of this club. According to R. Rajakrishnan, some of them include: N. M. Vasagam, M. Jegathesan, G. Rajalingam, K. Selvaratnam, and M. Rajamani in athletics; R. P. S. Rajasooria, P. Alagendra and Sundram Robert in cricket; S. C. E. Singham in soccer; the Appucutty brothers Samuel and Leslie in badminton; and G. Vijayanathan, A. Durairatnam, K. Aryaduray, and Sri Shanmuganathan in hockey.

C. Kunalan

Canagasabai Kunalan was inducted into the Singapore Sports Council's Hall of Fame as a double Olympian (Tokyo, 1964; Mexico, 1968). During his sprinting career, which lasted almost 20 years, there were several special moments that explain why he is heralded as a sporting legend in Singapore. In the 1968 Mexico Olympics, Kunalan, clocked a time of

Canagasabai Kunalan, better known as C. Kunalan, is regarded as one of Singapore's sporting heroes most notable for being the country's national sprinting king.

10.38 seconds for 100 metres, setting a record for Singapore that remained unbroken for 33 years.

Mani Jegathesan

Fondly regarded as the 'Flying Doctor', Mani Jegathesan has had an illustrious career both as a doctor and as a national icon of Malaysian athletics. In 1962, he won Malaysia's first ever Gold (200m) at the Asian Games, and again in the 1966 Asian Games (Gold for 100m, 200m, 4x100m). In the same year, he was crowned 'Asian Athlete of 1966' and titled the 'Fastest Man in Asia'.

Mani Jegathesan, Chairman of the OCA medical committee, speaks to reporters during a press conference at the Asian Youth Games in Singapore, 2009.

M. Rajamani

Rajamani Mailvaganam, in just four short years between 1964-68, won seven gold medals in two Southeast Asian Peninsular (SEAP) Games, one Asian Games Gold (400m)—becoming the first Malaysian female athlete to clinch Gold at the Asian Games—and also the National Sportswoman of the Year Award in 1966 and 1967.

Hema Kiruppalini

M.Rajamani (right) receiving the National Sports Award from Malaysia's first Prime Minister, Tunku Abdul Rahman, 1966.

Prashanth Sellathurai of Australia competes on the pommel horse during the Apparatus Finals of the 2005 World Gymnastics Championships in Melbourne, Australia.

The Canadian tennis star, Sonya Jeyaseelan, was well-recognised on the Grand Slam circuit in the late 1990s and early 2000s.

Sanjayan Thuraisingam, playing for Canada against Kenya in the 2003 ICC Cricket World Cup.

testimony to the quality of Sri Lankan cricket. Since then players of Sri Lankan origins like Malcolm Francke and Dav Whatmore have played prominently, Whatmore playing for Australia and going on to an international coaching career.

Gamini Goonesena was the most distinguished Sri Lankan player of this period to reach Australia, and perhaps the last of the great 'amateurs' to emerge from the school and values based system. Born in 1931 he played for Royal College then went to Cambridge where he not only won Blues but captained the university side, scoring 211 in 1957. He also played successfully for Nottinghamshire and, tellingly, played for the Gentlemen (amateurs) against the Players (professionals) for several years. He then shifted to Australia and played for New South Wales from 1961–64 and was still playing Sydney club cricket in the 1970s. After later returning to Sri Lanka he then retired back to Sydney.

During that period Goonesena was joined by many other leading Sri Lankan sports people. By the turn of the 21st century well over 100 former Sri Lanka representatives were based in Australia. Among them were people like Lorna van Cuylenberg (netball), Melanie Vanderwert (nee Cuylenberg and also netball), Peter Ranasighe (soccer), Dick and Bobby Schoorman (table tennis and cricket), and Marlon Vonhagt who like his ancestor, J. A. Scharenguivel, also played cricket for Sri Lanka. Rupert Ferdinands, a Davis Cup tennis player and accomplished table tennis player came to Australia in 1972 and has had an enormous impact nationally as a coach. His great veterans table tennis teammates in Australia have been Buddy Reid who played cricket for Ceylon from 1964–70, Nimo Ramchand who came to Australia as a railway engineer in 1974, and Dick Schoorman.

Raif Jansz, the great Thomas Cup badminton star, shifted to Australia in the 1970s and died in 2010. The Jansz name is prominent in Australia because Geoff Jansz is a famous television chef, part of the wider Sri Lankan contribution to Australian life, along with singers so diverse as Keith Potger of The Seekers, pop star Guy Sebastian and opera diva Danielle de Niese, and public figures like the former Governor of Victoria David de Kretser.

Some of these Australian residents retain an enormous sports standing in Sri Lanka. Early in 2011 the great hockey goalkeeper, Freddie White, returned for a visit to Sri Lanka and attracted considerable attention. His brother Duncan White was Ceylon's first Olympic medallist, winning a silver for sprinting in 1948 in London, where he later lived.

As with other South Asian diasporas, the modern Sri Lankan sports one demonstrates a multi-dimensional picture. Shyam Sidek, for example, another Royal College graduate, is now a leading business figure who plays cricket for the Royal Bangkok Sports Club and for Thailand. Prashanth Sellathurai was born in Sydney in 1986 after his parents migrated there in 1983. He won a team gold in gymnastics for Australia and won the individual pommel horse gold medal, the apparatus on which he has won three world championship medals.

Dimitri Mascarenhas demonstrates the complexity in all this. His parents, from the Baratha community near Colombo, first migrated to the United Kingdom. He was born in England but grew up in Western Australia, where his parents ran a restaurant business. He returned to England to play cricket for Hampshire and later was part of the national team. Sanjayan Thuraisingam was born in Colombo in 1969 but his family shifted to Canada and he played for the national cricket side there between 2003 and 2006. Dilip Kumar went to Trinity College in Colombo but became based in Sydney and became Chairman of the Australian Rugby Union in 2005.

Sonya Jeyaseelan was born in Canada to Sri Lankan parents and was a professional tennis player for some time, beating Venus Williams earlier in her career. She once revealed her sense of a cultural conflict, feeling more 'Canadian' than her parents and consequently struggling with her development. If so, that was a logical consequence of two intersecting trends that had emerged over the previous century for those Sri Lankan and other global citizens, especially sporting personalities, now working at a broader than national scale.

The first trend is for elite sport to become more global than national. Muttiah Muralitharan and Kumar Sangakkara are good examples. They play cricket for Sri Lanka but also apply their trade all over the world, so that their view of citizenship changes. The second trend is for that sports experience to become increasingly embedded in more of a world-culture view and for those of Sri Lankan origin, but living elsewhere permanently, it becomes a question of which cultural heritage becomes the dominant one.

Brian Stoddart

RELIGIOUS NETWORKS

THE MYRIAD EMIGRATION streams from Sri Lanka have produced a vibrant diasporic religious tapestry. In the 21st century, all of Sri Lanka's major religious traditions —Buddhism, Hinduism, Islam and Christianity—are represented in the diaspora. The specific development of religious life and institutions in countries where the diaspora has settled is detailed in the 'communities' section of this volume. An examination of religious linkages in a 'transnational networks' frame is however, useful where manifestations of Sri Lanka's religious traditions have extended beyond specific 'host' countries. The segments that follow study transnational Buddhist and Muslim religious networks that have emanated from Sri Lanka. In the case of Buddhism, such connections— particularly with countries in South and Southeast Asia—extend to a period long before the presence of a settled diaspora. These linkages provide the backdrop for the deep religious connections that exist between these countries in the 21st century.

Rajesh Rai

SINHALA BUDDHIST RELATIONS WITH SOUTHEAST ASIA

The movement of Sinhala monks and nuns to the Southeast Asian region was facilitated by advances in navigation technology that witnessed a quantum leap in the 4th–5th centuries. By the middle of the T'ang period (618–907 CE), Sri Lankan ships, which were about 100 feet long and carried about six to seven hundred men, were, according to Chinese sources, the largest ships known to them (Wolters, 1927: 146–48). Sri Lanka influenced the culture of Southeast Asia from at least the 8th century when inscriptions relating to the 'town folk from Anuradhapura' and another on a well-known incident in the Sinhalese Chronicle *Mahavamsa* occur in what is today's Thailand, and in Anuradhapura style statues discovered in different parts of Southeast Asia.

The major impact, however, began from around the 11th century when the Sinhalese form of Buddhism was first accepted in Myanmar, parts of today's northern Thailand (12th century), Cambodia and southern Vietnam (13th century), Laos (14th century), and the south-western region of China around Yunnan (12th and 13th centuries). In these countries the order of monks adopted the Sinhalese form and were often called the Sinhala order (*Sinhala Vamsa*) or the Lanka order (*Lanka Vamsa*). The Sri Lankan imprint in these countries was not restricted only to matters of Buddhism, its philosophy and culture, but also impacted architecture, the writing of history, literature, sculpture and painting. In their historical chronicles, the preamble was almost always taken from the *Mahavamsa* and so related their history to that of Sri Lanka. With this background, the following describe Sinhala Buddhist interactions with specific Southeast Asian countries untill the 19th and 20th centuries.

Thailand

The earliest cultural exchange appears to have taken place in the lower Menam valley in the Dvaravati kingdom, established in lower Thailand in the 6th or 7th century with Nakorn Pathom ('First City') or Phra Pathom as the capital. A significant indication of the existence of relations between Sri Lanka and Dvaravati was the discovery of an old Mon inscription of Tham Narai or the Khao Wong cave in Saraburi province, dated 550–650 CE, which mentions *kamun anuradhapurakoak* (town people from Anuradhapura). This is a reference to a group of people from Anuradhapura who settled as a community in Dvaravati. The close relations between Dvaravati and Anuradhapura in Sri Lanka were further corroborated when three verses, written in old Khmer in the Noen Sa Bua inscription of Prachinburi, dated 761 CE, were identified by Rohanadeera as verses from the Pali work *Thelakatahagatha*, written in Sri Lanka.

By the 13th century, Sri Lanka had become the acknowledged 'holy land' in the contemporary Buddhist world, and it was considered a demonstration of the prowess of the rulers of Southeast Asia to possess a Buddha image made in Sri Lanka. The *Jinakalamali* and the *Sihinga Buddharupanidana* refer to a mission sent in the 13th century by the Sukhothai king, Rocaraja (identified as Rama Khamheng), jointly with the king of Siridhammanagara (present-day Nakhon Si Thammarat), to the Sri Lankan king, Parakramabahu II of Dambadeniya (1236–71) requesting a famous image.

King Lothai (1317–47), son of Rama Khamheng requested a Sinhala Mahathera, Udumbara Mahasami of the *Arannavasi* fraternity who had arrived in Pegu (lower Burma) to send a monk to perform ecclesiastical functions (he has been identified as Sangharaja Medhankara, the author of the *Lokappadipasara*). A monk from Sukhothai named Sumana, had by that time, gone to Pegu and with another Sukhothai monk, Anomadassi, studied under Udumbara Mahasami, and received *upasampada*. Udumbara Mahasami sent Sumana to Sukhothai where he established the 'Sinhala sangha'. Similarly, at the request of King Kilana (1355–85), Sumana established the Sinhala sangha in Nabbisapura (Chiang Mai) and in Haripunjaya (present-day Lamphun), Kilana built the Puppharama monastery (present-day Wat Suan Dok and Wat Phra Yun) for the Thera Sumana. He also initiated the building of an artificial cave (Wat Umong) in Chiang Mai to house the visiting monks from Sri Lanka. Thus the Sinhala sangha was well spread in Northern Thailand with centres flourishing in Sukhothai, Chiang Mai, Sajjanalaya and Haripunjaya. Sri Lankan style *cetis* were built all over Northern Thailand enshrining Buddha relics.

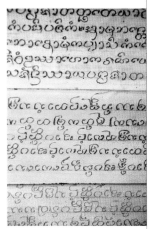

Pali tablets in Myanmar.

Built in a Sri Lankan style, Wat Chang Lom (Elephant temple) is an important historical site in Sukhothai, Thailand.

The architecture of Wat Mahathat in Sukhothai is said to be influenced by designs used at the Lankatilaka Vihara in Gampola.

Sri Sraddha (Si Satha), a nephew of King Rama Khamheng visited Sri Lanka some time before 1347. According to his own inscriptions, Sri Sraddha was a Buddhist monk and stayed in Sri Lanka at Gampola and Mahiyangana for 10 years, and also restored the Mahathupa and the Mahavihara of Anuradhapura and Mahiyangana Cetiya. On his return, Sri Sraddha got the Sri Lankan craftsmen whom he had brought back with him to add the stucco motifs to the four Khmer style towers of Sukhothai's main stupa, Mahathat, based on designs used at Lankatilaka Vihara at Gampola. He enshrined in it the collarbone relic and a hair relic he brought from Mahiyangana. He also built over a thousand *cetis*, planted 300 Srimahabodhi shoots, taken from the Bodhi tree at Anuradhapura, and founded a 'Footprint of the Buddha'. According to Gosling, after Sri Sraddha's return to Sukhothai, there was 'overwhelming adoption of Sinhalese styles… with a multitude of Sinhalese-style stupas' (1998: 121–3).

In the middle of the 14th century, Ayutthaya, which began to flourish as a Buddhist centre under royal patronage, continued religious and cultural ties with Sri Lanka. A major achievement was the composition of Thai histories (in Pali and Thai) by Thai monks. The famous Pali work *Saddhammasangaha*, a history of Buddhism in Sri Lanka, was composed by a monk from Ayutthaya who returned after studying under the Mahathera Dhammakitti Mahasami Sangharaja of Gadaladeni and receiving *upasampada* under the name of Dhammakitti. King Boromaraja (Paramaraja) (1370–88) built the Lankarama for him.

From the 16th century, the Sri Lankan Sangha had declined due to the Portuguese persecution of Buddhists. At the initiative of Venerable Welivita Saranankara, the 18th century Kandyan King Kirti Sri Rajasinghe sought the assistance of King Boromkot of Thailand to re-establish the higher ordination in Sri Lanka under the 'Siam' sect, which had a far-reaching impact on the religious, cultural and political history of Sri Lanka.

Close religious relations continued in the 19th century under the leadership of Venerable Waskaduwe Subhuti who had corresponded with and hosted several members of the royal household of King Chulalongkorn. Venerable Vajirananavarorasa of Wat Bonivet of Bangkok, the younger brother of King Chulalongkorn who had

also corresponded with Subhuti (in Pali), established the Mahamakut Rajavidyalaya in Bangkok in 1893, modelled after the two Monks' Colleges (Vidyodaya 1873, Vidyalankara 1875), established as part of the Buddhist Renaissance in Sri Lanka.

Prince Prisdang, the Siamese Ambassador to the UK, a grandson of Rama III, was ordained as Venerable Jinavaravamsa in 1896 in Sri Lanka under Subhuti. Jinavaravamsa built in the Dipaduttamarama in Colombo, the Ratana Ceti according to Thai architecture, and its gold pinnacle was sent by King Chulalongkorn. The ex-prince started a free Boys Buddhist English school in 1905, and remained at the forefront of the Sri Lanka Buddhist educational movement until he left Sri Lanka in 1911. Subhuti had a deep respect for the Siamese royalty, donating to the King of Siam one Buddha relic of the 21 relics he received from the Kapilavastu excavation in India in 1898. The connections between the Dipaduttamarama and the Thai royalty continue up to now, the Thai palace offering annually Katina robes to the Dipaduttamarama and all Thai dignitaries visiting Sri Lanka making a courtesy call here.

An idea mooted during the 19th century Buddhist Renaissance to bring together all Buddhists—Theravada, Mahayana and Vajrayana—became a reality in 1950 with the establishment of the World Fellowship of Buddhists (WFB) through an initiative of Malalasekera, the President of the All Ceylon Buddhist Congress. A Conference in Sri Lanka, with 129 Buddhist delegates from 27 countries from Asia, Europe and North America, saw Buddhists of all traditions assembled under one banner. At this gathering, the six-coloured Buddhist flag, designed in Sri Lanka in 1885, was accepted as the universal symbol of Buddhism, and the Dhammacakka, as the symbol representing the teachings of the Buddha. Since then, every two years, a conference is held in an Asian country. The WFB headquarters, initially located in Sri Lanka, was later moved to Burma and in 1963, its headquarters moved again to Bangkok where it remains till today.

Burma (Myanmar)

The major task undertaken by King Kyanzitta (1084–1113) was the revision of the *Tripitaka*, based on the Sinhala version with the assistance of a large number of Sinhala *bhikkhus*. Kyanzitta's son Rajakumar's paintings of *Mahavamsa* episodes in the Myankabau Kubyaki temple, covering the history of Buddhism in Sri Lanka marks the beginning of historiography in Burma.

According to the *Glass Palace Chronicle*, the Burmese king, Alaungsitthu (1112–67) visited Sri Lanka, married

A Thai delegation in Sri Lanka led by Princess Kalyani Vadhana in 2006. The delegation presented 40 volumes of Buddhist scriptures translated in English.

The Maya Devi temple in Lumbini, Nepal, is an important pilgrimage site for Sri Lankan Buddhists. In the complex, the Puskarini or Holy Pond is believed to be where Buddha's mother, Queen Maya Devi, took the ritual dip prior to the birth of Siddhartha Gautama.

Established in 1943, the Ananda Kuti Vihar was one of the earliest Theravada temples built in Kathmandu.

SRI LANKAN BUDDHISM AND NEPAL

Nepal's links with Sri Lanka were very important in the revival of Buddhism that took place there from the 1920s onwards. In 1900, Buddhists amounted to perhaps 10 per cent of the population of Nepal, mainly to be found in enclaves of Tibetan culture strung out along the north of the country and in certain pockets further south: among the Gurungs and Tamangs of the centre and centre-west regions of the middle hills, and among the Newars of the Kathmandu Valley. The only contact with Buddhists outside the country was with Tibet, where Newar traders dominated the bazaars of Lhasa, Shigatse and Gyantse, and where Gurungs, Tamangs, Sherpas and others committed to a path of learning and/or monasticism, would go for study. Tibetan pilgrims and traders also came south to Buddhist sites in the Kathmandu Valley and in India.

In 1921, Jagat Man Vaidya (1902–63) went to Calcutta to study commerce. He had a scholarship due to the fact that his father was the Ayurvedic doctor of Juddha Shamsher, younger brother of the then Prime Minister, Chandra Shamsher Rana. Jagat Man was a *shakya* by caste; a member of the hereditary 'householder monks' who controlled the monastic courtyard temples that are the main focus of Newar Buddhism (Gellner, 1992).

In Calcutta, he became a disciple of Anagarika Dharmapala and a member of the Maha Bodhi Society. He changed his name to Dharmaditya Dharmacharyya, began learning Pali and studying Buddhism, and devoted himself to the revival of Buddhism in his homeland. Despite the link with Dharmapala, it was only many years later that a direct connection with Sri Lanka was established.

In 1926, the Rana rulers of Nepal expelled five Buddhist monks and the monk who had initiated them, because one of the five came from a Hindu background and had therefore changed his religion. They

Many young Nepali boys, who are ordained as Buddhist monks, study in Sri Lanka.

were taken in by the Maha Bodhi Society, but they did not initially become Theravadin monks. One of the monks, Mahapragya (1901–79), the offending Hindu, went off to Tibet, returning to India a year later. Only then did he become a Theravada novice under the Venerable Chandramani (1876–1972), the Burmese monk who spent most of his life in Kushinagara and was preceptor to generations of South Asian Theravada monastics (including Ambedkar). Mahapragya then set off to study in Burma in 1931, as it was the closest Theravadin country.

It was a monk of the next generation who blazed a trail to Sri Lanka. Lal Kaji Shakya (1918–90), who later became *bhikkhu* Amritananda, studied for four years in Sri Lanka after becoming a novice in 1936. He was a charismatic and learned figure who founded the All-Nepal Bhikkhu Mahasangh in 1951, and remained its unchallenged leader until his death. After Amritananda, many other Nepali novices also went to Sri Lanka. As the home of Buddhist modernism, it is not surprising that many of the Sri Lankan-trained monks have been among the most active and reforming monks when they returned to Nepal.

By 1944, Theravada monastics were active in the Kathmandu Valley and Juddha Shamsher had by this time become Prime Minister. The regime, possibly uncomfortable with the growing Buddhist influence, decided to expel four monks and four novices, including Amritananda, accusing them of undermining family life by encouraging women to become nuns. The exiles gathered in Sarnath and founded the Dharmodaya Sabha, an organisation to fight for Buddhists' rights within Nepal.

In 1946, Amritananda persuaded the Venerable Narada Mahathera to come as an envoy from Sri Lanka to Nepal and intervene with the Rana government, and the monastics were allowed to return home. Narada returned for a second visit two years later and urged Nepalis

The Maha Bodhi Society in Lumbini (background) maintains close ties with Buddhist centres in Sri Lanka and India. Visits to Bodhgaya, Sarnath and Kushinagar in India, and then to Lumbini in Nepal is deemed to complete the Buddhist pilgrim circuit.

'to follow the rational and clear path of the historic Sakyamuni Buddha in preference to the mystical and complicated paths of mythological Buddhas' (LeVine and Gellner, 2005: 52).

From that time onwards links between Sri Lanka and Nepal have focused primarily on Buddhism, with Sri Lankan pilgrims visiting Lumbini and Nepali novices going for training in Sri Lanka (and sometimes disrobing and staying on there), and Sri Lanka providing support for the development of Lumbini. Diplomatic relations between Sri Lanka and Nepal were established in 1957, and there have been regular mutual visits at the highest level ever since (Shrestha, 2007). There have been periodic talks of reviving the direct flights between the two countries that existed between 1977 and 1986, but thus far these have been shelved due to concerns of economic viability. Consequently, the vast majority of Sri Lankan pilgrims travel to Nepal by land.

Trade between the two countries has remained at a relatively low level. Politically, however, both before and later within SAARC, which is headquartered in Kathmandu, there have been reasons (a shared need to stand up to India) to seek closer cooperation. Peace and conflict studies have been another growth area where Sri Lanka-Nepal cooperation has occurred in recent years

David N. Gellner

An engraving by Blanchard in 1863 depicting the Amarapura monastery, Mandalay, Myanmmar.

The construction of Shwezigon Paya, set between the villages of Wetkyi-in and Nyaung U, was completed in 1090. A copy of the Buddha's tooth relic of Kandy, Sri Lanka is enshrined in the structure.

The Kuthodaw pagoda was built during the reign of King Mindon. In the grounds of the pagoda are 729 stupas, each containing a marble slab inscribed on both sides with a page of text from the Tripitaka—the Pali Canon of Theravada Buddhism.

the Sri Lankan king's daughter, and returned to Burma with an image of Maha Kassapa Thera. The *Culavamsa* records that the Burmese king caught sight of a letter addressed to the King of Cambodia in the hands of the Sinhalese envoys, and suspecting that they were envoys sent to Cambodia, seized them and punished them. He also immediately stopped Sri Lanka's lucrative elephant trade with foreign countries, and captured the elephants, money and vessels of Sinhalese envoys.

In 1167, when King Narathu (1167–70) poisoned his elder brother who was the legitimate heir to the throne in a conspiracy, Sangharaja Panthagu of Burma sought refuge in Sri Lanka and stayed there for six years. A delegation of *bhikkhus* headed by Sangharaja Uttarajiva, who succeeded Panthagu, visited Sri Lanka in 1170 on a pilgrimage along with the Samanera, Chapata. Chapata who received *upasampada* from the Sinhala *bhikkhus*, mastered the *Tripitaka*, and after 10 years, returned to Myanmar along with four other monks, Tamalinda (son of Jayavarman VII of Cambodia), Sivali from Tamralipti in Bengal, Ananda from Kancipura and Rahula, a Sinhala *bhikkhu*, King Narapatisithu (1173–1210) who was impressed with these *bhikkhus* gave full patronage to set up a new sect, Sinhala Sangha. Thus in 1181, the Sinhala Sangha sect was established in Burma.

Close religious relations between Sri Lanka and Burma in the 19th century occurred due to two main factors. The restrictions imposed on the Siamese Sect by a decree of King Kirti Sri Rajasinha (of South Indian Hindu extraction) brought on a caste basis, resulted in other monks seeking higher ordination from Burma. A team of monks from the southern province received higher ordination in 1800 at Amarapura, the then capital of Burma under the patronage of King Bodawpaya. For the first time, a monastic lineage had been created not through royal patronage of a Sri Lankan king— but through the collective action of Buddhist laymen. Another team of Sinhala monks received higher ordination in Mandalay in 1861 under the patronage of King Mendung and a second 'Myanmar' sect, the Ramanna was established in Sri Lanka.

At the Buddha Jayanthi celebrating 2,500 years of Buddhism, Burma took the lead in bringing the Sangha

of Theravada countries together to edit, rehearse and publish the *Tripitaka*. Led by Prime Minister U Nu, the 6th Buddhist Council was inaugurated in Yangon in 1954 and completed in 1956. Scholar-monks of Sri Lanka played a major role, with Polwatte Buddhadatta who had studied in Burma serving as the general editor with overall authority. He was awarded the Myanmar Government ecclesiastical title of Agga Maha Pandita. This practice of awarding that title to outstanding Sinhala monks continues up to now. Burmese monks had been to Sri Lanka to teach the Abhidhamma and methods of meditation as practised in Burma while monks from Sri Lanka went to Burma to study.

Cambodia

About the same time Sinhala Buddhists had established relations with the Dvaravati kingdom in Thailand, Buddhist texts written in Sri Lanka were known in Funan, the earliest known kingdom of Cambodia. Funan with Oc Eo (in present-day Vietnam), as the central port, was a trading power, and known as the most powerful kingdom in mainland Southeast Asia, with Phnom Ksach Sa as the capital city in the province of present-day Prey Veng. The *Vimuttimagga* (a manual on *sila*, *samadhi* and *panna*), a Pali text of the Abhayagiri school of Sri Lanka, composed by Upatissa in the 2nd century CE, was known in Funan. At the invitation of the Chinese emperor, the Funanese monks, Mandrasena and Sanghapala, had taken many Theravada and Mahayana texts to China. Sanghapala translated the *Vimuttimagga* into Chinese in 505 CE. It should be noted here that several decades before this time, the Chinese Buddhist monk, Fa-Hsien stayed at the Abhayagiri Vihara, and went back to China with a large number of Buddhist texts written in Sri Lanka.

According to Wright, the stone stupa in the central tower of the vast temple Prasat Phra Khan, built by Jayavarman VII (1181–1215) in honour of his dead father is reminiscent of the then contemporary stupa style in Sri Lanka, as exemplified by the Kiri Vehera of Polonnaruwa. Although Jayavarman VII was certainly a Mahayana Buddhist, he would have been aware of Sri Lankan stupa architecture (2001). His son, Tamalinda was ordained in Sri Lanka, and probably held the view that a Sinhala style stupa was a suitable monument for his father.

Direct Sinhala Buddhist relations appear in Cambodia only in the 15th century. The five *wats* (*vihara*) King Ponhea Yat built in Phnom Penh—Buddhaghosachar, Wat Unnalom, Wat Koh, Wat Dhammalankara and Wat Lanka—were all associated with Sri Lankan monks. Two Mahatheras from Sri Lanka, Assajita and Buddhaghosa, lived in Cambodia during this time, and when Venerable Buddhaghosa passed away, the king built a temple in his honour, and named it Wat Boddhaghosachar. After

THE WORLD'S BIGGEST BOOK

Venerable Assajita's passing, the king built a stupa on the hill of Bodhilom enshrining Venerable Assajita's eyebrows. From that time, Bodhilom came to be known as Wat Unnalom, and became the abode of the Cambodian Sangharaja.

King Norodom (1860–1904), took the capital back to Phnom Penh and in 1863, the French imposed a protectorate over Cambodia. Norodom's mother remained in the former capital, Udong and had several *viharas* constructed in Sinhala style. The Buddha's ashes brought from Sri Lanka during this time were enshrined in Wat Unnalom, the main *vihara* in Phnom Penh. One of the most significant Cambodian religious events in the 20th century was the donation of Buddha relics from Sri Lanka to Cambodia in 1957.

In an effort to transform traditional monastic education at temples, a Pali high school was founded in Phnom Penh in 1914. The Preah Sihanouk Buddhist University began to function in 1961. After Pol Pot's destruction of Buddhism in 1975, a semblance of peace returned and Buddhist education was restored with the help of a Sri Lankan monk Vipulasara only in 1992. The Buddhist Institute, established by the French in 1930 and known as the 'soul of Cambodia' gained the services of a Sri Lankan advisor—Hema Goonatilake—who helped re-establish not only the Buddhist Institute, but also the Monks' University with monk-teachers brought from Sri Lanka. She also compiled a landmark Pali Grammar in Khmer language and helped establish training programmes with modern methods of teaching Pali. Some of the Cambodian monks whom she arranged to study in Sri Lankan monastic schools and universities have since been serving as Rector, Dean and staff members in the Monks' University. A district-based programme by the same advisor with training for Buddhist nuns linked them in a country-wide network under the patronage of Her Majesty Monineath Sihanouk.

Laos

The recorded history of Laos begins with its founding, in 1353, by Prince Fa Ngum, whose Cambodian Queen introduced Buddhism into Laos. Her father sent Fa Ngum's monk-teacher, three Sinhalese monks and his proudest possession, a Buddha image Prabang with 'miraculous powers' gifted to him by a Sinhalese king. This image became the national palladium of the country, and its capital was renamed after it as 'Luang Prabang'. A monastic complex Vat Po (Bo) Lanka was established with a Bodhi tree from a sprout of the Anuradhapura Bodhi tree. The chief Sinhalese monk Maha Tep Lanka and Fa Ngum's monk-teacher were designated as Sangharajas. By the end of Fa Ngum's reign, the city of Luang Prabang became an important centre of Buddhism in the region.

The statue of Prabang became the symbol for the sovereignty of the Lao state and remains so until now. With the French gaining ascendancy in 1893, and the Communist takeover in 1975, Buddhism suffered a setback, but after 1979, policy regarding Buddhism began to liberalise, and the number of monks and temples had returned almost to earlier levels with 17,990 monks and novices in 2,823 monasteries. Their main cultural influence is that originally transferred from Sri Lanka to the Yunnan region of China.

Conclusion

The cultural underpinnings of Sri Lanka's relations with Southeast Asia extend 1,000 years, and have had an impact on contemporary diaspora activities. In the 21st century, state-level and cultural exchanges have increased and are expected to intensify. In recent years, there has been an increase in tourist traffic from Sri Lanka to Thailand, Cambodia and Myanmar. The traffic to Thailand is largely to Bangkok for shopping or nightlife attractions while tourists go to Cambodia and Myanmar mostly to visit cultural sites. Visitors from these countries to Sri Lanka, however, have increasingly focused on travel to the ancient Buddhist centres. During the post-war period in Cambodia, Sri Lanka provided one of the largest contingents of foreign expertise, Sri Lanka being preferred to Thailand because of historical reasons.

The most visible Southeast Asian presence in Sri Lanka is the monk-students pursuing an education. The largest number of students come from Burma (they have three centres in Sri Lanka), followed by those from Cambodia and Thailand. A Cambodian Buddhist Centre was opened in July 2011. There are Sri Lankan Buddhist teachers in Thailand. While in Thailand, for several decades, Sri Lankan students in technology and related subjects have been studying in the Asian Institute of Technology in Bangkok.

Sri Lanka has, in the recent past, become more involved in Southeast Asian regional organisations, and is a dialogue partner in the Association of Southeast Asian Nations (ASEAN). Sri Lanka, Thailand and Burma are active members of the Bay of Bengal Initiative for Multi-sectoral Economic and Technical Cooperation while Sri Lanka and Thailand are members of the Indian Ocean Rim Association for Regional Cooperation. A joint venture between Sri Lanka and Laos has allowed them to position themselves as prime destinations for ecotourism in the South, Southeast Asia and the Pacific Regions.

Hema Goonatilake

One of Phnom Penh's five original wats, Wat Lanka was established in 1422 as a sanctuary for the Holy Writings and a meeting place for Cambodian and Sri Lankan monks. The Wat was named in honour of these meetings.

Novice Sri Lankan Buddhists in Colombo receive alms from Thai monks, 2003.

Muslims celebrating the end of Ramadan in Colombo.

SRI LANKAN MUSLIM DIASPORA

The story of the Sri Lankan Muslim diaspora is a subscript to the narrative of the Sri Lankan Tamil diaspora. Sri Lankan Muslims comprise of the Moors, Malays, Memons, Bohras and Khojas. Moors—whose ethnicity is subject to great controversy—form the vast majority, accounting for over 90 per cent of the total. The origins of a Sri Lankan Muslim diaspora of any notable scale begins only at the end of the 20th century. Although in terms of the Islamic *shariah*, migration from *Darul Harb* (the abode of war, which in reality refers to territories not under Muslim rule) to *Darul Islam* (the abode of peace or land under Muslim rule) is strongly recommended to the faithful, the Sri Lankan Muslims who fall under another category—*Dar-ul Sulh* (the Abode of Truce)—are so well integrated with the majority Sinhalese and minority Tamils that they neither had the need nor the inclination to emigrate. Even during the racial riots of 1915, when the Muslim community and particularly its Coast Moor (a sub-classification which the British colonialists introduced in order to separate the indigenous Muslims from those arrived from India during the 19th century) segment became the target of deadly violence from a politically motivated urban Buddhist mob, the Muslims never thought of leaving the country to settle elsewhere, but instead became even more wedded to the island's political, economic and socio-cultural landscape.

Genesis Of The Muslim Diaspora

In spite of the political tensions from the mid-1950s, the Muslim community, pragmatically adapted to the evolving ethno-political paradigm. Historically renowned for its business acumen, the Muslim community's attitude towards the deepening Sinhalese-Tamil ethnic divide remained business-like. For instance, when the Sinhala-Only language policy was introduced in 1956, the business-oriented Muslim community remained largely indifferent. Even though the vast majority of Muslims spoke Tamil at home, the community pragmatically accepted whatever the government of the day decided. This policy of siding with the government in power won the Muslims special privileges from the rulers especially in the fields of education, religion and culture. Even as Sri Lankan politics became more virulent, triggering over time a Tamil exodus to foreign soil, the Muslims, partly because of their cosy relationship with the majority community and partly because of a lack of saleable skills abroad, remained solidly-footed in native soil.

The political, economic and educational changes that took place from the 1950s to the 1980s, however, created a new generation of Muslims who felt increasingly uncomfortable with the situation at home and decided to emigrate when the opportunity availed. The 1983 Tamil pogrom, the growth and militarisation of the Liberation Tigers of Tamil Eelam (LTTE), the civil war that ensued, and a rising Sinhalese nationalism, placed the Muslims, especially those living in the north and east of the island—the

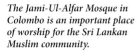

The Jami-Ul-Alfar Mosque in Colombo is an important place of worship for the Sri Lankan Muslim community.

Tamil heartland—in a political quagmire. Not only were they caught in the cross-fire between the confronting armed forces of the government and the LTTE, but the latter's policy of eliminating the Muslim intelligentsia and Muslim political leadership made life extremely dangerous to sections of this community. Dwindling business opportunities in the face of an aggressive Sinhalese economic nationalism after the 1980s made the situation worse for the business-minded Muslims.

The Muslim community had made notable gains in the field of professional and higher education from the 1970s. Thus, by the end of 1980s, a small class of educated and skilled Muslims were able to take up employment opportunities in the Arab Middle East and elsewhere. Their ultimate destination was the West. While some went directly to the United Kingdom, Australia, New Zealand, Canada and the United States of America, others took a circuitous route after sojourning in the Middle East. This diaspora was joined by a small number of refugees who fled from the war zone in the north and east of the island.

Size

The size of the Sri Lankan Muslim diaspora is difficult to determine. Census data in many Western countries do not provide a religious categorisation of their immigrant population. Even in Australia, where the census data provides such classification, because of prevailing negative images about Muslims in view of the 'War on Terror', many Muslim immigrants do not record their religious affiliation in census forms. This gap in official statistics has resulted in diasporic Muslims making their own population 'guestimates'. From such sources the size of the Sri Lankan Muslim diaspora, discounting those employed on temporary work permit in Saudi Arabia and the Gulf States, is according to Muslim community sources, estimated to be around 10,000–15,000, the majority of whom are concentrated in the United Kingdom and Australia.

Characteristics

In host countries, the majority of the Sri Lankan Muslims, like their Muslim brethren from other countries, live in 'parallel societies' having little contact with the mainstream community. Being Tamil or Sinhalese-speaking *sunni* Muslims of the Shafiite school, the Sri Lankan Muslims generally fall in the conservative end of the religious spectrum and some among them, especially those who came through the Middle East, have even embraced the strict Wahhabi code of Islamic beliefs and practices of Saudi Arabia. Frequent visits by members of the Tabligh Jamaat—a missionary movement started by Mawlana Ilyas in 1926 in India—from Sri Lanka further

SRI LANKAN SUFI TRANSNATIONAL NETWORKS

The origins of Sri Lanka's Muslim minority can be traced to Persian and Arab maritime trade routes across the Indian Ocean, and to the mixed Indo-Arab port settlements that arose along the Malabar and Coromandel coasts of South India in modern-day Kerala and Tamil Nadu. Similar transoceanic connections allowed Sufism, the mystical and devotional form of Islam, to take root in Sri Lanka and to flourish under British colonial rule. Today, only a small subset of Sri Lankan Muslims formally identify themselves as Sufis, yet the familiar elements of popular Sufi mysticism are seen in many local saintly tomb-shrines (*ziyaram*, *dargah*) and in weekly devotional meetings performed by initiated followers of spiritual leaders, or sheikhs, belonging to transnational Sufi orders (*tariqa*). A number of well-known *tariqas* are found in Sri Lanka, including Qadiriyya, Shaduliyya, Naqsbandiyya and Rifaiyya. Membership seems to have become widespread in the 19th and 20th centuries among the West Coast Muslim businessmen with commercial ties to South India and the Middle East. Urban Sufi chapter houses, often called *zavias*, can still be seen along the historic streets of the Galle Fort.

The larger social and geographical world of Sri Lankan Sufism includes South Indian port towns such as Calicut, Kayalpatinam, Kilakkarai and Nagapattinam, where seafaring Muslim merchants from the Mappila (Kerala Muslim) and Marakkayar (Tamil Nadu coastal Muslim) communities have had close trading ties with Colombo, Galle and other towns in Sri Lanka. As a part of these networks, Sri Lankan Muslims found it relatively easy to make seaborne pilgrimages across the Palk Strait to visit Sufi *dargahs* in Tamil Nadu such as Ervadi, Pasipattinam, Muttupettai and Nagoor, where they made religious vows to remedy illnesses and other problems.

Nagoor, located on the Bay of Bengal north of Nagapattinam, is perhaps the largest Sufi *dargah* in South India, attracting huge crowds to the annual death-anniversary festival (*kandoori*) commemorating the 16th-century saint Shahul Hameed. He is regarded as the divine patron of Tamil Muslim sea-traders, whose cargo ships sailed to Sri Lanka, Penang and Singapore during the colonial era. As a result, there are historic overseas 'branch office' shrines for the Nagoor saint in all of these locations, the largest of which in Sri Lanka is the 'Beach Mosque' near Kalmunai, Ampara District.

The dargah of Hazrat Seyyid Shahul Hameed in Nagoor, Tamil Nadu, South India. The flags celebrate the annual festival of this 16th-century Sufi saint.

Another Muslim saint popular in Sri Lanka is Abdul Qadir Gilani, a 12th-century mystic buried in Baghdad who, according to local legends, meditated for 12 years in a cliff-top cave at Daftar Jailani, a hermitage shrine in the southern Kandyan Hills near Balangoda, where throngs of Muslim devotees gather to celebrate his annual *kandoori*. Festivals for such widely renowned saints are counterbalanced by devotional practices at tomb-shrines for local Muslim holy men in many Sri Lankan Muslim towns and villages. Historical research has traced a number of these Sri Lankan saintly lineages back to the Hadramaut region of Yemen, an 18th and 19th century place of origin for Muslim families who claim the title of *maulana* or *seyyid*, meaning a lineal descendant of the Prophet Muhammad.

A less well-known Sufi connection can be traced between Sri Lanka and the Lakshadweep archipelago off the western coast of South India. Sheikhs of the Rifa'i order from Androth Island, who often bear the distinctive title of Tangal, have been visiting Sri Lanka at least since the middle of the 19th century, instilling a distinctive set of devotional practices such as the Rifa'i *ratib*, a kind of male group singing that is accompanied with tambourines. Semi-professional Rifa'i religious mendicants, who are called Bawas in Sri Lanka, travel the island staging ecstatic performances with sharp spikes and needles. Such self-mortifying Rifa'i traditions are shared across the globe from the Balkans to Indonesia, and Sri Lanka's Bawas obtain their highest levels of Rifa'i ordination in Tamil Nadu.

Historically, most Sri Lankan Sufis are initiated followers of sheikhs who visit the island from south India, but this may be changing. In recent decades, charismatic Sufi leaders with homegrown roots in the Batticaloa and Ampara Districts of the Eastern Province have attracted large lay followings while also arousing harsh opposition from Islamic reformist groups who condemn saint-veneration in any form.

Perhaps the most striking example of Sri Lankan-based diasporic Sufism is the late M. R. Bawa Muhaiyaddeen, popularly known as Guru Bawa, who founded a movement starting in the 1940s with followers in Jaffna, Matale and Colombo. In 1971, he began to share his Sufi wisdom with disciples in the USA, where he passed away in 1986. His peaceful tomb-shrine, located in the western suburbs of Philadelphia, is now the pilgrimage centre for a network of Sufi followers both in Sri Lanka as well as in Europe and North America.

Dennis B. McGilvray

Members of the Rifai'i order of Sufism venerate their saint at the Muslim hermitage shrine of Daftar Jailani, near Balangoda, in the central highlands of Sri Lanka.

The innermost part of the Beach Mosque shrine. The spiritual power of the Nagoor saint is believed to be present at this 'branch office', one of several located across the Bay of Bengal.

GROWING UP 'HALF-HALF' IN A MUSLIM FAMILY

In my mid-thirties I realised I had slipped past a childhood I had ignored and not understood.

Michael Ondaatje, *Running in the Family*

I was born 'half-half' in a Colombo suburb, the first issue of an Anglo-Welsh mother (Jameela Patricia Ann Salih) and a Ceylonese-Muslim father (Mohamed Farouk Salih).

My parents met on a ship. She was barely eighteen, bored with life in drab post-war Britain; and she took advantage of the Australian government's offer to populate Down Under with whites from the Old Country and elsewhere in Europe. She was a 'five-pound Pom': her passage cost her five pounds, the rest paid for by the Australian government. Black-and-white photos in the family album show her in full English bloom, setting out on her adventure brimming with hope and good cheer, enjoying every moment.

On that ship she met a group of Ceylonese Air Force cadets, only slightly older than her, returning home after three years of training in Britain. Among the cadets was Daddy. Mummy's photos of him, taken during the passage, show a thin but vigorous, good-looking, confident, wholesome young man.

Something clicked—a 'shipboard romance'. Daddy got off the boat in Colombo, but Mummy carried on to Australia. She lived there and in New Zealand for almost three years. They corresponded; she came back to Wales; they met again when he was back in England for Air Force training; they got engaged. Mummy's wedding day was the day she stepped onshore in Colombo—also the day she converted from the Church of England to Islam. She acquired a Muslim name, Jameela, although 'Pat' was what she remained. It was a pragmatic, not theological, conversion. She was marrying into a

Mohamed Farouk Salih on the ship Orian bound from Southampton to Colombo, 1955.

The Sally family, North Wales, Summer 1981.

Muslim extended family; there was no question of marriage without conversion.

There are about 1.8 million Muslims on the island—10 per cent of the population. Well over 90 per cent of Sri Lankan Muslims are Sunni 'Moors'; they trace their descent to Arab traders from the Gulf, who rode the monsoon winds to dominate Indian Ocean trade. In the southern coastal town of Beruwala there is the small Kechimalai mosque, believed to be the oldest in the island. It stands bleach-white on a promontory. Round the back is a *dargah*, the shrine, it is said, of a Yemeni trader who died in 1024 AD.

Muslims knitted the island together through trade before Portuguese *conquistadors* muscled in in the early 1500s. That is why there are Muslim settlements dotted all over the island, along the coast and in the interior, in towns large and small. The mosque, the shops; the men in prayer caps, white shirts and sarongs, sporting goatees or wispy beards; the women wrapped in saris, covering their heads as well as their bodies; these are tell-tale signs of a Muslim trading neighbourhood.

Trading is in the family blood. When I go back I meet innumerable male cousins and distant relatives who trade in one form or another. A plurality are in 'gems'— Muslims still dominate the gem-and-jewellery trade.

Some of my forefathers probably came as traders from the Gulf many centuries ago, although my grandmother had the fanciful notion that we are descended from Moroccan princes. But Sri Lankan Muslims often overlook the fact that they have South Indian blood coursing through their veins—the product of Arab settlement and miscegenation on the Malabar and Coromandel coasts, and subsequent intercourse with Muslim trading communities in Sri Lanka. Hence Tamil, not Sinhalese, is the mother tongue of most Sri Lankan Muslims. Indeed, my grandmother's family has such South Indian ancestry.

There is also a small Malay-Muslim minority. Most are descended from soldiers who came from Java and Malaya under Dutch and British rulers in the 18th and 19th centuries. Family lore has it that my grandfather's family hails from high-born Arabs who had privileged positions at a Javanese court. But there were allegations that they had sown dissension and strife—and were banished to Ceylon.

My grandfather was born rich, never did a serious day's work in his life, and frittered his inheritance away. He was also whimsical. The rest of the family is called 'Salih'—a Middle-Eastern name. 'Sally', a variant of 'Salleh', has a Malay provenance. My grandfather registered my father as 'Sally' because he thought it more fashionable to be Malay than Moor in the 1930s.

Daddy grew up in Badulla, once a thriving hill station in tea-clad Uva Province, which sits southeast of the middle of the island. His maternal grandfather was a wealthy tea transporter who sired 13 children. One of them inherited one of the largest tea estates in Ceylon, complete with two factories. He gambled the whole lot away over a game of billiards in the late 1920s.

My grandmother, cut out of the inheritance, bore six children who grew up as 'poor relations'. All made their way to Colombo. My aunts escaped relative poverty in Badulla through arranged marriages to richer men in Colombo. Daddy escaped to the Air Force at sixteen. My uncle Razeen, after whom I am named, met a Thai-Sinhalese heiress to a jewellery business while doing an internship in Hong Kong. He converted her to Islam; she and he ran the business in Bangkok; and by the late 1960s my uncle, barely thirty, was one of Ceylon's richest expatriates. That enabled him to buy lots of property in Colombo and elsewhere. His jewel in the crown was the Mount Lavinia Hotel, just outside Colombo—one of Asia's legendary colonial hotels. Daddy ran it for five years; I had the run of it as a little boy.

My memories of early and middle childhood are of a genuine extended family. My cousins and I were in and out of each others' houses every day; our house certainly was not our 'castle'. My brothers and I went to see my grandmother almost every day. There was always a family function to go to—betrothals, weddings, assorted religious functions, culminating in the two festival days, Ramadan and Hajj.

It is a wonder my private English mother fitted in so well. But she did. She adapted to Muslim mores, made friends with everybody, never gave offence, learnt 'kitchen Sinhalese', and, once in a blue moon, wore a sari for special occasions. And she did all this without changing her look or personality.

Effort and expense went to educating the boys in my extended family. Some went to public schools

Mohamed Farouk Salih and Jameela Patricia Ann Salih before they were married, Rhyl, North Wales, 1960.

in Britain; two of us went on to decent universities. But scant effort and expense went to educating the girls. They left school at sixteen and had marriages arranged a year or two later; by their early-to-mid twenties they had their complements of children.

In that sense I did not come from an extended-family tradition of books and high culture and 'progressive' values—not least educating the girls. As I grew into my teens I felt this keenly, envying the odd upper-class Sinhalese or Tamil family with such traditions. Later, I reacted against our religious tradition—lots of unquestioned rituals, dos-and-don'ts, prayer meetings, talk of spirits and *djinns*, and following this-or-that guru or 'bawa'. How I wished I was nurtured in a more learned, inquiring religious tradition. But, during my Sri Lankan childhood, I was content to learn the Qur'an by rote, accompany my father to *jummah* prayers on Fridays, and fast a few days during Ramadan.

Our life seemed dandy circa 1971. Then, one night, our world crashed. Police officers raided and ransacked the house; then they took Daddy away. Six years of turbulence followed. He and Uncle Razeen (safely away in Bangkok) were charged with foreign-exchange violations under draconian laws brought in by Sirimavo Bandaranaike's government. Daddy was held in remand. There was a protracted court case, at the end of which he was convicted and sent to jail. During those years Mummy, my brothers and I shuttled between Sri Lanka and Britain; I changed schools almost every year. In our *annus horribilis*—the year Daddy was in jail—Mummy home-schooled my brother Reyaz and I. Once a month we visited Daddy in Colombo's Welikada prison. And, almost every month, we spent an idyllic couple of weeks on the little tea estate Uncle Razeen bought, not far from Badulla. There I had morning 'class' with Mummy on the lawn, did my homework in the little bungalow, and wandered round tea trails in the afternoons.

Daddy was given a pardon and released in August 1977, two months after the opposition UNP won a landslide general-election victory. A few months later we left for the UK.

That was the end of my Sri Lankan childhood. Initially, I pined for Sri Lanka. But, gradually, that wore

Razeen Sally (seated on left), celebrates his 27th birthday in Colombo, January 1992.

off. I went back on infrequent holidays—once every four or five years on average. Sri Lanka—and my Muslim family there—dimmed in my memory. Other interests and other vistas took hold of my reality and imagination. In my mind, through my late teens, twenties and thirties, the country was a bothersome backwater. On my trips back I chafed at the restrictions, rituals and traditions of the extended family life I had grown up in, and at being in my father's shadow, constantly trailing him from one interminable business meeting and family visit to another.

But things changed in my forties. My father passed away; and, in the years that followed, it seemed that a mental block lifted. Sri Lanka revived in my imagination, as did memories of my childhood there. I started going back, no longer in Daddy's shadow but as a free agent. First I went back on a couple of short, touristy holidays. But that was not enough. I felt I was seeing the country anew, with fresh eyes and alert senses. I noticed things—people, buildings, landscapes, flora—I hardly noticed before. I became interested in Sri Lanka's history for the first time; I wanted to learn more about its religious and cultural mix. So I went back for two months on the next visit and brought my mother with me. We saw relations and old friends and relived old times, happy and sad. We did several trips out-station; we saw people and places we had not seen in decades. In 2011, before I moved to Singapore, I spent six months in Sri Lanka. I criss-crossed the island, south to north, east to west, and points in between. Now, living in Singapore, I go back every few months.

What do I see when I go back now? How does it differ from the Sri Lanka of my childhood? That is a subject for a book, not a short entry. But I will make a few observations about Muslim life in Sri Lanka today.

The Muslim community has not escaped a quarter-century of ethnic strife and civil war. The Muslims of Eastern Province—a third of the local population—and the much smaller Muslim minority in the Tamil North have suffered most. Many Muslims, like the bigger Tamil minority, have reacted to Sinhala chauvinism by retreating into their communal shell. Gone for them the easy multi-cultural mixing at school, workplace and after-hours social gatherings.

The mosques are several times bigger than they were in the 1970s; more men and boys look like they are wearing Arab religious uniforms, with stern, forbidding facial expressions; and more women and girls are draped in black from head to toe—some even with veils and black gloves. More Muslim children go to Muslim-only schools. There is pressure to rid Muslim life of Sufi influence and South Indian 'impurities'. These are the signs of a dourer, segregationist, Wahhabi-influenced Islam brought back by migrant workers from the Middle East, plus direct Saudi funding for mosques and madrasahs.

But I should not exaggerate. The moderate, Sufi-infused South Asian Islam of my childhood continues. Devotees continue to visit shrines of Sufi saints all over the island. One hopes that the old moderation will prevail, for it is indispensable for a small minority in a multi-religious country dominated by Sinhala Buddhists.

The extended Salih family, September 1972.

Razeen Sally

Meeran Jumma Mosque is also known as the Galle Fort Mosque.

A fund-raising dinner for the Breast Cancer Foundation organised by the United Sri Lankan Muslim Association of Australia in Melbourne, 2010.

Members of the Sri Lankan Muslim community in South Korea celebrating Eid Ul Fithr, 2010.

Sri Lankan Malay Cultural show in Toronto.

strengthens the community's religious conservatism. Even their outdoor activities such as sports and picnics are usually exclusive affairs. Moreover, a strong preference to send their children to Islamic schools and to keep them from mixing with children of non-Muslim communities, all in the name of preventing cultural pollution, makes social integration a nagging issue to this diasporic community. While the majority of the males are employed in skilled and unskilled work, the majority of women remain at home as economic dependents.

Ethnic and religious pluralism in Western democratic societies have given birth to ethnic-and-religious-based welfare associations among migrant communities. In countries like Australia, these organisations even receive state funding under various government schemes. Although the size of the Sri Lankan Muslim diaspora is small, it has a number of such organisations, all male dominated, notably in the United Kingdom and in Australia. In the former, the Sri Lanka Muslim Welfare Association in Crawley and the Sri Lankan Muslim Cultural Centre in Middlesex, and in the latter the Austra-Lanka Muslim Association in Sydney, the United Sri Lanka Muslim Association of Australia in Melbourne, and the Sri Lanka Muslim Society of Western Australia in Perth are the most prominent. Apart from engaging in religious activities, like organising *iftar* (breaking the fast) and *eid* (religious festival) celebrations, the key function of these organisations appears to be inculcating the young members of the diaspora with the community's received religious wisdom. Generally, these associations operate in isolation without even becoming part of the existing umbrella Muslim organisations such as the Union of Muslim Organisations of UK and Ireland (UMO) in Britain and the Australian Federation of Islamic Councils (AFIC) in Australia.

The lack of a common language of communication is one of the many challenges facing inter-Muslim ethnic organisations. Arabic, Urdu, Bengali and Turkish are the dominant languages spoken by the majority of first and second generation diasporic Muslims in the West. In this setting, the Tamil and Sinhalese-speaking Sri Lankan Muslims form a tiny minority and they find it difficult to socialise with the larger groups—a challenge that is especially evident amongst women. This language barrier further contributes to the isolation of the Sri Lankan Muslim diaspora. One consequence of this isolation however, is that the community hardly gets involved with issues pertaining to political Islam that straddles across several other Muslim communities in the West.

A key characteristic of first generation Sri Lankan Muslim migrants is their continued strong links with the 'mother' country. Although not deeply interested in the domestic politics of Sri Lanka, and in the course or outcome of the 26-year-old civil war that ended in 2009, they are not indifferent to the sufferings of the people there. Apart from periodic financial assistance to family members at home, a considerable proportion of the *zakath* (compulsory charity in Islam) collected during the fasting month of Ramadan, is sent to Muslim welfare institutions in Sri Lanka. Such fund-raising activities reached a peak after the 2004 tsunami, which devastated the southern and eastern coasts of Sri Lanka and impoverished tens of thousands of Muslims. Mosques, religious schools, and Muslim orphanages at home also receive financial aid from these migrants.

The Future

The economic, social and political environment in Sri Lanka that acted as the push factor for the Tamil and Muslim diaspora has not improved in spite of the government's victory in the civil war. Furthermore, increasing restrictions in the Western countries on immigration in general and Muslim migration in particular (because of a growing Islamophobic domestic public opinion) will keep the size of the Sri Lankan Muslim diaspora small. However, the most important problem confronting the Muslim diaspora, in general, is the issue of integration and assimilation. The Sri Lankan Muslim segment of this diaspora is no exception. Broadly the demand for assimilation, in the sense that Muslim communities in the West merge into the *weltanschauung* of the mainstream host community, may never be met. The preferred alternative therefore is integration without losing the community's religio-cultural identity. However, religion and language do present obstacles to many Muslims in socialising with mainstream communities. While language difficulties could be overcome in the long run, religious rigidities will continue to remain a nagging issue. This general observation applies equally to the Sri Lankan Muslim diaspora. While language presents no obstacle to Sri Lankan Muslims, the majority of whom are proficient in English, adherence to halal food consumption and aversion to gender-mixing, especially with non-Muslims, have become social barriers to integration. However, the Sri Lankan Muslim diaspora in the West is less than three decades old, and one can only hope that with the passage of time and with spread of secular education, the progenies of the current generation will adopt a more flexible attitude towards received religious rigidities and develop a more committed national identity than their parents.

Ameer Ali

POPULAR CULTURE

THE PRODUCTION AND distribution of Sri Lankan popular culture parallels the expansion of Sri Lankan diasporic communities across the globe, and is an increasingly important—and visible—aspect of the diaspora's cultural milieu. For emigrants, the consumption of specific forms of cultural matter enjoyed in the 'homeland' is intrinsically connected to the desire to sustain, in the new habituation, a link with the past. Such cultural matter—whether music, dance, television, film or fashion —can have myriad effects; it can connect diasporic Sri Lankan communities scattered in far-flung locations, or, sometimes even accentuate existing identity-based fissures. Over time, living in the diaspora can provide the creative impulse for the development of new 'hybrid' cultural forms that draw from both the old and the new 'homeland'. The segment that follows introduces artistes who are either emigrants, or descendants of emigrants from Sri Lanka, and are well known in the diaspora for the contributions in music, film and dance.

Rajesh Rai

ICONS

Mathangi 'Maya' Arulpragasam (M.I.A)

On 18 May 2009, as the war in Sri Lanka was reaching its bitter end, a report by Robert Mackey in *The New York Times* described Mathangi 'Maya' Arulpragasam as the 'most famous member of the Tamil diaspora' (*The New York Times*, 18 May 2009). Maya has become familiar to millions across the globe in her persona as the hip-hop performer M.I.A. The transformation of Mathangi 'Maya' Arulpragasam into M.I.A., for *Missing in Action*, is a story that is emblematic of a diaspora generation. As a military term, *Missing in Action* classifies someone who cannot be found in the theatre of war, but who also cannot be located outside it: the captive, the lost, the untraceable, the disappeared, the absconder, the escapee. The name M.I.A. speaks of a history of loss, damage, pain, displacement in which no clear distinction separates military from civilian casualties.

Maya was born on 18 July 1975 in London. According to an account in *Guardian*, her parents met in a pub in Hounslow (*The Guardian*, 13 June 2010). Upon completion of his engineering course in Russia, her father—Arulpragasam—moved to London during which time he married Kala. When M.I.A. was two months old, her father disappeared and was later known to have trained with the Palestinian Liberation Organisation (PLO) in Lebanon for a few months.

When her father returned, the family moved to Jaffna. Arulpragasam became a founding member of EROS (Eelam Revolutionary Organisation of Students), taking the *nom de guerre* Arular. Like many men in Jaffna in those years of growing support for militant separatism, he left the family to go underground. For their protection, the children were told their father was dead. On the rare occasions they saw him, he was introduced as an uncle. M.I.A.'s first album, *Arular* (2005) is often taken as a tribute to this absent fighter-father figure, but M.I.A. suggests the story is more complicated.

The many epic stories of M.I.A.'s formation are characteristic of an entire post-1983 Tamil diaspora generation. Kala and her children fled the war in Jaffna in the early 1980s, living as displaced people in South India before returning as refugees in 1986 to a council flat in London. The transformation of Mathangi 'Maya' Arulpragasam into M.I.A invokes not only the 'Missing in Action' of being both 'inside' and 'outside' the war in Jaffna, but also of being 'Missing in Action,' in the dubious refuge that London provided in the years following the Brixton riots: 'We were one of the two Asian families that lived there. I used to come home from school and see people burgling my house, just walk past with my telly. But it wasn't as horrible as being in Sri Lanka' (*The Guardian*, 20 March 2005).

It was when her radio was stolen that Maya first heard the music of Public Enemy playing on it from a neighbour's flat. The Afro-American voice from New York's main streets was instantly recognisable to a teenage Tamil refugee girl in South London. 'Hip-hop was the first thing that made me feel like I belonged to something in England' (*The Times of London*, 17 June 2005). Together with the formative rhythms of hip-hop and rap, M.I.A.'s music combines the sounds of the immigrant and the working class London in the 1980s—Jamaican dancehall, reggae, punk, bhangra—with echoes of Tamil film songs. Her first single, *Galang*, appeared in 2003, soon after she had graduated with a fine arts degree from the St Martins College of Art (she had originally gained entry because the academics recognised her 'chutzpah'). Her own designs and drawings featured prominently on M.I.A.'s website and her early music videos— bold motifs that, like her music, speak of the pop culture of South London, mixing Tamil political street art with images of Bollywood, London life and consumer culture. *Galang*, was followed soon after by another single, *Sunshowers*, both underground hits. The music video for the latter, filmed

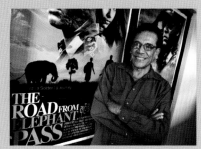

Chandran Rutnam: Born in Colombo to a Tamil father and a Sinhala mother, Rutnam fell in love with movie-making on the set of the World War II epic, *The Bridge on the River Kwai*, which was filmed in Sri Lanka. The film crew rented a house that belonged to his parents, and the teenaged Rutnam, inspired by his exposure to the set, moved to London to pursue a career in film. Eventually settling in Los Angeles, he attended the University of Southern California and the San Fernando Valley College of Law. Rutnam developed a reputation in Hollywood, convincing producers to film their movies on idyllic set locales in Sri Lanka. The award-winning director, producer, screenwriter and entrepreneur is well known to Hollywood moguls such as Steven Spielberg (who credits Rutnam for his marriage to Kate Capshaw, with whom he fell in love with on the Sri Lankan set of *Indiana Jones and the Temple of Doom*) and George Lucas, his former film school classmate. In 2008, he directed *A Road From Elephant Pass*. The film is based on Sri Lanka's decades-long ethnic conflict.

Patrick Mendis

Sri Lankan-American film director Chandra Rutnam promoting his movie—A Road From Elephant Pass— in Colombo, 2011.

Mathangi 'Maya' Arulpragasam also known as M.I.A. at the Vegoose Music Festival, Las Vegas, Nevada, 2007.

M.I.A. performs at the Outside Lands Music Festival 2009 at Golden Gate Park in San Francisco, California.

Neila Sathyalingam : Born in Jaffna in 1938, Neila Sathyalingam is among the pioneer Ceylon Tamil women in Singapore to achieve international standing in classical dance and choreography. She was trained in classical dance traditions such as *bharatanatyam*, *kathakali*, *kathak* and *manipuri* at Shanti Kumar School and Dance Kalaya School of Dance in Colombo, Sri Lanka. Prior to graduating with a first-class honours diploma in Bharatanatyam in 1957, Neila had already won the gold medal at the All Ceylon Dance Festival. At the age of 12, she was selected to perform for Queen Elizabeth II in Colombo. In 1974 she moved to Singapore. Three years later, together with her husband, Neila set up *Apsaras*—a dance institute. She has since been the company's Artistic Director while her late husband was the Music Director. In 1996, the couple received the Vishwakala Bharathi award from the Bharat Kalachar, a leading cultural organisation in South India. *Apsaras* is a regular feature at national events in Singapore, and the troupe has performed in myriad international dance, cultural and arts festivals. Neila has also received considerable acclaim for producing dance-dramas such as *Kannagi* in 1998 and *Aarupadia* in 2002; and for co-choreographing multi-racial dance programmes performed at the Children's Folklore Festival in France in 1995 and the International Folklore Festival in Spain in 1996. Neila was awarded the Singapore Cultural Medallion in 1989, and received the Kala Ratna award from the Singapore Indian Fine Arts Society in 1995.

YaliniDream is an Artist in Residence at the University of Michigan's Center for World Performance Studies. A well-known theatrical artist, she uses her entire body as a form to convey complex social and political issues through dance, poetry and song. Among other performances, one of YaliniDream's theatrical choreopoems include 'Wounds Unkisssed', which explores the unhealed pain of the Sri Lankan diaspora.

Hema Kiruppalini

CINEMA AND THE SRI LANKAN DIASPORA

The presence of Sri Lankan diasporic voices in cinema is frequently heard in films produced by the diaspora and in Indian Tamil cinema (Kollywood as it is popularly called). A number of these diasporic films have gained recognition in International film festivals, while those produced by Indian Tamil cinema have achieved considerable popular appeal.

One of the more famous Sinhalese directors is Vimukthi Jayasundara. A Paris resident, he travels frequently to Colombo. Jayasundara has gained world recognition for his films, which deal with the human tragedy of the civil war in Sri Lanka. His 2001 documentary *Land of Silence* earned considerable acclaim. *The Forsaken Land* (*Sulanga Enu Pinisa*), Jayasundara's first feature film, was screened in the 'Un Certain Regard' section at the 2005 Cannes Film Festival, where it won the Caméra d'Or. His 2009 production, *Between Two Worlds*, also received excellent reviews.

Indian Tamil cinema has also shown a marked fascination with the civil war in Sri Lanka and the Tamil 'other'—brothers in Sri Lanka with whom Tamil Nadu shares a linguistic affinity. During the civil war (1983–2009), Tamil cinema stars frequently protested through strikes and hunger fasts, demanding that the Indian central government protect the Tamils in Sri Lanka. In many Tamil movies one finds the presence of Sri Lankan characters that appear in the backdrop. For instance, in *Punnagai Mannan* (1986), Malini (played by Revathy) is a Sinhalese girl who is learning dance in Tamil Nadu. In *Pudhiya Mugam* (1993), Vineeth (played by Suresh Menon) is an assassin who works for the terrorists in Sri Lanka.

A recent, more popular Tamil movie that sympathises with the plight of Sri Lankan Tamils is *Thenali* (2000). In this movie, Kamal Hassan is a Sri Lankan Tamil who comes to Chennai for psychiatric treatment because of the trauma of the civil war. *Nandha* (2001) has in its midst, a heroine Kalyani (played by Laila) who is a Sri Lankan refugee in Rameshwaram. *Nala Dhamayanthi* (2003) is again built on the same idea where the heroine is a Sri Lankan immigrant living in Australia.

Both Santosh Sivan's *The Terrorist* (1999) and Mani Ratnam's *Kannathil Muthamittal* (2002) changed the representation of Sri Lankan Tamils in Tamil cinema. *The Terrorist*, a multi-award winning art film, was inspired by the assassination of Rajiv Gandhi in 1992 by a suicide bomber. It is an emotive and psychologically intense story of a pregnant militant woman on a suicide mission, who has to choose between life and death. Although the film does not name names or places, it is not difficult to surmise that the woman depicts a Sri Lankan Tamil Tiger soldier.

Kannathil Muthamittal (2002), a film by Mani Ratnam, tells the story of an urban Chennai family and their adopted daughter, Amudha. The story revolves around Amudha's search for her biological mother who is from Sri Lanka. *Kannathil Muthamittal* is haunted by the presence of Sri Lankan Tamil militancy, which is one of the film's central concerns. A more recent film that deals with Sri Lanka and the plight of the refugees who arrive in Tamil Nadu for protection is *Rameswaram* (2007). Directed by S. Selvam, this movie details the encounter between Indian Tamils and the refugees who temporarily fled the civil war.

Collectively, these cinematic works play a variety of roles. At one level, they are simply sources of entertainment for some in the diaspora. For others, these cinematic works are particularly important because they are viewed as powerful art forms that express stories of people's unremitting engagement with violence in everyday life. These are precisely the stories, which have not been sufficiently unravelled in contemporary journalistic accounts of the war.

Vasugi Kailasam

in South India, featured a jungle guerrilla camp, among ranks of women soldiers, reminiscent of the infamous LTTE female cadres, *Suthanthira Paravihal* (Birds of Freedom). In the video, the armed women march one way, while M.I.A. swaggers in the opposite direction, singing. Such images, together with M.I.A.'s frequent use of tiger motifs, have led to her being seen as a naive supporter of the LTTE. In interviews she is careful to distinguish between Tamil people and the LTTE.

M.I.A's provocations do not amount to a coherent political program—nor should they be taken as such. If she occasionally seems to miss the mark, as she did when she described herself as 'the only voice for Tamils' on an interview with Tavis Smiley on US public television (*The Tavis Smiley Show*, 2009), such statements are better understood as part of the bragadaccio and boasting conventions of hip-hop. Certainly, no one has played a greater part in bringing the invisible war in Sri Lanka into popular cultural consciousness. M.I.A.'s contribution as an unofficial spokeswoman for the Tamils through her music is acknowledged by her nominations for an Academy Award and two Grammy Awards. Indeed, her appearance on *Esquire* magazine's list of the 75 most influential people of the 21st century and *Time* magazine's annual 'Time 100' list for 2009 recognises a wider public significance, however fleetingly she closes the distance between 'here' and everywhere else.' That is her distinctive, perhaps unrivalled, achievement.

Suresh Joachim Arulanantham is a Tamil-Canadian film actor and producer from Colombo who has broken several world records for philanthropic purposes. The film he produced in 2009, Sivappu Mazhai, held the Guinness World Record for Fastest-Made Motion Picture.

Suvendrini Perera

TRANSNATIONAL SRI LANKAN TAMIL MARRIAGES

THE SOCIAL LANDSCAPE of the Tamil community in Sri Lanka has been ravaged by the prolonged civil war. As a result, the Tamil community is now widely dispersed both within Sri Lanka and around the world. In the context of this large-scale dispersion, marriage has emerged as a significant means by which people move out of places of insecurity. Tamil transnational marriages are primarily motivated by the desire to escape the civil war in Sri Lanka, and to help one's family do the same by opening up the possibility of chain migration. However, because transnational marriages are associated with leaving the site of violence or escaping from the war in Sri Lanka, this does not mean that such marriages are taking place in a random manner.

In this context, Tamil marriage brokers have emerged as 'mediators' between Tamil families across borders by 'holding' detailed information of prospective brides and grooms, and their family members. They are 'channels' or 'pathways' in the matchmaking process, keeping not only current and detailed information such as the expertise and educational levels of the prospective bride and groom. They are also knowledgeable about immigration rules and regulations in different countries. These mediators are thus crucial in transforming the anonymity and uncertainty of persons who have become distant by circumstance, into known persons with an identifiable history and biography and who can then be placed within the kinship network of the Tamil diaspora. The migration of Tamil women and men through marriage has indeed become one of the main links between the diasporic Tamils and those remaining in the homeland. In view of the difficulty faced by the prospective bride in gaining an entry visa to wed, these transnational marriages tend to take place in Colombo, India, Malaysia or Singapore.

There appear to be differences between the transnational marriages that have taken place prior to and after the war. These can be categorised in three distinct phases: 1) transnational marriages before the conflict; 2) transnational marriages that were contracted during the conflict and during the early refugee flow period that extended from the 1980s to the 1990s; and, 3) transnational marriages that took place after the asylum seekers gained permanent residence or citizenship in the host countries (in the 2000s). In the first phase, only a small segment of the upper caste or upper class Tamils took the step of migrating. Typically, the husband would

leave his wife in the natal village in Sri Lanka and visit frequently, or alternatively, over time, migrate with his wife when conditions are favourable.

The situation of Tamil refugees in the 1980s and early 1990s was quite different. Sri Lankan men had left their homeland but could not return or travel because, as refugees, they did not have the relevant travel documents. Consequently, in order to marry their prospective husbands, women had to travel abroad. Thus, during this second period, it was largely the Tamil brides who travelled out of Sri Lanka for marriage. In recent years, a further change has occured: many of the refugees who migrated in the late 1980s and early 1990s have now been granted either permanent residence or citizenship in their host countries. As a result, during the third phase, the grooms or brides travel to India, Singapore, Malaysia or Sri Lanka where the marriage ceremony is held. These countries are considered a transit site where most of the arranged or love marriages between Tamils actually take place. These sites play a vital role in creating a notion of community, kinship-network relatedness, and tradition through wedding-related events.

After the marriage ceremony, the spouse, who seeks to be reunited with their partner (husband or wife), has to make visits to the embassies and meet the required immigration regulations in these countries. Thus, transnational marriages involve not only arranging and contracting a marriage between parties of the Tamil community who are divided by geopolitical borders. There is also a requirement to conduct the wedding ceremony in such a way that it will convince the various state officials that the marriage is genuine. In an attempt to determine authenticity, immigration authorities question whether the wedding pictured in photographs provided to them were carried out according to 'Tamil traditions and customs'. Hence, wedding albums constitute an important source of reference for immigration officials attempting to ascertain the authenticity of a Sri Lankan Tamil marriage. Consequently, the processes and practices of a transnational Tamil marriages cannot be fully understood without taking into consideration the receiving state's practices and procedures for granting visas for marriage-migration.

Maunaguru Sidharthan

Sri Lankan Hindu wedding ceremony in Canada, 2009.

A Sri Lankan Tamil marriage in India between a groom from the United Kingdom and a bride from Sri Lanka.

Swiss national Alalasundaran Vinayagamoorthy's wife travelled from Jaffna to Basel for their wedding in 2012. Transnational marriage networks within the Sri Lankan community have aided in sustaining connections to the 'homeland'.

ENTREPRENEURSHIP AND REMITTANCES

Malaysian billionaire, T. Ananda Krishnan, controls Maxis Communications Bhd. His parents migrated from Jaffna to Malaya. Ananda Krishnan is one of the wealthiest entrepreneurs in Southeast Asia.

Arun Abey is the co-founder of IPAC securities in Australia. His co-authored book—How Much is Enough?—explores the interrelationship between money and happiness.

Susantha Shan Sisilchandra, received the 'International Businessman of The Year Award' from the Greater Dallas Asian American Chamber of Commerce in July 2011.

ACCORDING TO THE Sri Lankan Bureau of Foreign Employment estimates, about 1.7 million Sri Lankans were employed overseas in 2009 (SLBFE, 2009). More than 250,000 persons move out of the country annually with the objective of finding employment. Information on how many Sri Lankans settle abroad permanently is, however, not available as most Sri Lankans first migrate for studies or work, and it is unclear how many of these take up permanent residence overseas. Canada, the United Kingdom, Western Europe, the Middle East, and Australia comprise some of the major destinations for these Sri Lankans.

Middle Eastern countries have remained a major market for Sri Lankan labour since the late 1970s, followed by the East and Southeast Asian regions. For several decades, women, many of whom have been employed as domestic workers in the Middle East, constituted the majority of Sri Lankan migrant workers. However, the number of Sri Lankan men taking up employment overseas has increased over the past few years. The majority of the migrant workers range between 25 and 29 years old. In terms of the average age of workers, there is no major disparity between men and women.

According to the Annual Statistics Handbook of Foreign Employment, in 2010 skilled labour accounted for 26.69 per cent of migrant workers from Sri Lanka, while professionals comprised about 1.12 per cent, middle-level workers approximately 2.52 per cent and clerical workers about 2.93 per cent. With the exception of the domestic work sector, male migrants dominate all manpower categories.

Table 2.1 details the movement of Sri Lankans to the Organisation for Economic Co-operation and Development (OECD) countries. Since the beginning of the decade, the number of Sri Lankans moving to Australia and UK have increased substantially. A key factor for the high inflow of migration to these two countries is their attractiveness as destinations for higher education (*The Economist*, 17 February 2011).

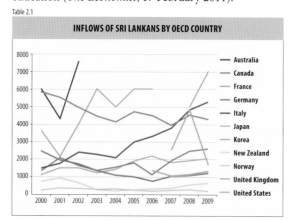

Table 2.1

INFLOWS OF SRI LANKANS BY OECD COUNTRY

— Australia
— Canada
— France
— Germany
— Italy
— Japan
— Korea
— New Zealand
— Norway
— United Kingdom
— United States

Source: OECD International Migration Database available at http://stats.oecd.org/Index.aspx?DataSetCode=MIG

The majority of Sri Lankans living in these OECD countries are Tamils, with the exception of Italy, where the majority are Sinhalese. The Sinhalese also comprise the majority of Sri Lankan labourers in the Gulf States (*International Crisis Group*, February 2010).

BUSINESSMEN IN THE DIASPORA

There has been little research on the employment status of Sri Lankan migrants in the diaspora. This may be due to the comparatively small number of enterprises, the more recent origins of the Sri Lankan migrant entrepreneurs, as well as the small size of the Sri Lankan and the Sri Lankan diasporic economy. Consequently, data limitation is a major barrier in analysing Sri Lankan migrant entrepreneurship. This section concentrates on studies of Sri Lankan entrepreneurship in Australia and Italy. In addition, individual cases of Sri Lankan migrant entrepreneurs have been used to document some impressions of the employment status of the Sri Lankan diaspora.

According to Peiris (2000), in Australia, a very large number of Sri Lankan independent businesses comprise professional consultants operating family-owned businesses in the form of a partnership or trust, with only a few resorting to a liability proprietary company (Pty.) structure. The study further posits that a substantial number of Sri Lankan medical practitioners, engineers, architects, lawyers and accountants in Australia were operating successful ventures by providing services to clients that included co-ethnics and others. An interesting feature of these enterprises is their success in managing small firms that often employ family members. Though they are operating on a small scale, most of these professionals are internationally qualified.

Moreover, Peiris explains that the motivation to start enterprises was the result of discrimination in finding employment and in keeping with the qualifications and skills of these migrants. Among the four explanatory hypotheses provided by Maria Vincenza Desiderio and John Salt (2010), it is clear that the choice of Sri Lankan entreprenuers to start enterprises falls under the 'disadvantage' or 'blockage' hypothesis. This hypothesis suggests that migrants enter self employment out of necessity that is usually the outcome of exclusion from salaried employment due to discrimination, language difficulties, low skills and lack of education. Seemingly, discrimination was possibly the important factor accounting for exclusion from salaried unemployment in the Sri Lankan case. Indeed, upon starting their enterprises, Salt (2010) suggests that their businesses have been successful and were able to reach out to Australian clients due to their language proficiency and international qualifications. Most Sri Lankan migrant entrepreneurs also used their networks of friends, family and business associates with ease, and through them, expand into overseas markets.

Some Sri Lankan entrepreneurs were engaged in the wholesale or retail trade and the restaurant business. Compared to Sri Lankans managing professional consultancy firms, Sri Lankan migrants engaged in these enterprises have not been as successful due to insufficient focus on co-ethnic customers and a general lack of background in retail trade and restaurant operations, which could differentiate their products and services from that offered by more experienced Chinese and Indian migrants. Apart from these fields, a few Sri Lankans were also engaged in the manufacturing sector.

According to Henayaka and Lambusta (2004), many Sri Lankans in Italy are employed in the domestic sector. However, a growing number have started their own businesses, setting up restaurants, cleaning agencies, call centres, video shops, traditional food shops and minimarkets. Most of these enterprises are located in Milan. In addition, some Sri Lankan men in Rome, after working for several years in the domestic sector, have started their own businesses, setting up, among others consumer cooperatives, handicraft shops and food shops. One of the biggest school-cleaning enterprises in Rome— the 'Cooperativa Multietnica di Pulizie Sud-Est'—is run by Sri Lankans.

A number of Sri Lanka-born entrepreneurs have begun to make a mark in the United States and the United Kingdom. Susantha Shan Sisilchandra, received the 'International Businessman of the Year Award' in 2011 from the Greater Dallas Asian American Chamber of Commerce (*Asian Tribune*, 20 August 2011). He migrated to USA in 2001 to work as a project manager and eventually started his own business on a new organic based growing medium product for the greenhouse industry. In 2009, the Sri Lanka-born entrepreneur, Ermila Smith, who is based in Cardiff, Wales, won the 'Best Product Design and Packaging' award, the 'Women in Product Development' award, and the 'Special Achievement' award in the British Female Inventor and Innovator of the Year competition.

As can be seen from the above cases, personal characteristics of migrant workers as well as the business environment of host countries, including the regulatory and institutional framework for immigrant entrepreneurship, are major determinants informing the immigrants decision to start new enterprises and sustain them successfully. For example, Sri Lankan migrants were able to start enterprises in Australia due to the relaxation of restrictions which hindered entry into many areas during the 'White Australia' period. Consequently, many Sri Lankan enterprises that commenced after the 1970s did not have to confront the restrictions that the

B. P. DE SILVA

Balage Porolis de Silva, better known as B. P. de Silva, was an exemplary jeweller who arrived in Singapore in the late 1860s. In 1874, he set up a jewellery shop—B. P. de Silva and Co.—in High Street. The firm employed well-trained Sinhalese craftsmen, salesmen and managers. Most of these personnel were recruited from Magalle and Bataduwa in Ceylon. During the early years, the shop had rooms that also provided boarding for Ceylonese immigrants. According to Richard Boyle— author of *B. P. de Silva: The Royal Jeweller of Southeast Asia*—the shop gradually became a centre of Sinhalese culture and custom and brought together the Sinhalese community in Singapore. Indeed, by the final decade of the 19th century, B. P. de Silva had come to be recognised as the leader of the Sinhalese community in the Straits Settlements (comprising Penang, Malacca and Singapore).

B. P. de Silva's firm was well known throughout the region for its exquisitely crafted jewellery, and by the early 20th century was patronised by the King of Siam, English royalty, Malayan Kings, royal princes and governors, not to mention some of the most wealthy European and Asian merchants in the Straits. A newspaper article in Singapore published in 1900 averred that 'Mr de Silva's jewellery creations, which are always artistic and often novel, are too well known to need commendation here'. His generosity towards public projects and charitable activities matched his business success. B. P. de Silva contributed a large sum to the construction of the local town hall in Singapore and while on a visit to Ceylon provided a significant donation for the development of a similar building in Galle.

In recognition of his position and contribution to the community, B. P. de Silva was elevated to the rank of honorary Mudaliyar in 1901 by the Governor of Ceylon, Sir West Ridgeway. That rank was preferred on the recommendation of the Governor of the Straits Settlements, Sir Frank Swettenham.

B. P. de Silva passed away in 1926, and his business has since been carried on by his kith and kin. From the 1990s his great-grandson, Sunil Amarasuriya, has held the position of the chairman of B. P. de Silva Holdings.

Hema Kiruppalini

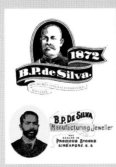

B. P. de Silva's logo has evolved to fit the tastes of the era it has found itself in, just like the businesses within the company.

In the 1960s, B. P. de Silva was 100 years old. Pictured above is its branch on Tanglin Road, Singapore.

early Chinese and Indian emigrants were subjected to (Peiris, 2000). In addition, demand, support and feedback from the diasporic community has also come to play an important role in the success of these migrant enterprises.

CONTRACT LABOUR AND THE DIASPORA; REMITTANCES AND ECONOMIC LINKS WITH SRI LANKA

Remittances sent by the migrant workers, both permanent and temporary, are one of the major foreign exchange sources for Sri Lanka. Alongside the increase in Sri Lankan migrant labour, there has been a steady rise in the inflow of remittances to Sri Lanka, from just US$9 million in 1975 to US$5.2 billion in 2011 (Central Bank of Sri Lanka, Annual Report). The developmental benefits of these remittances to the country of origin are manifested both at the macro and micro level.

Macro Level Impact

At the macro level, remittances to Sri Lanka have impacted macroeconomic stability and added to national savings. Remittance inflows are an important source of external financing for developing countries, often providing a

Bank of Ceylon at Devonshire Square in London.

Advertisement for money transfers to Sri Lanka in Uthayam, *an Australian magazine that provides news in both English and Tamil, November 2009.*

Table 2.2

TRENDS IN REMITTANCE INFLOWS (% OF GDP)

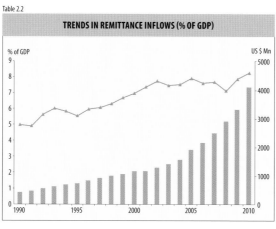

of import expenditure and 27 per cent of total current receipts in the balance of payments.

Sri Lanka has been able to maintain a higher rate of national savings and investment as a result of these remittance inflows. While remittances lead to increased investment and are likely to have an effect on economic growth, a good investment climate including the presence of a well developed financial system will determine the extent to which these remittances are utilised productively for the development of physical and human capital (Arunatilaka, *et al.*, 2011).

Micro Level Impact

Data from Sri Lanka's Household Income and Expenditure Survey (HIES) (2009/10) show that around 7 per cent of households in Sri Lanka receive remittances from overseas (author's calculations using HIES 2009/10 data). This has a direct bearing on consumpion patterns at the household level. On average, households in Sri Lanka that receive remittances spend over SLR7,000 more monthly compared to those that do not receive remittances. These remittances may be used to acquire land and improve household amenities. Having said that, Arunatilaka (2011) notes that in terms of school enrolment and morbidity levels indicators, there is no statistically significant difference between migrant and non-migrant households. From the above, it is clear that remittances have played a vital role in strengthening the Sri Lankan economy both at the macro and micro level.

Saman Kelegama and Roshini Jayaweera

steady source of capital in excess of funds generated through official development assistance (ODA), foreign direct investment (FDI), and portfolio flows. Remittance inflows to Sri Lanka increased to about 8 per cent of GDP in 2010—effectively the country's highest foreign exchange earner. Additionally remittances often play a counter-cyclical role, rising in times of global economic downturns and when a country faces a domestic shock.

As can be seen in Table 2.3, Sri Lanka's import expenditure has continuously outstripped export earnings, leading to considerable pressure on the country's trade balance. In this context, remittances have played an important role. In 2010, remittances contributed to 49 per cent of export earnings, 30 per cent

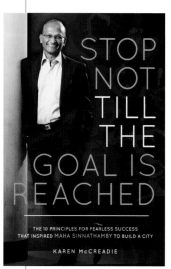

Malaysia-born Maha Sinnathamby is considered one of Australia's most successful immigrants. Best known for the 'Greater Springfield' development, he was influential in the transformation of thousands of hectares of inaccessible forest in Queensland into a city that is home to world-class educational, health, sports and recreational facilities.

Table 2.3

	SRI LANKA MIGRANT WORKER REMITTANCES IN RELATION TO SELECTED MACRO VARIABLES (1990–2010)								
Year	US $ Million					Worker Remittances as a % of			
	Remittances	Export Earnings	Import Payments	Total Current Receipt in Bop**	GDP	Export Earnings	Import Payments	Total Current Receipt in Bop**	GDP
1990	401	1,984	2,686	3,096	8,033	20.21	14.93	12.95	4.99
1991	443	2,040	3,037	3,287	9,000	21.72	14.59	13.48	4.92
1992	548	2,461	3,505	3,883	9,703	22.27	15.63	14.11	5.65
1993	627	2,864	4,011	4,405	10,354	21.89	15.63	14.23	6.06
1994	687	3,209	4,767	4,988	11,718	21.41	14.41	13.77	5.86
1995	727	3,807	5,311	5,822	13,030	19.10	13.69	12.49	5.58
1996	833	4,095	5,439	5,917	13,898	20.34	15.32	14.08	5.99
1997	921	4,639	5,864	6,715	15,092	19.85	15.71	13.72	6.10
1998	999	4,798	5,889	6,978	15,761	20.82	16.96	14.32	6.34
1999	1,056	4,610	5,979	6,826	15,712	22.91	17.66	15.47	6.72
2000	1,160	5,522	7,320	7,811	16,596	21.01	15.85	14.85	6.99
2001	1,165	4,817	5,974	7,457	15,750	24.19	19.50	15.62	7.40
2002	1,287	4,699	6,106	7,361	16,537	27.39	21.08	17.48	7.78
2003	1,414	5,133	6,672	8,164	18,882	27.55	21.19	17.32	7.49
2004	1,564	5,757	8,000	9,035	20,663	27.17	19.55	17.31	7.57
2005	1,918	6,347	8,863	9,983	24,406	30.22	21.64	19.21	7.86
2006	2,161	6,883	10,253	11,081	28,267	31.40	21.08	19.50	7.64
2007	2,502	7,640	11,296	12,463	32,351	32.75	22.15	20.08	7.73
2008	2,918	8,111	14,091	13,102	40,715	35.98	20.71	22.27	7.17
2009	3,330	7,085	10,207	12,500	42,068	47.00	32.62	26.64	7.92
2010*	4,116	8,307	13,512	15,266	49,551	49.55	30.46	26.96	8.31

* Provisional

** Total Current Receipt in BoP means sum of exports earnings, services receipts, income receipts, private transfers, and receipts and official transfers (net).

Source: Central bank of Sri Lanka, Annual Reports, Various Issues.

LITERATURE

As the Sri Lankan diaspora spread across the globe in the late 20th century creating significant migrant populations in Australasia, Europe and North America, the literature of the diaspora has evolved as a compelling and valuable corpus of writing. Testing the parameters of Sri Lankan literature, the writing of the diaspora has become increasingly concerned with exploring such themes as the twinned notions of belonging and alienation, the texture of memory, as well as the history and politics of the nation.

THE LITERATURE OF the Sri Lankan diaspora shares many concerns with synchronous diasporic literatures of South Asia, the Caribbean and Africa, many of which have also emerged from parallel histories of colonialism, post-colonial social and political conflict, and population displacement and dispersal. These diasporas have been caused concurrently, but not equally, by conflict and violence, economic deprivation, and the pursuit of personal and familial security, education and opportunity.

The proliferation of diasporas throughout the course of the 20th century and into the 21st has prompted an interrogation of the very concept of diaspora and the categories of people who claim habitation of the term. Aptly, diaspora is a term that 'travels' and the tensility of its borders has given rise to significant debates about its capacity to stretch from its locus of origin in the Jewish exodus, to accommodate the diverse trajectories of movement and migration that characterise an increasingly globalised world. In light of the proliferation of diasporas and the resultant debates over definition, one of the most useful ways to think about the term is 'as a category of practice, project, claim and stance, rather than as a bounded group' (Brubaker, 2005: 13). This 'protean' or 'plural' approach to the understanding of literary diasporas, with its emphasis on perspective and project, ultimately facilitates an analysis both within and across comparative diasporas that a more 'rigid diasporic grammar' (Walsh, 2003: 3) would preclude. In this context, 'diaspora' shifts from being a definitive noun to an expressive adjective, denoting the diasporic subject or diasporic consciousness, variable and diverse, which populates and shapes diasporic literature.

LITERARY DIASPORAS

Such openness to a variety of perspectives and projects is important in considering the literature of the Sri Lankan diaspora. This is especially true when we consider that analyses of this literature tend to valorise two particular ideological viewpoints. On one hand, the plurality of perspectives offered by the ethnically diverse writers of the diaspora are viewed by some literary critics as particularly valuable counterpoints to the nationalistic historical and social ideologies underpinning the Sri Lankan civil war. On the other, diasporic writers are often critiqued as being ignorant of the realities of contemporary Sri Lanka, as they are perceived to write not for a 'home' audience but to satisfy the desire for alterity and the exotic in global markets.

Certainly, diasporic Sri Lankan literature, whether it employs alterity as a commodity or not, enjoys significantly greater access to global markets, in contrast to the majority of Sri Lankan literature, whether written in English, Sinhala or Tamil. When the diaspora writes of 'home', its literature functions as a site upon which emotive issues of voice, representation and authenticity converge. Several diasporic writers have produced works that decidedly look away from Sri Lanka, such as Michael Ondaatje's exploration of immigrant stories in Canada in *In the Skin of a Lion* (1987) or his haunting multi-layered tale of displaced lives in the aftermath of World War II in *The English Patient* (1992); Bandula Chandraratna's study of justice and loss in an unnamed desert kingdom in *Mirage* (1999); Shiromi Pinto's *Trussed* (2006) that pulses with comic unpredictability as it encompasses prostitution, drugs and bounty hunters alike; and Michelle de Kretser's tale of a solipsistic Australian scholar in *The Lost Dog* (2007).

In texts such as these, the Sri Lankan origin of the author is more easily claimed as a source of value by readers in both Sri Lanka and in the diaspora. However, in other works, the 'relationship of the imagination' (Ghosh, 2002: 248) that maps the connections between the spatial and temporal past and present and between the homeland and the diasporic location, can become a key source of contention and even controversy, as diasporic writers are critiqued for authorising the most dominant representations of Sri Lanka in a global market, especially when these representations do not appear to cohere 'truthfully' with the experiences of readers and critics. Addressing the issue of audience and reception, Minoli Salgado, for example, had spoken about the legitimating power held

The Rice Mother (2002), the first book by novelist Rani Manicka, won the Commonwealth Writers' Prize in 2003.

Malaysia-born writer, Rani Manicka, with her third book, The Japanese Lover (2010).

Canadian Booker Prize-winning author and poet, Michael Ondaatje.

Poster of the Academy award-winning film, The English Patient (1996). This film was based on the novel by Michael Ondaatje that won the Booker Prize in 1992.

Singapore-based Sri Lankan author, Shehan Karunatilaka, won the Commonwealth Book Prize for his novel Chinaman in 2012.

Canadian writer Leah Lakshmi Piepzna-Samarasinha's Love Cake (2011) explores issues such as belonging and identity in the diaspora.

Colombo-born Chicago-based author, Mary Anne Mohanraj, founded DesiLit, an organisation which celebrates South Asian diasporic writers. Her book, Bodies in Motion (2005), was a finalist for the Asian American Book Awards.

Michelle de Kretser, of Burgher descent, migrated to Australia in 1972. Her writings draw on the polarities of diasporic identity.

The Hamilton Case (2003) and The Lost Dog (2007) authored by Michelle de Kretser.

by resident critics over a diasporic literature which has emerged during a period when 'the very boundaries of the nation and the basis of national affiliation are being tested and contested in the country' (Salgado, 2007: 3). As a result, Salgado claims that 'ex-patriate' texts are often 'ex-*patriot*ed' within the critical discourses of territoriality that she highlights in the Sri Lankan literary industry.

Indeed, preoccupations with belonging and authenticity can often override the awareness that thinking about the Sri Lankan diaspora, or for that matter, any diaspora, depends on being alert to context-dependent perspectives and inherent changeability. While writers may share a point of origin in Sri Lanka, this is staggered historically and spatially and then refracted according to the varied diasporic locations in which they live and write. Moreover, the continuing histories of violence in Sri Lanka, the ethnicised splitting of the diaspora as a mirror of nationalist politics, the various concepts of homeland in the Sri Lankan diasporic imaginary, as well as the multi-racial, cultural and gender politics in diasporic spaces all become the 'unstable points of identification and suture' (Hall, 1990: 226) that enable Sri Lankan writers to offer fresh perspectives on and from the diaspora.

The writers are most often taken as constituting a recognisable body called 'Sri Lankan diasporic literature'—Rienzi Crusz, Yasmine Gooneratne, Romesh Gunesekera, Chandani Lokuge, Michael Ondaatje, Shyam Selvadurai and Ambalavaner Sivanandan. It is clear that while they share certain overarching concerns with one another, and also with other bodies of diasporic writing (such as memory, the migrant's identity, the notion of home, the state of the nation), there is significant variation in the ways in which they explore and represent these concerns.

When other diasporic writers such as Bandula Chandraratna, V. V. Ganeshananthan, Michelle de Kretser, Ernest MacIntyre, Mary Anne Mohanraj, Leah Lakshmi Piepzna-Samarasinha, Shiromi Pinto, Karen Roberts, Shobasakthi, Roma Tearne, Marian Yalini Thambynayagam aka YaliniDream, are included in this grouping, it becomes clearer that Sri Lankan diasporic literature is best understood in terms of a matrix of multivalent positionings. The diversity of these writers' perspectives, projects and forms demands that diaspora be understood not simply as an elastic term which may or may not be in danger of losing analytical usefulness, but rather as a continually recalibrated term that will remain useful only if it reflects the rapid global changes wrought by technology, economics and cultural and political configurations.

BELONGING, IDENTITY AND LOCATION

Moreover, diasporic writers imagine modes of belonging and identity in ways that respond to their spatial and temporal location, drawing variously on facets of cultural and literary influence as well as inspired by the powerful ethnic, gender or class struggles that characterise their origins and present

positioning, imagining the diasporic subject as a complex embodiment of historical legacies, cultural influences and political impulses. In her first novel, *A Change of Skies* (1991), Yasmine Gooneratne, born in Sri Lanka in 1935 and a resident of Australia from 1972, explores the Horatian dictum that 'he who crosses the ocean may change the skies above him, but not the colour of his soul', through the lives of three generations of migrants in the Australian unknown. Gooneratne's 19th-century upper-class migrant initially views Australia as 'a blank pink space shaped like the head of a Scotch terrier with its ears pricked up and its square nose permanently pointed westward, towards Britain'. He is, however, compelled to transform his perspective as he begins to fill the relatively empty spatial signifier of Australia (albeit one oriented toward the colonial metropolis), with language and narrative that connects past and present, homeland and new world, when he discovers that the Western Australian town of Badagini derives its name from the words for 'hunger' in Sinhalese. The name functions as a creolised linguistic memorial to a group of hapless Sinhalese workers who, attracted by the 'rumour of employment' on a cattle farm, found themselves redundant and hungry during a time of drought. This tragic tale of migration, poverty and destitution is a 'burden' upon the narrator, yet it enables a connection with his Australian partner, a man of 'customary good-hearted kindness', whose friendship alleviates the pain of a troubled history of migration and who enables this moment of linguistic-historical recognition that acknowledges the interconnections between Sri Lanka and Australia.

Whether at home or away, several diasporic writers explore the colonial experience as a pre-condition of contemporary divisions and ruptures that shape diasporic identity. Michelle de Kretser, who was born in Sri Lanka in 1958 and relocated to Australia in 1972, sets her novel *The Hamilton Case* (2003) in pre-independence Ceylon. In the story, Sam Obeysekere is an elite lawyer and also a man with a penchant for a good detective story, and he becomes determined to solve a compelling murder mystery. Obeysekere, the product of an English public school education in the colonies, is a man with a 'gift of perfect mimicry', yet his embracing of imported forms and practices has resulted in a habit of self-deception. When his investigations lead him to the prime suspect, his notion of justice is battered, for he must deal with the colonial-era implications of 'putting a noose around an English neck'. As this local Sherlock Holmes tries to solve the case according to the principles of imported detective tales, the secrets of his own life begin to unravel. As the dark stories of Sam's childhood are detected, de Kretser explores the psychological damage wrought by colonialism. Alluding to her Burgher descent, de Kretser reveals that 'there is always this divided sense that the place you are living in is not actually where you belong', a realisation that compels her to focus on self-alienating characters such as Obeysekere.

While de Kretser's novel is not a tale of diasporic experience, it imbues subjectivity with the fracture and suppressed memory often allied with diasporic subjectivity. For instance, in a novel praised for its tangible evocation of place, de Kretser reveals that she felt that to return to Sri Lanka while writing the novel would weaken her capacity to write of the place; instead she draws upon her memory of a child's perspective, attuned to the lushness of flowers as well as the terror of snakes in a landscape that is 'utterly gorgeous on the one hand and faintly menacing on the other.' Her acknowledgement of the investment of the diasporic voice in distance and memory is also revealed in the work of other diasporic writers whose works are characterised by a similar capacity to combine beauty and barbarity in their representation of Sri Lanka, to both compelling and unsettling ends.

GEOGRAPHIES OF MEMORY

In her novel *Turtle Nest* (2003), Chandani Lokuge, born in Sri Lanka in 1952 and settled in Australia in 1987, evokes both the seduction and the violence of migration in lyrical language. The novel opens with an evocative description of a turtle hatchling yearning toward the safety of the sea, yet grasped by an eagle in flight—an analogy of the girl at the heart of the narrative, Aruni, adopted by Sri Lankan parents in Melbourne, who returns to Sri Lanka to find her roots. With her 'orphaned eyes', Aruni's perspective is bereft of the security of position, she is dispossessed of both mother and motherland, and through her story of return and discovery, Lokuge explores both the temptations and torments of belonging to places and people.

Lokuge's lyrical treatment of the painful allure of Sri Lanka, as memory and as geography, allies her writing with that of Romesh Gunesekera, born in Sri Lanka in 1954, and who grew up in the Philippines before settling in England in 1971. Sri Lanka's colours, tastes and sounds pervade Gunesekera's work, yet the epigraph to his collection of short stories, *Monkfish Moon* (1992) provocatively states, 'there are no monkfish in the ocean around Sri Lanka', enigmatically pointing to the paradoxical textures of his writing, which simultaneously draws directly on place, yet, refuses to be tied explicitly to the history or politics of it. His first novel *Reef* (1994) is the story about Triton, a young boy who becomes a cook for Mister Salgado, an amateur marine biologist; both cocooned by their respective preoccupations with the art of cooking and theorising about a vanishing reef in an era of increasing national conflict. Political tensions in Sri Lanka eventually lead to Triton's and Mister Salgado's emigration to England where they hear the news of the 1971 insurgency in which 'the heart of a generation was forever cauterized'. Later, in the flickering television images of the 1983 riots, Triton is unsettled by 'pictures of young men, who looked no different from

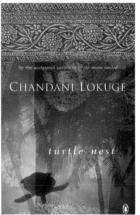

If the Moon Smiled *(2000)* and Turtle Nest *(2003) by the Australia-based novelist Chandani Lokuge.*

me', a disturbing moment of simultaneous recognition and disavowal that is echoed when he is faced with 'almost a reflection' of his own face in the young Tamil refugee manning the till in an English petrol station. In dislocated subjects such as Triton, Gunesekera effectively situates the disjunctions of perspective and identity of the diasporic subject in the violence and conflict dominating the Sri Lankan nation-state.

This dynamic is shared by Roma Tearne, another Sri Lankan-born and UK-based writer, who also merges beauty and brutality in provocative ways. Tearne was born in Sri Lanka in 1954 to Sinhala and Tamil parents, who migrated to England in 1964 with painful memories of betrayal and alienation born of the increasing ethnic tension, making their physical dislocation from the island simply 'a different kind of exile'. Tearne describes herself as always already displaced, 'the child of a disgraced union, neither Tamil nor Sinhalese, born with a foot in both worlds.' Her personal stories of displacement, loss and memory, powerfully infuse novels that register the intensely personal privations of an inescapable war; as Tearne reveals, her 'earliest memory was in 1958 when, aged four, I watched a Tamil man being set on fire in Colombo.' In *Mosquito* (2007), she recounts a story of diasporic return and loss as the widowed and middle-aged narrator, Theo, journeys back to Sri Lanka where he discovers a new, intense and scandalous love with teenaged artist Nulani. Their love is increasingly stained by a violence that spreads like a disease brought by a new kind of mosquito, bred alike in the North, the female suicide bomber: 'But unlike the mosquitoes, the women were full of a new kind of despair and a frightening rage.' In Tearne's novel, a gun-shot victim seeps out a grey substance from his head which 'in the early-morning light… spread like delicate fronds of coral on the sand'. The sound of a king coconut cracked open to release its cool, cloudy liquid reels the reader back to images of heads

Sri Lanka-born British novelist Romesh Gunesekera has won several awards including the inaugural BBC Asia Award for Achievement in Writing and Literature (1998); Premio Mondello Five Continents (1997); and the Yorkshire Post Best First Work Award (1995).

Illustrating the variety of Romesh Gunesekera's influential literary works. From left: The Match *(2006),* Heaven's Edge *(2002),* Monkfish Moon *(1992),* Reef *(1994),* Sandglass *(1998).*

Sri Lankan American Ru Freeman's first novel, **Disobedient Girl** *(2009), explores the lives of two Sri Lankan women and their struggle for freedom. She is also the author of* On Sal Mal Lane *(2013), which examines the years leading up to the civil war in Sri Lanka.*

Michael Ondaatje's critically acclaimed **Anil's Ghost** *(2000) won the Governor General's Award for English language fiction.* **Running in the Family** *(1982) is a fictionalised memoir that draws from his return to Ceylon in the 1970s.*

Roma Tearne, Sri Lanka-born author of Mosquito *(2007) and* Bone China *(2008).*

V. V. Ganeshananthan's first novel, Love Marriage *(2008), is set in Sri Lanka and North America.*

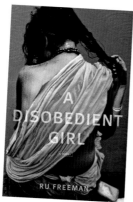

cracked like coconuts by guns and machetes. Tearne's writing presents the beauty and brutality of Sri Lanka as indivisible, in an unsettling conjunction that is a quality of much diasporic writing.

AESTHETICS AND POLITICS

In her work, Tearne, also an artist, consistently offers the value of art as a therapeutic and even cathartic act in the face of violence. Similarly, Michael Ondaatje, in his novel *Anil's Ghost* (2000), suggests the sublimity of art as a mode of working through trauma. Ondaatje was born in Sri Lanka in 1943 and has resided in Canada since 1962, after a period spent in England. In his first novel dealing explicitly with contemporary Sri Lanka, Anil, a US-based forensic scientist returns to the country of her birth as part of a United Nations human rights mission sent to investigate disappearances. Anil has 'lived abroad long enough to interpret Sri Lanka with a long-distance gaze' and the narrative charts her preoccupation with the existence and validity of truth. When she discovers a new skeleton buried amongst much older archaeological remains in a government-protected preserve, Anil provisionally names it Sailor and embarks on a dangerous process of investigation to discover its identity. To Anil, Sailor is the 'representative of all those lost voices' and she believes that 'to give him a name would name the rest'. For Anil, naming becomes an act that reinstates the identity obliterated in violence back into the memory of social relationship and human history. Yet, when the moment of naming finally becomes possible, it seems to have lost its sense of consequence. Instead, it is artisan Ananda's reconstruction of Sailor's face through innovative techniques rather than the identification of Sailor that is significant. In a novel structured by narrative strategies of fragmentation, elision, allusion and evasion, that underscore the challenges to knowledge, agency and recovery in a time of war, Ondaatje suggests the redemptive power of aesthetic and creative engagement in the face of an overwhelming and debilitating trauma.

In its focus on the therapeutic qualities of an imaginative response to the war, such writing encourages reflection on the forms and narrative strategies of literature and the need for new structures of reading—elliptical, allusive, even evasive—that take on particular resonance in the context of violent conflict, when speaking and censorship can have fatal consequences. This focus on the parameters of literary work is not exclusive to diasporic writing, yet much of that writing is concerned with the value of tangential positionings and perspectives. For example, in *Heaven's Edge* (2002), Gunesekera suggestively pushes the boundaries between realism and fantasy, authenticity and exoticism, in a novel set in the future on an unnamed island, a veiled Sri Lankan dystopia where beauty conceals violence and the

beguiling excesses of the landscape only serve to heighten the brutality of its inhabitants. By dislocating Sri Lanka in time and space (and even in genre as the novel combines elements of the *bildungsroman* and quest narrative with registers of fantasy and science fiction), Gunesekera urges the reader to leave aside questions about the politics of the exotic in the migrant's imaginative return and to examine instead, from a productively disoriented perspective, the continuities and discontinuities between past and present, reality and fantasy. In this novel he suggests the potential of exploring Sri Lanka through the spatial position of the 'edge', an imaginative equivalent of reality.

THE PERSONAL AS POLITICAL

Another mode through which diasporic writers explore their positioning in time and place is through the intergenerational family narrative. In such writing, interconnectivity structures narrative, rather than fragmentation and evasion, as writing about the past becomes a way of exploring one's own place in the present and the future. In memoirs and novels such as Ondaatje's *Running in the Family* (1982), Gunesekera's *The Sandglass* (1997), Sivanandan's *When Memory Dies* (1997), Selvadurai's *Cinnamon Gardens* (1998), Gooneratne's *The Sweet and Simple Kind* (2006), Tearne's *Bone China* (2008) and Ganeshananthan's *Love Marriage* (2008), the family and its interconnected stories, whether recounted in Sri Lanka or elsewhere, enable the construction of a viable authorial voice. Speaking with the 'small voice' (Guha, 1996) of history, the family fiction functions as an archive of unhistorical and unconventional stories. In the Sri Lankan context, in which history has often been written from the perspective of nationalist discourses, family fictions retrieve aspects of identity that do not necessarily align themselves neatly into projects of cultural and political nationalism.

A fine example is Sivanandan's *When Memory Dies*, which strives to represent the nation with remarkable historical range and analytical depth. Taking the span of the 20th century as his narrative field, Sivanandan contends with what he portrays as the loss of memory stemming from waves of European colonialism and intensified by the increasingly racialised politics of the nation. In Sivanandan's novel, which tells 'no one story', the intergenerational structure of narrative is based not simply upon bloodlines but upon shared social and political commitments. Structured on the premise that 'when memory dies a people die', the novel suggests that memory is not simply about recreating narratives

of history; rather, in retrieving stories of shared social and political affiliations arising from anti-colonial and post-colonial resistance to inequality and division, obscured by the manipulations of postcolonial politics, memory becomes an instrument of responsibility and resistance. Sivanandan left Sri Lanka in the wake of the 1958 race riots and arrived in Britain in the midst of the Notting Hill riots, suffering what he calls a 'double baptism of fire'. By 1972, he had become the director of the Institute of Race Relations (IRR) and the founding editor of the influential journal, *Race and Class*, in which, one year after the 1983 riots in Colombo, he published his powerful indictment of the state titled, 'Sri Lanka: Racism and the Politics of Underdevelopment'. In Sivanandan's political essays, as in the later novel, the strategy of imagining community through alternative narratives, or of using narrative as a technology for memory, creates powerful and incisive analyses of multi-racial Britain or ethnically-divided Sri Lanka alike.

WAR, VIOLENCE AND DISPLACEMENT

Diasporic responses to the social and ideological crises, both on a personal and public level, caused by the civil war are rich and varied. Both Selvadurai's *Funny Boy* (1994) and Roberts' *July* (2001) explore lives that are indelibly marked by the ethnic violence of July 1983, which functions in both novels as a pivotal point of fracture and alienation. Roberts, born in Sri Lanka in 1965 and settled in the US, explores the painfully personal inroads of racial and political division as lovers, families and neighbourhoods are riven by hatred and violence. Similarly, Selvadurai's *Funny Boy* imagines the personal as the political in the coming-of-age narrative of Arjie, whose queer identity is articulated against and in relation to the increasing ethnic tension and violence of the late 1970s and early 1980s. As ethnic tension mounts, Arjie begins to experience the home as an insecure place on several fronts as he develops consciousness of his 'funny' sexuality and also becomes a witness and actor in relationships that cross ethnic and gender boundaries. Finally, as ethnic violence erupts in the city around them, Arjie's family makes the difficult decision to leave their home for an unknown Canada.

Arjie's story reflects that of Selvadurai who was born into a Colombo Tamil family in 1965, and left the island in the wake of the 1983 riots for Canada.

In Selvadurai's fictional remembrance of childhood, space is constantly threatened by violence, either a violence enacted on personal identity or physical violence. Similar to *Funny Boy*, in that it explores the formation of identity and voice through the perspective and experience of childhood in the context of war, is Shobasakthi's *Gorilla* (2008), the tale of Rocky Raj, a young recruit of the Movement in Kunjan Fields and son of a locally infamous thug nicknamed Gorilla, whose name he unfortunately inherits. The narrative plays on naming and identity—Rocky is at once Gorilla, Arafat, Sanjay and Anthony Thasan (aka Shobasakthi) reflecting his dreams of who he wants to be and who he is made to be—and switches back and forth through asylum applications in France in the diasporic present and memory of conflict in family and community alike in the past. Shobasakthi explores the inescapability of violence for his protagonist, whether at the hands of his father, as a human instrument of the insurgent movement, or as a refugee. In this inventive 'auto-fiction'—the narrative is based on the author's own life, drawing on experiences as an LTTE child recruit and as a refugee in France—author, narrator and protagonist represent inextricable yet disjointed layers of identity.

As Shobasakthi reveals, the very act of writing in such a fraught context of personal and collective displacement is wrought with unpredictable contradictions: 'The moment I left Sri Lanka, my identity as a militant became that of a refugee. But when I began to write, I became a traitor to my race. I have been beaten up on the streets of Paris and on blogs by fellow Tamil refugees for my writings.' Writers such as Shobasakthi who persist in telling their stories despite the dangers of articulation, provide a valuable voice for those in the often invisible 'victim diaspora' of disenfranchised and stateless refugees and asylum seekers, as he asks 'What is more painful? Being a refugee first of all or then trying to prove to the authorities that one is actually a refugee?'

CONCLUSION

The relationship of the imagination that links past origin and present positioning gives rise to the desire to express the subjectivity of exile, the politics of memory, the idea of Sri Lanka, and what belonging means, especially in a context of conflict and violence, which is variously experienced according to race, gender and class. Dramatic social and political upheavals, experienced on both personal and collective levels, have shaped the contexts of diasporic literature. As the diaspora continues to expand and diversify and as new generations of writers trace their personal routes back to the island, or engage with their diasporic positioning in unconventional ways, there is always the promise of new, provocative, and refreshing approaches to memory and identity, personal and collective history, and the experience of contemporary global culture.

Sharanya Jayawickrama

Shobasakthi's novel, Gorilla, *narrates the story of Rocky Raj, a child who grows up in the village of Kunjan Fields during the height of the insurgency in Sri Lanka.*

Sri Lankan-Canadian author Shyam Selvadurai reading an excerpt from his critically acclaimed novel, Funny Boy *(1994), at the launch of the Samadhana 2012 Benefit Reading Series in Toronto.*

THE COMMUNITIES

T HROUGH REGION AND country based profiles, part IV of the encyclopedia discusses the conditions and specific features of the migration process leading to the formation of Sri Lankan diasporic communities; the community's social, cultural and political experience in the 'hostland'; the continued connections maintained with the country of origin; and the challenges that Sri Lankans based in these countries face at the beginning of the 21st century.

Pictured here is a religious procession in La Chappelle (sometimes referred to as 'Little Sri Lanka' or 'Little Jaffna') that is part of the annual Ganesh Festival organised by the Sri Manikar Vinayakar Alayam in Paris. The sustenance of religious traditions from the 'homeland' is an important feature of the Sri Lankan diaspora, and religious institutions are significant not only as places of worship but also for their wider role in community-building.

INDIA

I have lost the village home where
the sparrow will build its nest
the *cadjan* leaves will sing with the wind
the sun will enter the shoe flower
We crossed the seas dreaming of wealth
and a house
with a beach in front
and a garden along the red soil pathway
alas, we have lost our identities
in the wilderness of the refugee land

Selvam (Sri Lankan Tamil expatriate poet,
Chitralega Maunaguru, 1993)

O NE OF THE most fascinating and, at the same time, complex subject in the field of social sciences is the inter-relationship between the diaspora and their 'original homeland'. Does the Sri Lankan Tamil diaspora, scattered in different parts of the world, reflect the feelings and aspirations of their kinfolk in Sri Lanka? In what ways and to what extent can the Sri Lankan Tamil diaspora influence the political and economic developments in their original homeland?

This study reflects upon the living conditions and legal status of the Sri Lankan Tamils living in India, the Government of India's policy towards them and their linkages with Sri Lanka. Since the overwhelming majority of Sri Lankan Tamils live in the state of Tamil Nadu, attention is mainly focused on them.

PRELIMINARY OBSERVATIONS

The term 'diaspora' which is commonly used to refer to Chinese, Indians, Sri Lankans and other nationalities living outside their homeland is unsatisfactory. The term does not exactly convey the complexities of these people. 'Diaspora' was originally used to refer to the Jewish communities living in exile outside Palestine, consequent

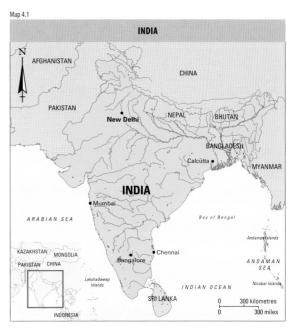

Map 4.1

Tamil refugees arrive in Rameshwaram, in the southern Indian state of Tamil Nadu, January 2006.

to the seizure of their homeland by external powers. The Jews were subjected to persecution and they fanned out to different parts of the world. However, throughout the centuries they hankered for their homeland. There was a special relationship between the land of Israel and the Jewish people. However, if one analyses the spread of the Sri Lankan Tamils, there were several 'pull' and 'push' factors. An even more relevant characteristic that differentiates is the fact that those who have settled in the developed world and have acquired citizenship in these host countries are unlikely to return to Sri Lanka on a permanent basis (Suryanarayan, 2005).

The second fascinating area is the cultural persistence among the diasporic communities. The Tamils, wherever they go, try to retain their cultural identity and, at the same time, adapt themselves to new situations. Cultural persistence and adaptation to new surroundings are twin facets of this dynamic group. The problem is rendered more complex in countries like Malaysia and Singapore where Sri Lankans are considered an integral part of the 'Indian' community, and where the label is used as a catch-all category for the descendants of those who originally migrated from the Indian sub-continent, which today comprises the nation-states of India, Pakistan, Bangladesh, Sri Lanka and Nepal. At the same time, the Sri Lankan Tamils try to retain their separate identity. Thus despite cultural linkages, inter-marriages between Tamils from India and those from Sri Lanka are very rare (Suryanarayan, 2005).

DIASPORA CONTRIBUTION TO NATIONALISM

In a recent article, Sri Lankan academic Kumar David raised certain interesting questions about the 'Tamils at home and the Tamil diaspora'. David rightly points out that there are two extreme views, first is the assertion of the Sri Lankan government that while the Tamils at home are 'content', the diaspora is intent on 'wreaking havoc'. The other extreme is represented by pro-Liberation Tigers of Tamil Eelam (LTTE) groups living abroad who maintain that the Tamils at home are 'too terrified and oppressed to speak up'. Both are inaccurate propositions but contain certain elements of truth (David, 2011).

One of the seminal contributions of the diaspora is to hold aloft the torch of nationalism and contribute to the advancement of freedom. The Sri Lankan Tamil diaspora not only internationalised the ethnic conflict, it also fuelled the LTTE war machine. Discriminated against by successive Sinhalese dominated governments, the Tamils, who left Sri Lanka, were in the forefront of Tamil struggle for a separate state (Santasilan Kadiragamar, 2010). They also expected that the government and people of Tamil Nadu would not only back them to the hilt, but would prevent the Sri Lankan government from accomplishing a military victory. In a conversation with Ambassador Lakhan Mehrotra, former Indian High Commissioner in Sri Lanka, Varatharaja Perumal, the leader of the Eelam People's Revolutionary Liberation Front (EPRLF) and the former Chief Minister of the North Eastern Province, said, 'The Eelam militants drew moral and material support from 20 times their number outside Sri Lanka—in Tamil Nadu and the Tamil diasporas spread over continents' (Mehrotra, 2011). What Perumal and other Tamil militant leaders did not realise is that despite sympathy for the Sri Lankan Tamil cause, what finally determined the stance of the Dravida Munnetra Kazagham (DMK)-led government in Tamil Nadu was the equation between India's central and the state governments. During the last stages of the fourth

Eelam War, the DMK, for reasons of political expediency, went along with the policies and programmes of the central government in New Delhi (Suryanarayan, 2010). The ultimate losers were the Sri Lankan Tamils.

SRI LANKAN TAMILS—A MIGRATORY COMMUNITY

The Sri Lankan Tamils were no strangers to migration. Since the Jaffna peninsula was relatively arid, it could not sustain a big population. Equally relevant, one of the benign aspects of British colonial rule was the introduction of education in the English medium. The American missionaries had established good schools in the Jaffna Peninsula and these schools contributed immensely to the intellectual advancement of the region. With the expansion of the British Empire, the British authorities required administrative personnel to serve in their far-flung colonies and the Sri Lankan Tamils availed themselves of this golden opportunity. The Jaffna economy thrived because of foreign remittances and that explains why it came to be known as the 'post office economy'.

During the British period, some Sri Lankan Tamils, especially from the Jaffna Peninsula, migrated to India, for education, employment and business. Gradually they settled down in India. Since both Ceylon and India were British possessions, travel between the two countries was very easy; it was not necessary to have a passport or apply for a visa. Most notable among the Sri Lankan Tamils who settled down in India during this period was the Hensman family. Rohini Hensman, the well known progressive writer, currently lives in Bombay, and writes regularly in the Indian and Sri Lankan media.

CYCLES OF MIGRATION TO TAMIL NADU

Given the geographical contiguity, there has been intense interaction between Tamil Nadu and Sri Lanka. The demographic structure in the island, its religion and philosophy, language and culture, political and economic development have all been influenced by constant interaction with Southern India. Relations between the two regions have been so close and intense that what afflicted one would affect the other. The educational advancement of Sri Lanka owed much to the contributions made by Indian teachers. A number of Sri Lankan students came for higher education to the Madras Presidency. Among the earliest graduates of Madras University, established in 1857, were two Sri Lankan Tamil students, C. Thamotharampillai and Visvanatha Pillai. The Indian national movement inspired political consciousness among sections of the Sri Lankan population. The Jaffna Youth Congress established close links with the leaders of the Indian National Congress. When the British government began detaining the leftist leaders in Sri Lanka, they found a safe haven in India and carried on their political work there. Mention should be made of Hector Abhayavardhana, N. M. Parera, Colvin R. de Silva, Anthony Pillai and others who not only escaped to India, but established fraternal relations with political leaders having socialist leanings (Philips, 2001).

Following Sri Lanka's independence in 1948, the nation-building experiment, with emphasis on Sinhala language and Buddhist religion, gradually led to the parting of the ways among Sri Lankan communities. The introduction of Sinhala as the official language; the policy of standardisation which made it difficult for the Tamils to get entry into engineering, medicine and agricultural sciences; and the policy of discrimination practised in

H. S. Hensman of the famous Hensman family from Ceylon served as the first Indian Superintendent of the Mental Health Hospital, Ayanavaram.

C. Thamotharampillai, from Jaffna, was the first graduate of the Madras University. He made significant contributions in the field of Tamil studies.

The grand dame and matriarch, Chellamuthu (9th great granddaughter of Singai Pararajasekaran Arya Chakravarty—King of Jaffna—1467–78); with her son, Thuraisingam (Chief Sanitary Engineer of Madras Presidency).

Sri Lankan President, J. R. Jayewardene (right), arrives in New Delhi in November 1987 for talks with the Indian Prime Minister, Rajiv Gandhi (left).

the recruitment to government services gave further fillip to a 'brain drain'. After 1983, when the ethnic conflict intensified, this situation triggered a vast migration of Sri Lankan Tamils to different parts of the world. An important point should be highlighted—whereas the migration in the 1950's and the 1960's consisted mainly of the educated people, the migration after 1983 involved those who did not know the English language. Contributing to the vast flow were two advantageous points. During this period, Western European countries and Canada were looking for cheap labour and they viewed these Tamils as a persecuted group, deserving sympathy and support (Suryanarayan, Sudrasen, 2000; Suryanarayan, 2003). The ardent support for the separate state of Tamil Eelam came from segments of those Sri Lankan Tamils who migrated after 1983. The formation of the 'Transnational Government of Tamil Eelam', after the defeat of the LTTE, is also due to the untiring efforts of this section of the Sri Lankan Tamil diaspora.

When the communal holocaust took place in July 1983, many Tamils came to India as refugees. The

Sri Lankan Tamils waiting to be rehabilitated in Indian refugee camps, March 1985.

geographical contiguity, cultural affinity and above all, New Delhi's liberal policy of granting asylum, made Tamil Nadu an attractive destination. Furthermore, since New Delhi was pursuing a 'mediatory-militant supportive policy' towards Sri Lanka during this period, the leaders of the Tamil political groups could carry on successful propaganda (Dixit, 1998). The administrative machinery rose to the occasion and a number of refugee camps came up in different parts of the state. Not one Sri Lankan Tamil was refused asylum and the Government of India provided not only essentials of life—shelter, food, medical aid and free education, but also financial doles. The refugees were allowed to work outside the camps to supplement their incomes.

Notwithstanding the support, the Sri Lankan refugees had moved from a poor country to a poorer country. The refugee camps in which most of them resided cannot be described as ideal. The camps were overcrowded, with asbestos roofing, had no proper sanitary facilities, scarce drinking water and no proper lighting. Nonetheless, what made Tamil Nadu attractive for these refugees was that there was no sense of insecurity here. There were no 'midnight knocks' by the armed forces and, what is more, their children were not forcibly conscripted into the 'baby brigade' of the LTTE. At the height of the fourth Eelam War, in April 2009, I visited the refugee camp in Mandapam at Rameshwaram and talked to a few refugees, who had arrived there from Mullaitivu after a lot of difficulties. When the war started in 2006, the Sri Lankan Navy began to consolidate its hold on the Sri Lankan side of the Palk Bay. The Indian Coast Guard had stepped up the vigil in the India-Sri Lanka maritime boundary; as a result, the Sri Lankan Tamils found it extremely difficult to come to Tamil Nadu as refugees. The refugees whom I interviewed told me that given an opportunity, all Tamils caught in the war zone between the Sri Lankan armed forces and the Tigers would have liked to come to India as refugees.

Sri Lankan refugees are the creation of a discriminatory political system and to expect them to be apolitical is an impossible task. All militant groups had their following, and in Tamil Nadu they could articulate their political views freely. However, the assassination of Rajiv Gandhi by the LTTE suicide squad in May 1991 radically changed the political situation. The Tigers were no longer welcome in India and the LTTE was banned. The Sri Lankan Tamils became very discreet in their comments about Sri Lanka and India's policy towards the island.

FOUR WAVES OF REFUGEES

The Sri Lankan refugees came to India in four waves. The first exodus of refugees began on 24 July 1983, soon after the communal holocaust. It continued until 29 July 1987, when the India-Sri Lanka Accord was signed. During this period, 134,053 Sri Lankan Tamils arrived in India. Following the Accord, the refugees began to return to the island by chartered ships or on their own. According to Indian government sources, 25,538 returned to Sri Lanka. The remaining Tamils either continued to live in Tamil Nadu or migrated to greener pastures in the Western world.

The second Eelam War commenced in June 1990 and a fresh exodus of refugees began. After 25 August 1989, 122,078 refugees went over to Tamil Nadu. The destitutes among them, numbering 115,680, were accommodated in refugee camps and the rest lived on their own. Following

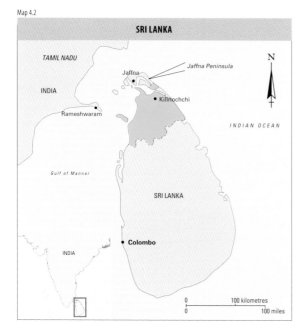

Map 4.2

SRI LANKA

TAMIL NADU

INDIA

Jaffna

Jaffna Peninsula

Killnochchi

Rameshwaram

INDIAN OCEAN

Gulf of Mannar

SRI LANKA

Colombo

INDIA

N

| 0 | | 100 kilometres |
| 0 | | 100 miles |

return of the refugees to Sri Lanka. According to UNHCR sources, from 2003 when UNHCR started facilitating the repatriation of refugees to Sri Lanka, 36,000 persons have returned to Sri Lanka. Most of them originally belonged to the Mannar and Trincomalee districts. The two districts have been declared as 'cleared areas' by the government of Sri Lanka. At the same time, many refugees who live in Tamil Nadu are uncertain about their future in Sri Lanka. Moreover, there is no demand either from the Tamil Nadu Government or from the political parties that the refugees should immediately return to the island. The political atmosphere in the Indian state remains congenial for the refugees and they can remain there until they voluntarily decide to return.

CATEGORIES OF SRI LANKAN TAMILS

The Sri Lankans living in Tamil Nadu can be divided into the following categories. 1) Refugees of Sri Lankan Tamil origin living in the camps; 2) Refugees of Indian Tamil origin, that is people from India who migrated to Sri Lanka at an earlier time and have returned as refugees, who live in the camps; 3) Refugees who live outside the camps; 4) Sri Lankan nationals; 5) Militant refugees in Special Camps and 6) Miscellaneous category.

1. *Sri Lankan Tamil refugees living in camps.* According to the policy note issued by the government of Tamil Nadu, 2009–10, there are 73,451 refugees belonging to 19,705 families in 115 refugee camps scattered throughout the state. Of these refugees, those of Indian origin number 28,500 (Suryanarayan, 2010). If one deducts this figure from the total, refugees belonging to the Sri Lankan Tamil category number 44,951.

2. *Refugees of Indian Tamil origin.* There are 28,500 people of Indian origin who live in the refugee camps. The legal distinction and the government's policy towards them should be clearly understood. The Sri Lankan Tamils are citizens of Sri Lanka and they do not belong to the Indian diaspora. Among the Indian Tamil refugees there are a few who were conferred Indian citizenship under the Sirimavo-Shastri Pact of 1964; but did not attempt to return to India until after July 1983. I came across a group of such people in the Kottappattu camp in Trichy; their representations

Map 4.2 shows the proximity of the northern peninsula of Sri Lanka and Tamil Nadu, India.

Rajiv Gandhi's assassination, the repatriation of refugees commenced on 20 January 1992. According to UNHCR sources, 54,188 refugees were voluntarily repatriated to Sri Lanka by chartered ships and flights.

The third Eelam War commenced in April 1995 and this initiated the third wave of refugee movement. With the signing of the ceasefire agreement in 2002, the flow of refugees dwindled. By the end of August 2003, 22,418 refugees had moved to Tamil Nadu. When the fourth Eelam War commenced in January 2006, the fourth wave of refugee movement began. However, due to the vigil exercised by the Sri Lankan Navy and the Indian Coast Guard, the flow did not become a mass exodus. Between January 2006 and May 2009, 24,823 refugees came to India (Suryanarayan, 2003).

The end of the war should have put an end to the flow of refugees, but that did not materialise. According to informed sources, nearly 20,000 Sri Lankan Tamils who were among the internally displaced persons (IDPs) living in the Mainik farm, after paying huge bribes to the Sri Lankan armed forces, escaped from Vavuniya. A number of them came to India after getting visas from the Indian High Commission through travel agencies operating in Colombo. According to these sources, hundreds of them came to Tamil Nadu. In fact, flights from Colombo to Chennai were heavily overbooked at the time. After arriving in India, a few of them approached the officials of the Rehabilitation Department to gain refugee status. Others just 'disappeared'. It is very likely many of them are hardcore members of the LTTE. Their presence in Tamil Nadu and neighbouring Indian states has serious security implications. Among others seeking asylum in Tamil Nadu are journalists and political dissidents who feel insecure under the present military dispensation. According to the Organisation for Eelam Refugee Rehabilitation (OfERR), 1,625 Sri Lankan Tamils sought asylum in Tamil Nadu from May 2009 to March 2011. This figure obviously does not include those mentioned earlier in this paragraph.

The Sri Lankan Deputy High Commission in Chennai, the Chennai office of the UNHCR and the Rehabilitation Department has started facilitating the

Sri Lankan refugee children, and Indian students sing the Indian national anthem at a school in the Mandapam refugee camp, near Rameshwaram, 2006.

Balu Mahendra, of Sri Lankan Tamil origin, is a veteran filmmaker. During his cinematic career from the 1970s to 1990s, he won several Indian Film Awards.

Ramachandra Sundaralingam, the former Additional Director-General of Police of Sri Lanka and Interpol drug expert, lectures on drug abuse and prevention in India.

S. C. Chandrahasan, a lawyer by profession, is the founder of OfERR (Organisation for Eelam Refugees Rehabilitation) in India. He is the son of the prominent Ceylonese political leader, S. J. V. Chelvanayagam.

to the Government of India and the Government of Tamil Nadu that their Indian citizenship should now be conferred have fallen on deaf ears. As a last resort, they sought legal remedies and filed a case in the Madurai bench of the Madras High Court. A few Indian origin Tamil refugees continue to remain stateless, but as a result of a recent legal enactment, they can get Sri Lankan citizenship when they return to Sri Lanka. However, most of these refugees would like to permanently settle down in India as Indian citizens. They do not own any property in Sri Lanka nor will they get any job on their return. There has been upward educational mobility among them; some of them have married into Indian families. The Citizenship Act of 1955 (57 of 1955) contains provisions for citizenship by registration, under which a person of Indian origin, who is ordinarily resident in India for seven years before making his/her application, is entitled to citizenship. As people of Indian origin, these refugees who want to settle down in India as Indian citizens in this category should receive sympathetic treatment from the government of India and the Government of Tamil Nadu.

3. *Refugees outside the camps.* This category comprises people who inform the Rehabilitation Department that they do not want government assistance and they have the means to look after themselves. The government officials advised them to register themselves with the nearest police station and also get a refugee certificate from the nearest Collector's office. According to the Government of Tamil Nadu there are 32,596 refugees who live outside the camps.

4. *Sri Lankan nationals.* These are people who came to India with valid travel documents and live in the state by their own means. They are required to register themselves with the nearest police station.

While some of them continue to stay in Tamil Nadu even after the expiry of their visas, others use Tamil Nadu as a transit point to go abroad. Some, through improper means, have acquired ration cards and property. According to informed sources, there are nearly 80,000 people under this category.

5. *Militants in Special Camps.* Those Sri Lankans who are alleged to have militant links are kept in two Special Camps in the Chengalpattu district. There are approximately 35 inmates in these two camps. The living conditions in these camps are abominable and the National Human Rights Commission has drawn the attention of the state government to improve the living conditions. The media has also reported that the inmates in these camps occasionally resort to hunger strikes to improve their status.

6. *Miscellaneous category.* Some Sri Lankan Tamils who are citizens of European countries have come to live in Tamil Nadu. R. Sundaralingam, who was former Chief Superintendent of Police, Northern Province, Sri Lanka, was deputed to INTERPOL in Paris, where he acquired French citizenship. He came to Chennai some years ago to give lectures on the narcotics trade. He and his wife have taken to the religious and cultural life of the city. Sundaralingam informed the author that he regularly extends his visa in order to continue to live in Chennai. Nirmala Chandrahasan, former Professor of Law in Colombo University, belongs to a different category. Daughter of Naganathan, the well known Federal Party leader and wife of Chandrahasan, the founding father of OfERR, Nirmala belongs to the well-known Hensman family, who migrated to India under British rule and became Indian citizens. Nirmala has recently acquired Overseas Indian Citizenship, while remaining a Sri Lankan citizen.

Sri Lankan Buddhist pilgrims at Dhamakh Stupa in Sarnath, India, March 2011.

Despite political uncertainties, Sri Lankan Tamil refugees continue to return to Sri Lanka from neighbouring India.

PILGRIMS AND STUDENTS

Although they do not strictly fall into the category of diaspora, mention should be made of approximately 200,000 Sri Lankan pilgrims who visit India every year. To a devout Buddhist, visiting the sacred places associated with Buddha's life—Gaya, where Buddha attained enlightenment; Sarnath, the site of his first sermon and Kushinagara, the site of Buddha's *Parinibbana*—is a cherished goal. Their visit is facilitated by the Mahabodhi Society, which provides lodging facilities in Chennai and New Delhi. Nearly 150,000 Buddhist pilgrims come to India every year. Similarly thousands of Hindus come to pray in Guruvayoor, Tirupati, Sabarimalai, Rameshwaram and Varanasi. The Christians come to India to pray in the Velankanni Church and the Muslims visit the Dargah in Nagore.

Equally important, Indian universities attract a large number of Sri Lankan students. While the fortunate few come to India under the scholarship programme of the Government of India, the majority arrive on their own initiative. Unfortunately, most Sri Lankan students do not register themselves in the Sri Lankan High Commission; and, therefore, the exact statistics of Sri Lankan students is not available. However, according to informed sources, nearly 5,000 Sri Lankan students are currently studying in India.

NEED FOR A NATIONAL REFUGEE LAW

India, like other SAARC countries, has neither signed the 1951 UN Convention on the Refugees nor the 1967 Protocol. In general, India has, so far, not enacted any national refugee law. There has been occasional demand that India should immediately enact a national refugee law, which combines the humanitarian concerns of the refugees and the security interests of the state (Suryanarayan, 2003).

As far as the policy of the Government of India is concerned, New Delhi looks at the problem strictly from a bilateral perspective. Unlike Western countries, where asylum is the first step towards citizenship and integration, the Government of India would like the refugees to return to their homeland once the situation improves there. Even though there is no national refugee law, the Government of India upholds the principle of *non-refoulment*, which is the basic principle of international refugee law. However, as described earlier, the Sri Lankan case is very complex, because there are refugees of Indian origin, who can claim Indian citizenship under the Indian Constitution.

The Government of India and the Government of Tamil Nadu can take credit that the treatment of Sri Lankan refugees had been praiseworthy. It needs to be highlighted that in the field of education, the refugees have excelled themselves; many refugee children enroll themselves in medical, engineering and other professional courses. An immediate survey, by the Governments of India and Sri Lanka, of manpower requirements in the Tamil areas of the island is recommended. After such a survey is done, technical training could be imparted to the refugees so that when they return to Sri Lanka, they can make constructive contributions towards the development of their country.

CONCLUSION

The experiences of refugees are traumatic illustrations of social change. They are uprooted from one social setting and thrown into another. In the process they undergo enormous suffering and irreparable tragedy. Torn between fear and hope, the refugee experience creates a void in their lives. As Benjamin Zephaniah, the refugee poet has written:

> We can all be refugees
> Nobody is safe
> All it takes is a mad leader
> Or no rain to bring forth food,
> We can all be refugees
> We can all be told to go
> We can be hated by some one
> For being some one. (Zephaniah, 2001)

*V. Suryanarayan**
This essay is partly based on the author's earlier writings on the subject.

Chelian Francis shows an application form for repatriation as he waits with his family and others at the Sri Lankan Deputy High Commission in Madras, June 2004.

MALAYSIA

Much has been written and said regarding the great contribution of the Chinese and Indians. The Ceylonese, however, have been grouped as Indians or as just 'Others'. Who were these significant 'Others' and what was their role in the development of this nation? ...As a former civil servant, the dedication and stability of the Ceylonese who worked in large numbers in almost every branch of public administration and in the plantation and industrial sectors, has left an indelible mark in my mind...

Foreword by Former Prime Minister of Malaysia,
Tunku Abdul Rahman Putra.
In S. Durai Rajasingham, A Hundred Years of Ceylonese in
Malaysia and Singapore: 1867–1967.

INTRODUCTION

Sri Lankan migrants came to Malaysia in multiple waves. In the modern period, records indicate that trade between the Malay Peninsula and Sri Lanka increased from the 1820s, and that the Straits Settlements (comprising of Penang, Malacca and Singapore) were employed as penal colonies for convicts from India, Sri Lanka and Burma. From the 1860s, Sri Lankans began immigrating to Malaysia in large numbers. Many Sri Lankans who set up their homes and businesses in the port cities of Singapore, Penang and Malacca were traders and jewellers.

The transfer of the Straits Settlements to the Crown in 1867 and the signing of the Pangkor Treaty in 1874 allowed for an expanded British involvement in the Malay states. To develop the Straits Settlements, there was a need for personnel who could build and manage a much needed infrastructure. Looking westward, Sri Lanka was an important place from where recruits could be procured as their knowledge of English and, more importantly, familiarity with the British colonial machinery made them a valuable workforce. Thus, in the 19th and 20th centuries many Sri Lankans were brought to Malaya to work on the railway as well as to build government

buildings, work in government offices, tend plantations, and develop public works projects.

Jeffrey Samuels

EARLY MIGRATION

The British took over the administration of Ceylon from the Dutch in 1795 and by the late 19th century a substantial number of children in the Jaffna peninsula had obtained an English education. This paved the way for their employment in the colonial civil service in various parts of the British Empire. Along with the Jaffna Tamils, Burghers and other Ceylonese communities also obtained English education and many sought employment in the British civil service abroad. English education was thus crucial in explaining the large-scale migration of the Ceylonese to Malaya.

In *A Hundred Years of Ceylonese in Malaysia and Singapore 1867–1967*, S. Durai Raja Singam gives a succinct account of Ceylonese emigration to Malaya. In the early days they travelled under considerable risk and danger. There were no regular steamers. If weather conditions were favourable, it would take between two and three hours for a sailing boat from Jaffna to reach Vedaraniyam in India. One would then proceed to Malaya by steamers that plied these waters. Another route was to travel from Jaffna to Kayts followed by taking a sailing vessel to Kodikarai and then to Negapatnam, a busy port in South India. From here they would take a steamer to

Map 4.3

Penang or Singapore. Sometimes Jaffna Tamils on their way to Malaya took the hazardous sea route, sailing from one of the Jaffna ports to Pamban, then to Colombo and thence to Penang and Singapore.

Many of the pioneers from Jaffna and other parts of Ceylon arrived in Malaya on the invitation of British administrators. They were recruited due to their English proficiency, work ethics, and the trust and confidence that the British had in them. For the British, the early migrants from Sri Lanka proved to be an invaluable asset in the administration and development of Malaya. They worked hard, suffered privation, endured loneliness and due to the hazardous conditions on the frontier, many even lost their lives. While many were educated personnel, there were Ceylonese emigrants who came with no English education at all. They entered the private sector as entrepreneurs, contractors, transporters, restauranteurs, shopkeepers, barbers, goldsmiths, etc. The migration process continued in spite of the Great Depression that severely impacted the Malayan economy in the 1930s.

ASSOCIATIONS

Even before the 20th century, the Ceylonese in Malaya had forged social organisations to represent their interests. Their early associations sought to promote the social, cultural, sporting, educational and welfare needs of the burgeoning Ceylonese community. Amongst the earliest to be set up by these emigrants was the Victoria Reading Room—situated in Barrack Road, Taiping—which by 1899 was already fully functioning. This was followed by the Ceylon Association in Taiping, formed in 1903. The building has now been declared a heritage building by the Malaysian government. Other organisations soon followed. Notable amongst these were the Selangor Ceylon Tamil Association (SCTA) in Kuala Lumpur, the Selangor Ceylon Saivites Association (SCSA) and the Negeri Sembilan Ceylonese Association (NSCA), while several active associations were also established in smaller towns in the Peninsula.

The Sinhalese, though small in number, formed the Sinhalese Association of Malaya in 1921. That organisation, however, dissolved a year later. They were only able to establish a more sustained social organisation in 1939 when the community came together to form the Malay States Sinhalese Association. Officially registered in April 1940, meetings of the Association were held on the premises of the Ceylon Bakery owned by P. H. Hendry. Shortly after its formation,

the activities of the Association were affected by the Japanese invasion of Malaya. It was only in 1946 that the organisation properly resumed its social functions.

CULTURAL ACTIVITIES

Alongside social organisations, the Ceylonese have shown a keen interest in developing and preserving their culture in the diaspora. For the purpose they set up several organisations in Kuala Lumpur, Ipoh, Seremban, Klang and Kuantan. Cultural organisations that have a long history in Kuala Lumpur include the Sangeetha Abivirthi Sabha in 1923—the brainchild of a group of devoted music lovers and leaders from the Jaffnese and South Indian community. Records suggest that the organisation was very active from 1925 until the outbreak of World War II. During this period, its activities included classical music and drama performances, literary activities, story-telling, and the rendering of the Thirukkural. A number of students trained at the association rose to become leading artistes in Malaysia. The Japanese Occupation, however, brought about a slowdown in the activities of the Sabha, which only fully resumed after 1947. The well-known Indian dancer, Gopal Shetty, has employed the Sabha premises to teach dance. Since then several successful public performances have been staged, and the Sabha is recognised by the government as a leading South Asian cultural institution in Malaysia.

The Ceylon Tamils' Kalavirthy Sangam (originally called the 'Chums' Amateur Dramatic Association Selangor), initiated by S. Rajaratnam and K. Chelliah in 1941, has also achieved prominence, like Sangeethalayam (founded in 1972). Although Ceylonese cultural exponents were involved in the founding of the latter, the organisation is not exclusive, and membership is open to all Malaysian communities. Many local students trained at these academies have

Members of the Sangeetha Abivirthi Sabha in Jalan Razario, Brickfields, Kuala Lumpur (circa 1940s). The photo clearly reveals that by this time women were already heavily involved in Ceylonese social and cultural organisations in Malaya.

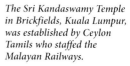

The Sri Kandaswamy Temple in Brickfields, Kuala Lumpur, was established by Ceylon Tamils who staffed the Malayan Railways.

SRI LANKAN BUDDHISM IN MALAYSIA

Sri Lankan Buddhist Temples in Malaysia

From the late 19th century, the increasing numbers of Sri Lankans living in Taiping and Kuala Lumpur led to the establishment of familiar places of worship. Thanks to the generous support of A. A. Gelis de Alwis and other Sri Lankans in Taiping, the first Sri Lankan Buddhist temple was established on the peninsula in 1889: Bodhi Langka Ram Vihara. Following that temple, three other Sri Lankan temples were built in Malaysia: one in the cosmopolitan section of Kuala Lumpur known as Brickfields (in 1895), one on the island of Penang (1914) and another in Kuala Lumpur where a number of railway employees lived and worked (1921). The Sri Lankan temples in Taiping and Kuala Lumpur were sponsored largely by Sri Lankans who regarded the temples as sites where their ethnic and Buddhist religious identity could be maintained.

Reaching Out

Despite the temples' ethnic origins, several Sri Lankan monastics have played a key role in the propagation of Buddhism in Malaysia beyond the Sri Lankan community. As chief incumbent of the Mahindarama Temple in Penang from 1933–64, Venerable Kamburupitiya Gunaratana reached out to new audiences by giving countless lectures as well as by preaching in both English and Hokkien.

Built in 1889 the Bodhi Lanka Ram Vihara in Taiping was the first Sri Lankan Buddhist temple to be established in Malaya.

Venerable Kirinde Sri Dhammananda, chief incumbent of the Sri Lankan temple in Brickfields from 1952 to 2006, also devoted his energy to broadening the reach of his temple to include Chinese Malaysians by giving regular talks on Buddhism as well as by publishing short tracts, books, and periodicals through his temple's Buddhist Missionary Society. Along with establishing a correspondence course in 1979, Venerable Dhammananda created youth sections of the Buddhist Missionary Society to educate Malaysian youth about their religion.

The Sri Lankan Catholic priest turned Buddhist monk, Venerable Wattala Ananda Mangala (the first resident monk of Seck Kia Eenh Temple in Malacca), also played a central role in propagating Buddhism in Malaysia. Like Venerable Dhammananda, he sought to increase the interest in Buddhism among Malaysian youth and university students. To achieve that objective, Venerable Ananda Mangala organised various youth-oriented activities: Buddhist youth seminars, holiday Buddhist training camps, drama shows, singing activities, hymn-singing competitions, youth sports meets, and so on.

The Taiping Bodi Langka Ram Buddhist Association is a symbol of the enduring Buddhist connections between Sri Lanka and Malaysia.

From Propagating Buddhism to Social Work

With the passing away of the above-mentioned Sri Lankan monks came a different group of monastics. Responding to the social and religious needs of their Chinese patrons—particularly their concern for social responsibility, sense of community interrelatedness, and penchant for philanthropy—several Sri Lankan leaders began transforming their temples into centres of social service.

Such a transformation is clearly evident at places such as Mahindarama, Buddhist Maha Vihara, Sri Lanka Buddhist Temple in Sentul, and the Seck Kia Eenh Temple. In recent years monastic leaders— E. Indaratana, K. Dhammaratana, B. Saranankara, and A. Ratanasiri respectively—have begun a host of social enterprises that include old age homes, cancer-care units, hospices, poverty-relief programmes, and free medical clinics. Inspired by the inroads made by Christian charity organisations and, partly, by the Mahayana Buddhist charity organisation Tzu Chi, the Sri Lankan temples have become very active in national and international aid, relief work, and social upliftment projects.

Jeffrey Samuels

The Buddhist Maha Vihara in Brickfields during Wesak Day celebrations in 2010.

Sri Lanka Buddhist Temple at Sentul, Kuala Lumpur.

Prize-giving day at Sentul Temple's Sinhala School, 1932.

achieved considerable recognition in the performing arts, specifically in classical music and dance. That success can, to some extent, be attributed to the initiative by these organisations to invite renowned exponents from abroad to train local students.

Religious Traditions

During the 1890s the Sinhalese community in Kuala Lumpur formed the first Theravada society known as the Sasana Abhiwurdhi Wardhana Society (SAWS). In January 1902, the Selangor Ceylon Saivites Association was instrumental in the establishment of the Sri Kandaswamy Temple in Brickfields, Kuala Lumpur [See boxed entry: Malayan Railways, page 82]. Jaffna Tamils also built temples in other parts of Malaya: in Klang, the Subramania Swamy Temple was established in 1912; in Taiping, Perak, the Vinayagar Temple was built in 1924; the Malaysian Saiva Siddhantha Sangam was formed in Sentul, Kuala Lumpur, and the foundation stone for the Ahthi Eeswaran Temple was laid in 1937. The Jaffna Tamil community also initiated the consecration of temples in Kuala Kangsar, Ipoh, Seremban and Kluang.

In addition to temple worship, Jaffna Tamils have also been involved in other socio-religious activities. They have played important roles in the formation of the Divine Life Society (Malaysia Branch), Malaysia Hindu Sangam, Pure Life Society, Hindu Youth Organisation (HYO) and the Young Men's Hindu Association. In the last three decades, many Ceylonese Tamils have been active participants in socio-religious organisations like

the Sathya Sai Baba Movement Malaysia and the Sathya Sai Central Council of Malaysia.

Ceylonese Christians were able to join churches of their respective denominations like the Wesleyan, Anglican and Catholic churches. From early on Jaffna Tamil Christians played key roles in their respective churches. Tan Sri Dominic Vendargon, the former Bishop of Kuala Lumpur, was subsequently elevated to Archbishop in 1975. He served the Roman Catholic Church in Malaysia for almost 50 years. Reverend Robert Velupillai Vethavanam (1850–1905), ordained as a priest in 1903, became the first Tamil priest of the St. Mary's Church Kuala Lumpur. Others like Reverend Samuel Abraham organised evangelistic meetings in Seremban, (Negeri Sembilan), Sungei Way, Puchong, Serdang, Serendah, Kuala Kubu Bahru, Rawang, Bukit Rotan and Carey Island. When Abraham was appointed the District Evangelist in 1909, there were already 17 preaching points in Selangor, four in Negeri Sembilan and three in Pahang.

EDUCATION

In the late 19th century, the Ceylonese were possibly the most educated Asian community in Malaya. The antecedents to that can be traced to American, Anglican and Roman Catholic missionaries who established schools and set up hospitals, and institutions in Sri Lanka, specifically on the Jaffna peninsula. On their part, the Tamils living in the region were quick to take up English education. They performed exceptionally in public service and professional examinations. Their success in this regard, collectively provided the background for their movement as educated personnel to Malaya.

In the diaspora, the Ceylonese took every opportunity to ensure that their children attended English schools. At the same time, Jaffna Tamils did not neglect their mother tongue. They ensured that after school hours, their children were provided a proper grounding in the Tamil language and in their religious traditions. The emphasis on education is crucial in explaining the upward socio-economic mobility evident in the Ceylonese community in Malaysia.

At the same time, Ceylonese educators have, since the beginning of the British administration in the Federated Malay States, occupied a prominent place in the provision and development of English education in Malaysia. Amongst notables in this sphere was Reverend Samuel Thambo Abraham from Jaffna, who in 1899 was invited to assist in the Tamil Church in Malacca Street, Kuala Lumpur, and to help in the school established by the Church. There was also an Episcopal Tamil Church that ran an Anglo-Tamil School, and in 1902 the two schools merged to form the Methodist Boys School, for which Reverend Abraham was the Headmaster. Foster E. Lee who came from Ceylon, served as Chief Assistant of the School.

The Victoria Institution—which emerged as the premier English medium school for secondary education in Kuala Lumpur from the final decade of the 19th century—had several Ceylonese teachers and students in its early days. Among notable educators at the Victoria Institution was R. Thambipillai who was also a student there and later retired as Senior Assistant. After World War II, Ceylonese educators also came to be involved in private schools that offered an alternative to students who could not find a place in government or mission schools. These private schools not only provided students an opportunity to gain education, but also allowed qualified Ceylonese teachers who could not get a job in government or mission schools to gain suitable employment.

Early Jaffna Tamil settlers in Negri Sembilan. S. Kanagasabai (seated on the left) arrived from Sri Lanka in 1904 and continued his ancestral profession of farming and rearing cattle. He supported his entire family of 12 children on the income he derived from selling milk and other garden produce. All his children were professionals. He had 26 grandchildren and 21 great-grandchildren.

The Selangor Ceylon Tamils' Association (SCTA) along Jalan Scott, Kuala Lumpur, 1926.

MEMORIES OF THE MALAYAN RAILWAYS

The railway service alone would testify to the efficient execution of duties by these (Ceylonese) subordinates who not only had a monopoly of this department, from guards and ticket collectors to station-masters and technical subordinates, but who very efficiently ran the railway service in pre-war Malaya. Before 1940, almost every station-master was invariably a Jaffnese, and many more were stationed in remote parts of the country to man the substations. As newly recruited clerks or appointed station-master, they were sent to underdeveloped parts of the country to live among people who were strangers and where health facilities were unheard of…

~ R. Rajakrishnan (1993)

Federated Malay States Railways (FMSR) collection and delivery service, 1930s.

The railway station at Tanjong Pagar in Singapore is a symbol of the inextricable historical link between Malaysia and Singapore—countries that once formed British Malaya. Built in the early 20th century, the railway station in Singapore—similar to the Kuala Lumpur railway station and Ipoh railway station (fondly regarded as the Taj Mahal of Ipoh by locals)—continues to have a majestic presence. These stations are among the very few landmarks in contemporary Singapore and Malaysia that exude the charm of a bygone and yet enduring British colonial era.

These railway stations have a special place in the hearts of many Ceylonese families. During the colonial period, the Ceylonese were heavily involved in the development and the administration of the Federated Malay States Railways (FMSR). Their descendants and their kith and kin continue to live in both Malaysia and Singapore, today.

Memories of that era inform a period when tiffin carriers with home-cooked Ceylonese food, like string hoppers and *sothi*, would travel the line for several stations, so much so that the train was termed

the 'Sothi Express'. Informants aver that this was a common practice among Jaffna Tamils across the Federated Malay States and the Straits Settlements. Another distinct item dispatched across the line was *Murungakkai* (vegetable drumsticks)—a favourite among the Ceylonese Tamils. The 'Murungakkai Mail', as it was sometimes called, would carry and distribute the 'drumsticks' to Ceylonese staff in Malaya. According to Indra Rani Iswaran, this resembled the practice on the 'Yarl Devi'—a train that continues to operate between Colombo and Jaffna.

The establishment of British rule in the Malay States and the concomitant development of the tin industry provided the backdrop for the construction of railroads in the country. By 1845, the Ceylon Railway Company (CRC) was already established in England. When the railway line connecting Taiping to Port Weld in Perak was disrupted by the lack of English educated staff and insufficient Indian labour, the Ceylon Government consented to loan two divisions of the Ceylon Pioneer Corps to Malaya. The corps that arrived in Perak between 1881 and 1883 aided

Table 4.1

Branch	Europeans	Eurasians	Indians and Ceylonese	Chinese	Malays	Others	Total 1946	Total 1939
General Managers	6	3	13	6	11	–	39	28
Way and Works and Construction	21	14	4,286	270	578	29	5,198	4,958*
Mechanical	17	35	1,215	450	473	112	2,302	2,104
Transportation	37	184	3,359	344	1,293	8	5,225	5,061
Accounts	6	10	91	37	52	–	196	180
Stores	4	–	131	6	41	4	186	149
Police	–	1	11	7	3	–	22	23
Health	–	–	147	1	10	–	158	105
Total (1946)	91	247	9,253	1,121	2,461	153	13,326	–
Total (1939)	90	195	9,292	1,001	1,812	218	–	12,608*

TOTAL NUMBER OF STAFF EMPOYED IN THE MALAYAN RAILWAYS (1946)

Source: Malayan Union: Railways Report for the period 1st April to 31st December, 1946. Kuala Lumpur: Printed at the Malayan Union Govt. Press, 1947 by H. T. Ross, Government Printer.

Class VI quarters that housed Ceylonese who staffed the Malayan railways.

A prominent judge and the author of Two Decades of Malayan Trials, *R. P. S. Rajasooria also served as a Malayan State and Municipal Councillor from 1948–1953.*

POLITICAL LIFE

The majority of the Ceylonese pioneers in Malaya were civil servants and had no intention of sustaining a long-term political engagement with their country of residence. It was only after World War II that there was a general awakening of political consciousness in the community. With growing opposition to British colonial rule evident from 1946, Ceylonese and other minority groups began to be concerned about their political rights in a future independent Malaysia. The prospect of decolonisation ushered in a variety of political responses from the Ceylonese community.

One response, catalysed by the zeal of nationalism nurtured during the war years, was manifest in Ceylonese involvement in non-communal institutions like

cooperatives, trade unions and professional associations. In many of these institutions, educated Ceylonese individuals comprised a key component of the leadership. Over time, they would play important roles in Malaysia's constitutional development, shaping national policies and developing programmes to encourage cordial race relations in independent Malaysia. In their position as leaders of trade unions, cooperative societies, and professional bodies, they would also represent Malaysia at international forums, and the Malaysian government remains cognisant of their views when formulating laws and regulations.

Another response, which followed from the predominantly race-based mode of politics in Malaysia, was the development of political parties organised in the successful completion of the first Malayan railway line, which was opened in 1885. While the majority of the labourers were from South India, the clerks, engineers, surveyors and overseers who formed part of the corps, were of Ceylonese origin.

In 1891, Charles Edwin Spooner brought with him a substantial number of Ceylonese from the Ceylon Public Works Department (PWD) when he became the State Engineer of the PWD in Selangor, Kuala Lumpur. According to the Selangor Establishment List, in 1900, almost 90 per cent of the Selangor State Railway was staffed by Ceylon Tamils and nearly all the station-masters in Selangor were Ceylon Tamils.

Railway lines were constructed in Singapore well after their development in the Malay States. A plan for the setup of a railway line was introduced in Singapore in 1865, but it was only in 1899 that the Legislative Council approved the building of a proposed railway from Singapore to the Johor Straits. Indian labourers, Ceylonese personnel and others were employed in the development of a railway line from Tank Road to Woodlands, which was completed in 1903. On 30 December 1903, the *Hindu Organ* recorded that there were 2,021 Jaffna Tamils and 84 Sinhalese employed in the FMSR.

A postcard issued by the FMSR, Kuala Lumpur, 1934.

C. E. Spooner became the first General Manager of the FMSR and was influential in extending the railway lines and connecting the various Malayan States. 'Spooner Road' in both Singapore and Ipoh are named after him. Spooner Road, just a few minutes away from the station in Singapore, marked the housing quarters for Ceylonese railway staff. Each flat was named after a Malay state (for example Negri Sembilan, Kedah, Perak, Pahang, etc.). These flats have since been demolished and new flats were built to accommodate the Keretapi Tanah Melayu (KTM) railway staff. However, the disused railway tracks behind the flats and the 'Running Bungalow' building at the entrance of Spooner Road serves as a nostalgic reminder of the contribution of the Ceylonese pioneers in Malaysia and Singapore.

In 1904, a central workshop establishment was set up at Sentul, Kuala Lumpur, to merge the repair establishments of the FMSR. The proximity of the administrative centre of the Malayan Railway and the Sentul workshop explains the erstwhile concentration of the Ceylon Tamil and Sinhalese diaspora in Brickfields and the Sentul area. The Sri Lankan Buddhist Temple in Sentul and the Buddhist Maha Vihara in Brickfields, both founded in the

early 20th century, allude to the early settlement of Sinhalese Buddhists who staffed the railways and colonial civil service. Similarly, the Sri Kandaswamy Temple in Brickfields was established by the Ceylon Tamils who staffed the railways. The construction of the Temple, which architecturally resembles the Nallur Kandaswamy Temple in Jaffna, commenced in 1902.

R. Rajakrishnan informs that despite a policy of favouring Malays in the government service after the 1920s, the Ceylonese, whose dedication and efficiency was admired by British officers, continued to be recruited, especially in the FMSR. The 1931 Census of British Malaya indicated that the 'Ceylon Tamil population of Kuala Lumpur is especially high since a very large proportion of the clerical staff of the railway department, and to a lesser extent, other government departments, is composed of Jaffna Tamils'. A year earlier, the Straits Settlements Legislative Council had approved a new railway line and station in Singapore. The new station in Singapore at Tanjong Pagar docks, named the Keppel Railway Station, was completed in 1932 and continued to operate till June 2011.

Hema Kiruppalini

The Railway Co-operative Thrift and Loan Society committee, Kuala Lumpur, 1947.

A portrait of Station Master Murugappa Krishner's (seated far left) family in Singapore (circa 1950).

Tank Road Station (circa 1910) which was Singapore's main rail terminus prior to the opening of the Tanjong Pagar Station.

specifically to represent the Ceylonese community. The Ceylon Federation of Malaya, formed in 1946, was an important attempt to bring together the Ceylonese in the Malay Peninsula under a common banner and to address their political concerns. Led by E. E. C. Thuraisingam, the Federation was joined by several prominent Jaffna Tamils. Members of the political organisation would come to be appointed in government bodies and accepted as *bona fide* representatives of the Jaffna Tamils. Thuraisingam was himself appointed a member of the Malayan Union Advisory Council and Member for Education in the Federal Legislative Council.

The attempt to bring together the Ceylonese community under a common political banner, however, faced serious impediments. A key problem in the mid-

1950s was the fact that Ceylonese personnel who were in government service were prohibited from taking an active part in politics. Active engagement in politics was thus left to either retired government pensioners or those in the private sector. Several organisations and notables from the community did not join the Federation, preferring instead to participate in other political parties. Indeed, the failure to bring together the myriad groups representing Ceylonese interests was crucial in explaining the dissolution of the Ceylon Federation in 1987.

Notwithstanding the dissolution of the Ceylon Federation, there remained several political parties representing Ceylonese interests at the state level. S. C. MacIntyre, a prominent lawyer, initiated the formation of the Central Council of Ceylonese Associations of

The eminent lawyer E. E. Clough Thuraisingham was a Member of the Malayan Advisory Council in 1946. In 1955, he was knighted by Her Majesty Queen Elizabeth II.

ENTREPRENEURSHIP

While much has been said about the Ceylonese involvement in the colonial civil service, less is known of their involvement in the private sector during that period. Although there was a preference towards securing employment in the civil service during British rule, many did venture out on their own. They were involved in acquiring landed properties and estates, banking and insurance, and various other business establishments.

Plantations

The Ceylonese involvement as entrepreneurs in the plantation sector emerged from their experience in working as middle-ranked managers and clerks for British coffee and rubber plantations. Some became proprietors of large rubber estates. Amongst these were Solomon Ramanathan (Kuala Kangsar, Perak); Vallipuram Sinnadorai (Perak); the Clough brothers (Batu Gajah, Perak); Dudleys (Cary Island, Selangor); Sabapathy Pillai Sinnathamby (Negeri Sembilan); William Arasaratnam Rogers of Ipoh and Nagamuthu Ganapathipillay (Sitiawan and Dindings).

Banking and Finance

The Oriental Bank of Malaya Ltd was the vision of Bastianpillai Paul Nicholas better known as B. P. Nicholas. The bank was incorporated on 31 December 1936. The Bank of Jaffna was founded in 1928 by another Jaffna Tamil, Kartigesu Arumugam. The latter failed partly because of its total dependence on Ceylonese or Tamil patronage, and also due to its inability to cope with competition from the Bank of Malaya Ltd. owned by Nicholas and his

family (*55th Anniversary Publication of Oriental Bank Berhad 1936–91*). R. Rajakrishnan informs that the Jaffnese Co-operative Society was established in 1924 to address some of the financial problems of the members of the Jaffnese community by granting loans to members for purchase of land or house and to finance their children's education. He adds that after 30 years of existence as a thrift and loan co-operative, the co-operative sponsored two other societies, namely the Jaffnese Co-operative Housing Society in 1954 which was responsible for the construction of houses in Taman Kanagapuram and Taman Yarl in Kuala Lumpur, and the Jaffnese Co-operative Stores Society in 1957 which ran a provision shop in Petaling Jaya.

Jewellery

Sri Lankan jewellers established a niche in the industry very soon after their arrival in the late 19th century. Their success was, in part, due to their connection to the gem industry in Sri Lanka and Southern India, as well as because they gained the trust of locals.

The Sinhalese jewellers were well patronised by the Malay royalty. Jewellers such as P. H. Hendry, M. B. Jinadasa, and T. A. Adris of Penang also made a mark for their excellent craftsmanship that was considered the best in the country. The trading houses started by them still remain to this day. The Jaffna Tamil jewellers known as *patthars* were equally skilled but had a smaller presence when compared to the well-established Sinhalese jewellers. They concentrated on a different clientele, usually serving generations of Tamil families.

P. H. Hendry (seated), founder of P. H. Hendry, Royal Jewellers (circa 1930s).

Estate Development

Developer A. S. Thambaiya (1908–74) went into business full time with no capital. With the help of venture capitalists he bought land, sub-divided it and sold it as residential plots with infrastructure. He also built and sold houses in Seremban. Four blocks of a 30-storey superstructure luxury condominium known as Villa Scott, a prominent landmark in the federal capital, was developed by a Sri Lankan Tamil, S. Saravanamuthu Indran. Three generations of this prominent family resided in the celebrated address of Jalan Scott. The family diversified into the construction industry by acquiring a stake in a leading glass manufacturer—products which were used in the construction of the Kuala Lumpur Convention Centre (KLCC) and the Kuala Lumpur International Airport (KLIA). During the late 1980s they took advantage of the property boom and ventured into property development in the Klang Valley.

In 1955, Samuel Chelvasingham MacIntyre became the first person of Ceylonese descent to be elected to the Federal Legislative Council. He later became Malaysia's first High Commissioner to India, Nepal and Sri Lanka.

D. R. Seenivasagam, popularly known as 'D. R.' was a legendary criminal lawyer. A public garden in Ipoh has been named after him.

Johor in August 1949, which brought together several Ceylonese organisations in the state. As a member of the State Council, he played an important role in reorganising Ceylonese associations and advocated the opening of community settlements to strengthen loyalty to the Malaysian state.

From January 1958, the Ceylon Association of Selangor—later renamed the Kongress Ceylonese Malaysia (Malaysian Ceylonese Congress [MCC])—began to play a more conscious political role. Like the Ceylon Federation that had been formed earlier, the MCC sought to unite all Malaysian citizens of Ceylonese origin under one political banner. From the fore, the MCC sought affiliation to the Alliance. The appointment of C. Sinnadurai, the President of MCC throughout the 1970s, to the Malaysian senate, reflected the close ties that the MCC forged with the erstwhile government.

The MCC continues to be a trusted ally of the government. The party has shown a specific interest in educational development, for which it set up the Malaysian Ceylonese Education Fund—now known as the Malaysian Community Education Fund—to grant scholarships and study loans to needy children of all races in Malaysia to pursue higher studies. Since December 2004, when N. K. S. Tharmaseelan was elected President of MCC, the organisation has focused on reaching out to the community by setting up more regional branches and increasing membership.

Although the Sri Lankans are numerically too small to muster enough support to get members elected into parliament, they have played important roles in different political parties. Some have been part of the government,

while others have joined opposition parties. Indeed, notable Sri Lankans such as S. P. Seenivasagam, D. R. Seenivasagam, S. Seevaratnam, S. Vijayaratnam and Sivarasa Rasiah have occupied leadership positions in several key multi-ethnic political parties in Malaysia such as the People's Progressive Party; Democratic Action Party; Parti Gerakan Rakyat Malaysia and Parti Keadilan.

CONCLUSION

Ceylonese emigrants played a key role in the British administration of colonial Malaya. In spite of their contributions to the development of the country, these pioneers largely saw themselves as sojourners. Moreover, because many were civil servants during the colonial period, they tended to remain outside the political arena.

However, in the radically changed Malaysian political landscape after World War II, not only were the indigenous people of the land increasingly conscious of the prospect of gaining their political freedom, Sri Lankans living in the diaspora were also motivated to seek their rights as citizens in the country of residence. That change in attitude, and of political affiliation, over time, has resulted in the community establishing deeper roots in Malaysia. This is clear in the engagement of Sri Lankan-Malaysians in a myriad fields of activity. While the younger generation of local-born Sri Lankans—with little or no connection to the ancestral 'homeland'—may not hold the same position in Malaysia's civil service as their predecessors did during the colonial period, they are well recognised for their role in the country's social, economic and political development.

Sinnapoo Apputhurai

SINGAPORE

All men are equal but some are more equal than the others and the Jaffnese are in the latter class. They work hard and faithfully wherever they go and have won not only general respect but affection so great that they have earned the nicknames such as 'The Aberdonians of Asia' and 'God's gift to the Government Official'.

Gerald Hawkins (Malayan Civil Service), excerpt in S. Durai Rajasingham, A Hundred Years of Ceylonese in Malaysia and Singapore: 1867–1967.

INTRODUCTION

Conventional historiography of the Ceylonese diaspora in Singapore is associated with the movement of Jaffna Tamils who staffed the public administration and rendered invaluable service to the development of modern Singapore. However, the composition of Ceylonese in Singapore is far more varied, comprising largely of Jaffna Tamils and Sinhalese, and to a lesser extent Burghers and Moors. While the Jaffna Tamils and Sinhalese are mostly Hindus and Buddhists respectively, there are significant numbers among both communities who are Catholics, and similar to the Burgher community they have, over time, integrated with the Eurasian diaspora in Singapore. A handful among the Sri Lankan diaspora are Bohras and Malays who have integrated with the wider Muslim community in Singapore.

The Ceylonese diaspora came to Singapore in five different migratory phases, spanning approximately a hundred and fifty years. The first phase began in the colonial period (late 19th century to early 20th century) during which time there was a movement of merchants (chiefly Sinhalese), Ceylon Pioneer Corps and English-educated Ceylonese (mainly Jaffna Tamils) who staffed the public administration in Malaya. The second phase, the post-war period (1945–50), was relatively brief. During this time thousands returned to Ceylon and at the same time, Singapore witnessed both the sojourn and settlement of the Royal Pioneer Corps (mainly Sinhalese). The post-colonial period (1960s and 1970s) that saw growing ethnic tensions in Sri Lanka, coincided with the time when newly-independent Singapore welcomed the arrival of Sri Lankan professionals. The fourth phase began from the 1980s—following the breakout of the civil war in Sri Lanka—which saw the arrival of domestic workers on temporary contracts. The contemporary phase commenced at the turn of the millennium, and has led to the gradual inflow of Sri Lankan professionals—referred to as 'foreign talent' in the Singapore context—who either take up permanent residency or venture abroad to another country.

The five phases of migration, with differentiated experiences of settlement, have added to the diversity of the community in Singapore. Notwithstanding the complexities, the identity of the Sri Lankan diaspora in Singapore is often defined and distinguished by a British colonial heritage, and descendents from that era continue to regard themselves as 'Ceylonese' despite being third or fourth generation settlers. The antiquated use of the term 'Ceylon' draws attention to the length of their settlement and at the same time, underpins the Sri Lankan community's social position, identity and sense of belonging in Singapore.

DEMOGRAPHIC PROFILE OF THE DIASPORA

Often (incorrectly) categorised as 'Indian'—a blanket term used in Singapore for all individuals who are either from the Indian subcontinent, or whose ancestors emigrated from the subcontinent—the Sri Lankan diaspora in Singapore is considered a 'minority within a minority'. This has made it difficult to ascertain precise numerical figures of the size of the community. While the population census of Singapore sometimes categorised the 'Singhalese' or 'Sinhalese' as distinct, Ceylonese Tamils have, at different periods of time, been broadly classified as either 'Tamil', 'Indian' or 'Others'. In the 1921 Census of British Malaya, the Ceylon Tamils were included in the 'Indian' category. In 1931, they were classified as 'Others' together with the Sinhalese and other 'Ceylon Peoples'. In the 2000 and 2010 population census they have largely been categorised as 'Indian'— the designated label for persons of Indian, Pakistani, Bangladeshi or Sri Lankan origin.

The 1871 Singapore Census states that there were seven Sinhalese in Singapore and 109 prisoners transported from Ceylon to Singapore. 10 years later, there were 42 Sinhalese and 10,475 Tamils in Singapore, the latter figure including Ceylon Tamils. It is plausible—given the occupational profile of Ceylon Tamils in Singapore—that the majority of the 738 Tamils that worked in the 'professional class' in 1881 referred to the Jaffna Tamils. In the 'professional class' many were employed as clerks

Ranee Supramaniam's Ceylonese passport. She applied for the passport in the 1950s so that she could travel to Scotland to join her husband, James Supramaniam, who was undertaking postgraduate medical studies there.

During his voyage from Jaffna to Singapore in the 1920s, all of Murugappa Krishner's belongings were contained in the 'trunk box' pictured above.

Murugasu Vaithilingam Pillai, popularly known as 'Singapore Vaithilingam', was one of the earliest Ceylonese to arrive in Singapore.

Map 4.4

SINGAPORE

MALAYSIA

SINGAPORE

Johor Strait

Pulau Ubin

Kallang

Rochor

Bedok

Singapore

Little India
Arab Street

Chinatown

Pulau Brani

Sentosa

Strait of Singapore

MALAYSIA

N

0   10 kilometres
0   10 miles

INDONESIA

Ceylonese ladies in Singapore pose for a picture with Lady Ramanathan (wife of Sir Ponnambalam Ramanathan), 15 March 1924. (Seated) Lady Ramanathan, (standing from left to right) Miss Sybil Gunatilleka, Mrs Handy, Miss Ramanathan, Mrs MacIntyre and Miss Gladys Gunatilleka.

During the Japanese Occupation (1942-45), the Ceylonese in Singapore were compelled to join the 'Ceylon Department' of the Indian Independence League (IIL).

The Ceylonese community in Singapore celebrate the Coronation of H.M. Queen Elizabeth II, 1953.

(170), in the civil service (137), and as physicians, surgeons and dentists (51) (*Miscellaneous Numerical Returns and Straits Settlements Population*, 1881: 13).

The 1931 census—when the categorisation of Ceylon Tamils shifted from 'Indians' to 'Others'—highlighted that there were 1,645 'Ceylon Peoples' in Singapore. That census identified that the Sinhalese belonged to the 'shopkeeping class, while the bulk of the Ceylon Tamils followed clerical occupations' (Vlieland, 1932: 87 and 200). The 1931 census also states that 165 Eurasians in Singapore were born in Ceylon. This numerical figure probably refers to the Ceylon Burghers who were broadly classified as Eurasians in the Malayan context. In postcolonial Singapore, the Sri Lankan Tamil community has been grouped as 'Indian', which in 2010 comprised 9.2 per cent of the total population. Non-official sources suggest the size of the Sri Lankan Tamil community to be between 10,000 and 15,000. The Sinhalese, categorised separately in the 2010 census, number 3,140. (*Singapore Census of Population 2000 and 2010*). These figures, however, do not include transient workers from Sri Lanka on temporary contracts.

EARLY CEYLONESE MIGRATION

The transfer of the Straits Settlements from British India to the Crown in 1867 was crucial in encouraging Ceylonese emigration to Singapore. Also important was the opening of the Suez Canal in 1869 and the British expansion in the Malayan Peninsular following the Pangkor Treaty in 1874. Collectively, these events laid the foundations for rapid socio-economic change in the region, which was paralleled by an expansion of the colonial bureaucracy.

In the late 19th century, the lackadaisical development of English education in Singapore resulted in a shortage of skilled staff proficient in English. This shortage underpinned the turn to Ceylon for educated personnel. American missionaries who came to Jaffna in the early 19th century had spread not just Christianity but also the English language and educational institutions. Educated Jaffna Tamils fared exceptionally well in the public service examinations and were able to

gain employment within the British administration in Ceylon and secure overseas postings. Beyond the Straits Settlements' civil service, the 'rubber rush' in Malaya saw British planters moving administrators from Jaffna to work as intermediaries with Indian labourers in the estates.

In the 1870s, the transfer of British administrator J. W. W. Birch from the Ceylon Civil Service to Malaya and the arrival of two divisions of the Ceylon Pioneer Corps to build the first railway line between Port Weld to Taiping in Malaya, led to the recruitment of hundreds of Ceylonese—Jaffna Tamils, Sinhalese, Burghers and Ceylon Malays—for white collar jobs. They filled up posts in the railways, harbour board, survey and geological departments, telegraphs, public works department, the medical field (doctors and apothecaries in hospitals), clerical services, and in rubber and tin estates (field supervisors, estate conductors, dispensary personnel, accountants, etc).

While the Jaffna Tamils were entrenched in the administrative and government services, the Sinhalese, with the exception of a few who staffed the railways, or worked as technicians and teachers, were otherwise chiefly merchants who specialised in the jewellery trade. During this period, Sinhalese gem merchants turned to new markets in cities and towns in the region, like Singapore and Penang, and later Ipoh and Kuala Lumpur. Exquisite gem stones from Ceylon and intricate craftsmanship were synonymous with Sinhalese jewellery merchants from the late 19th century.

The Ceylon Tamils hailed from areas in the Jaffna Peninsula such as Tellippalai, Vaddukoddai, Chankanai, Uduvil, Chulipuram, Punguduthivu, Kayts, Kokkuvil, Kondavil, Atchuvely, Karaveddy, Nelliady and Maviddapuram. The Sinhalese came mainly from Southern Ceylon—Galle, Matara and the hinterlands. The early migrants embarked on a perilous voyage to Singapore. According to Iswaran, migrants had to travel in small boats termed *surul kapal* or *pai kapal* from the Jaffna's ports of Kankrsanthurai, Velvetithurai and Point

Pedro. Another route was to travel from Jaffna to Kayts and then take a type of sailing vessel called an 'Uru' to Kodikarai and then to the Indian port Nagapatnam—before setting out for Malaya (i.e., Singapore or Penang) by steamships/streamers named SS *Lady Gordon*, SS *Lady Havelock*, SS *Ediatchy* and SS *Athaca*. Depending on the route, the journey took approximately five to nine days costing between 16 and 25 rupees (Lavan Iswaran, 2010: 32).

There were several Ceylonese educated in institutions such as Batticotta Seminary and American High School in Vaddukoddai who made important contributions to the development of Singapore in the late 19th and early 20th centuries. Among the pioneers include M. Vaithiyalingam Pillai (Overseer of Roads in the Municipality who came at the request of J. W. W. Birch); V. Murugesam Pillai (Chief Inspector of Roads); Arumugam Pillai Annamalay Pillai (Chief of the Survey Department of the Colony); Kuddiar Sinnappah (Government contractor responsible for reclaiming land in Telok Ayer); Vyravanather Sinnathamby (Overseer in the Singapore Municipality); Canapathipillai Namasivayam (Chief Inspector of Roads); Iampillai Waitilingampillai (Roads Engineering Assistant); and T. N. Mahalingam (Interpreter of Singapore Police Courts), etc. (Singam, 1968: 236–43).

While these pioneers from Ceylon played an important role in Singapore's administrative and economic development, the arrival of Ceylonese Christian clergymen in the late 19th century was crucial in the formation and expansion of mission schools and churches in Singapore. Singam states that Reverend Henry James Gomes founded a Chinese Mission School in 1871 and he is recorded as one of the earliest missionaries of the Anglican Church in Singapore (Singam, 1968: 239). Reverend Weerakarthy Underwood from Jaffna was the first pastor of the Methodist Tamil Church at Short Street in the late 1880s. Reverend H. L. Hoisington came to Singapore in 1891 and took charge of the Tamil church. His son, Henry Martyn Hoisington, was among the earliest students at the Anglo-Chinese School (ACS) and is better remembered as the teacher who penned the ACS anthem.

Like Henry Hoisington, Reverend James Arumugam Supramaniam, who came to Singapore in 1892, was among the pioneer batch of students schooled in ACS. He became a prominent educator in ACS and a notable preacher in Malaya who in 1934 was made the Southern District Superintendent of the Tamil Churches of the Methodist Mission. In light of their contributions to the growth of ACS, the 1936 Golden Jubilee commemorative magazine of the school records that 'James Supramaniam… and Henry Hoisington… are sterling men who have influenced many thousands of ACS boys'. Reverend James Supramaniam's son, James M. J. Supramaniam, was at the forefront of Singapore's fight against tuberculosis in the 1960s. He was also the Deputy Director of Medical Services and Deputy Permanent Secretary of Health from 1971 to 1981.

SOCIAL AND POLITICAL LIFE IN THE EARLY 20TH CENTURY

A strong sense of loyalty to the British was evident amongst the Ceylonese pioneers. During World War I, Ceylon Tamils from Singapore and the Peninsula, led by C. Alma Baker, Annamalai Pillai and James Muttiah Handy, made significant contributions to the Malayan

LEFT: *Reverend James Supramaniam and family pose for a photograph during Christmas celebrations in 1923.*

TOP: *15th-century Jaffna Kingdom coins brought by Ceylonese immigrants to Malaya in the early 20th century.*

Aircraft Fund and presented to British Malayan authorities a fighter plane named *The Jaffna*. In the same year, Ceylonese representatives from all ethnic groups collected funds to support the Red Cross Society. Following the advent of World War II in Europe, the Sinhalese Association in Singapore played a significant part in the collection of donations for the Malaya Patriotic Fund. In 1941, Ceylon Tamils collected money for the All-Malayan Ceylon Tamils Fighter Plane Fund. Press clippings in Singapore from 1939–40 recounts of how Ceylon Tamil women organised themselves into a 'Ceylon Women War Workers' Party' to stitch and supply pillow cases, handkerchiefs and roll bandages

Ceylonese immigrants often carried a 'mukku kolai', a cylindrical container to consume water and other liquids, during their ship journey from Ceylon.

LIKE DUCKS TO WATER: EDUCATION AND UPWARD MOBILITY

The Ceylonese diaspora in Singapore have been in constant pursuit of higher education that has sustained the upward mobility of this minority community. Despite the constraints of large families, single-wage incomes and limited savings, Ceylonese parents placed a premium on the provision of English education to their children. Even prior to World War II, there were a number of Ceylonese who graduated from King Edward VII Medical School and Raffles College in Singapore. Students were also known to 'return' to Colombo to further their education. With the establishment of the University of Malaya in 1949, the number of professionals in the community grew. The University of Malaya Register of Graduates (1960) recorded that the number of Ceylonese who graduated between 1949 and 1957 far exceeded the ratio of their population in the country at the time. In 1946, Jaffnese parents responded overwhelmingly to a call to donate towards the Malayan Ceylonese Endowment Fund and to provide scholarships to needy Sri Lankans entering the University of Malaya. According to Rajakrishnan (1993), many Sri Lankan government servants resolved to donate part of their salary towards the fund. The importance of higher education was regarded as a personal and social responsibility for Ceylonese parents. This mirrored the long-established tradition of pursuing education during the colonial period in Ceylon that, since the 19th century, was home to some of the earliest schooling institutions in Asia.

KING EDWARD VII COLLEGE OF MEDICINE

SINGAPORE

INDO-CEYLONESE
Freshmen's Dinner
1948

at Cathay Restaurant, Singapore

Wednesday 17th November, 1948.
at 7.30 p.m.

Menu card for the Indo-Ceylonese Freshman Dinner organised by students of the King Edward's VII College of Medicine, 1948.

University Fund
Generous Gift From The Ceylonese

THE Ceylonese community in the Federation have sent a first donation of $5,000 to the University of Malaya Endowment Fund. The latest list is as follows:

The Ceylonese community donated generously to the University of Malaya Endowment Fund, 26 August 1950.

DIASPORIC INSTITUTIONS

Several Ceylonese Tamil and Sinhalese institutions were formed in the early 20th century, a period that corresponded with the expansion in the size of the diaspora in Singapore. The Singapore Ceylon Tamils' Association (SCTA) was initiated in 1909, and registered in 1910. Four years later, in 1914, the Sinhalese formed the Aryan Sinhalese Fraternal Association, which, in 1923, came to be known as the Singapore Sinhala Association (SSA). Both the Ceylon Tamil Hindus and the Sinhalese have established their own places of worship, namely the Sri Senpaga Vinayagar Temple and the Sri Lankaramaya Temple. The Ceylon Sports Club (CSC) and the Lanka Lions Cricket Club are also key institutions linked to the Sri Lankan diaspora in Singapore (for further information on these organisations, see 'Sri Lankans and Sports in Malaysia and Singapore', page 47).

Singapore Ceylon Tamils' Association

During its formative years, the Ceylon Tamil Association (CTA), apart from serving the cultural and religious interests of the community, also provided financial assistance to Ceylon Tamils for weddings and funerals. A small number of Ceylon Tamil Christians—like J. Henry Ponnampalam who was the first president of the Association—were especially active in the early years of the organisation. James Muttiah Handy, one of the pioneers in the medical field from Ceylon, who arrived in Singapore in the late 1890s, served as the fourth president of the Singapore Ceylon Tamils' Association. He donated a piece of land—at what is now known as Handy Road—on which stood the Ceylon Tamils' Association Hall.

The initial Ceylon Tamils' Association (CTA) building at Handy Road.

The Ceylon Tamils' Association (CTA) was later renamed the Singapore Ceylon Tamils' Association (SCTA). The SCTA is closely connected to the Sri Senpaga Vinayagar Temple. In 1923, the SCTA provided assistance in acquiring the land for the temple at Ceylon Road where it stands today. The temple continues to be jointly managed by the temple committee and members of the SCTA.

Sri Senpaga Vinayagar Temple

The Sri Senpaga Vinayagar *kovil* at Ceylon Road is one of the oldest Hindu temples in Singapore. Some devotees believe that in the 1850s a figure of the Hindu deity, Lord Vinayagar, washed up on Singapore's shores and was found near a Chempaka (*Senpaga* in Tamil) tree. One of the early Ceylon pioneers, Ethirnayagam Pillai, built an attap shed under the tree and the temple became known as the Sri Senpaga Vinayagar Temple. The temple is currently

The kumbha abhishekam (consecration ceremony) of the Sri Senpaga Vinayagar temple in 2003 was attended by then Prime Minister Goh Chok Tong.

located at Ceylon Road and alludes to the large number of Ceylonese families that lived in the area. A short distance away is 'Nallur Road', named after an ancient city in Jaffna which was the seat of the Kings of Jaffna and the site of an old and significant Hindu temple—The Nallur Kandaswamy *kovil*. Over the years, the Sri Senpaga Vinayagar temple has undergone several renovations and consecration ceremonies. Celebrated as a 'world class' temple after the fifth *kumbha abhishekam* conducted in February 2003, the temple houses a collection of Lord Vinayagar images, figurines and statuettes.

The temple is involved in several community activities and includes a Ladies committee, a Music and Dance Academy, a Saiva Samaya school and a Saiva Siddhantha school, Thevaram classes, a Volunteers Committee and a Youth Wing. Each committee performs specific roles and collaborates in joint activities. Some of the major prayers and processions that witness the congregation of the

Ceylon Tamil Hindu diaspora include Thai Pongal, Tamil New Year, Maha Shivarathri, Singapore National Day prayers, 10 days Mahotsavam Festival, Vinayagar Chathurthi and Navaratri. The *Sanghu* is a quarterly magazine that showcases the initiatives of the temple committee and highlights the latest events organised by the Ceylon Tamil diaspora in Singapore. The temple has gained recognition for its efforts in conducting tours for visitors from abroad and for its important role in building inter-racial and religious harmony in Singapore. It is noteworthy that the temple has a number of Chinese devotees who partake in the religious events of the temple.

Some of the significant milestones in the history of the temple include the designation of the temple as a National Heritage Site in 2003; the unveiling of the first musical pillars in Southeast Asia in 2009; and the planting of two Palmyrah palms by the then Deputy Prime Minister and Minister of Defence, Teo Chee Hean, at the temple on 9 August 2010.

The Palmyrah palm or the *panai maram* is emblematic of the Jaffna Peninsula. The Palmyrah palm has several uses and it forms an integral part of the life and cuisine of the Jaffna people. Beyond symbolic identification with Jaffna, the community has also made concerted efforts to retain ties with the ancestral homeland through several initiatives including hosting visits of Hindu spiritual leaders from Sri Lanka, conducting a donation drive during the 2004 tsunami disaster, and donating books to the districts of Kilinochchi, amongst others.

Devotees gather at the Sri Senpaga Vinayagar Temple along Ceylon Road, 1954.

Singapore Sinhala Association

The Singapore Sinhala Association (SSA) was initially established in a shophouse at the junction of Orchard Road and Tank Road that served as a boarding house for Sinhalese immigrants. The composition of the membership has changed over the years. Most members today are Sinhalese Buddhists, whereas Sinhalese Christians comprised the majority in the past. The SSA organises the Sinhala New Year Dinner and Dance annually, an event that witnesses the congregation of the Sinhalese community irrespective of their religious orientation. The spirit of volunteerism and charity has long been a key element of the SSA's activities. As early as 1918, the Singapore Sinhalese Association had staged a drama in aid of victims of World War I and in 1947, the Association staged another drama titled *Wicked Master* at the Victoria Memorial Hall for charity. In 2005, the SSA with the assistance of the Singapore Red Cross was involved in rebuilding the tsunami-hit villages of Sinha in the Hambantota district of Sri Lanka. The project named Merlion Gammane (Merlion Village) sought to build houses and a community centre for displaced families. In 2006, 100 homes and a playground had been built and by 2007, a school named the Singapore-Sri Lanka Friendship College,

Sinha Gammane 'Lion Village' in Sri Lanka was initiated by the Singapore Sinhala Association (SSA) in 2005 to provide housing for those affected by the 2004 tsunami.

a S$2.78 million project, had been established for youths in the Hambantota district to pursue further education. In a speech by Vivian Balakrishnan, then Minister of Community Development, Youth and Sports and Second Minister for Information, Communication and the Arts, at the Sinhala Association's Dinner and Awards Nite 2007, he expressed that:

> …I am pleased that the Association has focused on volunteerism, philanthropy, cultural awareness, education and youth leadership in addition to meeting the social and recreational needs of the community… It has been partnering the Singapore Red Cross, grassroots organisations, Community Development Councils and the National Heritage Board in various community projects…

The Singapore-Sri Lanka Friendship Kindergarten in Hambantota, Sri Lanka.

SRI LANKAN BUDDHISM IN SINGAPORE

In the late 19th and early 20th centuries, Ceylonese migration to colonial Malaya accelerated. Most Buddhist migrants arrived from Sri Lanka's southern coast. It was initially a bachelor community but more settled Sri Lankan families formed in the 1920s. Prior to the 1930s, lay and monastic Ceylonese Buddhists crossed ethnic and linguistic lines to access Buddhist rituals and sermons. Sri Lankan Buddhists collaborated with Chinese Buddhists to establish the Shuang Lin Monastery in the late 19th century. This temple-monastery, focused on Sakyamuni Buddha, and attracted both Ceylonese and Singaporean Chinese patrons. In this period, Sri Lankan Buddhists also attended the Japanese Buddhist Mission and the English Buddhist Mission. Some may have attended the Burmese-run Kinta Road temple, opened in the early 1900s. The first distinctively Sri Lankan Buddhist ritual space dates to the late 1910s, on Spottiswoode Park Road, though there was no monk in permanent residence then. In the 1920s Ceylonese Buddhism became more visible in Singapore, along with sharper ethnic-nationalist self-identification. The Singapore Buddhist Association was founded in 1922–23. For rituals, Sri Lankan Buddhists in Singapore relied on monks in transit from Sri Lanka to Siam, invited from Ceylon for the rains retreat, or the Siamese monk at Wat Ananda Metyarama established in 1923. Some Ceylonese Buddhists attended the Tiger Sakyamuni Bodh Gaya temple. A Sri Lankan Buddhist temple opened at Outram Park Road in the mid-1930s, replacing the modest Spottiswoode Park Road locale. In 1934, Venerable Mahaweera arrived from Colombo, welcomed by Sri Lankans as well as Singaporean Chinese with Penang connections. Mahaweera served both Chinese and Ceylonese Buddhists in Singapore. By 1939, a Singapore Buddhist Association-English was formed for Chinese devotees, while the Singapore Buddhist Association served Sri Lankan Buddhists. Both groups attended the Outram Park Road temple and, later, Sri Lankaramaya Vihara, until the Mangala Vihara was established in 1960. This became the primary temple for Chinese Buddhists who followed Theravada Buddhism.

Anne M. Blackburn

The majestic reclining Buddha statue at the Sri Lankaramaya Vihara, 2012.

'Liberation of Birds' ceremony to mark Wesak Day at the Sri Lankaramaya Vihara, 1966.

Ceylonese women stitch pillow cases to help the British war effort, 1939. (L to R): Mrs Ambalavanar, Mrs Rajaretnam, Mrs P. Chelvanathan, Mrs Dana, Mrs Jayakkodi, and Miss F. A. Knight.

for the British military effort (*The Straits Times*, 13 February 1940; 1 March 1940).

During the Japanese Occupation, Japanese authorities tended to group the Ceylonese together with the wider Indian community. Consequently, when the Indian Independence League (IIL) and the Indian National Army (INA) were established in Singapore, the Ceylonese were included as members, and a 'Ceylon Department' and a 'Lanka Unit' comprised sub-units of the IIL in the struggle to liberate India and also Ceylon from British rule. According to Wimalatissa Indrasome, who worked at B. P. de Silva, the firm made the INA officers' silver badges with a map of India in the centre. Gladwin Kotalawela and T. A. Simon maintained close ties with Subhas Chandra Bose and played a key role in reaching out to the Sinhalese community in Singapore. Yet, the vast majority of Ceylonese remained silently loyal to the British. Indeed, given the strong relationship between the British administration and the middle and upper middle class orientation of the Ceylonese, ties with the Indian community remained perfunctory in spite of the pressure to join the INA and IIL. It came

as no surprise then that when the triumphant British forces returned to Singapore in late 1945, an article entitled 'Singapore Sinhalese' averred that the 'Sinhalese had preserved their allegiance to the British' (*The Straits Times*, 17 October 1945). According to a report by V. Coomaraswamy, a government representative of Ceylon in 1946, the 'interest of the Ceylonese in the IIL movement was lukewarm and [that] the INA itself received little support from the Ceylonese who did little or no harm to the British cause to which they were consistently loyal' (*The Straits Times*, 17 June 1946).

POST-WAR DEVELOPMENTS: SHIFTING NATIONAL LOYALITIES

A sense of uncertainty prevailed among the Ceylonese diaspora in the aftermath of World War II. The foremost question in the community was whether they should return to Ceylon or remain in Singapore. Singapore had suffered economically and the psychological wounds of the war ran even deeper. A press clipping reported that 1,127 Ceylonese left Malaya for their homeland immediately after the war (*The Straits Times*, 23 May

SINNATHAMBY RAJARATNAM

As a Singaporean, I have no difficulty, in a single lifetime, forgetting in turn that I was a Ceylon Tamil and Sri Lankan though I was born there... I had no difficulty forgetting I was a British subject, or the formative years as a Malayan... Being a Singaporean is not a matter of ancestry. It is conviction and choice...

~ S. Rajaratnam

Born in Jaffna on 25 February 1915, Sinnathamby Rajaratnam was Singapore's pioneer politician, philosopher, pressman and patriot. A former journalist, Rajaratnam was a founding member of the People's Action Party (PAP) in 1954. He comprised the initial 'Big Three of the PAP' with Lee Kuan Yew as the forerunner, Goh Keng Swee as the economist and Rajaratnam as the ideologue. In 1959, he contested in the first Legislative Assembly General Election and was elected as Member of Parliament representing the Kampong Glam constituency. He was appointed Singapore's Minister of Culture (1959–65) and served as the country's first Foreign Affairs Minister (1965–80) during which time he gave Singapore a louder voice in international affairs than its size merited. Till the late 1980s, he assumed various other political roles, including Minister for Labour (1968–71), Second

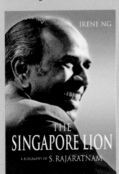

S. Rajaratnam's biography details the life of a political leader committed to the ideal of a meritocratic, multicultural and modern Singapore.

Deputy Prime Minister (Foreign Affairs) (1980–84) and Senior Minister, Prime Minister's Office (1984–88). He retired from the post as Senior Minister and Member of Parliament in 1988. According to *Singapore: The Encyclopedia*, he was admitted into the prestigious Order of Temasek (First Class) in 1990, and he received the ASEAN Heads of Governments Citation Award in 1997.

People's Action Party (PAP) candidate, S. Rajaratnam, addressing a crowd at Kampong Glam during the 1976 General Elections.

Among the ideas dearest to him was that of a 'Singaporean Singapore', a vision that he enshrined in the National Pledge in 1966, which he penned. At his state funeral on 25 February 2006, the first for a government minister, mourners recited the National Pledge in somber tribute to the man who embodied the notion of multiculturalism and helped to define the ideals of a meritocratic, modern and multiracial Singapore. In 2007, the Institute of Defence and Strategic Studies (IDSS) was renamed the S. Rajaratnam School of International Studies (RSIS) to honour the contributions of the late S. Rajaratnam.

S. Rajaratnam and the Ceylonese community

I have often wondered whether I could have attained the position I now hold in the Singapore Cabinet had I stayed on in Ceylon and ventured into politics. Let me hasten to add that I would be very distressed indeed were I made to understand that I am holding the position I now do in the Cabinet simply because I am a Ceylon Tamil. I like to think that I am where I am purely on basis of merit.

~ S.Rajaratnam (1985)

In numerous speeches made to the Ceylon Tamil community, Rajaratnam exhibited a deep concern about the future position of the Jaffna Tamils both in

Sri Lanka and in Singapore. His sentiments towards the land of his birth surfaced in the 1970s and 80s when violent ethnic clashes broke out in Sri Lanka. At the 75th anniversary celebration of the Singapore Ceylon Tamils' Association (SCTA) in 1985, Rajaratnam proclaimed that there will be a 'bright future for Ceylon Tamils 75 years from now even if—which I fervently hope will not happen—they become extinct in Ceylon'.

In 1976, he urged the Ceylonese in Singapore to take up skilled professions in science and technology to secure their future. He believed that the future of the Ceylon Tamils depended on the sustainability of multiculturalism in Singapore. In a speech made in 1985, it was poignant when he said that:

...if something should go wrong with Singapore's politics... then there is no escape hatch for Ceylon Tamils. Indian Tamils can, if they are lucky, go back to the vast continent they came from... But there is no place for Ceylon Tamils to run to short of a miraculous return to sanity in their ancestral homeland.

Rajaratnam was disconcerted by the ethnic conflict in Sri Lanka and was very concerned about their future as a minority community in Singapore. In an address to the Ceylonese community in 1989, he affirmed that the Ceylonese diaspora in Singapore 'should not end up like the Armenian community that was once very important'.

Minister of Foreign Affairs, S. Rajaratnam, speaking at the Singapore Ceylon Tamils' Association's 'Cheque Presentation' ceremony at the Ceylon Sports Club, 1976.

1946). Many Ceylonese were deeply concerned about their future and an article titled the 'Future of Malayan Ceylonese' in October 1946 drew attention to the emotional quandary of the Ceylon Tamil community who wanted to know if Malaya would be a land with equal rights and opportunities for all its inhabitants. Likewise, another article titled 'Sinhalese Want "Equal Rights" Guarantee', appealed for a suitable place for Sinhalese Buddhist worship, an appointment of a Sinhalese Registrar of Marriages, equal civil service rights and the provision of bilingual education for the Sinhalese in Singapore (*The Straits Times*, 1 May 1946).

In 1947 and 1948, even as a fraction of the resident Ceylonese population returned to the 'homeland', a military labour force from Ceylon was recruited for duty in Malaya and Singapore. 10,000 skilled and unskilled men constituted the 'Ceylonese Section' of the Royal Pioneer Corps. These men were housed at Colombo Camp in Reformatory Road (renamed Clementi Road) with their own cooks and welfare officers to take care of their needs (*The Straits Times*, 22 April 1946; 2 July 1947). The vast majority of the Ceylonese corps returned although a small percentage settled and later acquired Singapore citizenship.

Between the late 1940s to the mid-1960s, issues of nationality, citizenship, belonging and identity were key concerns for the Ceylonese community in Singapore. Following Ceylon's independence in 1948, the Ceylonese in Singapore were recognised as citizens of Ceylon. As the wave of decolonisation spread throughout South and Southeast Asia in the 1950s to 1960s, the Ceylonese in Singapore straddled their affiliation with Ceylon with their growing sense of political loyalty to Singapore.

When two Prime Ministers of Ceylon, D. S. Senanayake and Solomon Bandaranaike passed away in 1952 and 1959 respectively, the Singapore Sinhala Association, Ceylon Tamil Association, Ceylon Sports Club and the Singapore Sinhala Buddhist Association collectively mourned their deaths. Ceylonese businesses were closed as a mark of respect and special permission was sought from the Singapore government to allow all Ceylonese to fly the Ceylon flag at half mast. After the Sinhala Only Act of 1956 was passed in Ceylon, there was a gradual metamorphosis among the Ceylonese diaspora in Singapore. One response, in the midst of communal tensions in Ceylon, was for the community to grow increasingly politically aligned to Singapore. Indeed, the majority of those who remained after World War II, took up citizenship here.

SRI LANKANS IN INDEPENDENT SINGAPORE

Ceylonese professionals began streaming into Singapore from the late 1960s to the 1980s as ethnic tensions intensified in Sri Lanka. A sizeable number of engineers, doctors and other professionals emigrated. The new nation emphasised the need for these immigrants to contribute to the city-state's development and become 'Singaporean'. In a speech at the Ceylon Sports Club in 1973, Lee Kuan Yew, then Prime Minister of Singapore, expressed 'hope that the Singapore Ceylon Tamils' Association will become more Singaporean in its thinking and outlook, and become a valuable component of society' (*The Straits Times*, 7 October 1973).

From the 1980s, the outbreak of the civil war in Sri Lanka, and the need for foreign domestic workers in Singapore, catalysed the beginning of a new wave of Sri Lankan emigrants. By 1995, Sri Lanka and Indonesia were Singapore's top sources for domestic helpers. At the time, there were about 10,000 Sri Lankan domestic workers in Singapore and it was estimated that the monthly arrival had increased to about 1,000 from 400 in 1994. By 2004, of the 140,000 foreign domestic workers in Singapore, 12,000 were from Sri Lanka. According to the Sri Lankan High Commission based in Singapore, in 2011 there were between 2,500 and 3,000 registered and approximately 3,000 unregistered Sri Lankan domestic workers in Singapore; these were largely Sinhalese and to a lesser extent Tamils and Muslims.

The steady flow of Sri Lankan domestic workers to Singapore draws attention to the differentiated socio-economic status of the old and new wave of emigrants. The pioneer wave of Sri Lankan emigrants that came to Singapore were either British subjects who filled the upper echelons of the civil administration or businessmen. The movement of Sri Lankan domestic workers on temporary contracts, who occupy, arguably, the lowest socio-economic strata of Singapore society on the other hand presents a stark contrast. The difference between the two waves of emigrants is in many ways a manifestation of the disjuncture between a Ceylon that was once hailed as a model colony and whose emigrants comprised the elite of Asian society in Singapore, and the dark reality of the effects of the civil war in Sri Lanka. The interaction between the old and new movements of Sinhala emigrants is evident when they both visit the Sri Lankaramaya Buddhist Temple on Wesak Day, and where there is a tacit sense of a common Sri Lankan tradition that binds the two waves of emigrants. Yet that affiliation is temporary. Outside the corridors of worship, the differences of nationality, occupation, class, status and identity re-emerge—serving as a reminder of the complexity inherent in the Sri Lankan diaspora in Singapore.

BEING 'SRI LANKAN' IN CONTEMPORARY SINGAPORE

I was born in Jaffna and left when I was six months old. I spent most of my life in Seremban, Malaysia. Then I came here [Singapore]. So who am I? This is our problem. What is our identity?

~ *S. Rajaratnam (1991)*

The Sri Lankan diaspora in Singapore is textured by varying political, ethnic, cultural and religious identities.

Members of the Royal Pioneer Corps visit the Sri Lankaramaya Vihara in Singapore (circa 1950).

CEYLONESE TOLD: BE CITIZENS

The acting Commissioner for Ceylon in Malaya and Singapore, Mr. C. Gunasingham, last night called on all Ceylonese who intended making Singapore their home to register as citizens.

He was talking on "Citizenship" to the Ceylon Tamils' Association

He said citizenship would give Ceylonese new hopes.

He said Singapore citizenship was "more liberal in conception" than Ceylon's.

The decision to take up Singapore citizenship was a key issue in the late 1950s.

Sri Lankan domestic workers in Singapore celebrate Wesak Day, 2011.

Centennial celebration of the Singapore Ceylon Tamils' Association (SCTA) held at the Ceylon Sports Club, 2010.

PROMINENT SRI LANKANS IN SINGAPORE

Sunil Amarasuriya

Sunil Amarasuriya

Sunil Amarasuriya was born in Ceylon and migrated to Singapore in 1962. Chairman of one of the earliest and most prestigious jewellery firms in Singapore, Sunil Amarasuriya is the great-grandson of B. P. de Silva (for information on the famed jewellery merchant B. P. de Silva, see section on 'Entrepreneurship and Remittances', page 63). He joined the family business in 1972 and rose to head B. P. de Silva Holdings in the 1990s. Amasuriya's leadership was crucial in ensuring that the firm adapted well to the metamorphosis of Singapore's gem trade from skilled craftmanship to mechanised jewellery. He played a key role in the diversification of the business beyond the jewellery industry and developed a close relationship with the Audemars Piguet watch group based in Switzerland. B. P. de Silva Holdings has since expanded from jewellery, watches and silverware, to Asian gifts, tea, medical devices, environmental technologies and food and beverage. Over 140 years have passed since B. P. de Silva founded the firm in Singapore, and his family continues the proud legacy of maintaining the integrity and reputation of providing exquisite jewellery while keeping alive a generous philanthropic spirit that is evident in their support for several local and transnational charitable activities.

R. Theyvendran

R. Theyvendran is a well-known industrialist, investor, business and community leader. A unionist during his younger days, he is the Chairman and owner of the Stamford Press Group of Companies, which specialises in printing and publishing. Theyvendran is also the Secretary-General of the Management Development Institute of Singapore (MDIS). In the

R. Theyvendran

community-service sphere, he serves as the President of the Singapore Ceylon Tamils' Association (SCTA) and the Ceylon Sports Club (CSC). In 1998, he was conferred the prestigious Public Service Medal.

Eugene Wijeysingha

Eugene Wijeysingha

Eugene Wijeysingha, of Sinhalese and Burgher ancestry, is one of Singapore's most notable educators. He became the youngest school principal in the history of the country when, in 1967, at the age of 32, he was appointed principal of Changkat Changi Secondary School. Eugene Wijeysingha served as both teacher and principal of Singapore's premier school—Raffles Institution (RI). He was appointed Deputy Director for School Organisation (1973–76), Deputy Director of Staff and Training (Education) (1976–79) and Assistant Director of Education (1976–77). From 2003 to 2007, Wijeysingha served as the Chairman of the Compulsory Education Board (CEB). In recognition of his invaluable contribution to education, he received the Public Administration Medal (Bronze) in 1974, the Public Administration Medal (Silver) in 1978, and the Outstanding Singapore Sinhalese Award in 1992. Apart from being a celebrated educator, Eugene Wijeysingha is also well known for the books that he has authored and, in particular, for penning the history of Raffles Institution.

Tharman Shanmugaratnam

Tharman Shanmugaratnam was appointed Deputy Prime Minister, Minister for Finance and Minister of Manpower after the 2011 Singapore General Election. Before entering politics, Tharman served as the Chief Executive of the Monetary Authority of Singapore (MAS). After his resounding success in the 2001 elections, he was appointed Acting Minister

Tharman Shanmugaratnam

for Education, and subsequently Minister for Education (2004–March 2008) and Second Minister for Finance (2006–07). In addition to his heavy portfolio in government, Tharman in 2011 became the first Asian to be appointed Chairman of the key policy guiding unit of the International Monetary Fund (IMF), the International Monetary and Financial Committee (IMFC).

J. Y. Pillay

Born in 1934 in Klang, Malaya, Joseph Yuvaraj Pillay—J. Y. Pillay—is of Ceylonese-Indian heritage. His father hailed from Jaffna and worked as a government officer, while his mother, from Thirunnelveli, India, was a graduate teacher in Malaya. J. Y. Pillay is best known for his role as Chairman of Singapore Airlines (SIA). Under his leadership, the national carrier emerged as a premier global airline. Since 2005, he has served as the Chairman of the Council of Presidential Advisors (CPA). In 1996, J. Y. Pillay was conferred an honorary PhD in Law from the National University of Singapore (NUS) and in 2012 received the Order of Nila Utama (First Class)—the highest national award conferred that year in honour of public service.

S. S. Ratnam (left) and J. Y. Pillay (middle) at the National University of Singapore convocation ceremony, 1996.

As such, there is no monolithic 'Ceylonese' or 'Sri Lankan' identity. Moreover, in view of the racial categorisation in Singapore, there is also a broader identification with the Indian subcontinent. To some extent, like emigrants who arrived during the British period and regard themselves as 'Ceylonese', their descendants continue to identify themselves as either 'Singaporean Ceylonese/Sri Lankan', 'Sinhalese', 'Jaffna Tamil' or 'Ceylon Tamil'. Today, there are individuals from the community who prefer to regard themselves as either 'Indian' or in terms of hyphenated identities in view of the growing number of inter-marriages.

The prestige associated with being Ceylonese has sometimes led to tensions with the Indian diaspora in Singapore. To a considerable extent, the elite status of the community especially prior to Singapore's independence, has manifested in the desire to sustain differences vis-à-vis the Indian community. That desire was clearly evident in several letters to the press during the colonial era that sought to demarcate differences between the Ceylonese and Indian communities. Indeed, as early as 1917, a letter

to the press clearly expressed that the 'Ceylon Tamils of Malaya have not always identified themselves with the Indian Tamils… any representation of Indian races in the Federal Council must include Ceylonese in its scope' (*The Straits Times*, 12 March 1917). It is in this framework that the ethnic and racial categories of being 'Indian' and 'Ceylonese' have been contested and negotiated in the postcolonial era, and accounts for continued efforts towards gaining recognition and representation that is premised on the need to give separate credence to their contributions. At the same time, there are members who have bridged this gap by identifying themselves as 'Tamil' to mitigate an Indian-Lankan dichotomy.

In today's context, to regard oneself as 'Ceylonese' and 'Sri Lankan' may seemingly share similar meaning but these markers are loaded with difference. To identify oneself with Ceylon rather than Sri Lanka is to claim a heritage from an earlier era—a sense of pride in being connected to a 'remembered' land that was once heralded as being more advanced than Singapore—saturated with educated talent who made contributions

Kanagaratnam Shanmugaratnam

K. Shanmugaratnam

Kanagaratnam Shanmugaratnam is renowned for his path-breaking work in the field of pathology. He served as a pathologist in the Singapore Government Medical Service from 1948 to 1960. In 1960, he joined the University of Singapore, where he was appointed Head of the Department of Pathology, a position he held for 26 years. During his tenure at the University, he was also Dean of the Faculty of Medicine (1962–64). K. Shanmugaratnam played an important role in the establishment of the Singapore Cancer Registry, and served as its Director from 1968 to 2002. For his immense contribution to the medical field, K. Shanmugaratnam was awarded the Public Administration Medal (Gold) in 1976 and in 2001 became the inaugural recipient of the Lee Foundation-National Healthcare Group Lifetime Achievement Award. In 2006, he also received the Distinguished Fellow Award from the Royal College of Pathologists of Australasia.

Sittampalam Shanmugaratnam

Born in Chullipuram, Jaffna, in 1928, Sittampalam Shanmugaratnam better known as S.S. Ratnam, graduated with an MBBS from Sri Lanka in 1957. S. S. Ratnam gained international recognition for his ground-breaking achievements in the field of sex change operations and transsexualism, in vitro fertilisation (IVF) and embryo replacement. In 1971, S. S. Ratnam performed the first sex change operation in Asia at Singapore's Kandang Kerbau Hospital. For his contribution to medicine, he was awarded the Singapore Public Administration Medal (Gold) in 1977. He led the team that produced Asia's first IVF baby in 1983, and the world's first microinjection baby in 1989. In recognition of his unparalleled achievements in the field, S. S. Ratnam was elected President of the World Federation of Obstetricians and Gynecologists in 1982.

Ragunathar Kanagasuntheram

Ragunathar Kanagasuntheram has received considerable acclaim for his path-breaking work in

R.Kanagasuntheram

the field of anatomy. He gained his doctorate in anatomy from the University of Cambridge in 1952. From 1963–80, he headed the Department of Anatomy in the medical faculty of the University of Singapore. In 1981, he was conferred Emeritus Professorship by the National University of Singapore, the first anatomist to have received this title.

Ariff Bongso

Of Sri Lankan Muslim and Dutch Burgher heritage, Ariff Bongso was born in Colombo in 1946 and became a Singapore citizen in 1991. Recognised for his outstanding contribution to scientific research, some of the prestigious awards he has received include the Outstanding University Researcher Award by the National University of Singapore (1997), Asian Innovation Award (Gold) from the Far East Economic Review (2002), National Science Award from A-STAR (1988; 2002) and the ASEAN Outstanding Scientist Award (2005).

Ariff Bongso

Oliver Hennedige

Oliver Hennedige is well known for his work in orthodontics and implant dentistry. In 1981, he was elected the President of the Asian Pacific Dental Federation, the first time that a member of the Singapore Dental Association rose to the post (*The Straits Times*, 28 April 1981). He has served as the President of the Singapore Sinhala Association, and is Secretary General of the Asia Pacific Dental Federation/Asia Pacific Dental Regional Organisation.

A. V. Winslow

A. V. Winslow served the Singapore Bench from 1962 to 1977. He won the Queens Scholarship in 1935 to pursue legal studies and later joined the Straits

Among Singapore's Supreme Court judges in 1979, three were of Ceylonese descent—Justice T. Kulasekaram (3rd from left), Justice T. S. Sinnathuray (3rd from right) and Justice A. P. Rajah (1st from right).

Settlements Legal Service. In 1967, Justice Winslow was elected the first Chairman of the Board of Legal Education under the Legal Profession Act. A year later, he was elected the first President of the Singapore section of the International Commission of Jurists.

Justice A. V. Winslow

Joshua Benjamin Jeyaretnam

Born in Chankanai, Jaffna, in 1926, Joshua Benjamin Jeyaretnam—often referred to as J. B. J.—was widely recognised as an indomitable opposition figure in Singapore politics. In 1952, he was the youngest magistrate in Singapore to be appointed District Judge. In 1981, he won the Anson by-election, becoming the first opposition candidate to be elected after Singapore's independence.

J. B. J. following his landmark victory at the 1981 Anson by-election.

to the development of Singapore, well beyond their small number. During the 1950s and 60s, the community's identification with Ceylon gradually transformed due to changing circumstances in postcolonial Ceylon (renamed Sri Lanka), but also because many in the community took up Singapore citizenship. This changed further in the 1980s, when the civil war in Sri Lanka and the rise of the LTTE rendered the label 'Sri Lankan' laden with notoriety, terrorism and asylum seekers. The transformation in the political climate in Sri Lanka resulted in several Ceylonese in Singapore preferring instead to be referred to as 'Indian'.

By the 1980s local-born citizens gradually emerged as the majority of the Sri Lankan diaspora in Singapore. Most of those who were local-born maintained little affiliation with the war-stricken island-state. Furthermore, inter-marriage across racial lines has further attenuated identification with Ceylon. J. Y. Pillay considers that his 'grandchildren are 3/8th Lankan, 1/8th Indian and half American' and that arithmetic response goes a long way in encapsulating the complexity of Sri

Lankan identities in contemporary Singapore. During the pre-war years, inter-marriage in the community was an exception but now the reverse is probably true. One consequence has been the decreased involvement of subsequent generations in Sri Lankan socio-cultural activities, and the rapid attrition of the Jaffnese accent in spoken Tamil. Collectively, these have contributed to the loss of a distinct ethnic identity that once defined the Ceylonese diaspora in Singapore.

The present generation of Singaporean-Sri Lankans are comfortable carrying multiple identities. For some, there continues to be a cultural affiliation to Sri Lanka, mainly through the various diasporic institutions in Singapore which keep alive the religious and traditional heritage and sustain links with the ancestral land. However, the nostalgic sentiments that shaped their forefathers' connection to Ceylon has declined—remaining now primarily through the stories and memories that parents and grandparents share with the younger generation.

Hema Kiruppalini

BRUNEI DARUSSALAM

An early 20th-century photograph of a Sri Lankan Malay man with his son. The historical connection between the Malay archipelago and Sri Lanka has been documented in a book titled Lost cousins: The Malays of Sri Lanka *(1987).*

INTRODUCTION

The number of Sri Lankans currently domiciled in Brunei Darussalam is miniscule when compared to that of other South Asians from India, Bangladesh, Pakistan and Nepal. Like their South Asian counterparts, the Sri Lankans are a transient population in Brunei with little prospect of becoming permanent residents or citizens due to the strict immigration laws of Brunei. In 2011, approximately 150 to 200 Sri Lankan families lived and worked throughout the Sultanate. The largest number is based in and around Bandar Seri Begawan, the capital city of Brunei, while others lived in the Seria-Belait area, home to the oil industry. Many Sri Lankans are employed as expatriate officers in the government sector, but their number has dwindled when compared to the 1970s and 1980s. Others are engaged in private-sector work in the construction industry as engineers, quantity surveyors, or are engaged in minor clerical work. However, unlike the Indians and Pakistanis who abound in ubiquitous retail shops, tailoring and hairdressing occupations etc., not many Sri Lankans are engaged in unskilled jobs. Unlike in the Middle East, Sri Lankans are not recruited as domestic helpers due to the Brunei quota system which favours the import of workers recruited mainly from other ASEAN countries.

THE FIRST SRI LANKANS

There are no special historical links between Brunei and Sri Lanka (formerly Ceylon) which might have facilitated migration even on a small scale during pre-modern times. The earliest recorded contact between Sri Lankans and Bruneians occurred in 1846, when a recruiting party of Sri Lankan Malay soldiers led by Captain R.

Tranchell visited Brunei and Sultan Omar Ali Saifuddin II helped to enlist prospective Brunei Malay soldiers to serve in the Ceylon Rifle Regiment (1798–1873). For two years from 1869 to 1871 a detachment of Sri Lankan Malay soldiers was stationed in Labuan from where they interacted with the Brunei Malays from whom they obtained Malay manuscripts. The earliest reference to a Sri Lankan actually living in Brunei occurs in a colonial British report by a former British Consul, M. S. H. McArthur, in 1904 to a Sinhalese who served as a private secretary to the then Sultan Hashim Jalilul Alam (r. 1885–1906), the 25th Brunei Sultan. Similarly Sultan Ahmad Tajuddin (reigned 1929–50) was served by a Burgher from Sri Lanka named Miranda. Following the migration of Sri Lankan Burghers to Australia, the Sri Lankan Malays too tried to migrate to Brunei in the 1960s, but the proposal did not find favour with the British officials who were largely controlling the Brunei government administration at the time.

DEVELOPMENTS FROM THE 1950S

Workers of Sri Lankan origin began to trickle into the Sultanate in the 1950s and during the following decade, the number of Sri Lankan professionals steadily grew especially in the education, health, telecommunications sectors and the public works department. Their number saw a steady increase since early 1960s when Malaysian expatriates left Brunei following political tensions

Map 4.5

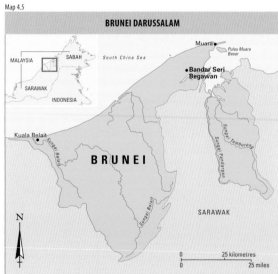

A sketch of the Ceylon Rifle Regiment soldiers. The Regiment had connections with Brunei while touring as members of a recruiting party in 1846 under Captain Tranchell.

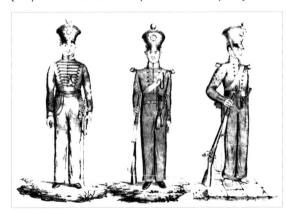

EMINENT SRI LANKANS IN BRUNEI

A Sri Lankan medical doctor, S. Sinnathamby, who rose to become the Medical Director General and a nurse, S. Thurairajah, who became the head of the nursing services, were both conferred the title 'Dato', a high state honour awarded by the Sultan. A Sri Lankan geographer, K. U. Sri Nanda became the founding Dean of the Faculty of Arts and Social Sciences when the University of Brunei Darussalam was established in late 1985. A Sri Lankan journalist of fame, Rex de Silva served from 1990 to 2011 as the chief editor of the country's oldest English-medium daily newspaper, *The Borneo Bulletin*. Another Sri Lankan, B. A. Hussainmiya, wrote several pioneering books on the history of Brunei Darussalam, including a political biography of the present Sultan's father—*Sultan Omar Ali Saifuddin III and Britain: The Making of Brunei Darussalam*—published by the Oxford University Press in 1995.

In 2007, the Sri Lankan scholar B. A. Hussainmiya was awarded the 4 Star (PSB) medal for his contributions to Brunei historiography by Sultan HM Haji Hassanal Bolkiah.

The famous Sri Lankan journalist, Rex de Silva, was the chief editor of Brunei's oldest English newspaper.

between the two countries after Brunei refused to join the Malaysian Federation in 1963. Sri Lankans made a good a name for themselves in their occupations and some rose to higher positions in their respective professions. The services of teachers like Tuan Bahar, K. C. Thangarajah, Tuan 'Tuna' Saldin and others are still fondly remembered by their students who have now come to occupy higher echelons of Brunei bureaucracy. Sri Lankan engineers were particularly conspicuous in the Public Works Department and in the telecommunications and health sectors. Lately there are about 10 Sri Lankan academics serving in the University of Brunei Darussalam, some of whom hold senior administrative positions.

THE SRI LANKA ASSOCIATION OF BRUNEI DARUSSALAM

The gradual increase in the size of the diaspora provided the backdrop for concerted efforts towards the formation of an organisation that could aid in bringing together members of the community in Brunei Darussalam. In 1968, Sri Lankans in Brunei formed their first association known as the Sri Lanka Association of

The Sri Lanka Association of Brunei Darusssalam, 2011.

Brunei Darussalam (SLABD). In 2011, the organisation, led by Ahmed Mackie, a surgeon attached to the main Brunei hospital, had more than 100 members. The Association is a focal point for Sri Lankan national and recreational activities. SLABD also periodically orgsanises cultural shows and welfare activities, and maintains close ties with other similar ethnic or national associations functioning in Brunei Darussalam.

B. A. Hussainmiya

Members of Sri Lankan Association who participated in the beach cleanup campaign

Sri Lankan Association in beach cleanup

By Liza Mohamad

EMPHASISING the importance of maintaining cleanliness and protecting the environment, the Sri Lankan Association in Brunei conducted a cleaning campaign at Belait Beach.

It was participated by over 100 members of the community who share the Sultanate's vision of a better and greener environment for the future generations.

Leading the campaign was the Honorary President, Dr Haji Ahmed Mackie, and the Executive Committee of the Belait Sri Lankan Association, Mr Saman Wickramasinghe.

Apart from preserving the cleanliness of the beach in Kuala Belait, the campaign hoped to bring about greater relationship between all members of the Sri Lankan community residing in Belait District and Brunei-Muara District.

In September 2011, members of the Sri Lanka Association in Brunei took part in a beach cleanup. The campaign sought to forge closer relations between members of the Sri Lankan community residing in Belait district and Brunei-Muara district.

THE GULF STATES

A Sri Lankan troupe from 'Chandana Wickramasinghe and the Dancers Guild' presented a dance show, 'Sri Lak Rangana', a fusion of contemporary and traditional choreography, on the opening night of the Sri Lanka Cultural Week in Kuwait City, 2010.

A job agency signboard in the UAE lists guest workers' countries of origin.

INTRODUCTION:
SOJOURNERS IN THE GULF

This volume examines groups of people living around the world who have identities rooted in Sri Lanka. Diasporic populations preserve links with their place of origin, but are less tightly tied to the homeland than are temporary travellers. In some cases, diasporic connections function symbolically in the realm of memory and myth. In others, the connections include active economic and political links with the homeland. Although individuals may return to the homeland temporarily or permanently, the term 'diaspora' inherently implies that the group in the destination will persist, collectively valuing and displaying cultural characteristics of the homeland but also firmly established as a minority community in the host country.

Within this framework, one might ask whether the large sojourner population of Sri Lankan guest-workers in West Asia counts as part of a diaspora. A growing number of Sri Lankans labour in the Gulf, but of these individuals, only a fraction has the time, mobility, or cultural capital to pursue connections with each other and to develop a sense of community in the host country. The majority of guest workers are male skilled or unskilled labourers and female domestic servants who sojourn abroad on short (often two-year) contracts. In the destination country, they are allowed

few, if any, political and social ties with each other or with the citizens of the host country; their ties to the host society are largely restricted to wage exchanges with their sponsor in their worksite location (factory, construction site, or sponsor's home). These individuals' identities are thoroughly Sri Lankan. They intend to return to Sri Lanka, and they maintain clear ties to Sri Lanka via citizenship, economic remittances, and connections to the extended family at home.

Guest workers' inability to form a stable, coherent community in the Gulf means that Sri Lanka's migrants may not qualify as a diaspora in the strictest sense of the word. Nevertheless, the phenomenon of transnational migration certainly merits scholarly consideration given the size of the migrant population, the extended duration of this migration stream, and the likelihood that growing numbers of migrants will continue to work abroad in the future.

This article briefly presents the history of Sri Lankan labour migration. It then considers government policies and labour relations in the main migrant destination countries, examining identity politics in the Gulf's segmented labour market and exploring labour conditions abroad. The article sets forth the economic context in Sri Lanka, examines the push factors for the current stream of transnational migration, and concludes with a discussion of the social consequences of migration for Sri Lanka and the families left at home. Throughout, emphasis falls on the political, economic, and social links that transnational migrants maintain with their homeland.

THE HISTORY OF SRI LANKAN LABOUR MIGRATION TO THE GULF

As other contributions to this volume have described, several waves of Sri Lankan migration have taken place since the country gained independence in 1948. Beginning in the mid 1950s, economic and social pressures have sent wealthy, educated, English-speaking émigrés to Europe, Australia, Canada and the United States. Ethnic violence, which surged into a civil war in 1983, spurred an out-migration of Tamil-speaking Sri Lankans from the North and East and augmented the return of Tamil plantation workers to South India from Sri Lanka's central highlands. These Sri Lankans have set up permanent communities in their destination countries.

In contrast with these permanent emigrants, since 1976 a significant and growing number of Sri Lankan guest workers have journeyed to the Gulf in a pattern of cyclical labour migration. The current pattern builds on a long history of interconnections in the region; South Asian

Map 4.6

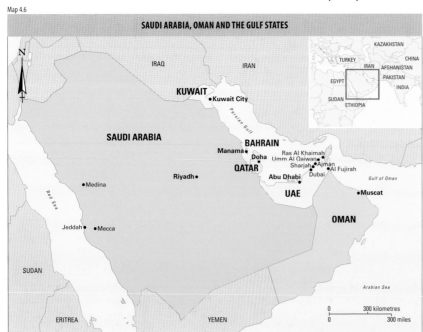

SAUDI ARABIA, OMAN AND THE GULF STATES

populations have dispersed throughout West, South, and Southeast Asia for several millennia along the rich and dynamic Indian Ocean trade routes. In earlier times, South Asia formed the centre of economic and cultural activity, with the Arabian peninsula relatively marginal in importance. Since the discovery of oil in the Gulf in 1930, and especially since the oil boom in the early 1970s, the regional balance of power has changed. As petroleum has flowed out of the Gulf, money has flowed in. The resultant development has brought millions of guest workers to the Gulf to realise the oil producing countries' plans for modernisation and development. These workers come from dozens of countries in Asia and beyond, and they bring a wide variety of skills and experience.

The Sri Lankan Bureau of Foreign Employment (SLBFE), the government's main administrative body regulating labour migration, estimates that half a million Sri Lankans worked abroad in 1994. The number doubled to one million in 2003, and by 2009 increased to 1.8 million. Most Sri Lankan labour migrants (93 per cent), both male and female, journey to the Gulf, with four countries (Saudi Arabia, the United Arab Emirates [UAE], Kuwait, and Qatar) absorbing over 80 per cent of Sri Lanka's guest workers. With over 1.6 million Sri Lankans (8 per cent of the island's 20 million people) in West Asia, Sri Lanka's well being is closely tied to policies and events in the Gulf (SLBFE, 2009).

GOVERNMENT POLICIES AND LABOUR RELATIONS IN MAIN DESTINATION COUNTRIES

Guest workers form a crucial aspect of local economies in the Gulf Cooperation Council (GCC) countries, which include Bahrain, Kuwait, Oman, Qatar, Saudi Arabia and the UAE. Most GCC countries have a *de facto* dual labour market, with well paying, non-strenuous, public-sector jobs created for 'nationals' and poorly paying, difficult, low-status, private-sector jobs performed by foreigners. Overall, foreigners make up an estimated 40 per cent of the population of the GCC countries and constitute 70 per cent of the workforce. Foreign representation in the workforce rises significantly higher in Kuwait (80 per cent), the UAE (85 per cent) and Qatar (93 per cent).

Dependence on guest workers worries government officials in the Gulf, and the GCC states have implemented policies to minimise the perceived threat. Most governments have instituted labour force 'nationalisation' plans to reserve employment in certain sectors for citizens of the country, achieving the most success in public sector jobs. In addition, stringent policies control workers on a number of fronts. The sponsorship system (*kafala*) serves as a primary mechanism of control. In the host country, an individual employer or sponsor (*kafeel*) assumes responsibility for that worker during his or her sojourn in the country. The worker can remain legally in the country only as long as he or she works for this sponsor. In addition, there are restrictions on length of stay, strict regulations prohibiting workers from changing jobs, and difficult-to-meet criteria for bringing in family members. For wealthy emigrant professionals, regulations restrict the ability to own land and businesses. It is nearly impossible for foreigners to obtain citizenship in the Gulf; even members of South Asian communities that have been based in the Gulf for generations are vulnerable to deportation and other forms of displacement. All of these factors function to keep guest workers' stays short, temporary or informal.

Sri Lankan domestic helpers return to Colombo, 2006.

Thus most Sri Lankan sojourners do not settle—and indeed are forbidden from settling—in the Gulf.

Neither citizens nor guest workers have many legal rights or protections in the Gulf. GCC states provide ample economic and social services to their citizens; in many countries, basic services such as healthcare and education are provided for free or at low cost, and housing and utilities such as water, sewage and electricity are free or highly subsidised. Citizens pay no taxes. But the political systems are not democratic, and ordinary people have little or no say in the governance of the country. Guest workers have even less political freedom; unions are not allowed, and troublemakers are sent home. In many GCC countries, labour laws sometimes cover male labourers but do not protect domestic workers in private households. Even laws that do exist may not be enforced against middle and upper class employers.

Diplomats from labour-sending countries can and do intercede for their citizens in the event of a crisis, but the Sri Lankan state is constrained in its ability to safeguard its citizens working in the Gulf. Diplomatic visas are limited in number, consular offices and embassies are expensive to maintain, and labour welfare officers have large case loads. In addition, foreign diplomats lack the authority to enforce contracts, demand the payment of back wages, or correct unsuitable working conditions. The power to inspect work sites and police labour codes lies with the Ministry of Labour in the host countries, but these government organs are often understaffed. Furthermore, host country officials are not obligated to protect foreign

Sri Lankan residents celebrate with Qatari citizens in the streets of Doha after the Qatari football team won the gold medal at the 15th Asian Games, 2006.

Emigration to the Gulf is seen as a major source of foreign exchange for Sri Lanka.

Nurses from Sri Lanka recruited by the Kuwaiti Ministry of Health, 2011.

citizens. Indeed, many officials may not be motivated to defend foreigners at the cost of local business interests.

The Sri Lankan state faces conflicting goals in mediating disputes between workers and sponsors in host countries. On the one hand, remittances are a primary source of foreign exchange, and making sure that workers receive their wages augments the inward flow of funds. On the other hand, advocating too energetically for labourers' rights could sour the market by making Sri Lankans 'difficult' to employ, which might result in sponsors seeking to recruit workers from other countries instead.

Under these circumstances, Sri Lanka has adopted a mixed strategy. Diplomatic missions often shelter and repatriate labourers in crisis. Sri Lanka has also negotiated labour agreements with host countries and has cautiously explored the possibility of multilateral agreements with other labour-sending nations. Labour law operates nationally but the labour market operates transnationally. Effectively, labour-sending nations cannot easily protect their citizens working abroad.

IDENTITY POLITICS IN A SEGMENTED LABOUR MARKET

In addition to the bifurcation between allocating public-sector jobs for citizens and private-sector jobs for guest workers, GCC labour markets are further segmented: employment sectors in various countries are dominated by people of particular ethnicities and nationalities. For example, Pashtuns from Pakistan and Afghanistan make up the majority of taxi drivers in Dubai, Filipinos work as concierges and run beauty parlours in Bahrain, and Indians, Pakistanis, and Bangladeshis do the majority of construction work in the Gulf. These divisions have arisen due to historic connections between particular manpower recruiting agencies in host and labour-sending countries, coupled with chain migration patterns whereby individuals bring their friends, relatives and countrymen to a particular employer, industry or destination country and thereby acquire a reputation of being the 'natural' community to do a particular sort of job.

Gender is another key element in allocating employment. Since the late 1980s, women have made up the majority of Sri Lanka's labour migrants. They accounted for 75 per cent of the migrant flow in the mid-1990s, down to just over 50 per cent by 2009 (SLBFE, 2009). Although a few Sri Lankan women find employment in garment factories in the Gulf, roughly 90 per cent work as domestic servants. Sri Lankan women share this market niche with women from Indonesia and the Philippines. Several other countries also send smaller numbers of female domestic servants to the Gulf.

Racial, ethnic, religious and national stereotypes predetermine wages. For example, in the UAE in 2004, housemaids from the Philippines were paid more than those from Indonesia, Sri Lanka, Ethiopia and Bangladesh, in that order; and sponsors paid job agencies more for recruiting Muslim than for non-Muslim employees.

Like their counterparts from India, Bangladesh and Pakistan, Sri Lankan male guest workers are engaged in construction and agriculture, cleaning and maintanence, or work as drivers, office assistants, shop clerks, nurses, doctors, engineers, technicians and teachers. In recent years, Sri Lankan officials have actively encouraged male migration. These male guest workers fill a diversity of roles, and skilled and unskilled labourers have made up roughly equal percentages of Sri Lanka's male migrants (each roughly 40 per cent) from 1994 to 2009.

Of the Sri Lankans working in the Gulf, less than 2 per cent are members of the professional, cosmopolitan, diasporic elite with business interests in the area, and less than 6 per cent are middle-level or clerical workers. Over 90 per cent are skilled, semi-skilled, or unskilled labourers or housemaids (male and female members of the transnational proletariat). These Sri Lankans work, remit money, and plan to return home once they have accomplished their financial goals.

LABOUR CONDITIONS ABROAD

Sri Lankans working abroad face a variety of labour conditions depending on their skills and qualifications. As mentioned, half of Sri Lanka's labour migrants are women working as domestic servants. As women in many industrialised and industrialising countries move into the workforce, they seek market proxies to perform domestic labour, often hiring women from less developed countries to perform these services. In contrast, in the Gulf, transnational domestic servants facilitate a socially significant lifestyle for their sponsors. Employing domestic servants has become a necessary element of household status in the Gulf. For example, 90 per cent of households in Kuwait employed at least one domestic servant in the late 2000s.

Although migrant domestic servants are referred to as 'housemaids,' these women's duties often exceed the narrow technical limits of the term. These domestic workers may be required to perform a variety of functions for their sponsors, including cooking, polishing, dusting, vacuuming, cleaning, washing and ironing the laundry, washing the cars, looking after children and elders, and taking care of pets, domestic animals, and gardens. Some homes have only one domestic servant; others have several.

Many migrant women borrow money from local moneylenders in order to pay the placement fees charged by manpower recruiting agencies, in addition to covering expenses for passports, medical exams and SLBFE insurance fees. Most women go abroad on two-year contracts. The labour contracts are written in English and Arabic, languages in which most housemaids are not highly literate. Contracts often specify the number of hours of work and days of holiday, but in practice housemaids are on call at all hours of the day, particularly during the Ramadan fasting period.

Most housemaids live in servants' quarters in their employers' residences. Throughout the world, live-in female servants have less autonomy and lower salaries than do women with part-time or live-out arrangements.

In the Gulf, domestic servants are often confined to the houses where they work, and are not allowed by employers (or by local gender norms) to travel alone or to associate freely with people outside the sponsor's family. Sponsors justify these restrictions by noting that they minimise the opportunities for employees to steal from or gossip about their employers, or to get into trouble. Many Sri Lankan women report that they value the 'protection' offered to their reputation by this work situation, but isolation can also lead to abuse and exploitation.

Male migrants usually pay higher agency fees than do female migrants, but their salaries are also greater. Because Sri Lankan men work in a wide range of skilled and unskilled positions, their work situations are more varied than those of housemaids. Many labourers live in barracks near their worksites, or in neighbourhoods of crowded, run-down buildings. Men have more chance to socialise with their compatriots and to get to know people from other countries than do female domestic workers. But because men's working hours are usually long and their days off are few, men's sociability revolves around their work site.

Sri Lankan professional level, middle level and clerical workers socialise with fellow countrymen and with members of the wider professional expatriate population. Relatively few in number, Sri Lankan professionals tend to integrate into the wider English-speaking expatriate population, networking with peers from India and other South Asian nations.

Workers encounter a number of difficulties while in the Gulf. The types of complaints most often received by the SLBFE in 2009 included breach of contract (3000), non-payment of wages (2000), lack of communication (1600), physical and sexual harassment (1500), sickness (1000), and not being sent back home after the completion of the contract (500). Comparing the total number of complaints (just over 12,000) with the total departures during 2009 for foreign employment (247,000) shows that fewer than 5 per cent of departing migrants, and fewer than 1 per cent of the total estimated stock of overseas migrant workers file complaints each year.

The relatively small number of complaints does not, however, reflect the totality of troubles encountered by migrants. The numbers reflect only the situations reported to consular offices and the SLBFE. Both men and women often borrow money to pay the agency fees to obtain their jobs abroad. These workers are thus virtually tied to their employment until they can pay back their debts. Due to the difficulty of changing sponsors while abroad, workers often accommodate to adverse labour conditions in order to keep their jobs and wages. Workers bear many minor and some major problems, and solve others informally rather than reporting them to the authorities. Migrant activists and advocates estimate that as many as 20 per cent of migrant workers encounter difficulties with their employment; of these problems, less than a quarter are addressed through official channels. Instead, migrants activate social networks and unofficial support structures to solve problems and weather crises while abroad.

ECONOMIC CONTEXT FOR SRI LANKAN TRANSNATIONAL MIGRATION

Many idiosyncratic factors motivate individuals' migration choices, but all decisions take place against a country-wide economic and political background. Despite its many development advantages and its high ranking in health, education, and other social indicators, Sri Lanka carries a high debt burden (due in part to military spending on its quarter-century-long civil war). Designed to reduce the national debt, neoliberal policies and structural adjustments have been imposed from outside and adopted voluntarily. The results have included cutting back government subsidies for essential goods, privatising government ventures, reducing public sector employment, and undercutting public expenditure for health care and other social services. These economic decisions have led to financial hardship for the poorer segment of Sri Lanka's population (estimated at 25–40 per cent of the people), among whom un- and underemployment are high, especially for women. Sri Lanka's transnational migrant workers come disproportionately from this poorer segment of society.

Migration not only alleviates unemployment among the nation's poor; it also provides hard currency with which Sri Lanka repays its international debts. Migrant labourers' remittances contribute significantly to Sri Lanka's foreign exchange earnings. In 2009, total remittances stood at Sri Lankan Rupees 383 billion or roughly US$3.4 billion. Nearly 60 percent of this total, Rupees 189 billion or US$2 billion came from the Gulf (SLBFE, 2009). In generating foreign earnings, in 2009 private remittances come first (47 per cent), followed by Sri Lanka's large garment industry (44 per cent) and the export of tea, rubber, and coconut. The country has a great financial stake in the remittances generated by migrant labourers, particularly those working in the Gulf.

Migrants registering with the SLBFE and travelling through the international airport come from most districts in Sri Lanka, though in the years up to and including 2009, few have come from the territories in the North held by the insurgent Liberation Tigers of Tamil Eelam. Low numbers of migrants also originate in the tea country or the far south. The greatest flow of migrants comes from Colombo district, followed by the districts of Gampaha, Kurunegala, and Kandy. Complex patterns in distributions of migrants' gender and skill-level appear in comparisons between rural and urban areas and between areas dominated by different religious and ethnic groups.

Remittances provide vital funds not only for the nation but also for many local families. Migrants from poor families consistently assert that they cannot make ends meet on local salaries, and that migration is their only available economic alternative. Slightly wealthier families suggest that although they can get by in Sri Lanka, they hope through migration to earn enough money for larger projects.

In 2010, Sri Lankans held placards outside the Saudi Embassy in Sri Lanka to demand that the life of a Sri Lankan housemaid convicted of killing an infant in Saudi Arabia be spared.

A Sri Lankan worker at the Shaybah oil site in Saudi Arabia, 2003.

99

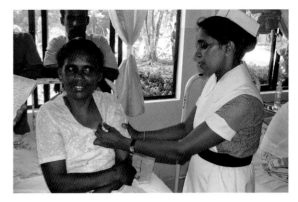

Sri Lankan housemaid L.T. Ariyawathi, who returned from Saudi Arabia with 24 nails inside her body, received treatment at a hospital in Batticaloa. She alleged that her Saudi employer had tortured her and drove nails into her body as punishment, 2010.

Locally available jobs are mostly poorly paid and temporary, particularly for women. Although transnational domestic workers earn only an average of US$ 100 a month while abroad, this is between two and five times what women could earn working in Sri Lanka, and equals or exceeds the wages earned by most village men. Migrant women often become the sole or most significant breadwinners for their families. Migrant men can also earn higher wages abroad than in Sri Lanka. Several studies suggest that each migrant supports four to five members of his or her family. The SLBFE estimates that in 1993, migrant labourers made up 9 per cent of the total number of employed Sri Lankans. By 2003, the figure stood at 14 per cent, and by 2009 it had jumped to 24 per cent. Thus, a significant and growing percentage of Sri Lankan families are directly dependent on the remittances from the Gulf.

Family motives for migration usually include getting out of debt, buying land, and building a house. Migrants (particularly women) also state that they would like to support their family's daily consumption needs, educate their children, and provide dowries for themselves or their daughters. Participants in the decision-making process (undergone repeatedly for migrants who return several times to the Gulf) weigh financial necessity and household improvements against separation, incursion of loans, and alternate arrangements for childcare.

SOCIAL CONSEQUENCES OF MIGRATION

Migrant workers who earn less than a particular threshold cannot bring their families with them to the Gulf, and thus most Sri Lankan guest workers are separated from their family members for the duration of their contract. These lengthy absences, particularly of migrant mothers, create a number of social challenges.

The family is a key institution supporting migration. Decisions about migration are made collectively, and family members often enable migration in a number of ways. Relatives in the extended family may find jobs for each other abroad. Migrants often pay fees to manpower recruitment agencies, and family members are instrumental in gathering the money or providing collateral for loans. In addition, family members enable workers to go abroad by filling in for them on the home front. This is especially important when women leave behind young children. In these cases, fathers

take over some of the domestic duties, but most often a grandmother or other female relative provides primary childcare. Migration strengthens extended families by actively reinforcing kinship bonds through the exchange of goods and services within the family.

As Sri Lankan families have adjusted to enable migration, gender roles have adapted and changed. After more than thirty years of female migration, men have assumed more care work and women have taken on some breadwinning responsibilities. Male migration has also affected gender roles, as their spouses at home have borne greater responsibilities in managing the family's interface with the wider world.

In many migration streams, migrants absorb cultural traits from abroad. Which host country they visit makes a difference in this regard. For example, Sri Lankan returnees often construct new houses with their earnings. Migrants who have been to the Gulf construct standard Sri Lankan homes with cement block walls and tile roofs. In contrast, migrants who have worked in Italy construct houses with distinctly Italian architectural styles. Key to this difference is the extent to which migrants are offered the opportunity to integrate in the host country. Working-class migrants in the Gulf are at best offered the opportunity to join a family as a servant. They are not offered a desirable place in the wider society, and thus their orientation remains toward their Sri Lankan family and culture. In contrast, many migrants who journey to Italy do so with the hope of settling there.

Current trends suggest that the next generation of Sri Lankan labour migrants will contain more men, that migrants will leave at younger ages and before marriage, that they will journey to destinations other than the Gulf, and that they will aspire to emigrate rather than sojourn abroad. In the future, care of children and aged will become a more significant issue than it is at present. Sri Lanka is currently undergoing a demographic transformation from a pyramid-shaped population structure with many younger people and few elders, to a columnar population structure characteristic of most developed nations. This demographic shift may eventually curtail migration or prompt the burgeoning of collective elder care arrangements such as nursing homes. As the percentage of elders increases in the society, there will be fewer members of the subsequent generations to look after them. In the future, prospective migrants may have to decide whether to work abroad and earn money for their family, or to remain in Sri Lanka to look after their elders. But as long as the Gulf continues to export petroleum to an oil-hungry world, migration from Sri Lanka to West Asia is likely to continue.

Michele Ruth Gamburd

Funds remitted from the Gulf enable female labour migrants to buy land and build homes for their families in Sri Lanka. The local expression 'Housemaid made house' sums up the situation below.

UNITED STATES OF AMERICA

THE UNITED STATES today is home to a small but growing population of Sri Lankans from Sinhalese, Tamil, Moor, Burgher and Malay ethnic communities, among others. Sri Lanka's 'best and brightest' have had a long history of taking up temporary residences in North America and Europe for advanced education and professional employment. Since the mid-1980s this profile has changed as a greater number of Sri Lankans, primarily Tamils, fled a lengthy civil war in their homeland to seek political asylum abroad, especially in Europe and Canada. Sri Lankans in the United States have shown themselves to be a versatile group of generally well educated and solidly middle class families active in the educational, medical, scientific, political, social, commercial, artistic and philanthropic realms of the American society.

HISTORICAL ORIGINS

Sri Lankan Americans descend from a variety of ethnic groups, and the Sinhalese make up roughly half of the community in the United States. Sri Lankan immigrants have been differentiated from other South Asian ethnic groups in public records in the United States only since 1975. Earlier immigrant Sri Lankans were classified either as 'other Asian' or 'South Asian', and the latter description remains on many data-collecting forms today. The first Sri Lankans may have arrived towards the end of the 19th century along with roughly 2,000 'other Asians', according to US immigration records—but it is impossible to confirm this. In 1975, fewer than 500 Sri Lankans immigrated to the United States (*American Fact Finder*, US Census Bureau, n.d.).

Violence at home intensified in the 1980s and caused many Sri Lankan Tamils to seek refuge abroad. Few arrived in the United States compared to other countries such as the United Kingdom, India and Canada. Of the estimated 25,000 Sri Lanka-born living in the United States in 2000, roughly 40 per cent were naturalised US citizens who mostly entered before 1989; by contrast, nearly three-quarters of non-naturalised citizens entered after 1990, when the number of Sri Lankan asylum seekers escalated as the danger of civil strife in their homeland grew stronger (*American Fact Finder*, US

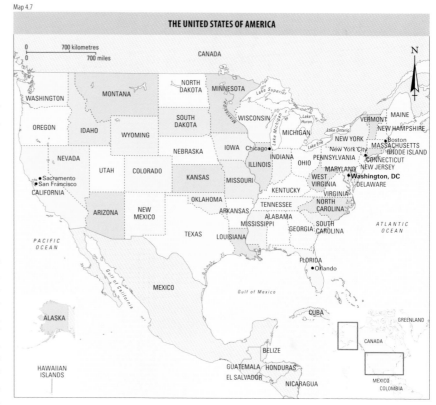

Map 4.7

THE UNITED STATES OF AMERICA

Census Bureau, n.d.). Notably, between 1989 and 1990, this number increased by a remarkable 27 fold in a 12 month span.

Over the past decade, an average of 1,300 refugees per year (mostly Tamils) have been granted asylum in the United States [with the exception of 2004–05, in which relatively small numbers were admitted for reasons that are not clear (*Statistics*, United Nations High Commissioner for Refugees, 2011)]. Various estimates suggest that roughly 35 to 40 per cent of the Sri Lankan American diaspora today is of Tamil origin, with the remainder largely being Sinhalese. Of the two groups, the former tends to hold a higher profile both within and outside of the United States for their political activism.

SETTLEMENT PATTERNS AND POPULATION CHARACTERISTICS

Sri Lankan Americans make up around 6 per cent of the entire Sri Lankan diaspora. The number of Tamil refugees accepted by the United States remains small especially when compared to Canada and Western Europe. Yet, notwithstanding stringent regulations on immigration, over the past 10 years the Sri Lankan population in the United States has grown by an estimated 60 per cent. Many newcomers settle near their corresponding religious communities, whether Buddhist or Hindu. In 2009, the top three states of permanent residence were California,

Don Francis Arichi from Sri Lanka takes his citizenship oath as more than 2,700 people are sworn in as US citizens during naturalisation ceremonies on 9 April 2009 in Montebello, California.

Sri Lankan fans celebrate during their match against New Zealand during the Pearls Cup T20 Series cricket game held at the Central Broward Regional Park in Fort Lauderdale, Florida, 2010.

Kandyan-style wedding portrait of Sri Lankan-American Manjula Dissanayake and Chara Gunawardhana, 2012.

The Sri Lanka Medical Association of North America booth at the 35th Annual Sri Lanka Day in Denville, New Jersey, 2010.

New York and Maryland, followed by New Jersey and Texas (*American Fact Finder*, US Census Bureau, n.d.). Sizeable populations exist in or near cities such as Boston, Chicago, Houston, Los Angeles, Las Vegas, Miami, Newark, New York, Seattle and San Diego, many of which already had established Indian communities. Of these, the New York City metropolitan area claims the largest community of Sri Lankans as well as the highest number of legal permanent resident immigrants. 'Little Sri Lanka' in Staten Island, New York City, is one of the largest Sri Lankan communities outside the homeland itself. Central New Jersey and Los Angeles metropolitan areas claim the next largest communities. Like their Indian counterparts, the Sri Lankan diaspora in the United States tends to be comprised mainly of highly educated professionals. Of those born in Sri Lanka, and over 25 years of age, more than half hold bachelors and professional or graduate degrees. The vast majority speaks a language other than English at home, but the same number also converses in English fluently. Sri Lankan families earn about one-fifth higher than the national median family income and have lower poverty rates than national averages as well. The majority of immigrants work in managerial and professional occupations in education, health, social, scientific and services industries (*American Fact Finder*, US Census Bureau, n.d.).

Many Sri Lankan Americans are successfully involved in business and demonstrate a strong sense of innovation and philanthropy (indeed, Sri Lankans in general were deemed the eighth most generous people in the world, according to the *World Giving Index* by the British-based Charities Aid Foundation). For example, the well-known non-profit organisation, The Indus Entrepreneurs (TiE), was started by South Asian-origin entrepreneurs and professionals in Silicon Valley with the intention of fostering free enterprise around the globe through networking, affiliation and intellectual capital pools.

ASSOCIATIONS

A growing number of Sri Lankan associations, language schools, charities, religious and cultural centres contribute to fostering a sense of collective identity and encouraging

the preservation of cultural traditions alongside the incorporation of American values.

Some of the earliest Sri Lankan associations in the United States were formed in the 1970s, and were primarily aimed at promoting the welfare of expatriate members. The very first Sri Lankan-American community organisation—Sri Lanka Association—was established in New York. The inaugural meeting on 2 October 1971 was attended by renowned Sri Lankan diplomat, Hamilton Shirley Amerasinghe, as well as Ceylon's High Commissioner to Canada, William Silva. The association remains an important forum for social and fraternal activities among members, and encourages the retention of Sri Lankan culture among younger generations. It hosts a number of events ranging from annual Christmas gala to dinner dances, Sri Lanka Day celebrations, picnics, sports days and Sri Lankan New Year festivities. Besides serving the largest Sri Lankan community in the US, the association also participates in charity activities and actively donates to government-recognised organisations in the homeland.

A similar organisation was formed in 1975 in the American capital. The Sri Lanka Association Washington, D.C. (SLAWDC) facilitates social and cultural interaction alongside the preservation of traditions. It organises three main events every year: the Sinhala-Tamil New Year in April, the Washington-New York Annual Cricket Encounter in the summer, and the New Year's Eve Gala. The association is also home to a plethora of smaller events including an annual children's Christmas party, sports tournaments, destination outings, food fairs, youth dances and career-oriented resources such as guidance seminars and professional events by notable speakers—all of which are intended to appeal to a diverse body of

members. While the organisation eschews political affiliation, it has from time to time participated in drought relief, medical assistance or charitable giving events for compatriots in Sri Lanka. An affiliate organisation, the tax-exempt Sri Lanka Association of Greater Washington (SLAGW), was set up in 2001 to field charitable and educational activities, and has received generous community support since its inception.

In recent years, the number of Sri Lankan organisations in the US has proliferated. That augmentation is largely the product of an increase in the size of the Sri Lankan-American population. While it is true that the growth of ethnic conflict in Sri Lanka has resulted in some Tamil emigrants distancing themselves from pan-Sri Lankan associations, at the same time there have been efforts by these organisations to foster a sense of fraternity. Amongst these include initiatives by the Sri Lanka Association of New England (SLANE). The organisation, created by 50 Sri Lankan Americans in 1998 in Cambridge, Massachusetts, has sought to promote friendship, goodwill, peace and unity among the Sri Lankan community within and in neighbouring regions of the state. SLANE has attempted to raise public awareness of and interest in Sri Lanka's political and economic situation; to welcome new arrivals from Sri Lanka, especially

students; to commemorate important national events; and to provide a forum for social, cultural and welfare community activities. Besides Christmas and National Day celebrations, the organisation hosts an annual Discover Sri Lanka project organised by young members for children to learn about their heritage in fun and interactive ways. The project simultaneously collects supplies to deliver to a school in Sri Lanka, and is one of three projects involving Sri Lankan-American youth in community service.

A distinctive feature of some of the more recent Sri Lankan American associations is the tendency to concentrate on educational and charitable activities. For example, the Educate Lanka Foundation(ELF), launched in 2007 by two young Sri Lankan student expatriates at the University of Maryland, has sought to empower Sri Lankan students through education. With advisory guidance from two Sri Lankan-American professors and the greater Washington, D.C. area Sri Lankan community, ELF has developed a unique web-centric peer-to-peer model to enable underprivileged students in Sri Lanka to continue their education through micro-financing. The foundation locates Sri Lankans around the world and awards individually generated scholarships to academically promising students. Currently, ELF

Cricket match organised by the Sri Lanka Association Washington, D.C. (SLAWDC).

Sri Lankan American Association of Houston (SLAAH) advertising a ballet workshop.

Dance performance by the Sri Lanka Foundation (SLF) at Santa Monica, California.

Sri Lankan cultural parade down the Third Street Promenade.

SRI LANKA FOUNDATION (SLF)

Located in Los Angeles, California, the SLF mission is to connect and aid Sri Lankan communities worldwide and advance international awareness of the cultural, artistic, philosophical and technical merits of Sri Lanka.

The non-profit organisation was created in 2003 by the well known Sri Lankan-American doctor Walter Jayasinghe. The SLF publishes *Expatriate Sri Lankan Good News*, a magazine that circulates to more than 10,000 Sri Lankan households around the globe and publicises relevant cultural and social events. An electronic version of the publication is available on the foundation's website alongside world news,

political events, analyses, editorials and opinions, among other categories that may be of interest to the Sri Lankan diaspora.

The SLF also hosts an annual one-day Sri Lanka Day Expo event on the Santa Monica Third Street Promenade, featuring Sri Lankan musicians, dancers, food and businesses. The expo attracted nearly a 100,000 Sri Lankans and Americans from around the world, and a cultural parade known as 'PERAHERA' was the main attraction. Additionally, the foundation holds an annual award ceremony in Los Angeles— the Sri Lanka Foundation Awards—to honour deserving members of the expatriate community in all disciplines. As part of a youth outreach focus,

the organisation hosts the Youth Expatriate Sri Lankans (YES!) World Youth Conference to foster networking, appreciation of Sri Lankan culture, and the development of plans to aid the island nation. To address other aspects of Sri Lankan assimilation, the SLF stages an annual Miss Sri Lanka-America beauty pageant and fashion show to showcase Sri Lankan ethnic beauty to the American mainstream. Another popular event is the Cultural Concert, which brings well known Sri Lankan performers before appreciative audiences. Finally, the foundation maintains social networking sites to facilitate community contact via platforms such as Facebook, MySpace, Flickr and Second Life.

Christmas nativity play by the Sri Lanka Association of New York (SLANY), 2010.

Scholarship recipients of the Educate Lanka Foundation (ELF) at Omanthai Central College, Vavuniya, 2013.

sponsors over 450 students of all ages, religion and ethnic groups in Sri Lanka, and has contributed over US$120,000 in scholarships. ELF also possesses a strong network of over a hundred volunteers both in the United States and Sri Lanka. The foundation participates in educational infrastructure development and other projects that improve the quality of education in the most needed areas of the country. In May 2011, ELF was among a handful of organisations selected to be part of US Secretary of State Hillary Clinton's 'Global Diaspora Forum', during which its financing platform was widely acknowledged as a successful working model.

Another organisation that has focused on educational initiatives is the New England Lanka Academy (NELA). The academy provides a gateway to Sri Lankan arts and sciences. The institution brings together academics, intellectuals and experts to share their experiences with the public, facilitating connections between specialists in the United States and their counterparts in Sri Lanka. It also aims to promote interaction and collaboration with the general public. Examples of activities include workshops on land robotics and Sri Lankan performing arts, hosted at Harvard University, and on Sri Lankan drumming and dancing, at Clark University.

DIASPORA POLITICS

While Sri Lankans identify themselves along various ethnic, linguistic, religious and regional identities, Tamils from the war-torn north and northeastern areas of the island have come to identify themselves as a distinct community both at home and abroad (Srikandarajah, 2005). Often sympathetic to the LTTE in the past, the Tamil diaspora has significant lobbies in the United States and generally maintains a higher profile around the world over their mostly Sinhalese counterparts.

For its part, the United States Department of State designated the LTTE, notorious for their use of suicide bombers, as a foreign terrorist organisation in 1997. The State Department then altered this characterisation to 'Specially Designated Global Terrorist' (SDGT) in

2001. One consequence of this has been that the United States declines to extend asylum to any of its members. Combined with the more stringent overall immigration procedures, these designations likely account for the far fewer numbers of Tamil immigrants admitted into the United States especially when compared to its northern neighbour, Canada.

Overall, transnational ties, political discourse and influence within a widespread Tamil diaspora were a critical mechanism for strengthening support for the Tamil cause within the homeland and direct Sri Lankan politics. The Tamil diaspora was intimately involved in the insurgency, using technology and social structures to mobilise and organise a specific diasporic identity that was strengthened over time (Fair, 2005). Tamils all over the globe tend to view themselves as members of a single diaspora shaped by the politics within their home country. Shared grievances linked to ethnic identity, subordination and war tactics have, at times, attracted the attention of both the media and authorities in their countries of residences, which in turn has led to some clashes with local governments.

PRO-LTTE NETWORKS IN THE UNITED STATES

The political activism of the Tamil American diaspora is undoubtedly shaped by the presence of well over 200,000

Demonstrators gathered at a park across the World Bank building in Washington, D.C. call for an end to the alleged genocide of Tamils by the Sri Lankan government, April 2009.

BUDDHIST VIHARAS, MEDITATION CENTRES & SOCIETIES

The Bhavana Society

Founded in 1985, the Bhavana Society began building a meditation centre in a mountainous forest region of West Virginia—not too far from Washington, D.C. The centre was opened in 1988, and expanded in the years that followed. With the aim of protecting the Theravada forest meditation tradition within the context of Western culture, the Society provides a monastery for ordained monks and nuns to live, as well as training and ordination for lay candidates. It also offers meditation retreats for the public, and is home to long-term resident laypersons.

The founding abbot, Venerable Bhante Henepola Gunaratana, was born in rural Sri Lanka and was fully ordained as a monk at age 20, in 1947. Popularly known as 'Bhante G,' the internationally-recognised author and teacher spent five years doing missionary work among the *harijans* (Untouchables) of India and 10 years in Malaysia before coming to the United States in 1968. He has worked as a chaplain at American University, where he obtained his PhD, and served as President of the Washington, D.C., Buddhist Vihara. He is the highest-ranking monk of his sect in North America.

The New England Buddhist Vihara and Meditation Center

Led by several Sri Lankan Theravada monks with experience practicing and teaching Buddhism and meditation techniques in Sri Lanka, South Korea and the United States, the centre is open to anyone who seeks solutions to life's problems in a peaceful and understanding environment regardless of personal beliefs. Registered as an official non-profit organisation in Framingham, Massachusetts, the centre emphasises loving kindness, compassion and caring. Along with meditation classes, it holds discussion sessions of Buddhist philosophy and counseling sessions based on Dhamma teachings and special instructional classes for teenagers and children. The centre occupies a 140-year old house, home to four resident monks, and serves over 100 New England families including those of Sri Lankan, Vietnamese, Bengali, Indian, Cambodian and Euro-American descent.

Ohio Buddhist Vihara

This Cincinnati, Ohio, temple lists its primary objectives as providing for the spiritual, religious and educational needs of men and women of all faiths. It is serving the diverse spiritual needs of Buddhists and non-Buddhists alike; teaching and practicing meditation techniques; and providing a cultural and social centre for Buddhists and non-Buddhist attendees. Inaugurated in October 2003, the Vihara is involved in educational and humanitarian relief activities in Sri Lanka, such as providing scholarships to local students as well as offering aid and helping reconstruction following the 2004 South Asian tsunami that devastated the island. Due to the growing attendance of worshippers, including the attendance and interest of Christians and other non-Buddhists, as well as Buddhists from all over the mid-western region, the temple intends to expand its physical accommodations.

Houston Buddhist Vihara

Founded in 1988, this Houston, Texas Vihara offers Dhamma classes and Pali (the language of ancient texts of the Theravada tradition) lessons to enable study. Other practices include instruction of Abhidhamma, an in-depth metaphysical analysis of the mind and mental factors to advance understanding of Buddha's teachings; chanting; and the observance of eight precepts over the more commonly held five (abstinence from killing living beings, from taking others' belongings, from sexual misconduct, from intoxicating drugs and drink). The stated purpose of the temple is to promote Buddhist practice and insight in the minds of people; to advance cultural understanding; to advocate peace among nations; and to propagate places for Buddhist fellowship. Ministering to a sizable Sri Lankan expatriate community, the scholarly venue offers classes in English and Vietnamese, and has opened its doors to all communities.

In 2005, about 175 students, faculty and residents were involved in a candlelight vigil on the campus of Arizona State University that was sponsored by the Sri Lankan Student Association, in remembrance of the victims of the tsunami.

Minnesota Buddhist Vihara

The Minneapolis-based Vihara has affiliate temples in North and South Dakota, Iowa, Wisconsin and Nebraska, all founded by the Minnesotan Temple abbot and President the Venerable Witiyala Seewalie Thera, established since 2004. The mission of the headquarters is to create a peaceful and harmonious world. Venerable Seewalie also serves as a volunteer chaplain in the local police department and holds monthly meditation sessions for penitentiary inmates. To acknowledge his services in disseminating the teachings of Buddha, he was invited by Sri Lankan president Mahinda Rajapaksa to visit the president's official residence in Sri Lanka. Temple classes are given in epistemology, theory of knowledge, ethics and basic teachings. Other services include counseling, running a Dhamma school, Dhamma discussions, *sil* observations, meditation sessions, visitations, giving blessings and offerings, opening a meditation retreat centre, providing language training and cultural activities to all communities in the area.

Berkeley Buddhist Vihara

Registered as a religious non-profit organisation in 2002, the Bay-area Vihara coordinated with another Sri Lankan temple, the nearby Dharmapala Institute, to use local connections for rescue, clean-up and reconstruction efforts following the 2004 Boxing Day tsunami through a Disaster Relief Fund. Together, the temples collected food, clothing and medical supply donations, helmed toy and backpack drives, and organised a team of doctors to visit remote villages of Sri Lanka. Donations and support from the surrounding community were received from groups such as the Church of Latter Day Saints, local elementary schools, the Jain community and the San Jose Sikh Gurwara Community. Weekly activities at the temple include a Sinhala-language Sunday School for children in addition to annual Wesak and Poson ceremonies, Vas Aradhana, Katina Pinkam, Atavisi Buddha *puja* and New Year's ceremonies alongside monthly sermons, Dhamma discussions and special Buddha *puja*.

Georgia Buddhist Vihara

Open in Atlanta, Georgia since the summer of 2000, the Vihara serves the religious needs of the region through daily chanting, *puja* and meditation, weekly Vipassana Meditation Dhamma school, Poya (Uposatha) full moon observance, Dhamma discussion and a meditation retreat alongside traditional temple services. Their aim is to educate the young and old in the cultural practices of Sri Lanka and other Buddhist countries, as well as encourage the practice of *dana* (generosity), *sila* (morality) and *bhavana* (meditation). The Vihara administers to Atlanta's large and growing South Asian population of well over 100,000.

Sri Lankan-Americans form a human-chain outside the Buddhist vihara in the Queens borough of New York City to pass along food and clothing for tsunami victims in Sri Lanka.

Tamils living in primarily the Greater Toronto area of Ontario, Canada—home to the largest Tamil community outside of Sri Lanka and India. Both within Canada and beyond, many Tamil organisations were set up explicitly to enable the LTTE's global outreach. Diasporic political activism was often realised through associations that worked to raise awareness of what was sometimes referred to as Tamil 'genocide' in Sri Lanka and aired grievances against anti-Tamil activities in the Sri Lankan capital, Colombo.

In Washington, Tamil expatriates formed lobbying groups such as Americans for Peace in Sri Lanka and Tamils for Justice. The New York Ilankai Tamil Sangam, the most active group representing Tamils in the United States, was formed in the aftermath of the 1977 anti-Tamil riots in Sri Lanka and was believed to be an umbrella organisation for the LTTE. Similarly, the World Tamil Coordinating Committee (WTCC) in the United States was revealed to be a satellite organisation of the LTTE, when the FBI arrested New York resident Karunakaran Kandasamy. He was reportedly orchestrating US-based LTTE support by using various charity fundraisers in the wake of the tsunami as a guise to channel funds through the WTCC. This was followed by earlier arrests of several Sri Lankan expatriates in Maryland, who were subsequently imprisoned and deported for providing material support to the LTTE. Other charities, such as the US branch of the Tamil Rehabilitation Organisation (TRO), was shut down by the US Treasury Department for their support to the LTTE.

Before the LTTE was designated as a terrorist organisation, a number of wealthy Tamil Americans and a network of pro-LTTE professionals gave generous support to the group. After 1997, such support necessarily assumed a covert profile in the United States, though it remained prolific in Canada. All US-based organisations naturally looked northward for funds and moral support. Taking advantage of the easy access afforded by the open border between the United States and Canada, American organisers mobilised Canadian LTTE sympathisers to travel by bus to Washington to participate in rallies and protests. Further punctuating the proximity between American and Canadian Tamils, New York-based lawyer Visvanathan Rudrakumaran—who maintained close ties with government officials in both countries—coordinated the Canadian Supreme Court defense of a notable leader of the LTTE imprisoned in Canada.

Yet, at certain times, the Tamil diaspora has exerted influence by pulling back funding to encourage the LTTE to seek out peace with Colombo. As the LTTE appeared to lose its military strategy, the diplomatic calculation of the pro-Tamil Tiger ideology grew more concrete. In a May 2010 interview with the well-known blog *Politico*'s Laura Rozen in Washington, D.C., Sri Lankan Minister of Foreign Affairs, Gamini Lakshman Peiris, summarised the current situation:

The war has come to an end in Sri Lanka, the military action is over, and the LTTE cannot rearm and regroup to fight a war again on the shores of Sri Lanka, but that doesn't mean that they have no influence elsewhere. The huge financial resources they have accumulated over ...[a] quarter of a century are still at their disposal, and they have a very sophisticated communication network. The diaspora is still very active in Western capitals and multilateral institutions, and they're basically waging an economic war with Sri Lanka—their activities have been transferred from the field of battle to the field of diplomacy.

According to the *Asian Tribune* (4 June 2010), the Tamil lobby reportedly infiltrated rights groups such as Human Rights Watch, Amnesty International and the International Crisis Group to gain access to principal agencies like the US State Department, Congressional committees, and even the Congressional Research Service and the Library of Congress. Well-educated siblings of Tamil expatriates held intern or staff positions at various offices of influential Senators and Congresspersons, and sympathisers occupied key posts for access. The newspaper took aim at the Sri Lankan embassy in particular, citing miscalculation of LTTE influence in the United States and decrying their failure to counter LTTE-backed propaganda. To a large extent, embassy diplomats reportedly outsourced their public and media relations responsibilities to a high-priced Washington, D.C., lobbying service in a last-ditch attempt to burnish the image of Sri Lanka in the eyes of Washington (*Asian Tribune*, 10 August 2008).

The non-governmental organisation (NGO) sector, which influences Washington's foreign policy agenda, and various US government agencies became sites of introduction to the Tamil narrative of brutal Sinhalese domination. This led to a seeming departure from standard procedures. While the State Department viewed the LTTE as a terrorist organisation, it did not seek to eliminate the group as it did with Al Qaeda. Instead, the American government hoped to use the LTTE as a pressure group to make changes in the Sri Lankan polity (US Senate Committee on Foreign Relations 2009). Another mechanism to advance the LTTE agenda in government and steer the perception of the Colombo administration's policy is through making use of bodies such as the United States Tamil Political Action Council. Meanwhile, former US Department of Justice attorney-turned-lobbyist Bruce Fein, once linked to the Tamils for Justice/Justice for Tamils organisation, publicly spearheaded a lengthy mission to remove the LTTE from the State Department's global terrorist list.

Yet in Washington, not all activities on behalf of Sri Lankans are organised by high-profile activist groups. For example, nationals of Sinhalese, Tamil and Muslim backgrounds and other supporters gathered near the

Sri Lankan Tamils in the United States organised several protests during the final days of the civil war in Sri Lanka.

NOTABLE SRI LANKAN-AMERICANS

Ananda Coomaraswamy
(1877–1947). Born in Sri
Lanka but raised in England,
Ananda Coomaraswamy was
a philosopher recognised
for his exploration of
the metaphysical realm.
Although he studied natural
sciences at university,
eventually earning a
doctorate in Ceylonese mineralogy, he went on to
cultivate an influence in the art world. With the aim
of introducing the West to Indian Art, he went on
to serve as curator of the Boston Fine Arts Museum
in 1917, where he remained until his death. There,
he amassed the first large collection of Indian Art in
the United States. Coomaraswamy made significant
contributions to the fields of philosophy, literature
and religion, and is credited with founding an esoteric
philosophical movement, Perennialism, alongside
French metaphysicist René Guénon and Swiss-
German philosopher Frithjof Schuon. Reportedly
fluent in 12 languages, Coomaraswamy used
intellectual exploration and anti-imperialist conviction
to build a two-way bridge between West and East that
served to cultivate appreciation for the richness of the
Indian heritage.

Muhammad Raheem Bawa Muhaiyaddeen

(Unknown–1986). The Tamil-
speaking Sufi mystic, Bawa
Muhaiyaddeen, retains a
numinous aura. Reportedly
emerging from the jungles of
Sri Lanka in the 1940s, Bawa
Muhaiyaddeen travelled to
various shrines in northern
Sri Lanka performing acts of
medical and spiritual healing. Invited to Philadelphia
in 1971, Bawa Muhaiyadden remained in the United
States teaching the doctrine of universal peace,
unity and equality until his death. People from all
walks of life would gather to hear him speak, and he
became known for doling out pacifist-oriented advice
to world leaders during the Iranian Hostage Crisis
in the late 1970s. A Philadelphia mosque bearing
his name continues to be a place of pilgrimage for
Muslims, Christians and followers of other religions
who admire his efforts towards forging unity through
understanding and empathy.

Cyril Ponnamperuma (1923–94). Born in Galle,
Sri Lanka, and educated in India and the United
Kingdom, Cyril Ponnamperuma researched the origin
of life at the University of California, Berkeley, where

he received his doctorate in 1962. The following
year, he took over the Chemical Evolution Division
at NASA, contributing directly to the Project Apollo,
Viking and Voyager space programs. His analysis of
moon dust for the Apollo Program earned him cover
stories in magazines and newspapers such as *Time*
and *Newsweek*. Ponnamperuma was associated with
a variety of academic institutions ranging from the
Arthur C. Clarke Centre for Modern Technologies in
Sri Lanka to the Chinese Academy of Sciences, the
World Academy of Art and Science, the Atomic Energy
Commission of India, United Nations Educational,
Scientific and Cultural Organisation (UNESCO) and the
University of Maryland. In 1994, he suffered a heart
attack while working at his laboratory for Chemical
Evolution at the University of Maryland in College

Park. Ponnamperuma
was widely known for
his sanguine belief that a
chemical explanation for
the origin of life could be
found. His *New York Times*
obituary stated that the
Sri Lankan-born scientist
had 'no doubt at all' that
life could some day be
created in a laboratory.

Rosemary Rogers (1932–). Dubbed 'the Queen of
Historical Romance' à la Harlequin style, Rosemary
Jansz was born in Ceylon to wealthy Dutch-
Portuguese settlers. She moved to London and
later to California. Putting pen to paper, Rogers, first
manuscript, 'Sweet Savage Love,' rose to the top of the
bestseller charts in record time. Known for themes
of violence against women, exotic travel and rags-
to-riches storylines, Rogers asserted that she herself
was her heroine and that her life story could easily be
one of her own plots. Having sold millions of novels
around the globe, Rogers continues to write and
dominate the world of historical romance.

Stanley Jeyaraja Tambiah (1929–). After being
raised in a Tamil Christian family and attending
the University of Ceylon, Tambiah earned a PhD
in anthropology from Cornell University. His field
work shifted from Sri Lanka to Thailand and back
to Sri Lanka, where ethnic conflict engaged his
interest. Fascinated by the interplay between
magic, science and religion, Tambiah studied the
role of competition between religious and ethnic
identities in the long-lasting conflict on the island,
and his original interpretations collectively formed
an invaluable contribution to Asian scholarship.
Tambiah served in various academic posts ranging
from a UNESCO teaching assistant in Thailand and the

National Research Council's
Committee for International
Conflict Resolution, to
positions at the Universities
of Ceylon, Cambridge,
Chicago and King's College
before joining the faculty
at Harvard University in
1976. The world-renowned
anthropologist has been
awarded three honorary
doctorates, prestigious fellowships and international
acclaim. In 2005, the Harvard Foundation
commissioned his portrait to grace the walls of the
institution at which he served.

Ananda W. P. Guruge (1928–). The Sri Lankan
diplomat, author and Buddhist leader graduated from
the University of Ceylon at the age of 19 and went
on to earn a PhD from the University of London. By
23, he took the Ceylon civil service exam and began
his career as a diplomat. He served as Sri Lankan
ambassador to France and the United States, and
then as a senior special adviser to the director-general
of UNESCO. Guruge is proficient in English, Sinhala,
French, Pali, Sanskrit, Tamil and Hindi, and has held a
variety of academic and leadership posts at the Los
Angeles-based University of the West, California State
University Fullerton, and the World Fellowship of
Buddhists, in addition to being Chairman of the World
Buddhist University Council, Patron of the European
Buddhist Union and winner of the 2004 Sri Lankan
Foundation Lifetime Achievement Award. He has
written over 50 books in English and Sinhala as well
as more than 175 research papers on Asian history,
Buddhism and education.

Danielle de Niese (1979–) Reportedly the youngest
singer to participate in the Young Artists Studio
at the Metropolitan Opera, Danielle de Niese is a
lyric soprano who developed a successful operatic
career from a very young age. Of Sri Lankan Burgher
heritage, she was only nine when she became the

youngest winner of the
Young Talent Time—an
Australian TV talent
competition. She moved
to America from Australia
as a teenager. Danielle
de Niese is renowned
for her performance as
Cleopatra in David McVicar's
staging of *Giulio Cesare* at
Glyndebourne in 2005, as
well as for various other
operatic productions.

White House in 2010 to protest the LTTE's treatment
of Tamil civilians. The *Asian Tribune* reported the
large gathering as assembling on 'short notice and little
organisation', and providing a visible counter to the
propaganda of 'pro-LTTE professionals and activists'
(*Asian Tribune*, 22 February 2009) in America. Congress
also funds groups such as The Asia Foundation, which
has occupied a 'quiet but important' role in strengthening
democratic institutions in the country and supporting the
Sri Lankan government long before the civil war broke
out and the Tamil diaspora took shape (Committee on
Foreign Relations United States Senate, 2009).

DIASPORA INFLUENCE ON US-SRI LANKAN RELATIONS

While Western countries with large Tamil diasporas grew
critical of Sri Lanka's handling of the war and human
rights record, non-traditional, no-strings-attached
sources of aid and investment—like China—stepped
in to fill the void left by Western donors that preferred
to qualify the terms of their loans (Mendis, 2010). This
shift was charted by a Senate Foreign Relations report,
the Kerry-Lugar Report, which noted the decisive
role China played in determining the outcome of the
conflict by providing massive funding to the Sri Lankan

Former US President Bill Clinton, US Senator Hillary Rodham Clinton and Buddhist monks listen as Venerable Pandit Piyatissa speaks during a visit to the New York Buddhist Vihara, 2004.

government that was then used to defeat the LTTE. Observing that the political environment in Sri Lanka was 'not as black and white as many outside observers believe', the report quoted Sri Lankan government officials citing American refusal to 'help Sri Lanka finish the war against the LTTE', for pushing the country to develop relationships with countries such as Burma, China, Iran and Libya (Committee on Foreign Relations United States Senate, 2009). Concerns for human rights and other humanitarian issues, whether overstated or legitimate, led the United States to curb aid to the Sri Lankan government. Colombo found it difficult to deal with the 'stick' approach employed by Washington and relations between the two countries soured. The report closed by noting that future US policy toward Sri Lanka ought not to be dominated by 'a single agenda' which 'shortchanges US geostrategic interests in the region' (Committee on Foreign Relations United States Senate, 2009).

In sum, although the civil war in Sri Lanka officially came to an end in 2009, the diaspora's self-perception remains largely ethno-centred. Despite residing mainly in liberal host countries, the community tends to stay tied to the traditional loyalties and social frameworks of their homeland. This highly politicised atmosphere is what migrants are welcomed into, which, while easing the process of integration into the local community, often simultaneously assimilates new arrivals into an anti-Colombo, pro-Tamil movement. However, in comparison to the Tamil Canadian diaspora (whose activities have received much scrutiny from Canadian media and authorities), the Tamil-American community goes largely unnoticed by the press. The United States'

early action to designate the LTTE as a terrorist organisation and prohibit fundraising on their behalf likely discouraged the formation of a robust and overtly politically active Tamil diaspora like that in Canada, which held no such view or prohibition against LTTE support until much later.

Participation rates in events such as protests and demonstrations were far fewer in the United States than in other countries with established Tamil diasporas. This is probably partly due to the fact that a larger percentage of Sri Lankan Americans arrived before 1990, looking for economic opportunity rather than political asylum. These immigrant professionals escaped the bulk of the violence in Sri Lanka and as a group they appear to identify less with Tamil identity than later migrants, which has allowed for a more complete integration into American society. One sign of this is that second generation Sri Lankan Americans tend to be highly Americanised and largely isolated from transnational diaspora politics. Young, second generation immigrants also help each other with assimilation, and a plethora of South Asian and Indian student associations and cultural groups exist to aid newcomers. Another reason for the seeming lack of interest in Tamil politics in general is that the dispersion of Sri Lankans across the country has led to the absence of large Tamil communities (to rectify this, the Tamil Sangams of North America, FeTNA, was established in 1987).

Finally, while international Tamil political activities are carried out in high-profile public forums designed to attract attention, pro-LTTE Americans seem to prefer a Washington-centric strategy of relying on key individuals in positions of influence, as well as a network of savvy elites and professionals, to advance their agenda. This has led to less militancy within the Tamil American community and Washington has been, for the most part, a big player in Sri Lankan politics. As Washington seeks to rework the power balance in its relations with Colombo, it may move away from advancing the Tamil agenda. This could cause a more noticeable split between Tamil Americans and the international Tamil diaspora, or could cause more radical Tamil Americans to reach out to a greater extent to their counterparts in Canada, where the LTTE retains a much stronger hold.

Patrick Mendis

Dinner and Dance night by the Sri Lanka Association Washington, D.C. (SLAWDC).

CANADA

SRI LANKANS IN Canada have continued to maintain their ethno-cultural identities even as they have come to appreciate and enjoy the unity and diversity that is evident in Canadian multicultural society. Canada has emerged as a preferred destination for Sri Lankan emigrants, and this is clearly evident in the size of the Sri Lankan diaspora here, which has grown exponentially over the last 25 years. Both the Tamil and Sinhala languages are widely spoken at the community level in Canada, and the former has earned a place in the top 25 languages spoken in Canada.

Tracing the exact number of Sri Lankans living in Canada, however, is a problematic exercise. Some in the diaspora do not identify themselves as Sri Lankan, Sinhala or Tamil in official census exercises. The difficulty in gaining a precise estimate is further complicated by the issue of multiple identities, particularly amongst the second generation who are Canadian citizens, those who may be of mixed ancestry or are descendants of 'twice migrants'. The 2006 Canadian Census indicates that there are over 103,000 Sri Lankans in Canada while the Sri Lankan high commission in Canada posits a figure of over 300,000 in 2012. Various scholarly works, based on data collected from Sri Lankan community organisations, suggest that in 2011, the Sri Lankan diaspora in Canada was 450,000 strong, comprising over 350,000 Tamils, over 75,000 Sinhalese, over 30,000 Muslims (Moors or Indo-Muslim and Malays or Malay-Muslim), and a tiny population of Burghers.

CANADA-SRI LANKA DIPLOMATIC RELATIONSHIP

As Commonwealth founding member-countries, Sri Lanka and Canada have had a history of development and mutual trade corporations from 1950. Canada opened its diplomatic mission in Sri Lanka in 1953. As an extension of this relationship, Sri Lanka was one of the few countries which received technical assistance from Canada under the Colombo Plan in the 1950s. The Canada-Sri Lanka Friendship Road leading to the international airport in Colombo is named in honour of Canada's generosity. In addition, Canada also established the Canadian International Development Agency (CIDA) in Sri Lanka in 1968. Since its inception, the CIDA has continuously provided assistance in the fields of education (working closely with the United Nations Children's Fund [UNICEF]), women's development, and humanitarian and rehabilitation assistance for civil war and tsunami-affected people. From the late 1980s in particular, Canada has been working very closely with the Tamil community in Sri Lanka. In 2009, the CIDA allocated C$22.5 million in humanitarian assistance for people who were affected by the civil war. It is in this context that people of all ethnic groups from Sri Lanka— but particularly Tamils—came to regard Canada as a resource-rich, generous and philanthropic country, with a relatively open policy vis-à-vis immigration.

The Ferdinands family at the Colombo jetty before embarking on their journey to Canada, 1958.

MIGRATION HISTORY

Sri Lankan emigration to Canada has largely been the product of changes in Canadian migration policies and the changing political and economic scenario in independent Sri Lanka. Sri Lankan emigration to Canada initially began as a trickle. The only available data in Canada showed that there were only 27 Sri Lankan Burghers and Sinhalese prior to 1955. Amongst these were the Tom Orchards family, considered the first Sri Lankan family to settle in Toronto.

From the second half of the 1960s, key reforms in Canadian migration policies encouraged the movement of Sri Lankans to Canada. During Trudeau's tenure as Prime Minister, the 'White Paper on Immigration' (1966) included non-discriminatory criteria and a point system

A Sri Lankan fan of the Canadian cricket team waves the Canadian national flag during a match in Colombo, 2011.

Map 4.8

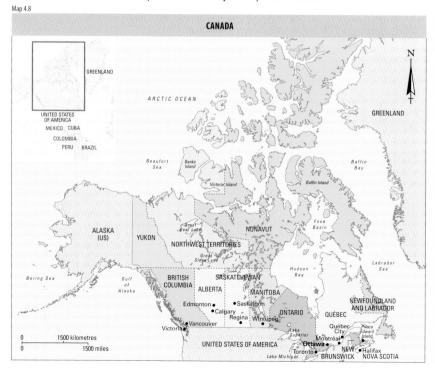

CANADA

Tamil asylum seekers look over the side of the MV Sun Sea, 13 August 2010. The small cargo ship, crammed with hundreds of Tamil refugees, arrived at a Canadian naval base after a grueling three-month journey.

Originally from Jaffna, Gomala Sivakumar and her husband first migrated to Germany and then to Canada.

A wide range of Sri Lankan foods and spices are available at the Yal Market in Scarborough.

The annual 'Roots for Reconciliation' tree planting event in 2010 organised by the Toronto-based Sri Lankans Without Borders (SLWB). The not-for-profit network provides young Canadians of Sri Lankan origin with opportunities to lead initiatives that promote dialogue, reconciliation and peace in Sri Lanka.

for entry. This resulted in the number of immigrants from Sri Lanka increasing substantially from 1967. Trade agreements, changes in recruitment policy, and the global economic situation after the 1970s also catalysed the emigration of Sri Lankan professionals and skilled workers to countries like Canada, Britain and Australia. In Canada, the introduction of the Federal Multiculturalism Policy in 1971, which gave official recognition to diverse cultures in a plural society, further encouraged emigration. Following the 1975 'Green Paper on Immigration', a new Canadian Immigration Act was introduced in 1976 that sought as well to encourage labour migration depending on provincial needs. The 1976 Act introduced new categories of immigrants including refugees, persecuted and displaced persons; immediate family members; and distant relatives sponsored by family members residing in Canada. The policy also persuaded those who had already migrated to another country to move to Canada.

The liberalisation of emigration policies in Canada coincided with deteriorating political conditions in Sri Lanka. The action taken by the Sri Lankan government against left-oriented militants in the early 1970s, the communal riots in 1977, and the break out of the civil war in the 1980s resulted in large numbers of Sri Lankans —particularly Tamils and Muslims—fleeing the country.

The first refugee boat arrived in Canada on 11 August 1986 with 155 Sri Lankan Tamil men, women and children on board (Mann, 2009). They were rescued by fishermen off the coast of Newfoundland. Once the formalities of immigration had been completed, they were allowed to stay with Tamil communities and individuals who offered them help to resettle in Toronto and Montreal. The settlement of these initial refugees was a key factor as to why, over time, Toronto has emerged as a home for the Tamil diaspora. Since it was found that almost all refugee claimants at that time were genuine, the Canadian government announced an amnesty for all refugees. After this incident, Sri Lanka emerged as one of the top three source countries for refugee claimants in Canada.

The reports of the steering committee on Immigration Policy Reform and its recommendations in 1989 greatly aided the immigration of Sri Lankans to Canada. The Canadian Immigration and Refugee Board was set up in 1989. Sympathy towards the plight of Tamils assisted the Tamil asylum seekers to possibly skip one or more stages of the refugee-hearings process. The asylum claims of Sri Lankan refugees lodged with the Board between 1989 and 1999 had an acceptance rate of approximately 85 per cent, when compared to the 60–70 per cent acceptance rate for all refugees. Canada maintained that any person who arrived at a Canadian port of entry had the right to claim refugee status. This provision was clearly the most suitable category of migrant status for the Sri Lankan Tamils and over 26,500 were accepted as refugees in Canada. This was more than any other country in the world. Canada also accepted a large number of Tamil, Sinhala and Muslim refugees from Sri Lanka who were affected by the 2004 tsunami.

In addition to refugees, three main categories of Sri Lankan Tamils were given priority

for immigration to Canada. This included: 1) family reunion to maintain emotional well-being of family in particular and community harmony in general; 2) independent skilled workers and; 3) internationally qualified professionals to contribute to the Canadian labour market. Sri Lankans who had migrated to Europe, particularly to countries where English was not an official and instructional language for their children, used these Canadian openings as a way for family and community reunion. Attractive Canadian social welfare and health care services, availability of employment and educational opportunities and the use of their own languages in the multicultural society were other reasons that led many Sri Lankans who first moved to Europe to choose Canada as their future home. Indeed, between 1990 and 1995, a large number of European Tamils, particularly from England, Germany, France, Switzerland and the Nordic countries, moved to Canada. Parallel to this trend, the Tamils who entered as asylum seekers and were accepted as refugees also gained citizen status. Many of them have sponsored their family members under the family reunion provision.

Although the humanitarian category has also played a role in the immigration history of Sri Lankan Sinhalese and Muslims, when compared to the Tamils, the number that moved under this category is smaller. In the 1980s, professionals and skilled workers from these communities started finding employment abroad due to the Open Economy Policy introduced in Sri Lanka in 1978, which allowed them to migrate for employment purposes. These workers had been employed for many years in Middle Eastern countries such as Saudi Arabia, Oman, Bahrain, United Arab Emirates, and Far Eastern countries, like Japan, Singapore, Malaysia, Thailand and South Korea. From the early 1990s, these transient workers, concerned over their prospects in Sri Lanka and their children's future there, began to emigrate in large numbers to Canada.

When compared to refugees, these emigrants were more qualified, with considerable work experience, and were financially better off.

SETTLEMENT PATTERNS

The overwhelming majority of Sri Lankans in Canada are settled in large cities such as Toronto, Montreal, Vancouver, Halifax, Calgary and Edmonton. Indeed, the Greater Toronto area and Montreal accounts for about 90 per cent of the diaspora. It is widely accepted that Toronto is the city with the largest number of Sri Lankans in the world outside Sri Lanka. From the 1990s, the Tamil population has been the fastest growing linguistic group in Metro Toronto. About two thirds of the Tamil population are male, while a large proportion of them consist of youths from 14 to 28 years of age, most of whom are students. This pattern is somewhat different from other ethnic groups in the diaspora. A dense pocket of Tamils, Sinhalese and Muslims is based in Scarborough in Toronto. In addition, several 'little Jaffnas' have emerged in suburbs of Toronto and Montreal. In these locales, economic enterprises and shopping complexes mostly consist of Tamil names and terms that are written in the Tamil language such as 'Arthi' shopping complex, 'Amma' restaurant and 'Rough vethuppaham'. In certain cases, such as 'Yal Market' and 'Sankanai Thalapadam', the names indicate villages in Jaffna or other parts of Sri Lanka from where these emigrants originated.

In recent years, there has been an increase in the number of Sri Lankans moving from cities in Ontario to the west, north and east. Preferred choices in the north are Markham and Richmond Hill, North York and Northern Mississauga, and in the east are Ajax, Hamilton, Waterloo, Niagara Falls, Windsor and Ottawa. In the west, Sri Lankan communities can be found scattered in East York, Brampton, Etobicoke and Pickering. Outside Ontario, high concentrations of Sinhalese are found in Saskatchewan and Alberta, especially Edmonton. Most of them are on work visas and employed in the hospitality sector. These Sinhalese—most of whom are from the Southern and North-western provinces of Sri Lanka—comprise of mainly skilled workers who moved to Canada after gaining several years of work experience abroad.

COMMUNITY LIFE

The early Sri Lankan immigrants to Canada struggled to develop a social support network. Their small number ushered a pragmatic outlook, pressing them to reach out and integrate with other collectives in Canadian society, including non-Sri Lankan South Asians and pan-ethnic Muslim communities. Economic, social and emotional interdependence has also facilitated a cohesive spirit amongst the Sri Lankan pioneers that often cut across Sri Lankan ethnic lines, in spite of the sharpening of divisions in the homeland.

Comparatively that pragmatism-induced integration is less evident amongst newer immigrants. Many arrivals from the late 1980s were refugee claimants, who moved because of specific political circumstances and with limited financial capital. While the generous allowances for Tamil asylum seekers contributed to the successful settlement of this diaspora, at the same time family reunification enabled the establishment of collectives and networks that were largely contained along ethnic lines. Indeed, collectives based along ethnic lines have emerged as key bases of community formation for this diaspora—

providing support in settlement and employment and enabling the development of specific cultural and religious institutions and celebrations. These networks have fostered, in both the Tamil and Sinhala communities, the development of associations of homeland schools and original villages in the diaspora, and also facilitated co-ethnic and co-religious transnational marriages.

Conditions in Sri Lanka have left a deep imprint on affiliations in the diaspora, and influenced group formation even amongst the second generation of settlers. Given the depth of the political divide, moderate voices have sometimes been silenced, and threats meted out to those who hold opposing views. Several episodes of youth gang violence in Toronto, from the latter half of the 1990s to the early 2000s, took ethnic lines and were influenced by the civil war in Sri Lanka. Even after May 2009, when the Sri Lankan civil war was 'officially' concluded, the political divide remains salient in the diaspora, affecting the nature of community relations.

ECONOMIC LIFE

The first generation of immigrants, i.e., those who came with their families to Canada from the 1950s until the mid-1980s, possessed higher levels of education and were fluent in English. They were predominantly of middle and upper middle class backgrounds, and most were able to sustain or improve on that position when they settled in Canada. The newer Sri Lankan Tamil migrants—those who arrived from the late 1980s—were not as well educated, and did not have the equivalent financial capital of the earlier emigrants. Indeed, given that the education of many of these Tamil immigrants had been disrupted by the civil war in Sri Lanka, they were pressed

In 2005, Indira Vasanthi Samarasekera became the first female President of Alberta University.

Janaka Ruwanpura, the developer of iBooth—a mobile information kiosk aimed at increasing productivity on construction sites—is the first Sri Lankan Canadian to receive the Brian D. Dunfield Educational Service Award.

The 'Tamileelam Challenge Cup' is an annual football tournament organised by the Canadian Tamil Youth Alliance.

CANADIAN-SRI LANKAN BUDDHISTS' ENGAGEMENT WITH THE 'HOMELAND'

Since the mid 1990s, Sri Lankan Buddhists in Toronto have been actively engaged in community services in Canada and in Sri Lanka. The community has sponsored a regular soup kitchen organised by the Buddhist youth for the homeless in the Toronto downtown area. Alongside this locally engaged Buddhist programme, a few ad hoc scholarships have been introduced for the benefit of school children from poverty-stricken families in Sri Lanka.

The Needy Children's Scholarship Foundation, established in 1997, exemplifies the generous support of numerous grassroot organisations within the Sri Lankan Buddhist community in Toronto. The Canada Sri Lanka Life Development Centre—a diasporic non-profit organisation and institution—has launched several successful charitable projects in southern Sri Lanka. Among these is an orphanage village named 'CanadaPura' that provides pre-school education programmes and house-building projects for low-income families.

The Canada Sri Lanka Life Development Centre (CSLDC) initiated an orphanage village named 'CanadaPura' in Hambantota.

D. Mitra Barua

The Canadian Tamils' Chamber of Commerce (CTCC) established in 1991 seeks to develop the entrepreneurial spirit of the Tamil community in Canada and promotes philanthropic activities.

to take up work in low-paying, unskilled jobs in Canada. Many did production-line work in factories, home-based self-employment, or worked in automobile repair shops and in the food and culinary industries. Like these Sri Lankan Tamils, a large proportion of Sinhalese who migrated to Canada from late 1980s also came from middle and lower middle class backgrounds. However, their comparatively higher education levels allowed them to take up jobs in the skilled worker category, which usually paid higher salaries.

Having said that, the tight social networks and connections that developed over the years—especially in the Sri Lankan Tamil diaspora—allowed them to tap job opportunities through community-based networks. Many took up employment in community-owned businesses. In cities such as Toronto and Montreal, Sri Lankans, particularly Tamils, have become major players in the business community, and own supermarkets, business complexes, convenience stores and franchise restaurants such as Tim Horton, Burger King and McDonalds. They also run real estate businesses, law firms, medical clinics, educational institutions and private financial institutions.

Members of the Saskatoon Sri Lankan Community have come together to organise a Sinhala Language School for children.

The Canadian Tamils' Chamber of Commerce (CTCC), established in 1991, has expanded its membership to over 500 in 20 years. These connections now extend transnationally—for example, the Tamils' Business Connection is an online resource that connects Tamil businesses around the world. The Sinhalese also possess businesses, many of which are located in Brampton and Scarborough. The Brampton Town Flea Market, which has a number of Sinhalese shops and cafes, is owned by a Sinhalese entrepreneur. As many Sinhalese shop at the Flea Market, the locale has turned into a gathering place for the members of the community.

Whatever may have been the starting point of the initial immigrants, the education of children has been a priority in the diaspora. That emphasis on education has strengthened the socio-economic position of the diaspora. A considerable proportion of the second generation have secured white collar jobs, and many are now engaged in the service sector.

Another feature of the Sri Lankan diaspora in Canada is the considerable sums that are remitted to the homeland. Transnational economic ties and contributions have been crucial for the care of families, immediate relations and community and ethnic groups in Sri Lanka, especially those affected by conflict, economic difficulties and natural disasters.

A priest blesses a devotee during the annual Vinayagar Chariot Festival in Toronto, 2010.

RELIGIOUS AND CULTURAL LIFE

All Sri Lankan ethnic groups in Canada have sought to preserve and cultivate their cultural and religious traditions in the diaspora. Sri Lankan Hindu temples, Buddhist *pansala*, mosques and religious and ethnic-specific cultural institutions and organisations have been crucial in sustaining their identity and heritage.

The first Sri Lankan *pansala* in Canada, built in 1978, is located at Kingston road in Scarborough (Toronto) and another was built in Mississauga in 1992. The Sinhalese have also been involved in the formation of several other cultural and religious institutions such as the Sri Lanka-Canada Association Ottawa (1970) and the West-End Buddhist Centre (1992). Teaching Sinhala language, Buddhist philosophy, organising cultural and religious-social events and celebration such as Aluth Avuruthu or Bak Maha Ulala (traditional celebration of New Year), Wesak or Buddha Jayanthi are some of the activities organised by these associations.

From the 1990s, a number of South-Indian-style Hindu temples have been established in Canada, particularly in the Greater Toronto Area. The Richmond Hill Hindu Temple, designed in 1987–88 and built with the help of Indian professionals in 1992, follows the sculptural and architectural style of Sri Lankan Hindu temples. To some extent, the Sri Lankan Hindu tradition of having temples for villages and for different Gods and Goddesses has also been reproduced in Canada. Temples that have maintained traditions include the Canada Sri Ayyappan Temple (1994), the Sri Muthumari Ambal Temple (1997), the Toronto Sridurka Hindu Temple, and the Thurketheswran Temple (2003). Beyond religious activities, these temples engage in charitable initiatives as well as spiritual education. The International Sivanantha Yoga Vedanta Centre, Montreal, established in 1957, with Indian collaboration, serves as an *ashram* as well as a

higher education institution, which provides residential lessons and courses on spiritual and Ayurvedic medical education. The key festivals celebrated by Sri Lankan Tamils in Canada include Thai Pongal (Harvest festival) in January, Puthuvarusham (Tamil/Hindu New Year) in April, and Deepavali (Festival of Lights) in October/ November. Reflecting the strong presence of the Tamil community in 2012, the Toronto and Peel region in the Greater Toronto Area declared January as the Tamil Heritage Month.

Upon their arrival in Canada, Sri Lankan Muslims were inclined to search for a home in an area close to a mosque. With the exception of Sri Lankan Malay Muslims, Sri Lankan Muslims usually opted to live in areas of Tamil concentration, as most spoke Tamil and came from the North-eastern province of Sri Lanka. While they had no hesitation in joining a mosque with a fellowship comprising different ethnic communities, there was a preference for South Asian mosques, and over time, these communities have come together to forge joint Islamic institutions. The first Sri Lankan Muslim mosque, Masjid-ut-Taqwa Islamic organisation, was established in Canada in 1996. Initially an Anglican church, the site was procured by Guyanese emigrants for the purpose of establishing a mosque, and later purchased by Sri Lankan Muslims. The Downtown Mosque (known also as Deedat Centre or Salatomatic) in Toronto was established in 2002 by the Muslim Association of Canada whose membership included Indians, Mongolians, Nepalese, Pakistanis and Sri Lankans. Masjid Al-Jannah—Sri Lanka Islamic Foundation of Ontario (SLIFO) in Scarborough was formally established in 2010. In addition to mosques, the Sri Lankan Muslim Association of Montreal (2003), the Canadian-Sri Lankan Muslim Association of Ontario (1997) and the BC-Sri Lankan Muslim Association (2006) are some of the key religious-cultural organisations that organise recreational activities, religious celebrations such as *Eid-ul-Fithr* (Festival after Fasting), *Eid-ul-Alha* (*Haj* festival), *Meelathun Nabi* (birthday of Prophet Mohamed), and religious education for children.

Given the size of the Tamil minority in Canada, Tamil language education is approved and accredited in the Canadian education system. For the second generation, Tamil language learning has developed through both formal and non-formal channels of education. At the same time, the development of Tamil language in Canada is subject to a myriad of challenges including differences in mainstream language cultures, language teaching methodologies and curriculum expectations. A disjuncture exists in the socio-cultural and linguistic tradition of Tamil language teachers and the macro social context of the second generation in the diaspora, which sometimes is revealed in pressures to dilute the 'purity' of the language so as to sustain the motivation of young learners.

SOCIAL ACTIVISM

Until the mid-1980s, Sri Lankan social activism largely took the form of organising cultural celebrations with the aim of sustaining Sri Lankan traditions in the diaspora. The arrival of large numbers of immigrants with lower levels of education however, and limited awareness

Volunteers of the Sinhalese Association in Canada distributing free spectacles to Sri Lankans.

of Canadian life from the late 1980s, marked an important turn in the nature of social activism in the diaspora. This created a demand for more programs and activities that sought to facilitate settlement, and meet socio-economic and welfare concerns. For this purpose, several not-for-profit organisations came to be established. Amongst these included the Tamil Eelam Society of Canada, which from 1983 served as a volunteer-based settlement agency with several branches in Canadian cities. Other notable organisations involved in such activities included the Ulaga Thamilar Iyakkam (World Tamil Movement), the Sri Lanka United National Association Canada (SLUNA), the Sinhalese Association of Canada (1998), the Canada Sri Lanka Muslim Association (1997), the Sri Lankan Muslim Association of Montreal (2003) and *Vizhippu* (Awakening) in Toronto who dealt exclusively with women's concerns.

Over the last decade, further transformations that reflect the maturing of Sri Lankan social activism in Canada have been visible. Several communications and media enterprises with Tamil and Sinhala content, that seek to capture the dynamics of community life in the diaspora, have emerged to disseminate information and identify community resources. For the Tamil community alone, there are now more than 25 weekly newspapers and magazines, seven radio channels and four nationwide TV channels. Beyond entertainment, the emergence of such media has enriched the artistic and literary life of the Sri Lankan diaspora, and facilitated economic enterprise, as well as political and social activism. In parallel, social activism of the Sri Lankan diaspora in Canada has evolved into addressing different issues and the concerns and interests of children, youth, adults and seniors. For example, the Canadian Tamil Youth Development (CanTYD) Centre established in 1998 by a group of 17 Tamil-Canadian university students focuses on empowering and developing Tamil Canadian youth, and addresses the needs of at-risk youth in the community through research,

There are a number of Sri Lankan newspapers and magazines published in Canada.

The Sri Lanka Malay Association of Toronto often organises 'Dikir Barat' musical performances. Its other activities include cultural fairs and events to promote the Malay language.

Sri Lankan supporters celebrate as Sri Lanka wins the Canada Cup 20/20 cricket tournament held in Ontario, 2008.

In 2013, a road in Markham, in the Greater Toronto area, was named Vanni Street after the Vanni region in Northern Sri Lanka. Councillor Logan Kanapathi and Mayor Frank Scarpitti officiated at the event.

Rathika Sitsabaiesan is the first person of Sri Lankan origin to be elected as Member of the Federal Parliament in Canada.

On 13 May 2009, thousands of Tamil protesters marched across Queen Street in Toronto to draw attention to alleged atrocities committed against Tamils in Sri Lanka.

education and advocacy. Intellectual dialogue, carried out through Tamil studies conferences, literary forums, and civic education and rights awareness, is another important dimension that has developed.

POLITICAL ACTIVISM

Until 2012, Sri Lankan participation in Canadian political parties and in legislative bodies at different levels of government has been nominal. In the 2011 Canadian General Election, the New Democratic Party candidate Rathika Sitsabaiesan, of Sri Lankan Tamil descent, was elected as representative to the Federal Government for the Scarborough-Rouge Valley Area. The elected city counsellor for Markham and a School board counsellor are also from the Tamil community.

Having said that, levels of political activism in other forms, through media, awareness-raising activities and participation at community level decision-making have been long-standing, dating to the arrival of the first Sri Lankan refugee ship in 1986. The organisational capacity of the Tamil community has also facilitated lobbying efforts so as to influence policy makers. These take place in a variety of fields. For example, in commerce and business, such influence may result in possible concessions in terms of recruitment policies and employment practices.

Another level of activism is based on ethnic lines. Informed of the conflict in Sri Lanka, the Tamils and the Sinhalese have long lobbied Canadian policy makers in favour of their preferred political positions. From January 2009, Tamil organisations staged a series of demonstrations to draw attention to the alleged war crimes perpetrated during the last phase of the civil war in Sri Lanka. Such demonstrations included protests in front of the Consulate General of Sri Lanka and the United States Consulate. This was followed by a 5-kilometre human chain in the streets in downtown Toronto and protests on Parliament Hill in Ottawa. Similar protests by Tamils in Montreal, Vancouver and Calgary appealed to the Canadian government for help to stop the war. On 27 May 2009, the Sri Lanka United National Association of Canada (SLUNA) organised demonstrations accusing the Canadian government of being sympathetic to the LTTE.

While the civil war in Sri Lanka may have ended, the conflict and its ramifications have continued to incite political activism in the diaspora. Beyond overt

demonstrations, a variety of social platforms including art and literary works, the media, human rights forums and community-based activities have contributed to public awareness of the political situation in Sri Lanka.

CHALLENGES

Over the last three decades, the relatively liberal Canadian stance towards Sri Lankan migration has resulted in the Sri Lankan diaspora in Canada growing extensively. That expansion is expected to continue in the near future. The emphasis on education, along with strong community networks have been crucial in supporting the upward mobility evident in the diaspora, even amongst those who came initially under desperate circumstances. Changes in Canadian multicultural policies have allowed for the preservation and development of Sri Lankan identities in the diaspora.

At the same time, there has been a tendency, in part due to the increase in the size of the diaspora, for communities to develop along narrow ethnic lines. In the context of the political conflict in the 'homeland', this has manifested in ethnic divisions forming within the diaspora. Especially for the diaspora of emigrants who arrived after the late 1980s, integration with Canadian society by reaching out across ethnic boundaries remains a challenge, as is the need to engage more deeply with mainstream socio-political ideals.

Also necessary, especially in light of the increasingly close-knit ethnic communities that have come to be forged in cities like Toronto, is the need for dialogue and understanding across generational lines. This may be a difficult process but it requires negotiation if a more sustainable balance between the demands of the older generation and the aspirations of young local-born Sri Lankan-Canadians is to be achieved.

Sithy Zulfika

UNITED KINGDOM

SRI LANKA HAS a long historical relationship with the United Kingdom. This relationship was formed primarily in a colonial context. British colonial rule over Sri Lanka, then Ceylon, lasted for 133 years (1815–1948). Even after independence in 1948, as a Commonwealth country, Sri Lanka continued to foster strong diplomatic and economic ties with the UK.

While the beginnings of Sri Lankan emigration to the UK can be traced to the colonial period, the arrival and settlement of Sri Lankans has intensified over the last five decades, shaped in part by UK immigration policies and the post-independence politics of Sri Lanka. The Sri Lankan diaspora in UK bears specific features in terms of religion and ethnic representation, and demonstrates significant diversity in social and economic status, as well as educational levels.

The four key ethno-religious communities of Sri Lanka—Sinhalas, Tamils, Muslims and Burghers—are all present in the UK. The former three groups have established strong and visible diaspora communities today. Established weekly newspapers such as *Newslanka* (founded in 1991) inform the diaspora community about details of member activities. Their ethnic and religious

centres promote religious and secular interests related to Sri Lanka. For these communities, the cultural and religious heritage of Sri Lanka remains important.

MIGRATION PROCESS AND DEMOGRAPHIC CHARACTERISTICS

Over the last three centuries, the UK gradually became home for many Asian communities. The earliest reports of South Asian migration to Britain date back to the 17th century, and over time with the expansion of the East India Company's trade, seamen from the subcontinent became more visible in British ports.

Although emigration during the colonial period was fragmentary, after World War II more Sri Lankans arrived in the UK, creating the basis for a settled diaspora. In particular, considerable numbers moved in the 1950s and 1960s. They were mostly professionals. In the 1960s, the UK's National Health Service opened up the opportunity for Sri Lankans to be employed as doctors. The immigration of professionals gave birth to organisations such as the Sri Lanka Medical and Dental Association UK, the Clinical Society of Sri Lankan Doctors and Dentists, and the Association of Sri Lankan Lawyers in the UK, amongst others. As in the case of other Asian communities, the Commonwealth Immigration Act that was passed in 1962 further accelerated Sri Lankan emigration to the UK. The Comptroller of Immigration records indicate that Sri Lankans arrived in Britain in great numbers between 1964 and 1966. The Immigration Act of 1968, however, reduced the numbers of immigrants by half and the Immigration Act of 1971 further constrained numbers, as it ensured that only a small number of immigrants could settle down in the UK on a permanent basis.

The Association of Professional Sri Lankans (APSL) in the UK held its annual 'We Sri Lanka' event for the third successive year in October 2012. The initiative seeks to nurture a plural and inclusive national consciousness within the Sri Lankan community by reconnecting people from the Sinhala, Tamil, Muslim and Burgher communities in the UK and in Sri Lanka.

Sri Lankans students at the Institute of Agriculture at Usk, Monmouthshire, 1946.

Map 4.9

UNITED KINGDOM

The Executive Committee of the Sri Lanka Medical and Dental Association (SLMDA) in the UK, 2010. Founded in 1982, SLMDA has been promoting medical and dental education in Sri Lanka.

The Sinhala newspaper, Lanka Viththi, *published in London.*

Members of the Association of Sri Lankan Lawyers in the UK.

In spite of these restrictions, the Sri Lankan population in the UK continued to increase as emigrants who settled aided in the movement of their families and kinsmen. Their numbers have increased due to asylum seekers who began to arrive in the mid-1980s following the civil war in Sri Lanka. Well-to-do families and temporary visitors, who may have come to the UK initially to pursue higher education, also began to settle down.

Defining the exact number of Sri Lankans who live in the UK is not an easy task. The Sri Lankan High Commission in London has no records. The National UK Census 2001 is also of limited use as a separate list for Sri Lankans is not included and they have been broadly classified as 'Other Asians.'

The Census and other sources such as the Labour Forces Survey aid only in deciphering the number of Sri Lanka-born individuals who are resident in the UK. These, however, do not provide figures of UK-born British-Sri Lankans of second, third or subsequent generations. The 1991 Census informs that there were 39,402 Sri Lanka born UK residents. This increased to 67,832 in the 2001 Census, an expansion of 72 per cent over one decade. The Labour Forces Survey (2006) posits that there were approximately 102,950 Sri Lanka born immigrants in the UK accounting for about 0.17 per cent of the total UK population—effectively making them the fourth largest group of Asian migrants in the UK (mighealth.net/uk). Of this number, 55 per cent were male and 45 per cent female, 6 per cent were aged 0–15 years, 8 per cent aged 16–24 years, 50 per cent were aged 25–44 years, 28 per cent were aged 45–64 years, and 7 per cent were aged over 65. In 2006, amongst Sri Lanka born immigrants in the UK, 73 per cent were listed as employed, 5 per cent as unemployed and 22 per cent were inactive. In the UK, 69 per cent of these Sri Lankans either owned property outright or have bought a home with a mortgage. The statistics aver that the most popular areas for Sri Lankan residence in London were Rayners Lane, East Ham South and Wembley. According to the BBC website 'Born Abroad', Sri Lankans tend to be moving from inner London to outer London (news.bbc.co.uk/2/shared/spl/hi/uk/05/born_abroad/countries/html/sri_lanka.stm).

The increase in Sri Lankan numbers is manifested not only in the diversity of ethnic groups but also in the variety of religious beliefs and practices that these immigrants have brought with them. Statistics of the ethnic and religious composition of Sri Lankans in the UK are not available. While the Comptroller of Immigration began to publish records pertaining to ethnic and religious differences amongst immigrants, these records are not satisfactory as they lack specific information on Sri Lankans. A further inadequacy of these records is that they do not distinguish Tamils from Sinhalas and thus complexities related to ethnicity have been ignored.

In spite of the lack of specific information, it is evident that Sinhalas, Tamils and Muslims, who collectively comprise the overwhelming number of immigrants from Sri Lanka, have forged distinct diasporas. UK was also a popular destination for the Burgher community, although, over time, larger numbers turned to Australia and other parts of Europe. Unlike Sinhalas, Tamils and Muslims, because of their European background, customs, and Christian religion, Burghers have easily assimilated into British society which has in turn attenuated their connections to Sri Lanka. Nonetheless, amongst the Burghers in UK include a few distinguished individuals such as Sir Christopher Ondaatje, a prominent businessmen, known for his philanthropy and in whose honour the new wing of the National Portrait Gallery is named.

CULTURAL EXPERIENCE

The cultural experience of the Sri Lankan community in the UK demonstrates diversity as well as strength. All ethnic communities in the UK have established religious and cultural representation. There are Buddhist temples, Hindu *kovils* and mosques representing specific religious orientations. Major events that are representative of Sri Lankan culture such as the Sinhala and Tamil New Year, Wesak Day celebration for the Buddhists, Ramadan for the Muslims, and Christmas for the Christians are widely celebrated. These celebrations have become occasions of unity and cooperation among members of the community. Cultural activities and festivals take place throughout the year. In particular, the Sinhala and Tamil New Year is the most visible Sri Lankan cultural festival held in contemporary London.

The monthly newspaper, *Lanka Viththi* (Lanka Affairs), patriotic in outlook and the first Sinhala language newspaper ever published outside Sri Lanka, provides vernacular materials for the Sinhala community since 1997. Contributing to the entertainment industry, the Sri Lankan community initiated TV channels in Sinhala such as Vectone TV and Kesara TV (July 2006–March 2009) and radio stations. Although most of these forays into the entertainment industry failed, perhaps due to financial reasons, the Sri Lankan Radio, an online radio station since November 2009 has continued. Notable Sri Lankans involved in the entertainment industry include the BBC TV presenter George Alagiah, among others.

Although the average Sri Lankan in the UK is a wage earner, and only a tiny minority in the diaspora has shown business prowess, they have nevertheless an established presence in the restaurant business. Sri Lankan restaurants have mushroomed in various parts of the UK, popularising Sri Lankan cuisine to the British. The history of Sri Lankan restaurants extends over eight decades. Peter Warnasuriya, a Sinhalese, brought to England

by the tea-merchant, Sir Thomas Lipton (1848–1931), established the Ceylon Restaurant in the West End of London in 1926 (Fernando, 'Sri Lankan Restaurants in London'). In the late 1960s, Charles Silva opened a restaurant in Earls Court. Since then several Sri Lankan restaurants—Prince of Ceylon, Lihiniya, Galla Café, Sekara, Papaya, Meeting Place, Rising Sun and Dosa World—have emerged. They cater for specific needs and tastes of a wider community of Sri Lankans representing cuisines of southern as well as northern Sri Lanka. The *UK Lanka Times* informs that Indika Jayasena, a gifted Sri Lankan female sugar crafter, has won four gold medals, including the British Open Cookery Championship for excellent culinary skills.

POLITICAL PARTICIPATION

By and large, the Sri Lankan community in the UK has remained a skilled labour force with a solid middle class background. In the earlier period, elite professionals were largely disinterested in active political participation in Britain or Sri Lanka. Lobbying in London for matters pertaining to Sri Lankan politics has now become more common. For example, on 29 May 2011, under the banner of the National Freedom Front, several diaspora organisations protested at No. 10 (British Prime Minister's Office) against the Darusman Committee Report Against Sri Lanka. Over the last two to three

decades, partly motivated by tensions created by the ethnic conflict in Sri Lanka, some members of the community have increased their participation in the political activities in Britain in order to influence the political process in Sri Lanka. Political activism of this nature is linked to members of the Tamil community.

The ethnic problem in Sri Lanka has had implications on community affairs, even in London. Some members of the Sinhala community were opposed to the public display of support for the LTTE by Tamil diaspora protesters in Westminster in 2009. On the eve of the Sri Lankan government's apparent success of militarily defeating the LTTE in May 2009, members of the LTTE were accused of engaging in arson attacks on a Buddhist temple in Kingsbury and several shops of the Sam Chicken chain in North London owned by a Sinhala businessman.

On the whole, the political participation of Sri Lankan diasporic communities has taken two forms—one that engages in 'homeland' politics and the other that involves participating in the 'host' country's party politics. Some members of the Sinhala community in Britain have organised branches of major Sri Lankan political parties such as the United National Party (UNP), Sri Lanka Freedom Party (SLFP) and Janatha Vimukthi Peramuna (JVP) in London. These organisations are geared towards raising funds, recruiting new members and thus promoting political interests and pursuing political agendas in Sri Lanka. Meanwhile activist members of the Tamil community have supported the diasporic political wing of the LTTE and other Tamil nationalist groups.

While some in the diaspora have concentrated on promoting political interests in Sri Lanka, others have participated in British politics, for example by contesting in local elections. In cities such as London where the Sri Lankan community is concentrated in areas such as Harrow and Brent, there are now councillors representing the community's interest. This involvement in local party politics has become a key instrument for representing the interests of the community. In recent years, during election campaigns in Britain, both the Labour and Conservative MPs have sought support of the Sri Lankan community in local elections. In this domain, the politics of the 'homeland' and the 'host' country are sometimes enmeshed because these MPs—dependent on Sri Lankan lobbies—have some interest in seeking political solutions to the ethnic problem in Sri Lanka.

CONTEMPORARY EXPERIENCE

The contemporary situation of the Sri Lankan community in the UK is promising. A significant segment of elite members of the Sri Lankan community contribute both intellectually and socially to the well-being of the local community. Economic benefits of living and working in the UK have gradually increased over the years. Members of the community are adjusting to the new challenges of the recession and expectations of the new economic environment. On the whole, even as some have continued their political activism, politics both in Britain and Sri Lanka continues to be an insignificant interest for most. In addition to the continuing successes of the elite, recent economic migrants are doing well in acquiring jobs and accumulating capital that will strengthen their position upon returning home. British government and local agencies have recognised the contributions of some leading members of the community to British society. In recent years, the Queen has conferred MBE and OBE

Supporters of the JVP Peoples Liberation Front at the 2008 May Day parade in Trafalgar Square, London.

In 2009, protestors occupied Bridge Street outside the British Parliament calling on the Sri Lankan government to end alleged atrocities committed against the Tamils.

The Sri Lankan New Year was celebrated at the Harrow Leisure Centre in April 2010.

ANAGARIKA DHARMAPALA

Eminent Sri Lankans were instrumental in laying foundations for the spread of the Sri Lankan form of Theravada Buddhism in the UK. The controversial revivalist and founder of the Mahabodhi Society in 1891, Anagarika Dharmapala (1864-1933), stands out due to his great interest in Britain. Dharmapala wrote:

I am resolved to give the remaining years of my life to enlighten the people of England by telling them of the sublime doctrine of the Tathagata' (Dharmapala, Return of Righteousness, 1965: 666).

These powerful words characterise the determination of Dharmapala and, translated into concrete action, opened a new chapter in the expansion of Theravada Buddhism outside Sri Lanka. Since Dharmapala's initial endeavours to introduce the Sri Lankan form of Theravada Buddhism to the UK, it has gradually consolidated its position there.

Anagarika Dharmapala's first visit to England was in 1890 as a guest of Sir Edwin Arnold (1832–1904), who wrote and published *The Light of Asia* in 1879. It was, however, during his second visit in 1925 that Dharmapala was able to contribute significantly to the growth of Buddhism in Britain. On 27 September 1925, Anagarika Dharmapala visited London in the hope of establishing a Buddhist mission in London. On that occasion, he met Christmas Humphreys (1901–83), the President of the Buddhist Lodge (now The Buddhist Society, founded in 1924) (http://www.thebuddhistsociety.org).

Dharmapala's objective was to set up a Buddhist centre, where the study and practice of Buddhism could be pursued. Subsequently, with the generous financial support of Mary Foster of Honolulu, on 24 July 1926, Dharmapala purchased No. 86, Madeley Road, Ealing, which became the beginning point of the current London Buddhist Vihara, the oldest Sri Lankan Theravada Buddhist temple in the West. In 1926, Dharmapala wrote:

I thought of the great work of preaching the Dhamma to the English people… Buddhists hitherto have not come to England with the determination to preach the Dhamma of the Lord Buddha to the English people (Dharmapala, 1965: 666).

Dharmapala's aim was to establish a Buddhist Vihara in London to spread Buddha's teaching among the English (http://www.londonbuddhistvihara.org). At that time, the support given to diaspora Sri Lankans was a minor objective.

The centennial celebration of the Buddhist legacy in UK showcasing Anagarika Dharmapala.

The Samarasinhe Healthcare and Rehabilitation for the Elderly (S.H.A.R.E) organisation in the United Kingdom has initiated several programmes to help the poor and disadvantaged in Sri Lanka.

The Prince of Ceylon restaurant and bar in London.

titles to several members of the Sri Lankan community in recognition of their contribution to British society.

RELIGIOUS ASPECTS

The defining factor in the life of the Sri Lankan community is the members' interest in their religion and cultural heritage. All major ethnic communities have attempted to develop their own religious centres. The outline below will indicate the development of religion in the community by focusing on religious places and activities of Sri Lankan Buddhists, Hindus and Muslims. Over the years, prominent Sri Lankans have given birth to new and innovative religious establishments in the UK.

(a) Sri Lankan Buddhist Diaspora in London

Early colonial encounters and developments in the study of Buddhism in Britain encouraged some Sri Lankan Buddhists, such as Anagarika Dharmapala (1864–1933), to take initiatives to expand knowledge of Buddhism in Great Britain and Europe. The gradual establishment of the Sri Lankan form of Theravada Buddhism in London has a history of nearly hundred years. Since the humble beginnings in the first quarter of the twentieth century, Theravada Buddhism has expanded to the rest of UK gradually by adapting to the new social, religious and cultural contexts in the last three decades. Over the years, Sri Lankan Buddhists have created several communities in London representing the diversity of the Sri Lankan Buddhist tradition. In London, among the Buddhist temples, three temples stand out: 1) London Buddhist Vihara, 2) Sri Saddatissa International Buddhist Centre (SSIBC), and 3) Thames Buddhist Vihāra.

Sri Lankan Buddhists, who embrace Great Britain as their adopted home, have brought with them diverse and rich beliefs and practices of various regions of Sri Lanka. This is demonstrated in ritual and cultural forms during festivals. These manifestations have reinforced the idea that the Sri Lankan Buddhist centres in London are organised along ethnic lines. The centres founded by the Sri Lankan communities still primarily operate as 'ethnic centres' for the Sinhalese community.

The broader picture of Buddhists in the UK today is as follows. The eighth edition of *The Buddhist Directory* recorded 372 Buddhist centres. According to Baumann, in the late 1990s, 130,000 out of 180,000 of the Buddhist population in the UK were from Asian countries. The National Statistics Census in 2001 estimated the total Buddhist population in England and Wales at 144,453.

The London Buddhist Vihara, reportedly the first Buddhist temple to be established outside the continent of Asia, has continued promoting Buddhist activities with resident *bhikkhus* (monks) mainly from Sri Lanka. In June 1928, Sri Lankan Buddhist monks headed by Venerable Parevehara Vajiranana (1893–1970) began to live in the Vihara. In the history of Buddhism in Britain, for the first time, the three monks of the first mission entered the rain retreat (*vassa*) on the Full Moon of 2 July 1928. Educated monks were invited to the UK from July 1928 until 1940 when the Vihara was officially closed down due to the World War II and only resumed its activities on 17 May 1954. On the eve of the Buddha Jayanthi celebrations on 5 July 1956, three British men were ordained as Buddhist novices at the Vihara. The London Buddhist Vihara entered a new phase in 1958, with the appointment of a distinguished Pali scholar, Venerable Hammalawa Saddhatissa (1914–90), as the Head of the Vihara, which strengthened its reputation. In 1963, the Mahabodhi Society of Sri Lanka took the responsibility of maintaining the London Buddhist Vihara and now The Anagarika Dharmapala Trust administers it. The late 1980s witnessed an expansion of Buddhist centres in London. Some of the *dhammaduta* (missionary) monks, who initially came to the London Buddhist Vihara, established the Thames Buddhist Vihara in 1982 and the Sri Saddhatissa International Buddhist Centre in 1989.

All these Buddhist centres primarily serve Sri Lankan communities but they include and embrace other ethnic groups and Buddhists from other nations. Many non-Sri Lankan Buddhists attend the religious activities during special festivals. Most of these Buddhist temples also function as cultural centres, which gather Sri Lankans for various social and cultural events. The *UK Lanka Times* (2007: 7) informs that the British Ministry of Defense has recognised the importance of Buddhism for citizens and recently appointed a Buddhist Chaplain to the British Armed Forces.

(b) A Modernised Sri Lankan Hindu Diaspora Tradition in Wales

The Community of the Many Names of God in Wales remains primarily a Hindu religious place. Sri Guru Subramaniam (1929–2007), a native of Panadura, known as Silva previously, stands out in the British religious landscape because of his founding of Skanda Vale: The Community of the Many Names of God in Camarthan, Wales in February 1971. Today, Skanda Vale attracts tens of thousands of devotees from the British Hindu diaspora. As an *ashram* (forest hermitage) made up of three temples in a 300 acre estate located in the remote and beautiful countryside of Carmarthen in West Wales, it has become a permanent abode to a community of 25 monks and nuns of Western origin and a few lay residents. The life at Skanda Vale is organised on the practice of *bhakti yoga* (path of devotion), *karma yoga* (path of work) and *ahimsa* (non-violence).

This community bears some eclectic aspects. The communal ethos of the monks and nuns who live there

Sri Lankan monks in Bath, 2002.

derives from adherence to Franciscan vows of obedience, poverty and chastity. Their daily religious lives from early mornings to late evenings revolve around performing *pujas* and worship services of Hindu type, working on the *ashram* land and farm, carrying out maintenance work in accommodation buildings, caring for rescued animals, preparing meals for residents and pilgrims, running the Skanda Vale Hospice that offers free day care to the terminally ill, and the nuns of the community work as staff. A simple lifestyle is required for upholding the ethos of the community.

Devotion, *ahimsa*, vegetarianism and care for animals are key features of the community. Animals are well treated and in 2007 the community entered into a media storm around Shambo, the cow, which contracted tuberculosis. When the authorities wanted to kill the cow, the monastics protested, drawing the attention of the British public.

The Sri Lankan Hindu diaspora in London is active in constructing temples and celebrating festivals. The diaspora runs three temples: the Saiva Eelapatheeswarar Aalayam in Wembley, Middlesex; the Shree Kanaga Durgai Amman Temple in Ealing, and the London Sivan Temple in Lewisham. Religious ceremonies such as the *kumbha abhishekam* (consecration) are conducted on a grand scale and witnesses the participation of the Sri Lankan Hindu diaspora. Eelapatheeswarar Alayam has conducted special prayers and rememberance services for those who were killed in the war.

Tamil News recorded 200,000 Hindu devotees in the Shri Kanaga Thurkkai Amman Temple's annual *Ter* (chariot) procession. The temple has donated large sums to help orphanages, old people's homes and widows in Sri Lanka. It is also notable that the presence of a Sri Lankan Hindu elite in the UK has led to the emergence of organisations such as the Jaffna Hindu College Old Boys Association (founded in the UK in 1987) that organises an annual cultural evening called *Kalai Arasi* and Hindu Night for fundraising.

(c) Muslims as a Sri Lankan Diaspora Community

Broadly speaking, there exists little information on Muslims of Sri Lankan origin in the UK due to their religious incorporation into the larger South Asian Muslim diaspora in the UK. In terms of population statistics, there is no conclusive evidence of their number in the UK. Informal accounts estimate the number to be around 50,000 although Muslims themselves believe the actual number to be much smaller ranging from approximately from 10,000 to 20,000 (Interview with the President of the Sri Lankan Muslim Cultural Centre, 5 June 2011). In contrast to other communities, this Muslim community has some distinguishing features,

The Sri Saddhatissa International Buddhist Centre's Wesak Day greeting card.

Queen Elizabeh The Queen Mother visiting the Master's Lodge at Christ's College.

CAMBRIDGE REFUGEE SCHOLARSHIP SCHEME

For over a decade after the outbreak of communal violence in Sri Lanka in 1983, Christ's College provided scholarships to a number of refugee students to pursue a University of Cambridge degree. Most of the recipients came from the Jaffna region and, unsurprisingly for a pragmatic community, they all chose engineering as their course of study. The scholarships, covering travel, tuition fees and maintenance, were awarded to selected applicants, all of whom completed their courses and graduated successfully, most with First Class Honours. Many of them went on to achieve higher research degrees and have established successful careers in academia or industry in the UK and other countries. The purpose of this refugee scholarship scheme was to establish a nucleus of highly talented scholars who could influence the education of Sri Lankans, both abroad and at home.

V. Navaratnam

Born in Sri Lanka, Guru Sri Subramaniam was the founder of Skanda Vale: The Community of the Many Names of God in Wales.

The Sri Lankan Muslim Cultural Centre (SLMCC) in Harrow, United Kingdom.

including an increasing number of professionals such as doctors and engineers.

Unlike the Sinhala and Tamil communities in the UK, the Sri Lankan Muslim community at large is trilingual; as much as 85 per cent of the community in London uses three languages (Sinhala, Tamil and English). It is evident that there are interesting linguistic shifts along with the changes in social circumstances in people's lives. Since most of the Muslims in Sri Lanka grow up largely alongside the Sinhala community, going to schools and universities together, most of the Muslim youth who arrive in the UK speak Sinhala with their friends. Their language use has shifted with changing social circumstances connected to marriage. After marriage, because of the language situation of the spouse (usually of Tamil-speaking background) and their family, they seem to speak Tamil more at home (Interview with Jawahir Marikkar, 5 June 2011). Traditionally, marriage has had a significant impact in the choice of religion. In this case, marriage has also become the crucial factor in the choice of the language used by the Sri Lankan Muslims.

The birth of Sri Lankan Muslim organisations in the UK can be traced to the 1970s. In 1972, The Sri Lanka Islamic (UK) Association (SLIA) was officially constituted, making it the oldest Sri Lankan Muslim organisation with a membership of some 400 families. A building purchased in July 1993 in Hanwell, London W7, became its headquarters. The Association undertakes many charitable services to relieve poverty and suffering in Sri Lanka.

Young UK-based Sri Lankan girls in their traditional dance costume.

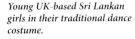

Some Sri Lankan Muslim associations in the UK have taken active roles in responding to crises at home. The Sri Lanka Muslim Refugee Assistance (UK) was formed in 1990. Its explicit objectives were providing relief to Muslims who were refugees or had suffered from ethnically motivated violence in Sri Lanka.

Recent emigrants established the Sri Lanka Islamic Forum UK (SLIF UK), a member of Muslim Council of Britain (MCB), in December 2000, with the aim of promoting an Islamic way of life and committing itself to the nation-building of Sri Lanka by promoting unity, peace, justice and mutual understanding (www.slif.org.uk). SLIF UK has been actively participating in political lobbying in order to highlight the plight of Sri Lankan Muslims to the international community.

The Masjidun-Noor (Rays of Light), popularly known as the Sri Lankan Mosque, located in Harrow, is the headquarters of the Sri Lankan Muslim Cultural Centre (UK) (www.slmcc.co.uk). On 19 May 2002, the premises was purchased and inaugurated as a Masjid and community centre on 25 August 2002. This property, worth more than one million pounds, has a land area of 0.42 acres with over 12,000 sq ft of building area. The London borough of Harrow is a densely populated area with over 30,000 Muslims living within a three-mile radius of the mosque. After the mosque was established, many Sri Lankan Muslims who were scattered around the Harrow area moved to the neighbourhood. Now there are around 400 Sri Lankan Muslim families in the Harrow area, with some 1,000 members of the community, most of whom turn up there for Friday *jummah* prayers. The cultural centre organises community activities and Islamic education classes.

A number of Sri Lankan Muslims have moved to Leicester where they form a distinct Tamil speaking Muslim community. These Sri Lankan Muslims began arriving in Leicester in 1998 and 1999 as students, individuals, and families. The community has grown over the years and now comprises of approximately 400–500 individuals who live largely around the two main roads of Melton and Catharine outside Leicester City Centre.

SIR CHRISTOPHER ONDAATJE

Born in Ceylon, Sir Christopher Ondaatje (b. 1933), arrived in England to study in 1947 and settled down in Canada in 1956 where he built a highly successful career in finance and publishing under Pagurian Corporation. In 1970, he was one of the co-founders of Lowen Ondaatjie McCutcheon (LOM) which is known to be the first independent research-based institutional equity firm in Canada.

In the late 1990s, Christopher Ondaatje moved to Britain. He is recognised as an acclaimed philanthropist, adventurer and writer (his younger brother, Michael Ondaatje is a world-renowned novelist). Some of the literary works of Christopher Ondaatje include *The Prime Ministers of Canada, 1867–1967* (1968); *The Man-Eater of Punanai: A Journey of Discovery to the Jungles of Old Ceylon* (1992); *Hemingway in Africa: The Last Safari* (2004); *Woolf in Ceylon: An Imperial Journey in the Shadow of Leonard Woolf, 1904–11* (2005); *The Last Colonial: Curious Adventures & Stories from a Vanishing World* (2011), etc.

In June 2000, he was conferred a CBE in the Queen's Birthday Honours List. Three years later, he was awarded a Knighthood in the Queen's Honours List. Some of his many philanthropic portfolios include 'The Sir Christopher Ondaatje Wing of the National Portrait Gallery' in London and 'The Sir Christopher Ondaatje South Asian Gallery' at the Royal Ontario Museum, Toronto.

Hema Kiruppalini

Sri Lankan dance performance at Princes Street Gardens, Edinburgh, 2005.

Sir Desmond Lorenz de Silva, of Sri Lankan and Anglo-Scottish origins, is one of England's most prominent Queen's Counsels. From 1980 to 1995, he was the elected councillor for the largest ward in the City of London.

CHALLENGES

Sri Lankan cultural and religious centres in the UK provide many services for the diaspora. Through their activities, they have aided in creating a sense of community and belonging. However, these centres face some important challenges. Foremost is the need for funds for the purchase and maintenance of buildings, and for the activities that they carry out throughout the year on a charitable basis. Despite financial difficulties, most centres have managed to survive over the last two or three decades. A number of centres have gradually and steadily expanded and have had a significant impact on Sri Lankan communities.

In the UK, Sri Lankan parents face another challenge. Their children attend regular schools and learn values, ideals and expressions from their environment. In this respect, parents rely on Sri Lankan centres to provide some traditional religious and cultural education with an introduction to the arts and aesthetics of Sri Lanka. For this purpose, in recent years schools for teaching dance and music of Sri Lanka have emerged in the London area. The Sri Lankan filmmaker, Tissa Madawela documents for the media, the cultural and religious events that take place in the community (Fernando, 2005). There are frequent concerts, musical shows and visits from Sri Lankan pop bands. While the first generation is satisfied with the practice of traditional religious rituals, the second generation is more inclined to learn and practice humanistic values of the respective religions. While struggling to preserve Sri Lankan cultural and religious heritage, a key challenge for these Sri Lankan centres is to find a balance to meet the differing needs of the first and the second generation of the diaspora.

Community relations between members of the Sri Lankan diaspora have largely been peaceful. Occasional violence, such as the 2011 shooting of five-year-old Thusha Kamaleswaran, shocked the community. Diasporic religious communities have increasingly come to participate in interfaith activities. There is a significant dialogue and exchange of ideas with Christian denominations and church organisations. For most festivals, Christian clergy and dignitaries such as MPs, MEPs, councillors and members of other faiths are invited so that there are significant interactions between the Sri Lankan diaspora and other communities in the UK. Sri Lankan communities in UK now have well-established networks in Sri Lanka so that they can send money and goods for participating in relief activities, which become important and prominent during periods of crisis such as the 2004 Tsunami.

THE FUTURE

Key challenges for the Sri Lankan community in Britain at the beginning of the 21st century pertain to issues of unity and political settlement at home. Rebuilding communities that were adversely impacted by the civil war remains a major concern both for the local and international community. Though there is political stability in Sri Lanka, the government's efforts for reconciliation and harmony among the divided communities has not yet been received favourably by the international community. The Sri Lankan government is encountering difficulty in convincing the international community that it has done well in securing a peaceful settlement with the Tamils. This is especially evident with regard to ensuring healthy economic progress for Sri Lanka and in particular to the war affected areas. These Sri Lankan political episodes and economic policies will determine the interactions and future cooperation among the Sri Lankan ethnic communities who have chosen Britain as their home.

Mahinda Deegalle

Sir Sabaratnam Arulkumaran is the President of the International Federation of Gynaecology and Obstetrics. In 2009, he was honoured as Knight Bachelor in the Queen's Birthday Honours List for his immense contribution in the field of medicine.

Sri Lanka-born Niranjan Joseph Nirj Deva-Aditya, better known as Nirj Dev, is a prominent politician in the United Kingdom. In 1999, he became the first Asian-born person to be elected as a Conservative Member of the European Parliament.

THE NETHERLANDS

In 1602, the Dutch naval officer, Joris van Spilbergen, met the King of Kandy, Vimala Dharma Suriya, and discussed the possibility of trade in cinnamon.

RELATIONS BETWEEN SRI LANKA and the Netherlands date back more than 400 years. On 30 May 1602, Admiral Joris van Spilbergen became the first Dutchman to set foot on Sri Lanka's shores in the neighbourhood of Batticaloa. From there he journeyed to Kandy, where he met the Ceylonese King Vimala Dharma Suriya.

In 1638, King Raja Sinha entered into an agreement with the Dutch on the understanding that they would help him to oust the Portuguese in exchange for trade benefits. In 1640, the Dutch captured Galle, the largest city in the south, followed by Colombo in 1656 and two years later Jaffna, the capital of the north.

The Dutch East Indies Company—Vereenigde Oost-Indische Compagnie (VOC)—maintained control over Ceylon till 1796. Over this period, the VOC's key concern was to optimise profits. The administrative and judicial reforms, expansion of agriculture and horticulture, and construction of canals were carried out in order to promote trade. In 1795, when France invaded the Netherlands, Prince William V, who took refuge in England, instructed the Dutch Governor in Colombo— Van Angelbeek—to hand over the VOC's possessions to the English. Consequently, the VOC surrendered Ceylon to the English in 1796 (Jongens, 2002: 7–12). The long-standing relations between Sri Lanka (then Ceylon)

Map 4.10

and the Netherlands had wider implications on the development of Sri Lankan society, and provides a backdrop for the advent of Sri Lankan emigration to the Netherlands.

BURGHERS

After their conquest, the Dutch founded colonies of Dutch citizens in Sri Lanka known as 'Burghers'. This was first attempted under Maetsuyker (governor from 1646 to 1650). However, at the end of his government and even under Rijcklof van Goens (governor from 1662–63 and 1665–75), there were only 68 married free-Burghers on the island. The policy was clearly a failure as only a few Dutch families settled on the island. In the first 30 years of Dutch rule in Ceylon, the Burgher community never exceeded 500 and mainly comprised of sailors, clerks, tavern-keepers and discharged soldiers.

Nonetheless, the VOC support did facilitate the strengthening of the Burgher position in Sri Lanka. Burghers alone had the privilege to keep shops, and were given liberal grants of land with the right of free trade. Whenever possible they were preferred to natives for appointment to office. Only Burghers had the rights to baking bread, butchering and shoemaking. Most were civil servants of the Company. Even after the English takeover of Sri Lanka, the Dutch Burghers maintained

Sri Lankans in the Netherlands posing for a group photograph after a cricket tournament, 2011.

their distinct profile. In 1899, the Dutch Burgher community formed the 'De Hollandsche Vereeniging' and later, in 1908, founded the Dutch Burgher Union of Ceylon. The 1981 Sri Lankan census listed 39,374 Burghers (both Dutch and Portuguese) accounting for 0.3 per cent of the total population.

IMMIGRATION AND SETTLEMENT

Officially, 10,346 Sri Lankans were resident in the Netherlands in 2010. However, unofficial estimates suggest that the figure is closer to 16,000. Sri Lankan emigration to the Netherlands can be divided into two distinct phases: the first, extending from Sri Lanka's independence to the early 1980s, comprises of mainly educated personnel, businessmen and students who took up residence in the Netherlands; and the second is made up overwhelmingly of asylum seekers and political refugees, mostly Tamils, who arrived from 1984 onwards.

Many Burghers left Sri Lanka after independence. Very few, however, settled in the Netherlands; most turning instead to Australia. Over time, a small group of Sri Lankans, mostly of Sinhalese background also migrated to the Netherlands. These Sri Lankans were usually businessmen and students, but also some lower-ranked personnel from the Sri Lankan Embassy. Some settled permanently in the Netherlands and many married a Dutch partner that facilitated their integration into the wider Dutch society.

Until 1984, the Sri Lankan community was small, because many students and businessmen did not settle permanently in the Netherlands. From 1984, however, Sri Lankans started to migrate to the Netherlands as asylum seekers. Although most were Tamils, some Sinhalese also moved. At the initial stage, Dutch policy was quite liberal and even Sinhalese migrants were easily able to acquire a residence permit.

Between 1984 and 1987, more than 3,500 Tamil men arrived in the Netherlands (*Tamil-asielzoekers in Nederland*, 2006). In the first three months of 1985, large numbers of Tamils arrived daily in the Netherlands. This led to huge pressures on settlement facilities, which in turn gave rise to an aversion towards Tamil asylum seekers. Hard pressed to cope with the influx, Dutch authorities implemented a policy of discouraging refugee migration. Tamil refugees were given a very basic arrangement known as the 'bed-bath-bread arrangement'. Very stringent asylum procedures and restrictions were imposed. Tamil men were confined to small rooms that they had to share with many others. Some Tamil refugees, not content with the asylum procedures and the facilities offered, went on hunger strike; and radicals set fire to a housing facility, which in turn generated even more hostility towards Tamils in the Netherlands.

The second wave arrived between 1990 and 1992. This group included women and children, reuniting with male household heads who had left earlier. In 1993, the Dutch government gave refugees the opportunity to apply for permanent residence; however, of the more than 14,000 Tamils who applied, only 2,200 were accepted (Verhallen, 2008; Geuijen, 2004). Nonetheless, the basis for a sizeable Tamil community was created and this was important for the future development of the diaspora.

The third wave of migrants arrived between 1995 and 2000. During this period, the net annual Sri Lankan migration (immigration minus emigration) was more than 500. In 1995, the net migration was 563, while in 2000, 623 Sri Lankans settled in the Netherlands (CBS, Statline, 2011). However, after 2000, immigration to the Netherlands declined, while the emigration of Sri Lankans from the Netherlands increased. For example, in 2009, while Sri Lankan immigration to the Netherlands was 343, net immigration was only 202.

UN refugee statistics posit that between 2000 and 2009, 13,231 refugees in total left Sri Lanka for the Netherlands. These were mostly Tamils, with the Sinhalese comprising a very small fraction. While most refugees chose to flee to Europe, some interviewed by Tessa Verhallen posited that their purpose was to settle in the Netherlands because of the positive view they held of the country. Women refugees went to the Netherlands because their husbands or acquaintances already lived there. The same was true of some Tamil men who fled after the first wave and chose to settle in the Netherlands because, as they explained to Verhallen, their 'brother', 'uncle', or 'friends' already lived there (Verhallen, 2008).

DEMOGRAPHIC PROFILE

Over the last 15 years, the Sri Lankan population in the Netherlands has almost doubled in size. In 1996, the Sri Lankan population was 5,600, while in 2010, more

Birthday celebrations in a Dutch-Sri Lankan family.

Table 4.2

SRI LANKANS IN THE NETHERLANDS BY AGE GROUPS IN 2010			
Age groups	Men	Women	Total
0–20 years	2,016	1,886	3,902
20–40 years	1,613	1,528	3,141
40–60 years	1,753	1,157	2,910
Above 60 years	204	189	393
	5,586	4,760	10,346

Source: Central Bureau of Statistics (CBS), Statline, The Hague, 2011.

Table 4.3

FAMILY STATUS OF SRI LANKANS IN THE NETHERLANDS IN 2010			
	Men	Women	Total
Unmarried	3,434	2,665	6,099
Married	2,012	1,885	3,897
Widowed	103		103
Divorced	120	127	247
	5,586	4,760	10,346

Source: Central Bureau of Statistics (CBS), Statline, The Hague, 2011.

Table 4.4

SRI LANKANS IN THE NETHERLANDS: FIRST AND SECOND GENERATIONS				
Year	Men First generation	Women First generation	Men Second generation	Women Second generation	Total
2000	3,635	2,339	860	851	7,685
2005	3,852	3,109	1,460	1,406	9,827
2010	3,697	2,959	1,889	1,801	10,346

Source: Central Bureau of Statistics (CBS), Statline, The Hague, 2011.

Table 4.5

SRI LANKANS IN THE NETHERLANDS BETWEEN 1996 AND 2010			
	Men	Women	Total
1996	3,611	2,025	5,636
2000	4,495	3,190	7,685
2005	5,312	4,515	9,827
2010	5,586	4,760	10,346

Source: Central Bureau of Statistics (CBS), Statline, The Hague, 2011.

Sri Lankan Muslims in the Netherlands pray before breaking their fast during the month of Ramadan, 2010.

than 10,000 Sri Lankans resided in the Netherlands. The proportion of men remains higher than women, but compared to 1996, the ratio has become more balanced (see Table 4.2 and Table 4.5).

The Sri Lankan population in the Netherlands is young. More than one-third (38 per cent) are under 20 years of age. The elderly—those above 60 years—comprise a small group of about 400 (less than 4 per cent of the Sri Lankan population in the Netherlands). In particular, the male political refugees who fled Sri Lanka more than 20 years ago and settled in the Netherlands are over-represented in the 40–60 year age group.

One notable feature is that a small group of men are listed as unmarried or widowed. Some men who fled Sri Lanka have probably not been able to find a spouse. This may partly be due to the very stringent Dutch procedures on immigration of a partner from a non-western country.

Although most Sri Lankans of the first generation have lived in the Netherlands for less than 25 years, in 2010 one in three Sri Lankans were born in the Netherlands. In 2000, only one of five Sri Lankans belonged to the second generation. It is clear from the above that the Netherlands-born Sri Lankans have come to comprise a growing segment of the Sri Lankan community.

Unlike other ethnic minorities in the Netherlands, most Sri Lankans do not live in big cities. For example, in 2007, only 485 Sri Lankans resided in Amsterdam. Sri Lankans are instead concentrated in towns in the centre of the Netherlands (Zeist, Utrecht and Nieuwegein), in the south (Roermond, Den Bosch and Breda) and in the northwest (Den Helder and Hoorn). This pattern is largely because government policies have consciously sought to settle (former) refugees away from big cities.

SOCIO-ECONOMIC POSITION AND EMPHASIS ON EDUCATION

While exact figures are not available, the overarching impression is that most Sri Lankan adults in the Netherlands are employed. When unemployed they acquire further qualifications through educational courses. Unemployed adults also get social benefits from the government in the Netherlands. Hence, every adult individual or family has an income. Tamils have taken advantage of the opportunities for earning a living in the Netherlands. Additionally, the low unemployment level in the community is also because Tamils have displayed a willingness to take on jobs below their qualifications (for example, in the cleaning and horticulture sector).

In Verhallen's study of the Tamil community, all respondents attached great value to education. Both boys and girls are raised with the idea that 'education is most essential in life'. A good education is seen as a key instrument for upward mobility. Consequently, even in the case of first generation immigrants, some have taken up advanced study in the Netherlands, which has made it possible for them to take up higher paid jobs than they had in Sri Lanka. There is a strong notion that through

Sri Lankan Hindu wedding in the Netherlands, 2011.

A traditional Sri Lankan dance performance in the Hague, 2010.

education, those in the diaspora will be best placed to aid in the development of their community in Sri Lanka.

CULTURAL INTEGRATION

Although Sri Lankans have (functional) contact with the white Dutch, and to some extent with other ethnic groups, the Tamils, in particular, have maintained a distinct identity. Indeed when compared to any other Sri Lankan immigrant community they have kept their culture and language intact; they maintain intensive relations with Sri Lanka and the Tamil diaspora; and there are very few inter-racial marriages within the group. Although the Tamil diaspora is scattered around the Netherlands, communications with others in the community have been maintained through mobile phone. They also gather frequently at community-based cultural and sports events organised in the different towns and cities where they reside. This has been possible because of the proximity of cities and towns, which are usually less than a three-hour drive away.

Classes are conducted for children to learn the Tamil language. Tamil television channels are easily accessible. Tamils also maintain close contact with their families in Sri Lanka and considerable sums are remitted to support them. The first generation of immigrants tend to keep abreast of news and developments about the Tamil minority in Sri Lanka. For the second generation, however, obligations towards Sri Lanka are less important. That is not to say that they are fully integrated into Dutch society. Many Tamils emphasise that integration does not mean that they have to give up 'their' culture totally, but to mix or practice both Dutch and Tamil culture.

Unlike the Tamil community, the other Sri Lankan diasporic groups have not maintained as distinctive an identity. This is in part due to their numbers. The Sinhalese comprise approximately 5–8 per cent of the Sri Lankan population and live in large cities like the Hague. When compared to the Tamils, they generally have more contact with the Dutch. The Sinhalese also maintain ties with Tamils as they share a Sri Lankan culture and sometimes work together in common organisations.

However, in spite of cordial relations, there are, from time to time, instances of conflict especially when more hardline Tamil activists and organisations are involved.

RELIGION

Although a small number of Tamils are Roman Catholic or have become members of evangelical churches such as Jehovah's Witnesses, the overwhelming majority are Hindus. Religion—in particular, Hinduism—is actively practised and functions as an important bond between most Tamils. 'Temples' have been established in towns where some 500 Tamil Hindus reside. Often the 'temple' is simply a room or rooms for their deities and a space for praying. Devotees visit the temple usually on weekends, and occasionally on weekdays.

The first temple space for Tamils from Sri Lanka was established in Den Helder, where Hindu ceremonies, meetings and celebrations are conducted. The temple is crucial in the establishment of the Tamil diasporic community in the Netherlands. Donations from private individuals aided in the establishment of a proper temple in 2005. In other towns, temples are usually based in community centres. For example in Zeist, Tamils rent small rooms on a second floor and two rooms have deities. Almost all Tamils in Zeist are members of the local temple organisation. The rent for the site (almost €2,500 monthly) is paid for by subscriptions.

The Sinhalese in the Netherlands are nearly all Buddhist or Catholic. The community is however, too small to have their own temple. Consequently, some visit the Vietnamese Buddhist temple in Hilversum. The Sri Lankan New Year on 14 April is celebrated by both Sinhalese and Tamils.

ORGANISATIONS

Sri Lankans in the Netherlands have formed various types of organisations. S. V. Den Helder was the first sports organisation founded in 1995 in Den Helder. In 2011, the sports body not only had a soccer team but also a cricket and volleyball team. In addition, soccer teams for women and youngsters have also been established. These soccer clubs have organised tournaments with one another. In 2011, there were eight officially registered soccer or football clubs in the different places where Tamils lived.

Tamil groups have also established websites. Together they organise activities, sometimes linked to Tamil ritual commemorative days. Often, the common denominator of nearly all of these events is fund-raising. For example, in 2007, funds were raised on Martyrs' Day commemorated by Tamils, in the town of Nieuwegein.

Tamils from the Netherlands participating in a Christian procession held in Belgium.

Only one Dutch town has a *Jumelage* (sister city relationship) with a counterpart in Sri Lanka. The *Jumelage* between the town of Velsen and Galle in Sri Lanka is more than 35 years old. Some organisations disseminate information about Sri Lanka and promote and organise tourism there. In 2010, a waste disposal project and a sports training programme was set up in Galle with financial assistance and advice from Velsen. Exhibitions of children's drawings from Galle in the Town Hall of Velsen have, in the past, attracted crowds of admirers. All the projects are coordinated and supervised by the Netherlands Alumni Association of Lanka (NAAL). Furthermore, the shopping centre of a new quarter in Velsen is also Galle Promenade, and surrounding streets are named after Sri Lankan cities.

IMAGE AND POLITICAL ACTIVITIES

The negative perception of the Tamils in the 1980s and 1990s is certainly less evident in the contemporary period. The 2004 tsunami increased compassion for Sri Lanka and Sri Lankan Tamils. The Tamil community has been working hard to build on this positive *Jumelage*. Having said that, until 2010 there continued to be reports of the LTTE being active in the Netherlands and pressuring the Tamil community for 'donations'. Fund-raising by the group has been undertaken through the organisation of events, and LTTE activists have also visited Tamils at their homes for the purpose. Periodically, demonstrations have been held against the oppression of the Tamils in Sri Lanka. For example, on 29 April 2009, some 600 Tamils protested in the Dutch capital, while smaller demonstrations have been organised in other towns such as Den Helder.

Now that the civil war in Sri Lanka has ended, the Tamils have come to be more focused on securing their future in the Netherlands. Their position has been helped by local newspapers which, after 2010, have provided more positive coverage of the community.

Chan E. S. Choenni

Prayer offerings for a chariot procession in Zeist.

This image—a drawing by a young Tamil student—released by the Dutch National Police Services Agency (KLPD), shows planes bombing thatched huts. In a report sent confidentially to Dutch municipalities in early 2011, police alleged that as many as 21 Tamil schools in the Netherlands were controlled by LTTE front organisations.

FRANCE

HISTORICAL OVERVIEW

France was not the favoured destination of Sri Lankan migrants at large, but for specific reasons it became important for Sri Lankan diasporas after the 1970s. The language barrier was initially a handicap, hence the first wave of Sri Lankan migrants, drawn from the English-speaking elite, chose Commonwealth countries instead and did not settle in France.

Yet pull factors in favour of emigration to France were already evident even before the great influx of the 1980s. France had a substantial community of French citizens of (Indian) Tamil origin (from the former French territories of Pondicherry and Karaikal, and also from Réunion and the French Caribbean islands) who could act as intermediaries. Most of them had opted for French citizenship and came to France in the late 1950s and early 1960s, after the transfer of Pondicherry and Karaikal to India, and following the independence of Vietnam and the subsequent communist take over there (there was a sizeable Tamil community in Saigon during the colonial period in police, army and trade).

Another factor effecting Sri Lankan emigration to France was that French Catholic priests (especially Oblates of Mary Immaculate) and nuns were numerous during the late British colonial period in the parishes of the Sri Lankan west coast, from Colombo to Chilaw, with Negombo as a major centre, and in the parishes of North Sri Lanka, from Mannar to Point Pedro, with Jaffna and the islands as focal points. The Catholic connection was an important resource for migrants from the Sri Lankan coasts, especially people from fishing communities, who were already commuting between Sri Lanka and India, and were most adversely affected by the growing conflict on the island. Italy was another possibility, but this was the favoured option of Sinhala-speaking Catholic migrants, while Tamil-speaking Catholic migrants preferred France.

The most important factor (or rather conjunction of factors) explaining the growth of Sri Lankan diasporas in France was the relative ease with which it was possible to obtain political refugee status during the Mitterrand Presidency (1981 to 1995), at a time when the Thatcher

A stall selling an array of Sri Lankan items during the 'Sri Lanka Day' celebrations in France, 2010.

Map 4.11

Wesak Day in Paris, 2010.

Government restricted Commonwealth emigration to the UK, even as the Eelam wars resulted in very large numbers of Tamils fleeing the country, and JVP activities and the harsh repression by the Premadasa government unsettled Southern Sri Lanka. Finally, various actors in French civil society were involved in aiding the movement of Sri Lankans to France: NGOs such as *France Terre d'Asile, Médecins sans Frontières* and *Caritas/Secours Catholique*, were ready to help migrants, while leftist groups supported liberation or revolutionary movements across the world.

Cultural exchange also played a role in aiding Sri Lankan emigration to France. Small groups of would-be French Buddhists who had spent time in meditation centres in Sri Lanka were ready to help set up Buddhist associations in France (although Tibetan Buddhism was much more popular with the French, especially women). Some Sri Lankans, particularly from the middle class, were able to learn the French language at Alliance Française institutes established first in Colombo (1955), then in Kandy, Matara and Jaffna. A small number of Sri Lankan students were granted scholarships in the 1970s, and when the grants dried up they found means to stay on and were followed by other students. The tourist business became a significant pull factor: with direct air connection between Colombo and Paris, Sri Lanka proved to be a favoured destination for French tourists in the 1970s, and some returning tourists invited Sri Lankan friends, especially hoteliers or tour guides to France. Finally, a small number of upper class French families employed Sri Lankan women as domestic helpers, although this never became an organised business as in the Middle East.

Map 4.12

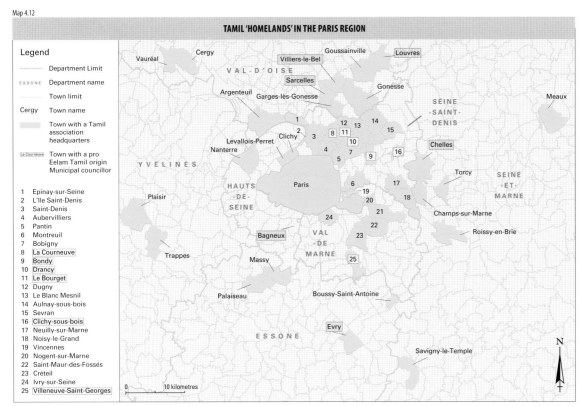

TAMIL 'HOMELANDS' IN THE PARIS REGION

Legend

Department Limit

ESSONE Department name

Town limit

Cergy Town name

Town with a Tamil association headquarters

La Courneuve Town with a pro Eelam Tamil origin Municipal councillor

1 Epinay-sur-Seine
2 L'Ile Saint-Denis
3 Saint-Denis
4 Aubervilliers
5 Pantin
6 Montreuil
7 Bobigny
8 La Courneuve
9 Bondy
10 Drancy
11 Le Bourget
12 Dugny
13 Le Blanc Mesnil
14 Aulnay-sous-bois
15 Sevran
16 Clichy-sous-bois
17 Neuilly-sur-Marne
18 Noisy-le-Grand
19 Vincennes
20 Nogent-sur-Marne
22 Saint-Maur-des-Fossés
23 Créteil
24 Ivry-sur-Seine
25 Villeneuve-Saint-Georges

Sources: G. Dequirez and E. Meyer; D. Madavan, 2011.

Most Sri Lankan emigrants arrived after 1983, with migration peaking during the 1990s, when political refugee status was still quite liberally granted. The restrictive policy of the French governments, especially after the 2002 Sri Lankan ceasefire and during the Sarkozy presidency from 2007, made it more difficult for migrants to obtain papers, but the inflow never ceased: bringing spouses or other members of the family from Sri Lanka is still common. The various routes to France and their attendant dangers are generally the same as for the rest of Europe, either through Eastern Europe or across the Mediterranean Sea, but circuitous itineraries through sub-Saharan Africa are also in use.

The Tamil Diaspora: Sociology and Politics

According to conservative estimates there are approximately 60,000 people of Sri Lankan origin in France. The estimate excludes children of emigrants born in France. More than 90 per cent of them are

Tamils. Tamils in France also comprise emigrants from the former French colonies, particularly Pondicherry, but as well from the Caribbean and from the Indian Ocean territories of Réunion and Mauritius. Because of the lack of statistics on ethnic groups in France (refer to the boxed feature on 'French census categories'), the geographical distribution of the Sri Lankan diaspora in French territory remains imprecise. Most of them are settled in Ile-de-France, and according to OFPRA (the French office for asylum seekers), in 2001, 89 per cent of Sri Lankan asylum seekers were located in this region. The urban concentration of Sri Lankan Tamils and their commercial and social dynamism have contributed to their visibility in the Paris region. The distribution of the Sri Lankan Tamil community associations in the Paris region provides interesting insight on the features of Tamil settlement in the city (see map 4.12).

Most Sri Lankan Tamils in France come from the Jaffna Peninsula and from the *vellala* and *karaiyar* castes. However, after the first arrivals in the 1970s, a greater diversity of geographical origin and caste has been manifested in the diaspora. Increasingly, Tamils from Mannar and the Vanni region applied for asylum.

FRENCH CENSUS CATEGORIES

Due to a specific integration tradition, it is very difficult to collect statistics on ethnic communities in France. Up to 1990, 'nationality' was the only criteria taken into account in the French census. Later the criteria 'immigrant' (defined as 'a person born abroad and living in France') was added. That category excluded the children of immigrants because the definition centred on the place of birth but not on the perceived 'ethnic' identity. Since 1978, French law forbids the collection of 'sensitive' data on racial or ethnic origin without the explicit consent of the interviewee. On the few occasions that deviations from this law are allowed, tight control is maintained by the state, and the data is organised in a way to preserve anonymity. It is for this reason that the figures for Sri Lankan diasporas in France are only estimates.

The wedding of Sri Lanka-born Purnima Athukorala and Roman Dragomirov was held at La Garenne Colombes, 2010.

The number of deprived caste groups such as the *pallars* and *nalavars* have also increased. Sri Lankan Tamil immigrants in France come mainly from middle and lower middle classes, as upper classes have shown a preference for Anglo-Saxon countries, while the lower classes generally cannot afford to pay the cost of the journey to the western world. In terms of employment prospects in France, language is a significant barrier. Consequently, Sri Lankan Tamils of the first generation have—in spite of their educational background and skills—often taken up employment in jobs not equivalent to their skills—as cooks, watchmen, domestic servants, and leaflet deliverers amongst others. Ethnic networks are crucial in facilitating access of Tamil newcomers to work and accommodation. *Cheetu* (a group saving and credit system common in Sri Lanka) is still used in the diaspora. Remittances are generally sent to Sri Lanka via informal money transfer systems.

In the Paris region an estimated 70 community-based associations are actively serving about 50,000 Sri Lankan Tamils. They are organised either at a national or at a local level. Most of them are officially called 'Associations-franco-tamoules' (French-Tamil associations) and are established at the level of one or several towns. They generally include a *Tamil cholai*, providing extra-school teaching for children; Tamil language courses and *bharatanatyam* dance courses. The development of these schools has been strengthened by the high level of investment in education, which is perceived as an avenue for upward social mobility.

Sri Lankan Tamils in France are either Christians or Hindus, and the latter have established nine temples. A Tamil sports club, 'Association sportive Eelavar' organises various sporting activities. There are youth and student organisations, aimed at the second generation; a women's organisation; humanitarian associations such as the ORT ('Organisation de Réhabilitation Tamoule'), a few home-village associations and an organisation of *dalits*, mainly focused on literary activities. The humanitarian section supports reconstruction projects particularly in relation to the damage caused by war and tsunami in the Tamil areas of Sri Lanka. All these associations are coordinated by head associations, which constitute the core of the system.

In France, a major part of the Sri Lankan Tamil associations are grouped in a federation. The Tamil Coordinating Committee (TCC) initially led this federation. In 2009, following a court ruling, the TCC was dissolved when some of its leaders were accused of collecting funds from Tamils for the LTTE. The Tamil Eelam House was established in 2009 in its place. Along with regular activities, the cultural and sports associations also set up collective events on various occasions (religious or traditional feasts, dance and music shows, sports competitions and so on). Almost every weekend, a Tamil event occurs in the Paris region. Grand annual events are very popular within the Tamil diaspora at large. *Salangai*, a bharatanatyam dance competition, which takes place in February, and *Tamilar Vilaiyattu Vizha*, a family friendly sports event held in July, are particularly notable.

Sri Lankan Tamil newspapers published in France include *Eelamurasu* and *Eelanadu*. Tamil literary magazines such as *Uyirnilal* and Tamil authors like the poet K. P. Aravindan and the writer Shoba Sakthi have contributed to Tamil literary productions in France. *TRT*, Tamil Radio and Television (renamed *TTN* Tamil Television Network in 2001) broadcasted from La Courneuve near Paris. The TV channel stopped broadcasting in 2007, but *TRT Tamil Olli*, a Tamil radio station, continues on the internet. Several websites are also based in France, like TamoulObs, or sites related to an association, like *ORT* France. But Sri Lankan Tamils in France also turn to international diasporic media that provide daily news from Sri Lanka. These diasporic media contribute to the construction of an 'imagined community', and they nourish a sense of transnational collective identity.

Tamil identity in France is reinforced by mass demonstrations in defence of the Tamil cause, such as

Tamils demonstrate in Paris to protest against the Sri Lankan government's offensive against strongholds of the LTTE, 2009.

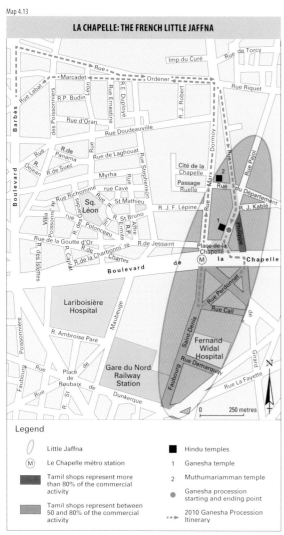

Map 4.13

LA CHAPELLE: THE FRENCH LITTLE JAFFNA

Legend

○ Little Jaffna

Ⓜ Le Chapelle métro station

■ Tamil shops represent more than 80% of the commercial activity

Tamil shops represent between 50 and 80% of the commercial activity

■ Hindu temples

1 Ganesha temple

2 Muthumariamman temple

● Ganesha procession starting and ending point

⇢ 2010 Ganesha Procession Itinerary

Source: Conception and mapping by A. Goreau-Ponceaud and D. Madavan, 2011.

the one that took place during the last phase of the LTTE fight in 2009. Regular political events or demonstrations are numerous: commemorations of important dates (July 1983, Prabhakaran's birthday), 'Martyr's Day' celebrations (*Maaveerar Naal, Annai Poopathy*) or international feasts (1st May, Women's Day). Second generation Tamils are now playing leading political roles in French society, thanks to their mastery of the French language. Local-elected representatives are the most receptive to Tamil associations and activism. Thus the more beneficial interactions for the Tamil militants have been at the local level, facilitated by electoral considerations. In 2008, a 'Tamil group' was formed with 12 elected representatives in different municipal councils of the Paris region. In 2010, a Tamil woman, the former secretary of the Tamil Coordinating Committee France, participated in the regional elections at the eighth position on the list of Europe Ecologie in Seine-Saint-Denis.

LA CHAPELLE, THE LITTLE JAFFNA IN PARIS

The French Little Jaffna, known as La Chapelle, is located in the 10th and 18th arrondissements of Paris around the La Chapelle metro station. Two zones can be distinguished (see map 4.13): the first, which extends south of the Boulevard de la Chapelle, is the most emblematic of the Sri Lankan Tamil population in the area, with a high concentration of commercial establishments or services

catering to the Tamil community. The second zone, north of the Boulevard de la Chapelle, is essentially known for the presence of two Hindu temples. One is dedicated to Ganesh, the other one to Maryamma. The larger Ganesh temple was founded in 1985, and, since 1996, is the only temple allowed to organise a procession in honour of Ganesh in the streets of La Chapelle. The colourful Chariot Festival, a tribute to the Hindu elephant god Ganesha, has become a popular annual procession eagerly anticipated by thousands of Parisians, including many non-Tamils.

The presence of many Sri Lankans of Tamil origin and the ethnic products offered in numerous shops strengthens what is perceived by the French at large as the 'Indianness' but is actually the 'Tamilness' of this neighbourhood. The display of Tamil cultural elements, especially from Sri Lanka, makes this district an ethnic territory and a minority centre. Thus, like in other 'Little Jaffnas' around the world, Tamil identity is evident by the pervasiveness of Tamil signs on store windows or posters pasted to walls (including obituary notices and movie posters). In addition, many shops carry a name that refers to Tamil cities (Jaffna/Yalpanam, Chennai/Madras, Pondicherry), or to Sri Lanka and India. The other Sri Lankan outlets are butcher's shops run by Sri Lankan Muslims and grocery stores run by the Sinhalese, which further reinforce the Sri Lankan character of this neighbourhood. Kollywood cinema and LTTE propaganda songs played in the stores are other elements that identify La Chapelle as a Sri Lankan Tamil district. All this distinguishes the neighbourhood from other areas of the city.

The commercial activity that developed in the area now caters to a much more diverse and widely spread community in the Paris region. The first immigrants, who were single men, lived in cheap hotels of 10th arrondissement. Later, with the arrival of their wives and children, they chose to settle in the suburbs that offered much lower rents or tried to buy houses to live with their entire family, especially in the northern suburbs well connected by rail to La Chapelle, such as La Courneuve, Garges and Sevran. Because of the diversity of businesses,

Map of the French Little Jaffna known as La Chapelle.

Ganesha Parade in Paris in 2007. The colourful chariot festival honoured Ganesha in the streets of 'Little Jaffna' where a large Sri Lankan community lives.

The 'Jaffna Boucherie' in Paris is one of the many stores and businesses that cater to the Sri Lankan diaspora in France.

Some retail outlets serve as a space for the projection of political sentiments. Aspirations related to 'Tamil Eelam' indicate the nature of the community's memory, longing and nostalgia towards their homeland.

La Chapelle has become a supply centre not only for the Tamils, but for other South Asian communities as well. There are restaurants, grocery stores, jewellers, travel agencies, bookstores, a driving school, a real estate agency, video shops, hairdressers and Indian beauty centres all catering to South Asians. Not only do these ethnic businesses attract the Tamil community, but more and more Parisians and tourists come to La Chapelle for the exotic character of the neighbourhood.

La Chapelle is also the centre of social networking and solidarity for Sri Lankan Tamils. It is a meeting place with other members of the community. The newly arrived, who do not know French and lack identity cards, can seek support and help in finding employment or housing within the community. Moreover, the neighbourhood has an important role in the transmission of culture and identity to the second and third generations. The district is also the place where youths born in France introduce their Tamil and/or Sri Lankan cultures to their friends from other origins through food or clothing.

Finally, the influence of the LTTE in La Chapelle is indisputable. Many shops have a portrait of Prabhakaran or the flag of the separatist movement. Many cultural and social institutions linked to the LTTE have their headquarters in the district (Tamil Youth Organisation, Tamil *cholai*, etc.). The stores display black banners to commemorate the death of a dignitary (Prabhakaran, Balasingham, Thamilselvam) or red and yellow banners during the celebrations of the separatist movement (*Maaveerar Naal*). In this district many demonstrations have been held in support of the LTTE and to denounce the military operations of the Sri Lankan army during the

Sri Lankan dance concert organised by the 'Sarasavi Ranga Nikethanaya' in France, 2012.

final military offensive in 2009, including the detention of Tamils in internment camps. The LTTE hold on the district is perceived as dangerous by the French authorities and has resulted in the local police raiding and arresting LTTE supporters for racketeering. The political function of La Chapelle clearly identifies this district as an Eelam Tamil diasporic territory.

Outside the Paris region, there are small Tamil communities in large cities such as Lyon and Rennes. Finally, two places of Catholic pilgrimage are very popular among Sri Lankans: Chartres mainly attracts Tamil faithful from Paris, while Lourdes attracts Tamils as well as Sinhalese.

The Sinhalese Diaspora

There is no homogeneous Sinhalese diaspora in France: their numbers are quite small (less than 5,000) and scattered. Broadly speaking, there is a group comprising middle class emigrants from Colombo, many of whom learnt French in Sri Lanka, who settled in France for studies, or to work in organisations such as UNESCO, or to do business (especially in tourism). Another group is made up of individuals or families who left Sri Lanka (notably the Southern province) during periods of political turmoil (especially 1989–93). Many applied for political refugee status in France as JVPers, but a few were ex-members of the armed forces.

While the first generation of migrants with a good command of English and French found employment in trade or services (often for the international community in Paris), newcomers sought odd jobs just like their Tamil counterparts. There are many cultural associations started by individuals or small groups, most of them short lived, which organise screenings of Sinhala films, music and dance performances, often with the support of the Sri Lankan embassy. There are also political associations—pro-UNP, pro-JVP, or pro-Rajapaksa—which became vocal during the Eelam wars and lobbied to counter the very effective demonstrations of the pro-LTTE groups. The Sinhalese diaspora generally seek to distance themselves from the history and culture of the much larger Tamil diaspora, and vice versa, although an attempt has been made to start a Sinhala-Tamil programme at university level at the National Institute for Oriental Languages and Civilisations (INALCO).

There is no specific Sinhalese area in Paris, but there are a few shops and restaurants, established alongside Tamil shops in La Chapelle, which the Sinhalas patronise. The only significant places of gathering for the Sinhala community are the Buddhist temples. The first to be established was the Centre Bouddhique International, founded in 1984 in Ermont by Parawahera Chandraratana, with the support of the then UNP government and of French Buddhists. In 1989, the temple was relocated to Le Bourget in the northern suburbs near Roissy Airport. The second temple is the Dhamma Chakra founded in Bobigny (also in the northern suburbs) by Ko Ananda, a well known pro-JVP monk and novel-writer, harassed by the Premadasa regime, who obtained political refugee status after 1989. Sri Lankans also attend the Vincennes Pagoda, which they share with other Buddhists, especially those from Southeast Asia. Finally, there are also a small number of Sinhala Catholics from the Negombo area, who have maintained connections with the former French missionaries.

Gaëlle Dequirez, Delon Madavan and Eric Meyer

GERMANY

THE SRI LANKAN diaspora constitutes the largest population of South Asians and of native Hindus in Germany. In 2011, there were 60,000 Sri Lankans residing in Germany, 33,000 of whom had attained German citizenship. The Federal Statistical Office does not distinguish Sri Lankan nationality and Tamil ethnicity, nor does it record religious membership. It is estimated that about 90 per cent of the Sri Lankan population is Tamil, approximately 70 per cent of whom are Hindus. Apart from the tiny Sinhalese Buddhist community which will be discussed in the final section due to its relatively different history, the Sri Lankan presence in Germany is recent and closely connected with the political situation of Sri Lankan Tamils in their homeland during the last four decades of the 20th century. In spite of difficult legal and labour conditions from 1985 to 2005, the refugees have successfully integrated without giving up their own cultural heritage.

Like other migrant communities, religion and religious institutionalisation are among the major factors of cultural reproduction and identity alongside family ties, ethnicity, common customs and language. This has been particularly true in Germany, where the largest temple in continental Europe was inaugurated in July 2002—the Tamil-Hindu Sri Kamadchi Ampal Alayam at Hamm-Uentrop (North-Rhine/Westphalia). The establishment of the temple has had a great impact, being the first in the style of traditional South Indian architecture. The temple and its yearly processions have

become a major meeting place for Sri Lankan Tamils both across the country and beyond. In addition, this has made the German majority population aware of a South Asian heritage within their own society, which has been exceptionally well received.

HISTORY

Unlike the countries of the British Commonwealth and the US, Germany is not a classical country for migrants from South Asia. The South Asian diaspora here is relatively small and recent. Between the 1950s and 1970s, the number of Indian citizens settling in Germany grew very gradually, reaching around 40,000. They were mainly medical students and professionals from North Western India; some came from Tamil Nadu and other Indian states. Both the number of South Asians and their social structure changed dramatically with the large-scale migration from Sri Lanka caused by civil war. Germany witnessed an influx of asylum seekers from Sri Lanka from the late 1970s onwards. Many of the first refugees came from land-owning *vellala* families or other higher

Tamil pilgrims light candles at the Catholic shrine of Madonna in Kevelaer, Germany. Since the late 1980s, the shrine in Kevelaer has become an important pilgrimage site for the Sri Lankan Tamil diaspora in Europe.

Map 4.14

GERMANY

The 'Ceylon Tearoom' at a fun fair in Bavaria, 1908.

A Sri Lankan dance troupe arrives for a performance at the Berlin Cathedral, 2003.

Sri Lankan Tamils selling 'exotic' fruits in Germany.

A recruitment campaign by the Duesseldorf police reaches out to young migrants in Germany, 2011.

castes in search of better labour conditions. By the 1980s and 1990s, however, most immigrants were from the lower and middle classes of rural Jaffna and were less educated. Most Sri Lankan Tamils experienced 'double migration', that is migration from their homeland to a foreign society and culture, and migration from rural areas to cities.

In 1978, only 1,299 Sri Lankan citizens were living in Germany, but in 1979 the number had already grown to 2,253. The influx augmented after the anti-Tamil riots in 1983. In 1985, a peak of 17,340 asylum seekers was recorded. As armed conflict in Sri Lanka continued, significant numbers continued to arrive. In the beginning this mainly comprised young men fleeing from persecution by the Sri Lankan army or forced recruitment by the LTTE (Liberation Tigers of Tamil Ealam). In the course of time wives, children and older family members were able to join them. In 1997, the Sri Lankan population in Germany reached a peak of 64,912 persons, 60,330 of whom still had Sri Lankan citizenship. About a third were below the age of 18, and about 63 per cent aged between 18 and 45. The percentage of males (63.5 per cent) was still much higher than that of females (36.5 per cent) (Baumann, 2003: 44, 49–51).

In the succeeding years there were very few new arrivals, with the exception of marriage partners. The total number of Sri Lankans in Germany decreased slightly, but remained more or less stable at about 60,000. A major reason behind the shrinking figure was the policy of tighter regulation on the part of the Federal Republic of Germany. This caused the applications for asylum to decline drastically from 1995. Other reasons included deportation to Sri Lanka, and migration to other countries, in particular Canada, where the legal and labour situations were more favourable. On the other hand, the legal situation of Sri Lankan migrants in Germany has stabilised since the mid-1990s, and a relatively large proportion have chosen to apply for German citizenship. Between 1998 and 2001, a total of 12,800 Sri Lankans exchanged their Sri Lankan passport for a German one

(Baumann, 2003: 52). By 2002, a quarter (27.2 per cent) of the Sri Lankan population was already legally German, and this number increased in the following years.

Over the last decade, the decrease in the number of Sri Lankan citizens corresponded approximately to the number taking up German citizenship. The legal situation for those who have kept Sri Lankan nationality has also become increasingly safe. The German Federal Statistical Office recorded a steady growth in the female proportion so that the gender profile of the Sri Lankan population in Germany has become increasingly balanced since 2003. In 2009, the dominant age groups ranged from 25 to 55, the average age being 35 to 45. The Sri Lankan Tamil diaspora in Germany is a young population with growing potential, since many are young families with at least two children. By 2000, 11,100 (75.5 per cent) of the 14,700 children below the age of 18 were born in Germany.

LEGAL AND LABOUR SITUATION

Although Germany effectively became a multicultural country in the 1960s—mainly due to the influx of a large number of labour migrants from Turkey—there was no policy of multiculturalism. Even at the end of the 20th century, federal policy did not view Germany as a classical country of immigration. The legal effects were a policy of avoiding double citizenship for nationalities outside the EU, and a rigorous distinction between Germans and non-Germans. All migrants seeking asylum have a difficult path, particularly if their application for asylum is unsuccessful. They face restrictions, legal insecurities, very complicated asylum proceedings, and a tangled situation regarding the right to stay and permission to work. Residence and labour depend on each other and are subject to time limits.

The legal status of the Sri Lankan citizens in Germany varies, and the conditions for remaining in the country have changed over time. 90 per cent of those who came before 1985 were granted asylum and the right to stay. Some even attained double citizenship. However, this no longer applied after 1985, when the Federal Administrative Court decided that Sri Lankan Tamils were not suffering targeted persecution. The proportion of applicants granted asylum sank to 1 per cent or less in the following years. Asylum seekers were not returned to their country of origin but instead, were placed under the Geneva refugee conventions and were given the status of 'toleration', which they had to renew every six months if they sought to remain.

Between 2000 and 2005, the legal position of approximately half of the German Sri Lankan population was uncertain, while the other half had secure rights to stay and work. Effectively, German jurisdiction created a double-track society in the Sri Lankan community. Those who enjoyed legal security were largely better-off and better educated Sri Lankans who had arrived before the mid-1980s, while the others, belonging almost without

Table 4.6

	RECENT SHIFTS IN FEMALE PROPORTION AND CITIZENSHIP			
End of the year	German population with Sri Lankan citizenship	Percentage of females	Sri Lankans who attained German citizenship	Percentage of females
2003	41,062	46.1	2,431	41.6
2004	34,966	48.9	1,968	44.8
2005	33,219	49.6	1,944	44.1
2006	31,440	49.8	1,765	47.9
2007	29,977	49.7	1,678	49.3
2008	28,780	49.6	1,492	49.1
2009	27,505	49.4	1,407	53.3
2010	26,628	49.5	[data not available as of April 2011]	

Source: German Federal Statistical office (accessed 19 April 2011).

Sri Lankan weddings in Germany are being organised on an increasingly grand scale.

exception to the lower classes, lived in fear of losing their toleration status and risked being sent back to Sri Lanka.

The types of temporary rights of residence granted by the courts varied considerably from person to person, and proceedings differed vastly among the various German states. After 1993, most of the asylum applications were refused. A particular difficulty for all immigrants in Germany is that a better resident status will only be granted if the applicant has a secure job. However, employment itself is subject to restrictions and requires a work permit from the Federal Ministry of Labour. Only those Sri Lankans whose asylum applications were successful were issued with a 'special permit', granting rights equal to those of Germans. They were given the opportunity to attend organised language courses and (re-)training. The others were usually granted only a 'general permit' which was restricted to certain fields of labour and valid for not longer than two years.

At the turn of the 21st century, the majority of Sri Lankan Tamils had no long-term secure employment. Most worked in low-income sectors, such as cleaning, selling flowers, or as kitchen staff in the local restaurants. The situation became more relaxed by 2005, when a new law and special privileges for Sri Lankans were granted, which ended the toleration status for most. Henceforth, five years of constant stay and labour instead of eight were enough for a person to be granted the right of residence, or even unlimited stay. The Sri Lankan migrants were extremely flexible and forbearing in the face of legal problems and labour discrimination. They quickly recognised the mechanisms of German society and developed a high level of inter-cultural and social competence. They earned a reputation as being kind and diligent, although economic participation remained unsatisfying for most Sri Lankans of the first generation. However, compared with other minority groups, a smaller percentage was out of work or dependent on social welfare. Up until 2005 their major problems were formal and informal obstacles and structural discrimination—insecure residence status, not being allowed to work, bad labour conditions, and hidden discrimination by administrative authorities.

One of the greatest impediments for the first generation was their lack of German language skills. Language abilities, education and participation in the labour market tremendously increased in the second-generation. They move freely between the two cultures and develop creative ways of 'double belonging'. Most were eager to play an active part in German life. By 2011, Sri Lankan entrepreneurship was no longer rare.

SETTLEMENT PATTERNS AND SOCIAL LIFE

The official policy of the German authorities was to distribute Sri Lankan asylum seekers all over Germany to prevent the formation of 'ethnic colonies'. Nevertheless, about 45 per cent of all Sri Lankans are concentrated in the West German state of North-Rhine/Westphalia, probably because the local jurisdiction was less rigid than in other German states. It was possible to work legally while the asylum proceedings were still ongoing. The state has the largest industries, the highest population density and the largest number of migrants (21 per cent of all 'foreigners' in Germany). A minor concentration of Sri Lankans can also be found in Baden-Württemberg and Hesse, whereas other federal states attracted significantly fewer refugees, and the new federal states of the former East Germany was almost none.

This situation has had an impact on the establishment and distribution of Tamil shops, cultural and political associations, religious institutions, sports clubs, supplementary schools for Tamil language, and tuition services for music and dance. North-Rhine/Westphalia is the principal area where a Tamil infrastructure has developed. By 2011, there were 113 registered Sri Lankan Tamil associations in the German states, 54 of them in North-Rhine/Westphalia. In addition, there are a number of non-registered associations. There exist 134 Tamil schools, 67 in North-Rhine/Westphalia. The number of places of worship is also greater. In North-Rhine/Westphalia, for instance, there were 20 temples by 2011 although only nine had been registered. The places of worship receive no public funds. They are supported by sponsorship and membership fees.

Sporting activities are very popular among the younger generation. Six of the 39 cultural associations

Born on 1939, in Kaddaively (Sri Lanka), Ian Kiru Karan studied in the UK and migrated to Germany in 1970. A leading entrepreneur, Ian Kiru founded his first company in 1977, and gradually came to be known as the 'Container King' of Hamburg. In 2010, he was elected Senator for Economic and Labour Affairs in Germany.

Popular dance troupes, Channa Upuli and Berlin Sri, perform at the 2012 'Carnival of Cultures' held in Berlin. The Sri Lanka Association of Berlin was instrumental in encouraging Sri Lankan participation at the parade.

Table 4.7

DISTRIBUTION OF TAMIL ESTABLISHMENTS IN GERMAN STATES			
	Cultural associations	Sports associations	Temples	Total
Baden-Württemberg	11	1	2	14
Bavaria	4	-	2	6
Berlin	5	1	3	9
Brandenburg	-	-	-	-
Bremen	2	1	2	5
Hamburg	-	-	-	-
Hesse	8	1	1	10
Mecklenburg-Western Pomerania	-	-	-	-
Lower Saxony	3	2	1	6
North-Rhine/Westphalia	39	6	9	54
Rhineland-Palatinate	1	2	-	3
Saarland	2	1	2	5
Saxony	-	-	-	-
Saxony-Anhalt	-	-	-	-
Schleswig-Holstein	1	-	-	1
Thuringia	-	-	-	-
Germany	76	15	22	113

Source: Survey of Ann-Kristin Beinlich, Sandhya Marla and Annette Wilke, 2011.

in North-Rhine/Westphalia are sports associations, besides the other six registered sports clubs. As well as cultural, religious and sports associations, Tamil schools provide education complementing compulsory German schooling, particularly Tamil language courses. Teaching Tamil became a major concern because of the second generation's lack of fluency in Tamil. Tuition in the common language simultaneously promotes friendships amongst those attending and has strengthened feelings of belonging to the same cultural background.

Although Sri Lankan Tamils have good relations with their native German neighbours and colleagues, and many inter-cultural friendships exist, particularly among school children, the closest relations are generally those with Tamil compatriots. This applies both to adults and to youths. Indeed, the Sri Lankans are the migrant group in which most intra-ethnic marriages occur.

The most urgent fears and hopes are naturally associated with the political situation in Sri Lanka, and one's current passport has had little influence on national identification with the original homeland.

Young Sri Lankan girls pose for a photograph before the bharatanatyam *performance in Schwelm.*

After Prabhakaran's death there remains, however, a sense of ambivalence among the migrants regarding 'Tiger politics' and the project of an independent Tamil Eelam. Nonetheless they continue to share experiences of discrimination, violence and death, and hope for a better future. Great Heroes' Day is regularly celebrated in Dortmund. Since 1980 the event has attracted 7,000 to 14,000 Tamil immigrants—a lesser number, however, than the *Ter* procession at the temple festival of Hamm-Uentrop that saw a gathering of 20,000 participants from all over Germany and other European countries in 2010 and 2011.

There remains a deep interest in Sri Lanka's developments and in transnational networking to build a better future. Part of the young generation is very involved in informing the German public about the conflict in Sri Lanka and promoting inter-cultural understanding. However, political engagement is difficult in Germany. Those seeking German citizenship must declare a list of associations that they are not affiliated to. The LTTE is a forbidden organisation in Germany and political activism has had to go undercover. This, along with the new aspirations for a 'Transnational Government of Tamil Eelam', has likewise aroused the suspicion of the Federal Office for the Protection of the Constitution. However, Sri Lankan politics is rarely discussed in public media, and there is little awareness in the majority culture about the reported atrocities against Tamils in 2009.

The 'diaspora awareness' of a multilocal being 'both here and there' pertains very much to the Sri Lankan Tamils in Germany. No contradiction is seen in being Tamil and living in Germany or even being German. There is loyalty to both. For most Tamil immigrants, integration means incorporation into the general framework of legal norms and laws, a secure economic situation and a close-knit family. Only a minority of the educated strata and a portion of the younger generation deliberately seek inter-ethnic attitudes and relations, or even complete cultural assimilation.

RELIGION AND RELIGIOUS INSTITUTIONS

According to a survey conducted in 2001 and analysed in 2006, 63.3 per cent of Sri Lankan Tamils living in Germany identify themselves as Hindus, 4.6 per cent as Catholics, 3.9 per cent as Protestants, and 8.1 per cent as being both Hindu and Catholic. Another 13 per cent do not consider themselves attached to any religion. The higher-income groups and the second generation tend to be more distanced from religion than those from the lower-income group and the first generation. On the other hand, data points to strong religious attachment amongst most migrants: 86.7 per cent feel 'strongly' (21.1 per cent) or 'very strongly' (65.6 per cent) Hindu, and two thirds share a high regard for temple culture. In 2011, approximately 40,000 Sri Lankans were Hindus. Most of them belonged to the Tamil Saiva devotional (*bhakti*) and Saiva Siddhanta traditions.

Early migrants contented themselves with domestic shrines and religious gatherings in private homes but, as wives and children joined them, there was a growing demand for life-cycle rituals and larger spaces for worship and celebrating festivals. Since the mid-1980s, a growing number of temporary and permanent places of worship have been established, the first in Schwerte in 1985. In 2002, 25 temples were recorded. By 2011, at least 38 more have been established. Initially, the temples were

Sri Lankan Christians comprised a large segment of participants at an intercultural mass in Germany, 2011.

practically 'invisible' to the German majority, being confined to basements, apartments, former factories and abandoned warehouses. But there have been ongoing efforts to make them more 'visible', larger, more temple-like, and to establish more prestigious structures in better locations. There has been a steady trend to expand the *puja* hours and the festival calendar, and to engage full-time priests. In 1993, the Kamadchi temple in Hamm initiated the first chariot processions in Germany, and a number of other temples have followed suit. None, however, could match the number of participants and vow-fulfillers that the Kamadchi temple has been able to attract. The older temple versions, which were not yet traditional temple structures, already drew 6,000 to 10,000 pilgrims for the chariot procession.

A newer phase has been the building of structures with traditional architectural elements. The most striking example is the newly-built Kamadchi temple in the industrial area of Hamm-Uentrop, which was established in 2002 and whose richly embellished *vimana* and *gopuram* towers can even be seen from the highway. It was built as a joint venture between a German architect and a South Indian *sthapati* and his team of artisans,

who spent nearly two years in Germany. The temple consecration lasted eight days and was performed by 11 priests from Sri Lanka, and the grand festivities on the final day in particular attracted much media attention with local VIPs and a crowd of several thousand guests from all over Europe. Having a 'real' temple was a very important step. It brought Sri Lanka closer to the younger generation, some of whom had no first-hand experience of traditional temple culture.

The Kamadchi temple has clearly managed to gain dominance on representing Hinduism in Germany. This is, however, not undisputed. Among the Sri Lankan Tamils, one reason for objection is the unusual organisational model diverging from the normal one of a temple committee employing a Brahmin priest. The temple triggered a rival project among Indian Tamil Hindus who sought to establish a traditional structure in Berlin, and inspired other temple projects and cultural centres among Afghani Hindus and Balinese Hindus. While temple-building activities are new amongst Indian Hindus in Germany, the political refugee communities—i.e. the Sri Lankan and Afghani Hindus—have been more active in institutionalising their religion and transferring

In mid-1957, a Theravada Buddhist mission from Sri Lanka arrived in Germany. The delegation, which included the Venerable Soma Thera, Venerable Kheminde and Venerable Vinitha, resided at the Das Buddhistische Haus in Frohnau, Berlin. Since then Sri Lankan Buddhist monks have from time to time visited the Berlin Vihara.

The Kamadchi temple was the first Hindu temple in Germany to organise large-scale processions during festivals.

THE KAMADCHI TEMPLE IN HAMM-UENTROP

The consecration of the Sri Kamadchi Ampal temple in Hamm-Uentrop triggered a host of local, national and transnational dynamic processes. Media reports made the temple known all over Germany. Since 2002 it has also attracted an impressive number of native Germans, some of whom even participate in the rituals (*puja* and *arcana*) like the faithful Hindus. The annual temple festival, chariot procession and festival market have enjoyed a growing number of participants and fulfillers of vows of self-affliction and in 2003 and 2004 even 'bird *kavadi*'—a practice that was abandoned after an accident with a broken swinging beam. From 2002 to 2011, the festival attracted an increasing crowd of 12,000 to 20,000 participants from Germany and the neighbouring countries (Netherlands, Switzerland and France), and it includes ritual specialists and sponsors from Sri Lanka, India, France and Great Britain. Meanwhile, the temple has become an internationally famous place of pilgrimage and its initiating chief priest and founder, Sri Paskaran *gurukkal* (priest), a Vira-Saiva, Shrividya-Upasaka and Agama specialist, gained a reputation as a holy man. By 2011, four regular priests were performing services three times a day.

Members of the German Dharmaduta Society, 1954. The World Fellowship of Buddhists (WFB), founded by Gunapala Malalasekera in 1950, encouraged a group of Sri Lankan Buddhists to form the Lanka Dharmadutha Society to propagate Buddhism in Germany.

regional forms of indigenous Hinduism into the German space. Before their advent only some smaller temples of the International Society for Krishna Consciousness (ISKCON) existed. Now, a very active Hindu temple life exists in Germany.

THE SINHALESE BUDDHIST DIASPORA

Buddhism in Germany has two strands, converts and immigrants. The former numbered around 100,000 in 2011, the latter approximately 120,000. Since the 1970s and 1980s, Zen and Tibetan Buddhism have attracted most converts and a large circle of interested Germans. More than half of the immigrant Asian Buddhists are Vietnamese who fled South Vietnam in 1975 and after. They established the largest Buddhist place of worship in continental Europe in 1991—Vien Giac pagoda in Hanover, which houses 15 monks.

However, the Buddhist presence in Germany goes back to the early and mid-20th century and over this period, Ceylon played a key role in establishing Buddhism in Germany. Prior to World War I and in the inter-war years, interest in Buddhism was already growing among German intellectuals. This resulted in the first German translations of Pali scriptures, the foundation of a number of Buddhist associations, and conversions to Sinhalese Buddhism. In 1904, the first German (Anton Gueth) to become a Buddhist monk, the Venerable Nyanatiloka, founded the Island Hermitage on Polgasduwa (Ceylon) in 1911. His most famous German student Nyanaponika (Siegmund Feniger) likewise became a great Buddhist scholar and a Sri Lankan citizen. Converts in Germany included Paul Dahlke (1865–1928), who built the Buddhist House in Indo-Buddhist style in Berlin-Frohnau in 1924. The Buddhist House was purchased in 1957 by the German Dhammaduta Society of Colombo to accommodate the first Buddhist monastery in Germany. The society was founded in 1956 by the Sinhalese Buddhist Asoka Weeraratna with the explicit aim to establish a Buddhist mission in Germany. A delegation of three Sinhalese monks arrived in 1957, and ever since at least one Sinhalese *bhikkhu* has resided permanently in the Buddhist House and conducted meditation and Dhamma classes. In 2011, the number of German participants ranged from 15 to 40, and on Sundays 20 to 25 native Sri Lankans were present, although there is no official membership.

Another key location where German converts and practitioners of Buddhism interact with the Sinhalese Buddhist mission and diaspora is Hamburg, where the local Buddhist Society was founded in 1954 by the Venerable Narada Mahathera. In 1960 Hamburg became the seat of the German Buddhist Union (DBU), which brought together seven Buddhist denominations and joined the World Fellowship of Buddhists. The Buddhist Society of Hamburg has adopted an increasingly ecumenical orientation. Overall, the Sinhalese Buddhist mission has had a minor impact in Germany. Zen Buddhism has exerted a far greater impact since the 1970s, and Tibetan Buddhism from the 1980s. The DBU has expanded to more than 20 member-organisations, most comprising Tibetan Buddhist groups.

Annette Wilke

'The Berlin Lions Team' was founded in 2009 by Sri Lankan cricket enthusiasts.

SWITZERLAND

PROFILE

The Sri Lankan diaspora in Switzerland is one of the largest, after Canada, UK and Germany. Almost 95 per cent of the Swiss Sri Lankan population are Tamils, most of whom emigrated during the ethnic crisis in Sri Lanka from the early 1980s. It is predominantly an 'asylum diaspora' and this has shaped its identity and activities. Switzerland has been a strategic point of settlement in Europe creating the conditions for expressions of Tamil political aspirations, political negotiations and humanitarian relief efforts. Being outside the European Union (EU), Switzerland as a host country was not bound by the ban on the Liberation Tigers of Tamil Eelam (LTTE) and moreover, Geneva, as a hub of the United Nations and other multilateral agencies, has often seen public mobilisations of Tamils from all over Europe, led by Swiss Tamils. Sri Lankans are among the largest migrant groups in Switzerland, numbering around 50,000 people. Generic data on Sri Lankans in Switzerland in effect reflects trends among Tamils, as Sinhalas comprise only a small minority of between 3,000 to 5,000. This study therefore deals largely with the Swiss Tamil population.

Caste exists among Tamils in Sri Lanka, although not in such an elaborate form as it does among Tamils in Southern India. While caste is not prominent in public social interactions in diasporic settings, it continues to have some role in domestic rituals and arranged marriages (Ganesh, 2011: 175–6). Precise figures on the caste composition of Swiss Tamils are not available, however, McDowell (1996) points out that the early migrants to Switzerland, who arrived in the 1980s

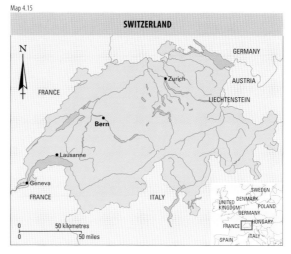

Map 4.15

SWITZERLAND

and early 1990s, comprised mainly high-caste *vellala* landowners, who controlled significant areas of farmland in Jaffna; *Theevans*—*vellala* traders from the island off the northwest coast of the Jaffna Peninsula; Roman Catholic urban *karaiyar* and some lower-castes from Jaffna Town (see also Luethi, 2005 and Marschall, *et al.*, 2003). Sri Lankan Tamils who sought asylum in Switzerland from 1995, tended to be mainly *karaiyar* and lower castes from predominantly rural areas.

McDowell's research also noted that early Tamil migrants in Switzerland tended to have lower educational attainment than Tamil migrants who settled in the UK, Australia or North America, reflecting, he argues, a migration strategy to match opportunity with ambition. Within Switzerland too, compared to Swiss citizens and other immigrants, Tamils above 25 years of age (usually first generation), are less educated (Moret *et al*, 2007: 51). However, it is noteworthy that there is very little gender disparity and clear indications that Tamil parents attach more importance to their children's educational qualifications than other recent migrant groups. The performance of Swiss Tamil students is improving, particularly in science and technical subjects.

Tamils—both men and women—are well integrated into the Swiss job market with more than 70 per cent working as unskilled labour, including educated migrants, a reflection of the restriction that work in the skilled sector is allowed only with stable residence permits. Around 20 per cent are white collar employees. Few are in skilled labour or senior service positions (Moret *et al*, 2007: 67). Over 40 per cent are employed in restaurants and hotels, and a good number are in care, maintenance and cleaning in hospitals, old age homes, etc.

FLIGHT TO SWITZERLAND

Between 1983 and 2007, almost 42,000 Sri Lankan Tamils sought refuge in Switzerland, the majority before 1994. Research suggests that Tamils initially used the asylum

Table 4.8

Caste of Migrant	Number	Percentage of Total	Proportion of Jaffna Caste Population in the 1960s
CASTE COMPOSITION OF TAMIL ASYLUM MIGRANTS ENTERING SWITZERLAND BETWEEN 1983 AND 1991			
'Touchable'			
Vellala (Cultivators)	162	62	50-57.0
Brahmin (Priests)	2	1	0.9
Karaiyar (Sea Traders)	34	13	10.0
Mukkiyar (Divers/Fishermen)	13	4	2.0
Timilar (Fishermen)	2	1	no entry
Tattar (Goldsmiths)	2	1	0.6
Taccar (Carpenters)	13	4	2.0
'Untouchable'			
Ampattar (Barbers)	5	1	0.9
Nalavar (Toddy-Tappers)	5	1	9.0
Pallar (Agrarian Labourers)	14	5	9.0
Parayer (Drummers)	3	1	2.7
Other Castes	15	6	5.9
Total	**270**	**100**	

Source: K. David, 1982; Survey of Swiss Federal Office for Refugees' Asylum Dossiers, Bern.

Residence quarters for asylum seekers from Sri Lanka, Steinbach, 2003.

Alalasundaran Vinayagamoorthy (far left) went to Basel following the outbreak of the civil war in Sri Lanka. Since the 1980s, he has been working as a chef in Switzerland.

route as a direct response to the ethnic conflict and fear of conscription or persecution from both the state military forces and the militants. Sometimes, cohorts of young men from the same village travelled together to seek asylum. Militant groups also funded passages for fighters to remove them from the battlefield. Most were single, but generally married within a few years of residence in Switzerland. These migrants were generally men in their 20s. By the mid-1990s, as young women were increasingly recruited as fighters, equal numbers of men and women sought asylum in Switzerland. The increase in the number of women migrants also reflected household migration strategies, whereby a male was sent first to gain asylum, and provided financial and logistical support for the emigration of other family members. Furthermore, marriage strategies evolved whereby brides would be chosen from Sri Lanka for men already established in Switzerland.

In addition to the length and intensity of the conflict, several other factors contributed to the high level of Tamil asylum migration. The emigration of educated Tamils during the colonial and immediate post-colonial periods had already established the rewards of relocating overseas. Following Sri Lanka's independence, Tamils viewed themselves as being persecuted and in need of refuge. Further, the professionalisation of asylum migration led to a network of agents who make arrangements for the asylum journey, the application process and early settlement, including provision of papers to support claims. During the 1980s and early 1990s, neither the Sri Lankan nor the Swiss government sought to stem the flow: the migration of some 500,000 Tamils considerably reduced humanitarian pressure on the former (and on international humanitarian agencies), and the latter initially remained either ambivalent or unable to respond to the growing asylum population.

By the late 1990s, with growth in the diapora population, a significant social division developed between the better established Swiss Tamil 'immigrant' population who arrived mainly in the 1980s and the asylum seekers of the 1990s. The relationships between the two shaped the dynamics of Tamil settlement in Switzerland during those first two decades. The 'immigrants' comprised mainly those from the lower middle class. A small number of high caste Tamils were employed with residence permits, and a few had gained Swiss citizenship. They had a longer-term view of their domicile in Europe and became an established ethnic minority in Switzerland.

In contrast, the 'asylum seekers' were a more diverse group and tended to be of lower caste background, from rural areas and less educated. They were seen to be more radical and unruly, having experienced the worst of the fighting in the north and east of Sri Lanka, and they provided a rich pool of recruits for LTTE activities. The former kept a distance from the latter, viewing them as a threat to their hard-earned relative stability in Switzerland.

Throughout this period, Swiss policy, in general, was characterised by tougher procedures, comprising of barriers to employment, serial granting of temporary

Kumutha Manivanan's grocery shop in Basel, set up in 2010, caters to Sri Lankan and Swiss clientele.

protection visas, restrictions on family reunion and ultimately, of unsuccessful attempts at repatriation.

Recent research suggests that only traces of this division remain, and only in the context of Eelam politics. Distinctions have become blurred due in part to the regularisation of immigrant status and a positive shift in the Swiss perception of Tamils. Throughout the 2000s, the Tamil population in Switzerland remained relatively stable as the rate of entry of new asylum seekers declined. During lulls in the fighting in Sri Lanka, increasing numbers of Swiss Tamils with regularised status made short return visits, though few returned home permanently. Most have chosen to remain in those German-speaking cantons (Zurich, Bern and Bale regions) where they first arrived, often remaining in the same suburbs of towns (Moret *et al*, 2006; *International Crisis Group*, 2010: 15).

POLITICS IN EXILE

Many commentators posit that the Tamil diaspora was a significant player in the Sri Lankan civil war by providing material and moral support to the LTTE, and influencing global opinion. Swiss Tamils in particular have been responsive to developments in Sri Lanka. During the first decade of settlement various Tamil nationalist groups were active in Switzerland. Over time, however, by sheer weight of numbers, resources, a competent leadership and an effective network that extended across Switzerland, the LTTE emerged as the dominant group by the early-1990s.

Tamils sympathetic to the cause of Eelam made doorstep collections at Tamil homes for the war and for humanitarian purposes. Profits from trading including a chain of 'people's shops' (convenience shops) were harnessed. While London and Paris emerged as the LTTE's political headquarters in Europe, Switzerland with its large and geographically concentrated population and high earning potential became, in effect, the LTTE's banker and a key location in Eelamist diaspora politics.

The LTTE's influence extended in other ways too, for example it was active in temple management, and had its own radio and TV channels, shops and restaurants. It organised events such as the annual Great Heroes Day to commemorate soldiers killed in the war, which frequently received coverage in the Swiss media. At the height of the war, there were reports (*Asian Tribune*, 3 June 2007) that LTTE cadres obtained Swiss visas by posing as victims of the LTTE in Colombo. However, upon entering Switzerland, these cadres re-entered the LTTE network and became especially active in the print and cyber media. Media stories of extortion of money using threats on relatives back home surfaced periodically.

Table 4.9

ASYLUM APPLICATION FROM SRI LANKA SUBMITTED TO THE SWISS FEDERAL AUTHORITIES BETWEEN 1983 AND 1991									
1983	1984	1985	1986	1987	1988	1989	1990	1991	Total
845	1,236	2,764	5,93	895	1,516	4,809	4,774	7,349	24,781

Source: Swiss Federal Office for Refugees, Bern.

The relative non-interference from the Swiss Federal Police enabled the LTTE to build its network. Occasional investigations into extortion and money laundering led to a limited number of prosecutions. However, in 2011, proceedings were initiated against 10 prominent Tamils for extortion and money laundering (*BBC News South Asia*, 12 January 2011).

With the exception of members of the centralised organising committees, hard core support for the LTTE among Swiss Tamils was limited. The majority, though appreciative of the LTTE's success in drawing world attention to the Tamil cause, and acknowledging that the Tigers were the only group capable of defending Tamils militarily against government actions, was deeply ambivalent about the violence. Many felt under pressure to show support and make donations while preferring not to acknowledge the war funding to which the so called 'humanitarian' donations were often linked.

From the outset, the politics of Tamil nationalism and separatism was energetically pursued in the public domain. Residents of Zurich and Geneva grew familiar with street demonstrations and occasional violence breaking out between rival liberation groups (LTTE, People's Liberation Organisation of Tamil Eelam [PLOTE], Tamil Eelam Liberation Organization [TELO]) ripping flags from their poles to use as weapons. Initially, protests were for establishing their own refugee status, later in open support of Tamil Eelam, and after the defeat, against genocide and in favour of international intervention and trade boycotts against Sri Lanka. Thus in 1984, a silent march was staged in Bern, against the repatriation of visa-rejected refugees.

In March 2000, approximately 6,000 Tamils held a silent demonstration at the UN Commission on Human Rights, to condemn war crimes and protest against repatriation. The red and black Eelam 'Tiger' flag has been a common sight at demonstrations since the early 1990s. However, it was in 2007 that the flag was raised for the first time, with considerable ceremony in a pro-Eelam rally attracting 8,000 people, in front of the Human Rights Council.

In February 2009, about 15,000 Tamils protested in front of UN buildings against genocide and in favour of western intervention. In one tragic incident a young Tamil set himself on fire as a form of protest and died from his injuries. The defeat of LTTE triggered several strong protests in Switzerland. Over the years, these demonstrations have become important and are often recalled as landmarks of community life, bringing the Tamil migrant populations and their causes to wider attention in Switzerland.

Partly due to the immigrants' efforts, Switzerland had been responsive to the unfolding political situation and at times played a low key mediatory role in international efforts to resolve the conflict. In 2003, representatives of the Sri Lankan government and LTTE attended a panel discussion in Bern in which Switzerland's federal system was proposed as a model for a political settlement in Sri Lanka (swissinfo.ch, 9 September 2003). In 2009, the Swiss Ministry for Development and Co-operation donated medical supplies for the internally displaced in Sri Lanka and reiterated its commitment to the welfare of the civilian victims (tamilnewsnetwork.com, 2009). The same year, the Swiss Federal Department of Foreign Affairs organised a conference with 17 Sri Lankan Tamil political parties, which committed itself to peaceful political solutions (Tamilnet.com, 2009).

The defeat of the LTTE presented important challenges to the global Tamil diaspora. Initially high profile campaigns against Sri Lankan military actions, internment of civilians in camps and calls for trade boycotts attracted media attention, but the political response was fractured and mostly incoherent. At the everyday level, Swiss Tamils no longer received demands for money as the LTTE structure became inactive. However, the political commitment to Eelam persisted in community discussions, although privately, many expressed support for a negotiated political settlement as the only practical way forward. In January 2010, a referendum was organised by pro-LTTE groups. 16,000 Tamils voted (out of an estimated 25,000 eligible voters in Switzerland) and gave overwhelming support for the creation of a separate Tamil state (*International Crisis Group*, 2010: 13–4). In the absence of international political support, however, this proved little more than a gesture. At this time of heightened politics, it is significant that among second generation Tamils, the overwhelming majority of whom have never visited Sri Lanka, there was a surge of activism across Europe and in the US. In Switzerland it was the younger members of the community who formed two-thirds of the members elected for the National Assembly of Swiss Council of Tamils in March 2010 (Tamilnet.com, 2010); elsewhere Swiss Tamil groups participated in the London-based Global Tamil Forum but overall the hub of diaspora political activity resided in the UK, the US and Canada rather than Switzerland, which remained somewhat marginalised.

Aside from Sri Lankan politics, Swiss Tamils have increasingly sought a role in domestic politics. In 2006, Rupan Sivaganesan was elected from the Sozialistisch-Gruene Alternative party (Socalist Green Alternative Zug) into the Kantonstrat of Zug, within 10 years of entering Switzerland and just six months after obtaining

Participants in Agni Thandavam *(Dance of Fire) organised by the Tamil Youth Organization (TYO) in Switzerland, 2011.*

Lathan Suntharalingam, who arrived as a refugee in Switzerland in the 1980s, is a representative of the Social Democratic Party.

Members of the Tamil community in Switzerland congregate for a protest march at the 'broken chair' monument in front of the UN Offices in Geneva, 2009.

citizenship, becoming the first assembly member to enter from a refugee background. Lathan Suntharalingam, who arrived in 1988 as a 14-year-old refugee became, in 2007, 'Gross Rat' in Luzern canton, representing the Social Democratic party. In 2009, he succeeded in getting the Commission for Foreign Affairs to approve motions for ceasefire and humanitarian aid, and against the repatriation of Tamil refugees.

SOCIAL ORGANIZATION AND CULTURAL ETHOS

The South Asian domestic ethos based on the centrality of marriage, family and patrilineal kinship is strong among the first generation Tamil migrants in Switzerland. The 2000 Census indicates that the largest proportion of Tamil households are made up of married couples with children, a distinctly higher proportion than among Swiss and other immigrant households (Moret *et al*, 2007: 100). Statistics for extended households are not available; however, fieldwork conducted by Ganesh suggests that they are not uncommon. The normative three generation household is rare, because the elderly parents of first generation migrants tend to only to come for short visits from Sri Lanka. Married siblings living in one household with their families or in close proximity within highly interactive kin networks is common. The reciprocal obligations of extended families include those in Sri Lanka and extend to other diasporic locations.

The high levels of debt amongst Tamil immigrants is partly the outcome of the tendency to distribute cash on visits home, sponsor visits or the migration of relatives to Switzerland, finance marriages of sisters or to provide funds to meet the medical expenses of aged parents. The pressure to fund the war was another factor. Those who do not have their own resources borrow from relatives and friends in Switzerland or from Tamil money lenders or agencies (Luethi, 2005: 50).

Members of the same family may be scattered in different countries, due to choice, or because of asylum procedures and residence permits. With cyber communications the transnational links of Swiss Tamils extend in multiple directions. Chain migration, visits back home, relocations to more favoured destinations such as the UK and Canada strengthen their links, firstly with the extended family and then with members of the same caste in several countries. For pilgrimage, the Tamil Hindu community forms the transnational unit, and for political and cultural mobilisation, the entire Tamil community itself. Marriage networks are transnational too but largely intra-caste. Tamil temples in Switzerland are closely linked to organisations in Sri Lanka and Tamil Nadu. Similarly, the products sold in shops owned by Tamils are imported from Sri Lanka and India.

Various studies (see Ganesh, 2011) indicate that first generation Swiss Tamils confine their social relations largely within the Tamil community. Leisure often revolves around the activities of temples, churches, Tamil cultural and sports associations, and celebrations of rites of passage and community-based film, dance and music programmes. Regular updates on the Sri Lankan situation are available through Tamil newspapers, magazines, radio and TV. In securing accommodation, Tamils prefer to live in areas with an existing Tamil population and to shop wherever possible in Tamil-owned stores.

According to Baumann, Tamils have higher rates of endogamous marriage when compared to the local Swiss population and other immigrant communities (2009a: 160) and arranged marriages are common. People tend to marry within their caste (even in non-arranged marriages) and marriage outside the Tamil community is rare. In 2004, only 521 people of Sri Lankan origin had a Swiss spouse (swissinfo.ch, 18 February 2006).

SRI LANKAN TAMIL RELIGIOUS INSTITUTIONALISATION

The process of religious institutionalisation in the early years of Tamil immigration was influenced by two main factors. On the one hand, the development depended on the specific religious tradition of the immigrants; on the other, these processes were shaped by Swiss social policies and the socio-economic status of these immigrant groups.

Whereas Christian Tamils were able to turn to already established Christian institutions in Switzerland, the Saiva Hindu majority found few, if any, organisations for Hindus. Only places of neo-Hindu movements, particularly the temple of the International Society for Krishna Consciousness (ISKCON), were important contact zones in the early 1980s. A result of the religious institutionalisation of Tamil Vaishnavas was the foundation of the Swiss Tamil Krishna Society in 1991.

Although the situation of the first Tamil immigrants was characterised by meagre financial resources, Tamil Hindu immigrants have invested much time and effort in constructing their own places of worship since the early 1980s. The first *puja* places were established in homes for asylum seekers. The predominantly male immigrants felt the need to demarcate places with visual symbols to worship their deities.

Map 4.16

HINDU TEMPLES IN SWITERLAND

Source: Rafaela Eulberg, Martin Bauman. Cartographer: Steffen Rink–TextWebGrafik, Marburg. Religionswissenschaftliches Seminar der Universität Luzern © 2010.

After the stabilisation of their legal situation, the Tamil immigrants rented their own flats that provided greater liberty in establishing a 'place for the Gods' in private space. Some of the *puja* rooms in private apartments were proclaimed as open places of worship for Tamil devotees. The migration of spouses and family members that followed in the 1990s, changed the family structure and, consequently, the religious life of the Tamil immigrants.

Religious experts, who had the ability to conduct life cycle rituals, became increasingly important. Male asylum seekers of the Brahmin caste were asked to function as priests during the rituals even if they had no training as religious experts. Effectively, these private flats in which Hindus practised regular *pujas* and certain rituals can be considered the first 'Saiva Hindu Temples' in Switzerland.

Renting rooms in industrial areas constituted the next step in Sri Lankan Tamil Hindu religious institutionalisation. Former halls were converted into temple-rooms and these rarely attracted the attention of the majority Swiss population. The first Sri Lankan Tamil Hindu Temple in Switzerland was inaugurated in the city of Basel in 1986 (relocated in 1989, 1994 and 2009) and others followed. During the 1990s and early 2000s, Hindu Tamils founded around 20 temples of varying size, the majority located in the conurbations of cities in the German-speaking cantons.

The latest development in the institutionalisation of Tamil Hindus is the building of the first purpose-built traditional Siva-temple with a high-rising *gopuram* in Trimbach (Northwest Switzerland). The inauguration was planned for 2012. This temple will be a milestone for Swiss Hindu Tamils.

Most Sri Lankan Tamil Christians have been integrated into Swiss parishes. The Roman Catholic Church has also established pastoral care in the Tamil language. During the 1990s the Swiss Conference of Catholic Bishops, together with the Catholic Bishops' Conference of Sri Lanka, decided to employ a Tamil priest to care for the Tamil-speaking believers. He is sent from the Sri Lankan district of Mannar to the parish centre in Wiedikon/Zurich and organises masses in Swiss cities such as Basel, Bern, Lucerne and

The Sri Sivasubramaniar temple in Zurich was established in 1994 by Sri Lankan Tamils living in Switzerland.

Zurich where a high percentage of Tamil Christians live. Numerous evangelical free churches, which are led by Tamil preachers and whose church services are held in the Tamil language, characterise the Protestant spectrum.

Compared to Christian and Hindu immigrants from Sri Lanka, the Sri Lankan Muslim community in Switzerland is considerably smaller with approximately 350 families. In the year 2000, only 0.1 per cent of the Muslim population of Switzerland was born in Sri Lanka. The institutionalisation of Sri Lankan Muslims in Switzerland began with the foundation of the Sri Lankan Muslims Association (SLMA), which is linked with other Muslim groups in Switzerland, for example as a member of *Umma*, the Muslim Cantonal Association of Bern. Connections to Tamil Christians or Tamil Hindus only exist on an individual basis. The SLMA classifies itself first as part of the Muslim diaspora rather than the Sri Lankan Tamil diaspora. Nevertheless, the foundation of the organisation was a reaction towards the situation in Sri Lanka—to organise emergency assistance to Muslims in Sri Lanka. In 2008, SLMA inaugurated the *Masjid-ul-Qghair* mosque in the capital of Switzerland, Bern. Like the majority of Tamil Hindu temples, this meeting place is not purpose-built but housed in a rented building.

Rafaela Eulberg

Through formal and informal social interactions, traditional 'Tamil values' are constantly emphasised. Leuthi describes how sponsoring *pujas* at temples, large-scale wedding and puberty ceremonies, etc., are sources of prestige in the community, though less so than in Sri Lanka (2005: 46–8). As though to compensate, children's birthday parties are celebrated lavishly. Personal reputation is closely linked with that of the family's and particular strictness is exercised on the behaviour of single women: premarital relationships, marriage outside the community, working in 'low' jobs (for example as cleaners) are said to tarnish an entire family's reputation and are sources of shame. Children are socialised to show deference to elders and senior males. Alcohol consumption, divorce and sex outside marriage are disapproved of. While Swiss society is considered to be socially traditional and conservative compared to other parts of Europe, Swiss Tamils tend to regard what they perceive as the more liberal attitudes of Swiss families as threatening to the maintenance of preferred social norms (Leuthi, 2005: 10–2). As with other diasporas, Swiss Tamils emphasise that language is as a vehicle of

culture. The first generation keenly promotes Tamil while the second generation is fluent in Swiss languages as well as Tamil. Although temple liturgy is largely in Sanskrit, a Tamil component is broadly insisted upon. All community gatherings are conducted in Tamil. Parallel education for children through weekend Tamil schools is strong, with

The Enrollment form for the examination organised by the Tamil Education Services in Switzerland. The organization runs around 90 schools in the country.

Children perform a traditional dance at a Tamil school in Switzerland, 2010.

The pastor and young members of the Katholische Tamilenseelsorge (Swiss Tamil Catholic Spiritual Service) during Saint Joseph's celebration, 2011.

Services conducted in the Tamil language are regularly held at the monastery of Einsiedeln.

a curriculum that includes Tamil language, literature, religion, culture and history, and also Swiss languages and practical information about Swiss society. A student may continue up to Standard 10 by passing annual exams which are a major community event. The Tamil Education Service Switzerland is the apex organisation. Its website (www.tamilschool.ch) reports that in 2010, the 16th year after inception, 4,600 children wrote the four-hour exam in 46 centres across the country. Interestingly, the exam began with a homage to the Tamils in Sri Lanka killed by the army.

RELIGIOUS AFFILIATION AND ACTIVITIES

Most Sri Lankan Tamil Hindus are Saivites from the Saiva Siddhanta tradition. Daily worship at the household altar and performance of domestic rituals for birth, puberty, death, etc., are important activities, somewhat adapted in the diasporic context. Swiss Tamils have also engaged actively in temple building. The anxieties of refugeehood and asylum have added impetus to what Baumann (2009a: 154) has termed 'templeisation among Tamil Hindus in Germany and Switzerland', by which he means a shift in the focus of religious activities from domestic to community scale, from the personal to congregational arena and from the control of older women to male priests. Vogeli (2006: 67) points out that women are more keenly religious than men. Out of the 19 temples found in Switzerland dedicated to Siva, Amman, Murugan and Pillaiyar, 16 are located in the German-speaking parts. Temples are also centres for community activity, celebration of rites of passage and festivals like Pongal, Navaratri and Deepavali as well as for the propagation of the Tamil language, music, dance, yoga, etc. through classes, competitions and performances.

Temple worship follows the norms for agamic temples in contemporary Tamil Nadu and Jaffna though slightly adapted. Thus some temples open only twice weekly while others have reduced the customary six daily *pujas* to two. However, worship is conducted with discipline and devotion and as is customary in agamic temples, eating meat and consuming alcohol are forbidden on the days of temple visits.

Priests or *gurukkal* are Brahmin *iyers* and part of the extensive informal priestly networks in Sri Lanka, India, the UK, Canada and elsewhere in Europe. They may sometimes be drawn from other castes such as *virasaivas* traditionally associated with temple service. They are typically trained in Jaffna, in the traditional *gurukulam* schools, or in Tamil Nadu with a middle level qualification. For special occasions like temple *kumbha abhishekam*, *Sivacaryas* or senior priests are invited from Sri Lanka or Tamil Nadu to officiate, often at quite considerable costs. Temple priests may also officiate at domestic rituals at homes. Most *gurukkals* are interrelated by blood or marriage, kinship lines reinforcing the professional network.

The annual festival includes an outdoor procession of the temple idols, drawing large crowds of devotees and curious onlookers. The first generation of Swiss Tamils tends to be more participative in these events though on special days, young people can also be seen in large numbers. At the spectacular street procession during its annual festival, the Sri Sivasubramaniar Temple at Adliswil, near Zurich, attracts thousands of devotees including Indians from all over Europe. Devotees perform difficult ascetic practices that are traditionally part of Tamil devotion (Baumann, 2009a:161).With only one Indian Hindu temple—in Lyss—inspired by the Melmaruvathur Aumshakti movement of Tamil Nadu and a Hare Krishna temple in Zurich whose followers are mainly European, Sri Lankan Tamils are the public face of Hinduism in Switzerland.

Eelam politics is not entirely absent from the temples, with some places having direct or indirect links with the militant Tamil movement supporting the rehabilitation of orphaned Tamil children and families in distress due to the civil war. It is noticeable that these temples carry posters for the Great Heroes Memorial Day, in remembrance of the LTTE cadres who lost their lives in the war.

The first Tamil temple in Switzerland—the Sithi Vinayagar temple—was established in 1986 in Basel canton. With an increase in women and children immigrants, the need was felt for additional temples but this building programme was met with some hostility on the part of the Swiss population. In 1994, when a Murugan temple was established at Bern-Bethlehem, residents complained to the police about the disturbance, and media coverage fuelled the debate on whether temples should be located in non-residential areas (*Schweizer Radio und Fernsehen* (SRF), 16 July 1994). Temples constructed in the first years of Tamil settlement had no visible architectural presence and were located in a fairly non-descript and out of the way industrial buildings, warehouses and in basements. Over time, however, attitudes changed and there is now wide public acceptance of temples, partly due to the Tamils' profile as 'good' migrants.

Post 9/11, the perception of Islam as a threat among sections of the Swiss public has resulted in a generally supportive attitude towards non-Muslim religious minorities (Beaumont, 2007). This is reflected in the debate over immigrants' visibility in public space through their religious monuments especially minarets adorning mosques (Baumann, 2009b: 148–50). While a referendum in 2009 banned construction of new minarets, the commune of Trimbach in 2006 approved plans for a temple with a prominent *gopuram* or tower which would reportedly on completion become the largest Hindu temple in Europe. The politics of temples has always been shaped by the diasporic culture and identity, and conflicts over temple management have frequently resulted in the breaking away and creation of new temples that reflects the changing dynamics within the community and is evidence of a complex Tamil community in the making.

For non-Hindu Tamils, the formal religious activities of Tamil Catholics are organised through the Katholische Tamilenseelsorge or the Swiss Tamil Catholic Spiritual Service (www.jesutamil.ch). There is no separate Tamil church but mass is conducted in Tamil regularly at different Catholic churches across Switzerland and the second generation often attends services in German. The organisation also conducts two pilgrimages, both to Maria shrines, attended by Catholics and Hindus and which Swiss Tamil Catholics consider to have miraculous powers. The Mariastein pilgrimage, on the first Saturday of August is in remembrance of their pilgrimage to

DEMOGRAPHIC PROFILE

In early 2010, almost 50,000 Sri Lankan people—including Swiss nationalised Sri Lankan citizens—lived in Switzerland, forming the largest Asian immigrant group in the country. Approximately 90–95 per cent of the Sri Lankan citizens are ethnically Tamil, amounting to about 45,000–47,500 Tamils in Switzerland. The Sinhalese form a comparatively small minority of some 3,000 to 5,000 immigrants.

The approximately 52,600 immigrants comprised different legal categories: 37.2 per cent have acquired Swiss nationality (19,600 persons), 55.1 per cent Sri Lankan citizens were on a continual and secure legal stay (29,000), and 7.6 per cent asylum seekers had been provisionally admitted (4,000). Thus, 92.3 per cent of immigrants and refugees were either nationalised or had acquired a legally secure stay. Significantly, since the late 1990s, the number of immigrants securing permanent status and those receiving Swiss citizenship grew exponentially. Whereas from 1974–2001 only 2,300 Sri Lankans had gained Swiss citizenship, from 2002–10 some 17,300 were nationalised. This significant development was based on three special state regulations to legalise the stay of Tamil refugees (after failed state repatriation programmes in the early 1990s), as well as to acknowledge their length of stay, as many had arrived in the mid-1980s.

Due to the great difference in the number of Sinhalese and Tamil people in Switzerland, the vast majority of Sri Lankans are Hindus (75 per cent). Catholics make up 10 per cent, while Protestants and Evangelical Christians collectively comprise about 5 per cent. There are also a few hundred Muslims. Sinhalese Buddhists probably make up less than 1 per cent of the total Sri Lankan population in Switzerland. The number of Sri Lankans without religious affiliation is estimated to be between 5 and 10 per cent (Baumann, 2003:276; Moret *et al*, 2007: 96).

In the 1970s, the Sinhalese established a *vihara* (an abode for monks) in Geneva. This was re-established in 1992 by the monk Tawalama Dhammika (www. geneva-vihara.org). In 2003, the Zurich Buddhist *vihara* (www.zb-vihara.ch) opened with two resident monks. The monks offer meditation programmes and Buddhist teachings in both *viharas* that are housed in former residences. The *viharas* are visited by both Sinhalese and Swiss Buddhists. In addition, the Sinhalese monks participate in activities of inter-Buddhist and inter-religious dialogue. Furthermore, the Sinhalese have set up two politico-cultural organisations—the Committee for Peace in Sri Lanka (Geneva) and the Committee for United Sri Lanka (Zurich)—though these organisations have become less active over the last few years (Stürzinger 2002: 21). Detailed information on occupational patterns and educational levels of the Sinhalese in Switzerland are not available.

In contrast, due to the much larger number of Sri Lankan Hindus (Tamils), the Swiss Census 2000 provides detailed figures. The educational and economic situation of Sri Lankan Hindus, i.e. mostly Tamils, is below average—only 17 per cent obtained an advanced education and 17.5 per cent a secondary education (compared to total Swiss national education 19 per cent and 51 per cent respectively), whereas a majority of 65 per cent of Hindu Tamils gained only primary education (total Swiss 29 per cent). With modest education and only a provisional legal status of admittance, these individuals had limited opportunities for upward mobility. This relegated Tamils to jobs in less prestigious sectors: in 2000, 38 per cent worked in the poorly paid sector

The Zurich Buddhist vihara *is an important centre for Sinhalese Buddhists in Switzerland.*

such as restaurant kitchens (total Swiss employed 5.4 per cent) and 11.9 per cent in the likewise inadequately paid health-care sector, as nurses and floor cleaners (total Swiss 10.9 per cent) (Bovay, 2004: 117; Baumann, 2009: 117). By acquiring a secure, legal stay, alongside a strong emphasis on education, Hindu Tamil people will be able to find better jobs.

As in Sri Lanka, Hindu Tamils in the diaspora kept strongly to endogamy. In Switzerland, Hindu Tamils scored as one of the highest of all immigrated people in the rate of endogamy (Bovay, 2004: 67). Recent figures point to a nascent change toward more inter-ethnic marriages between Tamils and the Swiss, indicating a process of acculturation in this as in other social and cultural areas. The importance of caste diminishes as well and is contested by education, wealth, occupation and socio-economic status.

Martin Baumann

Table 4.10

SRI LANKAN PERMANENT RESIDENTS IN SWITZERLAND 1981–2010														
1981	1982	1983	1984	1985	1986	1987	1988	1989	1990	1991	1992	1993	1994	1995
526	674	711	750	808	871	915	1,025	1,048	2,840	5,578	6,966	7,979	9,005	9,841
1996	1997	1998	1999	2000	2001	2002	2003	2004	2005	2006	2007	2008	2009	2010
10,786	11,939	14,400	17,978	20,215	24,895	29,628	31,772	32,284	31,8645	30,248	29,237	28,024	26,757	28,963

Source: PETRA (1980–2009), STATPOP (dès 2010). Information Centre, Demography and Migration section. FSO – Statistical Encyclopedia Switzerland.

'Madumatha', the only Maria shrine in Sri Lanka. The other pilgrimage—on the Saturday before Palm Sundayfis to Einsiedeln, to the world famous ancient church of the Black Madonna which McDowell (1996) noted has long been an important site of worship for Catholic and Hindu Tamils alike. On this occasion, devotees used to distribute parcels of food—much coveted due to a belief in its healing powers. However, this has been brought to an end by the Swiss Tamil Catholic Spiritul Service on account of the practice 'disturbing the normal routine'. According to priest Pater Christopar Anthonithas Dalima, Tamil Catholics are a close-knit community, regular in attending mass and performing Catholic rituals and ceremonies which incorporate elements common among Hindus, seen as part of Tamil culture—including mode of dress, rituals such as *aarathi* for welcoming important guests, boiling a pot of milk for housewarming and puberty ceremonies for girls. Thus while Swiss Tamil Hindus and Catholics are separately engaged in their respective religions, they have been closely and amiably interactive, as they are in Sri Lanka. The Tamil Pentecostal Free Church founded by three Tamil Hindu converts in 1989 is affiliated to the Evangelical Methodist Church of Switzerland (www. inforel.ch/i1245). Saravanabhavanantha, the priest of Sri Vishnu Durgaiamman temple near Zurich, noted that Tamil Catholics were different from such new groups, whose evangelical efforts were triggering a defensive reaction among Hindus.

Ganesh (2011) pointed out that, unlike sections of the Indian Hindu diaspora in the UK, US and Canada, Sri Lankan Tamils in Germany and Switzerland have not responded to the call of the Hindutva ideology from right-wing Hindu nationalist organisations. This may be due both to the Tamils' distinctive historical lineage from a regionally-rooted devotional form of Hinduism as well as the almost all-pervasive channeling of their cultural and religious resources for the Tamil ethno-nationalist project in Sri Lanka.

ISSUE OF INTEGRATION

A contract of reciprocity is important in Swiss society. Dependence on the state is eschewed, migrants need to

A Sri Lankan Tamil family along a lake in Zurich, 2004.

Kavithas Jeyabalan who learnt the art of building Arosa-style wooden sledges established his own carpenter workshop in Peist in 1996.

Jana Arunthavanathan, of Sri Lankan Tamil origin, is an internationally recognised dart player.

be seen as earning their way and adopting Swiss values. Integration is a major issue for the Swiss public, government and media. Neither immigrant nor Swiss society is static or internally homogenous, but such a notion is politically expedient and has gained currency over time.

Although Tamils were initially viewed with distrust and hostility, this perception changed to a mainly positive one by the late-1990s (Eulberg, 2008: 16). Currently, Swiss Tamils are perceived as better integrated than other immigrants (Swissinfo.ch, 30 January 2008)—law abiding, inconspicuous, hardworking, ready to do jobs shunned by others, and willing to make sacrifices for their family. The crime rate among Tamils in Switzerland is significantly lower than that recorded for other immigrants and only slightly higher than the Swiss average. Further, many convictions are for violation of residence permit rules (Moret *et al*, 2007: 75) rather than crimes against property or person. According to Luethi (2005: 60), structurally Tamils are well integrated; they know how to negotiate education, health and employment systems but socially and culturally, they tend to be aloof from Swiss life. Tamil society is highly cohesive with 'belongingness' to the extended family, caste and Tamil community crucial to Tamil identity. This relative social isolation may be compounded by the politics of being Tamil in Sri Lanka, the trauma of asylum and the dream of Tamil Eelam. Swiss Tamils have formed somewhat inward looking self-contained groups in their country of settlement, while maintaining outward looking and close transnational ties with Sri Lanka and the Tamil diaspora across Europe and beyond to North America, Southeast Asia and Australia.

When Sri Lankan Tamils first began arriving in Switzerland, exaggerated fears that large numbers would flood the country were exploited particularly by right-wing parties such as SVP (Schweizer Volkspartei), and deep reservations were expressed by trade unions concerned about cheap labour and the loss of local jobs. The sudden influx of dark-skinned people triggered xenophobic demands in the assembly to accommodate them not in hotels but army barracks (*Schweizer Radio und Fernsehen* (SRF), 12 March 1984). They were seen as making unreasonable demands on public money. However, the image became far more positive when Tamils were allowed to work (swissinfo.ch, 18 February 2006). They were recognised as migrants who were prepared to take employment in those areas often shunned by the Swiss population. Stuerzinger (2002) describes how Federal government policy in support of repatriation differed from the cantons and fluctuated depending on protests from immigrants, human rights campaigns and the situation in Sri Lanka itself. The public did not connect the immigration with the continuing unrest in Sri Lanka, intensifying the negative perception.

A study by Swiss Forum for Migration and Population Studies (Slater, 2005) partly blames the Swiss authorities for failing to give the Tamils a secure residence status, leaving them ineligible for training, pushing them into unskilled jobs, with little incentive to learn the language. It was only at the beginning of the 21st century that opportunities were created for economic integration, although Swiss Tamils still tend to have higher social assistance claimant rates compared to the other immigrant communities.

The early migrants harboured desires to return. They feared not being cared for by their children in Switzerland and being put in old age homes. But few actually returned, mostly those with parents or siblings in Sri Lanka, or those heavily dependent on Swiss social aid or with property in Sri Lanka. Several factors inhibited return: the continuing crisis in Sri Lanka, fear that their savings would dry up, and children's reluctance to uproot themselves. Some families have migrated to larger diasporic locations such as Canada, with the husband continuing to work in Switzerland. As the Tamils establish themselves economically, build temples and as children qualify professionally, they are less likely to want to return permanently (Luethi, 2005: 56–57).

One of the unusual stories of integration on Swiss terms is Kavithas Jeyabalan's. A carpenter by profession, he migrated in 1984 to Chur, a small mountain village. He is fluent in the region's dialect and is married to a Swiss woman. His workshop specialises in traditional handmade wooden sleds called 'StanfiggerSchlitten', with no screws. Kavithas is the only person in Switzerland who makes them now (Migros-Magazin, 2006: 14–17). Jana Arunthavanathan is a well-known dart player and regularly wins first prizes at Swiss and international dart competitions. Anton Ponrajah, an engineer and later an actor in Sri Lanka, is well known for his theatre production interpreting the Swiss hero William Tell's struggle against the 'Habsburger' as a metaphor for the Sri Lankan Tamils' fight for freedom. Saravanabhavanantha, a Marxist social activist in Sri Lanka, first worked in a factory in Switzerland and later returned to his hereditary occupation as priest. He is well known in the Swiss media, as a spokesperson on Tamil religious matters in multi-faith dialogues.

CHALLENGES IN THE 21ST CENTURY

By the 21st century, a whole new generation has grown up studying in Swiss schools and being exposed to Swiss life. But vis-à-vis the first generation, it is not a simple matter of Swiss values versus Tamil values. The Migration Office study (Slater, 2008) comments on how Tamil youth are at home with Swiss ways, but tend to marry within their own community and organise their family life around the values and conventions of Tamil culture. This orientation has been fostered by the LTTE through the culturalisation of politics. Particular exile-related problems have been observed with Swiss Tamil children, which distinguish them from the typical second generation immigrant syndrome. Achieving a balance in the second generation immigrants' approach vis-à-vis homeland and hostland remains an issue. Tamils in Switzerland also face the major challenge of delinking themselves from the violent past and harnessing their strategic global location for a just, peaceful and democratic resolution of the ethnic crisis in Sri Lanka.

Kamala Ganesh and Christopher McDowell

Acknowledgements to Ashish Upadhyay and Nicole Poyyayil for research assistance and to the latter also for the translation of German texts.

ITALY

I N SPITE OF long-standing relations between Italy and Sri Lanka, Italy was not a traditional destination for Sri Lankan emigrants. This, however, changed towards the end of the 1970s as Italy witnessed an inflow of Sri Lankan emigrants, the majority of whom were Sinhalese. Unlike many other European countries, Sri Lankan emigration to Italy was not simply an outcome of the civil war but also due to connections that existed between Sri Lankan Catholics and the Roman Catholic Church in Italy.

EARLY RELATIONS

I want you to understand that the island of Ceylon is, for its size, the finest island in the world, and from its streams come rubies, sapphires, topazes, amethyst and garnet.
Marco Polo's Diary, c. 13th Century CE

Long before the Italian national state was founded, Italy had trade contacts with Ceylon. Spices, pearls, gems and precious stones were valued by Europeans, and over time, major trade routes were developed on sea and land to the most important places where these commodities were found. These trade routes extended to the Persian Gulf, the Straits of Mannar between India and Ceylon, and even as far as China.

With the establishment of Constantinople as the seat of the Roman Empire and the gradual shift in the focus of trade to Ceylon from South India, Ceylon, by the 5th century CE, emerged as an important centre of trade in

Map 4.17

ITALY

Kandyan dancers at the international dance festival held in the City of Colina, Italy, greet Pope John-Paul II, Piazza San Pietro, July 1982.

the Indian Ocean. Artefacts such as the Roman and Indo-Roman coins of the 4th and 5th century found in Ceylon are evidence of the trade in precious items. During this period, Ceylon was often referred to by Europeans as the 'Jewel Box of the Indian Ocean'.

Following the advent of Portuguese colonial rule, many Sri Lankans on the west coast of the island and in the north embraced Catholicism. This paralleled the gradual permeation of Catholicism in Italian society. Although Italy had no direct bearing on Sri Lankan society, there was growing religious contact as both Ceylon and Italy had segments of their population united by a common faith. In addition, relations between the two countries were bolstered by the existing trade and economic linkages, in which Europeans sought to procure raw materials, minerals, spices, pearls, ivory and precious stones from Ceylon.

IMMIGRATION

By the 1960s, Italy became an attractive destination for Sri Lankan Catholics of lower middle class background. Young Sri Lankan Catholic women were the pioneers. After undergoing training provided by the Catholic Church in Sri Lanka and other church-based organisations, many were able to secure employment in the field of elderly care in Italy.

In parallel, the period witnessed growing interest amongst young Sri Lankan men to venture abroad for work. This was primarily due to the lack of employment opportunities in Sri Lanka although some were also keen because of a sense of adventure. Becoming a sailor was an option. Many young Sri Lankans who joined shipping companies were required to travel to distant locations. Upon arriving in European ports like Genoa, Hamburg, Athens and Marseille, some were known to 'jump ship' and over a period of time were able to secure employment in these cities.

The initial connections established by these pioneers facilitated the expansion of the Sri Lankan diaspora in Italy. In the early 1970s, Sri Lankan women working

The 13th-century Venetian traveller and merchant, Marco Polo, wrote about the treasures of Sri Lanka in his diary.

The Sri Lankan community in Milan, Italy during a special Eucharistic celebration of thanksgiving to welcome His Eminence Malcolm Cardinal Ranjith, 2011.

Newly-weds Alex Van Arkadie from Colombo and Lily d'sa from Mangalore with bridesmaids Stefania and Joyce, St. Peter's Square, Rome, October 1982.

in Italy were joined by their husbands and relatives. However, the extent of movement was constrained in part due to the Sri Lankan government's strict regulations on emigration prior to 1977.

In 1977, the Sri Lankan government began to deregulate, privatise and open up the economy to international competition. The effects of the change were wide-ranging as Sri Lankan society grew more conscious of the opportunities available abroad. Consequently, beyond women working in elderly care in Italy, the opportunity to work abroad became trendy even amongst other young people from a lower middle-class background. Their intention was to go abroad, find employment, increase savings over a short duration and return to the island.

However, without the assistance of informal networks, it was difficult to acquire visas to enter countries such as the UK, Australia or Canada in the 1970s. Consequently, in the 1970s lower middle class Sri Lankans turned to European countries that had more flexible visa requirements. Over time, a ranking system developed, with the first option being France, followed by the Netherlands and Germany and thereafter Switzerland and Italy.

When compared to the other key European destinations, Italy possibly had the least stringent entry regulations. France had established visa controls for Sri Lankans at the end of the 1970s, and the Netherlands and Germany followed suit. Only Italy did not require a visa. The Italian bureaucracy was also less demanding

on procedures for immigrant employment. If a migrant could prove his employment, a work permit was often issued quickly. When compared to Germany where many Sri Lankans required an asylum procedure to remain, the process was considerably less arduous in Italy.

Sri Lankan immigration to Italy accelerated following the outbreak of the civil war in the 1983. Going abroad increasingly became a necessity rather than an adventure. Youths were compelled by circumstances to look for prospects outside of their homeland. Like young Tamils, Sinhalese too began leaving the country due to the political instability that followed from developments in July 1983. The Sri Lankan diaspora in Italy that comprises mainly of Sinhalese is a testament to the impact that the 1983 riots had on the dislocation of the Sinhalese in Sri Lanka.

The initial social networks were crucial in explaining why the Sinhalese comprised the majority of Sri Lankans arriving in Italy. Relatives and friends informed them of the possibility of finding employment there. While initially the preferred country for Sri Lankan Catholic emigrants, Italy became a favoured destination for other Sinhalese as well. The way of life in Italy and the perceived easy-going atmosphere in Rome, Milan, Verona, Naples and other bigger cities were also important factors that drew these immigrants.

For the Sinhalese, migration to Italy was also attractive because they were not required to ask for asylum if they sought to remain. Indeed many of the Sinhalese immigrants could not justify their movement based on political grounds since most had not been critical of the politics of the Sri Lankan government. At the same time, the fact that they were not political refugees in Italy allowed them the freedom to visit their home country from time to time—a practice that would have been difficult to justify if one was an asylum seeker. Over time, however, the movement of Sinhalese also involved highly-politicised individuals. Amongst these were those who sympathised or had direct links with the Janatha Vimukthi Peramuna (JVP), whose insurrection in the late 1980s had been put down by the Sri Lankan government.

By this time several organisations had been setup in Italy offering assistance to Sri Lankan immigrants. Meeting points for Sri Lankans were established, for example near the station in Rome and in Milan. Those who needed help could avail to assistance from these centres. Through these avenues, new arrivals were given advice on how to source for employment oppotunities, secure accommodation and thus assisting in organising their day-to-day life in Italy.

THE SRI LANKA ASSOCIATION IN ITALY—A PERSONAL ACCOUNT

I was the founding secretary of the Sri Lanka Association in Italy in 1981. The association was established to promote culture and ensure common welfare, and it has today become an advisory-related-services-centre to help migrants. I came to Rome in 1977 and, in 1981, with a group of 18 friends began an 'association' for the Lankan migrant community. The first elected committee included Messrs. Mohideen Noufer (President), George Michael (Vice President), Wilfred Liyanagunawardena (Treasurer), Alex Van Arkadie (Secretary), and Messrs. Premadasa Ranasinghe and Thusita de Alwis (Organsing Secretaries).

From the late 1970s, Lankans often met together at the *Chiesa* San Sylvestro in Rome. Our regular get-togethers, on Thursday afternoons, Sundays, and public holidays, led to the founding of the parish LINK Group, to help enrich a fraternal mixture among all migrants: Filipinos, Indians, Sri Lankans, Irish, Scottish, South Americans, and Africans (with whom dozens of our families are linked to this day). The same venue also became the breeding ground for us (less than 100 Lankans) to sow the first seeds of an 'association'. In fact, thanks to the Irish Pallotine Fathers there future members congregated for worship and social get-togethers in dance, music, and song in the *cortile* of San Sylvestro! In later years as numbers grew, the Lankan communities gradually congregated also at the Twelve Apostles in *Roma Centro*, the *Santuario di Divina Rivelazione* in Laurentina, or Buddhists at the Santacittaramna in Sezze Latina and also at Prenestina Temple.

Early Sri Lankans who contributed specially to the welfare of their people in Italy include: the late Reverand Fr. Benedict Fernando, who spared no pain travelling between the northern and southern stretches of the Peninsula, getting Lankan student priests to attend to the spiritual needs of the Sinhala and Tamil speaking flock; and the late Therese Perera, a respected Lankan social worker, who in a voluntary capacity at San Sylvestro helped hundreds of migrants every Thursday afternoon. Two Lankans who introduced and promoted the game of cricket in Italy are coaches, Kariyawasam of the Lazio Cricket Club, and Jayarajah Alfonso of the Cappanelle Cricket Club.

A group of early migrants from Sri Lanka gather to celebrate the 10th wedding anniversary of Alex and Lisa at Capella Santa Anna, Vatican City, October 1992.

Alex Van Arkadie

Sinhalese women celebrate Wesak Day at the Lankarama Buddhist Temple in Milan.

The Catholic Church also became increasingly attentive of the needs of the growing Sri Lankan community. Many of these immigrants may have been able to find employment if they had adequate language skills. At the same time, there was a lack of trained staff for Sri Lankan Catholic congregations. Consequently, the church began to introduce Sri Lankan priests in the bourgeoning migrant communities. Trained priests with the requisite language skills were recruited, sometimes directly from Sri Lanka. In nearly all the bigger cities in Italy, there is now a Sri Lankan Catholic priest who, beyond performing religious duties, is also responsible for the Sri Lankan community and assists in ameliorating their concerns.

SOCIAL, ECONOMIC AND CULTURAL PRODUCTION

In 2011, approximately 80,000–100,000 Sri Lankans live in Italy, nearly 80 per cent of whom are Sinhalese. Some of these are temporary sojourners, while others have a more established position in the diaspora. Like most other countries, the Sri Lankan diaspora in Italy is organised along overarching Sinhala and Tamil ethnic lines.

The extent of social and cultural production in the Sinhalese community is considerable, partly due to the size of the community but also because of the longer duration of settlement that has resulted in the stability of their economic position. Centres have been established providing language instruction and training in traditional art and dance forms. Sinhalese Buddhists have founded temples in the bigger cities in Italy, such as Rome, Milan, Padua and Verona. At the initial stage, the development of these shrines did receive some support from the Catholic Church. During the annual Wesak Festival and the Katina Pinkam ceremonies, large numbers of

Sinhalese Buddhists congregate at these temples. The Sinhalese migrants have also come to organise several types of associations, including welfare groups, women's organisations and sports clubs—mainly for cricket. In Naples alone there are five different cricket clubs named after a particular school or town in Sri Lanka, like Chilaw, Nathtandi, Negombo or Kockchikade.

In 2011, there were approximately 25,000 Tamils living in Italy, most of whom have come as refugees and their numbers have increased considerably over the last few years. The Tamil diaspora is more concentrated in the southern part of Italy—Catania, Genoa, Modena, Rome and Milan being the main areas of settlement. In areas of Tamil concentration Hindu temples have been established, and Pongal celebrations are organised regularly in some cities. In these areas, Tamil language courses are run for children, and from time to time ethnic dance and cultural performances are also organised. However, when compared to France, Switzerland or Germany, the extent of religious and cultural activity in the Tamil community is limited. Nevertheless, many maintain a deep interest in Sri Lankan politics and during the 2006–09 conflict in Sri Lanka, the Tamil diaspora in Italy also protested, taking part in demonstrations in cities like Milan and Catania.

As the Sri Lankan diaspora became more established, the number of Sri Lankans venturing into business increased. Many have setup grocery stores, travel agencies, became lorry-drivers and specialised in cargo service transporting goods to Sri Lanka. Alongside these several businesses concentrated on the provision of 'ethnic ware'—including food products, clothes, costume jewellery, printed matter and media items directly imported from Sri Lanka. A small number of Sri Lankans have also joined municipal councils or city councils as community-level workers. Having said that,

Cardinal Albert Malcolm Ranjith Patabendige, Archbishop of Colombo, received the biretta cap from Pope Benedict XVI in St. Peter's Basilica, November 2010.

LEFT: *Sri Lankan monks and members of the Sinhalese community commemorate the Katina Pinkam festival in Milan.*

RIGHT: *Supporters of the Janatha Vimukthi Peramuna (JVP) in Rome.*

Team logo of the Sri Lanka Cricket Club in Milan.

however, the majority of migrants continue to work as domestic servants, in cleaning services, in gardening and clerical work, while others are engaged in the agricultural sector or in factories. Only a small segment of the Sri Lankan diaspora in Italy has been able to secure higher skilled jobs.

CONNECTING WITH THE 'MOTHERLAND'

Although they have lived and worked in Italy for many years, most in the Sri Lankan diaspora continue to hold onto the dream that they will one day return to Sri Lanka and live a comfortable life there. Consequently because of this overarching mindset that they are only sojourners, the possibility of integrating into Italian society has not been viewed as important. The continued focus on the 'motherland'—Sri Lanka—is evident in several of the diaspora's social and economic practices.

For one, significant sums are remitted or put aside with the aim of building a house in Sri Lanka. Additionally, a common practice is to send children to their grandparents in Sri Lanka. This practice is to some extent informed by the perception that some Sri Lankan emigrants have of Italian culture. The freedom and independence with which Italian children are brought up; the frequent contact between boys and girls; the attitude towards sexuality; and the perception that there is a lack of respect for the parents and elders in the local cultural milieu, is frowned upon. Once the children turn 16, they are brought back to Italy in order not to lose the permit to stay in the country.

Although Sri Lankans in Italy do not live in enclaves akin to that in several other European countries, a form of 'ghettoisation' is visible. On weekends there is a tendency to congregate in large groups—a process which aids in preserving community solidarity and retaining cultural identity. There continues to be a deep desire for information and cultural products from the homeland. At the early stages of the formation of the diaspora, newspapers and films (videos and CDs) from Sri Lanka facilitated that connection. However, over the years, vernacular newspapers have been published and in 2011 at least two television channels broadcast in Italy cater to the Sri Lankan diaspora.

SINHALESE NATIONALISM

Amongst Sinhalese immigrants in Italy, the erstwhile focus on Sri Lanka has underpinned the development of Sinhalese nationalism. The political developments in Sri Lanka particularly in the 1990s substantially contributed to the permeation of these affinities. Additionally, the turn to Sinhalese nationalist ideology was partly a reaction to the LTTE's considerable hold on the Tamil diaspora. In neighbouring European states the LTTE was well organised and held successful campaigns highlighting the situation of the Tamils in Sri Lanka. In comparison, the structural development of Sinhalese nationalism in other parts of Europe was far less significant.

Members of the JVP and the Sri Lanka-based Jathika Hela Urumaya (JHU) political party have been crucial in fostering the development of Sinhalese nationalism in Italy. To some extent their discourse of a distinctive Sinhalese culture and opposition to the LTTE provides a sense of identity for many in the Sinhalese diaspora, and an escape from their day-to-day reality of serving in Italian households. The increasing propaganda of these groups paralleled the escalation of the conflict in Sri Lanka from 2005, and the defeat of the LTTE has in turn further spurred the growth of nationalism in the Sri Lankan Sinhalese diaspora in Italy.

CONCLUSION

The first generation of Sri Lankan immigrants in Italy have held steadfastly to the dream of returning to Sri Lanka. The hold of the 'motherland' is perhaps an escape from the challenges they face in working and living in Italy. The turn towards the homeland has played a crucial role in shaping their political persuasions, social practices and cultural production in the diaspora. Perhaps some will indeed return to Sri Lanka. For the second generation, however, it is likely that they will not return and, over time, will have to come to terms with adapting to their new home-country and integrating into Italian society.

Ranjith Henayaka Lochbihler

Cricket remains a popular sport amongst Sri Lankans who settled in Italy.

NORWAY

INTRODUCTION

Official statistics in Norway do not separate immigrants from a particular country according to language-background or ethnic identity. Nevertheless, it is common knowledge that the large majority of the 8,500 immigrants and the 5,000 children of immigrants from Sri Lanka enumerated in 2009 are of Tamil background (Henriksen, 2010). Only around 500 are Sinhalese-speaking, the majority of these living in and around the capital Oslo, many of them having come to Norway by way of marriage to Norwegian citizens. Many of the Sinhalese-speaking in Norway meet and socialise in the Sri Lankan Association of Norway, established in 1984. This association is politically neutral, and also has a small number of Tamil and Muslim members. Most Sinhalese are Buddhists, and many are connected to the Tisarana Buddhist Association in Norway, established by Sri Lankan Buddhists in 1993.

The number of immigrants from Sri Lanka makes (Tamil) Sri Lankans the 13th largest immigration-based minority in Norway. The largest number came in the mid to late 1980s as a result of the war in Sri Lanka. In 1981, only 300 people of Sri Lankan background lived in Norway, in 1991, the number had grown to 5,300 (Henriksen, 2010). In 2009, half the population of Tamil background in Norway had lived in the country for more than 16 years while less than 10 per cent had lived in Norway for three years or less.

Immigration from Sri Lanka has over the years had a clear but changing gender profile: while only 552 out of 3,087 Tamil asylum seekers arriving between 1985 and 1992 were women (UDI, 1992), after 1992 more women than men have come, mainly for the purpose of marriage. However, a gender imbalance remains in the Tamil community. In 2009, there were between 140–150 men to 100 women amongst those above 40 years old (Henriksen, 2010). The generation raised in Norway is still young; in 2009, almost 60 per cent of the children of Sri Lankan immigrants in Norway were below 10, only 189 individuals were older than 20 years.

HISTORY OF IMMIGRATION

Tamil migration to Norway is part of a larger picture. With the implementation of Sinhala majoritarianism and Buddhist nationalism in all sectors of Sri Lankan society from the late 1950s, migration became a way for the

Map 4.18

Tamil middle class to safeguard what they saw as central elements of their own culture, especially the value of education. With an increasingly restrictive immigration policy in countries like Australia, United Kingdom, Germany and Switzerland, some fleeing from the troubles at home found their way to the cold North.

For the early Tamil migrants to Norway two institutions in particular were important. The first was the Cey-Nor Foundation, a Norwegian development project started in Jaffna in the 1960s. An interesting aspect of the Tamil-Norwegian immigration history is the fact that it is well known who the first person to arrive was. This man, Anthony Rajendram, left for Europe on a motor cycle and in 1956 ended up in Norway through a series of haphazard events. He married a Norwegian woman and settled in Norway for some time. He later went back to Sri Lanka to work for the benefit of his fellow Tamils. The enterprise established by him, called Malu Meen, eventually evolved into the Cey-Nor project, based at Karainagar in Jaffna. When it was taken over by the Sri Lankan government in 1986, Cey-Nor had several hundred employees involved in the production of fishing-nets and boat-building. With Norwegian leadership on the ground, the project became an important channel to present Norway as a rich and safe country to the Sri Lankan population. Most of the Tamil immigrants trickling in to Norway during the 1970s had been employed by Cey-Nor, and they were later joined by their families.

The Tisarana Sri Lankan Buddhist Association in Norway was established in 1993. Here, they are celebrating Wesak day, 2008.

A gathering organised by the Sri Lankan Association in Norway (SLAN).

From the late 1990s until 2008 Norway was an important player in the political and military game in Sri Lanka. The two parties asked Norway to act as facilitator for a peace process, and a cease-fire agreement was signed in 2002. A monitoring mission of Nordic observers was established to monitor the agreement. Led by Erik Solheim a series of meetings between the parties were held in 2002 and 2003. In 2003, the LTTE withdrew from the negotiations and there was an escalation of violence until the government forces started its decisive military campaign in the fall of 2007. The cease-fire agreement was formally abrogated in 2008. Even so, both Norway and Erik Solheim are household names in Sri Lanka, partly with a negative timbre because of the many controversies that were part of the peace process and its final failure.

The other institution of importance was the Folk High Schools, a chain of private colleges providing one-year classes to paying students, mainly in the humanities. For several reasons acceptance of students from the South to these schools were left as a loop-hole in the Norwegian immigration law after the general immigration ban was implemented in 1975. This school migration to a large extent became a continuation of the earlier family-based work-migration, in that Tamils who had already immigrated secured school admission for their own children and relatives' children still in Sri Lanka. When the students arrived in Norway the rules permitted admittance into the regular school-system, staying on temporary visas until they had finished their education. After the violence of 1983 in Sri Lanka and the escalation into civil war, the Norwegian immigration authorities found it increasingly difficult to deport students who had completed their education.

This migration history has provided the small Tamil community in Norway a very complex character. From the mid-1980s Tamils started to come to seek asylum, with 1987 seeing the largest number of arrivals in the history of immigration. Like the students, most asylum seekers arriving in the 1980s were young, but they had different experiences. What had caused their migration was often a wish to change society in their home country, and therefore loyalty to a particular party or militant group was prevalent. In addition, the turbulence in Sri Lanka's northeast in the 1980s and the internal violence between different Tamil organisations resulted in a complex pattern of caste, class and political loyalties in exile.

CHANGING SOCIAL FIELDS

In terms of community structures it is reasonable to look upon the short history of the small Tamil community in Norway as divided into two periods; the first from the late 1950s until the mid 1990s, the second from the late 1990s until today. During the first period the Tamil community was fragmented and fraught by internal conflicts. Members of the community may be seen as having participated in three 'social fields', a social field here seen as a delimited communication system with its own internal logic (Fuglerud, 1999). The fields were based on three separate, but partly overlapping, organisational principles structuring rivalry between groups and individuals: one field consisted of what Kuntz (1973) has called 'vintages' of migration. When conflicts arise as situations deteriorate, individual migrants have a tendency to leave their home country in distinct sets, often defending their own choice vis-à-vis people leaving before or staying longer. While such 'vintages' may often be invisible to outsiders, the timing of emigration may internally be important identity markers. Among Tamils in Norway one can—or could—identify four categories of migrants, each category carrying a social and political meaning beyond the timing itself:

1. Those leaving Sri Lanka in the period 1958–75 as working migrants;

Tamil demonstrators gathered outside the Norwegian Parliament in April 2009, calling on the Norwegian government to press for a ceasefire between Sri Lankan forces and the LTTE in Sri Lanka.

2. Those leaving Sri Lanka in the period 1975–88 as students at the 'Folk High Schools';

3. Those leaving Sri Lanka as refugees in the period 1980–86 and who were mostly granted refugee status in Norway;

4. Those leaving Sri Lanka after 1986 and who carry the identity of 'asylum seekers' in Norway.

This pattern is a result of the migrants' social background and the turn of political and military events in Sri Lanka. In simple terms one may say that with respect to rivalry for influence in the Norwegian-Tamil community the first two categories represent the Tamil pre-war elite groups who had the resources to leave in an orderly manner, while the latter two draw legitimacy from their participation in, or as victims of, the then ongoing war.

The next field was organised on the basis of politics. Until the mid 1990s political conflicts were deep and sometimes violent. The short version of a more complex picture was a division between those supporting and those not supporting the LTTE. Since LTTE's self-conception implied being the sole representative of the Tamil nation, also in exile, all members of the community were forced to take a stand on the organisation and its methods. As was the case elsewhere, criticism of the organisation or independent initiatives was not popular among LTTE supporters. For example, LTTE-supporters in Norway in the late 1980s stopped initiatives by independent groups to collect money for Tamil war-victims in Sri Lanka because the initiative was outside their own control. One Tamil informant explained at the time: 'All Tamils have either Tiger heads or Tiger tails—if you don't speak for them you must be silent'.

The third field was organised on the basis of traditional loyalties, especially family, village, and caste-membership. Most Tamils in Norway, especially in the early phase of immigration, come from the upper levels of the local caste hierarchy, and from a limited number of villages in Jaffna. Caste background is a sensitive question, and precise statistics are not possible. However, a fair approximation would be that more than 80 per cent of the Tamils who arrived in Norway before the mid 1990s were of *vellala*, *ceviyar* or *thimilar* background. Many came from Jaffna town or from the villages of Karayoor, Arialai and Navanthurai. The most important role of the network-relations and the communication within this social field was, and is, to facilitate the migration process itself. This is where money is borrowed and lent, where travel documents change owners, marriages are negotiated and responsibility transferred for children sent out of the war-zone on their own.

The main reason for dividing the history of the Tamil community into pre- and post-mid 1990s is that in the early period fragmentation and conflict was to a large extent structured along the lines organised by the social fields outlined above. In other words, one person's claim to status or influence on the basis of his caste-background could be met by another person's claim to seniority in terms of being an early immigrant and his knowledge of and contacts to Norwegian society. From the mid-1990s the situation changed. Perhaps because of LTTEs success on the battlefields in Sri Lanka, or because of a re-organisation of the militant movement's international activities, LTTE's supporters in the second part of this decade gradually gained hegemony and silenced all other Tamil voices in Norway. Paradoxically, this—at least to the external observer—also seemed to put a stop to the internal bickering and episodic violence as there was no longer any opposition. While internally there is no doubt of who are in charge, to the Norwegian society in general the politicised character of Tamil identity in Norway has—paradoxically—become less visible with the disappearance of internal turbulence.

WORK AND LIVING CONDITIONS

The early chain-migration through the Cey-Nor project has been important in several ways to the integration of Tamils from Sri Lanka in Norway. The establishment of contacts to Norwegian resource persons in the coastal areas through the project, and the knowledge of fisheries as such, brought many of the first migrants into contact with the Norwegian fish-processing industry upon their arrival in Norway. In particular, many travelled to Finnmark, the northernmost region of Norway, to work for a few years cutting fish and saving money before returning to the south. In the 1980s and 1990s, therefore, Tamil Sri Lankans were one of the immigrant groups with the most decentralised patterns of settlement in Norway. Today, however, the situation has changed. Having worked hard and saved money, Tamils have been able to compete on the real estate market, and around half of the total number has today settled in the capital Oslo where prices are high. As much as 85 per cent of the total population of Sri Lankan background today possess their own home, a number equivalent to the Norwegian population in general and much higher than among most other immigrant groups. The fact that this number has increased from 52 per cent in 1996 tells the story of a steep climb in social mobility for the Tamil group in the last ten years.

The rate of employment among Sri Lankans is high in Norway; in 2008, 61 per cent of women and 77 per cent of men were registered as employed (Henriksen, 2010). This number was the highest of all immigrant groups, among men, and 2 per cent above the Norwegian male population in general. As a result, income among Sri Lankans is higher than among almost all other immigrant groups in Norway. In a statistical survey from 2005/2006,

The 'Jaffna Food' grocery shop in Oslo is owned by Angelo, a Tamil from Jaffna who migrated to Norway in the 1980s.

Chekku Madu, 'Beast of Burden' by V. I. S. Jayapalan

No-one has better and more poetically captured the difficult experience of being a Tamil immigrant in Norway than the writer V.I.S. Jayapalan in the story *Chekku Madu*, 'Beast of Burden'. The story tells of Rajah and his mental problems. At his place of work these problems become externalised in a personalised relationship to a dish-washing machine, which 'having had much collaboration with Tamils over the years… had become quite fluent in Tamil'. At home Raja struggles with a demon disturbing his sleep by breaking his dinner-plates and doing all sorts of mischief. Through Rajah's battles with this demon the story communicates both the discrimination and racism faced by a non-white worker in the Norwegian labour market, the expectations of economic remittances from family-members left behind, and the difficulty and anguish of being separated from the ones close to him, making him unable to resolve the complications of past and ongoing family matters from his isolation in Oslo. The story reflects, in a magnificent way, the cognitive dissonance caused by traumatic memories and a liminal existence as an immigrant.

V.I.S. Jeyabalan, a Jaffna Tamil poet and writer who resides in Norway.

Staff and students of the Tamil School in Bergen, 2010.

63 per cent of immigrants from Sri Lanka said that they never experienced difficulties with expenses for food, transport and rent (Blom and Henriksen, 2008).

What lies behind this seemingly rosy picture, however, is a continued willingness to accept any employment that is available, often jobs for which they are over-qualified in terms of education. Many Tamil Sri Lankans are employed in low-status work such as office-cleaning and other unskilled services. It should be noted that even if their average income is high for immigrants, the median income for people of Sri Lankan background is only 80 per cent of that among Norwegians in general. Statistical surveys show that many immigrants from Sri Lanka find that Norway is a country where it is difficult for immigrants to make use of their qualifications and abilities. In one survey 41 per cent of Sri Lankans said that the experience of their work was a mental burden, as opposed to 27 per cent in the population as a whole. On the other hand, relatively few Sri Lankans report feeling discriminated or harassed in their work situation because of their immigrant status (Henriksen, 2010). While this is, of course, positive, one reason for this may be that many work within 'ethnic enclaves' where being an immigrant is the norm, not the exception.

NETWORKS, FRIENDS AND FAMILY

Empirical studies have suggested that there may be a link between particular networks, including political networks, prevailing in the Norwegian-Tamil community and their success in the labour market (Engebrigtsen and Fuglerud, 2006). As already indicated, many Tamils arriving in the early period of immigration were recruited into the fish-processing industry in Norway through personal acquaintances. An interesting study from the 1990s of labour-market participation in Norway among different groups of refugees shows that Tamils at that time were the group with the poorest command of the local language but with the highest rate of employment (Djuve and Hagen, 1995). This can be seen as confirming the instrumental value of ethnic networks with respect to finding work. While today the majority of Sri Lankans speak Norwegian well after years in Norway, internal networks are still important both economically and in other respects. The role of social networks, and the differences in the size, shape and quality of social networks between different immigrant groups, is a factor often neglected when integration is discussed. Among Tamils in Norway it may be argued that social networks have structured a form of enclave-integration; they have made possible labour-market integration but have prevented social integration in a wider sense.

While many Tamil immigrants from Sri Lanka have had one or more relatives already in Norway to assist them when they arrived, in general, social networks in Norway are not family-based. One reason for this is the very strict immigration and asylum policy preventing the assembling of families. Unlike in Canada and certain other countries, there has never been a system for sponsoring candidates for immigration in Norway. Family reunion is thus open only for spouses and children, and asylum is granted only on the basis of individual persecution by the government of the applicant's country of origin. During the years with the highest number of asylum seekers arriving from Sri Lanka, the Norwegian government did all it could to refuse granting asylum on the grounds that applicants were not individually persecuted, only reluctantly permitting people to stay when the public opinion became too strong (Fuglerud, 1997). As a result siblings have been divided between several countries; children settled in Norway have been unable to bring their parents from Sri Lanka. As a result empirical studies show that Tamils have very limited family-based networks in Norway, one random sample showed an average of 2.3 family-members per person, most of them distant relatives (Engebrigtsen and Fuglerud, 2007a). Instead, friendship-relations tend to take on the roles and functions normally filled by family-members. Some of these friendships, of course, are from a previous existence in Sri Lanka, but many are also initiated, shaped, or reproduced in Norway through membership in the Tamil community as such.

The most important arenas where such membership is expressed and sustained in Norway are organised by supporters of the LTTE: public rituals, cultural functions, political demonstrations, and—not the least—weekend schools teaching Tamil language and arts to children and youth. In Oslo only a handful of families do not send their children to the Tamil schools, making these an effective channel for political propaganda but also an important instrument for integration into Norwegian society. Parents spend hours at the school every weekend throughout the year watching and waiting for their children, conversing with other parents and sharing information about job opportunities and Norwegian society in general. In other words, according to the view put forward by Fuglerud and Engebrigtsen (2006), while in the ongoing public and political debate social integration and non-Norwegian cultural identity tend to be seen as inherently contradictory, Tamils have proved that this is not the case.

Not denying that tight networks may have negative consequences in terms of personal freedom (below), these networks are arguably a resource making possible the overcoming of barriers to social mobility. This is relevant to the future of the Tamil children now being raised in Norway. Internationally, in the last 15–20 years studies on 'segmented assimilation', particularly in the US, have attracted interest. Very briefly, the point these studies make is that in present-day immigration integration, outcomes vary across immigrant nationalities and rapid integration and acceptance into mainstream settlement society represents just one possible alternative, the other being 'downward assimilation into

A recital by Tamil school students in Bergen, 2012.

the urban underclass' (Portes and Zhou, 1993 and Portes and Rumbaut, 2005). One of the factors determining the outcome of the generational adaptation process is the family and community resources available for overcoming barriers in the form of discrimination and racism—in other words, social mobility through ethnic

cohesion. Such resources are in social science literature often spoken of as 'social capital'. These resources may be present to different degrees in different minority groups, and within the same group to different degrees in different regions and countries as a result of differences in the size, composition and complexity of the localised minority in question. In particular, mechanisms of what has been termed 'enforceable trust', the subordination of individual interests to collective expectations of long-term advantages, so important for establishing bonds of social capital, may work in different ways in different areas. In the Tamil case internal mechanisms of solidarity and homeland-orientation, and, through these, also of integration into mainstream society, seem in Norway to depend on the position and the strength of the LTTE-affiliated structures discussed above.

However, it is important to be clear that the positive effects of internal solidarity are matched by more problematic ones. In Norway, where the Tamil population is minute and the influence of the LTTE has been hegemonic, the situation of young Tamils was until the end of the war—apart from the imminence of violence and possible death—comparable with that of young people in the Tamil areas in Sri Lanka, described by Brun, (2008: 418) in terms of 'complex citizenship'. By this she refers to the fact that 'more than one actor represents "the government" and this forces people to relate to various governments, which materialise in abiding by different sets of rules'. While the level of social capital generated by this model of ethnic incorporation and social control had many positive consequences in terms of school discipline, prevention of criminal behaviour etc., the price they paid was submission. It should be noted that the interconnection between ethnic incorporation and integration into mainstream society has an important gender dimension.

While statistics show that both male and female second generation Tamils would like to have more interaction with mainstream Norwegian society than what is possible for them, the situation is particularly acute for girls and young women. Interviews show that many girls of Tamil background growing up in Norway are raised under very strict family regimes and rarely if ever leave the house after school (Engebrigtsen and Fuglerud, 2007b). The fact that girls of Tamil background in youth surveys score significantly higher on rates of 'contemplating suicide' and 'attempted suicide' than any other category of young people can be assumed to be related to this situation (Engebrigtsen and Fuglerud, 2007b). This is not simply a consequence of family dynamics but should be seen as a result of the particular national and/or regional minority dynamics. Many of the girls of Tamil background interviewed in Oslo pointed out that their parents' own norms and values were not the main problem but, rather, that both the girls and their parents were caught in a situation with no place to hide from the watching eye

of the larger ethnic community. To what extent this is changing as a result of a fragmentation of the Tamil community after the end of the war is still too early to tell. It is reasonable to assume that in the United Kingdom and Canada, which have considerably larger Tamil populations compared to Norway, there may be greater diversity of positions within the Tamil diaspora and, therefore, also more possibilities of establishing 'personal space'.

The Norway Tamil Sangam organises soccer matches to reach out to youngsters in the diaspora.

POST-WAR DEVELOPMENTS

As in most other countries where refugees of Tamil background live, the end-phase of the war in Sri Lanka was in Norway a difficult and traumatic period. It also led to political changes. On the one hand, it brought a formalisation of structures and an element of democracy into local political life. The Norwegian-Tamil community in May 2009, just before the ending of the war, was one of the first diasporic communities to hold a referendum on the Vattukottai-resolution of 1977. Approximately 95–98 per cent of the voting Tamils in Norway through this referendum confirmed the Vattukottai-resolution's aspiration for Tamil independence from Sri Lanka. In the local context this is known as the Norwegian-Tamil Mandate of 2009 (NTM-2009), serving as a political platform for the establishment of the Norwegian Council of Eelam Tamils (NCET). This was followed, one year later with elections to the 'Transnational Government of Tamil Eelam'. On the other hand, the establishment of these structures and the elections through which positions were filled, led to a replacement of the 'old guard' having served as loyal organisers for the LTTE over the last 10–15 years. A somewhat younger set of people took over. While the finer details of personal animosity and political opinions are difficult to discern for those not directly involved, there are indications that what lay behind was a more democratic strategy loosing out in internal struggles and a more 'hardline' philosophy with respect to political issues in Sri Lanka winning the support of voters. In 2012, a struggle along these various lines continues in most countries where people of Tamil background live. In itself, these differences are neither surprising nor wrong.

Øivind Fuglerud

Harvest festival (Pongal) celebrations in Norway, 2012.

SWEDEN

Sri Lankan Hindu devotees at the Sweden Ganesha Temple, 2008.

S RI LANKANS IN Sweden form a relatively small group of immigrants, and are scattered throughout the country. Unlike most other countries hosting migrants from Sri Lanka, there are more Sinhalese than Tamils in Sweden. In 2010, Sweden had 6,722 inhabitants born in Sri Lanka, and 4,008 born in Sweden with one or both parents from Sri Lanka. The question of who belongs to the Sri Lankan diaspora, however, is difficult to ascertain. About half of the Sri Lanka-born individuals in Sweden—3,326 in 2010—were adopted from Sri Lanka, and hence have grown up in a Swedish context with no or very limited contact with their country of birth.

For many of the ethnic Tamils, the violent conflict in their country of origin has alienated them from the Sri Lankan government and hence also from a Sri Lankan identity, and made them identify primarily as part of the Tamil, rather than the Sri Lankan, diaspora. Individuals born and raised in Sweden with Sri Lankan parents (both Sinhalese and Tamil) tend to primarily identify as Swedes, while also maintaining contact and identification with the homeland.

MIGRATION PATTERNS

The first Sri Lankans to migrate to Sweden arrived in the early 1970s, and came for various individual reasons, often linked to contacts with Swedes, for studies or work. Large-scale charter tourism from Sweden to Sri Lanka in the 1970s enabled interaction between Swedes and Sri Lankans, particularly in the coastal areas in Western and Southern Sri Lanka. This provided the groundwork for one of the most significant migration paths to Sweden: marriage. From the 1970s onwards there has been a continuous process of Sri Lankans—more women than men—moving to Sweden to marry Swedish partners. Sri Lankans already residing in Sweden, including second generation immigrants, have also found partners from Sri Lanka. Most Sri Lankans living in Sweden come from the coastal areas.

Before the commencement of the armed conflict between the Sri Lankan government and the Liberation Tigers of Tamil Eelam (LTTE) in 1983, very few Tamils lived in Sweden. The war provided both push and pull factors for Tamil migration. Although much fewer than in neighbouring Norway, large numbers of Tamils arrived in Sweden between 1983 and 2009. Whether they had formal refugee status or found other ways of entering Sweden, they identified themselves as refugees. Tamils came from all parts of northern and eastern Sri Lanka, but mostly from the Jaffna peninsula. Between 1987 and 1989 Sweden also received Sinhalese refugees.

Between 50 and 100 Sinhalese, affected by the violence between the Sri Lankan government and the socialist Janatha Vimukthi Peramuna (JVP) found refuge in Sweden.

Sri Lankans have also arrived in Sweden for studies, and stayed on after their graduation. While some have come on scholarships, more often students have relied on funds from their parents in Sri Lanka until they have found work to finance their own stay. Another migration path that has continued over the years is that of professionals—for instance within the fields of information technology or business—moving to Sweden for work.

The adoption of children from Sri Lanka took place in the 1980s and 1990s. Most of these children were born in southern and central Sri Lanka. A change in Sri Lankan government policy has, however, made Swedish adoption of children from Sri Lanka very rare in the 2000s.

INTEGRATION INTO SWEDISH SOCIETY

The Sri Lankan migrants in Sweden belong to four religious groups—Buddhism, Hinduism, Christianity (mostly Catholicism) and Islam. They have different class and caste background, although relatively few come from the upper-classes. While the Sinhalese live in various parts of Sweden, the Tamils are mostly concentrated in the Stockholm area.

Inspite of the difficulties in learning the Swedish language, the limited numbers of Sri Lankans in Sweden, the fact that they are geographically scattered and that many have married into Swedish families, has facilitated integration. Sri Lankans describe themselves as 'flexible' and 'adjustable' in relation to Swedish society, and they tend to prioritise hard work and studies. There are many examples of Sri Lankan migrants who have started in simple jobs and advanced to higher ranks, and a few examples of very successful careers, often in the private sector. Many Sri Lankans work in the tourism sector. While the first generation of immigrants has had to work hard to integrate, many second generation Sri Lankans, through higher studies, are engaged in professional occupations, including medical doctors and civil engineers.

LANGUAGE AND CULTURE

Most Sri Lankan migrants in Sweden maintain contact with the homeland. They communicate with family and friends, follow news media and, if possible, visit the island. Although many parents speak Sinhala or Tamil in their homes, their children's proficiency in these languages vary. Among the second generation, who usually identify themselves as Swedish rather than Sri Lankan, interest in learning written Sinhala and Tamil has been low. The Stockholm Buddhist Vihara offers Sinhala language training as part of the religious Dhamma school, and had between 10 and 12 participants in 2012, while about 60–70 children learnt Tamil on Saturdays

Map 4.19

through a Tamil heritage organisation in Stockholm. In 2008, *Tamilnet* reported that 95 students from Sweden had taken part in Tamil language exams conducted by the transnational Tamil Education Development Council.

With the exception of a Sinhala radio program that was broadcasted in the Stockholm area for several years, Sri Lankans in Sweden are too few and too scattered to sustain their own vernacular media. Having said that, a well-known English-language pro-government news site on Sri Lankan affairs, the *Asian Tribune*, is run by a Tamil who is based in Sweden.

Training in classical Tamil dance, *bharatanatyam*, is available in the Stockholm area, and the dance is often performed at special events. Sinhala dances also occasionally feature during cultural performances. There have been a few examples of restaurants serving Sri Lankan food in various parts of Sweden. In the 1990s and early 2000s a Stockholm-based cricket team dominated by Sri Lankans did very well in the local cricket circuit.

The Sri Lankan Association in Sweden (SLAIS) was established in 1993 and has since sought to draw the Sri Lankan community together, promote Sri Lankan culture and provide charity to Sri Lanka. It works closely with the Sri Lankan embassy—established in Sweden in 1970—as well as with the Buddhist temple. SLAIS has invited artists from Sri Lanka, and raised funds to support disabled Sri Lankans, education for children, tsunami housing projects, among many others. In 2012, SLAIS had 155 families as paying members, and their events drew up to 150–250 participants, mostly from the Stockholm area, but also from other parts of Sweden and Scandinavia. Beyond Stockholm, other organisations based in Umeå, Eskilstuna and southern Sweden, have played similar roles promoting Sri Lankan culture and engaging in charitable activities.

Persons adopted from Sri Lanka have their own organisations. A very active Facebook group had over 200 members in 2012. Most of those adopted are now young adults, and many display a keen interest in their country of birth. Some have travelled to Sri Lanka to search for their biological family members, while others only for the purpose of touring the country. Many have a very positive image of Sri Lanka, although a visit there, for most, usually acts as a reaffirmation of their Swedish, rather than Sri Lankan, identity.

RELIGION

The Sri Lankan diaspora in Sweden has been involved in the development of two religious shrines: The Stockholm Buddhist Vihara established in 1985; and the Sweden Ganesha Temple setup in 2000. Both these temples play an important role not only as a place for Sri Lankans to practice their religion, but also for the maintenance of social and cultural ties with others in the diaspora and in the homeland.

The Stockholm Buddhist Vihara has, since its inception, attracted Sri Lankan Buddhists from all parts of Scandinavia, although most visitors are from the Stockholm area. In 1995, it acquired a permanent temple building. A number of families provide the three residential monks with food according to a schedule. Main activities of the Vihara are *poya* day retreats, celebration of Wesak, New Year and Katina Pinkam (ritual offering of the robe). The Vihara has 25–30 more active visitors, while up to 100 take part in Wesak celebrations. The temple's chief incumbent, Bhante K. Siri Dhammaratana

Maha Thera, is also the Prelate of Scandinavia, and has played a significant role in the establishment of Buddhist temples in Copenhagen and Oslo in 2004 and 2011 respectively. In southern Sweden, the Sri Lanka Buddhist Cultural Association of Skaane was established in 2010, gathering 20–30 families from southern Sweden. A temple was inaugurated in Åstorp, but ceased to function after encountering problems related to building permits.

The Stockholm Buddhist Vihara was established by the Sri Lanka-Sweden Buddhist Association in 1985.

The Sweden Ganesha Temple is the only Tamil Hindu temple in Sweden. It draws mainly Sri Lankan Tamils, along with a smaller number of devotees of Indian or Swedish background. Its *puja*s held on Tuesdays and Fridays are frequented by worshippers of all ages, and play an important social integration role for Tamils, including the second generation. Among Tamil Hindus, Thai Pongal in January is an important important festive occasion.

The Christian Sinhalese and Tamils in Sweden—most of whom are Catholic—tend to be closely integrated with the Buddhist Sinhalese or Hindu Tamils respectively. Catholic church services in Tamil are conducted regularly in Stockholm.

GENDER

Women make up 56 per cent of the Sri Lanka-born persons in Sweden. The explanation for the imbalance can be attributed to the large number of women who arrived in Sweden and married Swedes. Women, especially first generation migrants, play an important role maintaining the traditions of the homeland, being religiously active and wearing traditional clothing on special occasions. Having said that, most Sri Lankan homes in Sweden reveal adjustments to Swedish cultural norms, in terms for example of the freedom second generation Sri Lankan girls' have in interacting with boys, and the growing parental acquisence to the right of young adults' to select their life partners. In Sweden, Sri Lankan women often work, and the extent of their integration in Swedish society is evident in the fact that even in the older generation, only a small number have not learnt Swedish.

HOMELAND POLITICS

The protracted civil war in Sri Lanka has had far-reaching implications for the diaspora. Tamil migrants, in particular, have been heavily engaged in homeland politics. The ethnic divides in Sri Lanka extended also to Sweden when from the mid-1980s, Tamils ceased to be active in Sri Lankan organisations, as they wished to distance themselves from the political regime in Sri Lanka. While some Sri Lanka organisations and the Sri Lankan Embassy have made it a point to invite Sri Lankans of all ethnic backgrounds to their activities, many Tamils have chosen to boycott the events as a protest against the government's treatment of Tamils in the homeland.

Many Tamils have instead supported the Tamil separatist struggle. Although Sweden is a relatively marginal Tamil diaspora country, the LTTE was active here before its demise in 2009. Several LTTE-

The Sri Lankan Association in Sweden.

linked organisations, such as the Tamil Rehabilitation Organisation (TRO) and the Tamil Youth Organisation (TYO) had branches in Sweden. Like in the countries with a larger Tamil diaspora, Tamils in Sweden have attempted to lobby Swedish politicians and build public support for the Tamil cause. This has, however, been less successful than elsewhere. The Great Hero's Day in November, when martyrs of the Tamil struggle are commemorated, usually draws hundreds of diaspora Tamils. However, unlike in Canada or the UK where the Tamil vote base is significant, Swedish politicians usually decline invitations to participate. A number of demonstrations have been organised, mainly in central Stockholm, to raise awareness of the reported atrocities of the Sri Lankan government and gain support for Tamil separatism. On a few occasions, these have gathered 400–500 people, but usually the numbers have been smaller. In April 2009, a sit-in demonstration where around 40 Tamils blocked the traffic in central Stockholm received some media attention. During the war years, Tamils from Sweden also joined the larger rallies organised in Oslo, London and Geneva.

With the exception of Tamils supportive of the LTTE, most Sri Lankans have not been overtly politically active. However, in 2008, three demonstrations against the LTTE took place in central Stockholm. One of them, organised by a group called 'Campaign Against Separatist Terrorism in Sri Lanka', drew around 200 people. The Sri Lankan Embassy also initiated moves to counteract the Tamil nationalist campaign. Although the Sinhalese in Sweden have been less involved with the conflict in Sri Lanka, the end of the war in 2009 did see a strengthening of their identification with the homeland, as pride in the Sri Lankan government's success in defeating the LTTE extended also to the diaspora. Some Sri Lankan associations were involved in organising victory celebrations and raising funds to support the Sri Lankan government's fund for victims of war.

Following the demise of the LTTE in 2009, Tamil nationalist activism almost ceased. While the Tamil diaspora elsewhere continued to pursue a separatist goal and justice for war victims, several leading Tamils in Sweden have chosen a reconciliatory path. A division can be discerned between those advocating cooperation with the Sri Lankan government and those who continue to strive for an independent Tamil Eelam. Tamils in Sweden are represented in the recently forged 'Transnational Government of Tamil Eelam' and the Global Tamil Forum, but they have not been very active.

ECONOMIC CONTRIBUTIONS

Sri Lankans in Sweden have contributed economically to their homeland through various channels. Many support family members in the homeland, while others assist needy children either directly or through an organisation which, for instance, runs an orphanage or gives scholarships to poor students. Numerous charity organisations that focus on helping the needy in Sri Lanka—often children—exist in Sweden. While many are run by Swedes who have visited Sri Lanka, Sri Lankans are active in some. For both the Sinhalese and Tamils in Sweden, the tsunami disaster in late 2004 was a significant event. In the aftermath of the tsunami, the Sri Lankan diaspora played an important role in relief work. A collection center was organised in the Stockholm harbour with the cooperation of the Sri Lankan Embassy. Notable individuals, organisations and private companies—Swedish and Sri Lankan—were also engaged in the provision of aid to the victims.

FUTURE

Since the 1970s, the Sri Lankan population in Sweden has gradually increased. It is likely to continue growing through the migration of Sri Lankans to Sweden to marry or join relatives, as well as the immigration of professionals for work. Having said that, the introduction of fees for foreign students in Swedish universities in 2011 has largely closed this migration route, while the end of the war has meant an end to asylum migration.

There has hardly been any return migration from Sweden to Sri Lanka, and this is unlikely to change, despite the end of the war in Sri Lanka. Second generation migrants grow up identifying as Swedes and consequently the third generation are likely to sustain only a vague notion of a Sri Lankan identity. The ambivalence about identity felt by many first generation migrants from Sri Lanka—the sense of feeling neither Sri Lankan nor Swedish, expressed by many migrants—is less of an issue for the second generation who grow up with a more firm Swedish identification. The continued existence of a viable diaspora will hence depend on new immigrants and the extent to which they are able to sustain connections with Sri Lanka.

A key question is also whether the end of the war in Sri Lanka will lead to reconciliation and shared identification between Sinhalese and Tamils in Sweden. The Sri Lankan government seeks to promote a Sri Lankan diaspora identity instead of the Tamil diaspora identity which was so important for the LTTE's struggle. A number of Tamil organisations located in the diaspora, however, continue to advocate Tamil nationalism. The developments in Sweden are contradictory: while many Tamils still maintain a distance from 'Sri Lankan' activities and organisations, others have have begun to participate recently. Whether the Tamils in Sweden will continue to remain alienated from a Sri Lankan identity will also depend on the success of initiatives that seek to foster political reconciliation in Sri Lanka.

Camilla Orjuela

Table 4.11

RESIDENT PERMITS GRANTED TO SRI LANKANS BETWEEN 1986 AND 2011: FAMILY REUNIFICATION																									
1986	1987	1988	1989	1990	1991	1992	1993	1994	1995	1996	1997	1998	1999	2000	2001	2002[2]	2003	2004	2005	2006	2007	2008	2009	2010	2011
56	56	59	107	157	133	211	166	119	87	78	78	107	84	98	117	93	94	72	85	142	122	102	60	98	108

Source: Swedish Migration Board, 2011.

Table 4.12

RESIDENT PERMITS GRANTED TO SRI LANKAN ADOPTED CHILDREN BETWEEN 1986 AND 2011																											
1984	1985	1986	1987	1988	1989	1990	1991	1992	1993	1994	1995	1996	1997	1998	1999	2000	2001	2002	2003	2004	2005	2006	2007	2008	2009	2010	2011
322	274	255	197	28	31	67	127	79	35	13	15	2	2	1	4	1	-	1	-	3	1	3	-	1	-	-	-

Source: Swedish Migration Board, 2011.

DENMARK

THERE WERE 10,988 individuals with a Sri Lankan background living in Denmark in 2012 (according to the Ministry of Social Affairs and Integration's 2011 census). The majority of these (around 9,800) were Tamils; the remainder (about 1,200) Sinhalese. The two groups differ significantly in religious affiliation, in their reasons for coming to Denmark, and in their settlement patterns, although they are treated as one group in many measurements and statistics. This article will attempt to widen the perspective and deal with the Tamils and the Sinhalese separately, where possible. This can, however, be difficult when dealing with exact figures, as the Danish statistical agency that registers all newcomers to Denmark does not document religious or ethnic differences, but only geographical affiliation, treating them as a single group.

THE SRI LANKAN TAMILS

The first significant wave of Sri Lankan Tamils came to Denmark in 1983 as a result of the escalating conflict in Sri Lanka between the Liberation Tigers of the Tamil Eelam (LTTE) and the Sri Lankan armed forces. They were mostly men, and they were categorised as de facto refugees, understood as admitted temporarily with the

Map 4.20

Sri Lankan children holding Danish flags during a festival.

possibility of repatriation when the conditions in Sri Lanka would allow it. During the 1990s they married Tamil spouses coming from Sri Lanka, or claimed reunification with the family they had had to leave behind. Today around 4,000 Tamils are children or young people born and raised in Denmark, and it is obvious that their relationship to Sri Lanka differs from that of their parents' generation.

With regard to religious affiliation, approximately 8,500 Tamils identify themselves as Hindu, around 1,000 as Catholic, and the remainder (a few hundred) are either Muslim, atheist, or have converted to various Christian groups such as Jehovah's Witnesses, Troens Ord (the Word of Belief) or the Baptists.

Most Tamils live today in central Jutland in the cities of Herning, Brande, Holstebro, Tarm, Struer, Vejle and Billund, as these were areas with growing industrial sectors and a high demand for workers in the 1990s. Today they have a cultural association based in Struer and two consecrated temples in Herning and Brande. The temple in Herning is dedicated to Ganesh; while the temple in Brande is dedicated to the goddess Abirami.

THE SINHALESE

The Sinhalese did not follow the same immigration pattern as the Tamils. At least 60 to 70 per cent of Sinhalese immigrants were women. The immigration of the Sinhalese took place in at least two smaller waves. The first and biggest was in the late 1970s, when Sinhalese women came to Denmark to marry Danish men they had met in Sri Lanka, visiting as tourists there. The next wave, as with the Tamils described above, was caused by the political conflict in Sri Lanka.

With regard to religious affiliation, around 900 of the Sinhalese identify themselves as Buddhists. The remainder, about 300, have converted to Christianity, following the affiliation of their Danish husbands. The Sinhalese are scattered around Denmark, with a small concentration living on Zealand close to Copenhagen, where the Buddhists occasionally visit a *vihara* located there. The temple, situated in a private apartment, is run by lay people and occasionally visited by an ordained

Table 4.13

DIFFERING GATEWAYS TO DENMARK	
Refugees from Sri Lanka	5,086
Other kinds of residence permit	1,086
Unknown reason for residence permit	602
Descendants	4,214
Total	**10,988**

Source: Danish Statistics, December 2011.

Table 4.14

DESCENDANTS GROUPED BY AGE (IN %)	
0–9 years	40
10–19 years	51
20–29 years	9

Source: Danish Statistics, December 2011.

The Sri Lankan-Danish Association (DSDFK) organises a picnic for its members.

monk. There is also a Sinhalese temple, with an ordained monk, in Stockholm, Sweden. This is seen as a temple for all Scandinavian Sinhalese Buddhists, and the Danish Sinhalese Buddhists do visit it occasionally for the most important festivals, such as Wesak. The Sri Lankan-Danish Association (DSDFK), being a formal association, focuses on cultural events, such as Sri Lankan dance, but organise trips to Sweden.

CONDITION AND SPECIFIC FEATURES OF THE MIGRATION PROCESS

The Tamils and, in particular, the first wave of Sinhalese had very different gateways into Denmark and therefore very different experiences in relation to residence permits, settlement patterns and so on. While a number of Sinhalese women were given residence permits because of marriages to Danish men, the Tamils mostly came as refugees or, later, through family reunification. While seeking asylum, they were confined in the Sandholm refugee camp.

For both groups though, the migration process seems to have been a success. Today more than half the Sri Lankans have become Danish citizens, a hallmark of their intention to stay in Denmark and to become a part of Danish society. Compared to most other refugee and immigrant groups in Denmark, Sri Lankans are well integrated in Danish society; most are employed, their children are doing well in Danish schools, they often choose to converse with one another in Danish, and many have adopted some Danish traditions, such as Christmas eve celebration. This, however, has been done in such a way that the tradition becomes their own, or acquires a symbolic meaning that does not clash with what they consider to be core matters of their own heritage.

At the same time, great effort is put into keeping up the most important religious and/or cultural festivals during the year. Here, the temple has become the primary bearer of tradition, not only for the Tamil Hindus, but also for some Sinhalese, who visit the Hindu temple to socialise and eat Sri Lankan food. In 1994, the consecretion of the first temporary temple in Denmark was a major event for the Tamil Hindus. It enabled easy access to a place of religious worship that is close to their homes. Now they could live up to the old Tamil-Hindu saying: 'Do not live in a village where there is no temple', meaning that one should live only where communication with God and the manifestation of God are possible.

SOCIAL, CULTURAL, EDUCATIONAL AND ECONOMIC CHANGES

The first generation of Sri Lankans found mainly unskilled work. They had to learn Danish, and they found that education and training in Sri Lanka were not recognised by most Danish employers. Therefore, if workers were unsatisfied with unskilled work, they had to start over from the beginning in the Danish educational system. Despite a tough start, most Sri Lankans today are doing well economically. When compared to other immigrant groups, the percentage of Sri Lankans in the workforce, aged between 16 and 64 years is high: 3,104 (64 per cent) for men and 3,164 (56 per cent) for women, totalling 6,268 (60 per cent) (Danish Statistics, 2011). This, together with the percentage of homes owned by Sri Lankans (52.8 per cent)—the highest among all immigrant groups in Denmark—gives a good indication of their economic stability (Danmarks Statistik, 2010 figures).

An especially high percentage of second generation girls are entering further or higher education after finishing high school. This has created an educational gender bias that is openly discussed among several Tamil youth groups. It seems that educational level is taken more seriously than caste when considering a suitable marriage match. A small survey conducted in 2005 by one of the editors of the Tamil magazine *Brobyggeren* ('The Bridge Builder') showed that 62 per cent of a group of 50 young Tamils described their own marriages as a love-match, despite having been negotiated according to the parental norms of marrying within one's own caste. This negotiating process is a great challenge, and can lead to a clash between the first and second generations.

THE CONTEMPORARY SITUATION: ISSUES, CHALLENGES AND OPPORTUNITIES

Compared to most other immigrant groups, Sri Lankans have only a short history in Denmark. Despite this they seem well integrated when it comes to employment, learning Danish and being active members in local associations and organisations. The second generation, accounting for nearly 40 per cent of the Sri Lankan population in Denmark (see Table 4.14), are doing well in the school system. Having said that, the attempt to get more boys to pursue a university degree is a challenge. Politics even draws the attention of Tamil youngsters. Quite a few are active in politics, but mostly at the community level, and they spend considerable time discussing issues in relation to Tamils in Denmark and the situation in Sri Lanka. The editors of both *Brobyggeren* magazine and the chat forum 'Nizhal.dk' are very active in these matters.

Sri Lankans seem to want both to retain some kind of Sri Lankan authenticity by preserving their traditions and to have an open cultural communication with Danish society at large. This is a difficult task. The first and second generations often disagree as to the elements of tradition that should be retained and those that should be discarded. In Denmark, arranged marriages and the role of women remain contentious issues within the Sri Lankan diaspora. The failure to sustain tradition in this regard can sometimes lead to divisions within the family.

In spite of the differences in opinion, the first generation still have great ambitions for their children: girls are expected to stay home, do housework and at the same time train as doctors or lawyers. In the long run, this pressure can be counterproductive. Seemingly, the main challenge for the Sri Lankans in Denmark stems from the need to reconcile the differing expectations of the first and second generations.

Marianne Qvortrup Fibiger

Bharatanatyam performance during Saraswati puja in Denmark, 2007.

'Asian Sensation', comprising Daneshan Thaivendran (Niller), Danushan Theivendran (Danu) and Kautham Jeyakumar (Koko), won the Danish X-Factor challenge in 2009.

A student of Sri Lankan descent at Rygaards school in Copenhagen.

PORTUGAL

THE SRI LANKAN community in Portugal comprises part of the larger South Asian diaspora. In 2009, of the approximately 9,500 South Asians in the country, most were Indians, followed by Pakistanis and Bangladeshis. In comparison, Sri Lankan citizens with residence permits in Portugal, constitute a minor community formed out of individual movements and supported by family networks, that have over time aided in reuniting a small number of families in the diaspora.

PORTUGAL IN SRI LANKA

The Portuguese Armada, commanded by D. Lourenço de Almeida, first arrived in Sri Lanka (1505) on the proximities of Galle, in the southwest of the island. They later moved north and founded Colombo. Sri Lanka had almost 450 years of Western influence which gave the island a quite unique identity: first the Portuguese (1505-1658), then the Dutch (1658-1796) and finally the British (1796–1948). The Portuguese cultural imprint in Sri Lanka is visible in three different spheres: by Portuguese descent (Portuguese Burghers that live mostly on the eastern side of the island mainly in the cities of Batticaloa and Trincomalee); by the existence of the Roman Catholic faith (the Portuguese introduced Roman Catholicism to the island); and finally by the existence of a language (the Sri Lankan Portuguese Creole). The interaction of the Portuguese and Sri Lankans was the most important factor that led to the evolution of the new language, which flourished as a lingua franca in the island for over three and a half centuries. The Portuguese have left their stamp on Sri Lankan social administration, society, fine arts and language, which is evident in the Portuguese lexical borrowings in Sinhala.

SRI LANKA IN PORTUGAL

In the 1980s there was a transformation in immigration patterns in Europe. The southern European countries, that had been an important source of labour supply to the more developed countries, began receiving migrants as well. Initially they came from Portuguese-speaking

Birthday parties provide an opportunity for Sri Lankans in Portugal to gather.

African countries but by the mid-1990s new migrant groups emerged, including Brazilians, Chinese and Bangladeshis, amongst others. Unlike the Indian presence in Portugal—that has a long history linked to colonialism—the Sri Lankans are numerically few, and have had limited social impact. They comprise people that arrived in Portugal as economic migrants as well as asylum seekers, including both Sinhalas and Tamils. A report published by the *Serviço de Estrangeiros e Fronteiras* (Aliens and Borders Service) in 2009 reveals that asylum seekers in Portugal comprise a very diverse group in terms of origin, social and cultural background, of which the Sri Lankans constitute a very small segment.

The majority of Sri Lankans living in Portugal in 2010 were men aged between 18-45 years. Though small, the network of Sinhalese and Tamil Sri Lankans in Portugal offers considerable aid to immigrants arriving in the country. The search for a job or for a house is made possible by the contacts established within the community. This has helped to provide the basic needs of these new immigrants in a foreign environment where most have little hold over the Portuguese language. Most Sri Lankan immigrants share houses and work at the same places— usually in Asian fusion restaurants in the hip zone of Lisbon (Chiado). They live near the centre because it is closer to their working place and near the Martim Moniz, an area where a large number of Indian, Chinese and African shops can be found.

Given the small size of the Sri Lankan community in Portugal, the lack of family units and the lack of diasporic structures, transnational relations remain central to the lives of these immigrants. From the generalised usage of mobile phones, telephone cards, Facebook, Twitter and Skype, these Sri Lankan migrants remain deeply and constantly connected, not just with their families in Sri Lanka but also with Sri Lankans in other parts of the world. These de-territorialised networks and their commitment towards their family and familial relationships are of great importance in influencing their social, cultural and political affinities. Indeed, it is through these transnational reciprocities, that Sri Lankan immigrants in Portugal have managed to create some semblance of the 'homeland' abroad.

Umme Salma

The Galle Fort in Southern Sri Lanka was built by the Portuguese in the 16th century and later fortified during the Dutch period. Also known as the 'Rampart of Galle', the majestic and well-preserved fort is recognised as a World Heritage Site.

Map 4.21

RUSSIA

A delegation of the Communist Party of Ceylon that arrived for the 24th Communist Party of the Soviet Union (CPSU) congress, laid a wreath at the Lenin Mausoleum, 29 March 1971.

THE EMERGENCE OF a Sri Lankan diaspora in Russia is the product of long and varied relations between Russia and Sri Lanka. The first Russian Consul was sent to Galle in 1882 and subsequently, in 1891, the main Consulate of Russia was established in Colombo. In November 1890, the famous Russian writer and playwright Anton Chekhov stayed in Colombo. Another famous Russian, Nobel Prizewinner Ivan Bunin, visited Sri Lanka in 1911. He described Sri Lanka's natural beauty and richness in many of his verses and stories. Bunin, in his poetry, recalled the story of Eden or the Lost Paradise. Indeed, in medieval times, many Russians believed that the Garden of Eden was in Sri Lanka.

Positive feelings towards Sri Lanka resulted in the establishment of diplomatic relations between the Soviet Union and Sri Lanka in 1958. On 25 February 1958, the Soviet Union and Sri Lanka signed an agreement on Economic and Technical Cooperation. As a result of this and other agreements between the two countries, several Sri Lankan companies established links with Moscow. The first group of professionals from Sri Lanka arrived in Moscow in 1958. This was followed by the first batch of Sri Lankan students (31) who came to study Engineering and Medicine in the Soviet Union (Sri Lankan Embassy, Moscow). In 1959, the Friendship Society with Sri Lanka was established in Moscow. Direct air flights between Moscow and Colombo began in 1964.

SRI LANKAN STUDENTS

By the late 1960s, the number of students coming from Sri Lanka to the USSR grew to one hundred per year. Later,

the Sri Lankan students in Russia formed the Sri Lankan Students Union (KSMU). While most of these students were based in Moscow, some did join educational institutions in Leningrad (now St. Petersburg), Kursk, Kiev, Novgorod, Krasnodar and other cities of the Soviet Union. The majority specialised in engineering and medicine, although a few did take up the study of geology, Russian language and literature and chemistry. The Soviet state offered a stipend and boarding for those who came within this 100 persons quota.

Map 4.22

The educational standard of these Russian-taught engineers and doctors was so outstanding that Sri Lankan middle class parents also began sending their sons and daughters to the Soviet Union for higher education. Some young Buddhist monks came to study history and literature in Leningrad. Young Sri Lankan actors went to Leningrad as probationer students. Among them was the famous Sri Lankan theater and television star, Senaka Perera. The famous Sri Lankan geologist Anura Gunasekera was educated at Leningrad Gorniy (Mining) Institute. Some Leningrad students, like Padma de Silva, went on to achieve great distinction in their careers in countries such as New Zealand and Australia.

For the majority of Sri Lankans in the USSR, life was good, but bilateral agreements between the Soviet Union and Sri Lanka did not allow their longer stay in Soviet cities. The only exceptions were Sri Lankans who married Soviet citizens—nearly all of whom comprised Sri Lankan men who married local women.

The break-up of the Soviet Union affected old bilateral relations. As the successor state of the Soviet Union, the Russian Federation allowed Sri Lankan students to come for studies to Moscow, St. Petersburg, Kursk and some other Russian cities but financial help from the Russian state ended. Students had a difficult time and some often had to find illegal employment or establish an illegal business to support their education.

Currently, there are about 700 Sri Lankan students in Russia (Sri Lankan Embassy, Moscow). Approximately 200 Sri Lankan students study at Kursk and Tver State Medical universities. Over the past decade, Russian immigration control has become less strict. From the 1990s, many former students found it easier to stay in Russia after their graduation. This marked the beginning of a small community of Sri Lankans permanently settled in Russia.

THE 1990S ONWARDS

Over the last two decades, Sri Lankan businessmen have embarked on several new business ventures in Moscow; from tea-trade to establishing an international university. In 2011, the Sri Lanka Tea Board participated in the PRODEXPO trade show in Russia and Eastern Europe with the support of the Sri Lankan Embassy and major Sri Lankan tea exporters such as Ceylon Tea Land, Sri Lanka Tea Bags, Imperial Tea Export, Jafferjee Brothers, Dilmah Teas, Ceylon Fresh Tea Company, etc. During the 2011 Wesak Day celebrations, the Sri Lanka Tea Board also sponsored the distribution of free tea. Although the aim of establishing a university failed, the tea-trade has proven to be highly profitable. Other established

Ceylon doctors in the diagnostic laboratory of the Moscow City Hospital, 1969.

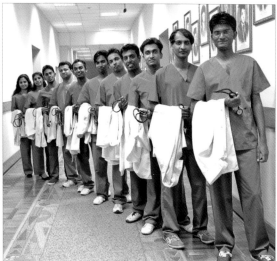

Sri Lankan medical students in Russia, 2012.

businesses included the import of fruits and vegetables and the export of Russian technology to Sri Lanka.

Illegal immigrants, mostly from areas affected by the civil war, also came to Moscow and St. Petersburg, using these cities as stepping stones to the refugee havens in Western Europe. However, there are some who have remained in Russia. Together with more successful Sri Lankans who married local citizens, they now form a settled community that expects to stay as long as possible in the Russian Federation.

CONCLUSION

A small expatriate community of Sri Lankans form the core of the existing Sri Lankan community in Moscow. They have established their own cultural centre and a Buddhist society. In parallel, in Sri Lanka, the Russian Cultural Centre in Colombo provides the opportunity for Sri Lankan children to learn Russian ballet, chess, art and music. These activities have aided in cultivating an interest in Russia amongst Sri Lankans. This may lead to an intention to visit Russia or a desire to settle there in the future.

The members of the Sri Lankan community in Russia are very active in the promotion of Sri Lankan culture. They have maintained close ties with the Sri Lankan Embassy in Moscow, which is an important venue in the celebration of Sri Lankan festivals. The small diaspora in Russia has also sustained its relationship with Sri Lanka, readily providing support to families of the victims of the 2004 tsunami.

Igor Kotin and Nina G. Krasnodembskaia

Wesak Day celebrated at the Sri Lankan embassy in Moscow, 2010.

EASTERN EUROPE

Sri Lankan students studying at Gomel State Medical University in Belarus.

International Festival of Youth and Students in Prague, August 1947. Students from Ceylon and other countries marched across the city with banners identifying their country of origin.

'THE TRANSIT ZONE'

Eastern Europe, that is the territory of the former Eastern Bloc countries (Hungary, German Democratic Republic (GDR) now part of Germany, Poland, Czechoslovakia now Czech and Slovak Republics, Romania) and the former republics of the Soviet Union (Estonia, Latvia, Lithuania, Ukraine, Belarus, Moldova) used to be a transit area between the Soviet Union and Western Europe. Until recently, these countries did not have any special importance for Sri Lankans. Refugees from Sri Lanka saw Western Europe as the asylum haven and Eastern Europe only as the porous border to it. For those students who wanted to find affordable and high-quality education, these countries were considered minor destinations in comparison with Russia. With the expansion of the European Community in 2008, temporary resident Sri Lankans were placed in a better position on their way towards the west. This was especially true in the case of Tamils from Sri Lanka who managed to gain asylum status in these countries.

GROWING TIES

Ukraine, a major importer of Sri Lankan tea and other products, with educational institutions comparable to Russia and a key supplier of arms, has attracted both Sri Lankan businessmen and students, mostly Sinhalese. The June 2010 visit of Sri Lankan President Mahinda Rajapaksa to Ukraine strengthened bilateral ties. Educational institutions in Ukraine are competing for fee paying Sri Lankan students. In Belarus, some 60 Sri Lankans were studying at the Gomel State Medical University in 2011. As costs of living in Russia are higher, these former Slavic Soviet republics provide an alternative to Sri Lankan students who have limited financial means.

In the 1990s, Tamil refugees in Eastern European countries were reported to have been engaged in drug and human-trafficking to Western Europe (United Nations Office on Drugs and Crimes, 2012: 18). At the same time, those connected with the banned terrorist organisations were also involved in the trade and supply of military equipment to the Tamil guerillas. These reports severely tarnished the image of Sri Lankan Tamils in Eastern Europe.

Consequently, countries in the region have become extremely vigilant towards Sri Lankan Tamil refugees, sometimes forcefully repatriating those who have crossed borders. In 2008, Ukraine was reprimanded by the United Nations for forcefully sending 11 Sri Lankan Tamil refugees back

to the island (*Ukraine News*, 31 March 2009). Popular opinion has continued to view these refugees negatively.

THE ATTRACTIVENESS OF EASTERN EUROPE

Nevertheless, establishment of tourist links with Sri Lanka and the rise of Eastern European tourism has given Sri Lanka a much better image as a 'tourist paradise'. All things related to Buddhism and Buddhist culture are quite warmly welcomed. There remain important factors that make Eastern Europe an attractive destination for Sri Lankan refugees and economic migrants. Cost of living is lower when compared to Western Europe. Immigration controls are less strict than in many other European countries. However, the rise of racism in these countries has raised safety concerns amongst Sri Lankans.

A number of Sri Lankans in Eastern Europe are engaged in the restaurant business although Sri Lankan cuisine is not as popular as Indian cuisine. Consequently, Sri Lankan Tamil restaurateurs have not stressed their national or ethnic identity in their business activities but have instead joined the 'Indian restaurants' segment of the ethnic cuisine market.

The small Sri Lankan communities in Eastern Europe use the development of communication technologies to sustain links with their relatives and friends in Sri Lanka. Contact is also maintained with compatriots in other parts of the world. Internet news sites keep Sri Lankans abreast of events in their motherland. Events and functions held at Sri Lankan embassies provide an important meeting place. Religious centres also act as key gathering places. For Sri Lankan Buddhists in Eastern Europe, Germany has a special importance as the location of the Berlin Vihara (Das Buddhistische Haus) and the European centre of the Ramanna sect of Buddhism. For Sri Lankan Tamils too, Germany is important because of its big Hindu temples, like the Kamadchi Temple in Hamm. To date, Eastern Europe remains nearly terra incognita for Sri Lankans, but global integration promises the emergence of 'little Sri Lankas' in Prague, Budapest and Kiev.

Igor Kotin and Nina G. Krasnodembskaia

Map 4.23

EASTERN EUROPE

AUSTRALIA

S RI LANKANS IN Australia are a diverse community—not only on the basis of their ethnicity, culture, class, identity, occupational structure, and education—but also in terms of their settlement experiences and the extent of their involvement in cultural and community practices. They do not reside in small enclaves, rather they are scattered in areas of ethnically and culturally mixed populations. Sri Lankan-Australians are well integrated in Australian work places, and educational and religious establishments. Saying that, however, many have continued to be involved in ethnic-specific religious, business, catering, cultural, media and performing organisations and events that are characterised by a degree of hybridity and multiplicity. Features of Sri Lankan-ness are evident in each of these areas, although adapted to the constraints and needs of the Australian context.

HISTORICAL ORIGINS AND THE MIGRATION PROCESS

The first immigrants from Ceylon arrived in Australia from the southern Sri Lankan town of Galle, which was an important port for the Peninsular & Oriental (P & O) Steam Company ships plying between Western European countries and the Australian colonies. From the 1870s, Sri Lankans (Ceylonese) were recruited to work in pearling centres on Thursday Island and established a Sinhalese community there. Burns Philp & Co. also recruited Sinhalese employees for various other services on Thursday Island and the Torres Strait. Others still were procured for labour on sugar and coffee plantations in Queensland.

The early Ceylonese emigrants faced numerous difficulties. When the first Ceylonese disembarked at Bundaberg on the Burnett River (Queensland) they met with violent opposition from the 'anti-Chinese Leaguers' and these Sinhalese labourers were prevented from travelling to the sugarcane estates. The terms of their indenture were arduous. They were required to work for three years before a return paid passage was provided, and were paid nominal wages of Sri Lankan Rupees 12 per month in the first year, and Rupees 15 and 20 per month in the second and third year respectively (Weerasooriya,1988).

Many of these early settlers left Australia around 1901 at the time when the Australian federation was established, and which also marked the advent of the 'White Australia' policy. Those who remained inter-married with Australian, Aboriginal and other populations and today their descendants live in cities such as Brisbane.

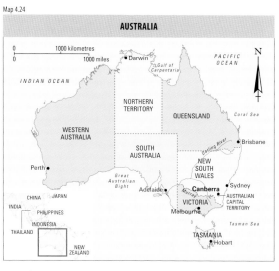

Map 4.24

AUSTRALIA

South Sea Islanders were brought to Queensland in the 1860s to work as farm labourers.

The next wave of Sri Lankan emigration began shortly after World War II. When Sri Lanka became independent in 1948, many Burghers sought to emigrate because they viewed themselves primarily as 'Europeans', but also due to concerns of their position in the newly independent state which had begun to display a majoritarian stance that emphasised the Sinhala language. Most of these Burgher emigrants moved to Australia. However, until 1964, only those who could prove that they had 'unbroken European ancestry' (with no less than 75 per cent European blood) were allowed entry because of the 'White Australia' policy. When conditions for the entry of people of non-European origin were relaxed in 1964, Burghers of mixed ancestry, and non-Burgher Sri Lankans married to Burghers were also allowed to reside in Australia.

Christie Eliezer (2001: 702) posits that in the late 1960s, the Eliezer family were the first Tamil emigrants from Sri Lanka to gain permanent residence in Australia.

In 1973, when the Labour Government of Australia put in place policies that effectively ended the 'White Australia' policy, more Sinhalese, Sri Lankan Tamils and Sri Lankan Muslims migrated. They were defined as 'distinguished and highly qualified Asians'. In the 1970s most of these comprised Sinhalese and Tamil professionals who migrated to Australia in search of better economic opportunities and because of growing political unrest in Sri Lanka.

In the 1980s migrants from Sri Lanka included large numbers of Tamil-speakers. Most came as humanitarian entrants following the 1983 ethnically motivated anti-

ORIENT LINE
MAIL STEAMERS TO
AUSTRALIA
TRAVEL ABROAD IN THE COMFORT OF A BRITISH SHIP
SPECIAL CHRISTMAS HOLIDAY TOURS TO
EGYPT and CEYLON
WINTER TIME IS SUMMER IN THE SOUTH SEAS

A 1931 advertisement for the cruise liner partly owned by the Peninsular and Oriental (P&O) Steam Navigation Company.

Bahirathy Devi Pathmanathan joined her husband in Australia soon after he arrived for his postgraduate studies at the University of New South Wales, under a Colombo Plan Award, 1962.

Members of the Ceylonese Students' Association of Melbourne, 1960.

Tamil unrest. This led to a substantial increase in the size of the Australian Tamil community, a collective that included Tamils not just from Sri Lanka but also those who arrived from India, Malaysia, Singapore, Fiji, and more distant locations such as Mauritius, South Africa and the Caribbean (Eliezer, 2001: 702). Additionally, in the 1980s and 1990s moderately educated, less affluent Sinhala, Tamil and to a lesser extent Muslim migrants from rural areas in Sri Lanka arrived in Australia. While many were middle class professionals with university degrees, a significant proportion were para-professional workers (such as mechanics), who were required to meet the changing economic, technical and professional needs of Australia. The family reunion category introduced in the 1980s also had a significant impact on the migration patterns of Sri Lankans, although because of the heavy scrutiny involved, migrants from Sri Lanka through family migration experienced more processing delays than they would have done in some other countries. Through family reunion, a number of immigrants with no recognised skills were able to gain entry into Australia.

In addition, another key emigrant stream emerged from the movement of students. Colombo Plan scholarships put in place after World War II enabled a number of outstanding Sri Lankan students to study in Australia. In the later decades of the 20th century, even more Sri Lankans arrived in Australia to pursue higher education. Over time, many of those who came as students remained and took up residency. In recent decades, the complexity of the Sri Lankan diaspora in Australia has also been added to by the advent of Sri Lankan 'twice migrants', comprising those who may have initially emigrated to England, America, New Zealand, Malaysia and Singapore, but have now relocated to Australia.

DEMOGRAPHIC CHARACTERISTICS AND SETTLEMENT PATTERNS

In 2006, Sri Lanka-born emigrants in Australia, numbering 62,256, comprised the 16th largest ethnic group in Australia, an increase of over 16 per cent from the 2001 Census. About 70 per cent of these, or just under 50,000 have acquired Australian citizenship. The census figure, however, clearly underestimates the full extent of the Sri Lankan diaspora in Australia as it excludes those born in Australia with Sri Lankan ancestry, and those who are 'twice migrants', born in Malaysia, Singapore and elsewhere, and who are descendants of earlier Sri Lankan emigrants.

Nonetheless the census is useful in identifying aspects of Sri Lankan settlement patterns in Australia, and providing an age-based profile. The 2006 distribution by state and territory revealed that Victoria had by far the largest number of Sri Lanka-born emigrants (31,482), most of whom live in and around the city of Melbourne. This was followed by New South Wales (19,086), Queensland (4,805) and Western Australia (3,285). According to the census, of those listed as Sri Lanka-born, 16.8 per cent were over 60 years of age, while 25 per cent were below 30 years. About 57.2 per cent belonged to the working-age category.

In the 2006 census, 76 per cent of Sri Lanka-born emigrants in Australia indicated Sinhalese ancestry although less than 39 per cent posited that they spoke Sinhala at home. This may imply a degree of language loss brought about by adopting English as the main language spoken at home. Indeed in that census, about 35 per

cent of Sri Lanka-born emigrants in Australia identified English as the main language spoken at home. The results for Sri Lanka-born Tamils are even more startling, only 8.8 per cent indicated Tamil ancestry whereas those who spoke Tamil at home accounted for 23.3 per cent of the total. A definitive reason for this paradox is unclear. One can conjecture that this may imply a reluctance on the part of Sri Lanka-born Tamils to acknowledge their ancestry for official purposes, at a time when the conflict in Sri Lanka has received worldwide attention.

SOCIO-ECONOMIC POSITION AND ADAPTATION

Various factors including, amongst others, socio-economic background, age, language proficiency and period of arrival, account for the differences in the socio-economic position of Sri Lankans in Australia. In general, however, when compared to most emigrant communities in Australia, Sri Lankans have fared well economically and achieved prominence in professional life. Their success can be attributed to the proficiency in English and high levels of educational achievements. While they comprise only a very small proportion of the total Australian population, they have gained distinction in medicine and in academia, sectors where the Sri Lankan representation is disproportionately high. The upward economic mobility evident in the community is to some extent also the outcome of a strong parental emphasis on children's education. Indeed, a survey by Ganewatta (2008) reveals that amongst Sri Lankan emigrants, concerns over children's education was cited as the most important factor accounting for immigration to Australia, higher than even 'seeking better employment opportunities' and 'avoiding the uncertain political situation in Sri Lanka'. The survey further revealed that the priority on children's education was especially high amongst academics and other professionals.

That is not to say that Sri Lankans have not faced serious challenges in adapting to Australia's economic environment. New immigrants have often faced serious difficulties finding employment that match their educational levels and work experience. This was especially prevalent during the economic recession of the late 1980's and early 1990's when many highly qualified Sri Lankan immigrants (including medical doctors, engineers, accountants and lawyers) had to change their career path and obtain other technical qualifications from Australian vocational education institutions (TAFE). According to Liyanaratchi (2006), one of the major reasons for the difficulty in finding suitable employment was the lack of Australian experience in the relevant occupation.

Table 4.15

SRI LANKA-BORN EMIGRANTS IN AUSTRALIA BY YEAR OF ARRIVAL 2006	
2006	2,186
2001-2005	10,954
1991-2000	18,484
Before 1991	28,508
Year of arrival not stated	2,120
Not accounted	4
Total	62,256

Source: Australian Bureau of Statistics, 2006 Census Community Profile Series.

Table 4.16

SRI LANKA-BORN EMIGRANTS IN AUSTRALIA BY STATE OF USUAL RESIDENCE 2006 (TOP 6)	
Victoria	31,282
New South Wales	19,086
Queensland	4,805
Western Australia	3,285
Australian Capital Territory	1,606
South Australia	1,486

Source: Australian Bureau of Statistics, 2006 Census Community Profile Series.

Table 4.17

SRI LANKA-BORN EMIGRANTS IN AUSTRALIA BY KEY RELIGIOUS AFFILIATIONS 2006	
Christianity	27,494
Buddhism	19,330
Hinduism	11,588
Islam	1,279
No religion	1,420

Source: Australian Bureau of Statistics, 2006 Census Community Profile Series.

SINHALA-BUDDHIST MIGRANT PROFESSIONALS IN AUSTRALIA

While the presence of Sinhala-Buddhist immigrants in sugar plantations in Queensland was recorded as early as 1870, the dominant stream of immigrant professionals arrived only after the end of the 'White Australia' policy in 1973. The increase in Sinhala-Buddhist migrant professionals from the late 1970s has resulted in the creation of a distinct ethnic, religious, cultural and political sub-group within the Sri Lankan diaspora in Australia.

The movement of these professionals from the 1970s was prompted by the difficult circumstances in Sri Lanka where unsuccessful socialist-oriented government policies had resulted in economic recession and large-scale graduate unemployment. The civil war and safety concerns due to possible suicide-bomb attacks exacerbated the push to migrate. Over time, students pursuing tertiary education in Australia—who upon graduation gained employment, obtained permanent resident status or Australian citizenship—added to the community of Sinhala-Buddhist migrant professionals.

The majority of Sinhala-Buddhists live in the suburbs of Melbourne while the second largest concentration is located in the suburbs of Sydney. While data specific to the occupational patterns of Sinhala-Buddhists in Australia is not available, according to the 2006 census 47.1 per cent of Sri Lankan-born emigrants in Australia were engaged in managerial and professional positions. These migrant professionals have sought to recreate their cultural practices and institutions, a process supported by Australia's multicultural policies in the 1980s and early 1990s. Buddhist shrines—a focal point for reconstructing Sinhala-Buddhist traditions—have increased from eight temples in the 1990s to 11 temples, four monasteries and five Dhamma (Buddhist knowledge) centres in 2010.

The migrant professionals have been actively involved in the development of Sinhala-Buddhist traditions, organising visits of Buddhist monks from Sri Lanka to Australia, establishing Dhamma and meditation centres and the publication of books in Sinhala and English.

From the early 1990s, these emigrants also began to establish 'Sinhala and Dhamma schools' for the purposes of educating young Sinhalese-Buddhists in Australia in the Sinhala language and Buddhist teachings. These schools are similar to the Sunday school held in Buddhist temples in Sri Lanka. In 2008, 12 Sinhala and Dhamma schools were active — the teachers comprising volunteers from the community, several of whom were university lecturers in Sri Lanka. In addition, annual celebrations of the Sinhala New Year, *Wesak* (celebration of the Lord Buddha's birth, enlightenment and passing), radio programmes, cultural shows, senior citizen events and alumni associations of Sri Lankan schools serve to maintain cultural cohesion within the community.

Although these migrant professionals are firmly settled in Australia they maintain close ties with Sri Lanka and have closely followed political developments in their country of origin. The reaction of these Sinhala-Buddhist emigrants to the civil war in Sri Lanka which ended in May 2009 has been varied, ranging from a hard-line Sinhala nationalist position to a moderate pro-reconciliation stance. Unlike the Tamil diaspora, the Sinhala community's engagement with the conflict has been fairly recent and only intensified towards the end of war when organisations were formed to bolster understanding between the Sinhala and Tamil communities in Australia.

In recent years, the Sinhala-Buddhist migrant professional community has participated actively in the post-war reconstruction work in Sri Lanka, for example by providing funds for the support of injured or disabled soldiers and their families. Other charitable ventures of these emigrants pre-date the post-war reconstruction efforts—including funds for the improvement of facilities in temples in rural and impoverished regions in Sri Lanka, establishing Buddhist libraries, sponsoring the education of Sri Lankan students and post-tsunami reconstruction projects. These organised forms of charity by the Sinhala-Buddhist migrant professionals serve to further unify the community in Australia even as these initiatives have aided in sustaining close ties with Sri Lanka.

Menusha de Silva

The Sinhala-Buddhist community in Australia participating in the annual Perahera festival.

A cultural concert organised by the Sinhala community in Melbourne, 2009.

Additionally, in recent years the Australian government has initiated measures to encourage employment visas for professionals willing to work in regional centres, country towns and rural areas (regional-skilled visas). Consequently, while most Sri Lankan professionals may prefer to work in big cities, the nature of the emigration regime has resulted in a number of recent emigrant professionals, particularly medical practitioners and engineers, working in regional centres and country towns like Tamworth, Armidale, Dubbo, Bundaberg, Gladstone.

COMMUNITY ORGANISATIONS

Sri Lankan community organisations form an integral part of Sri Lankan social life in Australia. The earliest of these organisations can be traced back to the 1950s. At the initial stage, the prime motivation to form a community group appeared to be the need for mutual support and assistance in the process of settlement in the new country. After the 1980s the motivation for establishing community organisations has become much broader, reflecting the needs and aspirations of the expanded community. In 2011, over 300 Sri Lankan clubs, societies and associations operated throughout Australia. These included old-school affiliations, professional associations, while other organisations are orientated towards community and welfare services, religious and cultural activities, and providing for vernacular educational needs. Some of

these organisations have also been precipitated by socio-political developments in Australia and Sri Lanka. The Sri Lankan Study Centre for the Advancement of Technology and Social Welfare (SCATS) and the Society for Peace Unity and Human Rights for Sri Lanka (SPUR) are two examples in this context.

The mainstay of Sri Lankan organisations in Australia have been forged along ethnic, religious and linguistic affiliations. The Dutch Burghers established their first community-based organisation, The Australian-Ceylon Fellowship, in 1957. As Burgher numbers increased, they formed many other associations including the Warblers Social Club, The Silver Fawn Club in Brisbane, The Bell Bird Club in Sydney, The Eighty Club and the Burgher Association (Australia) in Melbourne.

The earliest organisations formed by emigrant Tamils from Sri Lanka can be dated to the late 1970s. Since then their number has proliferated. Many of these organisations have been galvanised by the civil conflict in Sri Lanka, and have lobbied to protect the social, economic and cultural rights of Tamils living in Sri Lanka. Possibly the earliest amongst these was the Eelam Tamil Association (ETA) formed in Sydney in 1977. Similar associations were formed in other Australian states, and over time, they have connected to organisations in New Zealand that have come together to form the Australasian Federation of Tamil Associations. Most Tamil organisations have

Members of 'Sri Lanka Unites', Australia (SLUA) come together to 'Paint for Change' as part of their ongoing initiative to foster unity among Sri Lankans.

The Ceylon High Commission in Canberra celebrates Wesak, 1967.

The Sinhalese children choir in New South Wales, 1993.

Members of Australia's Tamil community hold a memorial in Sydney on 24 May 2009 to mourn the death of Tamil civilians killed in Sri Lanka's civil war.

focused mainly on the provision of Tamil language education, religious and cultural activities, and senior citizens' welfare. Kandiah (2003: 20–21) informs that some 32 Tamil language schools and study centres had been established in Australia by the early 21st century, although not all of these were run by Sri Lankan Tamil organisations. For example in New South Wales, of the nine Tamil Study Centres, five were run by the Sri Lankan Tamil community and four by the Indian Tamil Community (Kandiah, 2003: 20). There is some Australian government support for community language programs by way of funding, recognising teachers and students, and Tamil has been approved as a subject for year 12 examinations.

Sinhala organisations have tended to have a similar focus, concentrating also on Sinhala-language education, religious-cultural activities and senior citizens welfare. The emphasis on Sinhala-language education has been especially strong, given that a considerable number of Sinhala emigrants who have arrived from the late 1980s underwent Sinhalese-medium education in Sri Lanka. The Sinhala language teaching program was initiated in Melbourne in the late 1980s, and this was followed by New South Wales (NSW) where the Sinhalese Cultural forum established in 1990 began conducting language classes. Currently almost all states and territories have Sinhala language classes. In Victoria, Sinhalese has been recognised as a Higher School Certificate (HSC) community language subject.

PLACES OF WORSHIP

Sri Lankan Buddhists have established Theravada Buddhist temples across all Australian states and territories. In Melbourne alone in 2011, there were more than 10 Buddhist temples and meditation centres; with major temples located in Yuroke, Keysborough, Berwick and Dandenong. The major Theravada Buddhist temple in Sydney, Lankarama is located in the western suburb of Schofield, and in 2012 it opened a large meditation hall. Buddhist festivals like Wesak and Poson are celebrated with grandeur with the participation of thousands of devotees. Alms giving to monks on important occasions is a common practice. Sri Lankan Buddhist temples in Australia tend to perform a variety of functions. In addition to daily religious practice and the celebration of

festivals, they conduct Buddhism classes for school-aged children, and provide spiritual assistance to people when they are vulnerable in life, possibly due to the passing of parents or other relatives or stresses from modern life.

From the 1990s a number of Saivite Hindu temples structured according to Tamil traditions have been established in Australia. The mainstay of devotees at these temples comprise Sri Lankan and Indian Tamils, alongside a smaller number of Hindus who originate from other parts of India. Because of the prevalence of Murukan worship amongst Tamil Hindus from Sri Lanka (Kandiah, 2003: 50), the community has often played a key role in the establishment of temples dedicated to the deity. One example is the Murugan Temple in Sydney established in 1999 in the suburb of Mays Hill. Like Sri Lankan Theravada Buddhist shrines, these temple perform a variety of roles, including the running of Saiva religious classes, yoga practice, youth fairs, and numerous other charitable activities. Over the last two decades, with the increase in the number of Catholic and Christian Sri Lankan Tamils in Australia, a number of associations have been setup by these emigrants that enable the conduct of prayer meetings in Tamil, and as well an array of cultural activities including art, music, drama and dance (Kandiah, 2003: 48).

VERNACULAR MEDIA AND LITERATURE

A distinctive feature of the Sri Lankan diaspora in Australia has been the proliferation of ethnic-based radio-broadcasting stations. In 1979, the Australian government introduced the system of ethnic broadcasting, called the Special Broadcasting Service (SBS). From 1994, SBS radio, which had emerged as the largest community radio service in Australia, began broadcasting nationally. Immediately after the setup of SBS in 1979, Sinhalese and Tamil language programs started in Melbourne and this was followed soon after in Sydney.

With the expansion of SBS, Sinhala and Tamil ethnic radio programs mushroomed in Australian states and territories, and have emerged as by far the most popular stations for Sri Lankan listeners. Beyond entertainment, these programmes function as an avenue for announcing community events and organising discussions on issues relevant to community life (including taxation, health, and settlement issues). In Victoria there are now two Sinhala programs by Radio 3ZZZ every week, while thrice weekly Tamil radio programs are beamed through SBS, 3ZZZ and 3CR (Abeysekara, 1998). For Tamil listeners, the setup of the Australian Tamil Broadcasting

Corporation (ATBC) has been an especially significant milestone. Established with the help of volunteers, the radio station now broadcasts programs—primarily in the Tamil language—24 hours a day.

Beyond radio broadcasting, an increase in the production of Sinhalese and Tamil literature in Australia has been evident from the 1990s. Numerous magazines and newspapers in these languages have been published in Australia. Carrying articles, stories, poems and essays contributed by Sri Lankans, these publications, along with English language publications and community radio stations, provide opportunities to highlight uniquely Sinhalese and Tamil cultural expressions. In Melbourne, two Sinhala monthly magazines—*Pahans* (Light) and *Sannasa* (Message)—have been circulating since 2001. A Tamil community newspaper *Uthayan* was also regularly published till mid-2009. A number of novels, short story collections and poems depicting the lives of Sri Lankans

Outdoor broadcast of the SBS Radio Sinhalese program.

in Australia have been published from the 1990s. D. B. Kuruppu, has authored more than 50 books in Sinhala and English, while other prolific writers in these

THE BURGHERS IN AUSTRALIA

To me the 60th anniversary of Burgher settlement in Australia brings mixed feelings. I do remember the exodus of Burghers in the good old days. It was more or less a fad within the Burgher community to apply and emigrate to Australia. Those emigrating were in search of greener pastures in a land they heard of termed 'down under'... Ceylon's loss must surely be Australia's gain.
~ Neville Overlunde, Nugegoda—Sri Lanka, 11th October 2007.

Australia has been the most favoured destination for Burgher families emigrating from Ceylon after the island achieved its independence from Britain in 1948. The impetus for migration varied across families and time but the trickle of Burghers leaving the country grew to a flood after the passage of the 'Sinhala Only' Act in 1956. The minorities, Tamil, Muslim and Burgher, all felt disadvantaged by the rise of a virulent Sinhala Buddhist nationalism, and the Burghers, who were mostly Christian and English speaking, sought greener pastures for their children in the West.

The Australian connection had been developed for over a century when the ports of Galle and later Colombo became important stopping points for ships sailing to Australia. Residents of Galle became acquainted with Australians sailing to and from Australia in this way. Both Sri Lanka and Australia were former British colonies and had similar parliamentary and judicial systems, and trade between the two countries in Ceylon tea and Australian wheat was recognised as significant.

However, Sri Lankan emigration to Australia was very limited until 1948. The main reason was Australia's Immigration Restriction Act of 1901. This first act of the new Australian nation restricted immigration by race and colour, although this was always denied publicly. Thus only 'white' people were allowed into Australia until the mid-1960s when this *White Australia policy* began to be dismantled. In the 1950s and 1960s Burghers were the only Sri Lankans allowed to migrate to Australia, and then only if they had researched their genealogy and could prove their European pedigree. Up to 75 per cent European blood was required for immigration authorities to consider a potential Eurasian migrant. Further, they needed to be 'European in upbringing, outlook and

appearance' (Blunt, *http://home.alphalink. com.au/~agilbert/aijour~1.html*). Even so, stories abound of immigration staff in Fremantle turning away some Burghers who were adjudged to be '*not white enough*'.

Nevertheless, after World War II the Burgher community in Australia began to increase slowly. The Peninsular & Oriental (P & O) passenger liners such as *Arcadia*, *Oriana Himalaya* and *Canberra*, regularly sailed from the Colombo harbour carrying away the small but influential Burgher elite to new opportunities and new lives in Melbourne, Adelaide and Sydney. Even Burghers who had initially moved to Britain were sometimes attracted to Australia.

Once a few kinfolk and a few friends had moved to a new land, the connections were in place for yet more Burghers to follow them. The snowballing process of chain migration gathered momentum since the late 1950s. And it is possible for any Burgher to travel to any of the major Australian cities and find old friends and/or kinfolk in whose homes he or she would be made most welcome. These linkages have supported a fair proportion of intermarriages within the emigrant Burgher and Ceylonese 'communities' in Australia. (Roberts, 1989: 175)

In 2006, David de Kretser assumed office as the Governor of Victoria. A prominent figure in the Burgher community, he is recognised in Australia for his contributions in the field of medicine. He was the founding Director of the Monash Institute of Reproduction and Development (1991–2005) and Associate Dean for Biotechnology Development (2002–06).

Language forces 21 families to seek fresh lands abroad
By BOB PERIES
SINGAPORE, Tues. — The Burghers of Ceylon are faced with the choice of either integrating with the Sinhalese "and lose your identity, or you quit the country." "I chose to quit," said Mr. Vernon Francis Muller...

On 8 March 1960, an article in The Straits Times (Singapore) focused on the numerous Burgher families arriving in Singapore on transit to their new homes in Australia.

By 1966, the Sri Lankan community in Victoria had risen to 3,126, most of them Burghers. The preponderance of Burghers in the diaspora, and also those of the middle classes with strong English-speaking skills, is further underlined in the census statistics from 1986. They show that of the 23,800 Sri Lankans in Australia, 84 per cent used only English at home.

Many of the Burghers who migrated have since grouped together to form associations, with the accent on helping their old schools, universities and needy Burghers back home. The Burgher Association of Australia (1980) and the earlier Australian Ceylon Fellowship (1957) may have been initially set up to help new migrants assimilate into the Australian way of life but they have, paradoxically, led to a reaffirmation of their Burgher identity as proud Sri Lankan Australians.

We Burghers are ordinary people who are proud of our background and antecedents. The majority of us are also grateful to Australia and these characteristics have helped us to both preserve our identity as a cultural group and allowed us to integrate and become ONE in the true sense of Multicultural Australia.
~Doyne Caspersz, President of the Burgher Association (Australia) Inc., Dec 2011.

Larry Marshall

Sunil Govinnage's writings tend to deal with the experience of Sri Lankan immigrants in Australia.

Victor Melder holding his 'Sri Lankan Community Award' that was conferred to him in 2008 in recognition of his contribution to the Sri Lankan diaspora in Australia.

languages include Sunil Govinnage, Saman Mahanama Disanayake, Palitha Ganewatta and Jagath J. Edirisingha. In 2006, the *Sannasa* monthly published a collection of short stories written by Sri Lankan Australians, while the Sinhalese Cultural Forum of NSW published a collection of short stories and poems by Australian Sri Lankans in 2008 and 2010 respectively. Due to the contributions of these writers in vernacular languages, a rich corpus of Australian Sinhala and Tamil literature has gradually developed in Australia. Their diasporic works cover the challenges of living in an Anglo-Australian society and the dilemma of belonging to two countries and cultures with quite different characteristics.

PROMINENT PERSONALITIES HOLDING PUBLIC POSITIONS/ROLES

Numerous Sri Lankan-Australians have risen to prominence in Australian public life by holding positions in government or organisations. David Morritz de Kretser, a Sri Lankan Burgher, was the 28th Governor of Victoria. Randolph Alwis was the chairperson of the Federation of Ethnic Communities' Councils of Australia (FECCA). Fred Van Buren has contributed to Australian political life as a member of various Caucus committees of the Victorian Labour Party and a member of the Victorian parliament from 1985 to 1992. Jude Perera was elected to the Victorian parliament as an Australian Labour Party candidate for Cranbourne in November 2002, and was re-elected in November 2006.

The Sri Lankan community has made several significant contributions to the wider Australian community that have been recognised by the Australian government's Honours system. K. Kamalesevaran ('Kamahl'), Laksiri Jayasuriya, Olga Mendis, Christie Jayaratnam Eliezer, Yasmine Gooneratne, Moreley Perera, U. V. Wickrama, Karu Liyanarachchi have been honoured by Australia for their contribution to the Australian multicultural society. Victor Melder was honoured with a 'Sri Lankan Ranjana' award by the Sri Lankan government for his contribution to Sri Lanka through his efforts in the establishment of the Victor Melder Library in Melbourne. This library holds several thousand books and articles featuring Sri Lankan society, economy, politics, culture and history.

Academics

Christie Eliezer.

Almost all Australian universities and key national research centres (e.g. CSIRO) have on their staff Sri Lankan-Australians in teaching and research roles covering a range of discipline areas. The arrival of vernacular-educated Sinhalese and Tamil academics since the 1980s has buttressed the number of Sri Lankans in the ranks of the Australian academia. Some of the academics who came in the 1970s are renowned for their longstanding contributions.

Among the scholars who have made significant contributions in academic fields and the Sri Lankan diaspora in a multicultural setting are: Christie Eliezer, Laksiri Jayasuriya, S. Arasaratnam, Michael Roberts, Yasmine Gooneratne, G. Weeramanthri, Bernard Swan, Siri Gamage, S. Brathapan, Cynthia and Ian vanden Driesen. According to vanden Driesen (1998), about 150 Sri Lankans (Sinhalese, Tamil, Burgher and Muslims) held positions in Australian universities in 1998 and the number has continued to grow.

A number of these academics have displayed a distinct interest in Sri Lanka and the Sri Lankan diaspora. Specifically, Arumugam Kandiah published a book titled *Tamil Community in Australia* in 1997. Others include Olga Mendis of Melbourne who published a book titled *The Story of the Sri Lankans*, which is a useful reference of Sri Lankan history for Australians and for the second generation of Sri Lankan Australians.

Kandiah Kamalesvaran

Best known for his 1975 single 'The Elephant Song', Kandiah Kamalesvaran popularly known as 'Kamahl' is an Australian singer and recording artist. Of Sri Lankan Tamil heritage, he was born in Malaysia, and moved to Adelaide in early 1950s. He was requested by Queen Elizabeth II to give a Royal Command performance in Brisbane for the Commonwealth Games in 1982. He has been in the Australian music industry for half a century and was one of the early concert performers at the Sydney Opera House. Kamahl has released singles and albums around the world and some of his many awards include the Australian Father of the Year Award (1998), Australian Centenary Medal by Queen Elizabeth II (2004) and Australia's 'Our Entertainers of the 20th Century' (2006).

Australian-Sri Lankan singer and recording artist, Kandiah Kamalesvaran, popularly known as Kamahl.

CHALLENGES IN THE 21ST CENTURY

There are three major challenges facing the Sri Lankan diaspora in Australia, each reflecting a sense of identity loss among the older generation of immigrants. The first generation of Sri Lankan-Australian emigrants is ageing, and they require aged-care services which are provided by Australian welfare facilities. Unlike in the mother country, the dependence on children to take care of the aged is an increasingly rare phenomenon in Australia. Secondly, there are growing tensions between parents and children with regard to certain aspects of Australian culture, habits and practices that are considered normal by Australian standards but viewed by Sri Lankan parents with disdain—for example, sleepovers, regular visits to pubs and drinking alcohol. Some parents have come to accept these changes, reconciling to a degree of 'adult freedoms' for their older children. Others tend to advocate traditional Sri Lankan expectations even when their children have become adults. As a result of these tensions, a certain bicultural ethos is developing in the community that is produced from the compromises made by both parents and children.

The final challenge pertains to language loss. At the initial stage of settlement, parents, due to concerns of socio-economic mobility, tended to emphasise English learning for their children at the expense of the mother tongue. Many elders aver that that decision has haunted them later in life, as they have come to recognise how much is lost culturally. Inevitable comparisons tend to occur between those who retain a command of Sri Lankan languages and those who lose it, especially in the context of academic and employment success or failure, marriage, family formation, respect for elders and community involvement. What is perhaps hopeful is that there are now venues for English-speaking and vernacular-speaking individuals to interact and exchange 'cultural capital', and some make use of these opportunities for a meeting of minds. Through this, possibly the impact of culture and language loss can be minimised (Interview with Gamage, 2011).

Palitha Ganewatta

The author acknowledges the assistance received from Siri Gamage, University of New England, Australia, for reading and commenting on earlier drafts of this chapter.

NEW ZEALAND

HISTORICAL OVERVIEW

Sri Lankan immigration of any notable magnitude into New Zealand has been a relatively recent phenomenon. It was not until the change of the country's name to Sri Lanka in 1972 that immigrant numbers began showing an increase. Even by the mid-20th century, this number had barely crossed the 150 mark. The 1951 census figures were inclusive of the Europeans born in Ceylon. In fact, it is very likely that many of the early Ceylonese settlers were of European origin searching for fresh opportunities. The post-1950 totals included, however, a small quota of students and trainees, who mostly received postgraduate education in New Zealand, especially under the Colombo Plan for Cooperative Economic and Social Development in Asia and the Pacific.

During the 1960s the nature of immigration and the numbers involved remained static. The 1970s brought change. The new Labour Government in New Zealand decided in 1972 to pursue a more relaxed immigration policy. This resulted in a net influx of more than 100,000 immigrants during a short span of just two years between 1973 and 1975. Sri Lankans with the required skills and qualifications too could, along with other nationalities of the same calibre, avail themselves of this opportunity and easily choose to settle down in New Zealand.

SRI LANKAN MIGRATION

However, Sri Lankan migration into New Zealand did not start in earnest until the situation in Sri Lanka worsened. The major destination during this initial phase had been the UK. Even when Sri Lankans turned towards Australasia, the immediate preference had been, not New Zealand, but Australia. An underlying characteristic of this small number (less than one thousand in 1976) had been their professional qualifications mostly in the medical and engineering fields. It also meant that all Sri Lankan immigrants were legally qualified to enter New Zealand, bound by the mandatory stipulations under the 'general category'.

With the intensification of the civil war in Sri Lanka, overseas migration, hitherto considered as an alternate economic option, had suddenly transformed into a key

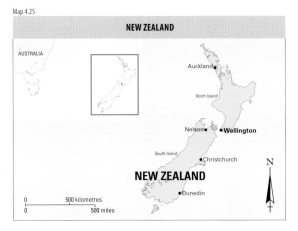

Map 4.25

means of survival providing an escape route. In the rush to flee, people were in no mood to weigh the pros and cons of migration. Their sole objective was to break away from the violence and the increased pessimism surrounding their lives in the homeland. When the choice of a country for Tamil migration became rather immaterial, they spread the net far and wide. New Zealand too came into reckoning and received more attention than earlier.

Under the 1984 economic reforms that emphasised efficiency and equity, immigration policies in New Zealand were more liberal and sought to promote the entry of skilled and business migrants. Similar to other nationalities, Sri Lankans were able to visit New Zealand upon receiving an offer from a sponsor and thereafter, apply for permanent residence or they could temporarily reside on study or work permits. The Immigration Act of 1987 encouraged more applications of this nature. This offered opportunities for a cumulative build-up of migrants. The professional category of migrants, who came to New Zealand during the earlier phase, played a comprehensive supportive role for those migrating in the post-1983 period.

The binding force in this process has been near and extended family connections, closely followed by intimate friendship links. The practice has been sustained, allowing for a perpetual rise in migrant numbers. Every set of new migrants considered helping kith and kin to get out of Sri Lanka as a prime obligation. This process of a cumulative build-up is not, however, confined to New Zealand alone. In every country, where there is a presence of Sri Lankan Tamil immigrants there exists, as Oivind Fuglerud posits, an 'international family network' within the community. While migration efforts have always been private and individual, this network provides a social façade that has helped Sri Lankan Tamils grow into a strong diasporic community.

It is estimated that at the beginning of the 21st century, over a million Sri Lankan Tamils are spread in 15 different countries. According to the 2006 Census, the share of New Zealand in this distribution was about

The Poonga Tamil Community Education organisation based in Auckland assists in integrating Sri Lankan migrants in New Zealand.

Sri Lankan refugees seeking to migrate to New Zealand, 2011.

New Zealand Thirumurugan Temple in Auckland during a festival held on 30 April 2010. Among those in attendance included former Temple President Puvanakumar Sundaramoorthy, Labour Party MPs Rajen Prasad and Phil Goff, and former Labour Party MP Carol Beaumont and Labour Party member Sunny Kaushal.

5,500—this comprised about two-thirds of the total Sri Lankan immigrants in New Zealand, which in 2006 was enumerated as 8,375.

On the other hand, Sinhalese migration to New Zealand has mainly been determined by economic factors alone. The major 'push' element has been the generally declining economic environment in Sri Lanka beginning almost from the time of its independence. Sections of the Sinhalese population, those belonging to the upper and upper middle classes in particular, were not only sceptical of state policies, but also totally abhorred the evolving violent environment. When their pessimism was translated into action, it gave rise to migratory tendencies. This explains why overseas migration of the Sinhalese had always remained strictly within the bounds of personal choice and initiative and was primarily confined to professional categories. The social facet so markedly displayed in Tamil migration is altogether absent or very negligible in the Sinhalese context. It was also devoid of the refugee element found in the Tamil migration.

The contrasting circumstances under which the two major ethnic communities of Sri Lanka engaged in migration extended to moulding the nature of the Sri Lankan diaspora wherever they settled. It could not, like many of the other diasporas, yield a singular entity with common attributes. Instead, the Sri Lankan diaspora has largely been split into two, Sinhalese and Tamil, with each conceiving its own characteristics.

OCCUPATIONAL PROFILE

A recent study on migration and career success by Nithya Tharmaseelan *et al* (2010) attempted to determine the degree to which Sri Lankan migrants were able to advance their careers after migration. In the process, it sought to find out whether pre-migration predictors in the form of human capital and motivation, or post-migration predictors like social integration and career self-management matter most. The study revealed that the career advancement of Sri Lankan migrants, despite about 66 per cent having tertiary qualifications and living in New Zealand for an average of six years,

actually declined. The education level attained in Sri Lanka is negatively related to career success after migration, leading to a good proportion of those with high-level academic and professional qualifications ending up doing manual jobs like stacking supermarket shelves, delivering junk mail, etc. The outcome suggests that New Zealand has not fully utilised the skills of Sri Lankan migrants in a way beneficial both to the migrants and the host country. The study describes this as 'a psychological form of brain waste'. With regard to the relative importance of pre-migration factors compared to those of post-migration, the study concluded that both sets were important to Sri Lankan migrants. While pre-migration knowledge, skills, and abilities complemented each other in predicting career success, post-migration acculturation and education were also equally salient. Yet, the Sri Lankans found that post-migration factors are more difficult to manage mainly because of discrimination against skilled migrants.

A large majority of Sinhalese diaspora belonged to various professions and were successful in finding lucrative positions with relatively minimum post-migration effort. When economic conditions in Sri Lanka deteriorated considerably in the 1990s, it is true that a number of Sinhalese from the lower strata of the society too ended up in New Zealand. But even this small number was largely skilled labour and mainly joined the technical, baking and hospitality industries.

The predicament of Tamil migrants was quite a contrast. Early Tamil migrants too were mostly professionals and did not encounter much hardship in their settling down process. But, with the rapidly declining political climate, the entire complexion of Tamilian migration underwent a drastic change. The need to migrate had suddenly become an urgent proposition, making migratory options very tight and restricted. Not all Tamil migrants coming into New Zealand after 1983 did so by choice. The author met a number of Tamil migrants, initially claiming refugee status, who did not even know that they were actually in New Zealand until they had reached the immigration counters at the airport. Foremost in their mind was to leave the shores of Sri Lanka, pushed by personal safety and the dire economic need to care for their families in a situation of war. Once they succeeded in entering a (developed) country, they did not hesitate to make their claim as a refugee. Between July 1997 and January 2011, 912 Sri Lankans were granted refugee status, which accounted for about 6 per cent of the total number who gained entry into New Zealand during this period under this category.

It is only after the emigration process was fulfilled that they had to weigh their options regarding settlement.

A young Sri Lankan supporter at the under-19 Cricket World Cup match between New Zealand and Sri Lanka, held in Christchurch, New Zealand, 2010.

In this compulsive course of establishment, at least initially, they could not be selective and were inclined to accept whatever employment options came their way. This was the prime reason for their choice of cities for settlement, where the job market is both big and versatile. It was possible to procure ready employment like factory or restaurant work without much difficulty. Moreover, opportunities for further study and training were better in cities. In New Zealand, most converged in Auckland, the largest city, where it is estimated that 90 per cent of the Sri Lankan migrants live. The balance have settled mainly in Wellington, the capital city, with a small proportion attracted to Christchurch on South Island. The occupational structure of the Tamil migrants in New Zealand has, unlike that of the Sinhalese, grown to be more penetrative and widespread. It is not, in other words, skewed towards the professional grades alone. To cite one example, in Auckland alone, there are about five retail grocery shops owned by Tamil migrants, whereas, there is a negligible Sinhalese presence in the sector.

Socio-Cultural Development

Early migrants from both communities were, mainly due to their exclusively professional-oriented character, prepared to downplay their ethnic distinctiveness and launch a common Sri Lankan identity. The New Zealand Sri Lanka Friendship Society, formed in 1972 was the first forum for expatriate Sri Lankans to meet socially. While the uniqueness of the Sinhalese and Tamil cultures was maintained, the Sri Lankan image was preserved through common objectives: promote close and friendly relations between New Zealand and Sri Lanka, foster in New Zealand an interest in Sri Lanka and its culture and, provide a centre for new arrivals from Sri Lanka and persons from New Zealand who propose to visit Sri Lanka. But the advent of the civil war in Sri Lanka in 1983 radically transformed the complexion of this society. The events of 1983 and its aftermath can, in this respect, be considered a watershed in Sri Lankan socio-cultural developments in New Zealand. Since then, no association of Sri Lankans has been able to bring about unity between the Sinhalese and Tamil settlers in New Zealand and promote a common Sri Lankan image. Instead, Sinhala migrants had their own gatherings with an emphasis on the Sinhala-Buddhist culture, whereas their Tamilian counterparts propagated separate forums to display their socio-cultural traits. The political underpinnings of the two groups were also markedly different, with the former supporting the ruling Sri Lankan governments while the latter vehemently opposed them.

A major qualitative change in this process of transformation has been the retention of the name 'Sri Lanka' by those associations floated by the Sinhalese with the underlining motto that the name symbolises one nation, one people. The germane slogan has been 'One Lanka' with diversity of cultures. The organisations were always careful in consciously incorporating this typical Sri Lankan image in their objectives and in all other activities. In 1983 when the rift between the Sinhalese and the Tamils widened, the latter became more open in seeking secession vis-à-vis the more aggressive discriminatory actions of the government.

At this time an organisation predominantly representing Sinhala Buddhist migrant interests was founded in New Zealand. The organisation called itself the United Sri Lanka Association (USLA) and established branches in Auckland and Wellington. Its prime objective has been to promote Sri Lanka as a single sovereign state in which all people have equal rights and can live in peace and harmony. In a similar vein, another Sinhala-dominated forum was established much later in 1998. Its newsletter still invites 'like-minded Sri Lankans to join...' and puts forward ideas to strengthen bonds between the Sri Lankan communities. Besides politics, these organisations have been active in promoting the Sri Lankan culture and heritage. Talented artists have been invited from time to time, in addition to regular craft festivals and food fairs. But, there has been modest participation of Tamils in New Zealand in these activities.

The events of 1983 had, on the other hand, instigated Tamil migrants in New Zealand to launch their own associations. The immediate concern in 1983 was for a forum to highlight their political plight and seek support from both the New Zealand government and the public. There was also an urgent need to meet the sudden influx of Tamil migrants and assist in their smooth absorption into the New Zealand community. Thus, when the New Zealand Tamil Society and the Wellington Tamil Society were established in 1983, the promotion of Tamil culture had not been foremost in the minds of

The New Zealand-Sri Lanka Friendship Society organises a cultural festival and a food fair.

A Sinhalese traditional dance alongside a bharatanatyam *performance, taken during a cultural show in 2010, depicts the ethnic diversity of the Sri Lankan community in New Zealand.*

In 2005, Sri Lankans in Auckland displayed a banner thanking those who contributed to the tsunami-relief efforts.

their architects. It had actually been overshadowed by other instant priorities. Cultural interests have, no doubt, subsequently been incorporated into the objectives of the two organisations and have constantly guided their functionary behaviour and activities. Yet, the pervading political undercurrent of an anti-Sri Lankan government stance together with support for the Tamilian struggle cannot in any way be concealed.

The organisations they formed sought, therefore, to retain a sense of their indigenous identity and keep (Tamil) nationalist hopes alive. They arranged regular Tamil language classes for children and periodically staged cultural programmes depicting Tamilian art forms. While a thematic representation of national issues was tailored to the latter, they also often served as a fund-raising device for the Tamilian struggle. A major event to mobilise the community organised annually by the Auckland and Wellington Tamil Societies has been the commemoration of Martyrs Day on 27 November in remembrance of Liberation Tigers of Tamil Eelam (LTTE) cadres who lost their lives. Even after the demise of the LTTE in May 2009, the celebrations have continued, albeit at a very low key. Nonetheless, these Societies have also come forward to conduct the elections for the newly floated 'Transnational Government of Tamil Eelam' (TGTE) in the aftermath of the downfall of the LTTE. It is an open secret that before the demise of the LTTE, two global Tamilian organisations, namely, the Tamil Coordinating Committee (TCC) and the Tamil Refugee Organisation (TRO), which were considered to be front organisations of the LTTE, lent their full-fledged backing for all politically oriented events of the Tamil societies. Both are now in a defunct state.

The involvement of the Tamil Societies in political issues and their open allegiance to the Tamil nationalist struggle has not, however, been welcomed by all members of the Tamil migrant community. There has always been a small section in the Tamil community, which is keen to keep clear of Tamilian politics, yet, interested in promoting literary and cultural activities. One such group in Auckland came forward to severe connections with the Tamil Society and floated the International Movement for Tamil Culture in December 1991. With less than 50 members on its roll this movement remains active, but fully divorced from any kind of political activism. There is

Recital by a group of Sinhala Buddhist children in Auckland, 2009.

another section of Tamil migrants, which is preoccupied with human rights issues and formed the Tamil Studies and Human Rights Trust in August 2003. Tamil migrants interested in Tamilian arts and literature, established the Arts and Literature Circle Trust in February 2004. At the other end of the spectrum, there is, yet, another group of Tamils, who shunned all other interests and confined themselves to issues dealing only with winning Tamilian rights in Sri Lanka. In their opinion, political rights of Tamils are fundamental to all others and, therefore, attention should now be concentrated on this matter. The Sri Lanka Tamil Forum initiated in 2009 functions with this objective. However, these smaller bodies cannot be compared to the Tamil Society either in size or in the array of activities performed. They could be described as adjunct to the Tamil Societies in Auckland and Wellington and to supplement their functionary role.

Sri Lankan settlers in New Zealand have, notwithstanding their ethno-political leanings, shown from the beginning an immense interest in the practice of their respective religions. This has resulted in the construction of several places of worship in the form of Buddhist shrines and Hindu temples both in Auckland and Wellington. These have, besides safeguarding respective religious rituals, also become in many ways centres propagating arts and culture belonging to the Sinhalese and Tamilian ilk. They have thus helped in preserving the respective cultural identities of the two ethnic communities.

Sinhalese migration has brought Theravada Buddhism to New Zealand, in addition to the Mahayana sect already there and practiced by the Chinese and Southeast Asian communities. But the opening of a Buddhist temple with a Sri Lankan (Sinhalese) contribution has, when compared to their socio-cultural formations, been somewhat a belated response. Sri Lankaramaya Temple (Auckland) inaugurated by the Sinhalese did not open its doors till 1999. Until then, the Sinhalese migrant community relied on Buddhist centres run by the Southeast Asian communities for religious observances. When the Lankaramaya Temple began functioning with a resident monk, a charitable trust called the New Zealand Sri Lanka Buddhist Trust was simultaneously setup to provide the necessary administrative support to the Temple. The Trust, which started with five trustees, now has 21 members working on a voluntary basis. Another formation of the Buddhist temple, Sri Mihindu Dhamma School, fulfils the need for Buddhist education for children. The Sri Lankaramaya Temple has seven committees taking care of various interests, including education and community projects.

While the Sinhalese migrants are drawn primarily from the upper hierarchy of the Sinhalese society in Sri Lanka, the Tamils hail from all sections of Tamilian society, with the bulk coming from the middle and lower strata. Again, it is normal to observe religious beliefs and practices ranking more highly among the lower ranges of a society than within the upper classes. To some extent, the religious performance of Sri Lankan immigrants in New Zealand depicts this tendency in terms of differences that can be observed along ethnic lines, with the Tamils seemingly exhibiting stronger participation in religious matters when compared to the Sinhalese.

The more robust religious conviction of Tamil migrants in New Zealand was manifested very early. Yet, conversion of their devotion in a physical form through temples of their own has been a late response. This was mainly due to the free availability of alternate facilities for worship. When a large majority of the Tamils were Hindus, it was easy for them to call upon the temples belonging to the Indian immigrant community in New Zealand. Although the rituals practiced in these temples did not always conform to the Saivite routines to which the Sri Lankan Tamils were accustomed to, they were, nevertheless, comfortable in adjusting to these minor variations. There were also several privately organised Friday (a holy day, especially for Saivite Hindus) prayer gatherings in selected centres as well as individual homes. In the meantime, the Tamil Christians, along with their few Sinhalese counterparts, were well-received and accommodated by all the churches in New Zealand.

Eventually, when the construction of Hindu temples with a Tamilian input commenced, the Wellington Tamils took the lead and started the Kurinji Kumaran Temple in 1992. From 1995 onwards, the temple gradually moved into a permanent structure located in the suburb of Newlands. The Tamil community in Auckland, moreover, lagged behind not only the Wellington Tamils but also the Sinhalese in not having a temple of their own. The New Zealand Thirumurugan Temple, its primary centre of worship, commenced functioning only in 2000 and moved into a permanent building in 2002. Until then, Auckland Tamils relied entirely on temples under Indian sponsorship. The Bharatiya Mandir in Balmoral attracted, for example, a large number of Tamil devotees. But, once the Thirumurugan Temple movement gained momentum, it quickly entrenched itself into almost the entire life pattern of the Sri Lankan Tamil migrant community in Auckland. The Temple performs all the religious functions of the Hindu calendar at its premises in the suburb of Mount Wellington. In addition to this, it has become a hive of activity in several other areas. The Temple has taken the lead role in promoting the traditional art forms of the Tamils, music and dance (*bharatanatyam*) in particular. It offers (Hindu) priest services for a variety of occasions in Tamil homes. It also organises health awareness and sports programmes. Above all, the Temple has demonstrated a keen interest in the field of education, to the extent of holding an annual Science Day with a number of competitions and other events. A major factor of encouragement has been its choice to honour Tamil students, who excel in tertiary examinations. In sum, it is not an exaggeration to say that the Thirumurugan Temple has become a way of life for a majority of Tamil immigrants in Auckland. Apart from the Thirumurugan Temple, there are two other temples: Auckland Sri Ganesh Temple in Papakura and Subramaniyam Temple in Ellerslie, primarily serving Tamil Hindus in Auckland.

Athough most Sri Lankan organisations in New Zealand function within the realms of politics, art and culture, and religion, there is however, one exception among the Tamil migrants. They have formed the New Zealand Tamil Senior Citizens' Association to look into the welfare of the senior citizens in the community. Formed in 1999 the Association is actively involved in a variety of pursuits. Their main objective is to keep the elders occupied and happy with leisure activities, in addition to providing them with useful information like funds transfer from Sri Lanka, taxes payable and tax exemptions, pension rights, superannuation, health matters, etc. Both the United Sri Lanka Association (USLA) and the New Zealand Tamil Society have also come to incorporate the welfare of the elders into their overall scheme of activity. The latter has even been successful in soliciting some funding for this purpose from the ASB Bank and has setup a section specialising in the management of issues affecting elders.

SIGNIFICANCE OF THE MEDIA

The role of community radio under the sponsorship of Planet FM is an important socio-cultural aspect of the Sri Lankan diaspora in New Zealand. In Auckland alone, there are approximately 10 weekly broadcasts with an airtime ranging from half to one hour catering mainly to listeners of Sri Lankan origin. Amongst these, only two—*Mowbima* (Mother Country) of USLA and *Shakthi FM Sri Lanka*—cater to the Sinhalese listeners. The remaining eight channels broadcast in the Tamil language is, incidentally, the highest number for any language under the ethnic radio broadcasts over the Planet FM. One of the eight is broadcast by the Tamils of South Indian origin. Yet, its programmes have a common clientele of all Tamils and is very relevant to Sri Lankan Tamil migrants too. There are three others which focus on religious aspects including one run by the Thirumurugan Temple. The remaining four are controlled by the various associations set up by Sri Lankan Tamil migrants. The content of broadcasting in all these channels is generally the same: news items of interest to Sri Lankan Tamils, community notices, films, songs, etc.

CONCLUSION

The most important feature of the Sri Lankan diapora in New Zealand is the duo nature of the community, divided into Sinhalese and Tamils. Although the ethnic division in itself is not uncommon to a migrant society, in the Sri Lankan diasporic case this has been made significant by the domestic political background from which it has emanated. An examination of the Sri Lankan community in New Zealand leads us to the conclusion that their behavioural pattern is, besides their direct material pursuits, highly conditioned by the ongoing socio-political developments on their home soil. Even individuals among the newly emerging second generation Sri Lankans are not altogether resistant to this tendency. A desirable change to this rather unfortunate climate is hard to achieve until some improvement occurs in the overall relationship between the Sinhalese and the Tamils in Sri Lanka.

Visaka Nithiyanandam

Children's performance at a Christmas party organised by the United Sri Lanka Association, 2008.

Lanka Nite Dinner and Dance is an important event in the calendar of the New Zealand Sri Lanka Foundation.

The New Zealand Sri Lanka Foundation celebrates 'Unity Cultural Day' at St Aidan's Church, Auckland, 2006.

GLOSSARY

aarathi: a Hindu ritual in which cotton wicks placed in clay lamps are lit, to worship deities or welcome an important individual.

abhidhamma: 'higher doctrine'; analysis and classification of Pali Buddhist canons.

ahimsa: 'non-violence'; a key precept in Buddhism, Hinduism and Jainism.

Aluth Avuruthu: The Sinhalese New Year festival, celebrated in April. Traditionally, the festival coincided with the end of the harvest season in Sri Lanka. Tamils celebrate their New Year (*Puthandu/Puthuvarusham*) on the same day.

Alayam: 'abode'; residence; Hindu temple.

ambul thiyal: sour fish (usually tuna) curry.

Annai Poopathy: 'Mother Poopathy'; remembrance day commemorated by supporters of the Liberation of the Tamil Tigers Eelam (LTTE) in memory of Poopathy Kanapathillai, who fasted to death in April 1988 protesting against alleged injustices committed by the Indian Peace-Keeping Force (IPKF) in Sri Lanka.

appa/appam: small wok-shaped crepe, with crispy edge and soft spongy centre, commonly referred to as 'hoppers'.

Arannavasi: Buddhist sect that emphasises living in isolation and practicing meditation.

āśram/ashram: 'abode'; Buddhist or Hindu hermitage for meditation, yoga, religious instruction and cultural activities.

Atavisi Buddha puja: the Buddhist ceremony during which offerings are made to the 28 Buddhas.

Ayurveda/Ayurvedic: the Hindu system of traditional medicine.

baila: a form of music popular among African-Sri Lankans where several notes are played simultaneously.

Bawa: 'father'; an honorific sometimes used for an elder, a teacher or a saint.

bhakti: devotion; Hindu devotional worship of a deity.

bharatanatyam: a classical dance form originating from South India.

Bhikkhu: an ordained Buddhist monk.

bibikkan: coconut cake made with jaggery.

bildungsroman: a literary genre focused on the coming of age of the main protagonist.

biryani: a rice-based dish prepared with spices and usually served with meat or vegetables.

bodhi: 'enlightenment'; the fig tree where Gautama Buddha was said to have gained enlightenment.

Bohra: a Muslim group traditionally engaged in trade, most of whom belong to the Shia branch of Islam.

brahman: member of the highest division of the Hindu caste system; the priestly caste.

Brāhmī script: ancient Indian script.

breudher: rich yeast cake of Dutch origin usually baked during Christmas by members of the Burgher community.

Buddha Jayanthi: *see Wesak*.

candala: 'untouchable' caste, traditionally associated with the disposal of corpses.

ceti: Buddhist religious edifice.

chalia: a Sri Lankan caste group traditionally engaged in cinnamon peeling and cultivation.

chambal: see sambol.

chapatti: a flatbread common in Sri Lanka and other parts of South Asia.

Chathurthi: a festival commemorating the birthday of the Hindu deity Ganesha who is also referred to as Vinayagar.

cheetu: an informal credit and saving system used in Sri Lanka.

cholai: Tamil school.

Cūlavamsa/Culavamsa: Chronicle of Sri Lankan monarchs from the 4th century C.E. to the early 19th century. *See also* Mahavamsa and Dipavamsa.

dagoba: *see stupa*.

dhal: a soup-like preparation usually made from different types of lentils.

dalit: a self-designated term used by people regarded as being of low-caste background.

dana: a charitable gift.

Dato: an honorific state title in Malaysia and Brunei, given to individuals who have made significant contributions to the country.

Deepavali: the Hindu festival of lights, which is celebrated in October or November.

dargah: a Sufi Muslim shrine usually built over the tomb of revered religious figure.

Dīpavamsa/Dipavamsa: Chronicle of Sri Lanka, compiled in the 3rd and 4th centuries C.E. *See also* Mahavamsa and Culavamsa.

durāva: a Sinhalese caste traditionally engaged primarily in agriculture.

Eelam: a term used by Tamil separatists to refer to their proposed Tamil homeland in Sri Lanka.

Eid: a short form for the Muslim festival Eid-ul-Fithr and/or Eid-ul-Alha.

Eid-ul-Fithr: 'the festival of fast breaking' celebrated by Muslims at the end of Ramadan.

Eid-ul-Alha: the 'festival of sacrifice' celebrated by Muslims in the final month of the Islamic lunar calendar.

garam masala: a blend of ground spices commonly used in South Asian cuisine.

geet: 'melody'; hymn.

godamba roti: a bread usually made from plain flour.

gopuram: gateway of Hindu temple complexes in Sri Lankan and South Indian architecture.

govigama: a dominant Sinhalese caste traditionally engaged in cultivation.

Guru: a teacher or guide; trusted counselor, adviser or mentor.

gurukkal: a Tamil honorific title for Hindu priests.

gurukulam: traditional residential school in South Asia run by a *guru*.

hoppers: *see appa/appam*.

idiyappam: a dish made of rice flour, pressed into a noodle-like cluster and steamed; commonly known as 'stringhoppers'.

jāti/jati: localised caste groups.

Jinakalamali: a Pali chronicle written in Thailand in the 16th century.

jummah: Muslim prayers held on Friday.

kafala: the sponsorship system used for migrant labourers in the Gulf States.

kangani: overseer or foreman; a labour recruitment system in the late 19th and early 20th century used primarily in Sri Lanka and Malaya.

karāva/karava: a caste group traditionally associated with fishing and seafaring.

kariyār/karaiyar: a Tamil caste traditionally engaged in seafaring.

Katina Pinkam: the Buddhist ceremony held following the monsoon season during which robes are offered to Buddhist monks.

Khoja: Muslim community originating from India, many of whom are followers of the Ismaili branch of Islam.

kiri bath: a Sri Lankan dish made with coconut milk and rice.

kithul: palm tree commonly found in Sri Lanka.

Kollywood: a popular term used for the Tamil film industry.

kookis: a traditional Sri Lankan sweetmeat made with deep-fried battered rice flour and coconut milk.

kottu roti: a popular street food in Sri Lanka, made from minced bread and/or vegetables, eggs and meat.

kovil: 'lord's home'; Hindu temple.

kshatriya: member of the second division of the Hindu caste system; the warrior caste.

kumbha abhishekam: Hindu temple consecration ceremony.

Maaveerar Naal: 'Great Heroes' Day; remembrance day held in memory of the LTTE cadres who lost their lives during the civil war in Sri Lanka.

Madrasah: a Muslim religious school.

Maha Sabha: 'Great assembly'

Mahasangh: 'Great union'

Maha Shivarathri: an annual Hindu festival during which Siva/Shiva is worshipped.

Mahāvamsa/Mahavamsa: Chronicle of Sri Lankan monarchs from the 6th century B.C.E. to the 4th century C.E. *See also* Culavamsa and Dipavamsa.

Maha Vihara: 'Great [Buddhist] monastery'

Mappila: a Muslim group predominantly based in the Indian state of Kerala, with smaller numbers in coastal regions of Sri Lanka and other parts of the Indian peninsula.

Marakkayar: a Tamil and/or Malayalam-speaking Muslim community traditionally engaged in seasfaring trade.

Masjid: mosque

Maulana: a title given to senior Muslim religious leaders.

Mahayana: 'Great vehicle'; a branch of Buddhism that is especially popular in many parts of East Asia.

Memons: a Muslim community from northwestern India, traditionally engaged in mercantile activities.

Mestiza/Mestizo: people of 'mixed' descent; mestiza refers to women, while mestizo is used for men.

Meelathun Nabi: the festival celebrating the birthday of Prophet Muhammad.

Moors: a Muslim ethnic community in Sri Lanka who trace their origins to Arab traders.

moong kavum: a sweet dish made with green gram, rice flour, treacle and deep-fried.

Mudaliyar: a title given to individuals who rose to prominence during the colonial period in Ceylon.

mukku kolai: bronze cylindrical container used to consume liquids.

Murungakkai: seed pods of the *Moringa oleifera* plant that is a popular ingredient in Sri Lankan and South Indian cuisine. *Murungakkai* is often referred to as 'drumsticks' and the leaves of the plant – *murunga* – are commonly used as a herbal spice in Sri Lankan dishes.

Murugan: a Hindu deity; the son of Siva and Parvathi.

Nāga/Naga: Snake deity.

Nagaraja: Snake King – King (*raja*) of the Snakes (*naga*) – who is worshiped as a deity.

nalavars: a caste group traditionally engaged in cultivation and toddy-tapping.

Navaratri: the nine-day festival during which Hindu Mother Goddess deities are worshipped.

Nirvana: 'to extinguish'; a Buddhist concept which refers to the liberation of the soul and an ineffable state of peace and bliss.

pachadi: a condiment commonly served in Sri Lankan and South Indian cuisine.

paitham paniyaram: a savoury snack made with green gram flour and coconut.

pallars: a Tamil caste traditionally engaged in cultivation.

pansala: Buddhist temple or monastery.

patthar: goldsmith

pittu: a steamed dish made from the granular mixture of coconut and rice flour.

Pongal: sweetened milk rice; also an abbreviation for the Tamil harvest festival, *Thai Pongal.*

poori: a fried bread popular in the Indian subcontinent.

Poson Poya: Held on a full moon day in June, the *Poson Poya* or *Poson* festival commemorates the arrival of Buddhism in Sri Lanka.

pūjā/puja : Hindu worship or ceremonial offering.

pulichatham: tamarind rice

Puthuvarusham: see Aluth Avuruthu.

Radala: high caste Kandyan aristocratic group.

Rājakāriya: a traditional labour service for the king based on caste obligations.

raasavali kelangu kanchi: yam pudding

Ramadan: the ninth month of the Islamic calendar, marked by a month of daytime fasting for muslims.

ratib: Sufi inspired music that is sung in Arabic and Urdu.

roti: bread

Sabha: assembly; organisation.

Saiva: Followers of Saivism.

Śaivism/Saivism: the Hindu sect which reveres Siva as the Supreme Being.

Saivite: *See* Saiva.

Sakyamuni: 'sage of the Sakya clan'; a term used to refer to the Buddha.

Salāgama/salagama: a caste group in Sri Lanka traditionally associated with cinnamon cultivation.

sambol: a spicy condiment served with various Sri Lankan dishes, such as stringhoppers and *idiyappam.*

sangha: 'union'; community of Buddhist monks and nuns.

sangharajas: the title given to the Buddhist monk who holds the most senior administrative position in the sangha.

Shariah: Islamic law

Sinhadipa: 'island of the Sinhala people'.

Sinhala Vamsa: Sinhalese order of monks adopted in some Southeast Asian countries from the 11th century.

Sivacaryas: Priests of the Saivite sect.

Sthapati: Temple architect.

stringhoppers: *see idiyappam.*

stupa: a domed reliquary; a large circular mound usually containing the relics of either the Buddha or Buddhist monks.

sothi: a coconut-based gravy that is usually served with *idiyappam*/stringhoppers.

sudra: the fourth division of the Hindu caste system; the castes within the division were traditionally engaged as artisans, labourers and/or other menial work.

Tabligh Jamaat: a Muslim reform movement that emerged in India in the 1920s.

Tamil Nadu: a southern state in India that lies in close proximity to Sri Lanka.

Ter: Hindu chariot procession

Thai pongal: Tamil harvest festival

Tesavalamai: the traditional Sri Lankan Tamil code of law.

Thanthai: 'father'; honorific for a senior figure.

theevans: *vellala* traders from the island off the northwest coast of the Jaffna Peninsula.

Theravāda/Theravada: the branch of Buddhism that is the predominant religion in Sri Lanka.

Theravādin/Theravadin: adherent of the Theravada branch of Buddhism.

Thevaram: Hymns sung in praise of Hindu deities.

thimilar: a Tamil caste traditionally engaged in fishing.

thosai: a crepe made with fermented black lentils and rice flour.

Umma: 'community' of Muslims

Upasampada: the rite of ordination for Sri Lankan Buddhist monastic life.

urad-dhal: a black lentil soup-like preparation.

vadai: a doughnut-shaped fried savoury.

vaisya: the third division of the Hindu caste system; the castes within the division were traditionally engaged in business or trade.

varna: the four-fold caste division of the traditional Hindu social order comprising *brahmans, kshatriyas, vaisyas* and *sudras.*

Vas Aradhana: a Buddhist ceremony held during the rainy season in which distinguished guest monks are invited to reside in a monastery, during which time they deliver sermons to lay practitioners.

vellala: a dominant Tamil caste traditionally engaged in cultivation and ownership of agricultural land.

Wesak: festival commemorating the birth, enlightenment and death of Buddha.

vihara: Buddhist monastery

vimana: temple; mythical aerial chariot.

Wahhabi: a strict, conservative branch of Sunni Islam.

watalappam: steamed pudding made with coconut and jaggery.

Yal/Yarl: a Tamil classical music instrument with strings and a circular base; also an abbreviation for Yalpanam.

Yālppāṇavaipavamālai: Book containing historical information of Jaffna written by the Tamil poet Mayilvagana Pulavar in the 18th century.

Yalpanam: the Tamil term that refers to the Jaffna peninsula in Sri Lanka.

Yoga: 'to unite': physical, mental and/or spiritual discipline.

zakath: 'to grow (in goodness)'; the contribution for social welfare that a Muslim is required to make to help the poor and the needy.

ziyaram: the tomb of a revered Muslim religious figure.

BIBLIOGRAPHY

GENERAL LIST OF REFERENCES

Agnew, Vijay, ed. *Diaspora, Memory and Identity: A Search for Home*. Toronto; Buffalo: University of Toronto Press, c2005.

Al-Ali, Nadje and Khalid Koser, eds. *New Approaches to Migration?: Transnational Communities and The Transformation of Home*. London; New York: Routledge, 2002.

Ananda, Kitana, V. V. Ganeshananthan and Ashwini Vasanthakumar. "Sri Lanka's Alternatives Abroad." *HIMAL South Asia*. December 2010.

Arambewela, R. and C. Forster, eds. *Glimpses of Sri Lankan and Australian Relations*. The Committee for Sri Lanka Inc., Melbourne, 1998.

Arasaratnam, Sinnappah. *Indians in Malaysia and Singapore*. Oxford University Press, Kuala Lumpur, Revised Edition, 1979.

Arseculeratne, S. N. *Sinhalese Immigrants in Malaysia and Singapore, 1860–1990: History Through Recollections*. K.V.G. De Silva & Sons, Colombo, 1991.

Ashcroft, Bill, Gareth Griffiths and Helen Tiffin, eds. *The Post-Colonial Studies Reader*. Abingdon, Oxford; New York: Routledge, 1995.

Athukorala, P. "International Contract Migration and the Reintegration of Return Migrants: The Experience of Sri Lanka." *International Migration Review* 24, 2 (1990): 323–46.

Basch, Linda, Nina Glick Schiller, and Cristina Szanton Blanc. *Nations Unbound: Transnational Projects, Postcolonial Predicaments, and Deterritorialized Nation-States*. Langhorn: Gordon and Breach, 1994.

Bates, Crispin, ed. *Community, Empire and Migration: South Asians in Diaspora*. New York, N.Y.: Palgrave, 2001.

Bauböck, Rainer and Thomas Faist. *Diaspora and Transnationalism: Concepts, Theories and Methods*. Amsterdam: Amsterdam University Press, 2010.

Baumann, Martin. "Sustaining 'Little Indias': The Hindu Diasporas in Europe." In *Religious Communities in the Diaspora*, edited by Gerrie ter Haar. Leuven: Uitgeverij Peeters, 1998.

_____, Brigitte Luchesi and Annette Wilke, eds. *Tempel und Tamilen in zweiter Heimat. Hindus aus Sri Lanka im deutschsprachigen und skandinavischen Raum*. Würzburg: Ergon Press, 2003.

Behera, Navnita Chadha, ed. *Gender, Conflict, and Migration*. New Delhi; Thousand Oaks: SAGE Publications, 2006.

Bertrand, Didier. "Going Back, But Where? Forced Repatriation of Tamil Asylum Seekers from Europe" *Refugee Watch*, 2000. Online at: http://www.safhr.org/medias/pdf/rw12/didier.pdf

Brah, Avtar. "Thinking Through the Concept of Diaspora." In *The Post-Colonial Studies Reader*, edited by Bill Ashcroft, Gareth Griffiths and Helen Tiffin, 443–46. Abingdon, Oxford; New York: Routledge, 2006.

Braziel, Jana Evans and Anita Mannur, eds. *Theorizing Diaspora: A Reader*. Malden, MA: Blackwell Pub, 2003.

Brettell, Caroline B. and James F. Hollifield, eds. *Migration Theory: Talking Across Disciplines*. New York: Routledge, 2008.

Brown, Judith M. and Rosemary Foot, eds. *Migration: The Asian Experience*. Palgrave Macmillan, 1994.

Brown, Judith M. *Global South Asians: Introducing the Modern Diaspora*. Cambridge: Cambridge University Press, 2006.

Brun, Catherine. "Sri Lankan Diaspora." In *Immigration and Asylum: From 1900 to the Present*, edited by Matthew J. Gibney and Randall Hansen. ABC-CLIO, Santa Barbara, California, 2005.

_____, and Nicholas Van Hear. "Between the Local and the Diasporic: The Shifting Centre of Gravity in War-Torn Sri Lanka's Transnational Politics." *Contemporary South Asia* 20, 1 (2012): 61–75.

Bütler, M. "Potentials and Limitations of the Second-Generation Tamil Diaspora to Engage in the Sri Lankan Peace Process." *Working Paper Series*, Intercultural Conflict Management, Berlin: Alice Salomon University of Applied Sciences, 2007.

Castles, Stephen and Mark J. Miller. *The Age of Migration: International Population Movements in the Modern World*. New York: Guilford Press, c2009.

Chandrahasan, Nirmala. "A Precarious Refuge: A Study of the Reception of Tamil Asylum-Seekers into Europe, North America and India." *Harvard Human Rights Yearbook* Volume 2, (1989): 55–96.

Chalk, Peter. "The Tiger's Abroad: How the LTTE Diaspora Supports the Conflict in Sri Lanka." *Georgetown Journal of International Affairs*, 2008.

Cheran, Rudhramoorthy. "Changing Formations: Nationalism and National Liberation in Sri Lanka and the Diaspora." Ph.D. diss., York University, Toronto, 2001.

_____, *The Sixth Genre: Memory, History and the Tamil Diaspora Imagination*. Marga Institute, Colombo, 2002.

_____, "Diaspora Circulation and Transnationalism as Agents for Change in the Post Conflict Zones of Sri Lanka." Berghof Foundation for Conflict Management, Berlin, Germany, 2004.

_____, ed. *Pathways of Dissent: Tamil Nationalism in Sri Lanka*. New Delhi, India; Thousand Oaks, Calif.: SAGE, 2009.

_____, and S. Guruge, eds. *Beyond Nations: Diasporas, Transnationalism and Global Engagement*. Colombo: ICES, 2010.

Choldin, H. M. "Kinship Networks in the Migration Process." *International Migration Review* 7, 2 (1973): 163–76.

Christophe, Guilmoto. "The Tamil Migration Cycle, 1830–1950." *Economic and Political Weekly* 28, 3/4, January 16-23 (1993): 111–20.

Clarke, Colin, Ceri Peach and Steven Vertovec, eds. *South Asians Overseas: Migration and Ethnicity*. New York: Cambridge University Press, 1990.

Clifford, James. "Diasporas." *Cultural Anthropology* 9, 3 (1994): 302–38.

_____, *Routes: Travel and Translation in the Late Twentieth Century*. Cambridge, Mass.: Harvard University Press, 1997.

Cochrane, Feargal, Bahar Baser and Ashok Swain. "Home Thoughts from Abroad: Diasporas and Peace-Building in Northern Ireland and Sri Lanka." *Studies in Conflict and Terrorism* 32, 8 (2009): 681–704.

Cohen, Robin, ed. *The Cambridge Survey of World Migration*. Cambridge; New York: Cambridge University Press, 1995.

_____, *The Sociology of Migration*. Cheltenham, UK; Brookfield, Vt., US: E. Elgar, c1996.

_____, *Global Diasporas: An Introduction*. London: UCL Press, 1997.

Cuny, F. and C. Cuny. "The Return of Tamil Refugees to Sri Lanka 1983–1989." In *Repatriation During Conflict in Africa and South Asia*, edited by F. C. Cuny, B. N. Stein and P. Reed. Dallas, The Centre for the Study of Societies in Conflict.

Daniel, E. Valentine and Y. Thangaraj. "Forms, Formations and Transformations of the Tamil Refugee." In *Mistrusting Refugees*, edited by E. Valentine Daniel and J. C. Knudsen, 225–56. Berkeley, CA: University of California, 1995.

Dissanayke, Manjula. "Beyond Remittances: A Case of Diaspora Addressing Global Issues in Sri Lanka." *Huffington Post*. April 5, 2013.

Eelens, F., T. Schampers and J. D. Speckmann, eds. *Labour Migration to the Middle East: From Sri Lanka to the Gulf.* K. Paul International, 1992.

Ember, Melvin, Carol R. Ember and Ian A. Skoggard, eds. *Encyclopedia of Diasporas: Immigrant and Refugee Cultures Around the World.* Springer, New York, 2005.

Fair, C. Christine. "Diaspora Involvement in Insurgencies: Insights from the Khalistan and Tamil Eelam Movements." *Nationalism and Ethnic Politics* 11, 1 (2005): 125–56.

_____, "The Sri Lankan Tamil Diaspora: Sustaining Conflict and Pushing for Peace." In *Diasporas in Conflict: Peace-Makers or Peace Wreckers?*, edited by Hazel Smith and Paul Stares, 172–95. Tokyo, New York, Paris: United Nation University Press, 2007.

Fontgalland, S. Guy de. *Sri Lankans in Exile: Tamils Displaced.* Madras, Cerro Publications, 1986.

"Formation of a Provisional Transnational Government of Tamil Eelam Report." TGTE Advisory Committee, 14 January 2010.

Fuglerud, Øivind. *Life on the Outside: The Tamil Diaspora and Long-Distance Nationalism.* London: Pluto Press, 1999.

Gamburd, Michele. *The Kitchen Spoon's Handle: Transnationalism and Sri Lanka's Migrant Housemaids.* Cornell University Press, Ithaca, 2000.

Gerharz, Eva. "Opening to the World: Translocal Post War Reconstruction in Northern Sri Lanka." In *The Making of World Society: Perspectives from Transnational Research*, edited by Remus Gabriel Anghel, et al., 173–94. Bielefeld: Transcript, 2008.

_____, "Reconstructing Jaffna: Transnational Tamil Activism at Local Interfaces." In *Ethnic Activism and Civil Society in South Asia*, edited by David N. Gellner, 83–114. Thousand Oaks, CA: SAGE Publications, c2009.

_____, "When Migrants Travel Back Home: Changing Identities in Northern Sri Lanka after the Ceasefire of 2002." *Mobilities* 5, 1 (2010): 147–65.

Gilroy, Paul. "Diaspora." *Paragraph* 17, 1 (1994): 207–12.

_____, "Diasporas." In *Migration, Diasporas, and Transnationalism*, edited by Steven Vertovec and Robin Cohen, 293–98. Northampton, Mass: Edward Elgar, 1999.

Glick Schiller, Nina, Linda Basch and Cristina Blanc-Szanton. "Transnationalism: A New Analytic Framework for Understanding Migration." In *Migration, Diasporas, and Transnationalism*, edited by Steven Vertovec and Robin Cohen, 26–49. Northampton, Mass: Edward Elgar, 1999.

Gunatilleke, Godfrey, ed. *Migration of Asian Workers to the Arab World.* Tokyo, Japan: United Nations University, c1986.

Gunewardena, Nandini. "Disrupting Subordination and Negotiating Belonging: Women Workers in the Transnational Production Sites of Sri Lanka." In *The Gender of Globalization: Women Navigating Cultural and Economic Marginalities*, edited by Nandini Gunewardena and Ann Kingsolver, 35–60. Santa Fe, N.M.: School for Advanced Research Press, 2007.

Hall, Stuart. "Cultural Identity and Diaspora." In *The Post-Colonial Studies Reader*, edited by Bill Ashcroft, Gareth Griffiths and Helen Tiffin, 428–34. Abingdon, Oxford; New York: Routledge, 2006.

Henayaka, Ranjith and Miriam Lambusta. "The Sri Lankan Diaspora in Italy." Berghof Research Center for Conflict Management, Berlin, 2004.

Hoole, Rajan. "Tamil Refugees in Sri Lanka and the West – Parts 1 and 2." *Tamil Studies* 12, 7–8, July and August, 1993.

Human Rights Watch. *Funding the "Final War": LTTE Intimidation and Extortion in the Tamil Diaspora.* New York: Human Rights Watch (HRW), 2006.

Iswaran, Indra Rani Lavan. *Celebrating 100 Years: The Singapore Ceylon Tamils' Association, Founded 1910.* Singapore Ceylon Tamils' Association, 2010.

Jacobsen, Knut A. and Kumar P. Pratap, eds. *South Asians in the Diaspora: Histories and Religious Traditions.* Leiden; Boston: Brill, c2004.

Jacobsen, Knut A. and Selva J. Raj, eds. *South Asian Christian Diaspora: Invisible Diaspora in Europe and North America.* Surrey, England; Burlington, USA: Ashgate Publishing Ltd, 2008.

Jeyaraj, D.B.S. "Diaspora LTTE Activists Posing as Human Rights Champions." March 8, 2013. Online at: http://dbsjeyaraj.com/dbsj/archives/17912

Jones, A. *Time for Decision: Sri Lankan Tamils in the West.* Washington DC: United States Committee for Refugees, 1985.

Jupp, James, ed. *The Australian People - An Encyclopedia of the Nation, its People and their Origins.* Cambridge University Press, 2001.

Kandiah, A. *Tamil Community in Australia: An Updated Survey Based on 2001 Census.* Natanalaya Publication, 2003.

Kiruppalini, Hema. "Of Diasporas and Displacements: What does it mean to be Sri Lankan?" *ISAS Insight No. 148.* Instutite of South Asian Studies (ISAS), Singapore, 14 December 2009.

Kottegoda, Sepali. "Bringing Home the Money: Migration and Poverty in Gender Politics in Sri Lanka." In *Poverty, Gender and Migration*, edited by Sadhna Arya and Anupama Roy. New Delhi; Thousand Oaks, Calif.: SAGE Publications, 2006.

Kumar, Pratap P., ed. *Religious Pluralism in the Diaspora.* Leiden; Boston: Brill, 2006.

Lal, Brij V., Peter Reeves and Rajesh Rai, eds. *The Encyclopedia of the Indian Diaspora.* Singapore: Editions Didier Millet, 2006.

Leonard, Karen Isaksen. *The South Asian Americans.* Westport, Conn.: Greenwood Press, 1997.

Lyons, Terrence and Peter Mandaville, eds. *Politics from Afar: Transnational Diasporas and Networks.* London: Hurst & Co., c2012.

Manoharan, K. *Tamil Refugees from Sri Lanka.* Oslo: PRIO, 1985.

McDowell, Christopher. *A Tamil Asylum Diaspora: Sri Lankan Migration, Settlement and Politics in Switzerland.* Berghahn, Oxford, 1996.

Migration, Urbanization, and Development in Sri Lanka. Economic and Social Commission for Asia and the Pacific New York : United Nations, 1980.

Muni, S. D. "Globalization and South Asian Insurgencies: With Special Reference to the Tamil Tigers and the Nepal Maoists." *ISAS Working Paper No. 64.* Institute of South Asian Studies (ISAS), Singapore, 10 June 2009.

Oakley, R. and V. I. S. Jayapalan. "Beast of Burden (Chekku Madu): The Power of the Wandering Poet Among the Sri Lankan Tamil Diaspora." *Journal of Poetry Therapy* 18, 1 (2005): 265–81.

Oberoi, Pia. *Exile and Belonging: Refugees and State Policy in South Asia.* New Delhi: Oxford University Press, 2006.

Orjuela, Camilla. "War, Peace and the Sri Lankan Diaspora: Complications and Implications for Policy." In *Diasporas, Armed Conflicts and Peacebuilding in Their Homelands*, edited by A. Swain. Uppsala: Department of Peace and Conflict Research, Uppsala University, 2007.

_____, "The Sri Lankan Tamil Diaspora: Warmongers or Peacebuilders?" In *Transnational South Asians: The Making of a Neo-Diaspora*, edited by S. Koshy and R. Radhakrishnan, 325–94. Oxford: Oxford University Press, 2008a.

_____, "Distant Warriors, Distant Peace Workers? Multiple Diaspora Roles in Sri Lanka's Violent Conflict." *Global Networks: A Journal of Transnational Affairs* 8, 4 (2008b): 436–52.

_____, "Tamil Nationalist Media (Sri Lanka/Transnational)" In *Encyclopedia of Social Movement Media*, edited by John D. H. Downing, 519–22. Thousand Oaks, Calif.: SAGE Publications, Inc., c2011.

_____, "Diaspora Identities and Homeland Politics: Lessons from the Sri Lanka/Tamil Eelam Case." In *Politics from Afar: Transnational Diasporas and Networks*, edited by Terrence Lyons and Peter Mandaville, 91–116. London: Hurst & Co., c2012.

_____, and Dhananjayan Srikandarajah. "The Sri Lankan Tamil Diaspora." In *Transnational South Asians: The Making of a Neo-Diaspora*, edited by Susan Koshy and R. Radhakrishnan. Delhi; New York: Oxford University Press, 2008.

R. Hinnells, John. *Religious Reconstruction in the South Asian Diasporas: From One Generation to Another.* Hampshire; New York: Palgrave Macmillan, c2007.

Rai, Rajesh and Peter Reeves, eds. *The South Asian Diaspora: Transnational Networks and Changing Identities.* London; New York, NY: Routledge, 2009.

Rajasingam, Nirmala. "The Stimulated Politics of Diaspora." *HIMAL South Asia.* January 2011.

Rajasingham Senanayake, Darini. "Diaspora and Citizenship: Forgotten Routes of Identity in Lanka." In *Culture and Economy in the Indian Diaspora*, edited by Bhikhu Parekh, Gurharpal Singh and Steven Vertovec, 81–101. London; New York: Routledge, c2003.

Ramasamy, Rajakrishnan. *Sojourners to Citizens: Sri Lankan Tamils in Malaysia, 1885–1965*. Kuala Lumpur, 1988.

_____, "Social Change and Group Identity Among the Sri Lankan Tamils." In *Indian Communities in Southeast Asia*, edited by Kernial Singh Sandhu and A. Mani, 541–57. Institute of Southeast Asian Studies, Singapore, 1993.

Rambukwella, Harshana. "In Search of the Nation: When Memory Dies and The [Im]possibility of a National Imaginary in Postcolonial Sri Lanka." *The Sri Lanka Journal of the Humanities* 33, 1–2 (2007): 57–70.

Ranganathan, Maya. "Nurturing a Nation on the Net: The Case of Tamil Eelam." *Nationalism and Ethnic Politics* 8, 2 (2002): 51–66.

_____, "Understanding Eelam Through the Diaspora's Online Engagement." *Continuum Journal of Media and Cultural Studies* 23, 5 (2009): 709–21.

Rex, John. "Ethnic Mobilization in a Multicultural Society." In *The Sociology of Race and Ethnicity*, edited by Malcom Cross, 593–602. Edward Elgar Publishing, 2000.

_____, "The Second Project of Ethnicity: Transnational Migrant Communities and Ethnic Minorities in Modern Multicultural Societies." In *The Sociology of Race and Ethnicity*, edited by Malcom Cross, 602–13. Edward Elgar Publishing, 2000.

Robinson, Francis, ed. *The Cambridge Encyclopedia of India, Pakistan, Bangladesh, Sri Lanka, Nepal, Bhutan, and the Maldives.* Cambridge University Press, 1989.

Rodgers, M. "Refugees and International Aid. Sri Lanka: A Case Study." Report Written for joint ILO-UNHCR Meeting on International Aid as a Means to Reduce the Need for Emigration, Geneva UNHCR, 1992.

Safran, William. "Diasporas in Modern Societies: Myths of Homeland and Return." *Diaspora* 1, 1 (1991): 83–99.

Sathiaseelan, S. *Malayan Migration and Jaffna Society.* United Kingdom: UK-Ceylon Malaysian Forum, 2007.

Schalk, Peter. "Beyond Hindu Festivals: The Celebration of Great Hopes' Day by the Liberation of Tigers of Tamil Eelam (LTTE) in Europe." In *Tempel and Tamilen in zweiter Heimat:hindus aus Sri Lanka im deutschprachigen und skandinavischen Raum*, edited by Martin Baumann, Brigitte Luchesi and Annette Wilke, 391–420. Wurzburg: Ergon Verlag, 2003.

Schneider, Alexandra. 2005. "'Jackie Chan is Nobody, and So am I': Juvenile Fan Culture and The Construction of Transnational Male Identity in the Tamil Diaspora." In *Youthscapes: The Popular, The National, The Global*, edited by Sunaina Maria and Elisabeth Soep. Philadelphia: University of Pennsylvania Press.

Searching for a Future: Tamil Refugees from Sri Lanka. Analysis and Propositions. Tamil Project Group. Caritas Switzerland, 1984.

Selvaratnam, Thillaiampalam and Sinnappo Apputhurai. *Legacy of the Pioneers: 125 Years of Jaffna Tamils in Malaysia*. Kuala Lumpur: Thillaiampalam Selvaratnam and Sinnapoo Apputhurai, 2006.

Sheffer, Gabriel. *Diaspora Politics: At Home Abroad.* Cambridge: Cambridge University Press, 2003.

Shukla, Sandhya. "Locations for South Asian Diasporas." *Annual Review of Anthropology* 30 (2001): 551-72.

Singam, S. Durai Raja. *A Hundred Years of Ceylonese in Malaya and Singapore, 1867–1967.* Kuala Lumpur, 1968.

Smith, Smith and Paul Stares, eds. *Diasporas in Conflict: Peace-Makers or Peace-Wreckers?*. Tokyo; New York : United Nations University Press, c2007.

Sri Lanka & Diasporas: Observatoire Pluridisciplinaire. Online at: http://slkdiaspo.hypotheses.org

Sriskandarajah, Dhananjayan. "The Migration-Development Nexus: Sri Lanka Case Study." *International Migration* 40, 5 (2002): 283–307.

_____, "Tamil Diaspora Politics." In *The Encyclopedia of Diasporas: Immigrant and Refugee Cultures Around the World,* edited by Melvin Ember, Carol R. Ember, and Ian Skoggard, 492–500. New Haven: Yale/Kluwer, 2004.

Steen, Ann Belinda. "Variations in Refugee Experience: Studying Sri Lankan Tamils in Denmark and England." Ph.D. diss., Institute of Anthropology and Ethnology, Copenhagen, 1992.

Suryanarayan, V. and V. Sudarsen. *Between Fear and Hope: Sri Lankan Refugees in Tamil Nadu.* T. R. Publications, Chennai, 2000.

Tambiah, Stanley J. "Transnational Movements, Diaspora and Multiple Modernities." *Daedalus* 129, 1 (2000): 163–94.

The Committee for the Formation of a Provisional Transnational Government of Tamil Eelam, "A Booklet on the Transnational Government of Tamil Eelam."15 September 2009.

Tekwani, Shyam. "The Tamil Diaspora, Tamil Militancy, and the Internet." In *Asia.com: Asia Encounters the Internet*, edited by K. C. Ho, Randolph Kluver and Kenneth C. C. Yang, 175–192. London; NewYork: Routledge Curzon, 2003.

"The Sri Lankan Tamil Diaspora after the LTTE." *International Crisis Group*, Asia Report Nº186, February 23, 2010.

Tölölyan, K. "Rethinking Diaspora(s): Stateless Power in the Transnational Moment." *Diaspora* 1, 1 (1996): 3–36.

Vaitheespara, Ravi. "Beyond 'Benign' and 'Fascist' Nationalisms: Interrogating the Historiography of Sri Lankan Tamil Nationalism." *South Asia: Journal of South Asian Studies* 29, 3 (2006): 435–58.

vanden Driesen, Cynthia and I. H. vanden Driesen, eds. *Celebrations: Fifty Years of Sri Lanka-Australia Interactions.* Government Press, Sri Lanka, 1998.

van der Veer, Peter, ed. *Nation and Migration: The Politics of Space in the South Asian Diaspora.* Philadelphia: University of Philadelphia Press, 1995.

van Hear, Nicholas. *New Diasporas: The Mass Exodus, Dispersal and Regrouping of Migrant Communities.* London: University College London Press, and Seattle: University of Washington Press, 1998.

_____, "Sustaining Societies under Strain: Remittances as a Form of Transnational Exchange in Sri Lanka and Ghana." In *New Approaches to Migration: Transnational Communities and the Transformation of Home*, edited by K. Koser and N. Al-Ali, 202–23. London and New York: Routledge, 2002.

_____, "Refugee Diasporas or Refugees in Diaspora." In *Encyclopedia of Diasporas: Immigrant and Refugee Cultures Around the World*, Vol. I: Overviews and Topics, edited by Melvin Ember, Carol R. Ember and Ian Skoggard, 580–89. New York: Kluwer Academic/Plenum Publishers, 2004.

_____, "The Rise of Refugee Diasporas." *Current History*, 108, 717, 2009.

_____, "Diaspora and Migration." In *Diasporas: Concepts, Intersections, Identities*, edited by Kim Knott and Seán McLoughlin. Zed Books, 2010.

_____, and Darini Rajasingham-Senanayake. "From Complex Displacement to Fragile Peace in Sri Lanka." In *Catching Fire: Containing Forced Migration in a Volatile World*, edited by Nicholas Van Hear and Christopher McDowell, 44–71. Lanham MA: Lexington/Rowman and Littlefield, 2006.

Varadarajan, Latha. *The Domestic Abroad: Diasporas in International Relations.* New York: Oxford University Press, 2010.

Velamati, Manohari. "Sri Lankan Diaspora Itching for a Greater Tamil Eelam?: Views from the UK and India." *Journal of Peace Studies* 15, 3–4 (July–December 2008).

_____, "Tamil Migration and Settlement: Time for Reconsideration." *India Quarterly: A Journal of International Affairs* 65, 3 (2009): 271–94.

Vertovec, Steven, ed. *Aspects of South Asian Diaspora*. Papers on India, Volume 2, Part 2, Delhi: Oxford University Press, 1991.

Vidanage, Harinda. "Cyber Cafes in Sri Lanka: Tamil Virtual Communities." *Economic and Political Weekly Commentary* 39, 36 (September 2004): 3988–91.

Vimalarajah, Luxshi and Rudhramoorthy Cheran. "Empowering Diasporas: The Dynamics of Post-war Transnational Tamil Diaspora." Berghof Occasional Paper No 31, Berghof Conflict Research, Berlin, 2010.

Wayland, Sarah. "Immigrants into Citizens: Political Mobilization in France and Canada." Ph.D. diss., University of Maryland, 1995.

_____, "Ethnonationalist Networks and Transnational Opportunities: The Sri Lankan Tamil Diaspora." *Review of International Studies* 30 (2004): 405–26.

Whitaker, Mark P. "Tamilnet.com: Some Reflections on Popular Anthropology, Nationalism, and the Internet." *Anthropological Quarterly* 77, 3 (2004): 469–98.

Wiemann, Dirk. "South Asian Christian Diaspora: Invisible Diaspora in Europe and North America." *South Asian Diaspora* 1, 2 (2009): 197–99.

Wijesinha, Ranjith. "Reconciliation between the Sinhala and Tamil Diasporas: A Possibility?" *Shanthi-An Online Journal Promoting Peace in Sri Lanka*. Online at: http://members.fortunecity.com/shanti/reconciliation_between_the_sinha.htm.

Yasuro, Hase, Miyake Hiroyuki and Oshikawa Fumiko, eds. *South Asian Migration in Comparative Perspective: Movement, Settlement and Diaspora*. The Japan Center for Area Studies, National Museum of Ethnology, 2002.

Zunzer, Wolfram. "Diaspora Communities and Civil Conflict Transformation." Berghof Occasional Paper No. 26, Berghof Research Center for Constructive Conflict Management, Berlin, 2004.

Part 1: The Sri Lankan Context

Alagappa, Muthiah, ed. *Civil Society and Political Change in Asia: Expanding and Contracting Democratic Space*. Stanford, Calif.: Stanford University Press, 2004.

Ali, Ameer. "The Muslims of Sri Lanka: An Ethnic Minority Trapped in a Political Quagmire." *Inter-Asia Cultural Studies* 5, 3 (2004): 372–83.

Allen, Douglas. "Religious-Political Conflict in Sri Lanka: Philosophical Considerations." In *Religion and Political Conflict in South Asia: India, Pakistan, and Sri Lanka*, edited by Douglas Allen, 181–204. Westport, Conn.: Greenwood Press, 1992.

Arasaratnam, Sinnappah. "Sri Lanka's Tamils: Under Colonial Rule." In *The Sri Lankan Tamils: Ethnicity and Identity*, edited by Chelvadurai Manogaran and Bryan Pfaffenberger, 28–53. Boulder: Westview Press, 1994.

Ariyapala, M. B. *Society in Mediaeval Ceylon*. Department of Cultural Affairs, Colombo, 1956.

Asad, Kamil. "The Communal Violence between Sinhalese and Muslims in Sri Lanka (The Puttalam Riots 1976: A Case Study)." *Journal of the Pakistan Historical Society* (Karachi) 47, 1 (1999): 55–56.

Bandarage, Asoka. *The Separatist Conflict in Sri Lanka: Terrorism, Ethnicity, Political Economy*. iUniverse, Inc: New York, Bloomington, 2009.

Bandaranayake, Senake. "The Peopling of Sri Lanka: The National Question and Some Problems of History and Ethnicity." In *Ethnicity and Social Change in Sri Lanka*, edited by the Social Scientists Association, ai–aixx. Colombo: The Social Scientists Association, 1984.

_____, and Gamini Jayasinghe. *The Rock and Wall Paintings of Sri Lanka*. Lake House, Colombo, 1986.

Bansal, Alok, M. Mayilvaganan and Sukanya Podder, eds. *Sri Lanka: Search for Peace*. New Delhi: Institute for Defence Studies and Analyses: Manas Publications, 2007.

Blackburn, Anne and Jeffrey Samuels, eds. *Approaching the Dhamma: Buddhist Texts and Practices in South and Southeast Asia*. Washington: Pariyatti Publications, 2003.

Blackburn, Anne. *Locations of Buddhism: Colonialism and Modernity in Sri Lanka*. The University of Chicago Press, 2010.

Bose, Sumantra. *States, Nations, Sovereignty: Sri Lanka, India and the Tamil Eelam Movement*. Sage Publications, New Delhi, 1994.

_____, "Sri Lanka." In *Contested Lands: Israel-Palestine, Kashmir, Bosnia, Cyprus, and Sri Lanka*, edited by Sumantra Bose, 6–54. Cambridge, Mass.: Harvard University Press, 2007.

Brohier, Deloraine. "Flashback to the Dutch Burghers of Ceylon in the Mid-Fifties." *Journal of the Royal Asiatic Society of Sri Lanka* 43 (1998): 33–38.

Brun, Cathrine. "Women in the Local/Global Fields of War and Displacement in Sri Lanka." *Gender, Technology and Development* 9, 1 (2005): 57–80.

_____, "Birds of Freedom: Young People, the LTTE, and Representations of Gender, Nationalism, and Governance in Northern Sri Lanka." *Critical Asian Studies* 40, 3 (2008): 399–422.

_____, and Tariq Jazeel, eds. *Spatialising Politics: Culture and Geography in Postcolonial Sri Lanka*. Sage, New Delhi, 2009.

Candappa, Reggie, ed. *History of the Colombo Chetties: As Featured in Two Exhibitions held to Celebrate the 75th and 80th Anniversaries of the Colombo Chetty Association of Sri Lanka*. Foremost Prooductions, 2000.

Codrington, Humphrey William. *A Short History of Ceylon*. London: Macmillan, 1947.

Coningham, R. A. E. "Monks, Caves and Kings: A Reassessment of the Nature of Early Buddhism in Sri Lanka." *World Archaeology* 27, 2 (1995): 222–42.

_____, and N. Lewer. "The Vijayan Colonization and the Archaeology of Identity in Sri Lanka." *Antiquity* 74 (2000): 707–12.

Coomaraswamy, Radhika. "Nationalism: Sinhala and Tamil Myths." *South Asia Bulletin* 6, 1986.

_____, "Myths Without Conscience: Tamil and Sinhalese Nationalist Writings in the 1980s." In *Facets of Ethnicity in Sri Lanka*, edited by Charles Abeysekera and Newton Gunasinghe. Colombo: Social Scientists Association, 1987.

_____, *Ideology and the Constitution: Essays on Constitutional Jurisprudence*. International Centre for Ethnic Studies, Colombo, 1996.

Da Silva, O M. *Fidalgos in the Kingdom of Kōtte*. Colombo: Harwoods Publishers, 1990.

Daniel, E. Valentine. *Fluid Signs: Being a Person the Tamil Way*. Berkeley: University of California Press, 1984.

Deegalle, Mahinda. *Buddhism, Conflict, and Violence in Modern Sri Lanka*. New York; Abingdon, Oxon: Routledge, 2006.

De Mel, Neloufer. *Militarizing Sri Lanka: Popular Culture, Memory and Narrative in the Armed Conflict*. Sage Publications, New Delhi, 2007.

Deraniyagala, S. U. "A Theoretical Framework for the Study of Sri Lanka's Prehistory." *Ancient Ceylon* 5 (1984): 81–104.

_____, and Sirima Kiribamune, eds. *Asian Panorama: Essays in Asian History, Past and Present: A Selection of Papers Presented at the 11th Conference of the International Association of Historians of Asia*. Vikas Pub. House, New Delhi, 1990.

de silva, Chandra Richard. "Sri Lanka in the Early Sixteenth Century: Political Conditions." In *University of Peradeniya, History of Sri Lanka*, edited by K. M. de Silva, 11–36. University of Peradeniya, Peradeniya, Vol. II, 1995.

_____, "Sri Lanka in the Early Sixteenth Century: Social Conditions." In *University of Peradeniya, History of Sri Lanka*, edited by K. M. de Silva. University of Peradeniya, Peradeniya, Vol. II, 1995.

_____, "The Rise and Fall of Sitawaka." In *University of Peradeniya, History of Sri Lanka*, edited by K. M. de Silva, 61–104. University of Peradeniya, Peradeniya, Vol. II, 1995.

_____, "Expulsion of the Portuguese from Sri Lanka." In *University of Peradeniya, History of Sri Lanka*, edited by K. M. de Silva, 163–81. University of Peradeniya, Peradeniya, Vol. II, 1995.

_____, "State Support for Religion in Contemporary Sri Lanka: Some Ideological and Policy Issues." In *The Post-Colonial States of South Asia: Democracy, Identity, Development and Security*, edited by Amita Shastri and A. Jeyaratnam Wilson, 183–95. Richmond: Curzon, c2001.

_____, and S. Pathmanathan. "The Kingdom of Jaffna up to 1620." In *University of Peradeniya, History of Sri Lanka*, edited by K. M. de Silva, 105–21. University of Peradeniya, Peradeniya, Vol. II, 1995.

de Silva, K. M. "The Burghers in Sri Lanka History: A Review Article." *Ethnic Studies Report* (Kandy, Sri Lanka) 8, 2 (1990): 44–47.

_____, ed. *Sri Lanka: Problems of Governance*. Konark Publishers, New Delhi, 1993.

_____, "Sri Lanka: Background to Ethnic Conflict in a Functioning Democracy." In *Democracy in Asia*, edited by Michèle Schmiegelow, 399–426. New York: St. Martin's Press, 1997.

_____, *A History of Sri Lanka*. Oxford University Press, New Delhi, 1999.

_____, *Sri Lanka and the Defeat of the LTTE*. Colombo, Sri Lanka: Vijitha Yapa, 2012.

_____, and G.H. Peiris, eds. *Pursuit of Peace in Sri Lanka: Past Failures and Future Prospects*, edited by K. M. de Silva and G. H. Peiris. Kandy: International Centre for Ethnic Studies, 2000.

de silva, Manik. "Sri Lanka's Civil War." In *South Asia*, edited by Sumit Ganguly, 68–76. New York : New York University Press, c2006.

DeVotta, Neil. *Blowback: Linguistic Nationalism, Institutional Decay, and Ethnic Conflict in Sri Lanka*. Standford University Press, California, 2004.

_____, "Sinhalese Buddhist Nationalist Ideology: Implications for Politics and Conflict Resolution in Sri Lanka." *Policy Studies* 40. Washington D. C.: East-West Center, 2007.

_____, "Liberation Tigers of Tamil Eelam and the Lost Quest for Separatism in Sri Lanka." *Asian Survey* 49, 6 (November/December 2009): 1021–51.

Eller, Jack David. *From Culture to Ethnicity to Conflict: An Anthropological Perspective on International Ethnic Conflict*. Ann Arbor: University of Michigan Press, c1998.

Fox, W. B. *A Dictionary of the Ceylon-Portuguese, Singalese and English Languages*. Colombo: Wesleyan Mission Press, 1819.

Fujinuma, Mizue. "Meanings of Ethnicity and Gender in the Making: A Case Study of Ethnic Change among Middle-Class Dutch Burghers in Post-Colonial Sri Lanka." Ph.D. diss., University of Washington, 1997.

Gamage, Siri and I. B. Watson, eds. *Conflict and Community in Contemporary Sri Lanka: 'Pearl of the East' or 'Island of Tears'?*. New Delhi: Sage Publications, 1999.

Geiger, Wilhelm. *The Dipavamsa and Mahavamsa and their Historical Development*. Government Printer, Colombo, 1908.

_____, ed., and trans. *The Mahavamsa or the Great Chronicle of Ceylon*. Information Department, Colombo, 1950.

_____, ed., and trans. *Culavamsa, Being the More Recent Part of the Mahavamsa*. 5 vols, Information Department, Colombo, 1953.

_____, "Culture of Ceylon in Mediaeval Times." Edited by Bechert Heinz. Wiesbaden O. Harrassowitz, 1960.

Genealogical Tables of Sri Lanka, Moors, Malays, and other Muslims. Colombo: Moor's Islamic Cultural Home, 1981.

Goodhand, Jonathan, Jonathan Spencer and Benedikt Korf, eds. *Conflict and Peacebuilding in Sri Lanka: Caught in the Peace Trap?* Abingdon, Oxon; New York: Routledge, 2011.

Grant, Patrick. *Buddhism and Ethnic Conflict in Sri Lanka*. Albany: SUNY Press, c2009.

Guilmoto, Christophe. "Démographie et Politique: Les Tamouls entre Sri Lanka et l'Inde." *Population (French Edition)* 42, 2 (1987): 283–303.

Gunaratna, Rohan. *Sri Lanka, A Lost Revolution?: The Inside Story of the JVP*. Kandy, Sri Lanka : Institute of Fundamental Studies, 1995.

_____, *Sri Lanka's Ethnic Crisis and National Security*. Colombo: South Asian Network on Conflict Research, 1998.

Gunasingam, Murugar. *Sri Lankan Tamil Nationalism: A Study of its Origins*. Sydney: MV Publications, 1999.

Gunatilleke, G. "The Economic, Demographic, Sociocultural and Political Setting for Emigration from Sri Lanka." *International Migration* 33, 3–4 (1995): 667–97.

Gunawardana, R. A. L. H. "Irrigation and Hydraulic Society in Ceylon." *Past and Present* 53 (1971): 3–27.

_____, "The People of the Lion: Sinhala Consciousness in History and Historiography." In *Ethnicity and Social Change in Sri Lanka*, edited by the Social Scientists Association, 1–53. Colombo: The Social Scientists Association, 1984.

_____, *Historiography in a Time of Ethnic Conflict: Construction of the Past in Contemporary Sri Lanka*. Colombo Social Scientist's Association, 1995.

_____, S. Pathmanathan and M. Rohanadeera. *Reflections on a Heritage: Historical Scholarship on Premodern Sri Lanka*. Central Cultural Fund, Ministry of Cultural and Religious Affairs, Colombo, 2000.

Haji Ismail Effendi, Mohamed Sameer bin. *Personages of the Past: Moors, Malays and Other Muslims of the Past of Sri Lanka*. Colombo: Moors' Islamic Cultural Home, 1982.

Harris, Elizabeth J. *Theravada Buddhism and the British Encounter: Religious Missionary and Colonial Experience in Nineteenth Century Sri Lanka*. New York: Routledge, 2006.

Hasbullah, S. H. and Barrie M. Morrison, eds. *Sri Lankan Society in an Era of Globalization: Struggling to Create a New Social Order*. New Delhi; Thousand Oaks, Calif.: Sage Publications, 2004.

Hellmann-Rajanayagam, D. "The Concept of a 'Tamil Homeland' in Sri Lanka: Its Meaning and Development." *South Asia* 13, 2 (1990): 79–110.

Hettiaratchi, S. B. *Social and Cultural History of Ancient Sri Lanka*. Studies on Sri Lanka Series No. 9, Sri Satguru Publications, Delhi, 1988.

Hettige, Siripala T., and Markus Maye, eds. *Sri Lanka at Cross Roads: Dilemmas and Prospects after 50 Years of Independence*. Macmillan, New Delhi, 2000.

Holt, John Clifford, ed. *The Sri Lanka Reader: History, Culture, Politics*. Durham [N.C.]: Duke University Press, 2011.

Hoole, Rajan. *The Broken Palmyra: The Tamil Crisis in Sri Lanka; An Inside Account*. Sri Lanka Studies Institute, 1992.

Howard, Wriggins. "Sri Lanka: Negotiations in a Secessionist Conflict". In *Elusive Peace: Negotiating an End to Civil Wars*, edited by I.

William Zartman, 35–58. Washington, D.C.: Brookings Institution, c1995.

Hyndman, Patricia. *Sri Lanka: Serendipity under Siege*. Nottingham, England: Spokesman, 1988.

Ilangasinha, H. M. B. *Buddhism in Medieval Sri Lanka*. Sri Satguru Publications, Delhi, 1992.

Indrapala, K. "Early Tamil Settlements in Ceylon." *Journal of the Ceylon Branch of the Royal Asiatic Society* 13 (1969): 43–63.

_____, ed. *The Collapse of the Rajarata Civilization and the Drift to the South-West*. Ceylon Studies Seminar, University of Ceylon, Peradeniya, 1971.

_____, *The Evolution of an Ethnic Identity*. Vijitha Yapa Publications, Colombo, 2007.

Ismail, Marina. *Early Settlements in Northern Sri Lanka*. Navrang, New Delhi, 1995.

J. Bullion, Alan. *India, Sri Lanka and the Tamil Crisis, 1976–94*. New York, NY; London: Pinter, 1995.

Jayasuriya, Laksiri. *The Changing Face of Electoral Politics in Sri Lanka (1994–2004)*. Marshall Cavendish Academic, Singapore, 2005.

Jayasuriya, Shihan de Silva. *Tagus to Taprobane: Portuguese Impact on the Socioculture of Sri Lanka from 1505 AD*. Sri Lanka: Tisara Prakasakayo, 2001a.

_____, *Indo-Portuguese of Ceylon: A Contact Language*. London: Athena Publications, 2001b.

_____, "An African Presence in Sri Lanka." In *The African Diaspora in the Indian Ocean*, edited by Shihan De Silva Jayasuriya and R. Pankhurst. New Jersey: Africa World Press, 2003.

_____, "The Afro-Sri Lankans: A Forgotten Minority." *Journal of African & Asian Studies* 6, 3 (2007): 227–42.

Jayawardena, K. *Nobodies to Somebodies. The Rise of the Colonial Bourgeoisie in Sri Lanka*. New Delhi, 2001.

Jazeel, Tariq. "Reading the Geography of Sri Lankan Island-ness: Colonial Repetitions, Postcolonial Possibilities." *Contemporary South Asia* 17, 4 (2009): 399–414.

Jenne, Erin K. "Sri Lanka: A Fragmented State." In *State Failure and State Weakness in a Time of Terror*, edited by Robert I. Rotberg, 219–44. Brookings Institution Press, c2003.

Johnson, Basil Leonard Clyde and M. LeM. Scrivenor. *Sri Lanka, Land, People, and Economy*. Scrivenor. London; Exeter, N.H.: Heinemann Educational Books, 1981.

Kaarthikeyan, Shari D. R. "Root Causes of Terrorism?: A Case Study of the Tamil Insurgency and the LTTE." In *Root Causes of Terrorism: Myths, Reality and Ways Forward*, edited by Tore Bjørgo. London; New York: Routledge, 2005.

"Kaffir Culture in Sri Lanka by Kannan Arunasalam." Online at: https://www.youtube.com/watch?v=BXvLYV9MZLI

Lakshman, Weligamage D. and Clement A. Tisdell. *Sri Lanka's Development since Independence: Socio-Economic Perspectives and Analyses.* Huntington, NY: Nova Science Publishers, 2000.

Lasagabaster, Esperanza, Samuel Munzele Maimbo and Sriyani Hulugalle. "Sri Lanka's Migrant Labor Remittances: Enhancing the Quality and Outreach of the Rural Remittance Infrastructure." *Policy Research Working Paper 3789.* Washington, D.C.: World Bank, 2005.

Leach, E. R., ed. *Aspects of Caste in South India, Ceylon, and North-West Pakistan.* Cambridge University Press, 1960.

Liyanagamage, Amaradasa. *The Decline of Polonnaruwa and the Rise of Dambadeniya, circa 1180–1270 A. D.* Department of Cultural Affairs, Colombo, 1968.

_____, *Society, State and Religion in Premodern Sri Lanka.* University of Kelaniya, 2001.

Madavan, Delon. Jaffna et le conflit intercommunautaire à Sri Lanka, Paris: Prodig/ Collection Grafigéo, 2007. Online at: http://f. hypotheses.org/wp-content/blogs.dir/846/ files/2012/08/delon_32_2007.pdf

_____, "Geography of 'Refugee Spaces' of Jaffnese since the Beginning of the War in Sri Lanka." Géographie de la ville en, 2011. Online at: http:// geographie-ville-en-guerre.blogspot.fr/2011/07/ geographie-des-espaces-refuges-des.html

_____, Gaëlle Dequirez and Eric Meyer, eds. Les communautés tamoules et le conflit sri lankais. Paris: L'Harmattan, 2011.

Mahroof, M. M. M. "The Muslims of Sri Lanka: The Maldivian Connection." *Pakistan Historical Society* 48, 3 (2000).

_____, "Spoken Tamil Dialects of the Muslims of Sri Lanka: Language as Identity-Classifier." *Journal: Islamic Studies* 34, 4 (1995): 407–26.

Malalgoda, K. *Buddhism in Sinhalese Society, 1750–1900: A Study of Religious Revival and Change.* Los Angeles, 1976.

Manogaran, Chelvadurai. *Ethnic Conflict and Reconciliation in Sri Lanka.* Honolulu: University of Hawaii Press, c1987.

_____, "Space-Related Identity in Sri Lanka." In *Nested Identities: Nationalism, Territory, and Scale*, edited by Guntram H. Herb and David H. Kaplan, 199–217. Lanham, Md.: Rowman & Littlefield Publishers, c1999.

_____, and Bryan Pfaffenberger, eds. *The Sri Lankan Tamils: Ethnicity and Identity.* Boulder: Westview Press, 1994.

Manor, James, ed. *Sri Lanka in Change and Crisis.* London: Croom Helm, c1984.

_____, *The Expedient Utopian: Bandaranaike and Ceylon.* Cambridge: Cambridge University Press, 1989.

McGilvray, Dennis B. "Dutch Burghers and Portuguese Mechanics: Eurasian Ethnicity in Sri Lanka." *Comparative Studies in Society and History (New York)* 24, 2 (1982): 235–63.

McGowan, William. *Only Man is Vile: The Tragedy of Sri Lanka.* New York: Farrar Straus Giroux, 1992.

Mendis, Garrett Champness. *The Early History of Ceylon or the Indian Period of Ceylon History.* 4th ed, YMCA Publishing House, Calcutta, 1940.

Mendis, Vernon L. B. "Sri Lanka." In *Counterterrorism Strategies: Successes and Failures of Six Nations*, edited by Yonah Alexander, 152–89. Washington, D.C.: Potomac Books, c2006.

Meyer, Eric. *Sri Lanka, Biography of an Island: Between Local and Global.* Negombo, Viator Publications, 2006.

Moore, Mick. "Sri Lanka: The Contradictions of the Social Democratic State." In *The Post-Colonial State in Asia: Dialectics of Politics and Culture*, edited by Subrata Kumar Mitra, 155–91. Wheatsheaf, New York, 1990.

_____, "Thoroughly Modern Revolutionaries: The JVP in Sri Lanka." *Modern Asian Studies* 27, 3 (1993): 593–642.

Nubin, Walter, ed. *Sri Lanka: Current Issues and Historical Background.* New York: Nova Science Publishers, 2002.

O'balance, Edgar. *The Cyanide War: Tamil Insurrection in Sri Lanka, 1973–88.* Brassey's, 1989.

Obeyesekere, Gananath. "The Vicissitudes of the Sinhala-Buddhist Identity through Time and Change." In *Collective Identities, Nationalism and Protest in Modern Sri Lanka*, edited by M. Roberts. Colombo, 1979.

_____, *The Cult of the Goddess Pattini.* The University of Chicago Press, Chicago, 1984.

Oldenberg, Hermann, ed., and trans. *The Dipavamsa: An Ancient Buddhist Historical Record.* Williams and Norgate, London, 1879.

Ollapally, Deepa M. "Sri Lanka's Violent Spiral." In *The Politics of Extremism in South Asia*, edited by Deepa M. Ollapally, 145–76. Cambridge; New York: Cambridge University Press, 2008.

Orjuela, Camilla. *Civil Society in Civil War: Peace Work and Identity Politics in Sri Lanka.* Goteborg: Padrigu, 2004.

Palanithurai, Ganapathy and K. Mohanasundaram. *Dynamics of Tamil Nadu Politics in Sri Lankan Ethnicity.* New Delhi: Northern Book Centre, 1993.

Parker, Henry. *Ancient Ceylon: An Account of the Aborigines and of Part of the Early Civilization.* Luzac & Co, London, 1909.

Pathmanathan, S. *The Kingdom of Jaffna.* Arul M. Rajendran, Colombo, 1978.

Paul, A. T. S. *The Colombo Chetty Community: Their History, Branches and Roots.* M.D. Gunasena, 2001.

Peebles, Patrick. *The History of Sri Lanka.* Greenwood Press, Greenwood, CT, 2006.

Perera, J. "Political Development and Ethnic Conflict in Sri Lanka." *Journal of Refugees Studies* 5, 2 (1992): 136–48.

Perera, Lakshman S., Sirima Kiribamune and Piyatissa Sēnānāyaka. *The Institutions of Ancient Ceylon from Inscriptions.* Kandy: International Centre for Ethnic Studies, 3 vols, 2001–2005.

Perera, N. "Colonialism and National Space: Representations of Sri Lanka." In *Conflict and Community in Contemporary Sri Lanka: 'Pearl of the East' or 'Island of Tears'?*, edited by S. Gamage and I. B. Watson, 23–48. New Delhi: Sage Publications, 1999.

Peacock, Olive. "The Burghers of Sri Lanka during Dutch and British Regime: A Socio-Economic-Political Profile." *South Asian Studies (Jaipur)* 19, 2 (1984): 48–59.

_____, *Minority Politics in Sri Lanka: A Study of the Burghers.* Jaipur: Arihant Publishers, 1989.

Pfaffenberger, Bryan. "The Cultural Dimension of Tamil Separatism in Sri Lanka." *Asia Survey* 21, 11 (1981): 1145–57.

_____, "Fourth World Colonialism, Indigenous Minorities and Tamil Separation in Sri Lanka." *Bulletin of Concerned Asian Scholars* 16 (1984): 15–22.

Ponnambalam, Satchi. *Sri Lanka: National Conflict and the Tamil Liberation Struggle.* Tamil Information Centre, 1983.

Rahula, Walpola. *History of Buddhism in Ceylon: The Anuradhapura Period, 3rd Century B. C. –10th Century A. C. M. D. Gunasena, Colombo, 1956.

Rajasingham-Senanayake, Darini. "Sri Lanka: Transformation of Legitimate Violence and Civil-Military Relations." In *Coercion and Governance: The Declining Political Role of the Military in Asia*, edited by Muthiah Alagappa, 294–316. Stanford, Calif.: Stanford University Press, 2001.

_____, "Between Tamil and Muslim: Women Mediating Multiple Identities in a New War." In *Gender, Conflict, and Migration*, edited by Navnita Chadha Behera, 175–204. New Delhi; Thousand Oaks: SAGE Publications, 2006.

_____, "Buddhism and the Legitimation of Power: Democracy, Public Religion and Minorities in Sri Lanka." *ISAS Working Paper No.99*, Institute of South Asian Studies (ISAS), Singapore, 26 November 2009a.

_____, "From National Security State to Human Security: The Challenge of Winning Peace in Sri Lanka." *ISAS Working Paper No.72*, Institute of South Asian Studies (ISAS), Singapore, 9 July 2009b.

Rasanayagam, C. *Ancient Jaffna: Being a Research into the History of Jaffna from very Early Times to the Portuguese Period.* Everymans Publisher, Madras, 1926.

Roberts, Michael, ed. *Collective Identities, Nationalisms and Protests in Modern Sri Lanka.* Colombo: Marga, 1979.

_____, *Caste Conflict and Elite Formation: The Rise of a Karava Elite in Sri Lanka, 1500–1931.* Cambridge University Press, 1982.

_____, *Exploring Confrontation: Sri Lanka Politics, Culture and History.* Chur, Switzerland: Harwood Academic Publishers, c1994.

Rohan, Edrisinha. "Religion and Nationalism in Recent Peace Initiatives in Sri Lanka." In *Religion and Nationalism in Iraq: A Comparative Perspective*, edited by David Little and Donald

K. Swearer with Susan Lloyd McGarry, 87–96. Cambridge, MA: Center for the Study of World Religions, c2006.

Ryan, Bryce Finley. *Caste in Modern Ceylon; The Sinhalese System in Transition.* New Brunswick, Rutgers University Press, 1953.

Sabaratnam, Lakshmanan. *Ethnic Attachments in Sri Lanka.* New York: Palgrave, 2001.

Sahadevan, P. "Political Trends in Post-War Sri Lanka." In *Ethnic Reconciliation and Nation Building in Sri Lanka: Indian Perspectives,* edited by V. Suryanarayan and S. Nambiar, 9–34. T.R. Publications, Chennai, 2010.

_____, and Neil DeVotta. *Politics of Conflict and Peace in Sri Lanka.* Manak Publications, New Delhi, 2006.

Saldin, B. D. K. *The Sri Lankan Malays and Their Language = Organ Melayu Sri Lanka dan Bahasanya.* Nedimala, Dehiwala: Printed by Mahendra Senanayake, Sridevi Printers, 1996.

Samaranayaka, Gamini. *Political Violence in Sri Lanka, 1971–1987.* Gyan Publishing House, Delhi, India, 2008.

Samuels, Jeffrey. "Establishing the Basis of the Sasana: Social Service and Ritual Performance in Contemporary Sri Lankan Monastic Training." In *Approaching the Dhamma: Buddhist Texts and Practices in South and Southeast Asia,* edited by Anne M. Blackburn and Jeffrey Samuels. Washington: Pariyatti Publications, 2003.

_____, "Monastic Patronage and Temple Building in Contemporary Sri Lanka: Caste, Ritual Performance, and Merit." *Modern Asian Studies* 41, 4 (2007): 757–94.

Saparamadu, Sumana D., ed. *The Polonnaruva Period.* Tisara Prakasakayo, Dehiwala, 1973.

Saravanamuttu, Paikiasothy. "Sri Lanka – The Intractability of Ethnic Conflict." In *The Management of Peace Processes,* edited by John Darby and Roger Mac Ginty, 195–227. Basingstoke, Hant: Macmillan Press; New York : St. Martin's Press, 2000.

Scott, David. "Religion in Colonial Civil Society: Buddhism and Modernity in 19th-Century Sri Lanka." *Cultural Dynamics* 8, 1 (1996): 7–23.

Senaratne, S. P. F. *Prehistoric Archaelogy in Ceylon.* Ceylon National Museums (Handbook Series No. 2), Department of National Museums, Colombo, 1969.

Seneviratne, H. L. "The Malaise of Contemporary Sri Lankan Society." In *Religion and Nationalism in Iraq: A Comparative Perspective,* edited by David Little and Donald K. Swearer with Susan Lloyd McGarry, 81–86. Cambridge, MA: Center for the Study of World Religions, c2006.

Shamugaratnam, N. "Caste Struggles in Northern Sri Lanka." *Pravada* 2, 3 (1993): 19–23.

Shastri, A. "Sri Lanka's Provincial Council System: A Solution to the Ethnic Conflict." *Asian Survey* 32, 8 (1992): 723–43.

Silva, Neluka, ed. *The Hybrid Island: Culture Crossings and the Invention of Identity in Sri Lanka.* London: Zed, 2002.

Sirisena, W. M. *Sri Lanka and South-East Asia: Political Religious and Cultural Relations.* E. J. Brill, Leiden, 1978.

Siriweera, W. I. *History of Sri Lanka from the Earliest Times up to the Sixteenth Century.* Dayawansa Jayakody & Company, Colombo, 2002.

_____, *A Study of the Economic History of Pre-Modern Sri Lanka.* Vikas Pub. House, New Delhi, 1994.

Spencer, Jonathan, ed. *Sri Lanka: History and the Roots of Conflict.* New York: Routledge, 1990a.

_____, *A Sinhala Village in Time of Trouble: Politics and Change in Rural Sri Lanka.* Oxford University Press, 1990b.

Shastri, Amita. "Estate Tamils, The Ceylon Citizenship Act of 1948 and Sri Lankan Politics." *Contemporary South Asia* 8, 1 (1999): 65–86.

Sri Lanka National Bibliography (Retrospective): English Publications 1901–1910. Colombo: National Library & Documentation Centre, 2000.

Sriskandarajah, Dhananjayan. "The Returns of Peace in Sri Lanka: The Development Cart before the Conflict Resolution Horse?" *Journal of Peacebuilding and Development* 1, 2 (2003): 21–35.

Suraweera, A. V., ed., and trans. *Rajavaliya: A Comprehensive Account of the Kings of Sri Lanka.* Vishva Lekha, Ratmalana, 2000.

Tambiah, S. J. *Sri Lanka: Ethnic Fratricide and the Dismantling of Democracy.* Chicago: University of Chicago Press, 1986.

_____, *Buddhism Betrayed? – Religion, Politics and Violence in Sri Lanka.* University of Chicago Press, 1992.

Tennakoon, Ajitha, ed. *Sri Lanka Economy in Transition: Progress, Problems, and Prospects.* Colombo: Vijitha Yapa Publications, 2009.

Thiranagama, Sharika. "Moving on?: Generating Homes in the Future for Displaced Northern Muslims in Sri Lanka." In *Ghosts of Memory: Essays on Remembrance and Relatedness,* edited by Janet Carsten, 126–49. Malden, MA; Oxford: Blackwell Publ., 2007.

Tiruchelvam, Neelan. "The Politics of Federalism and Diversity in Sri Lanka". In *Autonomy and Ethnicity: Negotiating Competing Claims in Multi-Ethnic States,* edited by Yash Ghai, 197–218. Cambridge: Cambridge University Press, 2000a.

_____, "Devolution and the Elusive Quest for Peace in Sri Lanka." In *Pursuit of Peace in Sri Lanka: Past Failures and Future Prospects,* edited by K. M. de Silva and G. H. Peiris, 183–202. Kandy: International Centre for Ethnic Studies, 2000b.

Thomas, M. A. "Sri Lanka: Political Uncertainty under the Threat of Insurgency." In *Asian Security Handbook: Terrorism and the New Security Environment,* edited by William M. Carpenter and David G. Wiencek, 273–82. Armonk, N.Y.: M.E. Sharpe, 2004.

Uyangoda, Jayadeva. "Ethnic Conflict in Sri Lanka: Changing Dynamics." *Policy Studies* 32, East West Center, Washington, 2007.

_____, *The Way We Are: Politics of Sri Lanka 2007–2009.* Social Scientists' Association, Colombo, 2008.

Vitharana, Vini. "Karapotta [Sinhalese Epithet ('Beetles') for Poor, Uneducated Burghers in Ceylon." *Journal of the Royal Asiatic Society of Sri Lanka,* 47 (2002).

Wickramasinghe, Nira. *Ethnic Politics in Colonial Sri Lanka 1927–1947.* New Delhi: Vikas Publ., 1995.

_____, "Sri Lanka: The Many Faces of Security." In *Asian Security Practice: Material and Ideational Influences,* edited by Muthiah Alagappa, 367–89. Stanford, Calif.: Stanford University Press, 1998.

_____, *Civil Society in Sri Lanka. New Circles of Power.* New Delhi, London, Thousand Oaks: Sage Publ., 2001.

_____, *Dressing the Colonised Body: Politics, Clothing and Identity in Colonial Sri Lanka.* New Delhi: Orient Longman Publ., 2003.

_____, *Sri Lanka in the Modern Age. A History of Contested Identities.* London: C. Hurst and Honolulu: University of Hawaii Press, 2006.

Wijeyeratne, Roshan de Silva. *Nation, Constitutionalism and Buddhism in Sri Lanka.* Routledge, 2011.

Wilson, Alfred Jeyaratnam. *Politics in Sri Lanka, 1947–1973.* Macmillan, London, 1974.

_____, *The Break-up of Sri Lanka: The Sinhalese-Tamil Conflict.* London, C. Hurst and Co, 1988.

_____, *Sri Lankan Tamil Nationalism: Its Origin and Development in the Nineteenth and Twentieth Centuries.* C. Hurst & Co, London, 2000.

Winslow, Deborah and Michael D. Woost. *Economy, Culture, and Civil War in Sri Lanka.* Bloomington: Indiana University Press, c2004.

Yalman, Nur. *Under the Bo Tree: Studies in Caste, Kinship, and Marriage in the Interior of Ceylon.* Berkeley, University of California Press, 1967.

Part 2: Life and People in the Diaspora

Aboosally, M. L. M. *Dafther Jailany: A Historical Account of the Dafther Jailany Rock Cave Mosque.* Sharm Aboosally, Colombo, 2002.

Ahmad, Nureza. "Neila Sathyalingam." *Singapore Infopedia,* National Library Board, August 25, 2004.

Ali, Ameer. "Assimilation, Integration or Convivencia: The Dilemma of Diaspora Muslims from 'Eurabia' to 'Londonistan', from 'Lakembanon' to Sri Lanka." *Journal of Muslim Minority Affairs* 30, 2 (2010): 183–98.

_____, "The Genesis of the Muslim Community in Ceylon (Sri Lanka): A Historical Summary." *Asian Studies* 19 (1981): 65–82.

_____, "The 1915 Racial Riots in Ceylon (Sri Lanka): A Reappraisal of its Causes." *South Asia* 4, 2 (1981): 1–20.

Arunatilaka, Nisha, Priyanka Jayawardena and Dushni Weerakoon. "Sri Lanka." In *Migration,*

Remittances and Development in South Asia, edited by S. Kelegama, 112–40. New Delhi, Sage India, 2011.

Black, Shameem. "Recipes for Cosmopolitanism Cooking Across Borders in the South Asian Diaspora." *Frontiers: A Journal of Women Studies* 31, 1 (2010): 1–30.

Boyle, Richard. *B. P. de Silva: The Royal Jeweller of South-East Asia.* Singapore: B.P. de Silva Investments Pte. Ltd., 1989.

Canagarajah, A. Suresh. "Language Shift and The Family: Questions from the Sri Lankan Tamil Diaspora." *Journal of Sociolinguistics* 12, 2 (2008): 143–76.

Carr, W. I. Sri Lanka: *Economic Indicators.* Hong Kong: ASB Ltd, 1993.

Ceylon Sports Club, Singapore. Online at: http://www.cscsingapore.org.sg/

Charuk Nai Prathet Thai (Inscriptions in Thailand), Volume 2, Bangkok, 1986.

Demieville, Paul, Hubert Durt and Anna Seidel. *Repertoire du Canon Bouddhique Sino-Japonais.* edition de Taisho, Tokyo, Maison Franco-Japonais, 1978.

Department of Census and Statistics, Household Income and Expenditure Survey (HIES), Colombo, 2009/10.

Deraniyagala, S. U. *The Pre-History of Sri Lanka: An Ecological Perspective.* Part 1, Department of Archaeological Survey, Colombo, 1992.

Desiderio, Maria Vincenza and John Salt. *Entrepreneurship and Employment Creation of Immigrants in OECD Countries.* OECD, Paris, 2010.

de Silva, Padmasiri and Trevor Ling. "Buddhism in Sri Lanka and South-East Asia." In *Companion Encyclopedia of Asian Philosophy*, edited by Brian Carr and Indira Mahalingam, 394–413. London; New York : Routledge, 1997.

"Dr Jega is Still Asia's Fastest Man." *The Straits Times* (Singapore), January 8, 1990.

Eliezer, Nesa, ed. *Recipes of the Jaffna Tamils.* Orient Longman Ptd. Ltd., India, 2003.

Fernando, C. M. "The Music of Ceylon." *Journal of the Royal Asiatic Society (Ceylon)* 13, (1894): 83–189.

"Flash-Forward." *The Observer* (United Kingdom), March 20, 2005.

Frere-Jones, Sasha. "Bingo in Swansea: Maya Arulpragasam's World." *The New Yorker*, November 22, 2004.

Gellner, David N. *Monk, Householder and Tantric Priest: Newar Buddhism and its Hierarchy of Ritual.* Cambridge University Press, 1992.

Goonatilake, Hema. "Laos." In *Encyclopaedia of Buddhism*, edited by W.G. Weeraratne. Vol. VI, Fascicle 2, Department of Buddhist Affairs, The Government of Sri Lanka, Colombo, 1999.

_____, "Cultural Exchanges Between Thailand and Sri Lanka." Proceedings of the Conference on Cultural Exchange between Thailand and Sri Lanka, Nakorn Sri Thammarat, October, 2001.

_____, "Sri Lanka-Cambodia Relations with Special Reference to the Period 14th-20th Centuries." *Journal of the Royal Asiatic Society of Sri Lanka* 48, Special Number. Colombo, Royal Asiatic Society, 2003.

_____, "Sri Lanka-Myanmar Historical Relations in Religion, Culture and Polity." *Journal of the Royal Asiatic Society of Sri Lanka* 55. Colombo, Royal Asiatic Society, 2009.

Gosling, Betty. *A Chronology of Religious Architecture at Sukhothai.* Silkworm Books, Chiang Mai, 1998.

Henayaka, Ranjith and Miriam Lambusta. "The Sri Lankan Diaspora in Italy." Berghof Research Center for Conflict Management, Berlin, 2004.

Holt, Clifford. "Muslim Identities: An Introduction." In *The Sri Lanka Reader: History, Culture, Politics*, edited by Clifford Holt, 409–57. Duke University Press, Durham and London, 2011.

International Migration Outlook Sri Lanka. Colombo: International Organization of Migration, IOM, 2008.

"It Ain't Broke." *The Economist*, February 17, 2011.

Jayasuriya, Shihan de Silva. "Portuguese Impact on Sri Lankan Language, Music and Dance." 3rd Congress of Réseau Asie – IMASIE, September 26–28, Paris, France, 2007.

Kumar, Peiris. "Sri Lanka-Australia Business Interactions." In *Celebrations: Fifty Years of Sri Lanka-Australia Interactions*, edited by Cynthia Vanden Driesen and I. H. Vanden Driesen, 26–32. Government Press, Sri Lanka, 2000.

LeVine, Sarah Ethel and David N. Gellner. *Rebuilding Buddhism: The Theravada Movement in Twentieth-Century Nepal.* Harvard University Press, Harvard, 2005.

Lohuizen-de Leeuw, J. E. van. "An Aspect of Sinhalese Influence in Thailand." In *Senarat Paranavitana Commemoration Volume*, edited by Prematilleke, Leelananda, et al. Leiden: Brill, 1978.

Luce, Gordon H. *Old Burma – Early Pagan.* Artibus Asiae, New York, 3 vols, 1969.

Mackey, Robert. "Outside Sri Lanka, Tamil Diaspora Not Ready to Surrender." *New York Times*, May 18, 2009.

McGilvray, Dennis B. "Households in Akkaraipattu: Dowry and Domestic Organisation among the Matrilineal Tamils and Moors of Sri Lanka." In *Society from the Inside Out: Anthropological Perspectives on the South Asian Household*, edited by John N. Gray and David J. Mearns, 192–235. New Delhi: Sage Publications, 1989.

_____, "Arabs, Moors and Muslims: Sri Lankan Muslim Ethnicity in Regional Perspective." *Contributions to Indian Sociology (Delhi)* 32, 2 (1998): 433–84.

_____, "Jailani: A Sufi Shrine in Sri Lanka." In *Lived Islam in South Asia: Adaptation, Accommodation, and Conflict*, edited by Imtiaz Ahmadand and Helmut Reifeld, 273–89. Delhi Social Science Press, New York and Oxford, 2004.

_____, *Crucible of Conflict: Tamil and Muslim Society on the East Coast of Sri Lanka.* Duke University Press, Durham and London, 2008.

_____, "Sri Lankan Muslims: Between Ethno-Nationalism and the Global Ummah." *Journal of Nations and Nationalism* 171 (2011): 45–64.

"M.I.A. Interview with Tavis Smiley." Public Broadcasting Service, 2009. Online at: http://www.youtube.com/watch?gl=SG&v=0VDff6crf8U&hl=en-GB

Meegaskumbura, P. B. "Sinhala Language and Literature Since Independence." In *Sri Lanka's Development since Independence: Socio-Economic Perspectives and Analyses*, edited by Weligamage D. Lakshman and Clement A. Tisdell, 259–74. Huntington, NY: Nova Science Publishers, 2000.

"Mr B. P. de Silva." *The Straits Times* (Singapore), October 3, 1900.

Nagara, Prasert Na and A. B. Griswold. *Epigraphic and Historical Studies.* The Historical Society, Bangkok, 1992.

Nizam, A. A. M. "A Sri Lankan Born Entrepreneur gets Honored as 'International Businessman of the Year' in Dallas, Texas." *Asian Tribune*, August 20, 2011.

Nuhman, M. A. *Sri Lankan Muslims: Ethnic Identity within Cultural Diversity.* International Centre for Ethnic Studies, Colombo, 2007.

Organisation for Economic Cooperation and Development (OECD), *StatExtracts*, "International Migration Database". Online at: http://stats.oecd.org/Index.aspx?DataSetCode=MIG

Tin, Pe Maung and Gordon H. Luce. *Glass Palace Chronicles of the Kings of Burma.* Rangoon University Press, Rangoon, 1960.

Rai, Hakikat. "Kunalan is All-Time SEA Best Sprinter." *The Straits Times* (Singapore), February 21, 1982.

Rohanadeera, Mendis. "Telakatahagatha in a Thailand Inscription of 761 A.D." *Vidyodaya Journal of Science* 1, 1 (1987).

Sawyer, Miranda. "MIA: 'I'm here for the people'" *The Observer* (United Kingdom), June 13, 2010.

Schulenkorf, Nico. "Sport Events and Ethnic Reconciliation: Attempting to Create Social Change between Sinhalese, Tamil and Muslim Sportspeople in War-Torn Sri Lanka." *International Review for the Sociology of Sport* 45, 3 (2010): 273–94.

Seddon, David. "South Asian Remittances: Implications for Development." *Contemporary South Asia* 13, 4 (2004): 403–20.

Sheeran, A. *Baila Music: European Modernity and Afro-Iberian Popular Music in Sri Lanka.* London: Zed Books, 2002.

Shekaran, Kana. "Respectable Dancer." *The Straits Times* (Singapore), October 25, 1992.

Shrestha, H. L. *Nepal – Sri Lanka Relation.* Janamaitri Prakashan, Kathmandu, 2007.

Siebel, Norman. "Jegathesan and Rajamani Star in Malaysian Meet." *The Straits Times* (Singapore), August 16, 1964.

Sirisena, W. M. *Sri Lanka and South-East Asia: Political, Religious and Cultural Relations from A.D. c.1000 to c.1500*. Leiden: Brill, 1978.

Speech by Senior Minister of State Tharman Shanmugaratnam at the "Ceylon Sports Club New Year's Eve Celebrations" 31 December 2001, National Archives of Singapore.

Sri Lanka Bureau of Foreign Employment (SLBFE). "Annual Statistical Report of Foreign Employment." Colombo, Sri Lanka, 2009.

"The Sri Lankan Tamil Diaspora after the LTTE." *International Crisis Group*, Asia Report N°186, February 23, 2010.

Ven, Som Chan. *History of Wat Unnalom*. Office of Information and Propagation and Office of Development of Culture, Tourism and Education, compiled by Somdeh Preah Bodhivong Sohai, Phnom Penh, 2002.

Vimuttimagga (Path of Liberation). Buddhist Text Society, Kandy, Sri Lanka, 1969.

Viravong, Maha Sila. *The History of Laos*. Joint Publication Research Service, New York, 1964.

Wolters, Oliver William. *Early Indonesian Commerce: A Study of the Origins of Śrivijaya*. Ithaca, N.Y.: Cornell University Press, 1967.

Wright, Michael. "The Arrival of Lankavamsa Theravada in Siam." Proceedings of Conference on Cultural Exchange between Thailand and Sri Lanka, Nakorn Sri Thammarat, October, 2001.

PART 3: DIASPORIC LITERATURE

Barbour, Douglas. *Michael Ondaatje*. New York: Twayne, 1993.

Brubaker, Rogers. "The 'diaspora' diaspora." *Ethnic and Racial Studies* 28, 1 (2005): 1–19.

Burnett, P. "The Captives and the Lion's Claw: Reading Romesh Gunesekera's 'Monkfish Moon'" *Journal of Commonwealth Literature* 32, 2 (1997): 3–16.

Burton, A. "Archive of Bones: *Anil's Ghost* and the Ends of History." *Journal of Commonwealth Literature* 39, 1 (2004): 39–56.

Chandraratna, Bandula. *Mirage*. Boston: Black Sparrow Press, 1999.

Crusz, Rienzi. *Elephant and Ice*. Erin, Ont.: The Porcupine's Quill, 1980.

_____, *Singing Against the Wind*. Erin, Ont.: The Porcupine's Quill, 1985.

de Kretser, Michelle. *The Hamilton Case*. London: Chatto & Windus, 2003.

_____, *The Lost Dog*. London: Chatto & Windus, 2008.

Gamlin, Gordon. "Trans-Pacific Multicultural Historiography: Sri Lankan Diaspora as Family History in Michael Ondaatje's *Running in the Family*." *Ritsumeikan Journal of Asia Pacific Studies* (Beppu-shi, Oita, Japan) 9 (Sep 2002): 71–80.

Ganeshananthan, V.V. *Love Marriage*. London: Weidenfeld & Nicolson, 2008.

Ghosh, Amitav. *The Imam and the Indian: Prose Pieces*. New Delhi: Permanent Black, 2002.

Gooneratne, Yasmine. *A Change of Skies*. Sydney: Picador, 1991.

_____, *The Sweet and Simple Kind*. Colombo: Perera-Hussein Publishing House, 2006.

Goonetilleke, D. C. R. A. *Sri Lankan English Literature and the Sri Lankan People, 1917–2003*. Colombo: Vijitha Yapa Publications, 2005.

Guha, Ranajit. "The Small Voice of History." In *Subaltern Studies IX: Writings on South Asian History and Society*, edited by Shahid Amin and Dipesh Chakrabarty, 1–12. Oxford University Press, 1996.

Gunesekera, Romesh. *Monkfish Moon*. London: Granta, 1992.

_____, *Reef*. London: Granta Books, 1994.

_____, *The Sandglass*. London: Granta, 1998.

_____, *Heaven's Edge*. London: Bloomsbury, 2002.

Hall, Stuart. "Cultural Identity and Diaspora." In *Identity: Community, Culture, Difference*, edited by Jonathan Rutherford, 222–37. London: Lawrence and Wishart, 1990.

Halpe, Ashley. "Sri Lankan Literature in English." In *Sri Lanka's Development since Independence: Socio-Economic Perspectives and Analyses*, edited by Weligamage D. Lakshman and Clement A. Tisdell, 275–84. Huntington, NY: Nova Science Publishers, 2000.

Ho, Elaine Y. L. and Harshana Rambukwella. "A Question of Belonging: Reading Jean Arasanayagam through Nationalist Discourse." *The Journal of Commonwealth Literature* 41, 2 (2006): 61–81.

Jazeel, Tariq. "Unpicking Sri Lankan 'Island-ness' in Romesh Gunesekera's *Reef*." *Journal of Historical Geography* 29, 4 (2003): 582–98.

_____, "Because Pigs Can Fly: Sexuality, Race and the Geographies of Difference in Shyam Selvadurai's *Funny Boy*." *Gender, Place and Culture* 12, 2 (2005): 231–49.

_____, "Geography, Spatial Politics, and Productions of the National in Michael Ondaatje's *Anil's Ghost*." In *Spatialising Politics: Culture and Geography in Postcolonial Sri Lanka*, edited by Cathrine Brun and Tariq Jazeel, 122–45. Los Angeles: Sage, 2009.

Jussawalla, Feroza. "South Asian Diaspora Writers in Britain: 'Home' versus 'Hydridity'" In *Ideas of Home: Literature of Asian Migration*, edited by Geoffrey Kain, 17–38. East Lansing: Michigan State University Press, c1997.

King, Russell, John Connell and Paul White, eds. *Writing Across Worlds: Literature and Migration*. London; New York : Routledge, 1995.

Knowles, Sam. "Sri Lankan 'Gates of Fire': Michael Ondaatje's Transnational Literature, from *Running in the Family* to *Anil's Ghost*." *Journal of Commonwealth Literature* 45 (2010): 429–41.

Lokuge, Chandani. *Turtle Nest*. Camberwell: Penguin Books Australia, 2003.

Nyman, Jopi. *Home, Identity, and Mobility in Contemporary Diasporic Fiction*. Textext, Studies

in Comparative Literature 59, Amsterdam; New York : Rodopi, 2009.

Oakley, R. and V. I. S. Jayapalan. "Beast of Burden (Chekku Madu): The Power of the Wandering Poet Among the Sri Lankan Tamil Diaspora." *Journal of Poetry Therapy* 18, 1 (2005): 265–81.

Ondaatje, Michael. *Running in the Family*. New York: W. W. Norton, 1982.

_____, *In the Skin of a Lion*. London: Secker & Warburg, 1987.

_____, *The English Patient*. London: Bloomsbury, 1992.

_____, *Anil's Ghost*. London: Bloomsbury, 2000.

Pinto, Shiromi. *Trussed*. London: Serpent's Tail, 2006.

Roberts, Karen. *July*. London: George Weidenfeld & Nicholson, 2001.

Salgado, Minoli. "Complexity and the Migrant Writer: Chaotics in Michael Ondaatje's Fiction." In *Unhinging Hinglish: The Languages and Politics of Fiction in English from the Indian Subcontinent*, edited by Nanette Hale and Tabish Khair, 89–106. Copenhagen: Museum Tusculanum Press, 2001.

_____, "Writing Sri Lanka, Reading Resistance: Shyam Selvadurai's *Funny Boy* and A. Sivanandan's *When Memory Dies*." *Journal of Commonwealth Literature* 39, 1 (2004): 5–18.

_____, "Writing Home" In *Writers on Writing: The Art of the Short Story*, edited by Maurice Lee. Greenwood, 2005.

_____, *Writing Sri Lanka: Literature, Resistance and the Politics of Place*. Routledge: Oxford, 2007.

Sarvan, Charles P. "Carl Muller's Trilogy and The Burghers of Sri Lanka." *World Literature Today* 71, 3 (1997): 527–32.

Selvadurai, Shyam. *Funny Boy*. London: Vintage, 1995.

_____, *Cinnamon Gardens*. Toronto: McClelland and Stewart, 1998.

Shobasakthi. *Gorilla*. Random House: New Delhi, 2008.

Silva, Neluka. "Situating the Hybrid 'Other' in An Era of Conflict: Representation of the Burgher in Contemporary Writings in English." In *The Hybrid Island: Culture Crossings and The Invention of Identity in Sri Lanka*, edited by Neluka Silva, 104–26. London: Zed Books, 2002.

Sivanandan, A. "Sri Lanka: Racism and the Politics of Underdevelopment." *Race and Class* 26, 1 (1984): 1–37.

_____, *When Memory Dies*. New Delhi: Penguin, 1998.

Sivanarayanan, Anushiya. "From Militant to Writer: Sri Lankan Tamil Author Shobasakthi." *Currents* (November-December 2008): 49–52.

Srikanth, Rajini. *The World Next Door: South Asian American Literature and The Idea of America*. Philadelphia: Temple University Press, c2004.

Tearne, Roma. *Mosquito*. London: Harper Collins, 2007.

_____, *Bone China*. London: Harper Collins, 2008a.

_____, "October 8 1950 ..." *The Guardian* (United Kingdom), June 14, 2008b.

Thiruchandran, Selvy. *Stories from the Diaspora. Tamil Women, Writing*. Colombo: Vijitha Yapa Publications, 2006.

Thillainathan, S. "Tamil Creative Writing in Sri Lanka: Post-Independence Trends." In *Sri Lanka's Development since Independence: Socio-Economic Perspectives and Analyses*, edited by Weligamage D. Lakshman and Clement A. Tisdell, 275–84. Huntington, NY: Nova Science Publishers, 2000.

Walsh, Rebecca. "Global Diasporas." *Interventions: International Journal of Postcolonial Studies* 5, 1 (2003): 1–11.

Whitaker, Mark. P. "The Sri Lankan Tamil Diaspora: Three Tamil Family Narratives." *Ethnic Studies Report* 21, 1 (January 2003): 61–80.

Part 4: Communities

India

Chandrahasan, Nirmala. "Access to Justice and Aliens: Some Insights into Refugee Groups in India." *Harvard Human Rights Yearbook* 16, (1998): 135–48.

Chitralega, Maunaguru. "The Immigrant Literature of Sri Lankan Tamils: Some Reflections." *Pravada* (Colombo May – June 1993): 30–33.

DeVotta. Neil. "When Individuals, States, and Systems Collide: India's Foreign Policy toward Sri Lanka." In *India's Foreign Policy: Retrospect and Prospect*, edited by Sumit Ganguly, 32–61. New Delhi: Oxford University Press, 2010.

Dixit, Jyotindra Nath. *Assignment Colombo*. Delhi: Konark Publishers, 1998.

Government of Tamil Nadu, 'Policy Notes of Department', 2009-2010.

J. Bullion, Alan. *India, Sri Lanka and the Tamil Crisis, 1976–94*. New York, NY; London : Pinter, 1995.

Jayaraj, D. B. S. "Tamil Nadu. Taamil Eelam and Greater Eelam." *HIMAL*. June 2000.

Kadiragamar, Santasilan. *The Tamils of Sri Lanka: Their Struggle for Justice and Equality with Dignity*. Kanyakumari, India, 2010.

Kodikara, S. *Indo-Sri Lankan Agreement of July 1987*. Sri Lanka: University of Colombo, 1989.

Kumar, David. "Sri Lanka: The Tamils at Home and the Tamil Diaspora." *South Asia Analysis Group* 4444, April 24, 2011.

Mehrotra, Lakhan. *My Days in Sri Lanka*. Har-Anand Publications, New Delhi, 2011.

Muni, S. D. *Pangs of Proximity: India and Sri Lanka's Ethnic Crisis*. Oslo, Norway: PRIO; New Delhi : SAGE publications, 1993.

Organisation for Eelam Refugee Rehabilitation (OfERR). Online at: http://www.oferr.org/home.php

Philips, Rajan, ed. *Sri Lanka: Global Challenges and National Crises: Proceedings of the Hector Abhayavardhana Felicitation Symposium*. Colombo, Sri Lanka, 2001.

Sahadevan, P. "Forced to Flee: Sri Lankan Tamil Refugees in India." In *The Elsewhere People: Cross-Border Migration, Refugee Protection and State Response*, edited by Omprakash Mishra and Anindyo J. Majumdar. New Delhi: Lancer's Books, 2003.

_____, "Globalisation and Sri Lanka." In *Globalisation and South Asia: Multidimensional Perspectives*, edited by Achin Vanaik, 118–37. New Delhi: Manohar Publishers, 2004.

Samaddar, Ranabir, ed. *Refugees and the State: Practices of Asylum and Care in India, 1947–2000*. New Delhi; Thousand Oaks, Calif.: Sage Publications, 2003.

Shamugaratnam, N. "Seven Days in Jaffna: Life under Indian Occupation." *Race and Class* 31, 2 (1989): 1–15.

Suryanarayan, V. and V. Sudarsen. *Between Fear and Hope: Sri Lankan Refugees in Tamil Nadu*. T.R. Publications, Chennai, 2000.

Suryanarayan, V. "Sheltering Civilians and Warriors: Entanglements in the South." In *Refugees and the State: Practices of Asylum and Care in India, 1947–2000*, edited by Ranabir Samaddar, 321–54. New Delhi; Thousand Oaks, Calif.: Sage Publications, 2003.

_____, "Reflections on Indian Communities in the Littoral States of the Indian Ocean." In *Lectures on Maritime Studies*, edited by V. Suryanarayan and E.K.G. Nambiar, 43–70. University of Calicut Publication, Kozhikode, 2005.

_____, "Is Tamil Nadu the Villain in India-Sri Lanka Relations?" In *Foreign Policy of India: Continuity and Change*, edited by M. B. Pillai and L. Premasekhara, 285–97. New Delhi, 2010a.

_____, "Reflections on Indian and Chinese Communities in Southeast Asia." In *Indian Perspectives on China*, edited by D.S. Rajan, 109–31. Chennai, 2010b.

_____, "Refugees Deserve Support." *New Indian Express*, June 11, 2010c.

_____, "When will the Tamil Refugees Return to Sri Lanka?" In *Ethnic Reconciliation and Nation Building in Sri Lanka: Indian Perspectives*, edited by V. Suryanarayan and S. Nambiar, 113–30. T.R. Publications, Chennai, 2010d.

Vijayathilakan, J. *A Study of Sri Lankan Tamil Refugees in Tamil Nadu*. Madras Christian College, 1985.

Zephaniah, B. "We Refugees." Online at: http://www.poemhunter.com/poem/we-refugees

Malaysia

Arasaratnam, Sinnappah. *Indians in Malaysia and Singapore*. Oxford University Press, Kuala Lumpur, Revised Edition, 1979.

Arseculeratne, S. N. *Sinhalese Immigrants in Malaysia and Singapore, 1860–1990: History Through Recollections*. K.V.G. De Silva & Sons, Colombo, 1991.

Bharatha Nesan, S. T. *Ceylon's Place in Asian Culture*. Bharatha Kam, Vaddukoddai, Jaffna, 1925.

Butcher, John G. *The British in Malaya, 1880–1941: The Social History of a European Community in Colonial South-East Asia*. Oxford University Press, Kuala Lumpur, 1979.

Cartman, James. *Hinduism in Ceylon*. M.D. Gunadasa and Co. Ltd, Colombo, 1957.

"Ceylon Tamils Kalavirthy Sangam." Golden Jubilee Celebrations, 1939–1988, Malaysia.

Commemorative Volume of Centenary Celebration of Swami Vivekananda's Chicago Addresses. Vivekananda Ashrama, Kuala Lumpur, 1993.

Das, Cyrus V., ed. *Justice Through Law: Fifty Years of the Bar Council of Malaysia 1947–1997: A Pictorial Biography of the Legal Profession*. Bar Council of Malaysia, 1997.

"Divine Life Society (Malaysia) Branch." Golden Jubilee Souvenir, 2003.

de Silva, K. M. "Immigrants in Malaysia and Singapore: The Sinhalese." *Ethnic Studies Report (Kandy, Sri Lanka)* 9, 1 (1991): 56–64.

Fifty Years of Railways in Malaya, 1885–1935. Federated Malay States Railways, Kyle, Palmer & Co., Ltd., 1935.

Hyatt, David. *Railways of Sri Lanka*. Wembley, Middlesex: Communications Research and Consultancy Ltd., 2000.

Jayasooria, Denison. *Politics and Services: The Experience of Banting Jaya*. JJ Resources, K.L. 2002.

Journey of the Andersonians Who's Who. Old Andersonians Club Ipoh, Anderson School Old Boys' Association,Wilayah Persekutuan and Selangor, 2004.

Karunaratne, Kusuma E. "A Comparative Study of the Traditions and Taboos Practiced by Malays in Malaysia and the Sinhalese." *Journal of the Royal Asiatic Society of Sri Lanka* 33 (1988-1999): 48–72.

Kuala Lumpur 100 Years: Centenary 1859–1959. Kuala Lumpur Municipal Council, 1959.

Kulasingham, Christine. The Hallel-Yah Florence Abraham Muttu Trust. Percetakan P. J. Sdn. Bhd, 1998.

"Malayan Ceylonese Association, Jaffna." Silver Jubilee Number, 1962.

"Malayan Railway Co-operative Society Limited." Golden Jubilee Souvenir (1924–1973), 1973.

"Malaysian Cricket Association, Malaysian in the I.C.C. Trophy 1979." United Kingdom, 1979.

"Malaysian Cricket Association, Malaysian in the I.C.C. Trophy, 1982." United Kingdom, 1982.

Mendis, G.C. *The Early History of Ceylon*. Asian Educational Services, New Delhi, 1998.

Mootootamby, Pillai. *Jaffna History*. Asian Educational Services, New Delhi, 2001.

National Railway Cooperative Ltd., Laporan Tahunan, 2004.

Navaratnam, C. S. *A Short History of Hinduism in Ceylon and Three Essays on the Tamils*. Sri Sammuganatha Press, 1964.

"Negeri Sembilan Ceylonese Association." Centenary Souvenir (1904–2004), Malaysia, 2004.

Oriental Bank Berhad, 55th Anniversary, 1936–1991. Kuala Lumpur, 1991.

Parameswaran, N. *Early Tamils of Lanka – Ilankai.* Kuala Lumpur, 1999.

_____, *Medieval Tamils in Lanka – Ilankai.* Kuala Lumpur, 2003.

Paranavitana, Senarat. *Ceylon and Malaysia.* Colombo, Lake House Investments, 1966.

Pathfinder, Quarterly magazine of Jaffnese Co operative Society Ltd, 1984 –2000.

Pathmanathan, S. *The Laws and Customs of the Sri Lankan Tamils.* Kumaran Book House, Colombo-12, 2002.

Persatuan Pure Life Rumah Kebajikan Sukarela Untuk Kanak-Kanak Yatim Piatu. The Pure Life Society A Spiritual Sanctuary, 2000.

Pieris, P.E. *The Kingdom of Jafnapatam 1645.* Asian Educational Services, New Delhi, 1955.

Ponniah, Edward I. and A.T. Kulasingam. *Spotlights on The Jaffna Tamils in Malaysia.* Kuala Lumpur, 1935.

Ponniah, Pillai K. *Isaiyiyal.* Annamalai University, Phidamparam, 1956.

Popley H. A. *The Music of India.* Y.M.C.A. Publishing House, New Delhi, 1966.

Raghavan, M.D. *Tamil Culture in Ceylon: A General Introduction.* Kalai Nilayam, Colombo, 1971.

Raghavan, V. *Tyagarasar.* Sahitya Akademi, New Delhi, 2000.

Ramasamy, Rajakrishnan. *Sojourners to Citizens: Sri Lankan Tamils in Malaysia, 1885–1965.* Kuala Lumpur, 1988.

_____, "Social Change and Group Identity Among the Sri Lankan Tamils." In *Indian Communities in Southeast Asia*, edited by Kernial Singh Sandhu and A. Mani, 541–57. Institute of Southeast Asian Studies, Singapore, 1993.

Rasanayagam, C. *Ancient Jaffna: Being a Research into the History of Jaffna from very Early Times to the Portuguese Period.* Everymans Publisher, Madras, 1926.

_____, *History of Jaffna.* Asian Educational Services, New Delhi, Tamil Edition, 1999.

"Sangeetha Abivirithi Sabha." Annual Reports, 1930–2000, Kuala Lumpur.

"Sangeetha Abvirthi Sabha." Diamond Jubilee Souvenir (1923–1983), Kuala Lumpur, 1983.

"Sangeethalayam." Silver Jubilee Souvenir Magazine, 2001, Malaysia.

"Sangeethalayam." Silver Jubilee Souvenir Magazine, 1971–2001, Malaysia.

Saravanamuttu, Manicasothy. *The Sara Saga.* Penang, 1969.

"Sai News." Sathya Sai Baba Centre, Petaling Jaya, June 2001.

"Selangor Ceylon Tamils' Association." Golden Jubilee Souvenir (1900–1950), Malaysia, 1951.

"Selangor Ceylon Tamils' Association." Platinum Jubilee Souvenir, Malaysia, 1972.

"Selangor Cricket Association." 50th Anniversary of Stoner Shield, 1925–1975, Souvenir Programme.

Selvaratnam, Thillaiampalam and Sinnappo Apputhurai. *Legacy of the Pioneers: 125 Years of Jaffna Tamils in Malaysia.* Kuala Lumpur: Thillaiampalam Selvaratnam and Sinnapoo Apputhurai, 2006.

Singam, A. R. *Sixty Years of Soccer by Tamils and Nationals in Malaysia, 1904–1964.* Di-Chetak oleh N. Thamotharam Pillay, 1965.

Singam, S. Durai Raja. *A Hundred Years of Ceylonese in Malaya and Singapore, 1867–1967.* Kuala Lumpur, 1968.

Tanjong Pagar: A Pictorial Journey (1819–1989). Singapore: Tanjong Pagar Citizens' Consultative Committee, c1989.

Tamilan Physical Cultural Association (T.P.C.A.), Golden Jubilee Souvenir, 1914–1964, Malaysia.

Tamilan Physical Cultural Association. Klab Sukan T.P.C.A., Annual General Meeting Report, 2000–2002, Malaysia.

Thambiah, H. W. *The Laws and Customs of the Tamils of Jaffna.* Women's Education & Research Centre, Colombo, Revised Edition, 2001.

Singapore

Amarasuriya, Sunil. Interview by author. Singapore, May 2011.

Arseculeratne, S. N. *Sinhalese Immigrants in Malaysia and Singapore, 1860–1990: History Through Recollections.* K.V.G. De Silva & Sons, Colombo, 1991.

"Back-Ground of Dr. R. Theyvendran, PBM: A Life-Time of Giving." *Stamford Media International.* Online at: http://www.stamford.com.sg/highlight/lifetime.htm

"Be Totally Loyal Call to Ceylon-Tamil Citizens of S'pore." *The Straits Times* (Singapore), September 25, 1972.

Bongso, Ariff. Interview by author (email). Singapore, 2011.

Census of Ceylon, 1946. Colombo: Ceylon. Department of Census and Statistics, 1950–2.

"Ceylon Men for Duties in Malaya." *The Straits Times* (Singapore), July 2, 1947.

"Ceylonese Hold Mass Meeting." *The Straits Times* (Singapore), March 27, 1952.

"Ceylonese Leave Malaya." *The Straits Times* (Singapore), April 22, 1946.

"Ceylonese Reaction to I.N.A." *The Straits Times* (Singapore), June 17, 1946.

"Ceylonese Told: 'Choose Now'" *The Straits Times* (Singapore), January 16, 1951.

"Ceylonese Told: Time to Look for Skilled Work." *The Straits Times* (Singapore), April 6, 1976.

"Colombo to Recognise Nationality: Ceylonese in Malaya." *The Straits Times* (Singapore), November 15, 1949.

Dass, Sulochana. "Sinhalese Jewellers Still Tops in Terms of Craftsmanship and Design." *The Straits Times* (Singapore), December 18, 1987.

"Doing their bit for the Fighting Forces." *The Straits Times* (Singapore), December 14, 1939.

"Far East: Formation of a Ceylonese Labour Force to Replace Japanese Surrendered Personnel in Malaya." Colonies General Supplementary Original Correspondence, 1759–1955. Great Britain, Colonial Office, CO 537/2503, 1947.

"Future of Malayan Ceylonese." *The Straits Times* (Singapore), October 23, 1946.

Gascon, George. "Tribute to 'Father of Pathology', 80." *The Straits Times* (Singapore), April 3, 2001.

Gulam, S. "From Unionist to Businessman: One Man's Road to Success." *The Straits Times* (Singapore), May 1, 2001.

Han, Gabriel Chan Eng. *The Volunteer Corps: Contributions to Singapore's Internal Security and Defence, 1854–1984.* Singapore Command and Staff College, 1990.

"Indian Representation." *The Straits Times* (Singapore), March 12, 1917.

Iswaran, Indra Rani Lavan. *Celebrating 100 Years: The Singapore Ceylon Tamils' Association, Founded 1910.* Singapore Ceylon Tamils' Association, 2010.

Koh, Tommy, Timothy Auger and Jimmy Yap. *Singapore: The Encyclopedia.* Singapore: Editions Didier Millet, 2006.

"Lee's Call to S'pore Ceylon Tamils." *The Straits Times* (Singapore), October 7, 1973.

Long, Susan. "The Multicultural Man." *The Straits Times* (Singapore), February 23, 2006.

Manukularatne, P.L.B. Nirmali. "The Sinhalese in Singapore: Facets of Change and Continuity in Ethnicity." Honours Thesis, National University of Singapore, 1993.

McNair, J.F.A. *Miscellaneous Numerical Returns and Straits Settlements Population.* Singapore, 1871.

Miscellaneous Numerical Returns and Straits Settlements Population, Singapore, 1881.

"More Troops from Ceylon." *The Straits Times* (Singapore), May 18, 1948.

Nathan, J. E. *The Census of British Malaya, 1921.* London: Dunstable and Watford, 1922.

"NUS to Honour Pillay and Ratnam." *The Straits Times* (Singapore), August 16, 1996.

Ong, Y. D. *Buddhism in Singapore: A Short Narrative History.* Singapore: Skylark Publications, c2005.

Pararajasingam, S. "Marriage and Community: The Ceylon Tamils of Malaya – A Study of Relationships and Values Among the Ceylon Tamils in Malaya and Singapore." Honours Thesis, University of Singapore, 1966.

Pek, Sarah Leng Leng. "S. Shan Ratnam." *Singapore Infopedia*, National Library Board, December 24, 2008.

"Petition: Ceylonese Community in Malaya." Straits Settlements Original Correspondence,

1940 to 1946. Great Britain, Colonial Office, CO 273/660/50007/183, 1940.

Pillay, J. Y. Interview by author. Singapore, 2011.

"Raja: Education is the Key for Minorities." *The Straits Times* (Singapore), November 9, 1989.

"Raja's Communal Politics Lesson." *The Straits Times* (Singapore), February 11, 1985.

Rajah, G. "The Ceylon Tamils of Singapore." Honours Thesis, University of Malaya, Singapore, 1958.

Ramasamy, Rajakrishnan. *Sojourners to Citizens: Sri Lankan Tamils in Malaysia 1885–1965*. Kuala Lumpur, 1988.

_____, "Social Change and Group Identity Among the Sri Lankan Tamils." In *Indian Communities in Southeast Asia*, edited by Kernial Singh Sandhu and A. Mani, 541–57. Institute of Southeast Asian Studies, Singapore, 1993.

"Ratnam's World Honour." *The Straits Times* (Singapore), December 30, 1982.

"S'pore Group to Rebuild Sri Lanka Village." *The Straits Times* (Singapore), April 25, 2005.

Sathiaseelan, S. *Malayan Migration and Jaffna Society*. United Kingdom: UK-Ceylon Malaysian Forum, 2007.

"Should the Ceylonese Join the Indians." *The Straits Times* (Singapore), November 27, 1946.

Singam, S. Durai Raja. *A Hundred Years of Ceylonese in Malaysia and Singapore, 1867–1967*. Kuala Lumpur, 1968.

Singapore Census of Population 2000. "Statistical Release 1: Demographic Characteristics, Education, Language and Religion." Department of Statistics, Ministry of Trade and Industry, Republic of Singapore.

Singapore Census of Population 2010. "Statistical Release 1: Demographic Characteristics, Education, Language and Religion." Department of Statistics, Ministry of Trade and Industry, Republic of Singapore.

"Singapore Ceylonese Women War-Workers." *The Straits Times* (Singapore), March 1, 1940.

Sinhalese Buddhist Missionary in South East Asia, 1959–1969. Singapore R. Pwee Kong Joo, 1970.

"Sinhalese want 'Equal Rights' Guarantee." *The Straits Times* (Singapore), May 1, 1946.

Sinnappah, Arasaratnam. *Indians in Malaysia and Singapore*. Oxford University Press (revised edition), Kuala Lumpur, 1979.

Speech by Dr Vivian Balakrishnan, Minister for Community Development, Youth and Sports and Second Minister for Information, Communication and the Arts at the "Singapore Sinhala Association's Dinner and Awards Nite" 21 April 2007, National Archives of Singapore.

Speech by Mr S. Rajaratnam, Senior Minister (Prime Minister Office) on the occasion of the "75th Anniversary celebration of the Singapore Ceylon Tamils' Association" 10 February 1985, National Archives of Singapore.

Sri Pemaloka, Ven. K. *Great Hero: Mahaweera*. Singapore: Mangala Vihara (Buddhist Temple), 2003.

"The 'Jaffna' Aircraft." *The Straits Times* (Singapore), August 24, 1915.

"The Singapore Rifles: How the Ceylon Corps was Organised." *The Straits Times* (Singapore), February 13, 1900.

Thulaja, Naidu Ratnala. "Sri Senpaga Vinayagar Temple." *Singapore Infopedia*, National Library Board, 23 May 2002.

"Trouble if People Do Not Unite as S'poreans: Raja." *The Straits Times* (Singapore), August 10, 1991.

Tufo, M. V. Del. *Malaya, Comprising the Federation of Malaya and the Colony of Singapore: A Report on the 1947 Census of Population*. Singapore: University of Singapore Library, 1975.

"University Fund: Generous Gift from the Ceylonese." *The Straits Times* (Singapore), August 26, 1950.

Vlieland, C. A. *British Malaya (The Colony of the Straits Settlements and the Malay States): A Report on the 1931 Census and on Certain Problems of Vital Statistics*. London: Crown Agents for the Colonies, 1932.

_____, *British Malaya (the Colony of the Straits Settlements and the Malay States): A Report on the 1931 Census and on Certain Problems of Vital Statistics*. Singapore: University of Malaya Library, 1957.

"Why I Would Rather be Called Indian (Letters)." *The Straits Times* (Singapore), October 5, 1991.

Wijeysingha, Eugene and Vincent Wijeysingha. Interview by author. Singapore, May 2011.

Winsley, T. M. *A History of the Singapore Volunteer Corps 1854–1937*. Singapore: Govt. Print. Off., 1938.

"Winslow to Head Board of Legal Education." *The Straits Times* (Singapore), May 22, 1967.

Yogarajah, Yogini. "Unity and Diversity in the Ceylonese Community in Singapore." Honours Thesis, University of Singapore, 1979.

Brunei Darussalam

Hussainmiya, B. A. *Orang Rejimen: The Malays of the Ceylon Rifle Regiment*. Bangi, Universiti Kebangsaan Press, 1991.

Sri Lanka Association of Brunei Darussalam (SLABD), Newsletters, 1997–2009.

Gulf States

Brochmann, Grete. *Middle East Ave: Female Migration from Sri Lanka to the Gulf*. Boulder: Westview Press, 1993.

Chang, Grace. *Disposable Domestics: Immigrant Women Workers in the Global Economy*. South End Press, Cambridge, Mass., 2000.

Constable, Nicole. *Made to Order in Hong Kong: Stories of Migrant Workers*. Cornell University Press, Ithaca, Second Edition, 2007.

_____, *Migrant Workers in Asia: Distant Divides, Intimate Connections*. Routledge, London, 2010.

Ehrenreich, Barbara and Arlie Russell Hochschild, eds. *Global Woman: Nannies, Maids, and Sex Workers in the New Economy*. Henry Holt, New York, 2002.

Flanigan, Shawn Teresa. "Nonprofit Service Provision by Insurgent Organizations: The Cases of Hizballah and the Tamil Tigers." *Studies in Conflict & Terrorism* 31, 6 (2008): 499–519.

Gamburd, Michele. "Advocating for Sri Lankan Migrant Workers: Obstacles and Challenges." *Critical Asian Studies* 41, 1 (2007): 61–88.

_____, *The Kitchen Spoon's Handle: Transnationalism and Sri Lanka's Migrant Housemaids*. Cornell University Press, Ithaca, 2000.

_____, "Milk Teeth and Jet Planes: Kin Relations in Families of Sri Lanka's Transnational Domestic Servants." *City and Society* 20, 1 (2008): 5–31.

Gardner, Andrew. *City of Strangers: Gulf Migration and the Indian Community in Bahrain*. Cornell University Press, Ithaca, 2010.

Hettige, S. T. "Migration to the Middle East, Social Stratification and Social Mobility: Case Studies from Sri Lanka." *Sri Lanka Journal of Social Sciences* 10, 1-2 (1987): 83–120.

_____, "Migration of Sri Lankan Workers to the Middle East - A Sociological Viewpoint." *Sri Lanka Journal of Social Sciences* 11, 1–2 (1988): 79–93.

Huang, Shirlena, Brenda S. A. Yeoh and Noor Abdul Rahman, eds. *Asian Women as Transnational Domestic Workers*. Marshall Cavendish, Singapore, 2005.

Human Rights Watch Report, "As if I Am Not Human: Abuses Against Asian Domestic Workers in Saudi Arabia." New York, 2008.

_____, "Exported and Exposed: Abuses Against Sri Lankan Domestic Workers in Saudi Arabia, Kuwait, Lebanon and the United Arab Emirates." New York, 2007.

Ismail, Munira. "'Maids in Space' Gendered Domestic Labour from Sri Lanka to the Middle East." In *Gender, Migration and Domestic Service*, edited by J. Momsen, 229–41. York: Routledge, 1999.

Jayaweera, Swarna, Malsiri Dias and Leelangi Wanasundera. *Returnee Migrant Women in Two Locations in Sri Lanka*. CENWOR, Colombo, 2002.

Khalaf, Sulayman N. "Gulf Societies and the Image of Unlimited Good." *Dialectical Anthropology* 17, 1 (1992): 53–84.

_____, and Saad Alkobaisi. "Migrants' Strategies of Coping and Patterns of Accommodation in the Oil-Rich Gulf Societies: Evidence from the UAE." *British Journal of Middle Eastern Studies* 26, 2 (1999): 271–98.

Leonard, Karen. "South Asian Workers in the Gulf: Jockeying for Places." In *Globalization under Construction: Governmentality, Law, and Identity*, edited by Richard Warren Perry and Bill

Maurer, 129–70. University of Minnesota Press, Minneapolis, 2003.

Longva, Ahn Nga. *Walls Build on Sand: Migration, Exclusion, and Society in Kuwait.* Westview Press, Boulder, 1997.

Middle East Institute. "Migration and the Gulf." Viewpoints Special Edition, February 2010.

Nagy, Sharon. "Making Room for Migrants, Making Sense of Difference: Spatial and Ideological Expressions of Social Diversity in Urban Qatar." *Urban Studies* 43, 1 (2006): 119–37.

Nichols, Robert. *A History of Pashtun Migration, 1775–2006.* Oxford University Press, Oxford, 2008.

Parrenas, Rhacel Salazar. *Servants of Globalization: Women, Migration, and Domestic Work.* Stanford University Press, Stanford, 2001.

Shaw, Judith. "From Kuwait to Korea: The Diversification of Sri Lankan Labour Migration." *Journal of the Asia Pacific Economy* 15, 1 (2010): 59–70.

Sri Lankan Bureau of Foreign Employment (SLBFE), "Annual Statistical Report of Foreign Employment 2009." Battaramula, Sri Lanka, 2010.

Thangarajah, C. "Veiled Constructions: Conflict, Migration and Modernity in Eastern Sri Lanka." *Contributions to Indian Sociology* 37, 1-2 (2003): 141–62.

Wanasundera, Leelangi. *Migrant Women Domestic Workers: Cyprus, Greece and Italy.* Colombo, CENWOR, 2001.

Weerakoon, Nedra. "Sri Lanka: A Caste Study of International Female Labour Migration." In *Legal Protection for Asian Women Migrant Workers: Strategies for Action,* edited by Maria Amparita S. Sta (et. al.), 97–118. Ateneo Human Rights Center, Makati City, Philippines, 1998.

United States of America

Cadge, Wendy. *Heartwood: The First Generation of Theravada Buddhism in America.* Chicago: The University of Chicago Press, 2005. Online at: http://www.sangam.org/articles/view2/?uid=1136

"Canada and Terrorism." *Anti-Defamation League,* January 2004. Online at: http://archive.adl.org/terror/tu/tu_0401_canada.asp

Dissanayake, Malathie P. "A Comparative Investigation of the Self Image and Identity of Sri Lankans in Sri Lanka and in North America." M.A., West Chester University, 2006.

Fair, Christine C. "Diasporic Involvement in Insurgencies: Insights from the Khalistan and Tamil Eelam Movements." *Nationalism and Ethnic Politics* 11, 1 (2005): 125–156.

Gamage, Daya. "How Tamil Tigers Increased their Influence in U.S. under Professional Sri Lankan Diplomats in Washington." *Asian Tribune,* August 10, 2008.

_____, 'Sri Lankan Expatriate Rally in Washington Airs Plight of Tamil Civilians Trapped by LTTE', *Asian Tribune,* February 22, 2009.

_____, "Globalization of Sri Lanka Issues: Minister Peiris Versus 'The Rest'" *Asian Tribune,* June 4, 2010.

Laura, Rozen. "Interview with Sri Lanka's FM." *Politico.com,* May 27, 2010.

Mendis, Patrick. "The Washington and Beijing Consensus in South Asia: How the Colombo Consensus Emerged with New Global Realities." Paper Presented at the Sixth International Conference on South Asia, Institute of South Asian Studies, National University of Singapore, 10-12 November 2010.

Numrich, Paul David. *Old Wisdom in the New World. Americanization in Two Immigrant Theravada Buddhist Temples.* Knoxville: The University of Knoxville Press, 1996.

Prebish, Charles S. *Luminous Passage. The Practice and Study of Buddhism in America.* Berkeley: University of California Press, 1999.

Srikandarajah, Dhananjayan. "Tamil Diaspora Politics." In *Encyclopedia of Diasporas: Immigrant and Refugee Cultures Around the World,* edited by Melvin Ember, Carol R. Ember and Ian A. Skoggard, 492–99. Springer, New York, 2005.

"Sri Lanka: Re-charting U.S. Strategy After the War", *Committee on Foreign Relations United States Senate,* U. S. Government Printing Office, Washington, D.C., 7 December 2009.

United Nations High Commissioner for Refugees (UNHCR), 'Statistics and Operational Data', 2011.

United States Census Bureau, 'American Fact Finder', 2011.

Wuthnow, Robert and Wendy Cadge. "Buddhists and Buddhism in the United States: The Scope of Influence." *Journal for the Scientific Study of Religion* 43, 3 (2004): 361–78.

Canada

Abrahams, Caryl and Lisa Steven. "Self-Perceived Success of Adjustment by Sri Lankan Immigrants in Metropolitan Toronto: A Preliminary Report." *Polyphony* 12 (1990): 30–34.

Aiken, Sharryn J. "National Security and Canadian Immigration: Deconstructing the Discourse of Trade- Offs." In *Les Migrations Internationals Contemporaines: Une Dynamique Complexe au Coeur de la Globalisation,* edited by F. Crépeau, 172–99. Presses de l'Université de Montréal, Montreal, 2009.

Amarasingam, Amarnath. "Religion and Ethnicity Among Sri Lankan Tamil Youth in Ontario." *Canadian Ethnic Studies* 40, 2 (2008): 149–69.

Aruliah, Arul S. "Accepted on Compassionate Grounds: An Admission Profile of Tamil Immigrants in Canada." *Refuge: Canada's Periodical on Refugees* 14, 4 (1994): 10–14.

Besseling, Dave. "Toronto Eelam." *HIMAL South Asia.* October 2009.

Buchignanani, Norman, Doreen Marie Indra and Ram Srivastiva. *Continuous Journey: A Social History of South Asians in Canada.* McClelland and Steward Ltd, Toronto, 1985.

Chandrasekere, Sarath. "Inventing the Sri Lankans: Construction of Ethnic Identity by Immigrants to Ontario." Ph.D. diss., University of Toronto, 2008.

Cheran, Rudhramoorthy. *The Sixth Genre: Memory, History and the Tamil Diaspora Imagination.* Marga Institute, Colombo, 2002.

_____, "Diaspora Circulation and Transationalism as Agents for Change in the Post Conflict Zones of Sri Lanka." Berghof Foundation for Conflict Management, Berlin, Germany, 2004.

_____, "Multiple Home and Parallel Civil Societies." *Refuge: Canada's Periodical on Refugees* 23, 1 (2006): 4–8.

_____, "Transnationalism, Development and Social Capital: Tamil Community Networks in Canada." In *Organizing the Transnational: Experiences of Asian and Latin American Migrants in Canada,* edited by Luin Goldring and Sailajah Krishnamurti, 277–305. UBC Press, Vancouver, 2007.

_____, ed. *Pathways of Dissent: Tamil Nationalism in Sri Lanka.* Sage Publications, London, 2009.

_____, and S. Guruge, eds. *Beyond Nations: Diasporas, Transnationalism and Global Engagement.* Colombo: ICES, 2010.

Citizenship and Immigration Canada. Recent Immigrants in Metropolitan Areas: Canada-A Comparative Profile Based on the 2001 Census.

Coomarasamy, Sudha. "Sri Lankan Tamil Women: Resettlement in Montreal." *Canadian Women Studies* 10, 1 (1989): 69–72.

Coward, Harold. "The Religions of the South Asian Diaspora in Canada." In *A New Handbook of Living Religions,* edited by John Hinnells, 775–95. Oxford, Cambridge, Mass.: Blackwell, 1997.

_____, John Hinnells and Raymond Brady Williams, eds. *The South Asian Religious Diaspora in Britain, Canada, and the United States.* Albany, NY: State University of New York Press, 2000.

Das, Sonia Neela. "Between Text and Talk: Expertise, Normativity, and Scales of Belonging in the Montreal Tamil Diasporas." Ph.D. diss., University of Michigan, 2008a.

_____, "Between Convergence and Divergence: Reformatting Language Purism in the Montreal Tamil Diasporas." *Journal of Linguistic Anthropology* 18, 1 (2008b): 1–23.

De Silva, Samangi Narmada. "The Contested Terrain of Citizenship and Exclusion in Canada: Sri Lankan Women's Narrative Accounts of School and Social Experience in the Diaspora." M.A., University of Toronto (Canada), 2003.

Hyndman, J. "Aid, Conflict and Migration: The Canada-Sri Lanka Connection." *Canadian Geographer-Geographe Canadien* 47, 3 (2003): 251–68.

Israel, M., ed. *The South Asian Diaspora in Canada: Six Essays.* The Multicultural History Society of Ontario, Toronto, 1987.

Kandasamy, Balagouri Vicky. "Findings on the Tamil Community City of York." York Community Services, 1995.

Kendall, Perry Robert William. "The Sri Lankan Tamil Community in Toronto." City of Toronto Department of Public Health, Health Promotion and Advocacy Section, 1989.

La, John. "Forced Remittances in Canada's Tamil Enclaves." *Peace Review* 16, 3 (2004): 379–85.

Lahneman, William J. "Impact of Diaspora Communities on National and Global Politic: Report on Survey of the Literature." CIA Strategic Assessment Group, Centre for International and Security Studies at Maryland (CISSM), University of Maryland, 5 July 2005.

Lal, Brij V., Peter Reeves and Rajesh Rai, eds. *The Encyclopedia of the Indian Diaspora*. Singapore: Editions Didier Millet, 2006.

Magocsi, Paul R. *Encyclopedia of Canada's Peoples*. Multicultural History Society of Ontario, Toronto, 1999.

Manogaran, Chelvadurai and Bryan Pfaffenberger. *Sri Lankan Tamils: Ethnicity and Identity*. Westview Press, Boulder, Colo, 1994.

McDonough, Sheila, and Homa Hoodfar. "Muslims in Canada: From Ethnic Groups to Religious Community." In *Religion and Ethnicity in Canada*, edited by Paul Bramadat and David Seljak, 133–53. Pearson Education Canada, 2005.

McLellan, Janet. *Many Petals of the Lotus: Five Asian Buddhist Communities in Toronto*. University of Toronto Press, 1999.

Moghissi, Haideh, Saeed Rahnema and Mark J. Goodman. *Diaspora by Design: Muslim Immigrants in Canada and Beyond*. University of Toronto Press, Toronto, 2009.

Naidoo, J. C. "South Asian Canadian Women: A Contemporary Portrait." *Psychology and Developing Societies* 15, 1 (2003): 51–67.

Nanayakkara, Sanjaya. "The Sinhala Transnational Community in Canada." In *Beyond Nations: Diasporas, Transnationalism and Global Engagement*, edited by R. Cheran and S. Guruge. Colombo: ICES, 2010.

"Recent Immigrants in Metropolitan Areas: Canada - A Comparative Profile Based on the 2001 Census." In *Citizenship and Immigration Canada*. Strategic Research and Statistics in Collaboration with Informetrica Limited, Government of Canada, 2001.

Sekar, Radhika. "Global Reconstruction of Hinduism: A Case Study of Sri Lankan Tamils in Canada." Ph.D diss., University of Ottawa, Canada, 2001.

Statistics Canada, *Home Language and Mother Tongue*, Ottawa, 1992.

Sugunasiri, Suwanda, H. J. "'Sri Lankan' Canadian Poets: The Bourgeoisie That Fled The Revolution." *Canadian Literature* 132 (Spring 1992): 60–79.

Tambiah, Stanley Jeyaraja. *Sri Lanka: Ethnic Fratricide and the Dismantling of Democracy*. University of Chicago Press, 1986.

"Thamilar Thagaval, 21st Anniversary Issue - Tamil's Information." Ealam Thamil Information Centre (ETHIC), Toronto, 2012.

Vimalarajah, Luxshi, and Rudhramoorthy Cheran. "Empowering Diasporas: The Dynamics of Post-war Transnational Tamil Diaspora." Berghof Occasional Paper No 31, Berghof Conflict Research, Berlin, 2010.

Wayland, Sarah. "Immigration and Transnational Political Ties: Croatians and Sri Lankan Tamils in Canada." *Canadian Ethnic Studies* 35, 2 (2003): 61–85.

_____, "Ethnonationalist Networks and Transnational Opportunities: The Sri Lankan Tamil Diaspora." *Review of International Studies* 30 (2004): 405–26.

_____, "Transnational Nationalism: Sri Lankan Tamils in Canada." In *Organizing the Transnational: Labour, Politics and Social Change*, edited by Lucin Goldring and Sailaja Krishnamurti. UBC Press, 2007.

William, J. Lahneman. *Impact of Diaspora Communities on National and Global Politics*. Report on Survey of the Literature, 2005.

Wong, Lloyd L. "Transnationalism, Diaspora Communities and Changing Identities: Implications for Canadian Citizenship." In *Street Protest and Fantasy Parks: Globalization, Culture and the State*, edited by David R. Cameron and Janice Gross Stein, 49–87. UBC Press, Vancouver, 2002.

Zulfika, Sithy F. "Sri Lankan Muslim in Canada." In *Beyond Nations: Diasporas, Transnationalism and Global Engagement*, edited by R. Cheran and S. Guruge. Colombo: ICES, 2010.

United Kingdom

Ali, N., V. S. Kalra and S. Sayyid, eds. *A Postcolonial People: South Asians in Britain*. New York: Columbia University Press, 2008.

Alles, Vijitha. "The Phoenix: The Remarkable Story of the Rise and Rise of the Extraordinary Sir Christopher Ondaatje." *UK Lanka Times* 7, 2007: 18–23.

Amsa, P. M. Acting High Commissioner of Sri Lanka. Interview by the author, June 2011.

"Arson Attack of Kingsbury Buddhist Temple." *Daily Mirror*, January 6, 2009.

Bald, Sureth Renjen. "Negotiating Identity in the Metropolis: Generational Differences in South Asian British Fiction." In *Writing Across Worlds: Literature and Migration*, edited by Russell King, John Connell and Paul White, 70–88. London; New York: Routledge, 1995.

"Born Abroad: An Immigration Map of Britain." *BBC News*, United Kingdom. Online at: http://news.bbc.co.uk/1/shared/spl/hi/uk/05/born_abroad/countries/html/sri_lanka.stm

"Buddhist Monk Honoured by Her Majesty the Queen Elizabeth II." Online at: http://homepage.ntlworld.com/ssibc/Head.htm

Christopher Ondaatje. Online at http://www.ondaatje.com/author.htm

Cochrane, Feargal, Bahar Baser and Ashok Swain. "Home Thoughts from Abroad: Diasporas and Peace-Building in Northern Ireland and Sri Lanka." *Studies in Conflict and Terrorism* 32, 8 (2009): 681–704.

Cowley-Sathiakumar, Shanthini Rebecca. "The Sri Lankan Tamils: A Comparative Analysis of the Experiences of the Second Generation in the UK and Sri Lanka." Ph.D. diss., University of Leeds, 2008.

Daniel, E. Valentine. *Charred Lullabies: Chapters in an Anthropography of Violence*. Princeton, N.J.: Princeton University Press, 1996.

Deegalle, Mahinda. "Sri Lankan Theravada Buddhism in London: Religiosity and Communal Activities of a Diaspora Community." *Studies in the History of Religions* 101 (2004) 52–76.

_____, ed. *Dharma to the UK: A Centennial Celebration of Buddhist Legacy*. London: World Buddhist Foundation, 2008.

_____, "Multi-faceted Theravada Buddhism in the United Kingdom." In *Buddhism, Buddhists and Buddhist Studies*, edited by Hari Shankar Shukla and Lalji Shravak, 37–57. Delhi: Buddhist World Press, 2012.

Fernando, Thilak S. "Sri Lankan Restaurants in London." Online at: http://www.infolanka.com/org/diary/71.html

Fernando, Tilak S. "Face 2 Face with Tissa Madawela." *Swadheena* 1, 9 (January 2005): 15.

Geaves, Ron. *The Community of the Many Names of God: Sampradaya Construction in a Global Diaspora or New Religious Movement*. London: Equinox, 2007.

"Girl, Five, Shot in Stockwell: 'Target' Contacts Police." *BBC News*, United Kingdom, March 30, 2011.

Guruge, Ananda W. P., ed. *Return to Righteousness: A Collection of Speeches, Essays and Letters of the Anagarika Dharmapala*. Colombo: Ministry of Educational and Cultural Affairs, 1965.

"Highgate Hill Murugan Temple." Online at: http://www.highgatehillmurugan.org/index.html

Herbert, Joanna. *Negotiating Boundaries in the City: Migration, Ethnicity, and Gender in Britain*. Ashgate Publishing, Ltd., 2008.

"Hunger Strike." *Daily Mirror*, November 17, 2008.

"International Buddha Procession." *Newslanka*, March 1, 2001.

"Jaffna Hindu College Old Boys Association." Online at: http:// http://www.jhc-oba.org.uk/

Jazeel, Tariq. "Postcolonial Geographies of Privilege: Diaspora Space, The Politics of Personhood and The 'Sri Lankan Women's Association in the UK'" *Transactions of Institute of British Geographers* 31, 1 (2006): 19–33.

Kirk, Tristan. "Sinhalese Chicken Shops under Attack." *This is Local London*, May 25, 2009.

"London Buddhist Vihara." Online at: http://www.londonbuddhistvihara.org/

"London Buddhist Vihara Vesak 2008." Online at: http://www.youtube.com/watch?v=ZK2V-GTpP4g&feature=related

"London Eating: Prince of Ceylon." Online at: http://www.london-eating.co.uk/3044.htm

"London Kingsbury 2011 Bakmaha Ulela (Sinhala New Year)' - Part 1." Online at: http://www.youtube.com/watch?v=E15INzU57pM&feature=related

"London Kingsbury Vesak 2008 – Part 1." Online at: http://www.youtube.com/watch?v=c8v1-vLJT1Y

Maheesha, Kottegoda. "'Christmas, Vesak': Celebration of Cultural Contradiction." *Swadheena* 1, 1 (April 2004): 22.

MIGHEALTHNET. "Asian Migrants in the UK - including the Chinese, Indians and Pakistanis." Online at: http://mighealth.net/uk/index.php/Asian_Migrants_in_the_UK-including_the_Chinese,_Indians_and_Pakistanis

Mubarak, Fathima Fatheena. "Tradition and Modernity: A Sociological Comparison between Sri Lankan Muslim Women in Colombo and London in the Late 1990s." Ph.D. diss., London School of Economics and Political Science, University of London, 2003.

"Nari Bena" and "Kamare Pore" at the Commonwealth Institute, *Newslanka*, March 1, 2001: 12.

President and Secretary of the Sri Lanka Muslim Cultural Centre (UK). Interview by the author, 2011.

Office for National Statistics, United Kingdom. Online at: http://www.statistics.gov.uk/statbase/Expodata/Spreadsheets/D6588.xls

"Ranaviruwo", *Voice of Lanka*, August 2000: 9.

Robinson, Vaughan. *Transients, Settlers and Refugees: Asians in Britain*. Oxford University Press, 1986.

"Sambuddha Jayanti", *Newslanka*, June 9, 2011: 16–17.

"Save our Shambo! Hindus to Form Human Chain to Save Sacred Welsh Bull from Slaughter." *Daily Mail*, United Kingdom, May 9, 2007.

Shah, Prakash Amritlal. *Refugees, Race and the Legal Concept of Asylum in Britain*. London: Cavendish Publishing Ltd., 2000.

"Shambo is Removed for Slaughter." *BBC News*, United Kingdom, July 26, 2007.

"Sir Christopher Ondaatje has Moved to London and Given Away Millions: Is a Little Respect Too Much to Ask for?" *The Daily Telegraph*. Online at: http://www.rootsweb.ancestry.com/~lkawgw/chrisond.html

Skanda Vale: The Community of the Many Names of God. Online at: http://www.skandavale.org/

Sky High Live Band. Online at: http://www.skyhighband.co.uk

Slivarrrow – For UK Sri Lankans. Online at http://www.silvarrow.com

"Spreading the Message: Meet the Sri Lankan who's Taking the Message of the Buddha to the British Military." *The Lanka Times: UK Sri Lankan Business and Community* 7, 2007: 36–38.

Sri Lanka Islamic Forum UK. Online at: http://slif.org.uk

Sri Lankan Artiste Visharada Nanda Malini for "Sravana Aradhana," *Newslanka*, April 3rd, 2008: 19–25.

Sri Lankan Radio. Online at: http://www.srilankanradio.co.uk/

Sri Saddhatissa International Buddhist Centre. Online at: http://www.ssibc.org.uk/

"Sweet Tooth Trade." *The Lanka Times: UK Sri Lankan Business and Community* 3, 2008: 64–65.

Taylor, Donald Alastair. "The Symbolic Construction of the Sri Lankan Hindu Tamil Community in Britain." Ph.D. diss., School of Oriental and African Studies, University of London, 1994.

Thames Buddhist Vihara. Online at: http://www.thamesbuddhistvihara.org/

The Sekara Restaurant: Specialists in Authentic Sri Lankan Cuisine. Online at: http://www.sekara.co.uk/html/sekara_home.html

van Hear, Nicholas, Frank Pieke and Steven Vertovec. "The Contribution of UK-Based Diasporas to Development and Poverty Reduction." A Report for the Department for International Development (DFID), April 2004.

The Netherlands

Brohier, Richard Leslie. *Links Between Sri Lanka and the Netherlands: A Book of Dutch Ceylon*. Netherlands Alumni Association of Lanka, Den Haag, 1978.

Central Bureau of Statistics (CBS), *Statline*, The Hague, 2011.

Coolhaas, W. Philippus and G. J. Schutte. *A Critical Survey of Studies on Dutch Colonial History*. Den Haag: Martinus Nijhoff, 1980.

Gaastra, Femme S. *The Dutch East India Company, Expansion and Decline*. Walburg Pers, Zutphen, 2003.

Goor, Jurrien van. *Jan Kompenie as Schoolmaster. Dutch Education in Ceylon 1690–1796*. Groningen, 1979.

Heintze, M. *Tamils in Nederland*. Amsterdam : J. Mets, 1985.

Jongens, E. *Het Nederlands-Ceylonese erfgoed*. Den Haag: Stichting Nederland-Sri Lanka, 2002.

Ramerini, Marco. "The Dutch Burghers of Ceylon." *Colonialvoyage.com*. Online at: http://www.colonialvoyage.com/eng/asia/sri_lanka/burghers.html

Rath, J. "Political Action of Immigrants in the Netherlands: Class or Ethnicity." *European Journal of Political Research* 16 (1988): 623.

van Gelder, Han. *Asielzoekers in Nederland*. Amsterdam: J. Mets, 1993.

van der Burg, C. J. G. "The Hindu Diaspora in the Netherlands: Halfway Between Local Structures and Global Ideologies." In *South Asians in the Diaspora: Histories and Religious Traditions*, edited by Knut A. Jacobsen, and Kumar P. Pratap. Leiden; Boston: Brill, c2004.

Verhallen, Tessa. "Between Bollywood and Suicide: A Case Study on the Limitations of Dutch Tamils' Integration Processes in the Netherlands." Master's Thesis, Radboud University Nijmegen, 2008.

Wagenaar, Lodewijk. *Galle VOC-vestiging in Ceylon. Beschrijving van een koloiale samenleving aan de vooravond van de Singalese opstand tegen het Nederlandse gezag, 1760*. Amsterdam: de Bataafsche Leeuw, 1994.

France

Bouillier, Véronique. "Interaction entre les institutions judiciaires françaises et les communautés sri-lankaises. Des affaires familiales en cour d'assises en région parisienne." *Hommes et Migrations* N°1291 (mai-juin 2011): 52–61.

Dequirez, Gaëlle. "Tamouls sri-lankais. Le Little Jaffna de La Chapelle." *Hommes et migrations* 1268-1269 (2007): 82–91.

_____, "Nationalisme à longue distance et mobilisations politiques en diaspora: le mouvement séparatiste tamoul en France, 1980–2009." Ph.D Thèse, Université de Lille 2, 2011a.

_____, "L'histoire de Sri Lanka vue par les associations nationalistes tamoules en France." *Hommes et Migrations* N°1291 (mai-juin 2011b): 72–81.

_____, "Les mobilisations politiques transnationales de la diaspora tamoule." In *Les communautés tamoules et le conflit sri lankais*, edited by Delon Madavan, Gaëlle Dequirez and Eric Meyer, 153–72. Paris, L'Harmattan, 2011c.

Etiemble, Angelina. *Les ressorts de la diaspora tamoule en France: associations, medias, politique*. Rennes, Aderiem/Mire, 2001.

Gazagne, Philippe. "Les Tamouls de La Chapelle. Entre solidarité et dependence." *Hommes et Migrations* N°1291 (mai-juin 2011): 82–93.

Goreau-Ponceaud, Anthony. "L'immigration sri-lankaise en France: Trajectoires, contours et perspectives." *Hommes et Migrations* N°1291 (mai-juin 2011): 26–39.

_____, "La diaspora tamoule: lieux et territoires en Ile de France." *L'espace politique* 4 (2008): 21–35.

_____, "La diaspora tamoule, trajectoires spatio-temporelles et inscriptions territoriales en Ile de France." Ph.D. Thèse, University Bordeaux 3, 2008.

_____, "Visibilité et mobilisation politique: quand diaspora rime avec reconnaissance." In *Les communautés tamoules et le conflit sri lankais*, edited by Delon Madavan, Gaëlle Dequirez and Eric Meyer, 127–52. Paris, L'Harmattan, 2011.

Madavan, Delon, Gaëlle Dequirez and Eric Meyer, eds. *Les communautés tamoules et le conflit sri lankais*. Paris, L'Harmattan, 2011.

Mantovan, Giacomo. "Faire parler: réflexions autour de l'écriture des récits de vie pour la demande d'asile des Tamouls sri lankais." In *Les communautés tamoules et le conflit sri lankais*, edited by Delon Madavan, Gaëlle Dequirez and Eric Meyer, 183–212. Paris, L'Harmattan, 2011.

_____, "Les récits de vie des demandeurs d'asile tamouls: Vers une mémoire collective?" *Hommes et Migrations* N°1291 (mai-juin 2011): 40–51.

Meyer, Eric. "Migrations sri lankaises. Origines et étapes." *Hommes et Migrations* N°1291 (mai-juin 2011): 12–21.

Robuchon, Gérard, Marie Percot and Andrea Tribess. *Tamouls sri lankais en France*. Rapport pour le Ministère de la Ville et des Affaires Sociales, Paris, 1995.

Sri Lanka & Diasporas: Observatoire Pluridisciplinaire. Online at: http://slkdiaspo. hypotheses.org

Tison, Brigitte. "Les mineurs et les jeunes majeurs isolés venus de Sri Lanka:Le traumatisme de l'exil." *Hommes et Migrations* N°1291 (mai-juin 2011): 62–71.

Germany

Alex, Gabriele. "Integration und Parallelgesellschaften am Beispiel von Tamilen." In *masala.de: Menschen aus Südasien in Deutschland*, edited by Christiane Brosius and Urmila Goel, 16–26. Heidelberg: Draupadi, 2006.

Baumann, Martin. *Deutsche Buddhisten. Geschichte und Gemeinschaften*. Marburg: Diagonal-Verlag, 1995.

_____, *Migration-Religion-Integration. Buddhistische Vietnamesen und hinduistische Tamilen in Deutschland*. Marburg: Dialognal-Verlag, 2000.

_____, and Kurt Salentin. "Migrant Religiousness and Social Incorporation: Tamil Hindus from Sri Lanka in Germany." *Journal of Contemporary Religion* 21, 3 (2006): 297–323.

Baumann, Martin. Brigitte Luchesi and Annette Wilke, eds. *Tempel und Tamilien in zweiter Heimat. Hindus aus Sri Lanka im deutschsprachigen und skandinavischen Raum*. Würzburg: Ergon, 2003.

Hecker, Hellmuth. *Buddhismus in Deutschland. Eine Chronik*. Hamburg: Deutsche Buddhistische Union, 1973.

Luchesi, Brigitte. "Leaving Invisibility: The Establishment of Hindu Tamil Religiosity in German Public Space." *New Kolam* 9 and 10 (2004).

_____, "Parading Hindu Gods in Public: New Festival Traditions of Tamil Hindus in Germany." In *South Asian Religions on Display: Religious Processions in South Asia and in the Diaspora*, edited by Knut A. Jacobsen. London: Routledge, 2008a.

_____, "Seeking the Blessing of the Consolatrix Afflictorum: The Annual Pilgrimage of Sri Lankan Tamils to the Madonna in Kevelaer (Germany)." In *South Asian Christian Diaspora: Invisible Diaspora in Europe and North America*, edited by Knut A. Jacobsen and Selva J. Raj, 75–96. Surrey, England; Burlington, VT: Ashgate, 2008b.

_____, "Immigrant Hinduism in Germany: Tamils from Sri Lanka and their Temples." The Pluralism Project, Harvard University.

Statistisches Bundesamt (German Federal Statistical Office), "Ausländische Bevölkerung," FS 1, R 1, 2010. Online at: http://www.destatis.de/jetspeed/portal /cms/Sites/destatis/Internet/DE/Content/Publikationen/Fachveröffentlichungen/Bevoelkerung/MigrationIntegration

Wilke, Annette. "Tamil Hindu Temple Life in Germany: Competing and Complimentary Modes in Reproducing Cultural Identity, Globalized Ethnicity, and Expansion of Religious Markets." In *Religious Pluralism in the Diaspora*, edited by Pratap P. Kumar, 235–68. Leiden; Boston: Brill, 2006.

Switzerland

Baumann, Martin. "Buddhism in Switzerland." *Journal of Global Buddhism* 1 (2000): 154–59.

_____, "Templeisation: Continuity and Change of Hindu Traditions in Diaspora." *Journal of Religion in Europe* 2 (2009a): 149–79.

_____, "Temples, Cuppolas, Minarets: Public Space as Contested Terrain in Contemporary Switzerland." *ReligioStudie* 17, 2 (2009b): 141–52.

_____, Brigitte Luchesi, Annette Wilke and Peter Schalk, eds. *Tempel und Tamilen in zweiter Heimat. Hindus aus Sri Lanka im deutschsprachigen und skandinavischen Raum*. Würzburg: Ergon Verlag, 2003.

Beaumont, Adam. "Some Religion are more Welcome than Others." *swissinfo.ch*, International Service of the Swiss Broadcasting Corporation, August 20, 2007.

Bovay, Claude. "Eidgenössische Volkszählung 2000: Religionslandschaft in der Schweiz." Federal Office of Statistics, Neuchâtel: Federal Office of Statistics, 2004.

Castles, Stephen and Mark J. Miller. *The Age of Migration: International Population Movements in the Modern World*. Palgrave Macmillan, London, 2003.

Doole, Claire. "Switzerland Asked to Probe Tamil Groups." *BBC News South Asia*, July 14, 2000.

Eulberg, Rafaela. "Hindu-Traditionen in der Schweiz." In *Handbuch der Religionen*, edited by Michael Klöcker and Udo Tworuschka. München, Germany: 19 Ergänzungslieferung, OlzogVerlag, 2008.

Ganesh, Kamala. "Diaspora, A Mirror to Indian Diversity? Caste, Brahmanism and the New Diaspora." In *Diversities in the Indian Diaspora: Nature, Implications and Responses*, edited by N. Jayaram. Oxford University Press, Delhi, 2011.

_____, "No Shri Ram in Lanka: Hinduism, Hindutva and Diasporic Tamils in Exile." In *Journal of the Asiatic Society of Mumbai*, edited by Arvind Jamkhedkar, N.B. Patil and K. Sankaranarayanan, Vol. 85, 2013 (forthcoming).

Guha, Ramachandra. "Tigers in the Alps." *World Policy Journal* 20, 4 (2003): 63–74.

"Hindu Tempel in Bern-Bethlehem." *Schweizer Radio und Fernsehen* (SRF), July 16, 1994.

Online at: http://www.videoportal.sf.tv/video?id=0c35add2-ef89-41ce-ae00-c04fd8cf87a9

"Independent Tamil Eelam Flag Hoisted in Switzerland." *Asian Tribune*, June 12, 2007.

Kailasapathy, K. "Cultural and Linguistic Consciousness of the Tamil Community." In *Ethnicity and Social Change in Sri Lanka*, edited by the Social Scientists Association. Colombo: The Social Scientists Association, 1984.

Lüthi, Damaris. *SozialeBeziehungen und WerteimExilbewahren: TamilischeFluechtlingeaus Sri Lanka imRaum*. Bern: Arbeitsblatt No.30, Arbeitsblatter des Institutes fur Ethnologie, 2005.

_____, "Perpetuating Religious and Social Concepts in the Extended Motherland: Tamil Christians in Berne (Switzerland)." In *South Asian Christian Diaspora: Invisible Diaspora in Europe and North America*, edited by Knut A. Jacobsen and Selva J. Raj, 97–116. Surrey, England; Burlington, VT: Ashgate, 2008.

MacNamee, Terence. "Swiss Tamils Look to the Future." *swissinfo.ch*, June 4, 2010.

Marschall, Wolfgang, Damaris Lüthi, Marie-Anne Fankhauser and Johanna Vögeli. *Social Change Among Sri Lankan Tamil Refugees in Switzerland*. Project by InstitutfürSozialanthropologie, Universitat Bern funded by Swiss National Science Foundation, 2003.

McDowell, Christopher. *A Tamil Asylum Diaspora: Sri Lankan Migration, Settlement and Politics in Switzerland*. Berghahn, Oxford, 1996.

_____, "The Point of No Return: The Politics of the Swiss Tamil Repatriation Agreement." In *The End of the Refugee Cycle?: Refugee Repatriation and Reconstruction*, edited by Richard Black and Khalid Khoser, 126–41. New York: Berghahn Books, 1999.

_____, "An Asylum Diaspora: Tamils in Switzerland." In *Encyclopedia of Diasporas Immigrant and Refugee Cultures Around the World*, Part Two: Topics - Types of Diasporas, edited by C. Ember, M. Ember and I. Skoggard. Kluwer, Yale, 2005.

Moret, Joëlle, Denise Efionayi-Mäder and Fabienne Stants. *Diaspora Sri Lankaise en Suisse*. Berne, Office Fédéral des Migrations, 2006.

_____, *Die srilankische Diaspora in der Schweiz*. Bern: Federal Office for Migration, 2007. Online at: http://www.bfm.admin.ch/content/dam/data/migration/publikationen/diasporastudie-srilanka-d.pdf

Nissan, E. and R. L. Stirrat. "The Generation of Communal Identities." In *Sri Lanka: History and the Roots of Conflict*, edited by Jonathan Spencer. Routledge, New York, 1990.

Slater, Julia. "Swiss Tamil Meets Integration Challenges." *swissinfo.ch*, January 30, 2008.

Sriskandarajah, Dhananjayan. "The Migration-Development Nexus: Sri Lanka Case Study." *International Migration* 40 (2002): 284–307.

"Suspected Tamil Tiger Members Held in Switzerland." *BBC News South Asia*, January 12, 2011.

"Swiss Tamil Look to Preserve their Culture." *swissinfo.ch*, February 18, 2006.

Tamil Education Services Switzerland. www. tamilschool.ch.

"Tamil Speaking Political Parties Conference in Switzerland." *Tamilnet.com*, November 25, 2009.

"Tamile in der Schweiz." *Migros-Magazin*, 35 (2006): 14–17. Online at: http://www. graubuenden.ch/fileadmin/user_upload/winter/ schlitteln/geschichte_peist_schlitten.pdf

"Tamilische Asylbewerber." *Schweizer Radio und Fernsehen* (SRF), March 12, 1984. Online at: http://www.videoportal.sf.tv/video?id=fb0a170c-ffad-492d-ad06-3fd5764d0969

"The Sri Lankan Tamil Diaspora after the LTTE." *International Crisis Group*, Asia Report N°186, February 23, 2010.

"Tigers Slipped into Switzerland through the Backdoors." *Asian Tribune*, June 3, 2007.

Tonkin, Samantha and Joanne Shields. "Conflicting Sri Lankan Sides Meet in Switzerland." *swissinfo.ch*, September 9, 2003.

Vertovec, Steven. "Migrant Transnationalism and Modes of Transformation." In *Rethinking Migration: New Theoretical and Empirical Perspectives*, edited by Alejandro Portes and Josh DeWind. Berghahn, Oxford, 2007.

Vimalarajah, Luxshi and Rudhramoorthy Cheran. "Empowering Diasporas: The Dynamics of Post-war Transnational Tamil Diaspora." Berghof Occasional Paper No 31, Berghof Conflict Research, Berlin, 2010.

Vogeli, J. "Ohnesaktiist Siva nichts: TamilischeGeschiechterbeziehngen in der Schweiz." Arneitsblat 28, Bern: Institutfur Ethnologie, 2006.

Warnapala, W. W. A. *The Sri Lankan Political Scene*. Navrang Press, New Delhi, 1993.

Italy

Arkadie, Alex Van. "Sri Lankan Migrants in Italy." 2011. Online at: http://burgherwrite.blogspot. sg/p/academic-writing.html

Balding, John William. *One Hundred Years in Ceylon, or, the Centenary Volume of the Church Missionary Society in Ceylon, 1818–1918*. Madras: Diocesan Press, 1922.

Henayaka, Ranjith and Miriam Lambusta. "The Sri Lankan Diaspora in Italy." Berghof Research Center for Conflict Management, Berlin, 2004.

"Indo-Roman Coins Found in Ceylon." *The Ceylon Coin Web*. Online at: http://ceylonweb. tripod.com./Roman.htm

Moule, A. C., and Paul Pelliot. *Marco Polo: The Description of the World*. Ishi Press, 2010.

Sivasupramaniam, V. "History of the Tamil Diaspora." Online at: http://murugan.org/ research/sivasupramaniam.htm

Sri Kantha, Sachi. "Marco Polo's Visit to Medieval Eelam." Online at: http://www.sangam.org/ ANALYSIS_ARCHIVES/Sachi05_08_02.htm

Norway

Annual Report for the Directorate of Immigration 1992, UDI, Oslo: Utlendingsdirektoratet, 1992.

Bivand Erdal, Marta. "Contributing to Development? Transnational Activities among Members of the Tamil Diaspora in Norway." M.A., University of Oslo, 2006.

Blom, Svein and Kristin Henriksen. "Levekår blant innvandrere i Norge 2005/2006." *Statistisk sentralbyrå*, Rapport 2008/5, 2008.

Brun, Cathrine. "Birds of Freedom: Young People, the LTTE, and Representations of Gender, Nationalism, and Governance in Northern Sri Lanka." *Critical Asian Studies* 40, 3 (2003): 399–422.

Djuve, A. B. and K. Hagen. "'Skaff meg en jobb!': Leverkår blant flyktninger i Oslo." *Fafo-rapport*, nr. 184, Fafo: Oslo, 1995.

Engebrigtsen, Ada and Øivind Fuglerud. "Culture, Networks and Social Capital: Tamil and Somali Immigrants in Norway." *Ethnic and Racial Studies* 29, 6 (November 2006): 1118–34.

_____, "Ekteskap, slektskap og vennskap – Netverksanalyse som inntak til kulturelle prosesser." In *Grenser for kultur?*, edited by Øivind Fuglerud and Thomas Hylland Eriksen, 209–26. Pax: Oslo, 2007a.

_____, *Ungdom i flyktningfamilier. Familie og vennskap – trygghet eller frihet?*, NOVA Rapport 03/07, 2007b.

Fuglerud, Øivind. "Ambivalent Incorporation: Norwegian Policy towards Tamil Asylum-Seekers from Sri Lanka." *Journal of Refugee Studies* 10, 4 (1997): 443–61.

_____, *Life on the Outside: The Tamil Diaspora and Long Distance Nationalism*. Pluto Press: London, 1999.

Henriksen, Kristin. "Levekår og kjønnsforskjeller blant innvandrere fra ti land." *Statistics Norway*, Report No. 6, 2010.

_____, "Creating Sri Lankan Tamil Catholic Space in the South Asian Diaspora in Norway." In *South Asian Christian Diaspora: Invisible Diaspora in Europe and North America*, edited by Knut A. Jacobsen and Selva J. Raj, 117–32. Surrey, England; Burlington, VT : Ashgate, c2008.

Jacobsen, Knut A. "Establishing Tamil Ritual Space: A Comparative Analysis of the Ritualisation of the Traditions of the Tamil Hindus and the Tamil Roman Catholics in Norway." *Journal of Religion in Europe* 2, 2 (2009): 180–98.

Kunz, E. F. "The Refugee in Flight: Kinetic Models and Forms of Displacement." *International Migration* 7, 2 (1973): 125–46.

Portes, Alejandro and Julia Sensenbrenner. "Embeddedness and Immigration: Notes on the Social Determinants of Economic Action." *American Journal of Sociology* 98, 6 (1993): 1320–50.

Portes, Alejandro and Min Zhou. "The New Second Generation: Segmented Assimilation and its Variants Among Post-1965 Immigrant Youth."

The Annals of the American Academy of Political and Social Sciences 530 (1993): 74–96.

Portes, Alejandro and Rubén G. Rumbaut. "Introduction: The Second Generation and the Children of Immigrants Longitudinal Study." *Ethnic and Racial Study* 28, 6 (2005): 983–99.

Sigfrid Grønseth, Anne. "In Search of Community: A Quest for Well-Being Among Tamil Refugees in Northern Norway." *Medical Anthropology Quarterly* 15, 4 (2001): 493–514.

Sweden

"Diaspora Children Attend Europe-Wide Exams in Tamil", *Tamilnet*, May 4, 2008. Online at: http://www.tamilnet.com/art. html?catid=13&artid=25522

Gaellmo, Gunnar. "Buddhism in Ceylon and Sweden." *Studia Orientalia* 50 (1980): 43–49.

Plank, K. "Buddhism i Sverige - om asiatiska buddhister, konvertitbuddhister, kristna zenmeditatörer och sympatisörer." In *Det mångreligiösa Sverige: Ett landskap i förändring*, edited by Daniel Andersson and Åke Sander, 221–84. Lund, Studentlitteratur, 2009.

Schalk, Peter. *God as a Remover of Obstacles: A Study of Caiva Soteriology Among Ilam Tamil Refugees in Stockholm, Sweden*. Acta Universitatis Upsaliensis, Uppsala, 2004.

Denmark

Fibiger, Marianne Qvortrup. "Young Tamil Hindus in Denmark and their Relationship to Tradition and Collective Memory." *The Finnish Journal of Ethnicity and Migration* (2011): 24–32.

_____, "When the Hindu-Goddess Moves to Denmark: The Establishment of a Sakta-Tradition." *Bulletin for the Study of Religion* 41, 3, Equinox (2012): 29–36.

Jacobsen, Knut A. "Establishing Ritual Space in the Hindu Diaspora in Norway." In *South Asians in the Diaspora: Histories and Religious Traditions*, edited by Knut A. Jacobsen and Pratap P. Kumar, 134–48. Leiden: Brill, 2004.

_____, and Pratap P. Kumar. "Introduction." In *South Asians in the Diaspora: Histories and Religious Traditions*, edited by Knut A. Jacobsen and Pratap P. Kumar, ix–xxiv. Leiden: Brill, 2004.

Jensen, Tim. *Religionsguiden. En vejviser til flygtninges og indvandreres religioner og trossamfund*. Danmark, Copenhagen: Danks Flygtningehjaelp, 1994.

Statistics Denmark. Online at: http://www.dst. dk/en

Steen, Ann-Belinda. *Varieties of the Tamil Refugee Experience in Denmark and England*, Copenhagen: Minority Studies, University of Copenhagen and Danish Centre for Human Rights, 1993.

Portugal

Esteves, Maria do Céu, ed. *Portugal: País de Imigração*. Lisboa, Instituto de Estudos para o Desenvolvimento, 1991.

Garcia, José Luís, eds. *Portugal Migrante: Emigrantes e Imigrados. Dois Estudos Introdutórios.* Oeiras: Celta, 2000.

Pires, Rui Pena. *Migrações e Integração: Teoria e Aplicações à Sociedade Portuguesa.* Lisboa, ISCTE, 2003.

Serviço de Estrangeiros e Fronteiras, *Relatório de Imigração, Fronteiras e Asilo – SEF,* 2009.

Serviço de Estrangeiros e Fronteiras, *Relatório de Imigração, Fronteiras e Asilo – SEF,* 2010.

Russia and Eastern Europe

Krasnodembskaya, N. G. *From the Lion's Island to the Abode of Snow.* Moscow: Nauka, 1983.

Ramet, Sabrina P. *Politics, Culture and Society since 1939.* Indiana University Press, Bloomington, Indiana, 1998.

"Sri Lanka Commemorates Its Chekhov Connection." *BBC News South Asia,* December 29, 2010.

Zagorodnikova, T.N. *Russians in Ceylon: Archive Documents.* Moscow, Vostochnaya Literatura, 2009.

Australia

Arambewela, R. and C. Forster, eds. *Glimpses of Sri Lankan and Australian Relations.* The Committee for Sri Lanka Inc., Melbourne, 1998.

Australian Bureau of Statistics, Census of Population and Housing, 2006.

Bilimoria, Purushottama. *Hinduism in Australia: Mandala for the Gods.* Melbourne: Spectrum Publication, Deakin University Press, 1989.

_____, "The Australian South Asian Diaspora." In *A New Handbook of Living Religions,* edited by John Hinnells, 728–55. Oxford, Cambridge, Mass.: Blackwell, 1997.

Eliezer, C. "Sri Lanka-Tamils." In *The Australian People - An Encyclopedia of the Nation, its People and their Origins,* edited by James Jupp, 702–3. Cambridge University Press, 2001.

Gamage, Siri. "Curtains of Culture, Ethnicity and Class: The Changing Composition of the Sri Lankan Community in Australia." *Journal of Intercultural Studies* 19, 1 (1998): 37–56.

_____, and K. Liyanaratchie. "Glimpses of Sri Lankan and Australian Relations." In *Glimpses of Sri Lankan & Australian Relations,* edited by R. Arambewela and C. Forster, 109–25. The Committee for Sri Lanka Inc., Melbourne, 1998.

Gamage, Siri. "Sri Lanka-Sinhalese." In *The Australian People - An Encyclopedia of the Nation, its People and their Origins,* edited by James Jupp, 684–85. Cambridge University Press, 2001.

_____, "Between School and Home: Sense of Self and Belonging and Their Contestations among Australian-Sri Lankan Children in Metropolitan Australia." 35th Annual Conference of Australia and New Zealand Comparative and International Education Society, University of Auckland, Auckland, November-December, 2007.

_____, "The Sri Lankan Diaspora in Australia: Identity and Integration Issues." 17th Biennial Conference, Asian Studies Association of Australia, Melbourne, July 2008.

Ganewatta, Palitha. *Adapting to a World of Difference: Attitudes of Sri Lankan Immigrants to Australia.* Pahana Publishers, Melbourne, 2008.

Jayasuriya, Laksiri. *Racism, Immigration and the Law: The Australian Experience.* University of Western Australia, School of Social Work and Administration, 1999.

Jupp, James, ed. *The Australian People - An Encyclopedia of the Nation, its People and their Origins.* Cambridge University Press, 2001.

Kapferer, Bruce. *Legends of People, Myths of State: Violence, Intolerance and Political Culture in Sri Lanka and Australia.* Washington: Smithsonian Institution Press, 1988.

Liyanaratchi, K. "Employment Problems of Recent Sri Lankan Skilled Immigrants in Australia." Ph.D. diss., University of Melbourne, 2006.

Mendis, Olga. "Sri Lanka: An Overview." In *Glimpses of Sri Lankan & Australian Relations,* edited by R. Arambewela and C. Forster, 1–12. The Committee for Sri Lanka Inc., Melbourne, 1998.

Pinawela, S. K. "Sri Lankans in Melbourne: Factors Influencing Patterns of Ethnicity." Ph.D. diss., Australian National University, 1984.

Rabot, M. "Sri Lanka: Dutch Burghers." In *The Australian People - An Encyclopedia of the Nation, its People and their Origins,* edited by James Jupp, 694–95. Cambridge University Press, 2001.

Roberts, Michael, Ismeth Raheem and Percy Colin-Thomé, eds. *People In Between: The Burghers and the Middle Class in the Transformations within Sri Lanka, 1790s–1960.* Sarvodaya Vishva Lekha Publications, Ratmalana, 1989.

The Burgher Association (Australia) Inc. Online at: http://www.burgherassocn.org.au/index.html

vanden Driesen, Cynthia. "A Chorus of Women's Voices: Sri Lankan Writing in Australia." 3rd International Conference, Rydges Hotel, Canberra, 3-6 December, 1999.

_____, and Ralph Crane. *Diaspora – The Australasian Experience.* Prestige Books, 2005.

vanden Driesen, I. H. "The Sri Lankan Diaspora and the Academic Scene in Australia." In *Celebrations: Fifty Years of Sri Lanka-Australia Interactions,* edited by Cynthia Vanden Driesen and I.H. Vanden Driesen, 341–43. Government Press, Sri Lanka, 1998.

Weerasooriya, W.S. *Links Between Sri Lanka and Australia.* Government Press, Colombo, 1988.

Wickrama, U. V. "The Sinhalese Migrants to Sydney: A Case Study of Family Migration to Australia, 1978–2000." Ph.D. diss., University of New England, Australia, 2005.

New Zealand

De Silva, K. M. *A History of Sri Lanka.* Oxford University Press, New Delhi, 1981.

Fuglerud, Øivind. *Life on the Outside: The Tamil Diaspora and Long-Distance Nationalism.* Pluto Press, London, 1999.

Lal, Brij V., Peter Reeves and Rajesh Rai. *The Encyclopedia of the Indian Diaspora.* University of Hawaii Press, Honolulu, 2006.

Leckie, Jacqueline. "South Asians: Old and New Migrations." In *Immigration and National Identity in New Zealand: One People, Two Peoples, Many Peoples?,* edited by Stuart William Greif. Palmerston North: Dunmore, 1995.

Nithiyanandam, V. "An Analysis of Economic Factors Behind the Origin and Development of Tamil Nationalism in Sri Lanka." In *Facets of Ethnicity in Sri Lanka,* edited by C. Abeysekera, and N. Gunasinghe, 100–70. Social Scientists Association, Colombo, 1987.

_____, "Ethnic Politics and Third World Development: Some Lessons from Sri Lanka's Experience." *Third World Quarterly* 21, 2 (2000a): 283–311.

_____, "Scenarios of Tamilian Culture: Some Thoughts on the Cultural Dimensions of the Ethnic War in Sri Lanka." *Asian Ethnicity* 2, 1 (2000b): 35–54.

_____, "The Economic Activities of the Sri Lankan Diaspora: An Overview of Their Spread and Impact." Keynote Address at the Conference - The Sri Lankan Diaspora: The Way Forward, University of Malaya, Kuala Lumpur, August 2008.

Ponnambalam, Satchi. *Dependent Capitalism in Crisis: The Sri Lankan Economy, 1948–1980.* Zed Press, London, 1981.

Rice, Geoffrey W., William Hosking Oliver and Bridget R. Williams, eds. *The Oxford History of New Zealand.* University Press (second edition), Auckland: Oxford, 1992.

Rudd, Chris and Brian Roper, eds. *The Political Economy of New Zealand.* Oxford University Press, Auckland, 1997.

Sheffer, Gabriel. *Diaspora Politics: At Home and Abroad.* Cambridge University Press, Cambridge, 2003.

Swarbrick, Nancy. "Sri Lankans – Immigration." *Te Ara – The Encyclopedia of New Zealand,* 13 July 2012. Online at: http://www.TeAra.govt.nz/en/sri-lankans/page-1

Tambiah, Stanley Jeyaraja. *Sri Lanka: Ethnic Fratricide and the Dismantling of Democracy.* I. B. Tauris & Co Ltd, London, 1986.

Tharmaseelan, Nithya, Kerr Inkson and Stuart C. Carr. "Migration and Career Success: Testing a Time-Sequenced Model." *Career Development International* 15, 3 (2010): 218–38.

Wilson, Alfred Jeyaratnam. *The Break-Up of Sri Lanka: The Sinhalese-Tamil Conflict.* London: Hurst, 1988.

_____, *Sri Lankan Tamil Nationalism: Its Origin and Development in the Nineteenth and Twentieth Centuries.* C. Hurst & Co, London, 2000.

193

INDEX

Note: Page numbers in *italic* refer to illustrations; page numbers in **bold** refer to maps; page numbers <u>underlined</u> refer to figures/tables.

LIST OF FIGURES, TABLES AND MAPS

PICTURE CREDITS

A. Sivanandan/*When Memory Dies* 69 (top)

Adrianne Koteen/YaliniDream 60 (centre)

AFP/Getty Images 33 (bottom)

Alalasundaran Vinayagamoorthy 61 (bottom), 138

Alex Van Arkadie 145 (top), 146

Alinari/Getty Images 27 (top)

Allen & Unwin Book Publishers/Michelle de Kretser 66 (bottom left)

Annette Wilke 132 (top left), 134, 1 (top and bottom)

AP Photo/Dinamalar 72

AP Photo/Eranga Jayawardena 27 (bottom)

AP Photo/Gemunu Amarasinghe 35 (bottom)

AP Photo/Jeffrey M. Boan 102 (top)

AP Photo/Julia Drapkin 77 (top)

AP Photo/KLPD 125 (bottom)

AP Photo/Liu Heung Shing 74 (top)

AP Photo /LTTE 36 (bottom centre)

AP Photo/M. Lakshman 75

AP Photo/The Canadian Press, Chris Young 114 (top)

AP Photo/The Canadian Press, Darren Calabrese 114 (bottom)

AP Photo/The Canadian Press, Jonathan Hayward 110 (top)

AP Photo/Wong Maye–E 92 (top right)

Apic/Getty Images 83 (top)

Apsaras Arts Ltd/Aravinth 60 (top)

Araya Diaz/WireImage 59 (bottom)

Ariff Bongso 93 (centre)

Arshak C. Galstaun/Courtesy of the National Archives of Singapore 83 (bottom left)

Arun Abey 62 (centre)

Arun Abey/Greenleaf Book Group/*How Much Is Enough?* 62 (centre)

Atlantide Phototravel/Corbis 19 (bottom)

B. A. Hussainmiya 94 (bottom), 95 (top), 95 (centre), 95 (bottom)

B. P. de Silva Group of Companies/Navin Amarasuriya 63 (centre), 92 (top left)

Bartosz Hadyniak/iStockphoto 58 (top)

Berlin Lions (Reinickendorfer Füchse e.V.), cricket team 136 (bottom)

Berlingske Media/Denmark 158

Bettmann/Corbis 16 (centre right), 23 (top), 33 (centre)

Bloomsbury Publishing/*Anil's Ghost*/Michael Ondaatje 68 (centre)

Bloomsbury Publishing/*The Match*/*Heaven's Edge*/Romesh Gunesekera 67 (bottom)

Bruno Cossa/Grand Tour/Corbis 52 (centre)

Cameron Spencer/Getty Images 45 (bottom)

Canada Sri Lanka Life Development Centre/Reverend Panasara 111 (bottom)

Canadian Tamils Sports Association (CTSA)/Kanthan 45 (top)

Canadian Tamil Youth Alliance (CTYA)/Ilan 111(centre)

Canadian Tamil's Chamber of Commerce (CTCC)/Navajeevan 112 (top)

Central Press/Getty Images 168 (top right)

Centre Bouddhique International–France/Sedaraa John 126

Ceylon Spices and Cargo Services, Adelaide/Keerthi Dharmabandu 41 (bottom centre)

Chan E. S. Choenni 122 (bottom), 123, 125 (top and centre)

Chandani Lokuge/*Turtle Nest*/*If the Moon Smiled* 67 (top)

Cheryl Selvanayagam 89 (bottom left)

Christiaan van Krimpen 29 (top left)

Christie Eliezer 168 (bottom)

Christophe Boisvieux/Corbis 18 (bottom), 19 (top)

City Image/Alamy 22 (bottom)

Clive Mason/Getty Images 48 (bottom)

Colin McPherson/Sygma/Corbis 65 (bottom right)

Courtesy of Hippocrene Books/Rice & Curry: Sri Lankan Home Cooking/S. H. Fernando Jr 42 (left)

Courtesy of National Library Board (Singapore)/*Malayan Saturday Post* 86 (top)

Courtesy of the University of Texas Libraries, The University of Texas at Austin 25 (bottom)

CTK/Alamy front cover (bottom right), 162 (left)

Dasatha Publications/Gamini Abeysinghe 113 (centre right)

Dave Bartruff/Corbis 17 (top left)

Dave Tyler 62 (bottom)

David Levenson/Getty Images 68 (bottom left)

David Munden/Popperfoto/Getty Images 46 (bottom)

Dennis B. McGilvray 55, 107 (left)

Dibyangshu Sarkar/AFP/Getty Images 77 (bottom)

Domini Sansoni 20 (top), 25 (centre), 30 (bottom), 38 (bottom)

Doug Houghton/Alamy 121 (top)

Durai Raja Singam, S/*A Hundred Years of Ceylonese in Malaysia and Singapore (1867–1967)* 81 (bottom), 86 (bottom)

Dutch Burgher Union, Sri Lanka/Joachim Caspersz 29 (centre)

Embassy of Sri Lanka in Moscow/Deputy Ambassador Major General Nandana Udayatta 161 (bottom)

Embassy of the Democratic Republic of Sri Lanka in the Netherlands 124 (top), 124 (bottom)

Enzo Tomasiello/Getty Images 167 (bottom)

Erick Nguyen/Alamy front cover (top left)

Eugene Wijeysingha/*The Eagle Breeds a Gryphon: The Story of Raffles Institution, 1823–1985* 92 (centre)

Eye Glamour Photography/Sri Lanka Association of New York 43 (top), 104 (top)

Eye Glamour Photography/Sri Lanka Medical Association of North America (SLMANA) front cover (bottom, second from right), 102 (bottom)

Frances Ferdinands 109 (top)

Franco Origlia/Getty Images 147 (bottom)

From the Collection of the National Archives of Australia 163 (bottom), 164, 166 (top)

Gamma-Keystone/Getty Images 27 (centre right)

George Osodi/AFP/Getty Images 121 (top right)

Gerard Cerles/AFP/Getty Images 121 (bottom)

Getty Images 46 (top)

Gloria Spittel 43 (bottom left), 43 (bottom centre)

Goh Seng Chong/Bloomberg via Getty Images 62 (top)

Gomala Sivakumar 110 (top left)

Granta Books/*Monkfish Moon*/*Reef*/*Sandglass*/Romesh Gunesekera (67 bottom)

Greg Wood/AFP/Getty Images 166 (bottom)

Hardie Grant Books/The Complete Asian Cookbook/Charmaine Solomon 43 (centre)

Hema Kiruppalini 22 (left), 23 (right and bottom), 51, 89 (centre), 91 (bottom left)

Heritage Images/Corbis 145 (centre)

Hodder & Stoughton Publishers/*The Rice Mother*/Rani Manicka 65 (top)

Horst Ossinger/dpa/Corbis 132 (centre)

Horst Tappe/Hulton Archive/Getty Images 67 (centre)

Hugh Sitton/Corbis 20 (centre left)

Igor Prahin/Alamy 53 (top)

Images of Asia.com/Omar Khan 7 (right), 26 (top right), 30 (bottom, second right)

Images of Ceylon/Palinda de Silva 26 (top left), 32 (centre left), 94 (top)

Imagestate Media Partners Limited–Impact Photos/Alamy 26 (centre left), 54 (top)

Institute of Southeast Asian Studies, Singapore/*The Singapore Lion: A Biography of S. Rajaratnam*/Irene Ng 90 (bottom left)

Interfoto/Alamy 131 (bottom)

Ishara S. Kodikara/AFP/Getty Images 37 (centre), 38 (centre), 59 (top), 98 (top), 109 (right)

Jaffna Food, Oslo 151 (top)

Jaffna House restaurant, United Kingdom 41 (top centre)

James Burke/Time Life Pictures/Getty Images 34 (top)

Janaka Ruwanpura 111 (right)

Jean-Francois Deroubaix/Gamma-Rapho via Getty Images 129

Jeff Morgan 07/Alamy 66 (top)

Jeffrey Samuels 80 (top right and bottom left)

Jeremy Horner/Corbis 17 (bottom)

Johannes Eisele/AFP/Getty Images 132 (top)

Jon Hicks/Corbis 159 (top)

Jose Fuste Raga/Corbis 17 (centre right)

'JVP Italy' on Facebook 148 (top right)

Kamala Ganesh 144 (bottom)

Kannan Arunasalam 29 (centre left), 29 (centre left), 29 (bottom), 31 (centre), 31 (bottom right)

Karl Walter/Getty Images 59 (centre)

Kathy deWitt/Alamy 63 (bottom)

Kaushi Rajah/Logan Kanapathi 114 (centre left)

Keystone/Hulton Archive/Getty Images 34 (bottom)

Krishner Rajadevi 83 (centre right), 85 (centre), 87 (centre right)

Kumutha Patpanathan 138 (left)

Lakruwan Wanniarachchi/AFP/Getty Images 36 (top right and bottom), 37 (top), 97 (top)

Lakruwana restaurant, Staten Island/Lakruwana Wijesinghe 43 (bottom right)

Lankaramaya, Milan/Shamith Mudalige 147 (top and centre), 148 (top left)

Larry Marshall 28 (centre), 29 (top right)

Lathan Suntharalingam 139 (centre)

Leah Lakshmi Piepzna-Samarasinha/TSAR Publications/*Love Cake* 66 (centre)

Lebrecht Music and Arts Photo Library/Photographersdirect.com 116 (centre)

Lee Kip Lin/Courtesy of the National Archives of Singapore 82 (top)

Little, Brown and Company–Hachette Book Group, Inc/*The Hamilton Case*/*The Lost Dog*/Michelle de Kretser 66 (bottom)

London: Hurst & Company/*S. J. V. Chelvanayakam and The Crisis of Sri Lankan Tamil Nationalism, 1947–1977*/Alfred Jeyaratnam Wilson 35 (centre)

Lordprice Collection/Alamy 163 (centre)

Luca Tettoni/Corbis 16 (left), 21 (right)

Maeers/Fox Photos/Getty Images 115 (bottom)

Mahinda Deegalle 117 (bottom), 118 (centre and bottom), 119 (top, centre and bottom), 120 (top)

Mahir Mohideen 58 (bottom centre)

Manjula Dissanayake 102 (centre), 104 (centre)

Marianne Qvortrup Fibiger 157 (top), 158 (top)

Mark Dadswell/Getty Images 48 (top)

Martin Bureau/AFP/Getty Images 128

Martin Rose/Bongarts/Getty Images 133 (centre)

Mary Anne Mohanraj/Colombo Chicago 66 (left)

Matt Campbell/AFP/Getty Images 48 (left centre)

Maunaguru Sidharthan 61 (top and centre)

Menusha de Silva 165 (centre)

Michael Freeman/Corbis 22 (top)

Michele Ruth Gamburd 96 (left), 100 (bottom)

Ministry of Information, Communication and the Arts/ Courtesy of National Archives of Singapore 88 (top), 90 (bottom right)

Moviestore Collection Ltd/Alamy 65 (bottom)

Muhammad Yusuf Bin Yacob 40 (bottom right)

Museum of Fine Arts, Boston Photograph ©2013 front cover (top, second from right), 107 (top left)

New Zealand Sri Lanka Foundation/Sydney Fernando 40 (left), 42 (centre), 173 (centre and bottom)

New Zealand-Sri Lanka Friendship Inc/Gregory de Costa 171 (centre)

Nicholas Ratzenboeck/AFP/Getty Images 139 (bottom)

Nicolas Asfouri/AFP/Getty Images 52 (bottom)

North Wind Picture Archives 26 (bottom right)

Norway Tamil Sangam/Ramesh Sivakolunthu 153

'Old Ceylon' on Facebook/Gehan Pinto 28 (bottom), 30 (centre right, 'London Calling' poster), 32 (top)

Oliver Berg/dpa/Corbis 131 (top)

Olivier Mentha/Patrick Grass 144 (centre)

Ong Teng Cheong/Courtesy of National Archives of Singapore 92 (top)

Organisation for Eelam Refugees Rehabilitation/S. C. Chandrahasan 76 (bottom centre)

Orient Blackswan Pvt Ltd, India/Recipes of the Jaffna Tamils/Nesa Eliezer (ed) 40 (centre)

Palitha Ganewatta 166 (centre left), 167 (top)

Pasan Chandrasekara 45 (centre)

Paul Kleiven/AFP/Getty Images 150 (bottom)

Paul Russell/Corbis 54 (bottom)

Paul Supramaniam 73 (bottom), 85 (top), 87 (top and bottom left)

Peter Macdiarmid/Getty Images 117 (right)

pf/Alamy 16 (bottom)

Phil Walter/Getty Images 170 (bottom)

Pictures from History/David Henley 24 (left and bottom), 25 (top), 26 (bottom left), 33 (top), 122 (top)

Popperfoto/Getty Images 18 (top), 35 (top)

Prasanna, Ukraine 162 (right)

Prashant Panjiar/The India Today Group/Getty Images 74 (bottom)

Preston Merchant/V. V. Ganeshananthan 68 (bottom)

Purnima Imiya front cover (top right), 127 (bottom), 130 (bottom)

R. Theyvendran 85 (bottom), 88 (centre), 92 (bottom left)

Rabih Moghrabi/AFP/Getty Images 97 (bottom)

Rafaela Eulberg 141 (top)

Raffles Institution/Courtesy of National Archives of Singapore 91 (top centre)

Rathika Sitsabaiesan 114 (bottom centre)

Ray Roper/iStockphoto 32 (bottom), 34 (centre)

Raynuha Sinnathamby 64 (bottom)

Razeen Sally 56, 57

Registry of Co-Operative Societies/Courtesy of the National Archives of Singapore 83 (right)

Reza/Getty Images 99 (bottom)

RIA Novosti–Russian News and Information Agency 160, 161 (top)

Roanna Jayasinghe 28 (top)

Robert Harding Picture Library Ltd/Alamy 49 (top)

Robert Nickelsberg/Time Life Pictures/Getty Images 36 (top centre)

Roberto Herrett Photography/Photographersdirect.com 117 (top)

Roger Viollet/Getty Images 30 (top), 52 (top)

Roslan Rahman/AFP/Getty Images 47 (centre)

Ru Freeman/Atria Books/A Disobedient Girl 68 (top)

S. Muttiah front cover (top, second from left), 73 (top and centre)

S. N. Aresecularetne/Sinhalese Immigrants in Malaysia and Singapore 80 (top left), 80 (bottom, centre and right), 84 (top), 86 (centre), 91 (top)

Sabaratnam Arulkumaran 121 (centre)

Samasinghe Healthcare and Rehabilitation for the Elderly (S.H.A.R.E), UK/Celine Samarasinhe 118 (left)

Sandra Teddy/Getty Images 172 (top)

Sanjeewa 46 (centre)

Sanka Vidanagama/AFP/Getty Images 50 (bottom)

Saskatoon Sri Lankan Community, Canada/Withana Gamage, Thushan Sanjeewa 42 (top), 112 (centre)

Sdrsreddy/Inmagine 39 (bottom)

Sena Vidanagama/AFP/Getty Images 53 (bottom)

Seralathan Sivagnanasuntharam/Kursk State Medical University 161 (centre)

Shankar Photography/Shankar 124 (centre), 133 (top left), 133 (top right)

Shihan de Silva Jayasuriya 31 (top and bottom left)

Shobasakthi/Gorilla 69 (centre)

Simon Lewis/Demotix/Corbis 37 (bottom)

Singapore Ceylon Tamils' Association/Eliyathamby Narasinghan 91 (bottom right)

Singapore Sinhala Association/Siri Amarasuriya 89 (top right)

Sinhalese Association of Canada/Jayasundara 113 (top)

Sinnapoo Apputhurai/Legacy of the Pioneers: 125 Years of Jaffna Tamils in Malaysia front cover (bottom, second from left), 41 (top), 47 (bottom right), 78, 79, 81 (top), 82 (bottom), 83 (bottom), 84 (left)

Special Broadcasting Service (SBS), Australia/ Julieanne McCormack-Brown/ Henry Motteram 40 (bottom left)

Spicy Bistro Tabrobane, Tokyo 39 (top)

Sri Lanka Association Berlin/Lankananda Perera/Sudath Thenuwara 133 (bottom)

Sri Lanka Association in Sweden/Harry Withana 156

Sri Lanka Association of Washington D. C. (SLAWDC)/ Roy T Braine 40 (top), 103 (top), 108 (bottom)

Sri Lanka Buddhist Temple/Bhante B. Sri Saranankara Nakya Maha Thera 80 (bottom centre)

Sri Lanka Cricket Club Milano/Nimal Hettiarachchi 148 (centre and (bottom)

Sri Lanka Daily News/Rajpal/Champika 146 (bottom)

Sri Lanka Danish Cultural Association/Ismail 157 (bottom)

Sri Lanka Unites Australia (SLUA)/Gayathri Hemachandra 165 (bottom)

Sri Lanka Unites/Prashan De Visser/Chrisjit Xavier 6

Sri Lankan Association of Norway/Harsha Ratnaweera 150 (top)

Sri Lankan Embassy in Kuwait 98 (centre)

Sri Lankan Malay Association of Toronto (SLAMAT)/ Rheana Lye 113 (bottom)

Sri Lankan Medical and Dental Association in the UK/ Champa Sumanasuriya 116 (top)

Sri Lankan Muslim Association (SLMA Korea)/Althaf Faiz 58 (bottom left)

Sri Lankan Study for the Advancement of Technology and Social Welfare (SCATS), Australia/Anjula Godakumbura 41 (bottom)

Sri Lankans Without Borders/Kumaran Nadesan 69 (bottom), 110 bottom

Sri Lankaramaya, New Zealand/Rev K. Chandrawimala 172 (bottom)

Stan White/Alamy 49 (bottom)

State Library of Queensland 163 (top)

Stephane de Sakutin/AFP/Getty Images 70–1, 130 (top and centre)

Steve Russell/ZUMA Press/Corbis 120 (centre)

Stockholm Buddhist Vihara/Bhante K. Dhammaratana Thera 155

Strdel/AFP/Getty Images 100 (top)

Sundaralingam Ramachandra 76 (top centre)

Sunil Govinnage/Black Swans and Other Stories/Perth: My Village Down Under, A Collection of Australian Poetry 168 (top left)

Supreme Court/Courtesy of the National Archives of Singapore 93 (top right)

Sweden Ganesh Temple/Mohan Sharma 154

Swiss Tamil Catholic Spiritual Service 142 (centre)

Sworup Nhasiju 7 (left)

Tamil Education (Poogna)/Uma George 169 (centre)

Tamil Education Services in Switzerland 141 (bottom), 142 (top)

Tamil School in Bergen/Aloycius Santhiapillai 152

Tamil Youth Organisation (TYO) in Switzerland/Thuva 139 (top)

Tan May Lee 65 (centre right)

Tara Walton/ZUMA Press/Corbis 60 (bottom)

The Art Archive/Alamy 20 (bottom)

The Association of Professional Sri Lankans in the UK/ Leslie Dep/Don Gihantha Jayasinghe 115 (top)

The Association of Sri Lankan Lawyers in UK/Surya Samaraweera 116 (bottom)

The Hindu Archives/Ashok Kumar/SK Subrramanya 76 (top)

The National Archives, United Kingdom/Paul Johnson 14–5

The National Archives/SSPL/Getty Images 20 (centre left, 'Our Allies The Colonies' poster)

The Protected Art Archive/Alamy 24 (top)

The Straits Times ©Singapore Press Holdings Limited 47 (bottom left), 78 (left), 87 (centre right), 88 (bottom), 89 (bottom right), 90 (top and centre), 91 (centre right), 93 (top left, centre right and bottom right), 167 (centre), 140 (bottom)

Thomas Tolstrup/Getty Images 158 (bottom)

Tim Graham/Getty Images 76 (bottom)

Tisarana Sri Lankan Buddhist Association in Norway/ Nirmala Eidsgård 149

TPG Images/Click Photos 21 (bottom)

Travel Pictures/Alamy 50 (top)

Umme Salma 159 (bottom)

United Sri Lanka Association, New Zealand (USLA)/ Channa Ranasinghe 171 (bottom), 173 (top)

United Sri Lankan Muslim Association of Australia/ Mohamed Mohideen 58 (centre)

Universal History Archive/Getty Images 19 (centre right)

University of Alberta/Aubrey Chau 111 (top right)

Used by permission of McClelland and Stewart/Random House of Canada Limited/Running in the Family/ Michael Ondaatje 68 (centre)

Uthayan Newspaper, Canada 113 (centre left)

Uthayan Newspaper, Canada 64 (top)

V. Navaratnam/ Chloe Applin 119 (left)

V. I. S. Jayapalan/Amaladas 151 (bottom)

Venkat Rahman/New Zealand Thirumurugan Temple 170 (top)

Vera Markus 137, 140 (top), 142 (bottom), 144 (top)

Victor Melder 168 (centre)

Web Administrator-Sinhala Hot News/Das Buddhistische Haus - Berlin-Frohnau 135 (bottom), 136 (top)

Wellington Tamil Society Inc/Mani Maniparathy 171 (top)

William West/AFP/Getty Images front cover (bottom left), 44 (top)

xinhua/Xinhua Press/Corbis 99 (top)

Yadid Levy/Corbis 21 (top)

Yal Market/Siva 110 (centre left)

Yasser Al-Zayyat/AFP/Getty Images 96 (top)

Yogesh Mehta 39 (centre right), 40 (bottom left), 47 (top)

Yuli Seperi/Getty Images 169 (bottom)

Zuma Wire Service/Alamy 112 (bottom)

Zurich Buddhist Vihara/Bhante Anuruddha 143

ACKNOWLEDGEMENTS

Without the support of many individuals and organisations, a project of this size and complexity could not have come about. It is with gratitude that the editorial team wishes to acknowledge these contributions. First and foremost are the numerous writers whose texts make up the substance of the volume. From all parts of the globe, contributors have given their time and expertise to the project with patience and goodwill. We have also had advice and encouragement from numerous colleagues and friends as readers and discussants. Our families have endured the inevitable stresses and strains of this production with humour and tolerance and for that we thank them sincerely. Finally, there are some people and institutions that we would like to specifically mention.

- The Sixth President of the Republic of Singapore, Mr S. R. Nathan, for initiating the development of the project.

- Deputy Prime Minister of Singapore and Minister of Finance, Mr Tharman Shanmugaratnam, for his sustained interest and encouragement.

- Our sponsors, Standard Chartered Bank, The Prima Group of Companies, Singapore Ceylon Tamils' Association, Mr Sat Pal Khattar and B P de Silva Holdings Pte Ltd, for their financial support.

- The International Advisory Panel, Chairman, Sir Professor Arulkumaran Sabaratnam, Professor David de Kretser, Mr J. Y. Pillay, Professor Patrick Mendis , Dr Razeen Sally and Professor V. Navaratnam for their valuable inputs and guidance.

- Our editorial reviewers, Professor Wang Gungwu, Professor Robin Jeffrey, Professor Brij Lal and Professor Laksiri Jayasuriya for their advice and endorsement of the project.

- Mr Didier Millet and the staff of Editions Didier Millet, Singapore, especially Mr Charles Orwin, Mr Douglas Amrine, Mr Francis Dorai, Ms Valerie Ho and Ms Lisa Damayanti

- Ambassador Gopinath Pillai, Chairman, Institute of South Asian Studies (ISAS) for his interest and involvement in the project.

- Professor Tan Tai Yong, Director, Institute of South Asian Studies (ISAS) and Vice-Provost (Student Life), National University of Singapore whose unfailing support and encouragement was important to the project.

- Mr Johnson Paul Devasagayam, Senior Associate Director, Institute of South Asian Studies (ISAS) for handling various aspects of the project spontaneously and efficiently.

- All research staff of ISAS who read and provided valuable feedback on the manuscript of the volume.

- The administrative team at ISAS, especially Ms Puspa Thangavelu, Ms Mohanarangam Vinitha Priyadhar, and Ms Asha Choolani for ensuring that the administrative tasks were completed smoothly; Ms Kamarunnisa Shaul Hameed and Mr Muhammad Yusuf for their assistance in facilitating overseas phone calls for the picture research; Mr Kirby Khoo for handling the financial aspects of the volume; and Ms Sithara Doriasamy for taking charge of corporate communications and sponsorship related matters.

- The staff and management officers of the South Asian Studies Programme (SASP) at the National University of Singapore for their support towards the project and for their generosity in providing a venue for the team to work together at various stages of the project.

- Ms Thavamani Prem Kumar, NUS Resource Librarian, for addressing requests for books and articles and graciously providing her support.

- Ms Ambika Ragavan and Ms Sivashangari Kiruppalini for voluntarily providing assistance for the tedious segments of the endlims.

- The project was supported by those who attended the 'Workshop on Approaches to The Development of a Projected Volume: The Encyclopedia of The Sri Lankan Diaspora', which was held in Singapore on 17 June 2010. We are especially thankful to the panelist—Professor S. D. Muni, Dr Dayan Jayatilleka, Dr C. Anandakumar—for sharing their insights during the conceptualization of this project.

- In the final stages, for the indexing of the volume, we had support from Ms Trendy Tan and Ms Sophy Tio.

- Finally, Prof Peter Reeves, would like to add a special mention of the work of the editorial team in Singapore. In addition to their often demanding roles, Dr Rajesh Rai and Ms Hema Kiruppalini have taken on the major tasks of communicating with writers internationally and the Singapore-based publisher EDM. With the unfailing support of Prof Tan Tai Yong, NUS and ISAS, they have been the day-to-day managers of the production of the volume. I thank them most sincerely for their commitment and their personal support.

Peter Reeves, Rajesh Rai, Hema Kiruppalini